Mathematical Modeling and Analysis of Problems in Ecology, Epidemiology and Oncology

Mathematical Modeling and Analysis of Problems in Ecology, Epidemiology and Oncology

Editors

Sophia Jang
Jui-Ling Yu

Basel • Beijing • Wuhan • Barcelona • Belgrade • Novi Sad • Cluj • Manchester

Editors
Sophia Jang
Department of Mathematics
and Statistics
Texas Tech University
Lubbock, TX
USA

Jui-Ling Yu
Department of Data Science
and Big Data Analytics
Providence University
Taichung
Taiwan

Editorial Office
MDPI AG
Grosspeteranlage 5
4052 Basel, Switzerland

This is a reprint of articles from the Special Issue published online in the open access journal *Mathematics* (ISSN 2227-7390) (available at: https://www.mdpi.com/journal/mathematics/special_issues/math_model_analysis_ecology).

For citation purposes, cite each article independently as indicated on the article page online and as indicated below:

Lastname, A.A.; Lastname, B.B. Article Title. *Journal Name* **Year**, *Volume Number*, Page Range.

ISBN 978-3-7258-2719-0 (Hbk)
ISBN 978-3-7258-2720-6 (PDF)
doi.org/10.3390/books978-3-7258-2720-6

© 2025 by the authors. Articles in this book are Open Access and distributed under the Creative Commons Attribution (CC BY) license. The book as a whole is distributed by MDPI under the terms and conditions of the Creative Commons Attribution-NonCommercial-NoDerivs (CC BY-NC-ND) license.

Contents

Preface vii

Sudeshna Mondal, Guruprasad Samanta and Manuel De la Sen
Dynamics of Oxygen-Plankton Model with Variable Zooplankton Search Rate in Deterministic and Fluctuating Environments
Reprinted from: *Mathematics* 2022, 10, 1641, https://doi.org/10.3390/math10101641 1

Ahmed M. Elaiw, Abdulla J. Alsaedi, Afnan Diyab Al Agha and Aatef D. Hobiny
Global Stability of a Humoral Immunity COVID-19 Model with Logistic Growth and Delays
Reprinted from: *Mathematics* 2022, 10, 1857, https://doi.org/10.3390/math10111857 25

Manuel Molina-Fernández and Manuel Mota-Medina
Some Contributions to the Class of Branching Processes with Several Mating and Reproduction Strategies
Reprinted from: *Mathematics* 2022, 10, 2061, https://doi.org/10.3390/math10122061 53

Usman Sanusi, Sona John, Johannes Mueller and Aurélien Tellier
Quiescence Generates Moving Average in a Stochastic Epidemiological Model with One Host and Two Parasites
Reprinted from: *Mathematics* 2022, 10, 2289, https://doi.org/10.3390/math10132289 67

Fatin Nadiah Yussof, Normah Maan, Mohd Nadzri Md Reba and Faisal Ahmed Khan
Mathematical Modelling of Harmful Algal Blooms on West Coast of Sabah
Reprinted from: *Mathematics* 2022, 10, 2836, https://doi.org/10.3390/math10162836 89

Rodrigo Crespo-Miguel and Francisco J. Cao-García
Predictability of Population Fluctuations
Reprinted from: *Mathematics* 2022, 10, 3176, https://doi.org/10.3390/math10173176 118

Wenhui Luo, Xuewen Tan, Xiufen Zou and Qing Tan
Optimal Treatment of Prostate Cancer Based on State Constraint
Reprinted from: *Mathematics* 2023, 11, 4025, https://doi.org/10.3390/math11194025 131

Julia Sergeeva, Dmitry Grebennikov, Valentina Casella, Paula Cebollada Rica, Andreas Meyerhans and Gennady Bocharov
Mathematical Model Predicting the Kinetics of Intracellular LCMV Replication
Reprinted from: *Mathematics* 2023, 11, 4454, https://doi.org/10.3390/math11214454 148

Amani S. Baazeem, Yasir Nawaz, Muhammad Shoaib Arif, Kamaleldin Abodayeh and Mae Ahmed AlHamrani
Modelling Infectious Disease Dynamics: A Robust Computational Approach for Stochastic SIRS with Partial Immunity and an Incidence Rate
Reprinted from: *Mathematics* 2023, 11, 4794, https://doi.org/10.3390/math11234794 174

Maxim Kuznetsov and Andrey Kolobov
Antiangiogenic Therapy Efficacy Can Be Tumor-Size Dependent, as Mathematical Modeling Suggests
Reprinted from: *Mathematics* 2024, 12, 353, https://doi.org/10.3390/math12020353 196

Till D. Frank
Mathematical Analysis of Four Fundamental Epidemiological Models for Monkeypox Disease Outbreaks: On the Pivotal Role of Human–Animal Order Parameters—In Memory of Hermann Haken
Reprinted from: *Mathematics* 2024, 12, 3215, https://doi.org/10.3390/math12203215 211

Preface

This reprint originated from the Special Issue Mathematical Modeling and Analysis of Problems in Ecology, Epidemiology, and Oncology of the MDPI journal *Mathematics* that aimed to bring together cutting-edge research in the field of Mathematical Ecology, Epidemiology, and Oncology. The collection of articles presented herein reflects the latest developments and insights into the subjects, offering a comprehensive overview of the challenges and advances in the field. The insights presented in this reprint will not only inform contemporary research but also lead the way for future investigations. As the challenges in mathematical biology continue to evolve, we hope this reprint will serve as a reference for researchers looking to deepen and broaden their knowledge and innovate in the field.

We are very grateful to all the authors who contributed their innovative work to this Special Issue. Their dedication to advancing the field is clearly reflected in each article. We also extend our sincere thanks to the reviewers and our editorial team for their invaluable input, which has greatly enriched the quality of the final product.

We sincerely hope that this reprint will stimulate further research and inspire collaborations across disciplines. We are excited to see the impact that this work will have on the ongoing development of mathematical biology.

Sophia Jang and Jui-Ling Yu
Guest Editors

Article

Dynamics of Oxygen-Plankton Model with Variable Zooplankton Search Rate in Deterministic and Fluctuating Environments

Sudeshna Mondal [1], Guruprasad Samanta [1] and Manuel De la Sen [2,*

[1] Department of Mathematics, Indian Institute of Engineering Science and Technology, Shibpur, Howrah 711103, India; sudeshna.rs2017@math.iiests.ac.in (S.M.); g_p_samanta@yahoo.co.uk or gpsamanta@math.iiests.ac.in (G.S.)

[2] Institute of Research and Development of Processes, University of the Basque Country, 48940 Leioa, Bizkaia, Spain

* Correspondence: manuel.delasen@ehu.eus

Citation: Mondal, S.; Samanta, G.; De la Sen, M. Dynamics of Oxygen-Plankton Model with Variable Zooplankton Search Rate in Deterministic and Fluctuating Environments. *Mathematics* 2022, 10, 1641. https://doi.org/10.3390/math10101641

Academic Editors: Sophia Jang and Jui-Ling Yu

Received: 3 April 2022
Accepted: 5 May 2022
Published: 11 May 2022

Publisher's Note: MDPI stays neutral with regard to jurisdictional claims in published maps and institutional affiliations.

Copyright: © 2022 by the authors. Licensee MDPI, Basel, Switzerland. This article is an open access article distributed under the terms and conditions of the Creative Commons Attribution (CC BY) license (https://creativecommons.org/licenses/by/4.0/).

Abstract: It is estimated by scientists that 50–80% of the oxygen production on the planet comes from the oceans due to the photosynthetic activity of phytoplankton. Some of this production is consumed by both phytoplankton and zooplankton for cellular respiration. In this article, we have analyzed the dynamics of the oxygen-plankton model with a modified Holling type II functional response, based on the premise that zooplankton has a variable search rate, rather than constant, which is ecologically meaningful. The positivity and uniform boundedness of the studied system prove that the model is well-behaved. The feasibility conditions and stability criteria of each equilibrium point are discussed. Next, the occurrence of local bifurcations are exhibited taking each of the vital system parameters as a bifurcation parameter. Numerical simulations are illustrated to verify the analytical outcomes. Our findings show that (i) the system dynamics change abruptly for a low oxygen production rate, resulting in depletion of oxygen and plankton extinction; (ii) the proposed system has oscillatory behavior in an intermediate range of oxygen production rates; (iii) it always has a stable coexistence steady state for a high oxygen production rate, which is dissimilar to the outcome of the model of a coupled oxygen-plankton dynamics where zooplankton consumes phytoplankton with classical Holling type II functional response. Lastly, the effect of environmental stochasticity is studied numerically, corresponding to our proposed system.

Keywords: oxygen-plankton model; modified Holling type II; stability analysis; local bifurcations

MSC: 37M05; 92D25; 92D40

1. Introduction

Plankton are the numerous series of organisms observed in water or air that are not able to propel themselves against water currents or wind, respectively. The individual organisms constituting plankton are known as plankters. In the ocean, they offer a vital source of meals to many small and massive aquatic organisms, including bivalves, fish and whales. The plant types of the plankton community are referred to as phytoplankton, they acquire their strength through photosynthesis, as do trees and different plants on land. This means phytoplankton need to have solar light, so they live within the properly-lit floor layers of oceans and lakes. Zooplankton are the animal components of the planktonic network, and they are the principle food supply for fish and other aquatic animals. Phytoplankton are not the best meal source for zooplankton; however, they offer a massive quantity of oxygen for human and different dwelling animals after soaking up carbon dioxide via photosynthesis from the environment. Some of this oxygen production is consumed by both phytoplankton and zooplankton because of respiration [1,2]. Furthermore, a decrease in the oxygen production rate by phytoplankton may have a disastrous effect for living animals, including humankind. Therefore, the study of the possible range of oxygen production rates is important to sustain system dynamics.

Mathematical modeling is a research tool that can reveal the dynamic properties of the oxygen-plankton model. Recently, researchers have analyzed a mathematical model of oxygen-plankton interactions with a Holling type II functional response [3–5], where the search rate of the predator population was constant, i.e., independent of the prey population [6–8]. However, it seems reasonable that predators can vary their search rates based on the availability of prey. In 1977, Hassel et al. [9] experimentally observed that the search rate of various invertebrate predators, specifically zooplankton, depended on the biomass of the prey (phytoplankton) population. In 2020, Dalziel et al. [10] analyzed the dynamics of a predator–prey model with a variable predator search rate. In 2021, Mondal and Samanta [11] studied the dynamic nature of a predator–prey model with the impact of a predator's fear, where the search rate of the predator depended on the biomass of the prey species. Recently, they also investigated the dynamic behavior of a toxin-producing plankton model where the zooplankton's search rate depended on the biomass of the phytoplankton population, rather than being assumed constant [12]. Motivated from the above discussions, we proposed and analyzed the dynamic behavior of the oxygen-plankton model with a variable zooplankton search rate, rather than constant, where oxygen is produced by the photosynthetic activity of phytoplankton during the daytime and consumed by phyto and zooplankton for their respiration.

This article is organized as follows: we have focused on the construction of the basic model in Section 2. The derivation of positivity and uniform boundedness is shown in Section 3. Section 4 describes the feasibility criteria and stability conditions of all the equilibria. Furthermore, the occurrence of local bifurcations are exhibited in Section 5. In Section 6, we conduct numerical simulations using MATLAB to validate the analytical findings. The impact of the oxygen production rate on the existence of the interior equilibrium point as well as the main qualitative difference between the proposed model and the system analyzed by Sekerci and Petrovskii [3] are discussed. This section also consists of the effect of environmental stochasticity on the proposed oxygen-plankton model by perturbing some parameters of the system with Gaussian white noise terms. This work ends with a discussion and the outcomes of the analytical consequences.

2. Construction of Basic Model

A marine ecosystem is a complicated system with many nonlinearly interacting species, organic substances, and inorganic chemical components. Correspondingly, a "realistic" ecosystem model can consist of many equations. In this article, we are mostly interested in the dynamics of the oxygen-plankton model, where oxygen is produced by the photosynthetic activity of phytoplankton.

Revisiting an oxygen-plankton model system given in [3,5] and taking a modified Holling type II functional response, where the search rate of the predator (zooplankton) depends on the biomass of the prey (phytoplankton), rather than being constant (for details, see [10–12]), we consider the following model (for details see Figure 1):

$$\begin{aligned}
\frac{dc}{dt} &= \frac{Ac_0 p}{c + c_0} - \frac{\delta c p}{c + c_2} - \frac{\nu c z}{c + c_3} - mc \\
\frac{dp}{dt} &= \left(\frac{Bc}{c + c_1} - \gamma p\right) p - \frac{ap^2 z}{ahp^2 + p + g} - \sigma p \\
\frac{dz}{dt} &= \left(\frac{\eta c^2}{c^2 + c_4^2}\right) \cdot \frac{ap^2 z}{ahp^2 + p + g} - \mu z
\end{aligned} \quad (1)$$

with initial conditions:

$$c(0) > 0, p(0) > 0, z(0) > 0. \quad (2)$$

Here, c is the amount of oxygen, and p and z are the biomass of phytoplankton and zooplankton, respectively. All the parameters are positive due to their biological meaning and are described in Table 1:

Table 1. Description of biologically meaningful parameters.

Parameters	Descriptions
A	effect of environmental factors on the rate of oxygen production due to the photosynthesis of phytoplankton
δ	maximum per capita phytoplankton respiration rate
ν	maximum per capita zooplankton respiration rate
m	rate of oxygen loss due to the biochemical reaction in a marine ecosystem
B	maximum phytoplankton per capita growth rate in the high oxygen limit
$c_i, i = 0,1,2,3,4$	half saturation constant of the corresponding processes
γ	mortality rate due to intraspecific competition among individual phytoplankton
a	maximally achievable search rate of zooplankton
h	handling time of zooplankton
g	half saturation constant
σ	natural mortality rate of phytoplankton. It is assumed that $B > \sigma$
$\eta \in (0,1)$	maximum feeding efficiency
μ	mortality rate of zooplankton

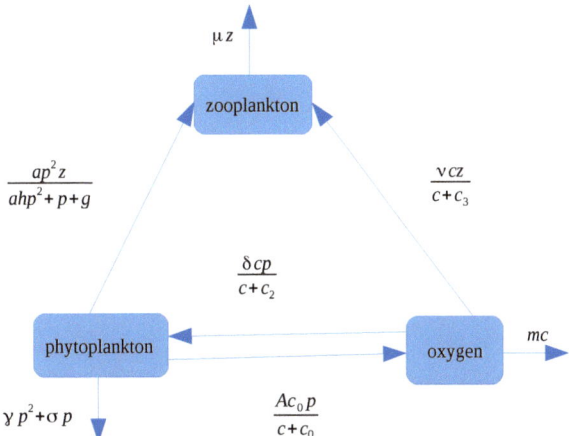

Figure 1. Graphical scheme representing the interactions among oxygen, phytoplankton, and zooplankton, where phytoplankton produce oxygen through photosynthetic activity in sunlight and consume it during the night for their respiration; zooplankton depend on phytoplankton for their growth and consume oxygen for their respiration.

Description of system (1):

- The term $\frac{Ac_0}{c+c_0}$ describes the rate of oxygen production per unit of phytoplankton biomass during the daytime by photosynthetic activity; $\frac{\delta cp}{c+c_2}$ and $\frac{\nu cz}{c+c_3}$ indicate the respiration of phytoplankton and zooplankton, respectively, and mc is the loss of oxygen due to natural depletion in a marine ecosystem.
- The term $\frac{Bcp}{c+c_1}$ describes the growth of phytoplankton depending on the amount of available oxygen. The function $\frac{ap^2}{ahp^2+p+g}$ is named as a modified Holling type II functional response, based on the premise that the zooplankton's search rate is dependent on the biomass of phytoplankton, rather than being constant (for details, see [10,11]). Again, the consumed phytoplankton biomass is transformed into zooplankton biomass

with an efficiency of $\frac{\eta c^2}{c^2+c_4^2}$, which depends on the oxygen concentration (zooplankton die due to insufficient oxygen).

The following are properties of a modified Holling type II functional response $H(p) = \frac{ap^2}{ahp^2+p+g}$

1. $H(p)$ is a smooth function, and $H(p) = 0$ for $p = 0$.
2. $H'(p) = \frac{ap(p+2g)}{(ahp^2+p+g)^2} > 0$, i.e., H increases with p and $\lim_{p \to \infty} H(p) = \frac{1}{h}$, i.e., $H(p)$ saturates at $\frac{1}{h}$ for a large prey population.
3. $H''(p) = \frac{-2a^2hp^3 - 6a^2ghp^2 + 2ag^2}{(ahp^2+p+g)^3}$, and $H''(p)|_{p=0} = \frac{2a}{g} > 0$. Therefore, $H''(p)$ has a unique positive root, and it changes sign from positive to negative at the unique inflection point. A graphical representation of $H(p)$ and $H''(p)$ is presented in Figure 2.

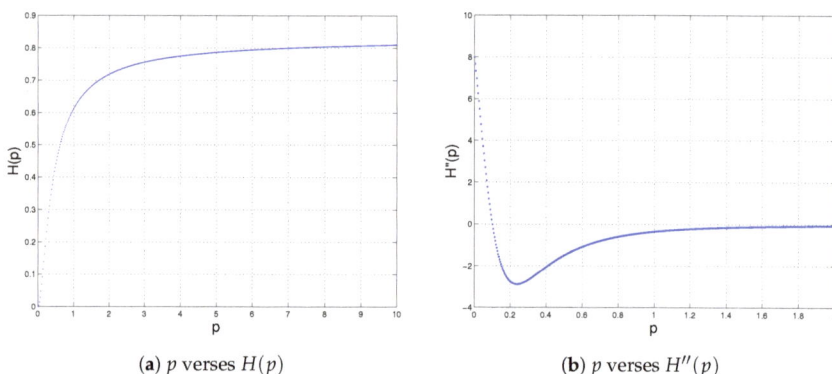

(a) p verses $H(p)$ (b) p verses $H''(p)$

Figure 2. Graphical representations of (a) $H(p)$ and (b) $H''(p)$ for the parametric set $\{a = 3, h = 1.2, g = 0.3\}$.

3. Positivity and Uniform Boundedness

Theorem 1. *Solutions of (1) with (2) exist uniquely and are positive for all $t \geq 0$.*

Proof. Since the right hand sides of (1) are completely continuous functions and locally Lipschitzian in the domain $\mathbb{R}_+^3$, solutions of (1) with (2) exist uniquely in $[0, \xi)$, where $0 < \xi \leq \infty$ [13].

From the first equation of (1), we have:

$$c(t) = c(0) \exp\left[-\int_0^t \left(\frac{\delta p(\theta)}{c(\theta)+c_2} + \frac{vz(\theta)}{c(\theta)+c_3} + m\right) d(\theta)\right]$$
$$+ \int_0^t \frac{Ac_0 p(u)}{c(u)+c_0} \left[\exp\left(\int_t^u \left(\frac{\delta p(\theta)}{c(\theta)+c_2} + \frac{vz(\theta)}{c(\theta)+c_3} + m\right) d(\theta)\right)\right] du > 0,$$

since $c(0) > 0$.

From the second equation of system (1), we have:

$$p(t) = p(0) \exp\left[\int_0^t \left\{\frac{Bc(\theta)}{c(\theta)+c_1} - \gamma p(\theta) - \frac{ap(\theta)z(\theta)}{ahp^2(\theta)+p(\theta)+g} - \sigma\right\} d\theta\right] > 0,$$

since $p(0) > 0$.

From the last equation of system (1), we have:

$$z(t) = z(0) \exp\left[\int_0^t \left\{\left(\frac{\eta c^2(\theta)}{c^2(\theta)+c_4^2}\right) \cdot \frac{ap^2(\theta)}{ahp^2(\theta)+p(\theta)+g} - \mu\right\} d\theta\right] > 0, \text{ since } z(0) > 0.$$

Therefore, $c(t) > 0$, $p(t) > 0$ and $z(t) > 0$ for all $t \geq 0$.
Hence, the theorem is proved. □

Theorem 2. *Solutions of (1) with (2) are uniformly bounded.*

Proof. From the second equation of system (1), we obtain:

$$\frac{dp}{dt} \leq Bp - \gamma p^2 - \sigma p$$

$$= (B - \sigma)p\left\{1 - \frac{p}{\frac{B-\sigma}{\gamma}}\right\}$$

$$\Rightarrow \limsup_{t \to \infty} p(t) \leq \frac{B - \sigma}{\gamma}.$$

Let
$$\Omega = c + p + z.$$

Then,

$$\begin{aligned}
\frac{d\Omega}{dt} &= \frac{dc}{dt} + \frac{dp}{dt} + \frac{dz}{dt} \\
&= \frac{Ac_0 p}{c + c_0} - \frac{\delta c p}{c + c_2} - \frac{\nu c z}{c + c_3} - mc + \left(\frac{Bc}{c + c_1} - \gamma p\right)p - \frac{ap^2 z}{ahp^2 + p + g} - \sigma p \\
&\quad + \left(\frac{\eta c^2}{c^2 + c_4^2}\right) \frac{ap^2 z}{ahp^2 + p + g} - \mu z \\
&\leq \frac{Ac_0 p}{c + c_0} + \frac{Bcp}{c + c_1} + \frac{ap^2 z}{ahp^2 + p + g}\left(\frac{\eta c^2}{c^2 + c_4^2} - 1\right) - \gamma p^2 - \{mc + \sigma p + \mu z\} \\
&\leq \frac{Ac_0 p}{c + c_0} + \frac{Bcp}{c + c_1} - \gamma p^2 - \{mc + \sigma p + \mu z\}, \text{ since } 0 < \eta < 1 \\
&\leq (A + B)p - \gamma p^2 - \{mc + \sigma p + \mu z\} \\
&\leq \frac{(A + B)^2}{4\gamma} - \{mc + \sigma p + \mu z\}.
\end{aligned} \quad (3)$$

Let
$$\kappa = \min\{m, \sigma, \mu\}.$$

Then, from (3), we obtain:

$$\frac{d\Omega}{dt} + \kappa \Omega \leq \frac{(A + B)^2}{4\gamma}.$$

Using the differential inequality:
$0 < \Omega(c(t), p(t), z(t)) \leq \frac{(A+B)^2}{4\gamma\kappa}\left(1 - e^{-\kappa t}\right) + e^{-\kappa t}\Omega(c(0), p(0), z(0))$.
$\therefore 0 < \Omega(c(t), p(t), z(t)) \leq \frac{(A+B)^2}{4\gamma\kappa} + \epsilon$, for any $\epsilon > 0$, as $t \to \infty$.
Hence, every solution of (1) enters into the region:

$$W = \left\{(c, p, z) \in \mathbb{R}_+^3 : 0 < p(t) \leq \frac{B - \sigma}{\gamma}; \ 0 < c(t) + p(t) + z(t) \leq \frac{(A + B)^2}{4\gamma\kappa} + \epsilon, \ \epsilon > 0\right\}.$$

□

4. Existence of Equilibria of (1) with Stability Analysis

4.1. Equilibrium Points

System (1) has the following equilibrium points (steady states):

1. Trivial equilibrium point $E_0(0,0,0)$ corresponding to depletion of oxygen and the extinction of plankton;
2. Planer equilibrium point $E_1(\tilde{c}, \tilde{p}, 0)$ (zooplankton free), where $\tilde{p} = \frac{1}{\gamma}\left(\frac{B\tilde{c}}{\tilde{c}+c_1} - \sigma\right)$, and $\tilde{c}$ is a positive root of the following equation:

$$X_1 c^4 + X_2 c^3 + X_3 c^2 + X_4 c + X_5 = 0.$$

Here, $X_1 = -m\gamma$, $X_2 = -(c_1+c_2) - c_0 + (B-\gamma)\delta$, $X_3 = -c_1c_2 - c_0(c_1+c_2) + (B-\gamma)(A-\delta)c_0 + \delta\gamma$, $X_4 = -c_0c_1c_2 + (B-\gamma)Ac_0c_2 - \gamma c_0(A-\delta)$, $X_5 = -\gamma A c_0 c_1 c_2$.

3. Interior (coexistence) equilibrium $\hat{E}(\hat{c}, \hat{p}, \hat{z})$, where $\hat{c}$, $\hat{p}$, and $\hat{z}$ can be obtained by solving the following system of equations using the software MATHEMATICA:

$$\frac{Ac_0 p}{c+c_0} - \frac{\delta cp}{c+c_2} - \frac{vcz}{c+c_3} - mc = 0,$$

$$\left(\frac{Bc}{c+c_1} - \gamma p\right) - \frac{apz}{ahp^2+p+g} - \sigma = 0,$$

$$\left(\frac{\eta c^2}{c^2+c_4^2}\right) \cdot \frac{ap^2}{ahp^2+p+g} - \mu = 0.$$

4.2. Local Stability

Now, we will determine the stability behavior of the biologically feasible equilibrium points of system (1).

The Jacobian matrix J_0 at $E_0(0,0,0)$ is given by:

$$J_0 = \begin{bmatrix} -m & A & 0 \\ 0 & -\sigma & 0 \\ 0 & 0 & -\mu \end{bmatrix}.$$

Here, the eigenvalues are $\lambda_1 = -m < 0$, $\lambda_2 = -\sigma < 0$, and $\lambda_3 = -\mu < 0$. Since all eigenvalues are negative, so $E_0(0,0,0)$ is always locally asymptotically stable (LAS).

The Jacobian matrix J_1 at $E_1(\tilde{c}, \tilde{p}, 0)$ is given by:

$$J_1 = \begin{bmatrix} -\frac{Ac_0 \tilde{p}}{(\tilde{c}+c_0)^2} - \frac{\delta c_2 \tilde{p}}{(\tilde{c}+c_2)^2} - m & \frac{m\tilde{c}}{\tilde{p}} & -\frac{v\tilde{c}}{\tilde{c}+c_3} \\ \frac{Bc_1 \tilde{p}}{(\tilde{c}+c_1)^2} & -\gamma\tilde{p} & -\frac{a\tilde{p}^2}{ah\tilde{p}^2+\tilde{p}+g} \\ 0 & 0 & \left(\frac{\eta\tilde{c}^2}{\tilde{c}^2+c_4^2}\right)\frac{a\tilde{p}^2}{ah\tilde{p}^2+\tilde{p}+g} - \mu \end{bmatrix}.$$

Here, one eigenvalue is $\lambda_1 = \left(\frac{\eta\tilde{c}^2}{\tilde{c}^2+c_4^2}\right)\frac{a\tilde{p}^2}{ah\tilde{p}^2+\tilde{p}+g} - \mu$, and the other eigenvalues can be obtained by solving the equation:

$$\lambda^2 - Q_1 \lambda + Q_2 = 0, \tag{4}$$

where $Q_1 = -\frac{Ac_0\tilde{p}}{(\tilde{c}+c_0)^2} - \frac{\delta c_2 \tilde{p}}{(\tilde{c}+c_2)^2} - m - \gamma\tilde{p} < 0$ and $Q_2 = \gamma\tilde{p}\left[\frac{Ac_0\tilde{p}}{(\tilde{c}+c_0)^2} + \frac{\delta c_2 \tilde{p}}{(\tilde{c}+c_2)^2} + m\right] - \frac{Bc_1 m\tilde{c}}{(\tilde{c}+c_1)^2} > 0$.

Hence, we have the following theorem:

Theorem 3. $E_1(\tilde{c}, \tilde{p}, 0)$ is LAS if $\left(\frac{\eta\tilde{c}^2}{\tilde{c}^2+c_4^2}\right)\frac{a\tilde{p}^2}{ah\tilde{p}^2+\tilde{p}_2+g} - \mu < 0$.

The Jacobian matrix $\widehat{J}$ at $\widehat{E}(\widehat{c}, \widehat{p}, \widehat{z})$ is given by:

$$\widehat{J} = \begin{bmatrix} a_{11} & a_{12} & a_{13} \\ a_{21} & a_{22} & a_{23} \\ a_{31} & a_{32} & a_{33} \end{bmatrix}$$

where $a_{11} = -\frac{Ac_0\widehat{p}}{(\widehat{c}+c_0)^2} - \frac{\delta c_2\widehat{p}}{(\widehat{c}+c_2)^2} - \frac{vc_3\widehat{z}}{(\widehat{c}+c_3)^2} - m < 0$, $a_{12} = -\frac{\delta \widehat{c}}{\widehat{c}+c_2} + \frac{Ac_0}{\widehat{c}+c_0} = \frac{\widehat{c}}{\widehat{p}}\left\{\frac{v\widehat{z}}{\widehat{c}+c_3} + m\right\} > 0$, $a_{13} = -\frac{v\widehat{c}}{\widehat{c}+c_3} < 0$, $a_{21} = \frac{Bc_1\widehat{p}}{(\widehat{c}+c_1)^2} > 0$, $a_{22} = \frac{B\widehat{c}}{\widehat{c}+c_1} - 2\gamma\widehat{p} - \frac{a\widehat{p}\widehat{z}(\widehat{p}+2g)}{(ah\widehat{p}^2+\widehat{p}+g)^2} - \sigma = -\gamma\widehat{p} - \frac{a\widehat{p}\widehat{z}(g-ah\widehat{p}^2)}{(ah\widehat{p}^2+\widehat{p}+g)^2}$, $a_{23} = -\frac{a\widehat{p}^2}{ah\widehat{p}^2+\widehat{p}+g} < 0$, $a_{31} = \frac{2\eta c_4^2\widehat{c}}{(\widehat{c}^2+c_4^2)^2}\frac{a\widehat{p}^2\widehat{z}}{ah\widehat{p}^2+\widehat{p}+g} > 0$, $a_{32} = \frac{\eta \widehat{c}^2}{(\widehat{c}^2+c_4^2)}\frac{a\widehat{p}\widehat{z}(\widehat{p}+2g)}{(ah\widehat{p}^2+\widehat{p}+g)^2} > 0$ and $a_{33} = 0$.

The characteristic equation corresponding to $\widehat{E}(\widehat{c}, \widehat{p}, \widehat{z})$ is

$$\lambda^3 + C_1\lambda^2 + C_2\lambda + C_3 = 0$$

where $C_1 = -(a_{11} + a_{22})$, $C_2 = -a_{23}a_{32} - a_{13}a_{31} + a_{11}a_{22} - a_{12}a_{21}$, and $C_3 = -\{-a_{11}a_{23}a_{32} + a_{12}a_{23}a_{31} + a_{13}(a_{21}a_{32} - a_{22}a_{31})\}$.

By Routh-Hurwitz's criteria [14], $\widehat{E}(\widehat{c}, \widehat{p}, \widehat{z})$ has three eigenvalues with negative real parts if $C_1 > 0$, $C_3 > 0$, and $C_1C_2 > C_3$. So, the local stability condition of $\widehat{E}(\widehat{c}, \widehat{p}, \widehat{z})$ is described in the following theorem:

Theorem 4. $\widehat{E}(\widehat{c}, \widehat{p}, \widehat{z})$ is LAS if $a_{22} < 0$ and $a_{11}a_{22} > a_{12}a_{21}$.

5. Local Bifurcations

A local bifurcation occurs when a parameter change causes the stability (or instability) of an equilibrium (or fixed point) to change. In continuous systems, this corresponds to the real part of an eigenvalue of an equilibrium passing through zero.

5.1. Transcritical Bifurcation

Theorem 5. *System (1) undergoes a transcritical bifurcation if* $\mu^{[tc]} = \left(\frac{\eta\widetilde{c}^2}{\widetilde{c}^2+c_4^2}\right)\frac{a\widetilde{p}^2}{ah\widetilde{p}^2+\widetilde{p}+g}$.

Proof. To prove a transcritical bifurcation, we apply Sotomayor's theorem [14] by considering μ as the bifurcation parameter. According to this theorem, one eigenvalue of J_1 at the bifurcation point must be zero.

The eigenvectors of $J_1 = [p_{ij}]$ and $(J_1)^T$ corresponding to the zero eigenvalue are obtained as: $V = (0, v_2, 1)^T$ and $W = (0, 0, 1)^T$, respectively, where $v_2 = -\frac{p_{13}}{p_{12}}$ and $p_{11} = -\frac{Ac_0\widetilde{p}}{(\widetilde{c}+c_0)^2} - \frac{\delta c_2\widetilde{p}}{(\widetilde{c}+c_2)^2} - m$, $p_{12} = \frac{m\widetilde{c}}{\widetilde{p}}$, $p_{13} = -\frac{v\widetilde{c}}{\widetilde{c}+c_3}$, $p_{21} = \frac{Bc_1\widetilde{p}}{(\widetilde{c}+c_1)^2}$, $p_{22} = -\gamma\widetilde{p}$, $p_{23} = -\frac{a\widetilde{p}^2}{ah\widetilde{p}^2+\widetilde{p}+g}$, and $p_{31} = p_{32} = p_{33} = 0$.

Compute Δ_1, Δ_2, and Δ_3 as follows:

$$\Delta_1 = W^T \cdot F_\mu\left(\widetilde{c}, \widetilde{p}, 0; \mu^{[tc]}\right) = (0, 0, 1) \cdot \begin{pmatrix} \frac{\partial F_1}{\partial \mu} \\ \frac{\partial F_2}{\partial \mu} \\ \frac{\partial F_3}{\partial \mu} \end{pmatrix}_{(E_1(\widetilde{c},\widetilde{p},0); \mu^{[tc]})}$$

$$\Rightarrow \Delta_1 = (0, 0, 1) \cdot \begin{pmatrix} 0 \\ 0 \\ -z \end{pmatrix}_{(E_1(\widetilde{c},\widetilde{p},0); \mu^{[tc]})} = 0,$$

where $F = (F_1, F_2, F_3)^T$, and F_1, F_2, and F_3 are given by:

$$F_1 = \frac{Ac_0p}{c+c_0} - \frac{\delta cp}{c+c_2} - \frac{vcz}{c+c_3} - mc,$$

$$F_2 = \left(\frac{Bc}{c+c_1} - \gamma p\right)p - \frac{ap^2z}{ahp^2+p+g} - \sigma p,$$

$$F_3 = \left(\frac{\eta c^2}{c^2+c_4^2}\right) \cdot \frac{ap^2z}{ahp^2+p+g} - \mu z.$$

$$\Delta_2 = W^T \cdot \left[DF_\mu\left(\tilde{c}, \tilde{p}, 0; \mu^{[tc]}\right)V\right] = (0,0,1) \cdot \begin{bmatrix} \frac{\partial^2 F_1}{\partial c \partial \mu} & \frac{\partial^2 F_1}{\partial p \partial \mu} & \frac{\partial^2 F_1}{\partial z \partial \mu} \\ \frac{\partial^2 F_2}{\partial c \partial \mu} & \frac{\partial^2 F_2}{\partial p \partial \mu} & \frac{\partial^2 F_2}{\partial z \partial \mu} \\ \frac{\partial^2 F_3}{\partial c \partial \mu} & \frac{\partial^2 F_3}{\partial p \partial \mu} & \frac{\partial^2 F_3}{\partial z \partial \mu} \end{bmatrix}_{(E_1(\tilde{c},\tilde{p},0);\mu^{[tc]})} \cdot \begin{pmatrix} 0 \\ v_2 \\ 1 \end{pmatrix}$$

$$\Rightarrow \Delta_2 = (0,0,1) \cdot \begin{bmatrix} 0 & 0 & 0 \\ 0 & 0 & 0 \\ 0 & 0 & -1 \end{bmatrix}_{(E_1(\tilde{c},\tilde{p},0);\mu^{[tc]})} \cdot \begin{pmatrix} 0 \\ v_2 \\ 1 \end{pmatrix} = -1 \neq 0.$$

$$\Delta_3 = W^T \cdot \left[D^2 F\left(\tilde{c}, \tilde{p}, 0; \mu^{[tc]}\right)(V, V)\right] = (0,0,1) \cdot D \begin{pmatrix} \frac{\partial F_1}{\partial c}v_1 + \frac{\partial F_1}{\partial p}v_2 + \frac{\partial F_1}{\partial z}v_3 \\ \frac{\partial F_2}{\partial c}v_1 + \frac{\partial F_2}{\partial p}v_2 + \frac{\partial F_2}{\partial z}v_3 \\ \frac{\partial F_3}{\partial c}v_1 + \frac{\partial F_3}{\partial p}v_2 + \frac{\partial F_3}{\partial z}v_3 \end{pmatrix}_{(E_1(\tilde{c},\tilde{p},0);\mu^{[tc]})} \cdot \begin{pmatrix} v_1 \\ v_2 \\ v_3 \end{pmatrix}$$

$$\Rightarrow \Delta_3 = (0,0,1) \cdot \begin{pmatrix} \frac{\partial^2 F_1}{\partial^2 c}v_1^2 + \frac{\partial^2 F_1}{\partial^2 p}v_2^2 + \frac{\partial^2 F_1}{\partial^2 z}v_3^2 + 2\frac{\partial^2 F_1}{\partial c \partial p}v_1 v_2 + 2\frac{\partial^2 F_1}{\partial c \partial z}v_1 v_3 + 2\frac{\partial^2 F_1}{\partial p \partial z}v_2 v_3 \\ \frac{\partial^2 F_2}{\partial^2 x}v_1^2 + \frac{\partial^2 F_2}{\partial^2 y}v_2^2 + \frac{\partial^2 F_2}{\partial^2 z}v_3^2 + 2\frac{\partial^2 F_2}{\partial x \partial y}v_1 v_2 + 2\frac{\partial^2 F_2}{\partial x \partial z}v_1 v_3 + 2\frac{\partial^2 F_2}{\partial y \partial z}v_2 v_3 \\ \frac{\partial^2 F_3}{\partial^2 x}v_1^2 + \frac{\partial^2 F_3}{\partial^2 y}v_2^2 + \frac{\partial^2 F_3}{\partial^2 z}v_3^2 + 2\frac{\partial^2 F_3}{\partial x \partial y}v_1 v_2 + 2\frac{\partial^2 F_3}{\partial x \partial z}v_1 v_3 + 2\frac{\partial^2 F_3}{\partial y \partial z}v_2 v_3 \end{pmatrix}_{(E_1(\tilde{c},\tilde{p},0);\mu^{[tc]})}$$

$$\Rightarrow \Delta_3 = \frac{2a\tilde{p}(\tilde{p}+2g)}{(ah\tilde{p}^2+\tilde{p}+g)^2} \times \frac{\eta \tilde{c}^2}{(\tilde{c}^2+c_4^2)} v_2 \neq 0.$$

Thus, by Sotomayor's theorem [14], system (1) exhibits a trancritical bifurcation at $\mu = \mu^{[tc]}$. □

Remark 1. *Similarly, it can be proved that system (1) exhibits transcritical bifurcations taking any one of the parameters h, σ, m, η, a, and γ as a bifurcation parameter.*

5.2. Hopf-Bifurcation

The characteristic equation of system (1) at $\widehat{E}(\hat{c}, \hat{p}, \hat{z})$ is given by

$$\lambda^3 + C_1(A)\lambda^2 + C_2(A)\lambda + C_3(A) = 0, \tag{5}$$

where $C_i(A)$ for $i = 1, 2, 3$ were defined earlier.

To determine the Hopf-bifurcation around $\widehat{E}(\hat{c}, \hat{p}, \hat{z})$ of system (1), let us consider A as the bifurcation parameter. For this purpose, let us first state the following Theorem:

Theorem 6 (Hopf-Bifurcation Theorem [15]). *If $C_1(A)$, $C_2(A)$, and $C_3(A)$ are continuously differentiable functions of A in a small neighbourhood of $A^{[H]} \in \mathbb{R}$ such that Equation (5) has:*
(i) a pair of imaginary eigenvalues $\lambda = p_1(A) \pm ip_2(A)$ with $p_1(A) \in \mathbb{R}$, $p_2(A) \in \mathbb{R}$, so that they become purely imaginary at $A = A^{[H]}$ and $\frac{dp_1}{dA}|_{A=A^{[H]}} \neq 0$,
(ii) the other eigenvalue is negative at $A = A^{[H]}$, then a Hopf-bifurcation occurs around $\widehat{E}(\hat{c}, \hat{p}, \hat{z})$ at $A = A^{[H]}$ (i.e., a stability change of $\widehat{E}(\hat{c}, \hat{p}, \hat{z})$ accompanied by the creation of a limit cycle at $A = A^{[H]}$).

Theorem 7. *System (1) possesses a Hopf-bifurcation around $\widehat{E}(\hat{c}, \hat{p}, \hat{z})$ when A passes through $A^{[H]}$, provided $C_1(A^{[H]}) > 0$, $C_3(A^{[H]}) > 0$, and $C_1(A^{[H]})C_2(A^{[H]}) = C_3(A^{[H]})$.*

Proof. At $A = A^{[H]}$, the roots of the equation:

$$\left(\lambda^2 + C_2\right)(\lambda + C_1) = 0$$

are $\lambda_1 = i\sqrt{C_2}$, $\lambda_2 = -i\sqrt{C_2}$, and $\lambda_3 = -C_1$, where C_1, C_2 and C_3 are differential functions of A. Furthermore, in the deleted neighborhood of $A^{[H]}$, the roots (eigenvalues) are $\lambda_1(A) = p_1(A) + ip_2(A)$, $\lambda_2(A) = p_1(A) - ip_2(A)$, and $\lambda_3 = p_3(A)$ $(p_3(A) = -C_1)$, where $p_i(A)$ are real for $i = 1, 2, 3$.

Now, we will verify the transversality condition:

$$\frac{d}{dA}(Re\ \lambda_i(A))\bigg|_{A=A^{[H]}} \neq 0,\ i = 1, 2.$$

Substituting $\lambda(A) = p_1(A) + ip_2(A)$ into the characteristic Equation (5), we have:

$$(p_1 + ip_2)^3 + C_1(A)(p_1 + ip_2)^2 + C_2(A)(p_1 + ip_2) + C_3(A) = 0 \tag{6}$$

Differentiating with regard to A, we have:

$$3(p_1 + ip_2)^2(\dot{p}_1 + i\dot{p}_2) + 2C_1(p_1 + ip_2)(\dot{p}_1 + i\dot{p}_2) + \dot{C}_1(p_1 + ip_2)^2 \\ + C_2(\dot{p}_1 + i\dot{p}_2) + \dot{C}_2(p_1 + ip_2) + \dot{C}_3 = 0 \tag{7}$$

Comparing the real and imaginary parts, we obtain:

$$X_1\dot{p}_1 - X_2\dot{p}_2 + X_3 = 0 \tag{8}$$

and

$$X_2\dot{p}_1 + X_1\dot{p}_2 + X_4 = 0 \tag{9}$$

where

$$\begin{aligned} X_1 &= 3\left(p_1^2 - p_2^2\right) + 2C_1 p_1 + C_2 \\ X_2 &= 6p_1 p_2 + 2C_1 p_2 \\ X_3 &= \dot{C}_1\left(p_1^2 - p_2^2\right) + \dot{C}_2 p_1 + \dot{C}_3 \\ X_4 &= 2\dot{C}_1 p_1 p_2 + \dot{C}_2 p_2. \end{aligned}$$

From (8) and (9), we obtain:

$$\dot{p}_1 = -\frac{(X_1 X_3 + X_2 X_4)}{X_1^2 + X_2^2}.$$

Now,

$$X_3 = \dot{C}_1\left(p_1^2 - p_2^2\right) + \dot{C}_2 p_1 + \dot{C}_3 \neq \dot{C}_1\left(p_1^2 - p_2^2\right) + \dot{C}_2 p_1 + \dot{C}_1 C_2 + C_1 \dot{C}_2$$

[since $C_3 \neq C_1 C_2$ in a deleted neighborhood of $A^{[H]}$]

At $A = A^{[H]}$,

- **Case 1:** $p_1 = 0, p_2 = \sqrt{C_2}$
  $X_1 = -2C_2, X_2 = 2C_1\sqrt{C_2}, X_3 \neq C_1 \dot{C}_2, X_4 = \sqrt{C_2}\dot{C}_2$
  Therefore, $X_2 X_4 + X_1 X_3 \neq 2C_1 C_2 \dot{C}_2 - 2C_1 C_2 \dot{C}_2 = 0$
  So, $X_2 X_4 + X_1 X_3 \neq 0$ at $A = A^{[H]}$, when $p_1 = 0, p_2 = \sqrt{C_2}$.
- **Case 2:** $p_1 = 0, p_2 = -\sqrt{C_2}$
  $X_1 = -2C_2, X_2 = -2C_1\sqrt{C_2}, X_3 \neq C_1 \dot{C}_2, X_4 = -\sqrt{C_2}\dot{C}_2$
  So, $X_2 X_4 + x_1 X_3 \neq 2C_1 C_2 \dot{C}_2 - 2C_1 C_2 \dot{C}_2 = 0$
  So, $X_2 X_4 + X_1 X_3 \neq 0$ at $A = A^{[H]}$, when $p_1 = 0, p_2 = -\sqrt{C_2}$.
  $\therefore \frac{d}{dA}(Re\ \lambda_i(A))\big|_{A=A^{[H]}} \neq 0$, for $i = 1, 2$ and $p_3(A^{[H]}) = -C_1(A^{[H]}) < 0$.
  Hence, Theorem 7 is proved using Theorem 6. □

Note: *Imaginary eigenvalues are connected with any molecular process (e.g., collisions) and the reverse of that process [16].*

Remark 2. *Similarly, system (1) undergoes Hopf-bifurcations around $\hat{E}(\hat{c}, \hat{p}, \hat{z})$ taking any one of the parameters a, g, h, m, η, σ, and μ as a bifurcation parameter.*

6. Numerical Simulations

Here, numerical simulations were performed to verify the analytical outcomes of the oxygen-plankton model (1). We are mainly interested in the existence and stability analysis of the interior equilibrium point $\hat{E}(\hat{c}, \hat{p}, \hat{z})$. For this purpose, we fixed most of the parameters as follows:

$$\{c_0 = 1, \delta = 1, c_2 = 1, m = 0.5, B = 1.8, c_1 = 1.0, \gamma = 0.7, \sigma = 0.1, \nu = 0.01, \mu = 0.1,$$
$$h = 1.2, a = 3.0, \eta = 0.7, c_4 = 1, g = 0.3, c_3 = 1\}, \quad (10)$$

but varied A in a broad range. For the existence of $\hat{E}(\hat{c}, \hat{p}, \hat{z})$, we always take $A \geq B$ (otherwise, it does not exist; see Figure 3), it is also ecologically meaningful. If we choose $A = 1.8$, and the other parameters are selected from set (10), then, the interior equilibrium $\hat{E}(\hat{c}, \hat{p}, \hat{z}) \equiv \hat{E}(0.682267, 0.515313, 0.30855)$ exists uniquely and is locally asymptotically stable (LAS). Figure 4 depicts the stable nature of $\hat{E}(0.682267, 0.515313, 0.30855)$. If we increase A from 1.8 to 2 keeping the others fixed as in set (10), then $\hat{E}(\hat{c}, \hat{p}, \hat{z})$ is destabilized through Hopf-bifurcation. Figure 5 shows the oscillatory nature of system (1) around $\hat{E}(0.710824, 0.473597, 0.352043)$. If we take a very large value of $A (= 10)$, choosing the other parameters from set (10), then system (1) again enters into a stable interior equilibrium by excluding the existence of a periodic solution. Figure 6 presents the stability nature of $\hat{E}(\hat{c}, \hat{p}, \hat{z}) \equiv \hat{E}(1.48635, 0.218551, 0.866809)$ of system (1) when $A = 10$. In this manner, we have found two thresholds for the parameter A: when $1.8 \leq A < A^{[H]_1} = 1.966532$ (threshold value) and $A > A^{[H]_2} = 7.258206$ (threshold value), a stable interior equilibrium exists; when $A^{[H]_1} = 1.966532 < A < A^{[H]_2} = 7.258206$, the interior equilibrium becomes unstable, and a Hopf-bifurcation occurs, leading to the occurrence of a stable periodic solution (see Figures 7 and 8). Moreover, comparing Figures 6 and 9, we found that for very large values of A, the interior equilibrium of system (1) exists, but it does not exist in the plankton–oxygen model system analyzed by Sekerci and Petrovskii [3]. This is the main difference between the proposed system (1) and the model studied by Sekerci and Petrovskii [3] (it is shown that the coexistence steady state exists unless A is too large or too small).

Again, if we increase μ (the mortality rate of the zooplankton) from 0.1 to 0.5 selecting other parameters from Figure 4, the zooplankton population can not persist in the marine ecosystem. Therefore, the coexistence steady state $\hat{E}(\hat{c}, \hat{p}, \hat{z})$ goes to zooplankton free equilibrium $E_1(\tilde{c}, \tilde{p}, 0)$. Under the parametric values: $\{A = 1.8, c_0 = 1, \delta = 1, c_2 = 1, m = 0.5, B = 1.8, c_1 = 1.0, \gamma = 0.7, \sigma = 0.1, \nu = 0.01, \mu = 0.5, h = 1.2, a = 3.0, \eta = 0.7, c_4 = 1, g = 0.3,$ and $c_3 = 1\}$, we have obtained two planer equilibrium points $E_1^{(1)}(0.0680515, 0.0209829, 0)$ and $E_1^{(2)}(0.958588, 1.11567, 0)$. Here, $E_1^{(2)}(0.958588, 1.11567, 0)$ is LAS but $E_1^{(1)}(0.0680515, 0.0209829, 0)$ is a saddle (unstable). Figure 10a depicts the stable behaviour of $E_1^{(2)}(0.958588, 1.11567, 0)$. Similarly, if we take $A = 10$ (large), but the other parameters remain the same as in Figure 10a, then we have also obtained two planer equilibria $E_1^{(1)}(0.0602258, 0.00321199, 0)$ and $E_1^{(2)}(4.24865, 1.93865, 0)$, where $E_1^{(2)}(4.24865, 1.93865, 0)$ is LAS (see Figure 10b), but $E_1^{(1)}(0.0602258, 0.00321199, 0)$ is a saddle.

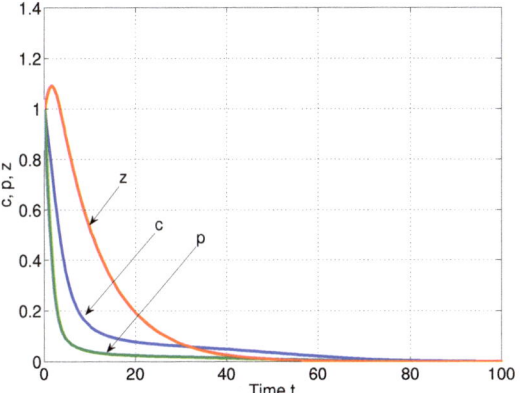

Figure 3. $\widehat{E}(\widehat{c}, \widehat{p}, \widehat{z})$ of system (1) does not exist when $A = 1.7 < B = 1.8$ and the remaining parameters are chosen from set (10), i.e., the dynamics of the system (1) change abruptly, resulting in oxygen depletion and plankton extinction for a small value of A.

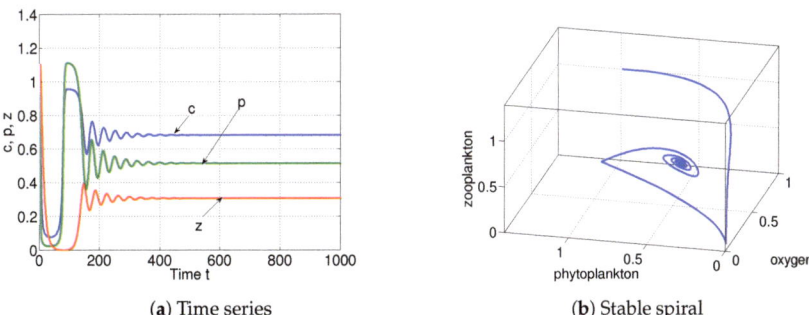

(**a**) Time series (**b**) Stable spiral

Figure 4. The stable nature of $\widehat{E}(\widehat{c}, \widehat{p}, \widehat{z}) \equiv \widehat{E}(0.682267, 0.515313, 0.30855)$ of system (1) under the parametric set: $\{A = 1.8, c_0 = 1, \delta = 1, c_2 = 1, m = 0.5, B = 1.8, c_1 = 1.0, \gamma = 0.7, \sigma = 0.1, \nu = 0.01, \mu = 0.1, h = 1.2, a = 3.0, \eta = 0.7, c_4 = 1, g = 0.3,$ and $c_3 = 1\}$. Initial conditions: $c(0) = p(0) = z(0) = 1$.

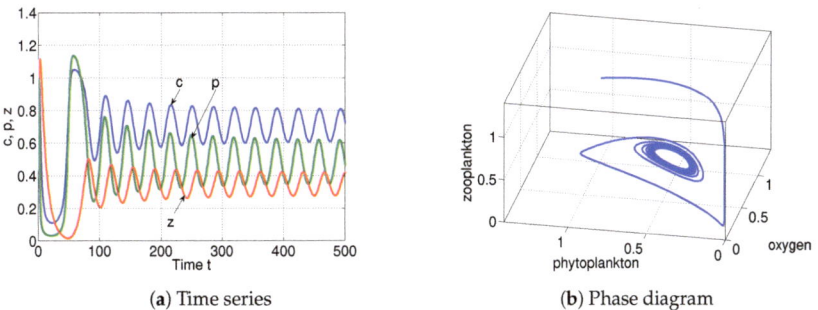

(**a**) Time series (**b**) Phase diagram

Figure 5. Oscillatory nature of system (1) around $\widehat{E}(0.710824, 0.473597, 0.352043)$, when $A = 2$ and the remaining parameters are same as in Figure 4. Initial conditions: $c(0) = p(0) = z(0) = 1$.

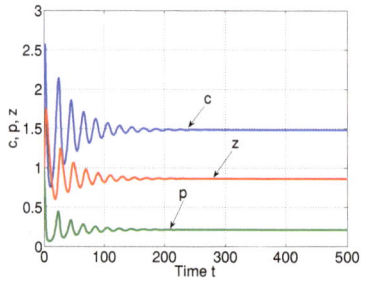
(a) Time series

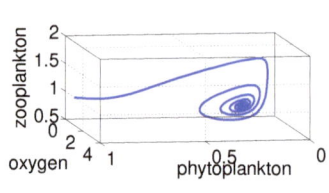
(b) Stable spiral

Figure 6. The stable nature of $\hat{E}(\hat{c}, \hat{p}, \hat{z}) \equiv \hat{E}(1.48635, 0.218551, 0.866809)$ of system (1), when $A = 10$ and the remaining parameters are same as in Figure 4. Initial conditions: $c(0) = p(0) = z(0) = 1$.

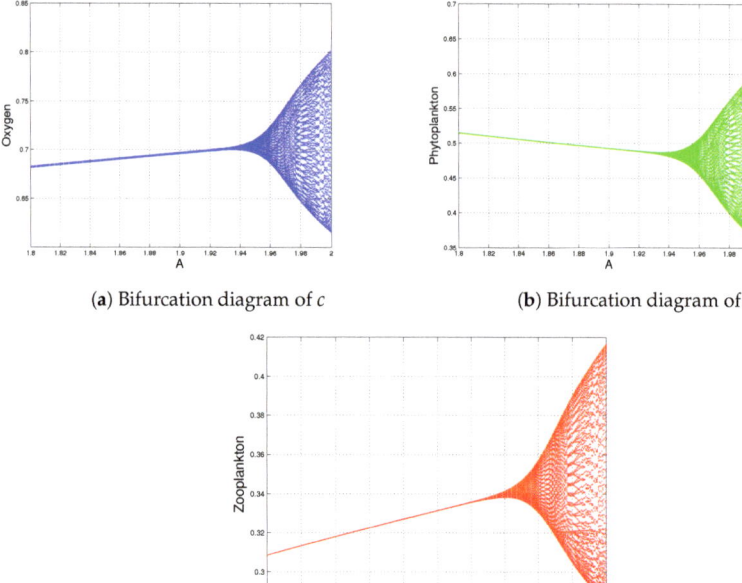

(a) Bifurcation diagram of c

(b) Bifurcation diagram of p

(c) Bifurcation diagram of z

Figure 7. Hopf-bifurcation diagrams of $\hat{E}(\hat{c}, \hat{p}, \hat{z})$ of system (1) while A varies in the interval $[1.8, 2]$ and the others remain unchanged as in Figure 6. Here, $A = A^{[H]_1} = 1.966532$.

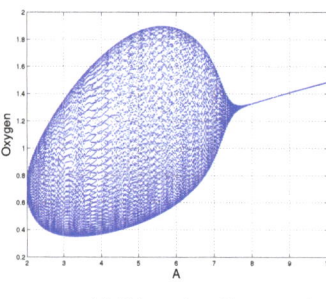
(a) Bifurcation diagram of c

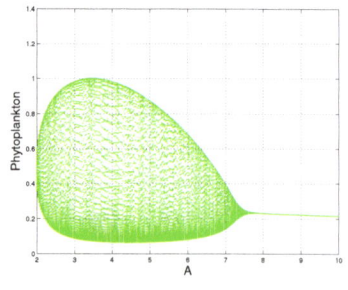
(b) Bifurcation diagram of p

Figure 8. Cont.

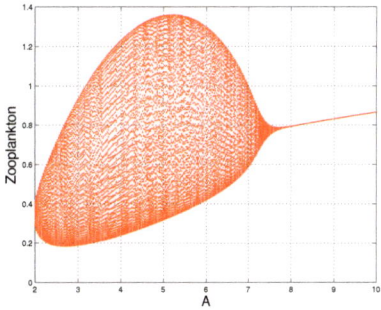

(c) Bifurcation diagram of z

Figure 8. Hopf-bifurcation diagrams of $\widehat{E}(\hat{c}, \hat{p}, \hat{z})$ of system (1) while A varies in the interval $[2, 10]$ and the others remain unchanged as in Figure 6. Here, $A = A^{[H]_2} = 7.258206$.

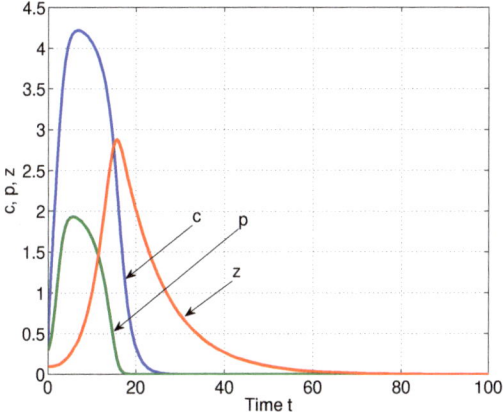

Figure 9. Interior equilibrium of the plankton–oxygen model studied by Sekerci and Petrovskii [3] does not exist under the parametric set: $\{A = 10, c_0 = 1, \delta = 1, c_2 = 1, m = 0.5, B = 1.8, c_1 = 1.0, \gamma = 0.7, \sigma = 0.1, \nu = 0.01, \mu = 0.5, h = 1.2, s = 1.0, \eta = 0.7, c_4 = 1, \text{ and } c_3 = 1\}$. Initial conditions: $c(0) = 0.385, p(0) = 0.3, z(0) = 0.1$.

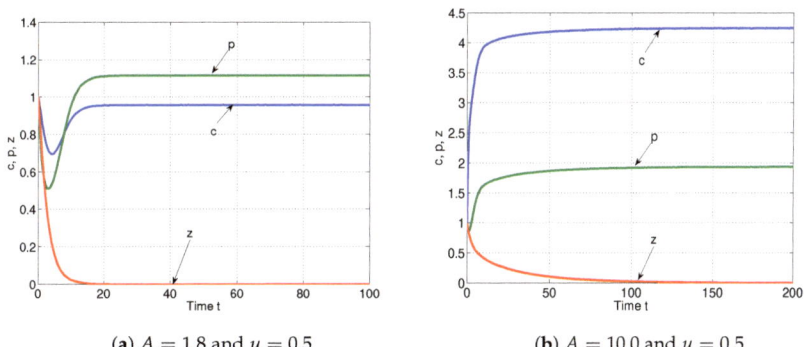

(**a**) $A = 1.8$ and $\mu = 0.5$ (**b**) $A = 10.0$ and $\mu = 0.5$

Figure 10. The stable nature of (**a**) $E_1^{(2)}(2.04036, 1.58281, 0)$ and (**b**) $E_1^{(2)}(4.24865, 1.93865, 0)$ of system (1) when the remaining parameters are same as in Figure 6. Initial conditions: $c(0) = p(0) = z(0) = 1$.

The qualitative nature of different steady states corresponding to bifurcation parameters σ, h, μ and m are depicted in Figures 11–14 respectively (for details see Table 2). Also, the qualitative nature of different steady states corresponding to bifurcation parameters g, η, a and γ are presented in Figures 15–18 respectively (for details see Table 2).

Table 2. Nature of the steady states when the parameters are chosen from Figure 6. Here, 'H' stands for the Hopf-bifurcation point, and 'tc' stands for the transcritical bifurcation point.

Bifurcation Parameter	Bifurcation Points	Nature of Equilibria
σ	$\sigma^{[H]} = 0.4216$ and $\sigma^{[tc]} = 0.4363$ (Figure 11)	$\widehat{E}$ is stable when $0 < \sigma < 0.4216$ $\widehat{E}$ is destabilized through Hopf-bifurcation when $0.4216 < \sigma < 0.4363$ $\widehat{E}$ goes to trivial equilibrium $E_0(0,0,0)$ when $\sigma > 0.4363$
h	$h^{[H]_1} = 1.442503$, $h^{[H]_2} = 5.917323$ and $h^{[tc]} = 6.434018$ (Figure 12)	$\widehat{E}$ is stable when $0 < h < 1.442503$ and $5.917323 < h < 6.434018$ $\widehat{E}$ is destabilized through Hopf-bifurcation when $1.442503 < h < 5.917323$ $\widehat{E}$ goes to stable zooplankton free equilibrium $E_1(\widetilde{c}, \widetilde{p}, 0)$ when $h > 6.434018$
μ	$\mu^{[H]_1} = 0.1311580$, $\mu^{[H]_2} = 0.354676$ and $\mu^{[tc]} = 0.474246$ (Figure 13)	$\widehat{E}$ is stable when $0 < \mu < 0.1311580$ and $0.354676 < \mu < 0.474246$ $\widehat{E}$ is destabilized through Hopf-bifurcation when $0.1311580 < \mu < 0.354676$ $\widehat{E}$ goes to stable zooplankton free equilibrium $E_1(\widetilde{c}, \widetilde{p}, 0)$ when $\mu > 0.474246$
m	$m^{[H]} = 0.6533$ and $m^{[tc]} = 2.287$ (Figure 14)	$\widehat{E}$ is stable when $0 < m < 0.6533$ $\widehat{E}$ is destabilized through Hopf-bifurcation when $0.6533 < m < 2.287$ $\widehat{E}$ goes to $E_0(0,0,0)$ when $m > 2.287$
g	$g^{[H]} = 0.226067$ (Figure 15)	$\widehat{E}$ is destabilized through Hopf-bifurcation when $0.09 < g < g^{[H]}$ (if $0 < g < 0.09$, $E_0(0,0,0)$ exists) $\widehat{E}$ is stable spiral when $g > g^{[H]}$
η	$\eta^{[tc]} = 0.147603$, $\eta^{[H]_1} = 0.198177$ and $\eta^{[H]_2} = 0.530864$ (Figure 16)	E_1 (zooplankton free equilibrium) is stable when $0 < \eta < \eta^{[tc]}$ $\widehat{E}$ is stable when $0.147603 < \eta < 0.198177$ and $0.530864 < \eta < 1$ $\widehat{E}$ is destabilized through Hopf-bifurcation when $0.198177 < \eta < 0.530864$
a	$a^{[tc]} = 0.109643$ and $a^{[H]} = 5.325675$ (Figure 17)	E_1 (zooplankton free equilibrium) is stable when $0 < a < a^{[tc]}$ $\widehat{E}$ is stable when $0.109643 < a < 5.325675$ $\widehat{E}$ is destabilized through Hopf-bifurcation when $a > 5.325675$
γ	$\gamma^{[tc]} = 4.479066$ (Figure 18)	$\widehat{E}$ exists and is stable when $0 < \gamma < \gamma^{[tc]}$ $\widehat{E}$ goes to stable zooplankton free equilibrium E_1 when $\gamma > \gamma^{[tc]}$

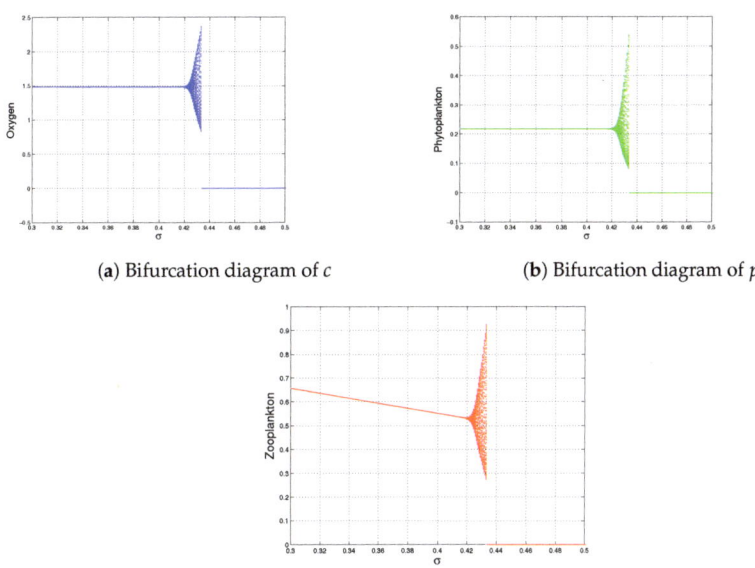

(a) Bifurcation diagram of c

(b) Bifurcation diagram of p

(c) Bifurcation diagram of z

Figure 11. Bifurcation diagrams of system (1) taking σ as the bifurcation parameter, while the others remain unchanged, as in Figure 6. Here, $\widehat{E}(\widehat{c}, \widehat{p}, \widehat{z})$ is stable when $\sigma \in (0.0, \sigma^{[H]} = 0.4216)$ and unstable with a periodic solution when $\sigma \in (0.4216, 0.4363)$. When σ (mortality rate of phytoplankton) $> 0.4363 = \sigma^{[tc]}$, the system dynamics change abruptly, resulting in the depletion of oxygen and the extinction of plankton in the marine ecosystem.

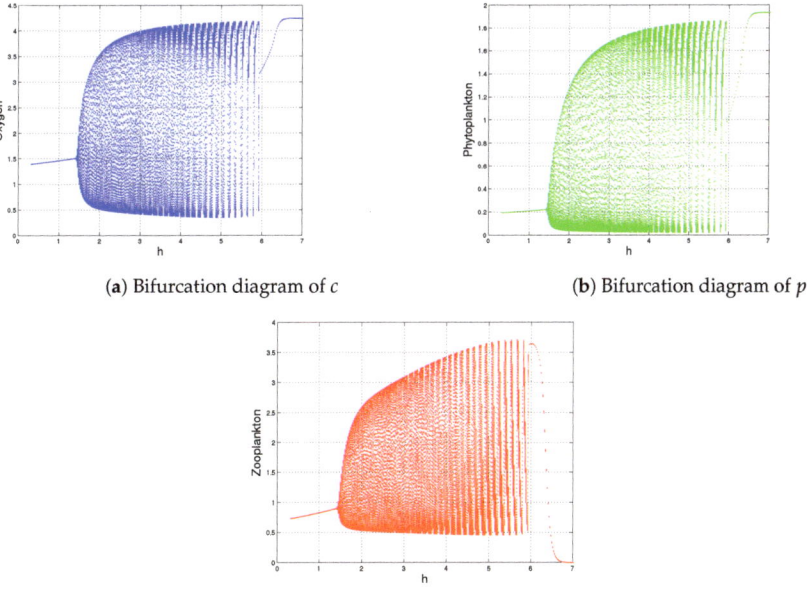

(a) Bifurcation diagram of c

(b) Bifurcation diagram of p

(c) Bifurcation diagram of z

Figure 12. Bifurcation diagrams of system (1) taking h as the bifurcation parameter, while the others remain unchange,d as in Figure 6. Here, $\widehat{E}(\widehat{c}, \widehat{p}, \widehat{z})$ is stable when $h \in (0.0, h^{[H]_1} = 1.442503) \cup (5.917323, h^{[tc]} = 6.434018)$ and unstable with a periodic solution when $h \in (1.442503, h^{[H]_2} = 5.917323)$. Again, $\widehat{E}(\widehat{c}, \widehat{p}, \widehat{z})$ goes to stable zooplankton free equilibrium $E_1(\widetilde{c}, \widetilde{p}, 0)$ when $h > h^{[tc]} = 6.434018$.

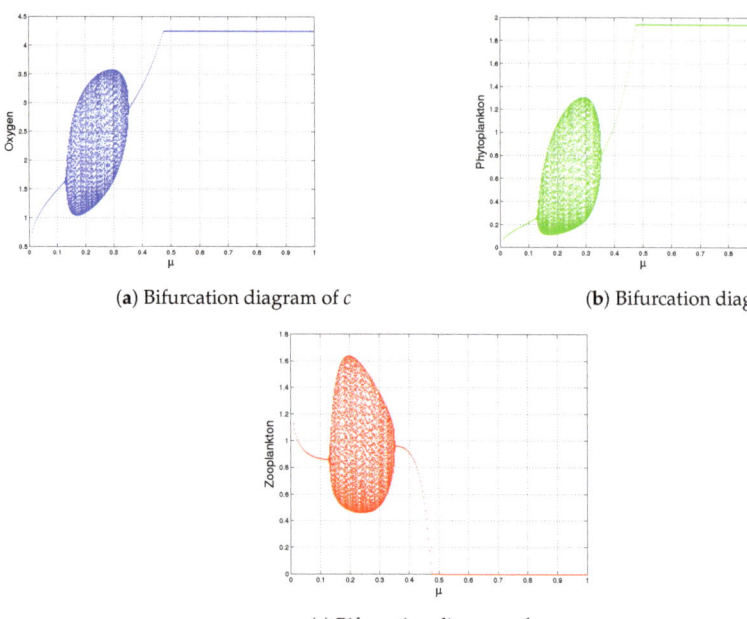

Figure 13. Bifurcation diagram of system (1) taking μ as the bifurcation parameter, while the others remain unchanged, as in Figure 6. $\widehat{E}(\widehat{c},\widehat{p},\widehat{z})$ is unstable with a periodic solution when $\mu \in (\mu^{[H]_1} = 0.131580, \mu^{[H]_2} = 0.354676)$ and stable when $\mu \in (0, 0.131580) \cup (0.354676, 0.474246)$. Again, $\widehat{E}(\widehat{c},\widehat{p},\widehat{z})$ goes to stable zooplankton free equilibrium $E_1(\widetilde{c},\widetilde{p},0)$ when $\mu > \mu^{[tc]} = 0.474246$.

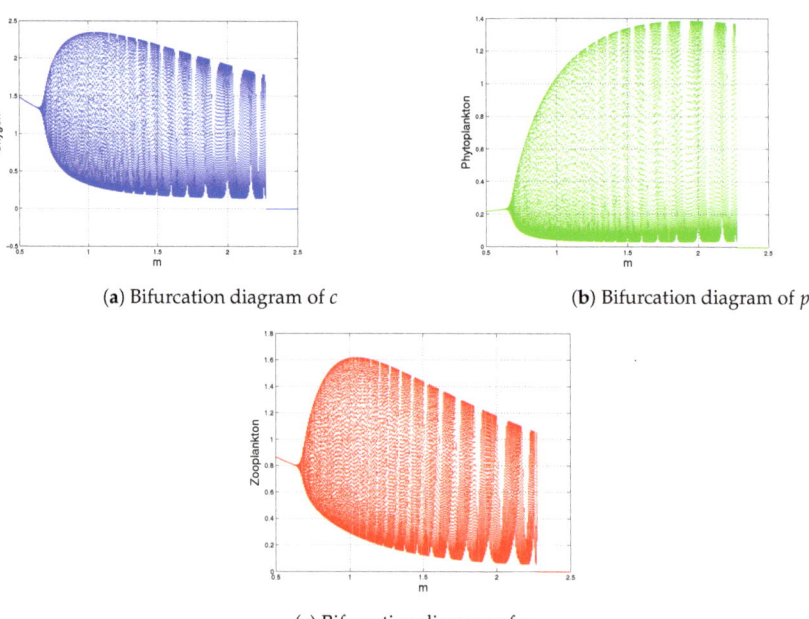

Figure 14. Bifurcation diagrams of system (1) taking m as the bifurcation parameter, while the others remain unchanged, as in Figure 6. Here, $\widehat{E}(\widehat{c},\widehat{p},\widehat{z})$ is stable when $m \in (0.0, m^{[H]} = 0.6533)$ and unstable with a periodic solution when $m \in (0.6533, 2.287)$. When $m > m^{[tc]} = 2.287$, trivial equilibrium $E_0 = (0,0,0)$ exists corresponding to the depletion of oxygen and the extinction of plankton.

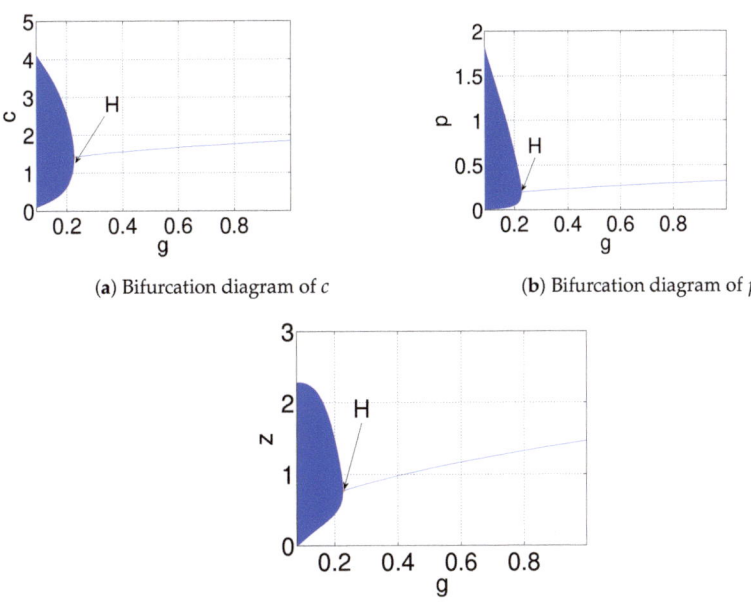

(a) Bifurcation diagram of c

(b) Bifurcation diagram of p

(c) Bifurcation diagram of z

Figure 15. Bifurcation diagrams of system (1) while g varies from $[0.09, 1]$ and the others remain unchanged, as in Figure 6. Here, the interior equilibrium $\widehat{E}(\hat{c}, \hat{p}, \hat{z})$ is unstable with a periodic solution when $g \in [0.09, g^{[H]} = 0.226067)$ and stable when $g > g^{[H]} = 0.226067$.

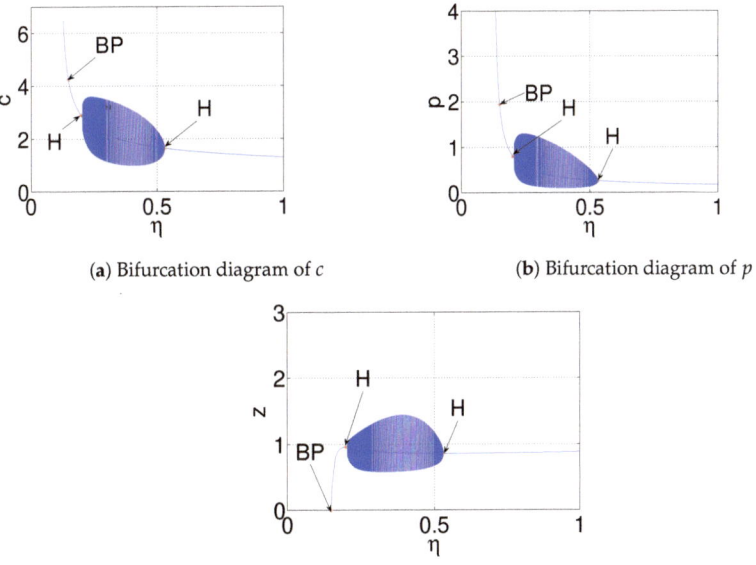

(a) Bifurcation diagram of c

(b) Bifurcation diagram of p

(c) Bifurcation diagram of z

Figure 16. Bifurcation diagrams of system (1) taking η as the bifurcation parameter, while the others remain unchanged, as in Figure 6. Here, the zooplankton free equilibrium $E_1(\tilde{c}, \tilde{p}, 0)$ is stable when $0 < \eta < \eta^{[tc]} = 0.147603$, and the interior equilibrium $\widehat{E}(\hat{c}, \hat{p}, \hat{z})$ is stable when $\eta \in (0.147603, \eta^{[H]_1} = 0.198177) \cup (\eta^{[H]_2} = 0.530864, 1)$ and unstable with a periodic solution when $\eta \in (0.198177, 0.530864)$. Here, 'BP' stands for the transcritical bifurcation point.

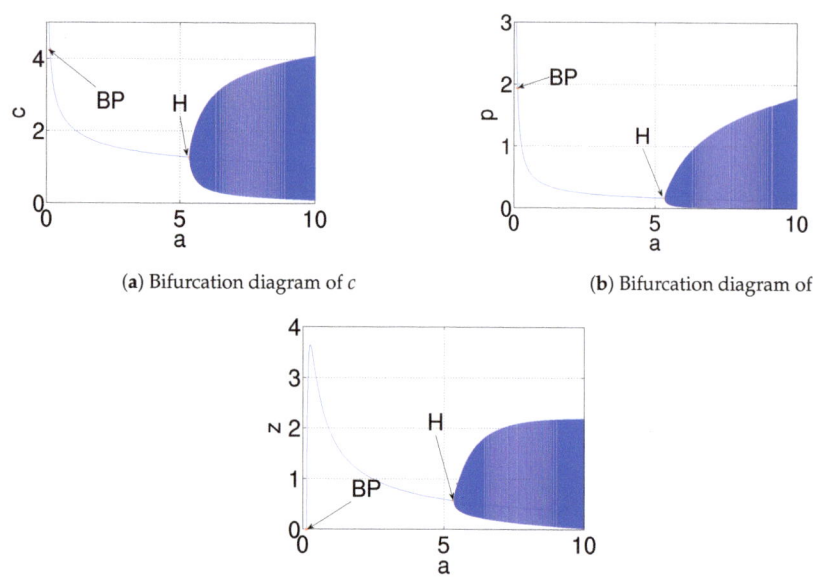

(a) Bifurcation diagram of c

(b) Bifurcation diagram of p

(c) Bifurcation diagram of z

Figure 17. Bifurcation diagrams of system (1) taking a as the bifurcation parameter, while the others remain unchanged, as in Figure 6. Here, the zooplankton free equilibrium $E_1(\tilde{c}, \tilde{p}, 0)$ is stable when $0 < a < a^{[tc]} = 0.109643$, and the interior equilibrium $\hat{E}(\hat{c}, \hat{p}, \hat{z})$ is stable when $a \in (0.109643, a^{[H]} = 5.325675)$ and unstable with periodic solution when $a > a^{[H]} = 5.325675$.

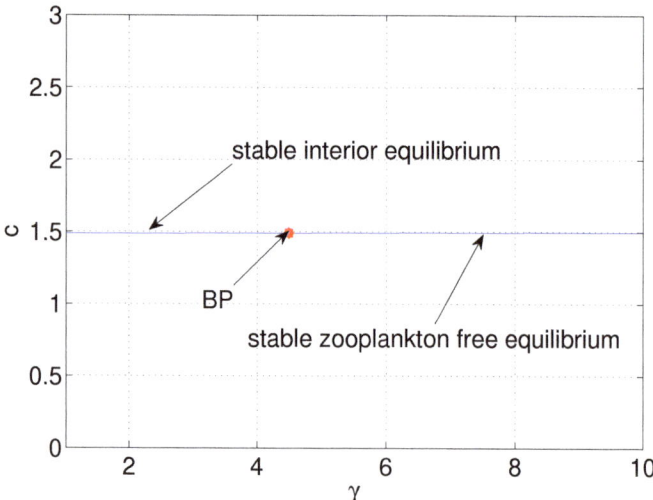

Figure 18. Bifurcation diagram of system (1) taking γ as the bifurcation parameter, while the others remain unchanged, as in Figure 6. Here, 'BP' appears at $\gamma = \gamma^{[tc]} = 4.479066$.

Effect of Environmental Noise on System (1)

In a marine ecosystem, the oxygen-plankton model is affected by the environmental noise due to the inherent stochasticity of the weather conditions. For environmental noise, some of the parameters of system (1) change randomly over time. In this study, we have assumed that the stochasticity affects the oxygen production term through parameter A, the phytoplankton growth term through parameter B, and the zooplankton mortality rate μ by turning A, B, and μ into random variables as follows:

$$
\begin{aligned}
A &\to A + \gamma_1(t) \\
B &\to B + \gamma_2(t) \\
\mu &\to \mu + \gamma_3(t)
\end{aligned}
\quad (11)
$$

where γ_1, γ_2, and γ_3 are independent Gaussian white noise terms and satisfy the following conditions:

$$<\gamma_j(t)> = 0 \text{ and } <\gamma_j(t_1), \gamma_j(t_2)> = \alpha_j^2 \delta_j(t_1 - t_2), \text{ for } j = 1, 2, 3$$

where α_j are the intensities or strengths of the random perturbations, δ is the Dirac delta function defined by:

$$\begin{cases} \delta(x) = 0, \text{ for } x \neq 0 \\ \int_{-\infty}^{\infty} \delta(x) dx = 1 \end{cases}$$

and $< \cdot >$ is the ensemble average of the considered stochastic process.

Introducing Gaussian white noises, system (1) can be formulated as:

$$
\begin{aligned}
\frac{dc}{dt} &= \frac{(A + \gamma_1(t))c_0 p}{c + c_0} - \frac{\delta cp}{c + c_2} - \frac{vcz}{c + c_3} - mc \\
\frac{dp}{dt} &= \frac{(B + \gamma_2(t))cp}{c + c_1} - \gamma p^2 - \frac{ap^2 z}{ahp^2 + p + g} - \sigma p \\
\frac{dz}{dt} &= \left(\frac{\eta c^2}{c^2 + c_4^2}\right) \cdot \frac{ap^2 z}{ahp^2 + p + g} - (\mu + \gamma_3(t))z
\end{aligned}
$$

i.e.,
$$
\begin{aligned}
\frac{dc}{dt} &= \frac{Ac_0 p}{c + c_0} - \frac{\delta cp}{c + c_2} - \frac{vcz}{c + c_3} - mc + \frac{\gamma_1(t) c_0 p}{c + c_0} \\
\frac{dp}{dt} &= \frac{Bcp}{c + c_1} - \gamma p^2 - \frac{ap^2 z}{ahp^2 + p + g} - \sigma p + \frac{\gamma_2(t) cp}{c + c_1} \\
\frac{dz}{dt} &= \left(\frac{\eta c^2}{c^2 + c_4^2}\right) \cdot \frac{ap^2 z}{ahp^2 + p + g} - \mu z - \gamma_3(t) z
\end{aligned}
$$

$$
\begin{aligned}
\frac{dc}{dt} &= \frac{Ac_0 p}{c + c_0} - \frac{\delta cp}{c + c_2} - \frac{vcz}{c + c_3} - mc + \left(\frac{c_0 p}{c + c_0}\right) \cdot \alpha_1 \frac{dw_1}{dt} \\
\frac{dp}{dt} &= \frac{Bcp}{c + c_1} - \gamma p^2 - \frac{ap^2 z}{ahp^2 + p + g} - \sigma p + \left(\frac{cp}{c + c_1}\right) \cdot \alpha_2 \frac{dw_2}{dt} \\
\frac{dz}{dt} &= \left(\frac{\eta c^2}{c^2 + c_4^2}\right) \cdot \frac{ap^2 z}{ahp^2 + p + g} - \mu z - \alpha_3 z \frac{dw_3}{dt}
\end{aligned}
$$

where $\gamma_1 = \alpha_1 \frac{dw_1}{dt}$, $\gamma_2 = \alpha_2 \frac{dw_2}{dt}$, and $\gamma_3 = \alpha_3 \frac{dw_3}{dt}$. Here, $w = \{w_1(t), w_2(t), w_3(t) | t \geq 0\}$ represents three-dimensional standard Brownian motion.

Hence, our proposed stochastic system is:

$$
\begin{aligned}
dc &= \frac{Ac_0 p}{c + c_0} - \frac{\delta c p}{c + c_2} - \frac{\nu c z}{c + c_3} - mc + \left(\frac{c_0}{c + c_0}\right)\alpha_1 p dw_1 \\
dp &= \frac{Bcp}{c + c_1} - \gamma p^2 - \frac{ap^2 z}{ahp^2 + p + g} - \sigma p + \left(\frac{p}{c + c_1}\right)\alpha_2 c dw_2 \quad (12) \\
dz &= \left(\frac{\eta c^2}{c^2 + c_4^2}\right) \cdot \frac{ap^2 z}{ahp^2 + p + g} - \mu z - \alpha_3 z dw_3.
\end{aligned}
$$

The effect of environmental noise on the dynamics of system (12) is analyzed numerically by the Euler Maruyama method in MATLAB. For this purpose, we chose the parametric set as follows:

$$
\begin{aligned}
\{c_0 = 1, \delta = 1, c_2 = 1, m = 0.5, B = 1.8, c_1 = 1.0, \gamma = 0.7, \sigma = 0.1, \nu = 0.01, \mu = 0.1, \\
h = 1.2, a = 3.0, \eta = 0.7, c_4 = 1, g = 0.3, c_3 = 1, \alpha_1 = \alpha_2 = \alpha_3 = 0.001\}, \quad (13)
\end{aligned}
$$

but varied A in a broad range.

When we took $A = 10$, while the other parameters remained the same as in set (13), then the effect of the Gaussian white noises on the stochastic system (12) were as depicted in Figure 19. Furthermore, Figure 19 shows that the oxygen, phytoplankton, and zooplankton varied around the deterministic coexistence steady-state values 1.48635, 0.218551, and 0.866809, respectively. Hence, system (12) is persistent. In this context, we repeated the stochastic simulations 20000 times, and the numerical results are depicted in Figure 20, which shows the stationary distribution of $c(t)$, $p(t)$, and $z(t)$ at time $t = 600$. Moreover, when we chose $A = 1.8$, while the remaining parameters remained the same as in set (13), then system (12) was also persistent (see Figure 21).

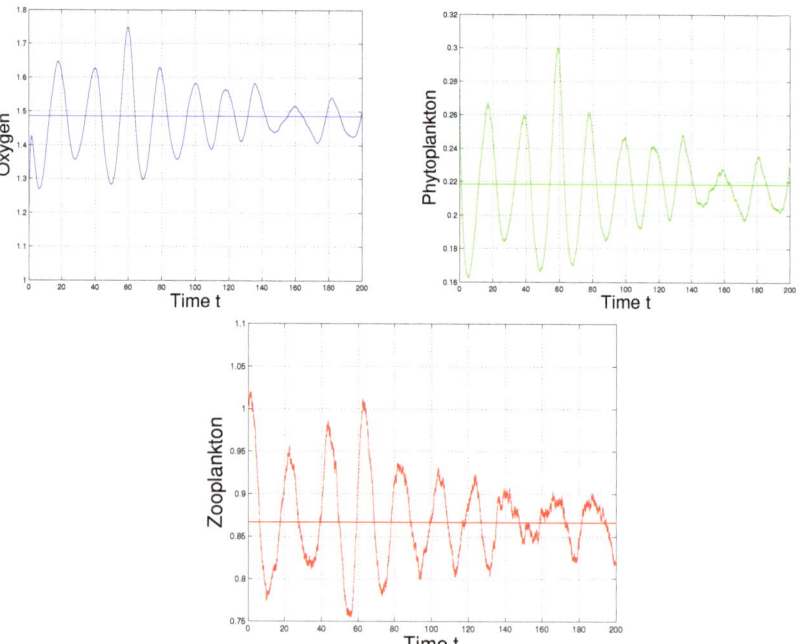

Figure 19. Stochastic trajectories of system (12) when $A = 10$ and the remaining parameters are same as in set (13). Initial conditions are $c(0) = 1$, $p(0) = 0.3$ and $z(0) = 1$.

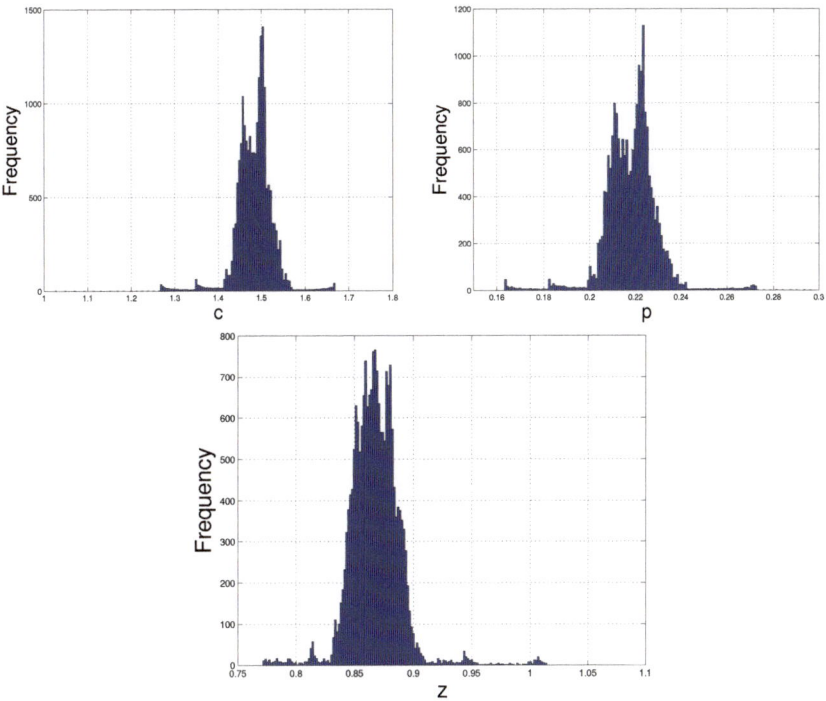

Figure 20. Histograms of system (12) with the parameters chosen from Figure 19.

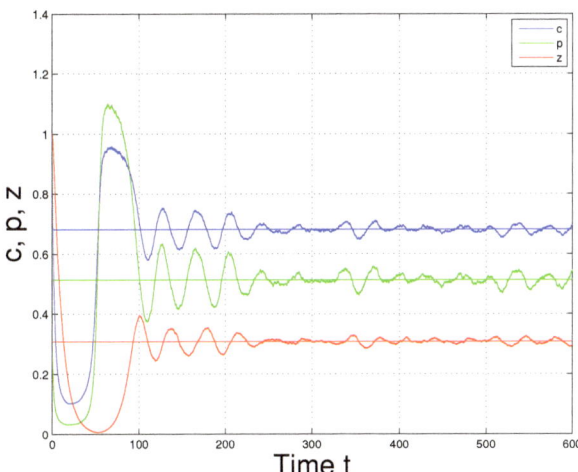

Figure 21. Persistence of system (12) when $A = 1.8$ and the remaining parameters stay unaltered as in Figure 19.

Again, if we take $\mu = 0.5$, while the other parameters remain the same as in set (13), then, it is noted from Figure 22 that the zooplankton population can not persist in system (12) for any of the following choices: (a) $A = 1.8$ and (b) $A = 10$.

Furthermore, it is observed from Figure 23 that system (12) becomes extinct for any of the following choices: (a) $A = 1.5$, (b) $\sigma = 1.0$, and (c) $m = 2.9$, while the other parameters remain the same as in set (13).

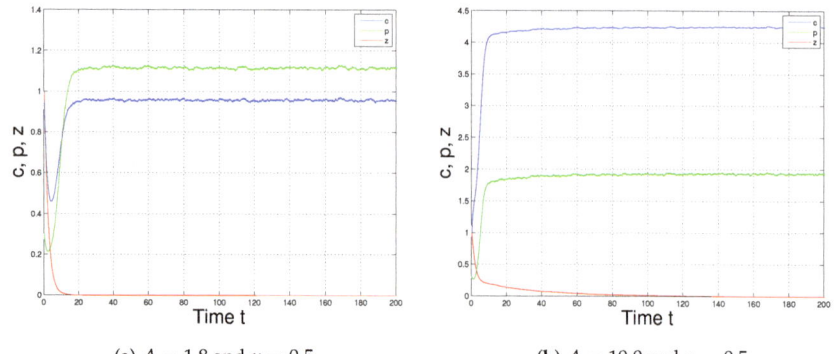

(**a**) $A = 1.8$ and $\mu = 0.5$

(**b**) $A = 10.0$ and $\mu = 0.5$

Figure 22. Extinction of the zooplankton in system (12) when (**a**) $A = 1.8$ and $\mu = 0.5$, (**b**) $A = 10.0$ and $\mu = 0.5$ and remaining parameters are chosen from set (13).

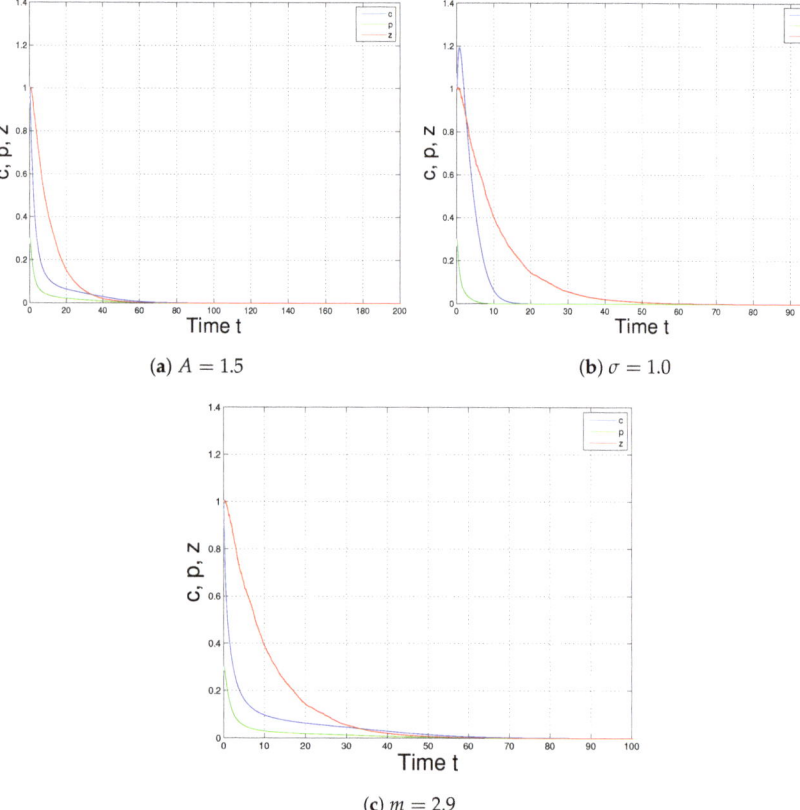

(**c**) $m = 2.9$

Figure 23. Depletion of oxygen and extinction of plankton corresponding to system (12) when (**a**) $A = 1.5$, (**b**) $\sigma = 1.0$, (**c**) $m = 2.9$ and the remaining parameters are chosen from set (13).

7. Discussion and Conclusions

A Holling type II functional response [6–8] is predicated on the assumption that the search rate of a predator is constant, i.e., independent of the prey population. However, it seems reasonable that the predator can vary their search rate based on the availability of prey. In particular, it is estimated that 50–80% of the oxygen production on Earth comes from the oceans due to the photosynthetic activity of phytoplankton. Some of this production is consumed by both phytoplankton and zooplankton for cellular respiration. Furthermore, zooplankton consume phytoplankton with a modified Holling type II functional response, based on the premise that the zooplankton search rate is dependent on phytoplankton (for details, see [10,11]). The goal of this article was to investigate the behavior of the oxygen-plankton model with a modified Holling type II functional response. The following summarizes our findings:

- The coexistence steady state is stable when $1.8 \leq A < 1.966532$, and it loses its stable nature through Hopf-bifurcation when $1.966532 < A < 7.258206$ (see Figures 7 and 8).
- The dynamic behavior of system (1) changes abruptly for a low oxygen production rate ($0 < A < 1.8$), resulting in the depletion of oxygen and plankton extinction (see Figure 3). This depletion of oxygen production will be a consequence of the global ecological disaster.
- System (1) always has a stable coexistence steady state for a high oxygen production rate (see Figure 6), i.e., the sustainability of oxygen production is possible when A is large ($A > 7.258206$). This result is opposite to the outcome shown by Sekerci and Petrovskii [3] because they observed that the system dynamics were not sustainable for a high oxygen production rate. This is the main qualitative difference between the modified Holling type II (variable search rate, as mentioned in the proposed model) and the Holling type II functional responses. Therefore, the study of the modified Holling type II functional response is ecologically meaningful for the sustainability of the dynamics of system (1), if the net oxygen production rate is above a certain critical valve ($A \geq 1.8$).

Moreover, the effect of environmental noise has a strong impact due to the inherent stochasticity of weather conditions. So, our proposed deterministic system (1) was compared with a corresponding stochastic model (12) incorporating Gaussian white noises in the system parameters A, B, and μ, as mentioned in (11).

In the future, a realistic model can be proposed to explore the effects of spatial diffusion in the pattern formation through diffusion-driven instability.

Author Contributions: Conceptualization, S.M., G.S. and M.D.l.S.; Methodology, S.M. and M.D.l.S.; Investigation, S.M., G.S. and M.D.l.S.; Formal analysis, S.M., G.S. and M.D.l.S.; Writing—original draft preparation, S.M., G.S. and M.D.l.S.; Writing—review and editing, S.M., G.S. and M.D.l.S. All authors have read and agreed to the published version of the manuscript.

Funding: This research was funded by the Spanish Government and European Commission for its support through grant RTI2018-094336-B-I00 (MCIU/AEI/FEDER, UE) and to the Basque Government for its support through grant IT1207-19.

Institutional Review Board Statement: Not applicable.

Informed Consent Statement: Not applicable.

Data Availability Statement: The data used to support the findings of the study are available within the article.

Acknowledgments: The authors are grateful to the anonymous referees, for their careful reading, valuable comments, and helpful suggestions, which have helped them to improve the presentation of this work significantly. The third author (Manuel De la Sen) is grateful to the Spanish Government and European Commission for its support through grant RTI2018-094336-B-I00 (MCIU/AEI/FEDER, UE) and to the Basque Government for its support through grant IT1207-19.

Conflicts of Interest: The authors declare that they have no conflict of interest regarding this work.

References

1. Harris, G.P. *Phytoplankton Ecology: Structure, Function and Fluctuation*; Springer: Dordrecht, The Netherlands, 1986.
2. Moss, B.R. *Ecology of Fresh Waters: Man and Medium, Past to Future*; Wiley: London, UK, 2009.
3. Sekerci, Y.; Petrovskii, S. Mathematical modelling of plankton-oxygen dynamics under the climate change. *Bull. Math. Biol.* **2015**, *77*, 2325–2353. [CrossRef] [PubMed]

4. Gokce, A.; Yazar, S.; Sekerci, Y. Delay induced nonlinear dynamics of oxygen-plankton interactions. *Chaos Solitons Fractals* **2020**, *141*, 110327. [CrossRef]
5. Sekerci, Y.; Petrovskii, S. Global Warming Can Lead to Depletion of Oxygen by Disrupting Phytoplankton Photosynthesis: A Mathematical Modelling Approach. *Geosciences* **2018**, *8*, 201. [CrossRef]
6. Holling, C.S. The components of predation as revealed by a study of small-mammal predation of the european pine sawfly. *Can. Entomol.* **1959**, *91*, 293–320. [CrossRef]
7. Holling, C.S. Some characteristics of simple types of predation and parasitism. *Can. Entomol.* **1959**, *91*, 385–398. [CrossRef]
8. Holling, C.S. The functional response of predators to prey density and its role in mimicry and population regulation. *Mem. Entomol. Soc. Can.* **1965**, *97* (Suppl. S45), 5–60. [CrossRef]
9. Hassell, M.P.; Lawton, J.H.; Beddington, J.R. Sigmoid functional responses by invertebrate predators and parasitoids. *J. Anim. Ecol.* **1977**, *46*, 249–262. [CrossRef]
10. Dalziel, B.D.; Thomann, E.; Medlock, J.; Leenheer, P.D. Global analysis of a predator-prey model with variable predator search rate. *J. Math. Biol.* **2020**, *81*, 159–183. [CrossRef] [PubMed]
11. Mondal, S.; Samanta, G.P. Impact of fear on a predator-prey system with prey-dependent search rate in deterministic and stochastic environment. *Nonlinear Dyn.* **2021**, *104*, 2931–2959. [CrossRef]
12. Mondal, S.; Samanta, G. Dynamics of a delayed toxin producing plankton model with variable search rate of zooplankton. *Math. Comput. Simul.* **2022**, *196*, 166–191. [CrossRef]
13. Hale, J.K. *Theory of Functional Differential Equations*; Springer: New York, NY, USA, 1977.
14. Perko, L. *Differential Equations and Dynamical Systems*; Springer: New York, NY, USA, 2001.
15. Murray, J.D. *Mathematical Biology*; Springer: New York, NY, USA, 1993.
16. Summers, D.; Scott, J.M.W. Systems of first-order chemical reactions. *Math. Comput. Model.* **1988**, *10*, 901–909. [CrossRef]

Article

Global Stability of a Humoral Immunity COVID-19 Model with Logistic Growth and Delays

Ahmed M. Elaiw [1,2,*], Abdullah J. Alsaedi [1,3], Afnan Diyab Al Agha [4] and Aatef D. Hobiny [1]

1. Department of Mathematics, Faculty of Science, King Abdulaziz University, Jeddah 21589, Saudi Arabia; aaalharbi@stu.kau.edu.sa (A.J.A.); ahobany@kau.edu.sa (A.D.H.)
2. Department of Mathematics, Faculty of Science, Al-Azhar University, Assiut Branch, Assiut 4293073, Egypt
3. Department of Mathematics, University College in Al-Jamoum, Umm Al-Qura University, Makkah 21955, Saudi Arabia
4. Department of Mathematical Science, College of Engineering, University of Business and Technology, Jeddah 21361, Saudi Arabia; a.alagha@ubt.edu.sa
* Correspondence: aelaiwksu.edu.sa@kau.edu.sa

Citation: Elaiw, A.M.; Alsaedi, A.J.; Al Agha, A.D.; Hobiny, A.D. Global Stability of a Humoral Immunity COVID-19 Model with Logistic Growth and Delays. *Mathematics* **2022**, *10*, 1857. https://doi.org/10.3390/math10111857

Academic Editors: Sophia Jang and Jui-Ling Yu

Received: 19 April 2022
Accepted: 26 May 2022
Published: 28 May 2022

Publisher's Note: MDPI stays neutral with regard to jurisdictional claims in published maps and institutional affiliations.

Copyright: © 2022 by the authors. Licensee MDPI, Basel, Switzerland. This article is an open access article distributed under the terms and conditions of the Creative Commons Attribution (CC BY) license (https:// creativecommons.org/licenses/by/ 4.0/).

Abstract: The mathematical modeling and analysis of within-host or between-host coronavirus disease 2019 (COVID-19) dynamics are considered robust tools to support scientific research. Severe acute respiratory syndrome coronavirus 2 (SARS-CoV-2) is the cause of COVID-19. This paper proposes and investigates a within-host COVID-19 dynamics model with latent infection, the logistic growth of healthy epithelial cells and the humoral (antibody) immune response. Time delays can affect the dynamics of SARS-CoV-2 infection predicted by mathematical models. Therefore, we incorporate four time delays into the model: (i) delay in the formation of latent infected epithelial cells, (ii) delay in the formation of active infected epithelial cells, (iii) delay in the activation of latent infected epithelial cells, and (iv) maturation delay of new SARS-CoV-2 particles. We establish that the model's solutions are non-negative and ultimately bounded. This confirms that the concentrations of the virus and cells should not become negative or unbounded. We deduce that the model has three steady states and their existence and stability are perfectly determined by two threshold parameters. We use Lyapunov functionals to confirm the global stability of the model's steady states. The analytical results are enhanced by numerical simulations. The effect of time delays on the SARS-CoV-2 dynamics is investigated. We observe that increasing time delay values can have the same impact as drug therapies in suppressing viral progression. This offers some insight useful to develop a new class of treatment that causes an increase in the delay periods and then may control SARS-CoV-2 replication.

Keywords: COVID-19; latent infection; humoral immunity; time delay; Lyapunov function; global stability

MSC: 34D20; 34D23; 37N25; 92B05

1. Introduction

Coronavirus disease 2019 (COVID-19) is considered one of the most severe epidemics that has spread throughout whole world. According to the COVID-19 weekly epidemiological update of 16 January 2022 by the World Health Organization (WHO), over 323 million confirmed cases and over 5.5 million deaths have been reported worldwide [1]. COVID-19 is caused by the severe acute respiratory syndrome coronavirus 2 (SARS-CoV-2). This virus can cause some symptoms including fever, cough, sputum production, fatigue, headache, diarrhea, dyspnoea, and hemoptysis [2]. The virus can be transmitted from an infected person to an uninfected person through coughing, sneezing, or talking [3]. To reduce SARS-CoV-2 transmission, preventive measures must be implemented, such as hand washing, the use of face masks, physical and social distancing, disinfection of surfaces, and vaccination.

Fortunately, the following vaccines are approved for use by WHO: Oxford/AstraZeneca, Janssen (Johnson & Johnson), Sinovac, Pfizer/BioNTech, Sinopharm (Beijing), Moderna, Serum Institute of India, Novavax, and Bharat Biotech [4]. In addition to vaccination, the scientific community needs to discover and develop effective drugs to treat the virus and help to address the COVID-19 pandemic.

SARS-CoV-2 is a single-stranded RNA virus, which belongs to the Coronaviridae family. Epithelial cells with angiotensin-converting enzyme 2 (ACE2) receptor are attacked by SARS-CoV-2 [5]. These target cells are found in the respiratory tracts, including the lungs, trachea/bronchial tissues, and nasal region [6]. The immune response plays an essential role in controlling the disease's progression and clearing SARS-CoV-2 infection. There are two main immune responses against viral infections: CTLs and antibodies. CTLs are responsible for killing virus-infected cells, while antibodies are responsible for neutralizing the virus.

Besides biological and medical research, the mathematical modeling of infectious diseases has attracted the interest of several researchers. Several epidemiological (between-host) mathematical models for COVID-19 were proposed to forecast disease severity and help policymakers in developing disease control interventions (see, e.g., [7–14]). Nevertheless, between-host models have occupied more attention than within-host models that study the infection within a human body [15]. Mathematical models of within-host COVID-19 dynamics can help researchers to understand the replication cycle of SARS-CoV-2 and the response of the immune system against viral infection. Moreover, these models enable the merits of different types of antiviral drug therapies to be assessed in individual COVID-19 patients [16]. Many scientists have been interested in modeling and analyzing COVID-19 dynamics within the host (see the review paper [17]). Du and Yuan [6] proposed a within-host model of COVID-19 infection. They studied the influence of the interaction between adaptive and innate immune responses on the viral load's peak in COVID-19 patients. Li et al. [18] developed a within-host COVID-19 infection model and estimated the model's parameters. Fatehi et al. [16] developed a within-host COVID-19 dynamics model with five components: healthy cells, latent infected cells, productively infected cells, SARS-CoV-2 particles, and antibodies and effector cells. Antiviral and convalescent plasma therapies were incorporated. It was shown that using a combination of both therapies in the early stage of infection can be very effective in reducing the duration of infection. Danchin et al. [19] formulated a within-host COVID-19 dynamics model under the effect of antibodies. Sadria and Layton [20] formulated a within-host COVID-19 infection model to simulate the effect of three drug therapies: Remdesivir, an alternative (hypothetical) therapy, and transfusion therapy convalescent plasma. It was suggested that therapies are more effective when they are applied early, one or two days after symptom onset [20]. Néant et al. [21] reported that the viral dynamics are associated with mortality in COVID-19 patients and that strategies that consider reducing the viral load can be more effective. Dual infection with SARS-CoV-2 and other viruses may appear in some patients. Mathematical models of co-infection with SARS-CoV-2 and other respiratory viruses within a host were developed in [22]. It was reported that SARS-CoV-2 progression can be suppressed by other viruses when the co-infections occur at the same time.

Mathematical modeling with available real data helps in extensively exploring the dynamical aspects of within-host COVID-19 infection. Hernandez-Vargas and Velasco-Hernandez [23] used the Akaike information criterion to compare between different within-host COVID-19 models. The models were fitted with real data from nine patients with COVID-19. It was shown that the model with an immune response was better fitting than logarithmic decay and exponential growth models, a target cell-limited model, and a latent target cell-limited model. The COVID-19 dynamics model with the immune response presented in [23] was used in many works (see, e.g., [24,25]). In [24], a differential evolution algorithm was applied to fit the model with experimental data. Blanco-Rodriguez el al. [25] elucidated the key parameters that define the course of COVID-19 developing from a severe to critical case. The impact of multiple types of treatment or vaccines on the dynamical

COVID-19 systems has been investigated by many researchers. Abuin et al. [3] studied the mathematical analysis of the target cell model presented in [23]. The effect of antiviral pharmacodynamic therapy that reduces the production of infectious SARS-CoV-2 particles was studied using control theory. Ke et al. [26] developed some mathematical models for the within-host dynamics of COVID-19 and fitted them to real data. They supported a quantitative framework for concluding the influence of vaccines and therapeutics on the infectiousness of COVID-19 patients and for assessing rapid testing strategies. Ghosh [27] formulated a mathematical model that describes the interaction between SARS-CoV-2, healthy cells, and the immune response within a host. The model was fitted with real data and the effect of different antiviral drugs was addressed. Wang et al. [28] introduced three within-host COVID-19 dynamics models: a basic model, a model with latency, and a model with two types of target cells (pneumocytes and lymphocytes). The effects of antiviral drugs or anti-inflammatory treatments combined with interferons on the viral load and recovery time were studied. The models were fitted with real data of COVID-19 patients and non-human primates. Most of these studies did not perform the mathematical analysis of the within-host COVID-19 models.

Stability analysis of within-host COVID-19 dynamics models is one of the most powerful tools that can provide researchers with a better understanding of the dynamics of the virus and how the immune system controls and clears the virus. The stability analysis of the COVID-19 dynamics model with the immune response presented in [23] was studied by Almocera et al. [29]. CTL and antibody immune responses play important roles in controlling COVID-19 infection. Hattaf and Yousfi [30] developed a COVID-19 dynamics model with the CTL immune response and cell-to-cell infection. The global stability of the three equilibria of the model was studied. Chatterjee and Al Basir [31] studied a COVID-19 infection model with treatment and a CTL immune response. Mondal et al. [32] developed and analyzed a five-dimensional within-host COVID-19 dynamics model that includes both CTL and antibody immune responses. Nath et al. [33] studied the mathematical analysis of the COVID-19 infection model presented in [18]. They established both the local and global stability of the two steady states of the model. The memory is an important characteristic of COVID-19 dynamics at both within-host [34] and between-host [35,36] levels. Ghanbari [34] extended the model presented in [30] and investigated the memory effect on the COVID-19 dynamics by using a fractional derivative. Mathematical analysis of COVID-19 and other diseases co-infection models has received considerable attention. Elaiw et al. [37] developed and proved the global stability of a COVID-19/cancer co-infection model with two immune responses: cancer-specific CTL immune response and COVID-19-specific antibody. Mathematical modeling and analysis of COVID-19/HIV co-infection were studied in [38]. The global stability of a SARS-CoV-2/malaria model with antibody immune response was studied in [39]. It was found that the SARS-CoV-2/malaria co-infection can be protective as the shared antibody immune response serves to eliminate SARS-CoV-2 particles from the body. This may cause less severe SARS-CoV-2 infection.

Optimal control theory (OCT) offers a means to understand how to apply one or more time-varying control measures to a within-host or between-host viral infection model in such a way that a given objective is optimized [40]. OCT was used for COVID-19 epidemiological models to determine optimal strategies for the implementation of interventions to control COVID-19 spread with optimal implementation costs (see, e.g., [40–44]). On the other hand, OCT was applied for within-host viral infection models to determine optimal antiviral drug schedules for infected patients with different viruses, such as HIV [45,46], HBV [47], and HCV [48]. On the basis of the basic within-host viral dynamics model presented by Nowak and Bangham [49], Chhetri et al. [50] formulated and analyzed a within-host COVID-19 dynamics model under the effect of immunomodulating and antiviral drug therapies. Optimal drug interventions were determined. It was suggested that the combination of immunomodulating and antiviral drug therapies is most effective. In [51], fractional differential equations were used in formulating a within-host SARS-CoV-2 model with non-lytic and lytic immune responses. Two types of antiviral drugs were included as control inputs, one for blocking the infection and the other for inhibiting viral production. Optimal antiviral drugs were determined by solving the fractional optimal control problem.

Most of the above-mentioned within-host COVID-19 dynamics models assumed that the dynamics of the target cells take one of the following forms:

(i) Target cell-limited [3,23,26,28]:

$$\dot{T}(t) = -\beta T(t)V(t),$$

(ii) Constant regeneration of target cells [6,18,19,27,32,38,50]:

$$\dot{T}(t) = \lambda - dT(t) - \beta T(t)V(t),$$

where $T(t)$ and $V(t)$ are the concentrations of healthy target cells and SARS-CoV-2 particles, at time t, respectively. Parameters λ, d, and β are the regeneration, death, and infection rates of target cells, respectively. In these works, the proliferation of the healthy target cells was not considered. Fatehi et al. [16] and Fadai et al. [52] developed COVID-19 dynamics models by assuming that the healthy epithelial cells follow logistic growth in the absence of the virus. However, mathematical analysis of these models was not studied. Moreover, time delays were not considered in these papers.

It was observed experimentally that there exits a time lag between the infection of a target cell and the release of new virions [53]. Therefore, several COVID-19 dynamics models were developed using ordinary differential equations (ODEs) by splitting the infected cells into two classes: latent infected cells and active (productive) infected cells (see, e.g., [16,20–23,26,28]). Latent infected cells contain viruses but do not produce them until they are activated. These models assume that, once infected, the cell immediately becomes a latent infected cell. Further, these models neglect the time needed for the latent infected cells to be activated [54]. Furthermore, the maturation time of the new viruses was not considered. To incorporate these time lags, we need to formulate the COVID-19 dynamics using delay differential equations (DDEs). DDEs models can characterize the effect of time delay on the dynamical behavior of the virus.

The aim of the present paper is to formulate and analyze a within-host COVID-19 model that includes: (i) a logistic growth term for the healthy epithelial cells, (ii) latent and active infected epithelial cells, (iii) the antibody immune response, (iv) four time delays, namely the time from the SARS-CoV-2 particles' contact with the healthy epithelial cells to the time that they become latent/active infected cells, the reactivation time of latent infected cells, and the maturation time of new virions. The basic and global properties of the model were studied. To support the theoretical results, we performed some numerical simulations. The effect of time delay on the dynamics of COVID-19 was addressed.

Overall, this analysis can help to better understand the dynamical behavior of within-host COVID-19 models with time delays and immune responses. In addition, our proposed model can be useful to develop co-infection dynamics models with more aggressive variants of SARS-CoV-2, such as Alpha, Beta, Gamma, Delta, Lambda, and Omicron.

2. Model Development

This section provides a brief description of the model under consideration. The model takes the form

$$\dot{T}(t) = \lambda - d_1 T(t) + rT(t)\left(1 - \frac{T(t)}{T_{max}}\right) - \beta T(t)V(t), \quad (1)$$

$$\dot{L}(t) = \eta \int_0^{\tau_1} f(\psi) e^{-n_1 \psi} \beta T(t-\psi) V(t-\psi) d\psi - \alpha L(t) - d_2 L(t), \quad (2)$$

$$\dot{I}(t) = (1-\eta) \int_0^{\tau_2} g(\psi) e^{-n_2 \psi} \beta T(t-\psi) V(t-\psi) d\psi + \alpha e^{-n_3 \tau_3} L(t-\tau_3) - d_3 I(t), \quad (3)$$

$$\dot{V}(t) = k e^{-n_4 \tau_4} I(t-\tau_4) - d_4 V(t) - u A(t) V(t), \quad (4)$$

$$\dot{A}(t) = q A(t) V(t) - d_5 A(t), \quad (5)$$

where $T(t)$, $L(t)$, $I(t)$, $V(t)$, and $A(t)$ represent the concentrations of healthy epithelial cells, latent infected cells, active infected cells, SARS-CoV-2 particles, and antibodies at time t, respectively. The healthy epithelial cells are regenerated at a constant rate λ and proliferate at a logistic growth rate $rT\left(1 - \frac{T}{T_{max}}\right)$, where r is the rate of growth and T_{max} is the maximum capacity of healthy epithelial cells in the human body. Healthy epithelial cells are assumed to be infected by SARS-CoV-2 at a rate βTV. Parameter $\eta \in (0,1)$ is the fraction of the healthy epithelial cells that enter the latent state, while α is the activation rate constant of latent infected cells. kI is the rate at which active infected cells produce SARS-CoV-2 particles. uAV is the neutralization rate of SARS-CoV-2, and qAV is the recruitment rate of antibodies. The parameters d_1, d_2, d_3, d_4, and d_5 symbolize the death rate constants of healthy epithelial cells, latent infected cells, active infected cells, SARS-CoV-2 particles, and antibodies, respectively. The factor $f(\psi)e^{-n_1\psi}$ denotes the probability that healthy epithelial cells contacted by SARS-CoV-2 particles at time instant $t-\psi$ survive ψ time units and become latent infected cells at time t. The factor $g(\psi)e^{-n_2\psi}$ is the probability that healthy epithelial cells contacted by SARS-CoV-2 particles at time instant $t-\psi$ survive ψ time units and become active infected cells at time t. Here, ψ is a random variable generated from probability distribution functions $f(\psi)$ and $g(\psi)$ over the intervals $[0, \tau_1]$ and $[0, \tau_2]$, respectively. τ_1 and τ_2 are the upper limits of the delay periods. τ_3 is the period of time during which latent infected cells are activated to produce active infected cells. τ_4 is the time it takes for the newly released viruses to become mature and then infectious. Factors $e^{-n_3\tau_3}$ and $e^{-n_4\tau_4}$ are the survival rates of latent infected cells and viruses during their delay periods $[t-\tau_3, t]$ and $[t-\tau_4, t]$, respectively. The functions $f(\psi) : [0, \tau_1] \to [0, \infty)$ and $g(\psi) : [0, \tau_2] \to [0, \infty)$ are the distribution functions, which satisfy the following conditions:

(i) $f(\psi) > 0$, $g(\psi) > 0$,

(ii) $\int_0^{\tau_1} f(\psi) d\psi = 1$, $\int_0^{\tau_2} g(\psi) d\psi = 1$,

(iii) $\int_0^{\tau_1} f(\psi) e^{-n_1 \psi} d\psi < \infty$, $\int_0^{\tau_2} g(\psi) e^{-n_2 \psi} d\psi < \infty$, $n_1, n_2 > 0$.

Let
$$F = \int_0^{\tau_1} f(\psi) e^{-n_1 \psi} d\psi \quad \text{and} \quad G = \int_0^{\tau_2} g(\psi) e^{-n_2 \psi} d\psi.$$

Hence, $0 < F, G \leq 1$.

The initial conditions of system (1)–(5) are:

$$T(\varkappa) = \varphi_1(\varkappa),\ L(\varkappa) = \varphi_2(\varkappa),\ I(\varkappa) = \varphi_3(\varkappa),\ V(\varkappa) = \varphi_4(\varkappa),\ A(\varkappa) = \varphi_5(\varkappa),$$
$$\varphi_i(\varkappa) \geq 0,\ \varkappa \in [-\kappa, 0],\ i = 1, 2, \ldots, 5, \quad (6)$$

where $\kappa = \max\{\tau_1, \tau_2, \tau_3, \tau_4\}$ and $\varphi_i \in \mathcal{C}([-\kappa, 0], \mathbb{R}_{\geq 0}), i = 1, 2, \ldots, 5$, and $\mathcal{C}$ is the Banach space of continuous functions mapping the interval $[-\kappa, 0]$ to $\mathbb{R}_{\geq 0}$ with

$$\|\varphi_i\| = \sup_{-\kappa \leq \varkappa \leq 0} |\varphi_i(\varkappa)| \text{ for } \varphi_i \in \mathcal{C}.$$

By the fundamental theory of functional differential equations [55], system (1)–(5) with initial conditions (6) has a unique solution.

3. Basic Properties

This section proves the basic properties of system (1)–(5), including the non-negativity and boundedness of solutions. We determine a bounded domain for the concentrations of the model's compartments to ensure that our model is biologically acceptable. In particular, the concentrations should not become negative or unbounded. Moreover, it lists all possible steady states and their existence conditions.

For the non-negativity and boundedness of solutions for the system (1)–(5), we state the following theorem:

Theorem 1. *Let $(T(t), L(t), I(t), V(t), A(t))'$ be an arbitrary solution of system (1)–(5) with initial conditions (6). Then, $(T(t), L(t), I(t), V(t), A(t))'$ are non-negative on $[0, +\infty)$ and ultimately bounded.*

Proof. Let us write system (1)–(5) in the matrix form $\dot{K}(t) = H(K(t))$, where $K = (T, L, I, V, A)'$, $H = (H_1, H_2, H_3, H_4, H_5)'$, and

$$H(K(t)) = \begin{pmatrix} H_1(K(t)) \\ H_2(K(t)) \\ H_3(K(t)) \\ H_4(K(t)) \\ H_5(K(t)) \end{pmatrix} = \begin{pmatrix} \lambda - d_1 T(t) + rT(t)\left(1 - \frac{T(t)}{T_{max}}\right) - \beta T(t) V(t) \\ \eta \int_0^{\tau_1} f(\psi) e^{-n_1 \psi} \beta T(t-\psi) V(t-\psi) d\psi - \alpha L(t) - d_2 L(t) \\ (1-\eta) \int_0^{\tau_2} g(\psi) e^{-n_2 \psi} \beta T(t-\psi) V(t-\psi) d\psi + \alpha e^{-n_3 \tau_3} L(t-\tau_3) - d_3 I(t) \\ k e^{-n_4 \tau_4} I(t-\tau_4) - d_4 V(t) - u A(t) V(t) \\ q A(t) V(t) - d_5 A(t) \end{pmatrix}.$$

We observe that the function H fulfills the following condition:

$$H_i(K(t))|_{K_i = 0, K(t) \in \mathbb{R}_{\geq 0}^5} \geq 0, \; i = 1, 2, \ldots, 5.$$

Using Lemma 2 in [56], any solution of system (1)–(5) with the initial states (6) is such that $K(t) \in \mathbb{R}_{\geq 0}^5$ for all $t \geq 0$. Hence, $\mathbb{R}_{\geq 0}^5$ is positively invariant for the system (1)–(5). Next, we prove the ultimate boundedness of the solutions. From Equation (1), we have

$$\dot{T}(t) = \lambda - d_1 T(t) + rT(t)\left(1 - \frac{T(t)}{T_{max}}\right) - \beta T(t) V(t) \leq \lambda - d_1 T(t) + rT(t)\left(1 - \frac{T(t)}{T_{max}}\right). \tag{7}$$

From the inequality (7) and the comparison principle, we obtain $\limsup_{t \to \infty} T(t) \leq T_0$, where T_0 is the positive root of $\lambda - d_1 T + rT\left(1 - \frac{T}{T_{max}}\right) = 0$ and is given by

$$T_0 = \frac{T_{max}}{2r}\left[r - d_1 + \sqrt{(r-d_1)^2 + \frac{4r\lambda}{T_{max}}}\right]. \tag{8}$$

Now, we define

$$W_1(t) = \int_0^{\tau_1} f(\psi) e^{-n_1 \psi} T(t-\psi) d\psi + \frac{1}{\eta} L(t).$$

Then, we obtain

$$\dot{W}_1(t) = \int_0^{\tau_1} f(\psi)e^{-n_1\psi}\dot{T}(t-\psi)d\psi + \frac{1}{\eta}\dot{L}(t)$$

$$= \int_0^{\tau_1} f(\psi)e^{-n_1\psi}\left[\lambda - d_1 T(t-\psi) + rT(t-\psi)\left(1 - \frac{T(t-\psi)}{T_{max}}\right) - \beta T(t-\psi)V(t-\psi)\right]d\psi$$

$$+ \int_0^{\tau_1} f(\psi)e^{-n_1\psi}\beta T(t-\psi)V(t-\psi)d\psi - \frac{\alpha}{\eta}L(t) - \frac{d_2}{\eta}L(t)$$

$$= \int_0^{\tau_1} f(\psi)e^{-n_1\psi}\left(-\frac{r}{T_{max}}T^2(t-\psi) + rT(t-\psi) + \lambda\right)d\psi - d_1\int_0^{\tau_1} f(\psi)e^{-n_1\psi}T(t-\psi)d\psi$$

$$- \frac{\alpha + d_2}{\eta}L(t).$$

Let us define $\Gamma(T) = -\frac{r}{T_{max}}T^2 + rT + \lambda$. Then, to find the maximum value of $\Gamma(T)$, we find

$$\Gamma'(T) = -\frac{2r}{T_{max}}T + r = 0 \Rightarrow T = \frac{T_{max}}{2}$$

and

$$\Gamma''(T) = -\frac{2r}{T_{max}} < 0.$$

Then,

$$\Gamma\left(\frac{T_{max}}{2}\right) = -\frac{r}{T_{max}}\left(\frac{T_{max}}{2}\right)^2 + r\left(\frac{T_{max}}{2}\right) + \lambda = \frac{rT_{max}}{4} + \lambda.$$

Let $N_1 = \frac{rT_{max} + 4\lambda}{4} > 0$ and $q_1 = \min\{d_1, \alpha + d_2\}$, then $\dot{W}_1(t) \leq FN_1 - q_1 W_1(t) \leq N_1 - q_1 W_1(t)$. Therefore, $\limsup_{t\to\infty} W_1(t) \leq \frac{N_1}{q_1}$. Since $T(t) \geq 0$ and $L(t) \geq 0$, then $\limsup_{t\to\infty} L(t) \leq \frac{\eta N_1}{q_1} = p_1$. To prove the ultimate boundedness of $I(t)$, we define

$$W_2(t) = \int_0^{\tau_2} g(\psi)e^{-n_2\psi}T(t-\psi)d\psi + \frac{1}{1-\eta}I(t).$$

Then, we obtain

$$\dot{W}_2(t) = \int_0^{\tau_2} g(\psi)e^{-n_2\psi}\dot{T}(t-\psi)d\psi + \frac{1}{1-\eta}\dot{I}(t)$$

$$= \int_0^{\tau_2} g(\psi)e^{-n_2\psi}\left[\lambda - d_1 T(t-\psi) + rT(t-\psi)\left(1 - \frac{T(t-\psi)}{T_{max}}\right) - \beta T(t-\psi)V(t-\psi)\right]d\psi$$

$$+ \int_0^{\tau_2} g(\psi)e^{-n_2\psi}\beta T(t-\psi)V(t-\psi)d\psi - \frac{d_3}{1-\eta}I(t) + \frac{\alpha e^{-n_3\tau_3}}{1-\eta}L(t-\tau_3)$$

$$\leq \int_0^{\tau_2} g(\psi)e^{-n_2\psi}\left(-\frac{r}{T_{max}}T^2(t-\psi) + rT(t-\psi) + \lambda\right)d\psi + \frac{\alpha e^{-n_3\tau_3}}{1-\eta}p_1$$

$$- d_1\int_0^{\tau_2} g(\psi)e^{-n_2\psi}T(t-\psi)d\psi - \frac{d_3}{1-\eta}I(t)$$

$$\leq \int_0^{\tau_2} g(\psi)e^{-n_2\psi}\left(\frac{rT_{max} + 4\lambda}{4}\right)d\psi + \frac{\alpha e^{-n_3\tau_3}}{1-\eta}p_1$$

$$- d_1\int_0^{\tau_2} g(\psi)e^{-n_2\psi}T(t-\psi)d\psi - \frac{d_3}{1-\eta}I(t)$$

$$= \frac{rT_{max} + 4\lambda}{4}G + \frac{\alpha e^{-n_3\tau_3}}{1-\eta}p_1 - d_1\int_0^{\tau_2} g(\psi)e^{-n_2\psi}T(t-\psi)d\psi - \frac{d_3}{1-\eta}I(t)$$

$$\leq \frac{rT_{max} + 4\lambda}{4} + \frac{\alpha}{1-\eta}p_1 - d_1\int_0^{\tau_2} g(\psi)e^{-n_2\psi}T(t-\psi)d\psi - \frac{d_3}{1-\eta}I(t).$$

Let $N_2 = \frac{rT_{max}+4\lambda}{4} + \frac{\alpha}{1-\eta}p_1 > 0$ and $q_2 = \min\{d_1, d_3\}$, then

$$\dot{W}_2(t) \leq N_2 - q_2 W_2(t).$$

This implies that $\limsup_{t\to\infty} W_2(t) \leq \frac{N_2}{q_2}$. Since $I(t) \geq 0$, then $\limsup_{t\to\infty} I(t) \leq \frac{(1-\eta)N_2}{q_2} = p_2$.

To prove the ultimate boundedness of $V(t)$ and $A(t)$, we consider

$$W_3(t) = V(t) + \frac{u}{q}A(t).$$

This gives

$$\begin{aligned}
\dot{W}_3(t) &= ke^{-n_4\tau_4}I(t-\tau_4) - d_4V(t) - uA(t)V(t) + uA(t)V(t) - \frac{ud_5}{q}A(t) \\
&= ke^{-n_4\tau_4}I(t-\tau_4) - d_4V(t) - \frac{ud_5}{q}A(t) \\
&\leq ke^{-n_4\tau_4}I(t-\tau_4) - q_3[V(t) + \frac{u}{q}A(t)] \\
&\leq kp_2 - q_3 W_3(t),
\end{aligned}$$

where $q_3 = \min\{d_4, d_5\}$. Hence, $\limsup_{t\to\infty} W_3(t) \leq \frac{kp_2}{q_3} = p_3$. We have $V(t) \geq 0$ and $A(t) \geq 0$, then $\limsup_{t\to\infty} V(t) \leq p_3$, and $\limsup_{t\to\infty} A(t) \leq \frac{q}{u}p_3$. The above analysis proves that $T(t), L(t), I(t), V(t)$ and $A(t)$ are ultimately bounded. □

Steady States

This subsection computes all possible steady states of system (1)–(5) and the threshold parameters that guarantee the existence of these steady states. Let $SS = (T, L, I, V, A)$ be any steady state of system (1)–(5) fulfilling the following system of nonlinear equations:

$$0 = \lambda - d_1 T + rT\left(1 - \frac{T}{T_{max}}\right) - \beta TV, \tag{9}$$

$$0 = \eta F\beta TV - (\alpha + d_2)L, \tag{10}$$

$$0 = (1-\eta)G\beta TV + \alpha e^{-n_3\tau_3}L - d_3 I, \tag{11}$$

$$0 = ke^{-n_4\tau_4}I - d_4 V - uAV, \tag{12}$$

$$0 = qAV - d_5 A. \tag{13}$$

By solving system (9)–(13), we find that system (1)–(5) has the following steady states:

- Healthy steady state $SS_0 = (T_0, 0, 0, 0, 0)$, where T_0 is given by Equation (8).

Now, we calculate the basic reproduction number $\mathcal{R}_0$ for system (1)–(5) by using the next-generation matrix method [57]. We define the matrices $\mathbb{F}$ and $\mathbb{V}$ as follows:

$$\mathbb{F} = \begin{pmatrix} 0 & 0 & \eta F\beta T_0 \\ 0 & 0 & (1-\eta)G\beta T_0 \\ 0 & 0 & 0 \end{pmatrix}, \quad \mathbb{V} = \begin{pmatrix} \alpha + d_2 & 0 & 0 \\ -\alpha e^{-n_3\tau_3} & d_3 & 0 \\ 0 & -ke^{-n_4\tau_4} & d_4 \end{pmatrix}.$$

The basic reproduction number $\mathcal{R}_0$, can be derived as the spectral radius of $\mathbb{F}\mathbb{V}^{-1}$, and we obtain

$$\mathcal{R}_0 = \frac{k\beta e^{-n_4\tau_4} T_0}{d_3 d_4}\left(\frac{\alpha\eta e^{-n_3\tau_3}}{\alpha + d_2}F + (1-\eta)G\right).$$

The parameter $\mathcal{R}_0$ estimates the number of secondary infections that arise from one infected cell over the course of its lifespan at the beginning of infection, when cells susceptible to infection are not depleted [58].

For convenience, let $\rho = \frac{\alpha\eta e^{-n_3\tau_3}}{\alpha+d_2}F + (1-\eta)G$. Then, $\mathcal{R}_0$ can be rewritten as

$$\mathcal{R}_0 = \frac{k\beta e^{-n_4\tau_4} T_0}{d_3 d_4}\rho.$$

- Infected steady state with inactive antibody immune response $SS_1 = (T_1, L_1, I_1, V_1, 0)$, where

$$T_1 = \frac{d_3 d_4 e^{n_4 \tau_4}}{k\beta\rho} = \frac{T_0}{\mathcal{R}_0},$$

$$L_1 = \frac{\eta}{\alpha + d_2} F\beta T_1 V_1,$$

$$I_1 = \frac{d_4 e^{n_4 \tau_4}}{k} V_1,$$

$$V_1 = \frac{\lambda k e^{-n_4 \tau_4} \rho}{d_3 d_4} + \frac{r}{\beta} - \left(\frac{d_1}{\beta} + \frac{r d_3 d_4 e^{n_4 \tau_4}}{k\beta^2 T_{max} \rho}\right).$$

Assume that $d_1 - r + \frac{rT_1}{T_{max}} > 0$; then, we obtain

$$d_1 - r + \frac{r}{T_{max}} \frac{d_3 d_4 e^{n_4 \tau_4}}{k\beta\rho} > 0 \implies \frac{r d_3 d_4 e^{n_4 \tau_4}}{k\beta T_{max} \rho} - (r - d_1) > 0. \tag{14}$$

We note that

$$\mathcal{R}_0 > 1 \iff \frac{T_{max}}{2r}\left[(r - d_1) + \sqrt{(r - d_1)^2 + \frac{4r\lambda}{T_{max}}}\right] > \frac{d_3 d_4 e^{n_4 \tau_4}}{k\beta\rho}$$

$$\iff \sqrt{(r - d_1)^2 + \frac{4r\lambda}{T_{max}}} > \frac{2r d_3 d_4 e^{n_4 \tau_4}}{k\beta T_{max} \rho} - (r - d_1).$$

From inequality (14), we have $\frac{2r d_3 d_4 e^{n_4 \tau_4}}{k\beta T_{max} \rho} - (r - d_1) > 0$. Then,

$$\mathcal{R}_0 > 1 \iff \frac{4r\lambda}{T_{max}} > \frac{4r^2 d_3^2 d_4^2 e^{2n_4 \tau_4}}{k^2 \beta^2 T_{max}^2 \rho^2} - \frac{4r d_3 d_4 e^{n_4 \tau_4}}{k\beta T_{max} \rho}(r - d_1)$$

$$\iff r\lambda > \frac{r^2 d_3^2 d_4^2 e^{2n_4 \tau_4}}{k^2 \beta^2 T_{max}^2 \rho^2} - \frac{r^2 d_3 d_4 e^{n_4 \tau_4}}{k\beta\rho} + \frac{r d_1 d_3 d_4 e^{n_4 \tau_4}}{k\beta\rho}$$

$$\iff \frac{\lambda k e^{-n_4 \tau_4} \rho}{d_3 d_4} + \frac{r}{\beta} - \left(\frac{d_1}{\beta} + \frac{r d_3 d_4 e^{n_4 \tau_4}}{k\beta^2 T_{max} \rho}\right) > 0$$

$$\iff V_1 > 0.$$

Thus, SS_1 exists when $\mathcal{R}_0 > 1$ and $d_1 - r + \frac{rT_1}{T_{max}} > 0$.

- Infected steady state with active antibody immune response $SS_2 = (T_2, L_2, I_2, V_2, A_2)$, where

$$T_2 = \frac{T_{max}}{2r}\left[r - d_1 - \frac{d_5 \beta}{q} + \sqrt{\left(r - d_1 - \frac{d_5 \beta}{q}\right)^2 + \frac{4r\lambda}{T_{max}}}\right],$$

$$L_2 = \frac{d_5 \eta \beta F T_2}{q(\alpha + d_2)}, \quad I_2 = \frac{d_5 \beta T_2}{q d_3} \rho, \quad V_2 = \frac{d_5}{q},$$

$$A_2 = \frac{d_4}{u}\left(\frac{k\beta e^{-n_4 \tau_4} T_2}{d_3 d_4} \rho - 1\right).$$

We define the antibody immune response activation number $\mathcal{R}_1$ as

$$\mathcal{R}_1 = \frac{k\beta e^{-n_4 \tau_4} T_2}{d_3 d_4} \rho.$$

We note that $A_2 > 0$ when $\mathcal{R}_1 > 1$. Thus, SS_2 exists when $\mathcal{R}_1 > 1$.

Lemma 1. *For system (1)–(5), we have the following:*

(i) *if $\mathcal{R}_0 \leq 1$, then there exists only one steady state SS_0;*
(ii) *if $\mathcal{R}_1 \leq 1 < \mathcal{R}_0$ and $d_1 - r + \frac{rT_1}{T_{max}} > 0$, then there exist two steady states SS_0 and SS_1;*
(iii) *if $\mathcal{R}_1 > 1$, then there exist three steady states SS_0, SS_1, and SS_2.*

4. Global Properties

Stability analysis is at the heart of dynamical analysis. Only stable solutions can be noticed experimentally. Therefore, in this section, the global asymptotic stability of SS_0, SS_1, and SS_2 will be presented by utilizing the direct Lyapunov method and applying LaSalle's invariance principle, following the works of Korobeinikov [59]. Denote $(T, L, I, V, A) = (T(t), L(t), I(t), V(t), A(t))$. Define a function $\mathcal{H} : (0, +\infty) \to [0, +\infty)$ by $\mathcal{H}(x) = x - 1 - \ln x$. Clearly, $\mathcal{H}(x) = 0$ if and only if $x = 1$.

The following result suggests that when $\mathcal{R}_0 \leq 1$, the COVID-19 infection is predicted to die out regardless of the initial conditions.

Theorem 2. *The steady state SS_0 of system (1)–(5) is globally asymptotically stable (GAS) when $\mathcal{R}_0 \leq 1$.*

Proof. Define a Lyapunov function $\mathcal{V}_0(T, L, I, V, A)$ as

$$\mathcal{V}_0 = \rho T_0 \mathcal{H}\left(\frac{T}{T_0}\right) + \frac{\alpha e^{-n_3 \tau_3}}{\alpha + d_2} L + I + \frac{d_3 e^{n_4 \tau_4}}{k} V + \frac{d_3 u e^{n_4 \tau_4}}{kq} A + \mathcal{U}_0(t),$$

where

$$\mathcal{U}_0(t) = \frac{\alpha \eta e^{-n_3 \tau_3}}{\alpha + d_2} \int_0^{\tau_1} f(\psi) e^{-n_1 \psi} \int_{t-\psi}^{t} \beta T(\phi) V(\phi) d\phi d\psi$$
$$+ (1 - \eta) \int_0^{\tau_2} g(\psi) e^{-n_2 \psi} \int_{t-\psi}^{t} \beta T(\phi) V(\phi) d\phi d\psi$$
$$+ \alpha e^{-n_3 \tau_3} \int_{t-\tau_3}^{t} L(\phi) d\phi + d_3 \int_{t-\tau_4}^{t} I(\phi) d\phi.$$

Clearly, $\mathcal{V}_0(T, L, I, V, A) > 0$ for all $T, L, I, V, A > 0$, and $\mathcal{V}_0(T_0, 0, 0, 0, 0) = 0$. The derivative of $\mathcal{U}_0(t)$ is computed as

$$\frac{d\mathcal{U}_0(t)}{dt} = \frac{\alpha \eta e^{-n_3 \tau_3}}{\alpha + d_2} F \beta TV - \frac{\alpha \eta e^{-n_3 \tau_3}}{\alpha + d_2} \int_0^{\tau_1} f(\psi) e^{-n_1 \psi} \beta T(t-\psi) V(t-\psi) d\psi$$
$$+ (1-\eta) G \beta TV - (1-\eta) \int_0^{\tau_2} g(\psi) e^{-n_2 \psi} \beta T(t-\psi) V(t-\psi) d\psi$$
$$+ \alpha e^{-n_3 \tau_3} L - \alpha e^{-n_3 \tau_3} L(t-\tau_3) + d_3 I - d_3 I(t-\tau_4)$$
$$= \rho \beta TV - \frac{\alpha \eta e^{-n_3 \tau_3}}{\alpha + d_2} \int_0^{\tau_1} f(\psi) e^{-n_1 \psi} \beta T(t-\psi) V(t-\psi) d\psi$$
$$- (1-\eta) \int_0^{\tau_2} g(\psi) e^{-n_2 \psi} \beta T(t-\psi) V(t-\psi) d\psi$$
$$+ \alpha e^{-n_3 \tau_3} L - \alpha e^{-n_3 \tau_3} L(t-\tau_3) + d_3 I - d_3 I(t-\tau_4).$$

Hence, $\frac{d\mathcal{V}_0(t)}{dt}$ in terms of the solutions of system (1)–(5) is given by:

$$\frac{d\mathcal{V}_0}{dt} = \rho\left(1 - \frac{T_0}{T}\right)\dot{T} + \frac{\alpha e^{-n_3 \tau_3}}{\alpha + d_2}\dot{L} + \dot{I} + \frac{d_3 e^{n_4 \tau_4}}{k}\dot{V} + \frac{d_3 u e^{n_4 \tau_4}}{kq}\dot{A} + \frac{d\mathcal{U}_0(t)}{dt}.$$

By using system (1)–(5), we obtain

$$\frac{d\mathcal{V}_0}{dt} = \rho\left(1 - \frac{T_0}{T}\right)\left[\lambda - d_1 T + rT\left(1 - \frac{T}{T_{max}}\right) - \beta TV\right]$$
$$+ \frac{\alpha e^{-n_3\tau_3}}{\alpha + d_2}\left[\eta \int_0^{\tau_1} f(\psi)e^{-n_1\psi}\beta T(t-\psi)V(t-\psi)d\psi - (\alpha + d_2)L\right]$$
$$+ (1-\eta)\int_0^{\tau_2} g(\psi)e^{-n_2\psi}\beta T(t-\psi)V(t-\psi)d\psi + \alpha e^{-n_3\tau_3}L(t-\tau_3) - d_3 I$$
$$+ \frac{d_3 e^{n_4\tau_4}}{k}\left[ke^{-n_4\tau_4}I(t-\tau_4) - d_4 V - uAV\right] + \frac{d_3 u e^{n_4\tau_4}}{kq}\left[qAV - d_5 A\right]$$
$$+ \rho\beta TV - \frac{\alpha\eta e^{-n_3\tau_3}}{\alpha + d_2}\int_0^{\tau_1} f(\psi)e^{-n_1\psi}\beta T(t-\psi)V(t-\psi)d\psi$$
$$- (1-\eta)\int_0^{\tau_2} g(\psi)e^{-n_2\psi}\beta T(t-\psi)V(t-\psi)d\psi$$
$$+ \alpha e^{-n_3\tau_3}L - \alpha e^{-n_3\tau_3}L(t-\tau_3) + d_3 I - d_3 I(t-\tau_4)$$
$$= \rho\left(1 - \frac{T_0}{T}\right)\left[\lambda - d_1 T + rT\left(1 - \frac{T}{T_{max}}\right)\right] + \rho\beta T_0 V - \frac{d_3 d_4 e^{n_4\tau_4}}{k}V - \frac{d_3 d_5 u e^{n_4\tau_4}}{kq}A.$$

At the steady state SS_0, we have $\lambda = d_1 T_0 - rT_0\left(1 - \frac{T_0}{T_{max}}\right)$, then

$$\lambda - d_1 T + rT\left(1 - \frac{T}{T_{max}}\right) = (T_0 - T)\left(d_1 - r + \frac{rT_0}{T_{max}} + \frac{rT}{T_{max}}\right).$$

Therefore, we deduce that

$$\frac{d\mathcal{V}_0}{dt} \leq -\rho\left(d_1 - r + \frac{rT_0}{T_{max}}\right)\frac{(T-T_0)^2}{T} + \left(\rho\beta T_0 - \frac{d_3 d_4 e^{n_4\tau_4}}{k}\right)V - \frac{d_3 d_5 u e^{n_4\tau_4}}{kq}A$$
$$= -\rho\left(d_1 - r + \frac{rT_0}{T_{max}}\right)\frac{(T-T_0)^2}{T} + \frac{d_3 d_4 e^{n_4\tau_4}}{k}\left(\frac{k\beta e^{-n_4\tau_4}T_0}{d_3 d_4}\rho - 1\right)V - \frac{d_3 d_5 u e^{n_4\tau_4}}{kq}A$$
$$= -\rho\left(d_1 - r + \frac{rT_0}{T_{max}}\right)\frac{(T-T_0)^2}{T} + \frac{d_3 d_4 e^{n_4\tau_4}}{k}(\mathcal{R}_0 - 1)V - \frac{d_3 d_5 u e^{n_4\tau_4}}{kq}A.$$

At the equilibrium, we have $\lambda = d_1 T_0 - rT_0\left(1 - \frac{T_0}{T_{max}}\right)$, which implies that $d_1 - r + \frac{rT_0}{T_{max}} > 0$. It follows that $\frac{d\mathcal{V}_0}{dt} \leq 0$ when $\mathcal{R}_0 \leq 1$. Moreover, $\frac{d\mathcal{V}_0}{dt} = 0$ when $T = T_0$, $V = 0$, and $A = 0$. The solutions of system (1)–(5) converge to M'_0, the largest invariant subset of $M_0 = \{(T, L, I, V, A) \mid \frac{d\mathcal{V}_0}{dt} = 0\}$. For any elements in M'_0, we have $T = T_0$ and $V = A = 0$, and hence $\dot{V} = 0$. From Equation (4), we obtain $0 = \dot{V} = ke^{-n_4\tau_4}I$, which gives $I = 0$ and $\dot{I} = 0$. From Equation (3), we obtain $0 = \dot{I} = \alpha e^{-n_3\tau_3}L$, which gives $L = 0$. It follows that $M'_0 = \{SS_0\}$. By LaSalle's invariance principle (LIP) [60], we find that SS_0 is GAS when $\mathcal{R}_0 \leq 1$.
□

The following result establishes that when $\mathcal{R}_1 \leq 1 < \mathcal{R}_0$ and $d_1 - r + \frac{rT_1}{T_{max}} > 0$, a COVID-19 infection with inactive antibody immunity is always established, regardless of the initial conditions.

Theorem 3. *The steady state SS_1 of system (1)–(5) is GAS when $\mathcal{R}_1 \leq 1 < \mathcal{R}_0$ and $d_1 - r + \frac{rT_1}{T_{max}} > 0$.*

Proof. Define a Lyapunov function $\mathcal{V}_1(T, L, I, V, A)$ as

$$\mathcal{V}_1 = \rho T_1 \mathcal{H}\left(\frac{T}{T_1}\right) + \frac{\alpha e^{-n_3\tau_3}}{\alpha + d_2}L_1 \mathcal{H}\left(\frac{L}{L_1}\right) + I_1 \mathcal{H}\left(\frac{I}{I_1}\right) + \frac{d_3 e^{n_4\tau_4}}{k}V_1 \mathcal{H}\left(\frac{V}{V_1}\right) + \frac{d_3 u e^{n_4\tau_4}}{kq}A + \mathcal{U}_1(t),$$

where

$$\mathcal{U}_1(t) = \frac{\alpha\eta e^{-n_3\tau_3}}{\alpha + d_2}\beta T_1 V_1 \int_0^{\tau_1} f(\psi)e^{-n_1\psi}\int_{t-\psi}^{t} \mathcal{H}\left(\frac{T(\phi)V(\phi)}{T_1 V_1}\right)d\phi d\psi$$
$$+ (1-\eta)\beta T_1 V_1 \int_0^{\tau_2} g(\psi)e^{-n_2\psi}\int_{t-\psi}^{t} \mathcal{H}\left(\frac{T(\phi)V(\phi)}{T_1 V_1}\right)d\phi d\psi$$
$$+ \alpha e^{-n_3\tau_3}L_1\int_{t-\tau_3}^{t}\mathcal{H}\left(\frac{L(\phi)}{L_1}\right)d\phi + d_3 I_1 \int_{t-\tau_4}^{t}\mathcal{H}\left(\frac{I(\phi)}{I_1}\right)d\phi.$$

It is seen that $\mathcal{V}_1(T,L,I,V,A) > 0$ for all $T,L,I,V,A > 0$, and $\mathcal{V}_1(T_1,L_1,I_1,V_1,0) = 0$. Then, $\frac{d\mathcal{U}_1(t)}{dt}$ is given by

$$\frac{d\mathcal{U}_1(t)}{dt} = \rho\beta TV - \frac{\alpha\eta e^{-n_3\tau_3}}{\alpha + d_2}\int_0^{\tau_1} f(\psi)e^{-n_1\psi}\beta T(t-\psi)V(t-\psi)d\psi$$
$$- (1-\eta)\int_0^{\tau_2} g(\psi)e^{-n_2\psi}\beta T(t-\psi)V(t-\psi)d\psi$$
$$+ \frac{\alpha\eta e^{-n_3\tau_3}}{\alpha + d_2}\beta T_1 V_1 \int_0^{\tau_1} f(\psi)e^{-n_1\psi}\ln\left(\frac{T(t-\psi)V(t-\psi)}{TV}\right)d\psi$$
$$+ (1-\eta)\beta T_1 V_1 \int_0^{\tau_2} g(\psi)e^{-n_2\psi}\ln\left(\frac{T(t-\psi)V(t-\psi)}{TV}\right)d\psi$$
$$+ \alpha e^{-n_3\tau_3}\left(L - L(t-\tau_3) + L_1 \ln\left(\frac{L(t-\tau_3)}{L}\right)\right)$$
$$+ d_3\left(I - I(t-\tau_4) + I_1 \ln\left(\frac{I(t-\tau_4)}{I}\right)\right).$$

By using the derivatives in Equations (1)–(5), we obtain

$$\frac{d\mathcal{V}_1}{dt} = \rho\left(1 - \frac{T_1}{T}\right)\dot{T} + \frac{\alpha e^{-n_3\tau_3}}{\alpha + d_2}\left(1 - \frac{L_1}{L}\right)\dot{L} + \left(1 - \frac{I_1}{I}\right)\dot{I} + \frac{d_3 e^{n_4\tau_4}}{k}\left(1 - \frac{V_1}{V}\right)\dot{V}$$
$$+ \frac{d_3 u e^{n_4\tau_4}}{kq}\dot{A} + \frac{d\mathcal{U}_1(t)}{dt}$$
$$= \rho\left(1 - \frac{T_1}{T}\right)\left[\lambda - d_1 T + rT\left(1 - \frac{T}{T_{max}}\right) - \beta TV\right]$$
$$+ \frac{\alpha e^{-n_3\tau_3}}{\alpha + d_2}\left(1 - \frac{L_1}{L}\right)\left[\eta\int_0^{\tau_1} f(\psi)e^{-n_1\psi}\beta T(t-\psi)V(t-\psi)d\psi - (\alpha + d_2)L\right]$$
$$+ \left(1 - \frac{I_1}{I}\right)\left[(1-\eta)\int_0^{\tau_2} g(\psi)e^{-n_2\psi}\beta T(t-\psi)V(t-\psi)d\psi + \alpha e^{-n_3\tau_3}L(t-\tau_3) - d_3 I\right]$$
$$+ \frac{d_3 e^{n_4\tau_4}}{k}\left(1 - \frac{V_1}{V}\right)\left[ke^{-n_4\tau_4}I(t-\tau_4) - d_4 V - uAV\right] + \frac{d_3 u e^{n_4\tau_4}}{kq}[qAV - d_5 A] \qquad (15)$$
$$+ \rho\beta TV - \frac{\alpha\eta e^{-n_3\tau_3}}{\alpha + d_2}\int_0^{\tau_1} f(\psi)e^{-n_1\psi}\beta T(t-\psi)V(t-\psi)d\psi$$
$$- (1-\eta)\int_0^{\tau_2} g(\psi)e^{-n_2\psi}\beta T(t-\psi)V(t-\psi)d\psi$$
$$+ \frac{\alpha\eta e^{-n_3\tau_3}}{\alpha + d_2}\beta T_1 V_1 \int_0^{\tau_1} f(\psi)e^{-n_1\psi}\ln\left(\frac{T(t-\psi)V(t-\psi)}{TV}\right)d\psi$$
$$+ (1-\eta)\beta T_1 V_1 \int_0^{\tau_2} g(\psi)e^{-n_2\psi}\ln\left(\frac{T(t-\psi)V(t-\psi)}{TV}\right)d\psi$$
$$+ \alpha e^{-n_3\tau_3}\left(L - L(t-\tau_3) + L_1 \ln\left(\frac{L(t-\tau_3)}{L}\right)\right)$$
$$+ d_3\left(I - I(t-\tau_4) + I_1 \ln\left(\frac{I(t-\tau_4)}{I}\right)\right).$$

Equation (15) can be simplified as

$$\begin{aligned}\frac{d\mathcal{V}_1}{dt} &= \rho\left(1-\frac{T_1}{T}\right)\left[\lambda - d_1 T + rT\left(1-\frac{T}{T_{max}}\right)\right] + \rho\beta T_1 V \\ &\quad - \frac{\alpha\eta e^{-n_3\tau_3}}{\alpha+d_2}\int_0^{\tau_1} f(\psi)e^{-n_1\psi}\frac{L_1\beta T(t-\psi)V(t-\psi)}{L}d\psi + \alpha e^{-n_3\tau_3}L_1 \\ &\quad - (1-\eta)\int_0^{\tau_2} g(\psi)e^{-n_2\psi}\frac{I_1\beta T(t-\psi)V(t-\psi)}{I}d\psi - \alpha e^{-n_3\tau_3}\frac{I_1 L(t-\tau_3)}{I} + d_3 I_1 - \frac{d_3 d_4 e^{n_4\tau_4}}{k}V \\ &\quad - d_3\frac{V_1 I(t-\tau_4)}{V} + \frac{d_3 d_4 e^{n_4\tau_4}}{k}V_1 + \frac{d_3 u e^{n_4\tau_4}}{k}V_1 A - \frac{d_3 d_5 u e^{n_4\tau_4}}{kq}A \\ &\quad + \frac{\alpha\eta e^{-n_3\tau_3}}{\alpha+d_2}\beta T_1 V_1\int_0^{\tau_1} f(\psi)e^{-n_1\psi}\ln\left(\frac{T(t-\psi)V(t-\psi)}{TV}\right)d\psi \\ &\quad + (1-\eta)\beta T_1 V_1\int_0^{\tau_2} g(\psi)e^{-n_2\psi}\ln\left(\frac{T(t-\psi)V(t-\psi)}{TV}\right)d\psi + \alpha e^{-n_3\tau_3}L_1\ln\left(\frac{L(t-\tau_3)}{L}\right) \\ &\quad + d_3 I_1\ln\left(\frac{I(t-\tau_4)}{I}\right).\end{aligned}$$

By using the steady-state conditions at SS_1,

$$\lambda = d_1 T_1 - rT_1\left(1-\frac{T_1}{T_{max}}\right) + \beta T_1 V_1,$$

$$\alpha e^{-n_3\tau_3}L_1 = \frac{\alpha\eta e^{-n_3\tau_3}}{\alpha+d_2}F\beta T_1 V_1,$$

$$d_3 I_1 = \rho\beta T_1 V_1,$$

$$\frac{d_3 d_4 e^{n_4\tau_4}}{k}V_1 = d_3 I_1.$$

we obtain

$$\lambda - d_1 T + rT\left(1-\frac{T}{T_{max}}\right) = (T_1-T)\left(d_1 - r + \frac{rT_1}{T_{max}} + \frac{rT}{T_{max}}\right) + \beta T_1 V_1.$$

Further, we obtain

$$\begin{aligned}\frac{d\mathcal{V}_1}{dt} &\leq -\rho\left(d_1 - r + \frac{rT_1}{T_{max}}\right)\frac{(T-T_1)^2}{T} + \rho\beta T_1 V_1 - \rho\beta T_1 V_1\frac{T_1}{T} \\ &\quad + \left(\rho\beta T_1 - \frac{d_3 d_4 e^{n_4\tau_4}}{k}\right)V - \frac{\alpha\eta e^{-n_3\tau_3}}{\alpha+d_2}\beta T_1 V_1\int_0^{\tau_1} f(\psi)e^{-n_1\psi}\frac{L_1 T(t-\psi)V(t-\psi)}{LT_1 V_1}d\psi \\ &\quad + \frac{\alpha\eta e^{-n_3\tau_3}}{\alpha+d_2}\beta T_1 V_1 F - (1-\eta)\beta T_1 V_1\int_0^{\tau_2} g(\psi)e^{-n_2\psi}\frac{I_1 T(t-\psi)V(t-\psi)}{IT_1 V_1}d\psi \\ &\quad - \frac{\alpha\eta e^{-n_3\tau_3}}{\alpha+d_2}\beta T_1 V_1 F\frac{I_1 L(t-\tau_3)}{IL_1} + \frac{\alpha\eta e^{-n_3\tau_3}}{\alpha+d_2}\beta T_1 V_1 F + (1-\eta)\beta T_1 V_1 G - \rho\beta T_1 V_1\frac{V_1 I(t-\tau_4)}{VI_1} \\ &\quad + \rho\beta T_1 V_1 + \frac{\alpha\eta e^{-n_3\tau_3}}{\alpha+d_2}\beta T_1 V_1\int_0^{\tau_1} f(\psi)e^{-n_1\psi}\ln\left(\frac{T(t-\psi)V(t-\psi)}{TV}\right)d\psi \\ &\quad + (1-\eta)\beta T_1 V_1\int_0^{\tau_2} g(\psi)e^{-n_2\psi}\ln\left(\frac{T(t-\psi)V(t-\psi)}{TV}\right)d\psi + \frac{\alpha\eta e^{-n_3\tau_3}}{\alpha+d_2}\beta T_1 V_1 F\ln\left(\frac{L(t-\tau_3)}{L}\right) \\ &\quad + \frac{\alpha\eta e^{-n_3\tau_3}}{\alpha+d_2}\beta T_1 V_1 F\ln\left(\frac{I(t-\tau_4)}{I}\right) + (1-\eta)\beta T_1 V_1 G\ln\left(\frac{I(t-\tau_4)}{I}\right) + \frac{d_3 u e^{n_4\tau_4}}{k}\left(V_1 - \frac{d_5}{q}\right)A.\end{aligned}$$

From the steady-state conditions of SS_1, we have $\rho\beta T_1 - \frac{d_3 d_4 e^{n_4\tau_4}}{k} = 0$.
Now, using the following equalities

$$\ln\left(\frac{T(t-\psi)V(t-\psi)}{TV}\right) + \ln\left(\frac{L(t-\tau_3)}{L}\right) = \ln\left(\frac{T_1}{T}\right) + \ln\left(\frac{L(t-\tau_3)V_1}{L_1 V}\right) + \ln\left(\frac{L_1 T(t-\psi)V(t-\psi)}{LT_1 V_1}\right),$$

$$\ln\left(\frac{T(t-\psi)V(t-\psi)}{TV}\right) + \ln\left(\frac{I(t-\tau_4)}{I}\right) = \ln\left(\frac{T_1}{T}\right) + \ln\left(\frac{I(t-\tau_4)V_1}{I_1 V}\right) + \ln\left(\frac{I_1 T(t-\psi)V(t-\psi)}{IT_1 V_1}\right),$$

we obtain

$$\frac{d\mathcal{V}_1}{dt} \leq -\rho\left(d_1 - r + \frac{rT_1}{T_{max}}\right)\frac{(T-T_1)^2}{T} + \rho\beta T_1 V_1 - \rho\beta T_1 V_1 \frac{T_1}{T}$$

$$- \frac{\alpha\eta e^{-n_3\tau_3}}{\alpha + d_2}\beta T_1 V_1 \int_0^{\tau_1} f(\psi)e^{-n_1\psi}\frac{L_1 T(t-\psi)V((t-\psi)}{LT_1 V_1}d\psi + \frac{\alpha\eta e^{-n_3\tau_3}}{\alpha + d_2}\beta T_1 V_1 F$$

$$- (1-\eta)\beta T_1 V_1 \int_0^{\tau_2} g(\psi)e^{-n_2\psi}\frac{I_1 T(t-\psi)V(t-\psi)}{IT_1 V_1}d\psi - \frac{\alpha\eta e^{-n_3\tau_3}}{\alpha + d_2}\beta T_1 V_1 F\frac{I_1 L(t-\tau_3)}{IL_1}$$

$$+ \frac{\alpha\eta e^{-n_3\tau_3}}{\alpha + d_2}\beta T_1 V_1 F + (1-\eta)\beta T_1 V_1 G - \rho\beta T_1 V_1 \frac{V_1 I(t-\tau_4)}{VI_1} + \rho\beta T_1 V_1 \quad (16)$$

$$+ \rho\beta T_1 V_1 \ln\left(\frac{T_1}{T}\right) + \frac{\alpha\eta e^{-n_3\tau_3}}{\alpha + d_2}\beta T_1 V_1 \int_0^{\tau_1} f(\psi)e^{-n_1\psi}\ln\left(\frac{L_1 T(t-\psi)V(t-\psi)}{LT_1 V_1}\right)d\psi$$

$$+ (1-\eta)\beta T_1 V_1 \int_0^{\tau_2} g(\psi)e^{-n_2\psi}\ln\left(\frac{I_1 T(t-\psi)V(t-\psi)}{IT_1 V_1}\right)d\psi + \frac{\alpha\eta e^{-n_3\tau_3}}{\alpha + d_2}\beta T_1 V_1 F\ln\left(\frac{L(t-\tau_3)V_1}{L_1 V}\right)$$

$$+ (1-\eta)\beta T_1 V_1 G\ln\left(\frac{I(t-\tau_4)V_1}{I_1 V}\right) + \frac{\alpha\eta e^{-n_3\tau_3}}{\alpha + d_2}\beta T_1 V_1 F\ln\left(\frac{I(t-\tau_4)}{I}\right) + \frac{d_3 u e^{n_4\tau_4}}{k}\left(V_1 - \frac{d_5}{q}\right)A.$$

By using the equality

$$\ln\left(\frac{L(t-\tau_3)V_1}{L_1 V}\right) + \ln\left(\frac{I(t-\tau_4)}{I}\right) = \ln\left(\frac{I_1 L(t-\tau_3)}{IL_1}\right) + \ln\left(\frac{V_1 I(t-\tau_4)}{VI_1}\right),$$

and rearranging the R.H.S. of (16), we obtain

$$\frac{d\mathcal{V}_1}{dt} \leq -\rho\left(d_1 - r + \frac{rT_1}{T_{max}}\right)\frac{(T-T_1)^2}{T} - \rho\beta T_1 V_1 \mathcal{H}\left(\frac{T_1}{T}\right) - \rho\beta T_1 V_1 \mathcal{H}\left(\frac{V_1 I(t-\tau_4)}{VI_1}\right)$$

$$- \frac{\alpha\eta e^{-n_3\tau_3}}{\alpha + d_2}\beta T_1 V_1 \int_0^{\tau_1} f(\psi)e^{-n_1\psi}\mathcal{H}\left(\frac{L_1 T(t-\psi)V(t-\psi)}{LT_1 V_1}\right)d\psi$$

$$- \frac{\alpha\eta e^{-n_3\tau_3}}{\alpha + d_2}\beta T_1 V_1 F\mathcal{H}\left(\frac{I_1 L(t-\tau_3)}{IL_1}\right)$$

$$- (1-\eta)\beta T_1 V_1 \int_0^{\tau_2} g(\psi)e^{-n_2\psi}\mathcal{H}\left(\frac{I_1 T(t-\psi)V(t-\psi)}{IT_1 V_1}\right)d\psi$$

$$+ \frac{d_3 u e^{n_4\tau_4}}{k}\left(V_1 - \frac{d_5}{q}\right)A.$$

Since $d_1 - r + \frac{rT_1}{T_{max}} > 0$, then we obtain

$$d_1 - r + \frac{rd_3 d_4 e^{n_4\tau_4}}{k\beta T_{max}\rho} > 0 \implies d_1 - r + \frac{d_5\beta}{q} + \frac{2rd_3 d_4 e^{n_4\tau_4}}{k\beta T_{max}\rho} > 0$$

$$\implies \frac{2rd_3 d_4 e^{n_4\tau_4}}{k\beta T_{max}\rho} - \left(r - d_1 - \frac{d_5\beta}{q}\right) > 0.$$

Then, we note that

$$\mathcal{R}_1 \leq 1 \iff \frac{T_{max}}{2r}\left[r - d_1 - \frac{d_5\beta}{q} + \sqrt{\left(r - d_1 - \frac{d_5\beta}{q}\right)^2 + \frac{4r\lambda}{T_{max}}}\right] \leq \frac{d_3 d_4 e^{n_4 \tau_4}}{k\beta\rho}$$

$$\iff \sqrt{\left(r - d_1 - \frac{d_5\beta}{q}\right)^2 + \frac{4r\lambda}{T_{max}}} < \frac{2rd_3 d_4 e^{n_4 \tau_4}}{k\beta T_{max}\rho} - \left(r - d_1 - \frac{d_5\beta}{q}\right)$$

$$\iff \frac{4r\lambda}{T_{max}} < \frac{4r^2 d_3^2 d_4^2 e^{2n_4 \tau_4}}{k^2 \beta^2 T_{max}^2 \rho^2} - \frac{4rd_3 d_4 e^{n_4 \tau_4}}{k\beta T_{max}\rho}\left(r - d_1 - \frac{d_5\beta}{q}\right)$$

$$\iff r\lambda < \frac{r^2 d_3^2 d_4^2 e^{2n_4 \tau_4}}{k^2 \beta^2 T_{max}\rho^2} - \frac{r^2 d_3 d_4 e^{n_4 \tau_4}}{k\beta\rho} + \frac{rd_1 d_3 d_4 e^{n_4 \tau_4}}{k\beta\rho} + \frac{rd_3 d_4 d_5 e^{n_4 \tau_4}}{kq\rho}$$

$$\iff \frac{\lambda k e^{-n_4 \tau_4}\rho}{d_3 d_4} + \frac{r}{\beta} - \left(\frac{d_1}{\beta} + \frac{rd_3 d_4 e^{n_4 \tau_4}}{k\beta^2 T_{max}\rho}\right) < \frac{d_5}{q}$$

$$\iff V_1 < \frac{d_5}{q}.$$

Thus, $\frac{d\mathcal{V}_1}{dt} \leq 0$ when $\mathcal{R}_1 \leq 1$ and $d_1 - r + \frac{rT_1}{T_{max}} > 0$. Moreover, $\frac{d\mathcal{V}_1}{dt} = 0$ when $T = T_1, L = L_1, I = I_1, V = V_1$ and $A = 0$. Thus, the largest invariant subset of $M_1 = \left\{(T, L, I, V, A) \mid \frac{d\mathcal{V}_1}{dt} = 0\right\}$ is $M_1' = \{SS_1\}$. By LIP [60], SS_1 is GAS when $\mathcal{R}_1 \leq 1 < \mathcal{R}_0$ and $d_1 - r + \frac{rT_1}{T_{max}} > 0$. □

The following result illustrates that when $\mathcal{R}_1 > 1$ and $d_1 - r + \frac{rT_2}{T_{max}} > 0$, COVID-19 infection with active antibody immunity is always established, regardless of the initial conditions.

Theorem 4. *The steady state SS_2 of system (1)–(5) is GAS when $\mathcal{R}_1 > 1$ and $d_1 - r + \frac{rT_2}{T_{max}} > 0$.*

Proof. Define a Lyapunov function $\mathcal{V}_2(T, L, I, V, A)$ as

$$\mathcal{V}_2 = \rho T_2 \mathcal{H}\left(\frac{T}{T_2}\right) + \frac{\alpha e^{-n_3 \tau_3}}{\alpha + d_2} L_2 \mathcal{H}\left(\frac{L}{L_2}\right) + I_2 \mathcal{H}\left(\frac{I}{I_2}\right) + \frac{d_3 e^{n_4 \tau_4}}{k} V_2 \mathcal{H}\left(\frac{V}{V_2}\right) + \frac{d_3 u e^{n_4 \tau_4}}{kq} A_2 \mathcal{H}\left(\frac{A}{A_2}\right)$$
$$+ \mathcal{U}_2(t),$$

where

$$\mathcal{U}_2(t) = \frac{\alpha \eta e^{-n_3 \tau_3}}{\alpha + d_2}\beta T_2 V_2 \int_0^{\tau_1} f(\psi) e^{-n_1 \psi} \int_{t-\psi}^t \mathcal{H}\left(\frac{T(\phi)V(\phi)}{T_2 V_2}\right) d\phi d\psi$$

$$+ (1 - \eta)\beta T_2 V_2 \int_0^{\tau_2} g(\psi) e^{-n_2 \psi} \int_{t-\psi}^t \mathcal{H}\left(\frac{T(\phi)V(\phi)}{T_2 V_2}\right) d\phi d\psi$$

$$+ \alpha e^{-n_3 \tau_3} L_2 \int_{t-\tau_3}^t \mathcal{H}\left(\frac{L(\phi)}{L_2}\right) d\phi + d_3 I_2 \int_{t-\tau_4}^t \mathcal{H}\left(\frac{I(\phi)}{I_2}\right) d\phi.$$

We have $\mathcal{V}_2(T, L, I, V, A) > 0$ for all $T, L, I, V, A > 0$, and $\mathcal{V}_2(T_2, L_2, I_2, V_2, A_2) = 0$. Then, we have

$$\begin{aligned}
\frac{d\mathcal{V}_2}{dt} =& \rho\left(1-\frac{T_2}{T}\right)\dot{T} + \frac{\alpha e^{-n_3\tau_3}}{\alpha+d_2}\left(1-\frac{L_2}{L}\right)\dot{L} + \left(1-\frac{I_2}{I}\right)\dot{I} + \frac{d_3 e^{n_4\tau_4}}{k}\left(1-\frac{V_2}{V}\right)\dot{V} \\
& + \frac{d_3 u e^{n_4\tau_4}}{kq}\left(1-\frac{A_2}{A}\right)\dot{A} + \frac{d\mathcal{U}_2(t)}{dt}. \\
=& \rho\left(1-\frac{T_2}{T}\right)\left[\lambda - d_1 T + rT\left(1-\frac{T}{T_{max}}\right) - \beta TV\right] \\
& + \frac{\alpha e^{-n_3\tau_3}}{\alpha+d_2}\left(1-\frac{L_2}{L}\right)\left[\eta\int_0^{\tau_1} f(\psi) e^{-n_1\psi}\beta T(t-\psi)V(t-\psi)d\psi - (\alpha+d_2)L\right] \\
& + \left(1-\frac{I_2}{I}\right)\left[(1-\eta)\int_0^{\tau_2} g(\psi) e^{-n_2\psi}\beta T(t-\psi)V(t-\psi)d\psi + \alpha e^{-n_3\tau_3}L(t-\tau_3) - d_3 I\right] \\
& + \frac{d_3 e^{n_4\tau_4}}{k}\left(1-\frac{V_2}{V}\right)\left[ke^{-n_4\tau_4}I(t-\tau_4) - d_4 V - uAV\right] + \frac{d_3 u e^{n_4\tau_4}}{kq}\left(1-\frac{A_2}{A}\right)[qAV - d_5 A] \quad (17)\\
& + \rho\beta TV - \frac{\alpha\eta e^{-n_3\tau_3}}{\alpha+d_2}\int_0^{\tau_1} f(\psi) e^{-n_1\psi}\beta T(t-\psi)V(t-\psi)d\psi \\
& - (1-\eta)\int_0^{\tau_2} g(\psi) e^{-n_2\psi}\beta T(t-\psi)V(t-\psi)d\psi \\
& + \frac{\alpha\eta e^{-n_3\tau_3}}{\alpha+d_2}\beta T_2 V_2 \int_0^{\tau_1} f(\psi) e^{-n_1\psi}\ln\left(\frac{T(t-\psi)V(t-\psi)}{TV}\right)d\psi \\
& + (1-\eta)\beta T_2 V_2 \int_0^{\tau_2} g(\psi) e^{-n_2\psi}\ln\left(\frac{T(t-\psi)V(t-\psi)}{TV}\right)d\psi \\
& + \alpha e^{-n_3\tau_3}\left(L - L(t-\tau_3) + L_2 \ln\left(\frac{L(t-\tau_3)}{L}\right)\right) + d_3\left(I - I(t-\tau_4) + I_2 \ln\left(\frac{I(t-\tau_4)}{I}\right)\right).
\end{aligned}$$

Summing the terms of Equation (17), we obtain

$$\begin{aligned}
\frac{d\mathcal{V}_2(t)}{dt} =& \rho\left(1-\frac{T_2}{T}\right)\left[\lambda - d_1 T + rT\left(1-\frac{T}{T_{max}}\right)\right] + \rho\beta T_2 V \\
& - \frac{\alpha\eta e^{-n_3\tau_3}}{\alpha+d_2}\int_0^{\tau_1} f(\psi) e^{-n_1\psi}\frac{L_2 \beta T(t-\psi)V(t-\psi)}{L}d\psi + \alpha e^{-n_3\tau_3}L_2 \\
& - (1-\eta)\int_0^{\tau_2} g(\psi) e^{-n_2\psi}\frac{I_2\beta T(t-\psi)V(t-\psi)}{I}d\psi - \alpha e^{-n_3\tau_3}\frac{I_2 L(t-\tau_3)}{I} + d_3 I_2 - \frac{d_3 d_4 e^{n_4\tau_4}}{k}V \\
& - d_3\frac{V_2 I(t-\tau_4)}{V} + \frac{d_3 d_4 e^{n_4\tau_4}}{k}V_2 + \frac{d_3 u e^{n_4\tau_4}}{k}V_2 A - \frac{d_3 d_5 u e^{n_4\tau_4}}{kq}A - \frac{d_3 u e^{n_4\tau_4}}{k}A_2 V + \frac{d_3 d_5 u e^{n_4\tau_4}}{kq}A_2 \quad (18)\\
& + \frac{\alpha\eta e^{-n_3\tau_3}}{\alpha+d_2}\beta T_2 V_2 \int_0^{\tau_2} f(\psi) e^{-n_1\psi}\ln\left(\frac{T(t-\psi)V(t-\psi)}{TV}\right)d\psi \\
& + (1-\eta)\beta T_2 V_2 \int_0^{\tau_2} g(\psi) e^{-n_2\psi}\ln\left(\frac{T(t-\psi)V(t-\psi)}{TV}\right)d\psi + \alpha e^{-n_3\tau_3}L_2 \ln\left(\frac{L(t-\tau_3)}{L}\right) \\
& + d_3 I_2 \ln\left(\frac{I(t-\tau_4)}{I}\right).
\end{aligned}$$

The steady state conditions at SS_2 are given by

$$\lambda = d_1 T_2 - r T_2 \left(1 - \frac{T_2}{T_{max}}\right) + \beta T_2 V_2,$$

$$\alpha e^{-n_3 \tau_3} L_2 = \frac{\alpha \eta e^{-n_3 \tau_3}}{\alpha + d_2} F \beta T_2 V_2,$$

$$d_3 I_2 = \rho \beta T_2 V_2,$$

$$d_3 I_2 = \frac{d_3 d_4 e^{n_4 \tau_4}}{k} V_2 + \frac{d_3 u e^{n_4 \tau_4}}{k} A_2 V_2,$$

$$V_2 = \frac{d_5}{q}.$$

and we obtain

$$\lambda - d_1 T + r T \left(1 - \frac{T}{T_{max}}\right) = (T_2 - T)\left(d_1 - r + \frac{r T_2}{T_{max}} + \frac{r T}{T_{max}}\right) + \beta T_2 V_2.$$

By using the above conditions, the derivative in (18) is transformed into

$$\frac{dV_2}{dt} \leq -\rho \left(d_1 - r + \frac{r T_2}{T_{max}}\right) \frac{(T - T_2)^2}{T} + \rho \beta T_2 V_2 - \rho \beta T_2 V_2 \frac{T_2}{T}$$

$$+ \left(\rho \beta T_2 - \frac{d_3 d_4 e^{n_4 \tau_4}}{k} - \frac{d_3 u e^{n_4 \tau_4}}{k} A_2\right) V$$

$$- \frac{\alpha \eta e^{-n_3 \tau_3}}{\alpha + d_2} \beta T_2 V_2 \int_0^{\tau_1} f(\psi) e^{-n_1 \psi} \frac{L_2 T(t - \psi) V(t - \psi)}{L T_2 V_2} d\psi + \frac{\alpha \eta e^{-n_3 \tau_3}}{\alpha + d_2} \beta T_2 V_2 F$$

$$- (1 - \eta)\beta T_2 V_2 \int_0^{\tau_2} g(\psi) e^{-n_2 \psi} \frac{I_2 T(t - \psi) V(t - \psi)}{I T_2 V_2} d\psi - \frac{\alpha \eta e^{-n_3 \tau_3}}{\alpha + d_2} \beta T_2 V_2 F \frac{I_2 L(t - \tau_3)}{I L_2}$$

$$+ \frac{\alpha \eta e^{-n_3 \tau_3}}{\alpha + d_2} \beta T_2 V_2 F + (1 - \eta)\beta T_2 V_2 G - \rho \beta T_2 V_2 \frac{V_2 I(t - \tau_4)}{V I_2} + \rho \beta T_2 V_2$$

$$+ \frac{\alpha \eta e^{-n_3 \tau_3}}{\alpha + d_2} \beta T_2 V_2 \int_0^{\tau_1} f(\psi) e^{-n_1 \psi} \ln\left(\frac{T(t - \psi) V(t - \psi)}{TV}\right) d\psi$$

$$+ (1 - \eta)\beta T_2 V_2 \int_0^{\tau_2} g(\psi) e^{-n_2 \psi} \ln\left(\frac{T(t - \psi) V(t - \psi)}{TV}\right) d\psi + \frac{\alpha \eta e^{-n_3 \tau_3}}{\alpha + d_2} \beta T_2 V_2 F \ln\left(\frac{L(t - \tau_3)}{L}\right)$$

$$+ \frac{\alpha \eta e^{-n_3 \tau_3}}{\alpha + d_2} \beta T_2 V_2 F \ln\left(\frac{I(t - \tau_4)}{I}\right) + (1 - \eta)\beta T_2 V_2 G \ln\left(\frac{I(t - \tau_4)}{I}\right).$$

From the steady-state conditions of SS_2, we have

$$\rho \beta T_2 - \frac{d_3 d_4 e^{n_4 \tau_4}}{k} - \frac{d_3 u e^{n_4 \tau_4}}{k} A_2 = 0.$$

Now, using the following equalities

$$\ln\left(\frac{T(t - \psi) V(t - \psi)}{TV}\right) + \ln\left(\frac{L(t - \tau_3)}{L}\right) = \ln\left(\frac{T_2}{T}\right) + \ln\left(\frac{L(t - \tau_3) V_2}{L_2 V}\right) + \ln\left(\frac{L_2 T(t - \psi) V(t - \psi)}{L T_2 V_2}\right),$$

$$\ln\left(\frac{T(t - \psi) V(t - \psi)}{TV}\right) + \ln\left(\frac{I(t - \tau_4)}{I}\right) = \ln\left(\frac{T_2}{T}\right) + \ln\left(\frac{I(t - \tau_4) V_2}{I_2 V}\right) + \ln\left(\frac{I_2 T(t - \psi) V(t - \psi)}{I T_2 V_2}\right),$$

we obtain

$$\frac{d\mathcal{V}_2}{dt} \leq -\rho\left(d_1 - r + \frac{rT_2}{T_{max}}\right)\frac{(T-T_2)^2}{T} + \rho\beta T_2 V_2 - \rho\beta T_2 V_2 \frac{T_2}{T}$$

$$- \frac{\alpha\eta e^{-n_3\tau_3}}{\alpha + d_2}\beta T_2 V_2 \int_0^{\tau_1} f(\psi) e^{-n_1\psi} \frac{L_2 T(t-\psi)V((t-\psi)}{LT_2 V_2} d\psi + \frac{\alpha\eta e^{-n_3\tau_3}}{\alpha + d_2}\beta T_2 V_2 F$$

$$- (1-\eta)\beta T_2 V_2 \int_0^{\tau_2} g(\psi) e^{-n_2\psi} \frac{I_2 T(t-\psi)V(t-\psi)}{IT_2 V_2} d\psi - \frac{\alpha\eta e^{-n_3\tau_3}}{\alpha + d_2}\beta T_2 V_2 F \frac{I_2 L(t-\tau_3)}{IL_2}$$

$$+ \frac{\alpha\eta e^{-n_3\tau_3}}{\alpha + d_2}\beta T_2 V_2 F + (1-\eta)\beta T_2 V_2 G - \rho\beta T_2 V_2 \frac{V_2 I(t-\tau_4)}{V I_2} + \rho\beta T_2 V_2$$

$$+ \rho\beta T_2 V_2 \ln\left(\frac{T_2}{T}\right) + \frac{\alpha\eta e^{-n_3\tau_3}}{\alpha + d_2}\beta T_2 V_2 \int_0^{\tau_1} f(\psi) e^{-n_1\psi} \ln\left(\frac{L_2 T(t-\psi)V(t-\psi)}{LT_2 V_2}\right) d\psi$$

$$+ (1-\eta)\beta T_2 V_2 \int_0^{\tau_2} g(\psi) e^{-n_2\psi} \ln\left(\frac{I_2 T(t-\psi)V(t-\psi)}{IT_2 V_2}\right) d\psi + \frac{\alpha\eta e^{-n_3\tau_3}}{\alpha + d_2}\beta T_2 V_2 F \ln\left(\frac{L(t-\tau_3)V_2}{L_2 V}\right)$$

$$+ (1-\eta)\beta T_2 V_2 G \ln\left(\frac{I(t-\tau_4)V_2}{I_2 V}\right) + \frac{\alpha\eta e^{-n_3\tau_3}}{\alpha + d_2}\beta T_2 V_2 F \ln\left(\frac{I(t-\tau_4)}{I}\right).$$

By using the equality

$$\ln\left(\frac{L(t-\tau_3)V_2}{L_2 V}\right) + \ln\left(\frac{I(t-\tau_4)}{I}\right) = \ln\left(\frac{I_2 L(t-\tau_3)}{IL_2}\right) + \ln\left(\frac{V_2 I(t-\tau_4)}{V I_2}\right),$$

and rearranging the R.H.S. of $\frac{d\mathcal{V}_2}{dt}$, we obtain

$$\frac{d\mathcal{V}_2}{dt} \leq -\rho\left(d_1 - r + \frac{rT_2}{T_{max}}\right)\frac{(T-T_2)^2}{T} - \rho\beta T_2 V_2 \mathcal{H}\left(\frac{T_2}{T}\right) - \rho\beta T_2 V_2 \mathcal{H}\left(\frac{V_2 I(t-\tau_4)}{V I_2}\right)$$

$$- \frac{\alpha\eta e^{-n_3\tau_3}}{\alpha + d_2}\beta T_2 V_2 \int_0^{\tau_1} f(\psi) e^{-n_1\psi} \mathcal{H}\left(\frac{L_2 T(t-\psi)V(t-\psi)}{LT_2 V_2}\right) d\psi$$

$$- \frac{\alpha\eta e^{-n_3\tau_3}}{\alpha + d_2}\beta T_2 V_2 F \mathcal{H}\left(\frac{I_2 L(t-\tau_3)}{IL_2}\right)$$

$$- (1-\eta)\beta T_2 V_2 \int_0^{\tau_2} g(\psi) e^{-n_2\psi} \mathcal{H}\left(\frac{I_2 T(t-\psi)V(t-\psi)}{IT_2 V_2}\right) d\psi.$$

We see that $\frac{d\mathcal{V}_2}{dt} \leq 0$ when $\mathcal{R}_1 > 1$ and $d_1 - r + \frac{rT_2}{T_{max}} > 0$. Moreover, $\frac{d\mathcal{V}_2}{dt} = 0$ when $T = T_2$, $L = L_2$, $I = I_2$, and $V = V_2$. The solutions of system (1)–(5) tend toward M_2', the largest invariant subset of $M_2 = \{(T, L, I, V, A, C) \mid \frac{d\mathcal{V}_2}{dt} = 0\}$. For each element in M_2', we have $V = V_2$ and then $\dot{V} = 0$, and from Equation (4), we have $0 = \dot{V} = ke^{-n_4\tau_4}I_2 - d_4 V_2 - uAV_2$, which gives $A(t) = A_2$. It follows that $M_2' = \{SS_2\}$. By LIP [60], SS_2 is GAS when $\mathcal{R}_1 > 1$ and $d_1 - r + \frac{rT_2}{T_{max}} > 0$. □

5. Numerical Simulations

In this section, we execute numerical simulations to enhance the results of Theorems 2–4. Moreover, we study the impact of time delays on the dynamical behavior of the system. Let us take a particular form of the probability distributed functions as

$$f(\psi) = \delta(\psi - \psi_1), \quad g(\psi) = \delta(\psi - \psi_2),$$

where $\delta(.)$ is the Dirac delta function. When $\tau_i \to \infty, i = 1, 2$, we have

$$\int_0^\infty f(\psi)d\psi = 1, \quad \int_0^\infty g(\psi)d\psi = 1.$$

We have

$$\int_0^\infty \delta(\psi - \psi_i)e^{-n_i\psi}d\psi = e^{-n_i\psi_i}, \quad i = 1, 2.$$

Moreover,

$$\int_0^\infty \delta(\psi - \psi_i)e^{-n_i\psi}T(t-\psi)V(t-\psi)d\psi = e^{-n_i\psi_i}T(t-\psi_i)V(t-\psi_i), \quad i = 1, 2.$$

Hence, model (1)–(5) becomes

$$\dot{T}(t) = \lambda - d_1 T(t) + rT(t)\left(1 - \frac{T(t)}{T_{max}}\right) - \beta T(t)V(t), \tag{19}$$

$$\dot{L}(t) = \eta\beta e^{-n_1\psi_1}T(t-\psi_1)V(t-\psi_1) - \alpha L(t) - d_2 L(t), \tag{20}$$

$$\dot{I}(t) = (1-\eta)\beta e^{-n_2\psi_2}T(t-\psi_2)V(t-\psi_2) + \alpha e^{-n_3\tau_3}L(t-\tau_3) - d_3 I(t), \tag{21}$$

$$\dot{V}(t) = k e^{-n_4\tau_4} I(t-\tau_4) - d_4 V(t) - u A(t)V(t), \tag{22}$$

$$\dot{A}(t) = q A(t)V(t) - d_5 A(t). \tag{23}$$

The threshold parameters $\mathcal{R}_0$ and $\mathcal{R}_1$ of model (19)–(23) are given by

$$\mathcal{R}_0 = \frac{k\beta e^{-n_4\tau_4}T_0}{d_3 d_4}\left(\frac{\alpha\eta e^{-n_3\tau_3}}{\alpha+d_2}e^{-n_1\psi_1} + (1-\eta)e^{-n_2\psi_2}\right), \tag{24}$$

$$\mathcal{R}_1 = \frac{k\beta e^{-n_4\tau_4}T_2}{d_3 d_4}\left(\frac{\alpha\eta e^{-n_3\tau_3}}{\alpha+d_2}e^{-n_1\psi_1} + (1-\eta)e^{-n_2\psi_2}\right). \tag{25}$$

To solve system (19)–(23) numerically, we use the MATLAB solver dde23 (see the Appendix A). Without loss of generality, let us consider for simplicity that $\psi_1 = \psi_2 = \tau_3 = \tau_4 = \tau$. The values of the parameters of model (19)–(23) are chosen as $\lambda = 0.11, r = 0.01, T_{max} = 13, \eta = 0.5, \alpha = 4.08, k = 0.25, u = 0.05, d_1 = 0.01, d_2 = 10^{-3}, d_3 = 0.05, d_4 = 4.36, d_5 = 0.04, n_1 = 10^{-3}, n_2 = 0.11, n_3 = 1$, and $n_4 = 1$. The remaining parameters of the model will be varied. We have chosen the parameters of the model in order to perform the numerical simulations. This is because the difficulty of obtaining real data from COVID-19 patients; however, if one has real data, then the parameters of the model can be estimated and the validity of the model can be established. To illustrate our global stability results provided in Theorems 2–4, we show that, from any chosen initial states (any disease stage), the solution of the system will converge to one of the three steady states of the system. Therefore, we select three different sets of initial conditions for system (19)–(23):

Initial-1 : $(T(\varkappa), L(\varkappa), I(\varkappa), V(\varkappa), A(\varkappa)) = (10, 0.007, 1, 0.04, 8),$
Initial-2 : $(T(\varkappa), L(\varkappa), I(\varkappa), V(\varkappa), A(\varkappa)) = (8, 0.008, 1.1, 0.05, 10),$
Initial-3 : $(T(\varkappa), L(\varkappa), I(\varkappa), V(\varkappa), A(\varkappa)) = (6, 0.009, 1.2, 0.06, 12),$

where $\varkappa \in [-\tau, 0]$.

5.1. Stability of Steady States

In this subsection, we address the stability of the three steady states with $\tau = 0.1$, while β and q are varied.

Scenario 1 (Stability of SS_0): $\beta = 0.05$ and $q = 0.1$. Using these values, we compute $\mathcal{R}_0 = 0.5874 < 1$ and $\mathcal{R}_1 = 0.2291 < 1$. According to Theorem 2, SS_0 is GAS and SARS-CoV-2 is predicted to be completely cleared from the body. From Figure 1, we see that the numerical results confirm the results of Theorem 2. We note that the concentration of healthy epithelial cells is increased and converges to its normal value $T_0 = 11.9583$, while the concentrations of latent infected cells, active infected cells, SARS-CoV-2 particles, and antibodies are decaying and tend toward zero. In this situation, the virus particles will be eliminated from the body.

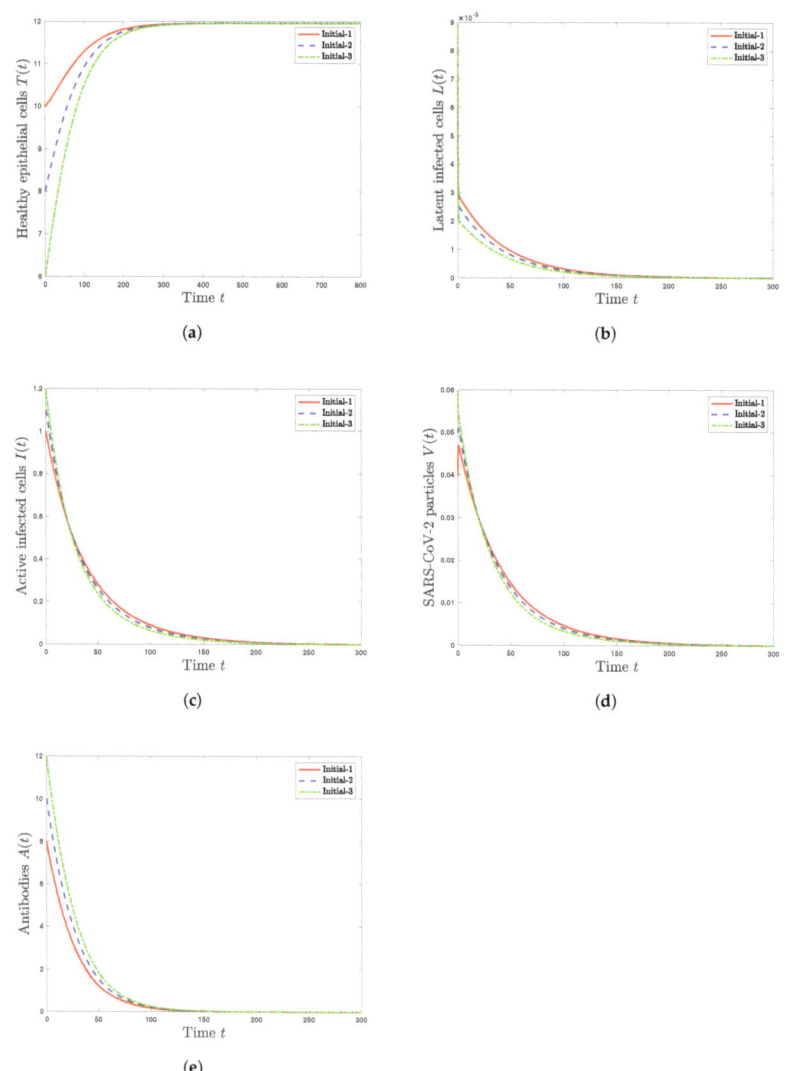

Figure 1. Solutions of system (19)–(23) with three initial conditions when $\mathcal{R}_0 \leq 1$. (**a**) Healthy epithelial cells; (**b**) latent infected cells; (**c**) active infected cells; (**d**) SARS-CoV-2 particles; (**e**) antibodies.

Scenario 2 (Stability of SS_1***):*** $\beta = 0.13$ and $q = 0.1$. This gives $\mathcal{R}_0 = 1.5273 > 1$, $\mathcal{R}_1 = 0.2622 < 1$, and $d_1 - r + \frac{rT_1}{T_{max}} = 0.006 > 0$. According to Theorem 3, SS_1 is GAS. From Figure 2, we can see that there is agreement between the numerical and theoretical results of Theorem 3. In addition, the solutions of the system converge to the steady state $SS_1 = (7.8298, 0.0077, 1.19, 0.0617, 0)$. In such a case, SARS-CoV-2 exists but with an inactive antibody immune response.

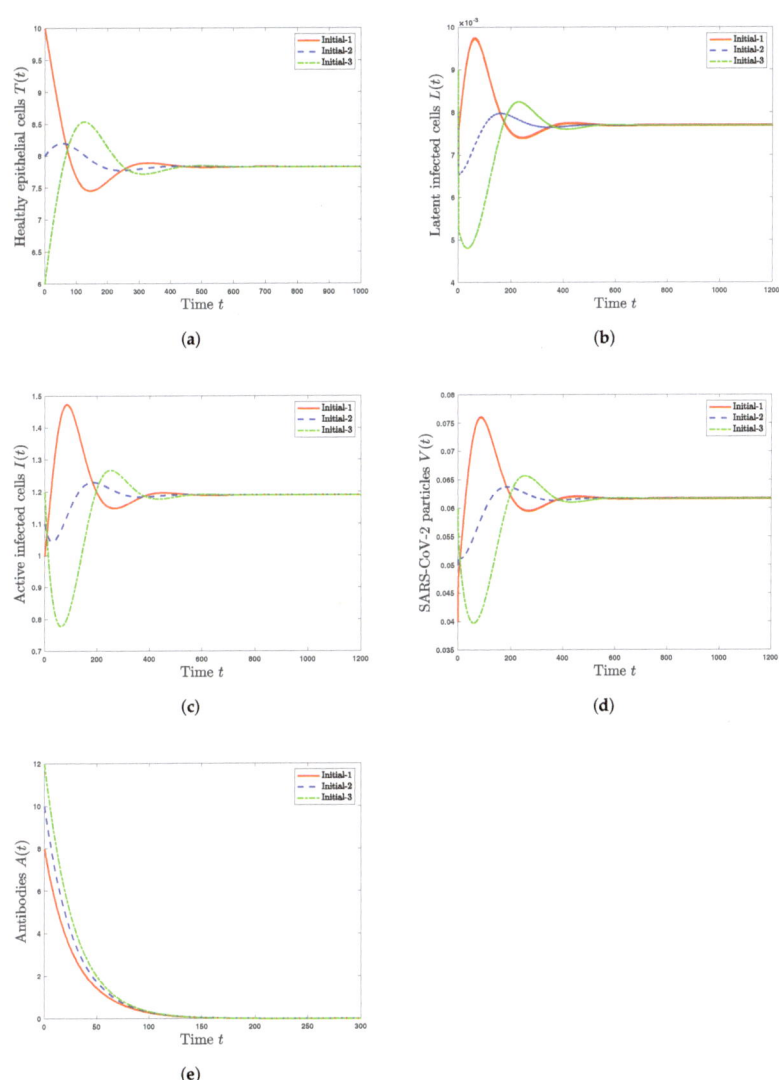

Figure 2. Solutions of system (19)–(23) with three initial conditions when $\mathcal{R}_1 \leq 1 < \mathcal{R}_0$ and $d_1 - r + \frac{rT_1}{T_{max}} > 0$. (**a**) Healthy epithelial cells; (**b**) latent infected cells; (**c**) active infected cells; (**d**) SARS-CoV-2 particles; (**e**) antibodies.

Scenario 3 (Stability of SS_2): $\beta = 0.13$ and $q = 0.9$. These values give $\mathcal{R}_0 = 1.5273 > 1$, $\mathcal{R}_1 = 1.1212 > 1$, and $d_1 - r + \frac{rT_2}{T_{max}} = 0.0068 > 0$. According to Theorem 4, SS_2 is GAS. Further, the solutions of the system converge to the steady state $SS_2 = (8.7786, 0.0062, 0.9604, 0.0444, 10.567)$. In this situation, SARS-CoV-2 exists with active antibody immunity (Figure 3).

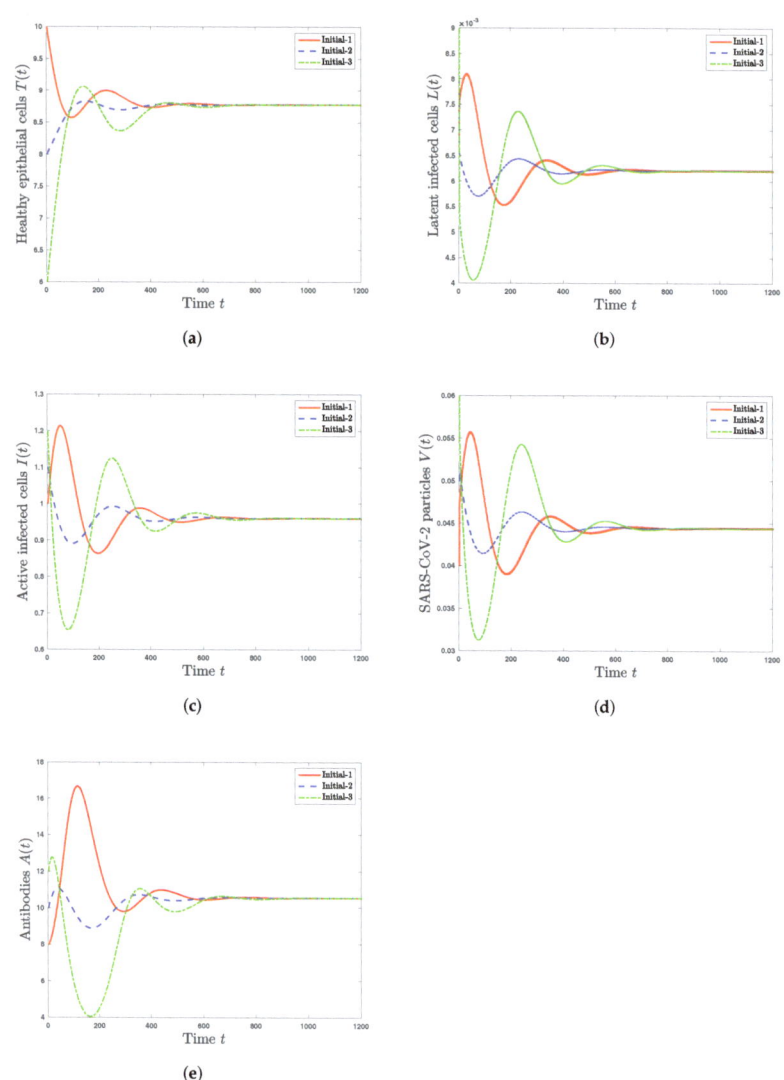

Figure 3. Solutions of system (19)–(23) with three initial conditions when $\mathcal{R}_1 > 1$ and $d_1 - r + \frac{rT_2}{T_{max}} > 0$. (**a**) Healthy epithelial cells; (**b**) latent infected cells; (**c**) active infected cells; (**d**) SARS-CoV-2 particles; (**e**) antibodies.

5.2. Effect of the Time Delay on the SARS-CoV-2 Dynamics

In this subsection, we explore the impact of time delays τ on the stability of the steady states. We note from Equations (24) and (25) that the parameters $\mathcal{R}_0$ and $\mathcal{R}_1$ rely on the delay parameter τ, which causes a significant change in the stability of the system. To clarify this situation, we choose $\beta = 0.13$, $q = 0.9$, and τ is varied. Moreover, we consider the initial state initial-3. Figure 4 shows the influence of the time delay on the solution of the system. We notice that as time delay τ is increased, the number of healthy epithelial cells is increased, while the numbers of latent infected cells, active infected cells, SARS-CoV-2 particles, and antibodies are decreased. Now, let us write $\mathcal{R}_0$ and $\mathcal{R}_1$ as

$$\mathcal{R}_0(\tau) = \frac{k\beta e^{-n_4\tau}T_0}{d_3 d_4}\left[\frac{\alpha\eta e^{-n_3\tau}}{\alpha + d_2}e^{-n_1\tau} + (1-\eta)e^{-n_2\tau}\right],$$

$$\mathcal{R}_1(\tau) = \frac{k\beta e^{-n_4\tau}T_2}{d_3 d_4}\left[\frac{\alpha\eta e^{-n_3\tau}}{\alpha + d_2}e^{-n_1\tau} + (1-\eta)e^{-n_2\tau}\right].$$

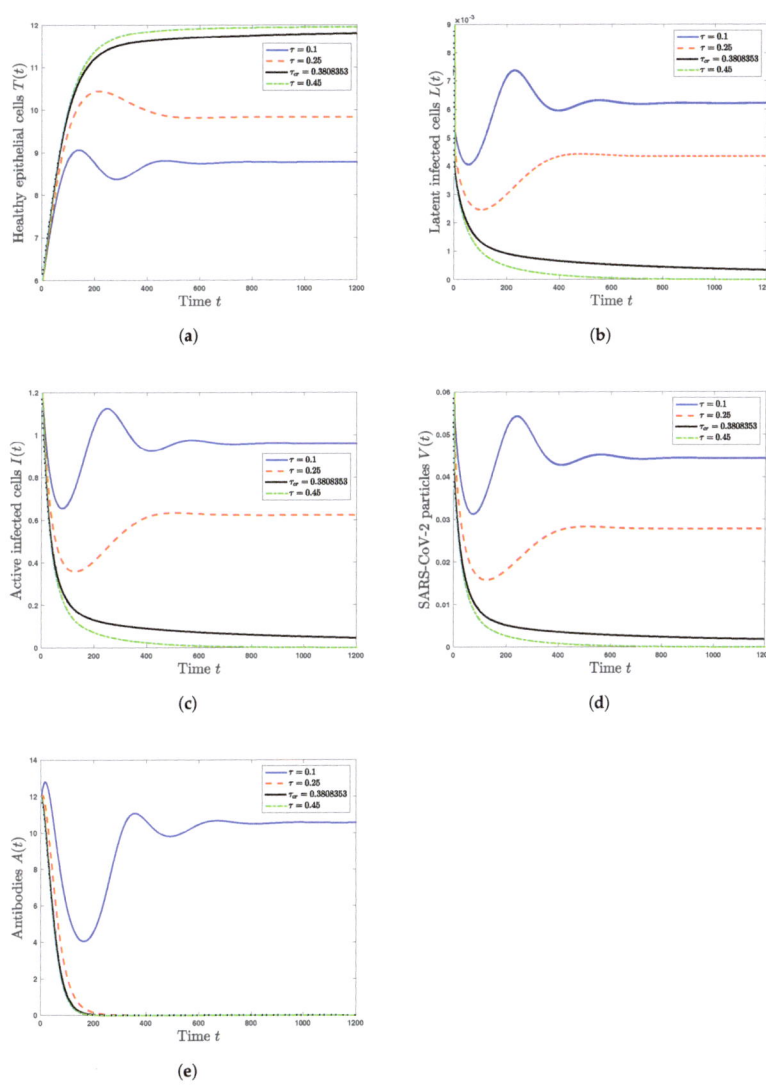

Figure 4. Solutions of system (19)–(23) under the influence of the time delay τ. (**a**) Healthy epithelial cells; (**b**) latent infected cells; (**c**) active infected cells; (**d**) SARS-CoV-2 particles; (**e**) antibodies.

We see that $\mathcal{R}_0$ and $\mathcal{R}_1$ are decreasing functions of τ. Let τ_{cr0} and τ_{cr1} be such that $\mathcal{R}_0(\tau_{cr0}) = 1$ and $\mathcal{R}_1(\tau_{cr1}) = 1$. Using the values of the parameters, we obtain $\tau_{cr0} = 0.380835$ and $\tau_{cr1} = 0.174848$. Therefore, we have the following cases:

(i) if $\tau \geq 0.380835$, then $\mathcal{R}_0 \leq 1$ and SS_0 is GAS;

(ii) if $0.174848 \leq \tau < 0.380835$, then $\mathcal{R}_1 \leq 1 < \mathcal{R}_0$ and $0.006753 \leq d_1 - r + \frac{rT_1}{T_{max}} < 0.009199$ and SS_1 is GAS;

(iii) if $0 \leq \tau < 0.174848$, then $\mathcal{R}_1 > 1$ and $d_1 - r + \frac{rT_1}{T_{max}} = 0.006753 > 0$ and SS_2 is GAS. We can see from the above argumentation that increasing time delay values can have the same impact as antiviral treatment.

6. Conclusions and Discussion

In this paper, we formulate a COVID-19 infection model with distributed and discrete delays and an antibody immune response. Four time delays are included in the model: a delay in the formation of latent infected cells, a delay in the formation of active infected cells, a delay in the activation of latent infected cells, a maturation delay of new SARS-CoV-2 particles. We consider a logistic term for the healthy epithelial cells. We prove the nonnegativity and boundedness of the solutions. We calculate all steady states and establish that their existence is governed by two threshold parameters: the basic reproduction number $\mathcal{R}_0$ and the antibody immune response activation number $\mathcal{R}_1$. The global stability of all steady states of the model is investigated by constructing Lyapunov functions and LaSalle's invariance principal. We prove the following:

- The healthy steady state SS_0 always exists and it is GAS when $\mathcal{R}_0 \leq 1$. This leads to the situation of an individual without SARS-CoV-2 infection.
- The infected steady state with an inactive antibody immune response SS_1 exists if $\mathcal{R}_0 > 1$ and $d_1 - r + \frac{rT_1}{T_{max}} > 0$. It is GAS when $\mathcal{R}_1 \leq 1 < \mathcal{R}_0$ and $d_1 - r + \frac{rT_1}{T_{max}} > 0$. This represents the situation of SARS-CoV-2 infection in a patient with an inactive immune response.
- The infected steady state with active antibody immune response SS_2 exists and it is GAS when $\mathcal{R}_1 > 1$ and $d_1 - r + \frac{rT_2}{T_{max}} > 0$. This leads to the situation of SARS-CoV-2 infection in a patient with an active immune response.

We performed numerical simulations for the model and found that both the numerical and theoretical results are consistent. We studied the effect of time delays on the global dynamical properties of the model. We note that $\mathcal{R}_0$ is a decreasing function on time delays τ_1, τ_2, τ_3, and τ_4. When all other parameters are fixed and delays are sufficiently large, $\mathcal{R}_0$ becomes less than one, which makes the healthy steady state SS_0 globally asymptotically stable. From a biological viewpoint, time delays play positive roles in the SARS-CoV-2 infection process in order to eliminate the virus. Sufficiently large time delays slow down SARS-CoV-2's development, and SARS-CoV-2 is controlled and disappears. This offers some suggestions on new drugs to prolong the time for the formation of latent infected epithelial cells, the time for the formation of active infected epithelial cells, the time for the activation of latent infected epithelial cells, or the time for SARS-CoV-2 particles to mature (infectious).

The model investigated in this work can be developed by (i) using real data to estimate the parameters' values and examine the validity of the model, (ii) considering the diffusion of SARS-CoV-2 particles and cells [61,62], (iii) expanding it to a multiscale model to obtain a deeper understanding of the SARS-CoV-2 dynamics [63,64], (iv) incorporating the role of CTLs in killing the active infected cells. If we consider system (1)–(5) under the effect of CTL immunity, system (1)–(5) is extended to the following model:

$$\dot{T}(t) = \lambda - d_1 T(t) + rT(t)\left(1 - \frac{T(t)}{T_{max}}\right) - \beta T(t)V(t),$$

$$\dot{L}(t) = \eta \int_0^{\tau_1} f(\psi) e^{-n_1 \psi} \beta T(t-\psi) V(t-\psi) d\psi - \alpha L(t) - d_2 L(t),$$

$$\dot{I}(t) = (1-\eta) \int_0^{\tau_2} g(\psi) e^{-n_2 \psi} \beta T(t-\psi) V(t-\psi) d\psi + \alpha e^{-n_3 \tau_3} L(t-\tau_3) - d_3 I(t) - \omega I(t) C(t),$$

$$\dot{V}(t) = k e^{-n_4 \tau_4} I(t-\tau_4) - d_4 V(t) - uA(t)V(t),$$

$$\dot{A}(t) = qA(t)V(t) - d_5 A(t),$$

$$\dot{C}(t) = \sigma I(t) C(t) - d_6 C(t),$$

where $C(t)$ represents the concentration of CTLs at time t. The active infected cells are killed by CTLs at rate ωCI. The terms σCI and $d_6 C$ refer to the proliferation and death rates of CTLs, respectively. Studying the SARS-CoV-2 dynamics model with such extensions is left to future work.

Author Contributions: Conceptualization, A.M.E. and A.D.A.A.; Formal analysis, A.M.E, A.D.A.A. and A.D.H.; Investigation, A.J.A.; Methodology, A.M.E. and A.D.H.; Writing—original draft, A.J.A.; Writing—review & editing, A.D.A.A. All authors have read and agreed to the published version of the manuscript.

Funding: This project was funded by the Deanship of Scientific Research (DSR), King Abdulaziz University, Jeddah, Saudi Arabia, under grant no. (KEP-PHD-95-130-42).

Institutional Review Board Statement: Not applicable.

Informed Consent Statement: Not applicable.

Data Availability Statement: Not applicable.

Acknowledgments: This project was funded by the Deanship of Scientific Research (DSR), King Abdulaziz University, Jeddah, Saudi Arabia under grant no. (KEP-PHD-95-130-42). The authors, therefore, acknowledge with thanks DSR technical and financial support.

Conflicts of Interest: The authors declare no conflict of interest.

Appendix A

```
MATLAB scripts
function H = COVID (t,y,Z)
global lambda beta eta tau1 tau2 tau3 tau4 alpha d1 d2 d3 d4 d5 r k u q n1 n2 n3 n4 Tmax
ylag1 = Z (:,1); ylag2 = Z (:,2); ylag3 = Z (:,3); ylag4 = Z (:,4);
H=zeros (5,1);
H (1)=lambda-d1*y (1)+r*y (1)*(1-y (1)/Tmax)-beta*y (1)*y (4);
H (2)=eta*beta*exp (-n1*tau1)*ylag1 (1)*ylag1 (4)-(alpha+d2)*y (2);
H (3)=(1-eta)*beta*exp (-n2*tau2)*ylag2 (1)*ylag2 (4)+alpha*exp (-n3*tau3)*ylag3 (2)-d3*y (3);
H (4)=k*exp (-n4*tau4)*ylag4 (3)-d4*y (4)-u*y (4)*y (5);
H (5)=q*y (4)*y (5)-d5*y (5);
end
Main Programm
global lambda beta eta tau1 tau2 tau3 tau4 alpha d1 d2 d3 d4 d5 r k u q n1 n2 n3 n4 Tmax
caseNumber=3;
j=1;
if caseNumber==1
beta=0.05;
```

```
                q=0.1;
                end
                if caseNumber==2
                beta=0.13;
                q=0.1;
                end
                if caseNumber==3
                beta=0.13;
                q=0.9;
                end
                %===== Fixed data =======
                lambda=0.11; r=0.01; Tmax=13; eta=0.5; alpha=4.08; k=0.25; u=0.05; d1=0.01; d2=1e-3;
                d3=0.05; d4=4.36; d5=0.04; n1=0.001; n2=0.11; n3=1; n4=1;
                %==== Delay parameters =====
                tau1=0.1; tau2=0.1; tau3=0.1; tau4=0.1;
                %===Initial conditions =====
                a0=10;b0=0.007;c0=1.;d0=0.04;e0=8;
                sol12 = dde23 ('COVID',[tau1 tau2 tau3 tau4],[a0; b0; c0; d0; e0], [0 1200]);
                figure (1)
                pp0=plot (sol12.x, sol12.y(j,:));
```

References

1. World Health Organization (WHO). Coronavirus Disease (COVID-19), Weekly Epidemiological Update. 2022. Available online: https://www.who.int/emergencies/diseases/novel-coronavirus-2019/situation-reports (accessed on 16 January 2022).
2. Huang, C.; Wang, Y.; Li, X.; Ren, L.; Zhao, J.; Hu, Y.; Zhang, L.; Fan, G.; Xu, J.; Gu, X.; et al. Clinical features of patients infected with 2019 novel coronavirus in wuhan, china. *Lancet* **2020**, *395*, 497–506. [CrossRef]
3. Abuin, P.; Anderson, A.; Ferramosca, A.; Hernandez-Vargas, E.A.; Gonzalez, A.H. Characterization of SARS-CoV-2 dynamics in the host. *Annu. Rev. Control* **2020**, *50*, 457–468. [CrossRef] [PubMed]
4. World Health Organization (WHO). Coronavirus Disease (COVID-19). Vaccine Tracker. 2021. Available online: https://covid19.trackvaccines.org/agency/who/ (accessed on 1 April 2022).
5. Varga, Z.; Flammer, A.J.; Steiger, P.; Haberecker, M.; Andermatt, R.; Zinkernagel, A.S. Endothelial cell infection and endotheliitis in COVID-19. *Lancet* **2020**, *395*, 1417–1418. [CrossRef]
6. Du, S.Q.; Yuan, W. Mathematical modeling of interaction between innate and adaptive immune responses in COVID-19 and implications for viral pathogenesis. *J. Med. Virol.* **2020**, *92*, 1615–1628. [CrossRef]
7. Currie, C.; Fowler, J.; Kotiadis, K.; Monks, T. How simulation modelling can help reduce the impact of COVID-19. *J. Simul.* **2020**, *14*, 83–97. [CrossRef]
8. Fredj, H.B.; Chérif, F. Novel corona virus disease infection in Tunisia: Mathematical model and the impact of the quarantine strategy. *Chaos Solitons Fractals* **2020**, *138*, 109969. [CrossRef]
9. Browne, C.J.; Gulbudak, H.; Macdonald, J.C. Differential impacts of contact tracing and lockdowns on outbreak size in COVID-19 model applied to China. *J. Theor. Biol.* **2022**, *532*, 110919. [CrossRef]
10. Anderson, R.M.; Heesterbeek, H.; Klinkenberg, D.; Hollingsworth, T.D. How will country-based mitigation measures influence the course of the COVID-19 epidemic? *Lancet* **2020**, *395*, 931–934. [CrossRef]
11. Davies, N.G.D.; Kucharski, A.J.; Eggo, R.M.; Gimma, A.; Edmunds, W.J.; Jombart, T. Effects of non-pharmaceutical interventions on COVID-19 cases, deaths, and demand for hospital services in the UK: A modelling study. *Lancet Public Health* **2020**, *5*, 375–385. [CrossRef]
12. Ferretti, L.; Wymant, C.; Kendall, M.; Zhao, L.; Nurtay, A.; Abeler-Dorner, L.; Parker, M.; Bonsall, D.; Fraser, C. Quantifying SARS-CoV-2 transmission suggests epidemic control with digital contact tracing. *Science* **2020**, *368*, eabb6936. [CrossRef]
13. Krishna, M.V.; Prakash, J. Mathematical modelling on phase based transmissibility of coronavirus. *Infect. Dis. Model.* **2020**, *5*, 375–385. [CrossRef] [PubMed]
14. Ferguson, N.M.; Laydon, D.; Nedjati-Gilani, G.; Imai, N.; Ainslie, K.; Baguelin, M.; Bhatia, S.; Boonyasiri, A.; Cucunubá, Z.; Cuomo-Dannenburg, G.; et al. *Impact of Non-Pharmaceutical Interventions (NPIs) to Reduce COVID-19 Mortality and Healthcare Demand*; Technical Report; Imperial College London: London, UK, 2020.
15. Bellomo, N.; Bingham, R.; Chaplain, M.A.J.; Dosi, G.; Forni, G.; Knopoff, D.A.; Lowengrub, J.; Twarock, R.; Virgillito, M.E. A multiscale model of virus pandemic: Heterogeneous interactive entities in a globally connected world. *Math. Model. Methods Appl. Sci.* **2020**, *30*, 1591–1651. [CrossRef] [PubMed]
16. Fatehi, F.; Bingham, R.J.; Dykeman, E.C.; Stockley, P.G.; Twarock, R. Comparing antiviral strategies against COVID-19 via multiscale within-host modelling. *R. Soc. Open Sci.* **2021**, *8*, 210082. [CrossRef]

17. Perelson, A.S.; Ke, R. Mechanistic modeling of SARS-CoV-2 and other infectious diseases and the effects of therapeutics. *Clin. Pharmacol. Ther.* **2021**, *109*, 829–840. [CrossRef] [PubMed]
18. Li, C.; Xu, J.; Liu, J.; Zhou, Y. The within-host viral kinetics of SARS-CoV-2. *Math. Biosci. Eng.* **2020**, *17*, 2853–2861. [CrossRef] [PubMed]
19. Danchin, A.; Pagani-Azizi, O.; Turinici, G.; Yahiaoui, G. COVID-19 adaptive humoral immunity models: Non-neutralizing versus antibody-disease enhancement scenarios. *medRxiv* **2020**.
20. Sadria, M.; Layton, A.T. Modeling within-host SARS-CoV-2 infection dynamics and potential treatments. *Viruses* **2021**, *13*, 1141. [CrossRef]
21. Néant, N.; Lingas, G.; Hingrat, Q.L.; Ghosn, J.; Engelmann, I.; Lepiller, Q.; Gaymard, A.; Ferrxex, V.; Hartard, C.; Plantier, J.-C.; et al. Modeling SARS-CoV-2 viral kinetics and association with mortality in hospitalized patients from the French COVID cohort. *Proc. Natl. Acad. Sci. USA* **2021**, *118*, e2017962118. [CrossRef]
22. Pinky, L.; Dobrovolny, H.M. SARS-CoV-2 coinfections: Could influenza and the common cold be beneficial? *J. Med. Virol.* **2020**, *92*, 2623–2630. [CrossRef]
23. Hernandez-Vargas, E.A.; Velasco-Hernandez, J.X. In-host mathematical modelling of COVID-19 in humans. *Annu. Rev. Control.* **2020**, *50*, 448–456. [CrossRef]
24. Blanco-Rodríguez, R.; Du, X.; Hernández-Vargas, E.A. Computational simulations to dissect the cell immune response dynamics for severe and critical cases of SARS-CoV-2 infection. *Comput. Methods Programs Biomed.* **2021**, *211*, 106412. [CrossRef] [PubMed]
25. Blanco-Rodríguez, R.; Du, X.; Hernández-Vargas, E.A. Untangling the cell immune response dynamic for severe and critical cases, of SARS-CoV-2 infection. *bioRxiv* **2020**. [CrossRef]
26. Ke, R.; Zitzmann, C.; Ho, D.D.; Ribeiro, R.M.; Perelson, A.S. In vivo kinetics of SARS-CoV-2 infection and its relationship with a person's infectiousness. *Proc. Natl. Acad. Sci. USA* **2021**, *118*, e2111477118. [CrossRef] [PubMed]
27. Ghosh, I. Within host dynamics of SARS-CoV-2 in humans: Modeling immune responses and antiviral treatments. *SN Comput. Sci.* **2021**, *2*, 482. [CrossRef] [PubMed]
28. Wang, S.; Pan, Y.; Wang, Q.; Miao, H.; Brown, A.N.; Rong, L. Modeling the viral dynamics of SARS-CoV-2 infection. *Math. Biosci.* **2020**, *1328*, 08438. [CrossRef]
29. Almoceraa, A.E.S.; Quiroz, G.; Hernandez-Vargas, E.A. Stability analysis in COVID-19 within-host model with immune response. *Commun. Nonlinear Sci. Numer. Simul.* **2021**, *95*, 105584. [CrossRef]
30. Hattaf, K.; Yousfi, N. Dynamics of SARS-CoV-2 infection model with two modes of transmission and immune response. *Math. Biosci. Eng.* **2020**, *17*, 5326–5340. [CrossRef]
31. Chatterjee, A.N.; Basir, F.A. A model for SARS-CoV-2 infection with treatment. *Comput. Math. Methods Med.* **2020**, *2020*, 1352982. [CrossRef]
32. Mondal, J.; Samui, P.; Chatterjee, A.N. Dynamical demeanour of SARS-CoV-2 virus undergoing immune response mechanism in COVID-19 pandemic. *Eur. Phys. J. Spec. Top.* **2022**. [CrossRef]
33. Nath, B.J.; Dehingia, K.; Mishra, V.N.; Chu, Y.-M.; Sarmah, H.K. Mathematical analysis of a within-host model of SARS-CoV-2. *Adv. Differ. Equ.* **2021**, *2021*, 113. [CrossRef]
34. Ghanbari, B. On fractional approaches to the dynamics of a SARS-CoV-2 infection model including singular and non-singular kernels. *Results Phys.* **2021**, *28*, 104600. [CrossRef] [PubMed]
35. Khan, H.; Ahmad, F.; Tunç, O.; Idrees, M. On fractal-fractional Covid-19 mathematical model. *Chaos Solitons Fractals* **2022**, *157*, 111937. [CrossRef]
36. Pandey, P.; Gómez-Aguilar, J.F.; Kaabar, M.K.; Siri, Z.; Allah, A.M.A. Mathematical modeling of COVID-19 pandemic in India using Caputo-Fabrizio fractional derivative. *Comput. Biol. Med.* **2022**, *145*, 105518. [CrossRef] [PubMed]
37. Elaiw, A.M.; Hobiny, A.D.; Agha, A.D.A. Global dynamics of SARS-CoV-2/cancer model with immune responses. *Appl. Math. Comput.* **2021**, *408*, 126364. [CrossRef] [PubMed]
38. Elaiw, A.M.; Agha, A.D.A.; Azoz, S.A.; Ramadan, E. Global analysis of within-host SARS-CoV-2/HIV coinfection model with latency. *Eur. Phys. J. Plus* **2022**, *137*, 174. [CrossRef] [PubMed]
39. Agha, A.D.A.; Elaiw, A.M. Global dynamics of SARS-CoV-2/malaria model with antibody immune response. *Math. Biosci. Eng.* **2022**, accepted.
40. Perkins, T.A.; España, G. Optimal control of the COVID-19 pandemic with non-pharmaceutical interventions. *Bull. Math. Biol.* **2020**, *82*, 1–24. [CrossRef]
41. Balcha, S.F.; Obsu, L.L. Optimal control strategies for the transmission risk of COVID-19. *J. Biol. Dyn.* **2020**, *14*, 590–607.
42. Libotte, G.B.; Lobato, F.S.; Platt, G.M.; Neto, A.J.S. Determination of an optimal control strategy for vaccine administration in COVID-19 pandemic treatment. *Comput. Methods Programs Biomed.* **2020**, *196*, 105664. [CrossRef]
43. Shen, Z.H.; Chu, Y.M.; Khan, M.A.; Muhammad, S.; Al-Hartomy, O.A.; Higazy, M. Mathematical modeling and optimal control of the COVID-19 dynamics. *Results Phys.* **2021**, *31*, 105028. [CrossRef]
44. Asamoah, J.K.K.; Okyere, E.; Abidemi, A.; Moore, S.E.; Sun, G.Q.; Jin, Z.; Acheampong, E.; Gordon, J.F. Optimal control and comprehensive cost-effectiveness analysis for COVID-19. *Results Phys.* **2022**, *33*, 105177. [CrossRef] [PubMed]
45. Kirschner, D.; Lenhart, S.; Serbin, S. Optimal control of the chemotherapy of HIV. *J. Math. Biol.* **1997**, *35*, 775–792. [CrossRef] [PubMed]

46. Elaiw, A.M.; Xia, X. HIV dynamics: Analysis and robust multirate MPC-based treatment schedules. *J. Math. Anal. Appl.* **2009**, *359*, 285–301. [CrossRef]
47. Alrabaiah, H.; Safi, M.A.; DarAssi, M.H.; Al-Hdaibat, B.; Ullah, S.; Khan, M.A.; Shah, S.A.A. Optimal control analysis of hepatitis B virus with treatment and vaccination. *Results Phys.* **2020**, *19*, 103599. [CrossRef]
48. Mojaver, A.; Kheiri, H. Dynamical analysis of a class of hepatitis C virus infection models with application of optimal control. *Int. J. Biomath.* **2016**, *9*, 1650038. [CrossRef]
49. Nowak, M.A.; Bangham, C.R.M. Population dynamics of immune responses to persistent viruses. *Science* **1996**, *272*, 74–79. [CrossRef]
50. Chhetri, B.; Bhagat, V.M.; Vamsi, D.K.K.; Ananth, V.S.; Prakash, D.B.; Mandale, R.; Muthusamy, S.; Sanjeevi, C.B. Within-host mathematical modeling on crucial inflammatory mediators and drug interventions in COVID-19 identifies combination therapy to be most effective and optimal. *Alex. Eng. J.* **2021**, *60*, 2491–2512. [CrossRef]
51. Chatterjee, A.N.; Basir, F.A.; Almuqrin, M.A.; Mondal, J.; Khan, I. SARS-CoV-2 infection with lytic and nonlytic immune responses: a fractional order optimal control theoretical study. *Results Phys.* **2021**, *26*, 104260. [CrossRef]
52. Fadai, N.T.; Sachak-Patwa, R.; Byrne, H.M.; Maini, P.K.; Bafadhel, M.; Nicolau, D.V., Jr. Infection, inflammation and intervention: mechanistic modelling of epithelial cells in COVID-19. *J. R. Soc. Interface* **2021**, *18*, 20200950. [CrossRef]
53. Bar-On, Y.M.; Flamholz, A.; Phillips, R.; Milo, R. Science Forum: SARS-CoV-2 (COVID-19) by the numbers. *elife* **2020**, *9*, e57309. [CrossRef]
54. Zhou, X.; Zhang, L.; Zheng, T.; Li, H.; Teng, Z. Global stability for a delayed HIV reactivation model with latent infection and Beddington-DeAngelis incidence. *Appl. Math. Lett.* **2021**, *117*, 1–10. [CrossRef]
55. Hale, J.K.; Lunel, S.M.V. *Introduction to Functional Differential Equations*; Springer: New York, NY, USA, 1993.
56. Yang, X.; Chen, S.; Chen, J. Permanence and positive periodic solution for the single-species nonautonomous delay diffusive models. *Comput. Math. Appl.* **1996**, *32*, 109–116. [CrossRef]
57. Driessche, P.V.; Watmough, J. Reproduction numbers and sub-threshold endemic equilibria for compartmental models of disease transmission. *Math. Biosci.* **2002**, *180*, 29–48. [CrossRef]
58. Ciupe, S.M.; Heffernan, J.M. In-host modeling. *Infect. Dis. Model.* **2017**, *2*, 188–202. [CrossRef] [PubMed]
59. Korobeinikov, A. Global properties of basic virus dynamics models. *Bull. Math. Biol.* **2004**, *66*, 879–883. [CrossRef]
60. LaSalle, J.P. *The Stability of Dynamical Systems*; SIAM: Philadelphia, PA, USA, 1976.
61. Bellomo, N.; Tao, Y. Stabilization in a chemotaxis model for virus infection. *Discret. Contin. Dyn. Syst. Ser. S* **2020**, *13*, 105–117. [CrossRef]
62. Elaiw, A.M.; Agha, A.D.A.; Alshaikh, M.A. Global stability of a within-host SARS-CoV-2/cancer model with immunity and diffusion. *Int. J. Biomath.* **2021**, *15*, 2150093. [CrossRef]
63. Bellomo, N.; Burini, D.; Outada, N. Multiscale models of Covid-19 with mutations and variants. *Netw. Heterog. Media* **2022**, *17*, 293–310. [CrossRef]
64. Bellomo, N.; Burini, D.; Outada, N. Pandemics of mutating virus and society: A multi-scale active particles approach. *Philos. Trans. Ser. A Math. Phys. Eng. Sci.* **2022**, *380*, 1–14. [CrossRef]

Article

Some Contributions to the Class of Branching Processes with Several Mating and Reproduction Strategies

Manuel Molina-Fernández [†] and Manuel Mota-Medina *,[†]

Department of Mathematics, Institute of Advanced Scientific Computation, University of Extremadura, 06006 Badajoz, Spain; mmolina@unex.es
* Correspondence: mota@unex.es
† These authors contributed equally to this work.

Abstract: This work deals with mathematical modeling of dynamical systems. We consider a class of two-sex branching processes with several mating and reproduction strategies. We provide some probabilistic and statistical contributions. We deduce general expressions for the probability generating functions underlying the probability model, we derive some properties concerning the behavior of the states of the process and we determine estimates for the offspring mean vectors governing the reproduction phase. Furthermore, we extend the two-sex model considering immigration of female and male individuals from external populations. The results are illustrated through simulated examples. The investigated two-sex models are of particular interest to mathematically describe the population dynamics of biological species with a single reproductive episode before dying (semalparous species).

Keywords: mathematical modeling; branching models; two-sex models; models with immigration; population dynamics

MSC: 60J80; 62M05

1. Introduction

In this work, we continue the research line about the class of two-sex branching processes with several mating and reproductive strategies introduced in [1]. Branching processes are usually used as mathematical models to describe the population dynamics of biological species, see, e.g., [2–4]. In particular, a fairly rich literature has emerged concerning discrete-time two-sex branching processes, see the surveys by [5,6], and discussions therein. Most of these stochastic models assume that all the couples female-male have identical reproductive behavior (they produce new female and male individuals according to the same offspring probability distribution) and also that mating and reproduction depend on the number of progenitor couples in the population, see, e.g., [7–11]. In many biological species, due to environmental factors, reproduction occurs in a non-predictable environment where both phases, mating and reproduction, usually are influenced by the current numbers of females and males in the population, see, e.g., [12]. In order to describe the probabilistic evolution of such species, branching processes had not been sufficiently investigated. To this purpose, in [1], a class of two-sex branching models was introduced. Several results about such a class of models have been derived in [13,14]. We continue this research line providing new probabilistic and statistical contributions.

The paper is organized as follows. In Section 2, we mathematically describe the probability model and we derive some theoretical contributions. In Section 3, we extend the probability model and the previous contributions incorporating immigration of females and males from external populations. We include illustrative examples. In Section 4, we present the concluding remarks and some questions for research.

2. Probability Model

In [1], on a probability space $(\Omega, \mathcal{A}, P)$, we introduced a two-sex branching process $\{X_n\}_{n=0}^{\infty}$, $X_n = (F_n, M_n)$ representing the number of female and male individuals at generation n. The probability model assumes $n_m \geq 1$ and $n_r \geq 1$ mating and reproduction strategies, respectively. It is described as follows, where $\mathbb{N}$ and $\mathbb{N}_+$ denote the non-negative and positive integers, respectively:

1. Mating phase is represented by a sequence of n_m two arguments integer-valued functions $\{L_l\}_{l \in \mathbb{N}_m}$, $\mathbb{N}_m := \{1, \ldots, n_m\}$. Each L_l is assumed to be non-decreasing and such that $L_l(f, m) \leq fm$, $f, m \in \mathbb{N}$. At generation n, according to the l-th mating strategy, $L_l(F_n, M_n)$ couples female-male are formed.
2. Reproduction phase is modeled by a sequence of n_r probability distributions (offspring distributions) $\{P_h\}_{h \in \mathbb{N}_r}$, $\mathbb{N}_r := \{1, \ldots, n_r\}$, $P_h := \{p^h_{(f,m)}\}_{(f,m) \in S_h}$, $S_h \subseteq \mathbb{N}^2$, $p^h_{(f,m)}$ being the probability that a given couple produces exactly f females and m males when P_h is the underlying reproductive strategy.
3. In each generation, the mating and reproduction strategies are determined through functions φ_m and φ_r, both defined on $\mathbb{N}^2$ and taking values on $\mathbb{N}_m$ and $\mathbb{N}_r$, respectively.

We start with $X_0 = (F_0, M_0) \in \mathbb{N}_+^2$. Then, given that at generation n, $X_n = x \in \mathbb{N}^2$, we obtain that $L_{\varphi_m(x)}$ and $P_{\varphi_r(x)}$ are the mating and reproductive strategies, respectively. Hence,

$$X_{n+1} = (F_{n+1}, M_{n+1}) := \sum_{i=1}^{L_{\varphi_m(x)}(x)} (F^{\varphi_r(x)}_{n,i}, M^{\varphi_r(x)}_{n,i}), \quad n \in \mathbb{N} \qquad (1)$$

with $F^{\varphi_r(x)}_{n,i}$ and $M^{\varphi_r(x)}_{n,i}$ denoting, respectively, the number of female and male individuals originated by the i-th couple at generation n. For each $h \in \mathbb{N}_r$, independently of n, the random vectors $(F^h_{n,i}, M^h_{n,i})$, $i = 1, \ldots, L_{\varphi_m(x)}(x)$, defined on $(\Omega, \mathcal{A}, P)$, are assumed to be i.i.d. with P_h being the offspring distribution,

$$P(F^h_{n,1} = f, M^h_{n,1} = m) = p^h_{(f,m)}, \quad (f, m) \in S_h$$

Given $x_0, \ldots, x_n, x_{n+1} \in \mathbb{N}^2$, by considering that independently of the generation n, the random vectors $(F^h_{n,i}, M^h_{n,i})$ are i.i.d., it is derived from (1),

$$P(X_{n+1} = x_{n+1} \mid X_0 = x_0, \ldots, X_n = x_n) = P\left(\sum_{i=1}^{L_{\varphi_m(x_n)}(x_n)} (F^{\varphi_r(x_n)}_{n,i}, M^{\varphi_r(x_n)}_{n,i}) = x_{n+1}\right)$$

$$= P(X_{n+1} = x_{n+1} \mid X_n = x_n)$$

Note that, the corresponding transition probabilities are independent of the generation n considered. In fact, for $x, z \in \mathbb{N}^2$,

$$P(X_{n+1} = z \mid X_n = x) = P\left(\sum_{i=1}^{L_{\varphi_m(x)}(x)} (F^{\varphi_r(x)}_{n,i}, M^{\varphi_r(x)}_{n,i}) = z\right) = \sum_{z_1, \ldots, z_d \in \Delta_z} \prod_{i=1}^{d} p^{\varphi_r(x)}_{z_i}$$

where $d = L_{\varphi_m(x)}(x)$ and $\Delta_z := \{z_1, \ldots, z_d \in \mathbb{N}^2 : \sum_{i=1}^{d} z_i = z\}$. Hence, $\{X_n\}_{n=0}^{\infty}$ is a homogeneous Markov chain with state space $\mathbb{N}^2$. Clearly, if for some n, $X_n = (0, 0)$ then $X_{n+j} = (0, 0)$, $j \geq 1$. Thus, $(0, 0)$ is an absorbent state.

Remark 1. *Two-sex Model (1) is particularly appropriate to mathematically describe the population dynamics of semalparous species, namely, biological species with a single reproductive episode before dying. Functions L_l, φ_m, and φ_r, should be flexible enough in order to fit the main features of* the species we pretend to describe. Usually, such functions will depend of biological/ethological parameters of interest in the demographic dynamics of the species.

Let $f_h(s,t) := E[s^{F_{0,1}^h} t^{M_{0,1}^h}]$ and $g_n(s,t) := E[s^{F_n} t^{M_n}]$, $s,t \in [0,1]$, be the probability generating functions (p.g.f.) of $(F_{0,1}^h, M_{0,1}^h)$ and (F_n, M_n), $h \in \mathbb{N}_r$, $n \in \mathbb{N}$, respectively. Clearly, $g_0(s,t) = s^{F_0} t^{M_0}$. Next result determines the general expression for g_n, $n \in \mathbb{N}_+$.

Proposition 1. *For $n \in \mathbb{N}$,*

$$g_{n+1}(s,t) = E\left[(f_{\varphi_r(X_n)}(s,t))^{L_{\varphi_m(X_n)}(X_n)}\right], \quad s,t \in [0,1]$$

Proof. Given $n \in \mathbb{N}$,

$$g_{n+1}(s,t) = E[s^{F_{n+1}} t^{M_{n+1}}] = E\left[E[s^{F_{n+1}} t^{M_{n+1}} \mid X_n]\right]$$

$$= \sum_{x \in \mathbb{N}^2} E\left[s^{\sum_{i=1}^{L_{\varphi_m(x)}(x)} F_{n,i}^{\varphi_r(x)}} t^{\sum_{i=1}^{L_{\varphi_m(x)}(x)} M_{n,i}^{\varphi_r(x)}}\right] P(X_n = x)$$

$$= \sum_{x \in \mathbb{N}^2} \left(E[s^{F_{0,1}^{\varphi_r(x)}} t^{M_{0,1}^{\varphi_r(x)}}]\right)^{L_{\varphi_m(x)}(x)} P(X_n = x)$$

$$= \sum_{x \in \mathbb{N}^2} \left(f_{\varphi_r(x)}(s,t)\right)^{L_{\varphi_m(x)}(x)} P(X_n = x)$$

$$= E\left[(f_{\varphi_r(X_n)}(s,t))^{L_{\varphi_m(X_n)}(X_n)}\right], \quad s,t \in [0,1]$$

□

We now provide some properties about the behavior of the states of $\{X_n\}_{n=0}^\infty$. To this purpose, we assume that L_l, $l \in \mathbb{N}_m$, are superadditive functions, i.e., given $n \in \mathbb{N}_+$,

$$L_l\left(\sum_{i=1}^n x_i\right) \geq \sum_{i=1}^n L_l(x_i), \quad x_i \in \mathbb{N}^2, \ l \in \mathbb{N}_m \qquad (2)$$

Superadditivity is a classical and logical requirement in two-sex branching process literature. Furthermore, for $x \in \mathbb{N}^2$, independently of n, let

$$C_x := \{y \in \mathbb{N}^2 : P(X_{n+m} = y \mid X_n = x) > 0 \text{ for some } m \geq 1\}$$

be the set of states which can be reached from x.

Proposition 2. *Assume $x_0 \in \mathbb{N}_+^2$ such that $p_{x_0}^h > 0$, $L_l(x_0) > 1$, $h \in \mathbb{N}_r$, $l \in \mathbb{N}_m$. Given $x \in \mathbb{N}^2$:*

(a) *There exists $x' \in \mathbb{N}^2$ with $L_{\varphi_m(x')}(x') > L_{\varphi_m(x)}(x)$ verifying that $x' \in C_{x_0}$.*

(b) *If $p_{(0,0)}^h > 0$, $h \in \mathbb{N}_r$, then $(0,0) \in C_x$.*

Proof.

(a) Let us introduce the sequence $\{x_n\}_{n=0}^\infty$, where

$$x_{n+1} := x_0 L_{\varphi_m(x_n)}(x_n), \quad n \in \mathbb{N}$$

By using (2) and the fact that $L_l(x_0) > 1, l \in \mathbb{N}_m$,

$$L_{\varphi_m(x_{n+1})}(x_{n+1}) = L_{\varphi_m(x_{n+1})}\left(x_0 L_{\varphi_m(x_n)}(x_n)\right)$$

$$= L_{\varphi_m(x_{n+1})}\left(\sum_{i=1}^{L_{\varphi_m(x_n)}(x_n)} x_0\right)$$

$$\geq \sum_{i=1}^{L_{\varphi_m(x_n)}(x_n)} L_{\varphi_m(x_{n+1})}(x_0)$$

$$= L_{\varphi_m(x_n)}(x_n) L_{\varphi_m(x_{n+1})}(x_0)$$

$$> L_{\varphi_m(x_n)}(x_n)$$

Hence $\{L_{\varphi_m(x_n)}(x_n)\}_{n=0}^{\infty} \nearrow \infty$. Consequently, given $x \in \mathbb{N}^2$, there exists x_n such that $L_{\varphi_m(x_n)}(x_n) > L_{\varphi_m(x)}(x)$. Thus, it is sufficient to check that $x_n \in C_{x_0}$. In fact, if for some $l \in \mathbb{N}_+$, $X_l = x_0$, then:

$$P(X_{l+n} = x_n \mid X_l = x_0) \geq \prod_{i=0}^{n-1} P(X_{l+i+1} = x_{i+1} \mid X_{l+i} = x_i) = \prod_{i=0}^{n-1} P(X_{l+1} = x_{i+1} \mid X_l = x_i) \quad (3)$$

Now, using that $x_{i+1} = x_0 L_{\varphi_m(x_i)}(x_i)$ and $p^h_{x_0} > 0, h \in \mathbb{N}_r$,

$$P(X_{l+1} = x_{i+1} \mid X_l = x_i) = P\left(\sum_{j=1}^{L_{\varphi_m(x_i)}(x_i)} (F^{\varphi_r(x_i)}_{l,j}, M^{\varphi_r(x_i)}_{l,j}) = x_{i+1}\right) \geq (p^{\varphi_r(x_i)}_{x_0})^{L_{\varphi_m(x_i)}(x_i)} > 0$$

Therefore, from (3),

$$P(X_{l+n} = x_n \mid X_l = x_0) \geq \left(p^{\varphi_r(x_i)}_{x_0}\right)^{\sum_{i=0}^{n-1} L_{\varphi_m(x_i)}(x_i)} > 0$$

(b) If for some $n \in \mathbb{N}$, $X_n = x$, then:

$$P(X_{n+1} = (0,0) \mid X_n = x) = P\left(\sum_{j=1}^{L_{\varphi_m(x)}(x)} (F^{\varphi_r(x)}_{n,j}, M^{\varphi_r(x)}_{n,j}) = (0,0)\right) = \left(p^{\varphi_r(x)}_{(0,0)}\right)^{L_{\varphi_m(x)}(x)} > 0$$

□

Let $\mu^h := (\mu^h_1, \mu^h_2)$ and $\Delta^h := (\sigma^h_{ij})_{i,j=1,2}$ be, respectively, the mean vector and the covariance matrix of $(F^h_{0,1}, M^h_{0,1}), h \in \mathbb{N}_r$,

$$\mu^h_i := \sum_{(k_1,k_2) \in S_h} k_i p^h_{(k_1,k_2)}, \quad \sigma^h_{ij} := \sum_{(k_1,k_2) \in S_h} (k_i - \mu^h_i)(k_j - \mu^h_j) p^h_{(k_1,k_2)}, \quad i,j = 1,2.$$

For $n \in \mathbb{N}$ and $x \in \mathbb{N}^2$, let us denote by μ^x_{n+1} and Δ^x_{n+1} the mean vector and the covariance matrix, respectively, of X_{n+1} given that $X_n = x$. From Proposition 1, it can be verified that, independently of n:

$$E[s^{F_{n+1}} t^{M_{n+1}} \mid X_n = x] = (f_{\varphi_r(x)}(s,t))^{L_{\varphi_m(x)}(x)}, \quad s,t \in [0,1]$$

$$\mu^x_{n+1} = L_{\varphi_m(x)}(x) \mu^{\varphi_r(x)}, \quad \Delta^x_{n+1} = L_{\varphi_m(x)}(x) \Delta^{\varphi_r(x)} \quad (4)$$

Next, we consider the estimation of μ^h, $h \in \mathbb{N}_r$. To this end, we will assume that, for some $n \in \mathbb{N}_+$, we know the observations of the variables:

$$X_0, L_{\varphi_m(X_k)}(X_k), X_{k+1}, k = 0, \ldots, n \quad (5)$$

For each $h \in \mathbb{N}_r$, let $T_h := \{k \in \{0, \ldots, n\} : \varphi_r(X_k) = h\}$, i.e., the set of generations (until generation n) where P_h has been the reproductive strategy.

Proposition 3. *Given $h \in \mathbb{N}_r$ such that $T_h \neq \emptyset$ and $\sum_{k \in T_h} L_{\varphi_m(X_k)}(X_k) > 0$, a conditional moment-based estimator for μ^h using the data sample (5), is given by:*

$$\widehat{\mu^h} = \left(\sum_{k \in T_h} L_{\varphi_m(X_k)}(X_k) \right)^{-1} \sum_{k \in T_h} X_{k+1} \tag{6}$$

Proof. From (4),

$$E[X_{k+1} \mid X_k] = L_{\varphi_m(X_k)}(X_k) \mu^{\varphi_r(X_k)} \quad a.s.$$

Hence, by using the moment estimation procedure, we can propose as estimate for $\mu^{\varphi_r(X_k)}$, based on the observations of $L_{\varphi_m(X_k)}(X_k)$ and X_{k+1},

$$\overline{\mu_{(k)}^{\varphi_r(X_k)}} := (L_{\varphi_m(X_k)}(X_k))^{-1} X_{k+1}, \; k = 0, \ldots, n \tag{7}$$

It is verified that,

$$E\left[\overline{\mu_{(k)}^{\varphi_r(X_k)}} \mid L_{\varphi_m(X_k)}(X_k) > 0 \right] = \mu^{\varphi_r(X_k)}$$

In fact,

$$E\left[\overline{\mu_{(k)}^{\varphi_r(X_k)}} \mid L_{\varphi_m(X_k)}(X_k) > 0 \right] = \frac{\sum_{z \in \mathbb{N}_+} z^{-1} E[X_{k+1} \mid L_{\varphi_m(X_k)}(X_k) = z] P(L_{\varphi_m(X_k)}(X_k) = z)}{P(L_{\varphi_m(X_k)}(X_k) > 0)}$$

$$= \frac{\sum_{z \in \mathbb{N}_+} z^{-1} E[\sum_{i=1}^{z} (F_{k,i}^{\varphi_k(X_k)}, M_{k,i}^{\varphi_k(X_k)})] P(L_{\varphi_m(X_k)}(X_k) = z)}{P(L_{\varphi_m(X_k)}(X_k) > 0)}$$

$$= \frac{\mu^{\varphi_r(X_k)} \sum_{z \in \mathbb{N}_+} P(L_{\varphi_m(X_k)}(X_k) = z)}{P(L_{\varphi_m(X_k)}(X_k) > 0)} = \mu^{\varphi_r(X_k)}$$

Thus, by considering (7), we propose as appropriate estimator for μ^h:

$$\widehat{\mu^h} := \sum_{k \in T_h} \beta_k^h \overline{\mu_{(k)}^h} \tag{8}$$

where $\sum_{k \in T_h} \beta_k^h = 1$. Taking $\beta_k^h \propto L_{\varphi_m(X_k)}(X_k)$, we deduce,

$$\beta_k^h = \left(\sum_{k \in T_h} L_{\varphi_m(X_k)}(X_k) \right)^{-1} L_{\varphi_m(X_k)}(X_k)$$

Consequently, from (7) and (8), we derive the Expression (6). □

Example 1. *Let us consider a two-sex model (1) where, given $(f, m) \in \mathbb{N}^2$,*
1. *Females and males form couples through the $n_m = 2$ mating strategies:*

$$L_1(f, m) = \lfloor K_1 f \min\{1, m\} \rfloor, \; L_2(f, m) = \lfloor K_1 m \min\{f, 1\} \rfloor$$

$\lfloor \cdot \rfloor$ denoting integer part and $K_1 \in (0,1)$ representing the estimated proportion of individuals in the population which disappears due to environmental factors.

2. The couples produce new female and male individuals according to the $n_r = 2$ reproductive strategies $P_h = \{p^h_{(f,m)}\}$, $h = 1, 2$, where:

$$p^1_{(f,m)} := P(F^1_{0,1} = f, M^1_{0,1} = m) = e^{-2.5}(1.3)^f(1.2)^m(f!m!)^{-1} \tag{9}$$

$$p^2_{(f,m)} := P(F^2_{0,1} = f, M^2_{0,1} = m) = e^{-2.4}(1.1)^f(1.3)^m(f!m!)^{-1} \tag{10}$$

Thus, we are considering two bivariate Poisson laws as offspring distributions. In fact, Poisson probability distribution is very used to describe the probabilistic evolution of biological species. From (9) and (10) we deduce,

$$\mu^1 = (1.3, 1.2), \quad \Delta^1 = \begin{pmatrix} 1.3 & 0 \\ 0 & 1.2 \end{pmatrix}$$

$$\mu^2 = (1.1, 1.3), \quad \Delta^2 = \begin{pmatrix} 1.1 & 0 \\ 0 & 1.3 \end{pmatrix}$$

Offspring distribution P_1 favors the birth of females, with a ratio females/males of the means equal to 1.083. This ratio has a value of 0.847 for the offspring distribution P_2 that consequently favors the birth of males.

3. In each generation, we assume the following functions φ_m and φ_r:

$$\varphi_m(f, m) = 1 I_{\{fm^{-1} > K_2\}}(f, m) + 2 I_{\{fm^{-1} \leq K_2\}}(f, m)$$

$$\varphi_r(f, m) = 1 I_{\{f \leq m\}}(f, m) + 2 I_{\{f > m\}}(f, m)$$

I_A being the indicator function of the set A and K_2 representing a suitable threshold for the ratio females/males.

As illustration, taking, e.g., $X_0 = (300, 80)$, $K_1 = 0.75$ and $K_2 = 1.05$, applying the computing programs we have implemented through the statistical software R, ([15]), we have simulated data for a total number of 30 generations, see Table 1.

Table 1. Females and males (X_n), mating strategy (l_n), couples ($Z_n = L_{\varphi_m(X_n)}(X_n)$) and reproductive strategy (h_n) in the successive generations.

Generation	X_n	l_n	Z_n	h_n	Generation	X_n	l_n	Z_n	h_n
0	(300, 80)	1	225	2	16	(154, 124)	1	115	2
1	(236, 302)	2	226	1	17	(130, 134)	2	100	1
2	(308, 275)	1	231	2	18	(124, 105)	1	93	2
3	(238, 298)	2	223	1	19	(104, 135)	2	101	1
4	(307, 269)	1	230	2	20	(128, 117)	1	96	2
5	(229, 301)	2	225	1	21	(122, 106)	1	91	2
6	(288, 271)	1	216	2	22	(86, 131)	2	98	1
7	(244, 240)	2	180	2	23	(125, 106)	1	93	2
8	(182, 239)	2	179	1	24	(106, 130)	2	97	1
9	(223, 218)	2	163	2	25	(122, 148)	2	111	1
10	(191, 214)	2	160	1	26	(131, 125)	2	93	2
11	(197, 205)	2	153	1	27	(89, 115)	2	86	1
12	(190, 169)	1	142	2	28	(119, 111)	1	89	2
13	(148, 195)	2	146	1	29	(96, 116)	2	87	1
14	(172, 183)	2	137	1	30	(112, 118)	2	88	1
15	(162, 175)	2	131	1					

From Table 1, we have that:

$$T_1 = \{1, 3, 5, 8, 10, 11, 13, 14, 15, 17, 19, 22, 24, 25, 27, 29, 30\},$$
$$T_2 = \{0, 2, 4, 6, 7, 9, 12, 16, 18, 20, 21, 23, 26, 28\}$$

Hence, by (6), we determine the following estimates for μ^h, $h = 1, 2$,

$$\widehat{\mu^1} = (1.266, 1.203), \quad \widehat{\mu^2} = (1.070, 1.291) \tag{11}$$

From (11),

$$\max_{h=1,2}\left\{\max_{i=1,2}\{|\widehat{\mu_i^h} - \mu_i^h|\}\right\} = 0.034$$

This value indicates good accuracy for the obtained estimates. See also Figure 1.

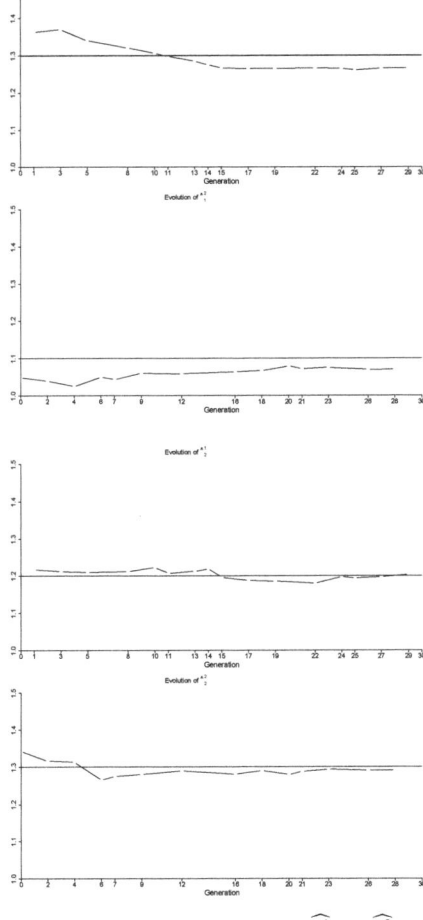

Figure 1. Evolution of the estimates $\widehat{\mu_i^1}$ and $\widehat{\mu_i^2}$, $i = 1, 2$, in the successive generations belonging to T_1 and T_2, respectively.

3. Probability Model with Immigration

In this section, the previous two-sex probability model is extended including immigration of females and males from external populations. On the probability space $(\Omega, \mathcal{A}, P)$ we now introduce the sequence $\{Y_n\}_{n=0}^{\infty}$, $Y_n = (F_n, M_n)$ representing the number of female and male individuals in the population at generation n. Initially we assume $Y_0 = (F_0, M_0) \in \mathbb{N}_+^2$. As in model (1), given that $Y_n = y \in \mathbb{N}^2$, then L_{l_n} and P_{h_n} with $l_n := \varphi_m(y)$ and $h_n := \varphi_r(y)$

are the mating and reproductive strategies at the n-th generation, respectively. At generation $n+1$,

$$Y_{n+1} = (F_{n+1}, M_{n+1}) := \sum_{i=1}^{L_{\varphi_m(y)}(y)} (F_{n,i}^{\varphi_r(y)}, M_{n,i}^{\varphi_r(y)}) + (F_{n+1}^I, M_{n+1}^I), \quad n \in \mathbb{N} \qquad (12)$$

where F_{n+1}^I (M_{n+1}^I) represents the number of immigrant females (males). It is assumed that, $\{(F_n^I, M_n^I)\}_{n=1}^{\infty}$ is a sequence of i.i.d non-negative variables (defined on $(\Omega, \mathcal{A}, P)$) independent of $(F_{0,1}^h, M_{0,1}^h)$, $h \in \mathbb{N}_r$. The probability distribution (immigration distribution) of (F_1^I, M_1^I) will be denoted by $\{q_{(f,m)}\}_{(f,m) \in \mathbb{N}}$, $q_{(f,m)} := P(F_1^I = f, M_1^I = m)$.

From (12), given $y_0, \ldots, y_n, y_{n+1} \in \mathbb{N}^2$, using that $\{(F_n^I, M_n^I)\}_{n=1}^{\infty}$ is a sequence of i.i.d random vectors independent of $(F_{0,1}^h, M_{0,1}^h)$, $h \in \mathbb{N}_r$,

$$P(Y_{n+1} = y_{n+1} \mid Y_0 = y_0, \ldots, Y_n = y_n) = P\left(\sum_{i=1}^{L_{\varphi_m(y_n)}(y_n)} (F_{n,i}^{\varphi_r(y_n)}, M_{n,i}^{\varphi_r(y_n)}) + (F_{n+1}^I, M_{n+1}^I) = y_{n+1}\right)$$

$$= P(Y_{n+1} = y_{n+1} \mid Y_n = y_n)$$

Again, the transition probabilities are independent of the generation n considered. In fact, for $y, z \in \mathbb{N}^2$,

$$P(Y_{n+1} = z \mid Y_n = y) = P\left(\sum_{i=1}^{L_{\varphi_m(y)}(y)} (F_{n,i}^{\varphi_r(y)}, M_{n,i}^{\varphi_r(y)}) + (F_{n+1}^I, M_{n+1}^I) = z\right) = \sum_{z_1, \ldots, z_d, w \in \Delta_z^*} \prod_{i=1}^{d} p_{z_i}^{\varphi_r(y)} q_w$$

where $d = L_{\varphi_m(y)}(y)$ and $\Delta_z^* := \{z_1, \ldots, z_d, w \in \mathbb{N}^2 : \sum_{i=1}^{d} z_i + w = z\}$. Thus, $\{Y_n\}_{n=0}^{\infty}$ is a homogeneous Markov chain with state space $\mathbb{N}^2$.

In what follows, we provide analogous results to Propositions 1–3 for this new class of two-sex branching processes with immigration of females and males.

For $s, t \in [0,1]$, let $\phi(s,t) := E[s^{F_1^I} t^{M_1^I}]$, $h_n(s,t) := E[s^{F_n} t^{M_n}]$, $n \in \mathbb{N}$, be the p.g.f. of (F_1^I, M_1^I) and $Y_n = (F_n, M_n)$, respectively. We have that $h_0(s,t) = s^{F_0} t^{M_0}$. The general expression for h_n, $n \in \mathbb{N}_+$, is given in the following result.

Proposition 4. *For $n \in \mathbb{N}$,*

$$h_{n+1}(s,t) = \phi(s,t) E\left[(f_{\varphi_r(Y_n)}(s,t))^{L_{\varphi_m(Y_n)}(Y_n)}\right], \quad s, t \in [0,1]$$

Proof. Given $n \in \mathbb{N}$,

$$h_{n+1}(s,t) = E[s^{F_{n+1}} t^{M_{n+1}}] = E\left[E[s^{F_{n+1}} t^{M_{n+1}} \mid Y_n]\right]$$

$$= \sum_{y \in \mathbb{N}^2} E\left[s^{\sum_{i=1}^{L_{\varphi_m(y)}(y)} F_{n,i}^{\varphi_r(y)} + F_{n+1}^I} t^{\sum_{i=1}^{L_{\varphi_m(y)}(y)} M_{n,i}^{\varphi_r(y)} + M_{n+1}^I}\right] P(Y_n = y)$$

$$= \sum_{y \in \mathbb{N}^2} E\left[s^{F_1^I} t^{M_1^I}\right] \left(E\left[s^{F_{0,1}^{\varphi_r(y)}} t^{M_{0,1}^{\varphi_r(y)}}\right]\right)^{L_{\varphi_m(y)}(y)} P(X_n = y)$$

$$= \phi(s,t) E\left[(f_{\varphi_r(Y_n)}(s,t))^{L_{\varphi_m(Y_n)}(Y_n)}\right], \quad s, t \in [0,1].$$

$\square$

For the next result, we assume again that L_l, $l \in \mathbb{N}_m$, are superadditive functions.

Proposition 5. Assume $y_0, z_0 \in \mathbb{N}_+^2$ such that $p_{y_0}^h > 0$, $q_{z_0} > 0$, $L_l(y_0) > 1$, $h \in \mathbb{N}_r$, $l \in \mathbb{N}_m$. Given $y \in \mathbb{N}^2$:

(a) There exists $y' \in \mathbb{N}^2$, with $L_{\varphi_m(y')}(y') > L_{\varphi_m(y)}(y)$, verifying that $y' \in C_{y_0}$.

(b) $z_0 \in C_y$.

Proof.

(a) Let us consider the sequence $\{y_n\}_{n=0}^{\infty}$, where
$$y_{n+1} := y_0 L_{\varphi_m(y_n)}(y_n) + z_0, \ n \in \mathbb{N}$$

By the superadditivity of L_l, $l \in \mathbb{N}_m$,

$$L_{\varphi_m(y_{n+1})}(y_{n+1}) = L_{\varphi_m(y_{n+1})}(y_0 L_{\varphi_m(y_n)}(y_n) + z_0)$$
$$= L_{\varphi_m(y_{n+1})}\left(\sum_{i=1}^{L_{\varphi_m(y_n)}(y_n)} y_0 + z_0\right)$$
$$\geq \sum_{i=1}^{L_{\varphi_m(y_n)}(y_n)} L\varphi_m(y_{n+1})(y_0) + L_{\varphi_m(y_{n+1})}(z_0)$$
$$= L_{\varphi_m(y_n)}(y_n) L\varphi_m(y_{n+1})(y_0) + L_{\varphi_m(y_{n+1})}(z_0)$$
$$> L_{\varphi_m(y_n)}(y_n)$$

Hence $\{L_{\varphi_m(y_n)}(y_n)\}_{n=0}^{\infty} \nearrow \infty$. Thus, given $y \in \mathbb{N}^2$, there exists y_n such that $l_{\varphi_m(y_n)}(y_n) > L_{\varphi_m(y)}(y)$. If for some $l \in \mathbb{N}_+$, $Y_l = y_0$, then:

$$P(Y_{l+n} = y_n \mid Y_l = y_0) \geq \prod_{i=0}^{n-1} P(Y_{l+i+1} = y_{i+1} \mid Y_{l+i} = y_i) = \prod_{i=0}^{n-1} P(Y_{l+1} = y_{i+1} \mid Y_l = y_i) \quad (13)$$

Now, using that $y_{i+1} = y_0 L_{\varphi_m(y_i)}(y_i) + z_0$,

$$P(Y_{l+1} = y_{i+1} \mid Y_l = y_i) = P\left(\sum_{j=1}^{L_{\varphi_m(y_i)}(y_i)} (F_{l,j}^{\varphi_r(y_i)}, M_{l,j}^{\varphi_r(y_i)}) + (F_{l+1}^I, M_{l+1}^I) = y_{i+1}\right)$$
$$\geq \left(p_{y_0}^{\varphi_r(y_i)}\right)^{L_{\varphi_m(y_i)}(y_i)} q_{z_0} > 0$$

Therefore, from (13),

$$P(Y_{l+n} = y_n \mid Y_l = y_0) \geq \left(p_{y_0}^{\varphi_r(y_i)}\right)^{\sum_{i=0}^{n-1} L_{\varphi_m(y_i)}(y_i)} (q_{z_0})^{n-1} > 0$$

We deduce that $y_n \in C_{y_0}$ and the result is proved.

(b) If for some $n \in \mathbb{N}$, $Y_n = y$, then

$$P(Y_{n+1} = z_0 \mid Y_n = y) = P\left(\sum_{j=1}^{L_{\varphi_m(y)}(y)} (F_{n,j}^{\varphi_r(y)}, M_{n,j}^{\varphi_r(y)}) + (F_{n+1}^I, M_{n+1}^I) = z_0\right)$$
$$\geq \left(p_{(0,0)}^{\varphi_r(y)}\right)^{L_{\varphi_m(y)}(y)} q_{z_0} > 0$$

□

Let us denote by μ^I and Δ^I the mean vector and the covariance matrix of (F_1^I, M_1^I), respectively. Furthermore, for $n \in \mathbb{N}$ and $y \in \mathbb{N}^2$, let η_{n+1}^y and Γ_{n+1}^y the mean vector and covariance matrix, respectively, of Y_{n+1} given that $Y_n = y$. From Proposition 4, it can be checked that, independently of n:

$$E[s^{F_{n+1}} t^{M_{n+1}} \mid Y_n = y] = \phi(s,t)(f_{\varphi_r(y)}(s,t))^{L_{\varphi_m(y)}(y)}, \ s,t \in [0,1]$$

$$\eta_{n+1}^y = L_{\varphi_m(y)}(y)\mu^{\varphi_r(y)} + \mu^I, \quad \Gamma_{n+1}^y = L_{\varphi_m(y)}(y)\Delta^{\varphi_r(y)} + \Delta^I \tag{14}$$

We now consider the estimation of μ^h, $h \in \mathbb{N}_r$ and μ^I. We will assume that, for some $n \in \mathbb{N}_+$, we know the observations of the variables:

$$Y_0, \ L_{\varphi_m(Y_k)}(Y_k), \ Y_{k+1}, Y_{k+1}^I \ k = 0, \ldots, n \tag{15}$$

where, by simplicity $Y_{k+1}^I := (F_{k+1}^I, M_{k+1}^I)$. Clearly, we can propose as estimator for μ^I, based on the data sample (15),

$$\widehat{\mu^I} = (n+1)^{-1} \sum_{k=0}^{n} Y_{k+1}^I \tag{16}$$

For each $h \in \mathbb{N}_r$, let $T_h^* := \{k \in \{0, \ldots, n\} : \varphi_r(Y_k) = h\}$ be the set of generations (until the generation n) where P_h has been the underlying reproductive strategy.

Proposition 6. *Given $h \in \mathbb{N}_r$ such that $T_h^* \neq \emptyset$ and $\sum_{k \in T_h^*} L_{\varphi_m(Y_k)}(Y_k) > 0$, a conditional moment-based estimator for μ^h using the data sample (15), is given by:*

$$\widehat{\mu^h} = \left(\sum_{k \in T_h^*} L_{\varphi_m(Y_k)}(Y_k) \right)^{-1} \sum_{k \in T_h^*} (Y_{k+1} - Y_{k+1}^I) \tag{17}$$

Proof. From (14),

$$E[Y_{k+1} \mid Y_k] = L_{\varphi_m(Y_k)}(Y_k)\mu^{\varphi_r(Y_k)} + \mu^I \quad a.s.$$

Hence, by moment estimation procedure, we propose as estimate for $\mu^{\varphi_r(Y_k)}$, based on the observations of $L_{\varphi_m(Y_k)}(Y_k)$ (assumed positive), Y_{k+1} and Y_{k+1}^I,

$$\overline{\mu_{(k)}^{\varphi_r(Y_k)}} = (L_{\varphi_m(Y_k)}(Y_k))^{-1}(Y_{k+1} - Y_{k+1}^I), \ k = 0, \ldots, n \tag{18}$$

It can be verified that,

$$E\left[\overline{\mu_{(k)}^{\varphi_r(Y_k)}} \mid L_{\varphi_m(Y_k)}(Y_k) > 0\right] = \mu^{\varphi_r(Y_k)}$$

Taking into account (18), an appropriate estimator for μ^h, based on the data sample (15), is given by:

$$\widehat{\mu^h} = \sum_{k \in T_h^*} \gamma_k^h \overline{\mu_{(k)}^h} \tag{19}$$

where $\sum_{k \in T_h^*} \gamma_k^h = 1$. Taking $\gamma_k^h \propto L_{\varphi_m(Y_k)}(Y_k)$, we deduce,

$$\gamma_k^h = \sum_{k \in T_h^*} (L_{\varphi_m(Y_k)}(Y_k))^{-1} L_{\varphi_m(Y_k)}(Y_k)$$

Hence, from (18) and (19), we obtain Expression (17). □

Example 2. Let the two-sex probability model (1) considered in Example 1. We now assume that, in each generation, immigrant females and males enter the population from other populations according to a certain probability distribution, for example, the trinomial distribution:

$$q_{(f,m)} = (50!)(f!m!(50-f-m)!)^{-1}(0.4)^f(0.4)^m(0.2)^{50-f-m}$$

$$f, m \in \{0, 1, \ldots, 50\}, \ f + m \leq 50$$

We deduce that,

$$\mu^I = (20, 20), \quad \Delta^I = \begin{pmatrix} 12 & -8 \\ -8 & 12 \end{pmatrix}$$

As illustration, taking $Y_0 = (300, 80)$, $K_1 = 0.75$ and $K_2 = 1.05$, we have simulated data for a total number of 30 generations, see Table 2.

Table 2. Females and males (Y_n), mating strategy (l_n), couples ($Z_n = L_{\varphi_m(Y_n)}(Y_n)$), immigrant females and males (Y_n^I) and reproductive strategy (h_n) in the successive generations.

Generation	Y_n	l_n	Z_n	Y_n^I	h_n	Generation	Y_n	l_n	Z_n	Y_n^I	h_n
0	(300, 80)	1	225	(0, 0)	2	16	(379, 356)	1	284	(20, 20)	2
1	(250, 343)	2	257	(17, 23)	1	17	(320, 396)	2	297	(18, 16)	1
2	(389, 314)	1	291	(24, 15)	2	18	(427, 384)	1	320	(16, 17)	2
3	(354, 387)	2	290	(23, 17)	1	19	(358, 428)	2	321	(20, 19)	1
4	(425, 366)	1	318	(17, 25)	2	20	(446, 386)	1	334	(18, 21)	2
5	(369, 411)	2	308	(14, 28)	1	21	(401, 455)	2	341	(24, 17)	1
6	(410, 369)	1	307	(17, 24)	2	22	(459, 452)	2	339	(19, 22)	2
7	(379, 412)	2	309	(22, 19)	1	23	(408, 465)	2	348	(20, 25)	1
8	(453, 411)	1	339	(17, 22)	2	24	(491, 419)	1	368	(19, 21)	2
9	(389, 444)	2	333	(17, 24)	1	25	(432, 501)	2	375	(24, 20)	1
10	(484, 410)	1	363	(21, 23)	2	26	(514, 433)	1	385	(20, 21)	2
11	(453, 445)	2	333	(21, 19)	2	27	(437, 509)	2	381	(18, 23)	1
12	(426, 425)	2	318	(27, 17)	2	28	(520, 524)	2	393	(20, 20)	1
13	(369, 408)	2	306	(16, 22)	1	29	(497, 509)	2	381	(23, 18)	1
14	(389, 374)	2	280	(13, 22)	2	30	(464, 496)	2	372	(22, 16)	1
15	(306, 375)	2	281	(14, 24)	1						

From Table 2, we have that:

$T_1^* = \{1, 3, 5, 7, 9, 13, 15, 17, 19, 21, 23, 25, 27, 28, 29, 30\}$,

$T_2^* = \{0, 2, 4, 6, 8, 10, 11, 12, 14, 16, 18, 20, 22, 24, 26\}$

Hence, by (16) and (17),

$$\widehat{\mu^I} = (18.633, 20.133), \quad \widehat{\mu^1} = (1.313, 1.198), \quad \widehat{\mu^2} = (1.115, 1.272)$$

We obtain,

$$\max_{i=1,2}\{|\widehat{\mu_i^I} - \mu_i^I|\} = 1.367, \quad \max_{h=1,2}\left\{\max_{i=1,2}\{|\widehat{\mu_i^h} - \mu_i^h|\}\right\} = 0.028$$

These values indicate good accuracy for the proposed estimates. See also Figures 2 and 3.

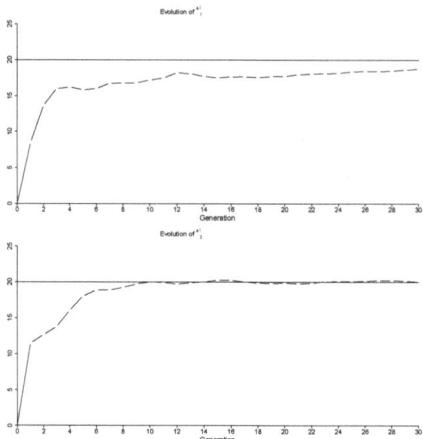

Figure 2. Evolution of the estimates $\widehat{\mu_i^l}$, $i = 1, 2$, in the successive generations.

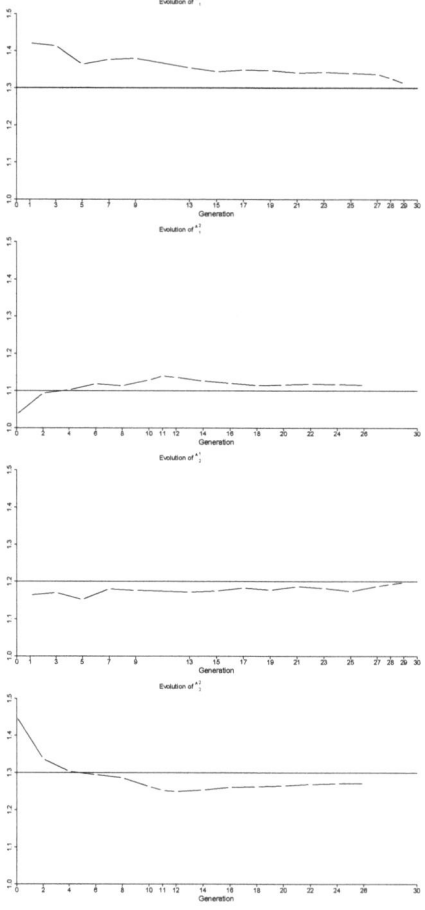

Figure 3. Evolution of the estimates $\widehat{\mu_i^1}$ and $\widehat{\mu_i^2}$, $i = 1, 2$, in the successive generations belonging to T_1^* and T_2^*, respectively.

4. Conclusions

In this research, we have focused attention to the mathematical modeling of the population dynamics in biological species with sexual reproduction. We have considered the possibility of multiple mating and reproductive strategies, thereby continuing the research line initiated in previous papers. Several probabilistic and statistical contributions have been derived. In particular, general expressions for the probability generating functions associated with the variables of interest in the underlying probability model have been deduced (Proposition 1), some properties about the behavior of the states of the process have been studied (Proposition 2) and estimates for the mean vectors of the offspring distributions have been proposed (Proposition 3). This class of two-sex branching models has been generalized by considering immigration of females and males from external populations. The previous results have been then extended to this new class of models with immigration (Propositions 4–6). As illustration, for both classes of two-sex models, simulated examples have been presented.

Some questions for future research are, e.g., consider alternative inferential procedures in order to estimate the main parameters governing the reproduction phase; determine the probability distribution associated with the number of generations elapsed before the possible extinction of the population; or explore potential applications of the investigated two-sex models in phenomena of ecological and environmental interest, for example, in mathematical modeling of the phenomenon concerning populating or re-populating a certain habitat with some semelparous species.

Author Contributions: Conceptualization, M.M.-F. and M.M.-M.; methodology, M.M.-F. and M.M.-M.; software, M.M.-F. and M.M.-M.; validation, M.M.-F. and M.M.-M.; formal analysis, M.M.-F. and M.M.-M.; investigation, M.M.-F. and M.M.-M.; resources, M.M.-F. and M.M.-M.; data curation, M.M.-F. and M.M.-M.; writing original draft preparation, M.M.-F. and M.M.-M.; writing review and editing, M.M.-F. and M.M.-M.; visualization, M.M.-F. and M.M.-M.; supervision, M.M.-F. and M.M.-M.; project administration, M.M.-F. and M.M.-M.; funding acquisition, M.M.-F. and M.M.-M. All authors have read and agreed to the published version of the manuscript.

Funding: The authors thank the support by the Junta de Extremadura (Grant GR21050) and the Fondo Europeo de Desarrollo Regional.

Institutional Review Board Statement: Not applicable.

Informed Consent Statement: Not applicable.

Data Availability Statement: Not applicable.

Acknowledgments: The authors also thank the support by the Ministerio de Ciencia e Innovación of Spain (Grant PID2019-108211GB-I00/AEI/10.13039/501100011033).

Conflicts of Interest: The authors declare they have no conflict of interest.

References

1. Molina, M.; Mota, M.; Ramos, A. Stochastic modeling in biological populations with sexual reproduction through branching models: Application to Coho salmon populations. *Math. Biosci.* **2014**, *258*, 182–188. [CrossRef]
2. Athreya, K.B.; Ney, P.E. *Branching Processes*; Dover Publications Inc.: Mineola, NY, USA, 2004.
3. Guttorp, P. *Statistical Inference for Branching Processes*; Wiley: New York, NY, USA, 1991.
4. Haccou, P.; Jagers, P.; Vatutin, V. *Branching Processes: Variation, Growth, and Extinction of Populations*; Cambridge University Press: Cambridge, UK, 2005.
5. Hull, D.M. A survey of the literature associated with the bisexual Galton-Watson branching process. *Extr. Math.* **2003**, *18*, 321–343.
6. Molina, M. Two–sex branching process literature. In *Lectures Notes in Statistics*; Springer: Berlin/Heidelberg, Germany, 2010; Volume 197, pp. 279–293.
7. Cornell, S.; Isham, V. Ultimate extinction of the promiscuous bisexual Galton–Watson metapopulation. *Aust. N. Z. J. Stat.* **2004**, *46*, 87–98. [CrossRef]
8. Daley, D.J.; Hull, D.M.; Taylor, J.M. Bisexual Galton–Watson branching processes with superadditive mating functions. *J. Appl. Prob.* **1986**, *23*, 585–600. [CrossRef]
9. Hull, D.M. A reconsideration of Lotka's extinction probability using a bisexual branching process. *J. Appl. Prob.* **2001**, *38*, 776–780. [CrossRef]

10. Ma, S. Bisexual Galton-Watson branching processes in random environments. *Acta Math. Appl. Sin. Engl. Ser.* **2006**, *22*, 419–428. [CrossRef]
11. Xing, Y.; Wang, Y. On the extinction of one class of population-size dependent bisexual branching processes. *J. Appl. Prob.* **2005**, *42*, 175–184. [CrossRef]
12. Fleming, I.A. Reproductive strategies of Atlantic salmon: Ecology and evolution. *Rev. Fish Biol. Fish.* **1996**, *6*, 379–416. [CrossRef]
13. Molina, M.; Mota, M.; Ramos, A. Two-sex branching processes with several mating and reproduction strategies: Extinction versus survival. In *Branching Processes and Their Applications*; Springer: Cham, Switzerland, 2016; Volume 219, pp. 307–317.
14. Molina, M.; Mota, M.; Ramos, A. Estimation of parameters in biological species with several mating and reproduction alternatives. *Math. Biosci.* **2020**, *329*, 108471. [CrossRef]
15. R Development Core Team. *A Language and Environment for Statistical Computing*; R Foundation for Statistical Computing: Vienna, Austria, 2009. Available online: http://www.r-project.org (accessed on 15 May 2022).

Article

Quiescence Generates Moving Average in a Stochastic Epidemiological Model with One Host and Two Parasites

Usman Sanusi [1,2,3], Sona John [1,2], Johannes Mueller [2,4] and Aurélien Tellier [1,*]

1. Population Genetics, Department of Life Science Systems, School of Life Sciences, Technical University of Munich, 85354 Freising, Germany; usman.sanusi@tum.de (U.S.); sona.john@tum.de (S.J.)
2. Department of Mathematics, Technical University of Munich, 85748 Garching, Germany; johannes.mueller@mytum.de
3. Department of Mathematics and Statistics, Umaru Musa Yar'adua University, Dutsin-Ma Road, Katsina P.M.B. 2218, Nigeria
4. Institute for Computational Biology, Helmholtz Center Munich, 85764 Neuherberg, Germany
* Correspondence: aurelien.tellier@tum.de

Citation: Sanusi, U.; John, S.; Mueller, J.; Tellier, A. Quiescence Generates Moving Average in a Stochastic Epidemiological Model with One Host and Two Parasites. *Mathematics* 2022, *10*, 2289. https://doi.org/10.3390/math10132289

Academic Editors: Sophia Jang and Jui-Ling Yu

Received: 25 May 2022
Accepted: 28 June 2022
Published: 30 June 2022

Publisher's Note: MDPI stays neutral with regard to jurisdictional claims in published maps and institutional affiliations.

Copyright: © 2022 by the authors. Licensee MDPI, Basel, Switzerland. This article is an open access article distributed under the terms and conditions of the Creative Commons Attribution (CC BY) license (https://creativecommons.org/licenses/by/4.0/).

Abstract: Mathematical modelling of epidemiological and coevolutionary dynamics is widely being used to improve disease management strategies of infectious diseases. Many diseases present some form of intra-host quiescent stage, also known as covert infection, while others exhibit dormant stages in the environment. As quiescent/dormant stages can be resistant to drug, antibiotics, fungicide treatments, it is of practical relevance to study the influence of these two life-history traits on the coevolutionary dynamics. We develop first a deterministic coevolutionary model with two parasite types infecting one host type and study analytically the stability of the dynamical system. We specifically derive a stability condition for a five-by-five system of equations with quiescence. Second, we develop a stochastic version of the model to study the influence of quiescence on stochasticity of the system dynamics. We compute the steady state distribution of the parasite types which follows a multivariate normal distribution. Furthermore, we obtain numerical solutions for the covariance matrix of the system under symmetric and asymmetric quiescence rates between parasite types. When parasite strains are identical, quiescence increases the variance of the number of infected individuals at high transmission rate and vice versa when the transmission rate is low. However, when there is competition between parasite strains with different quiescent rates, quiescence generates a moving average behaviour which dampen off stochasticity and decreases the variance of the number of infected hosts. The strain with the highest rate of entering quiescence determines the strength of the moving average and the magnitude of reduction of stochasticity. Thus, it is worth investigating simple models of multi-strain parasite under quiescence/dormancy to improve disease management strategies.

Keywords: parasite dormancy; moving average; epidemiology; stochasticity; coevolution; infectious diseases

MSC: 92D30; 34F05; 60H30

1. Introduction

Dormancy or quiescence is a bet-hedging strategy common to many bacteria, fungi [1,2], invertebrates [3], and plants which evolves to dampen off the effect of bad conditions and maximize the reproductive output under good conditions [4–6]. This bet-hedging in time occurs when the individual (bacteria, fungus, invertebrates) or the offspring of the individual (plants, invertebrates) enter dormancy with a low metabolic state for some period of time during which reproduction and evolution occurs in the active part of the population. The dormant individuals constitutes a reservoir, the so-called seed banks, and can re-enter the active population at a later time point. Dormancy (quiescence) evolves a bet-hedging strategy in response to unpredictable environments such as random variations of the abiotic conditions [7], competition under density-dependence regulation of the population [8], contact between a bacteria host and viruses [9], frequency- or density-dependent selection due to host-parasite coevolution [10] or prey-predator interactions. Dormancy (quiescence) introduces overlap between generation and a storage effect which generates a time delay in the generation time [11,12]. At the population level, dormancy is shown to slow down the rate of genetic drift, that is increasing the time to random loss or fixation of neutral alleles. Moreover, seed banks also slow down the action of natural selection by increasing the time to fixation (loss) of the positively (deleteriously) selected alleles [13–15]. We note the use of the term dormancy preferably for plant seeds or crustacean eggs (e.g., *Daphnia* sp.), while quiescence refers to individual bacteria or fungi switching between "on" and "off" metabolic states [16]. As we focus on microparasites in the following, we prefer the term quiescence from now on.

Parasite quiescence is a strategy of microparasites (bacteria, fungi) becoming inactive inside an infected host for some period of time. During this period, the disease does not progress in the host and the host can express symptoms or be asymptomatic. Importantly, quiescent parasites do not contribute to the disease transmission. In the medical community, the infections in which the parasite is quiescent or inactive are referred to as silent or dormant, and in the virology literature they are referred to as covert [17]. Parasite quiescence has well known but yet underappreciated consequences for disease management. During quiescence, the parasite are often resistant to the application of drugs, antibiotics or fungicides [18–21]. Furthermore, applying antibiotics can trigger the switching of bacteria from active to the inactive (quiescent) state. *Plasmodium falciparum*, the main agent of malaria, has the ability to lurk in the hepatocytes of some patients, remaining inactive but being resistance to drug treatments, causing later on disease relapse [10,21,22]. *P. vivax*, another malarial agent, exhibits also the ability to become dormant in the liver of a host for some weeks, months even up to a year or more, which makes the task to eradicate the disease difficult [23–25]. Therefore, it is important to determine the (1) conditions for the evolution of parasite quiescence, and (2) influence of quiescence on the sustainability of parasite populations. A key theoretical study on the evolution of quiescence in animal parasites [17] shows that silent/covert infection is not likely to be the optimal strategy (trait value) for the parasite (so-called Evolutionary Stable Strategy (ESS)) in an epidemiological model with one host and one parasite genotype. Parasite quiescence would only evolve if there were substantial fluctuations in the host population size or seasonal variations in transmission rates. Therefore, the authors state that their "models predict low rates of covert infection, which does not reflect the consistent high levels that are found in some host–parasite systems". Based on a modelling framework with fixed population sizes but two hosts and two parasite types, the host population can evolve dormancy as an optimal strategy (ESS) as a result of the parasite pressure and coevolutionary dynamics [4]. While more theoretical work is needed to decipher the conditions for the evolution of parasite quiescence/dormancy, likely involving a combination of temporally variable environmental and coevolutionary pressures, we focus in the present study on the consequence of quiescence for the stability and outcome of host-parasite coevolutionary dynamics. As a first step in this direction, we consider here a model with one host and two parasite strains (or types).

Indeed, one host population under pressure by several parasite strains, or even several parasite species, is the rule rather than the exception [26,27]. Considering the epidemiological dynamics under competition/co-infection between strains is important [7] to predict the evolution of parasite virulence, that is disease induced death rate of host [28]. We are interested here in understanding the epidemiological dynamics of a single host type infected by one of the two parasite strains exhibiting quiescence. We ask whether quiescence affects the parameters for which two strains can co-exist or competitively exclude one another. Furthermore, the maintenance of several strains, the persistence of disease as endemic or the persistence of the host population are affected by stochastic processes. Disease epidemics are subjected to stochasticity at various levels, the main one being in the transmission rate, and thus stochastic approaches are required to predict the outcome of epidemics. While the deterministic model of epidemiology successfully captures the behaviour when the size of host and parasite populations are large, stochasticity can affect the outcome of the dynamics for small sizes significantly [29–32]. Quiescence affects the size of the parasite active population and thus possibly the epidemiological dynamics. We hereby hypothesize that quiescence may also affects the outcome of stochasticity on the co-existence of our two parasite strains epidemiological model.

In the first part we describe our epidemiological model with changes in the number of healthy and infected host individuals over time under quiescence of both parasite strains. We then derive a stability condition for the dynamical ODE system. In the second part of the study, we introduce stochasticity in disease transmission and derive a Fokker-Planck equation of the Continuous Time Markov Chain model. Lastly, we perform some numerical study on the model behaviour under stochasticity. We show that for symmetric case i.e., when the infected class are identical and quiescence phases are also identical, quiescence increases the variance, and decrease it when the rate of infection is small. For asymmetric case i.e., when the infected class as well as the quiescence phases are not identical, quiescence has a major effect in reducing the intensity of the noise in the stochastic process, whenever the rate of entering (or exiting) quiescence differ between strains. By analogy, we term this phenomenon as moving average.

2. Deterministic Model with Quiescence

2.1. Model Description

Our model is similar in essence to classic epidemiological models [7,11,33–36]. Here we consider one host population and two parasite strains, thus the population is divided into five mutually exclusive compartments: one healthy susceptible host compartment H, two infected host, I_1 and I_2, infected by parasite of type 1 and 2 respectively, and two quiescence compartments Q_1 and Q_2, comprise the infected individuals I_1 and I_2 for which the parasite is in the quiescent state. We define the following system of ordinary differential equations describing the rate of change of the number of individuals in each compartment.

$$\begin{aligned}
\frac{dI_1}{dt} &= \beta_1 H I_1 - \rho_1 I_1 - d I_1 - \gamma_1 I_1 - \nu_1 I_1 + \zeta_1 Q_1 + \epsilon_1 \\
\frac{dI_2}{dt} &= \beta_2 H I_2 - \rho_2 I_2 - d I_2 - \gamma_2 I_2 - \nu_2 I_2 + \zeta_2 Q_2 + \epsilon_2 \\
\frac{dH}{dt} &= \Lambda - \beta_1 H I_1 - \beta_2 H I_2 - d H + \nu_1 I_1 + \nu_2 I_2 \\
\frac{dQ_1}{dt} &= \rho_1 I_1 - \zeta_1 Q_1 - d Q_1 \\
\frac{dQ_2}{dt} &= \rho_2 I_2 - \zeta_2 Q_2 - d Q_2
\end{aligned} \quad (1)$$

where Λ is the constant birth rate of healthy host and d to is the natural death rate, γ_1 and γ_2 are the disease induced death rate or (virulence) caused by parasite 1, and 2 respectively. Similarly all other parasite specific parameters such as disease transmission rate β, recovery rate ν, rate at which parasite switches to quiescence ρ and the switching back rate ζ are defined for each parasite strains separately. The parameters ϵ_1 and ϵ_2 are the rates of incoming migration of parasite 1 and 2 respectively from an outside compartment/population. These parameters are introduced to avoid the competitive exclusion principle, namely without the ϵ's, one parasite type necessarily excludes the other and there is no coexistence of both parasite types at the epidemic equilibrium, the same effect is expected if the migration of quiescent parasite would occur (not shown here). We assume (1) that the parasite lives and multiplies within its host, (2) the absence of multiple infection so that strains 1 and 2 of the parasite are mutually exclusive on one host, and (3) no latency period for the parasite, hence, the infected persons are infectious immediately after infection. Note that the model reduces to a simple model of one susceptible host and two infected host types (SI_1I_2S, referred to as system without quiescence) when setting the quiescence parameters equal to zero (Appendix C). In the present study we are particularly interested in following the number of hosts infected by parasite 1 or 2 and to study conditions for which both types of parasites are maintained. We therefore assume constant birth rate, to ensure a non-explosive process when moving to the stochastic version of our model. We finally introduce the parameters ϵ_1 and ϵ_2 to promote the coexistence of both strains at the equilibrium and to guarantee a unique steady state solution in the continuous time Markov chain version of the model (see below, Stochastic model).

2.2. Steady State Solutions

In this section we find the equilibrium solutions of the system. First, we analyse the system without inflow of new infection to the population ($\epsilon_1 = \epsilon_2 = 0$). This simple system generically has the three equilibrium states: (1) a disease free equilibrium in which both parasite strains die off and are removed from the system (yielding $I_1 = I_2 = Q_1 = Q_2 = 0$), (2) two-boundary equilibria at which a single parasite strain survive i.e., competitive exclusion when parameters of the model are non-symmetric (yielding in either $I_1 = Q_1 = 0$ or $I_2 = Q_2 = 0$). In the non-generic case that we have symmetric parameters, we have line of stationary solutions. By evaluating the Jacobian matrix of the system, one can evaluate the stability conditions for these equilibria. To ensure the existence of unique polymorphic equilibrium, we introduce two parameters for invasion/immigration rates namely, ϵ_1 and ϵ_2 which are greater than zero. The introduction of these two parameters results in moving the disease free as well as one of the boundary equilibria to the negative cone i.e., makes them to have negative values which is biologically meaningless. We are thereafter left with only one polymorphic equilibrium which is biologically meaningful. Henceforth, we focus on the analysis of the polymorphic equilibrium for which both parasite strains are maintained in the system. We show the existence and uniqueness of this endemic equilibrium under mild conditions (for more details, see Appendix A).

2.3. Stability Analysis

An $n \times n$ Jacobian matrix P is said to be stable, and thus an equilibrium being locally stable, if all its eigenvalues lie on the left half plane. As it may be impractical to determine the stability of a matrix analytically [11], by using the Lyapunov theorem to determine if the system is stable, it is easier to apply the Routh-Hurwitz criterion [11,37,38]. However, this criteria can be cumbersome if the matrix is of high dimension. In this section we therefore derive the stability condition for a generic 5×5 matrix G with parasite quiescence by reducing our system to 3×3 which is more easily amenable to computation.

The Jacobian of system in Equation (1) evaluated at equilibrium is given as follows

$$G = \begin{pmatrix} \beta_1 H^* - \rho_1 - \gamma_1 - \nu_1 - d & 0 & \beta_1 I_1^* & \zeta_1 & 0 \\ 0 & \beta_2 H^* - \rho_2 - \gamma_2 - \nu_2 - d & \beta_2 I_2^* & 0 & \zeta_2 \\ -\beta_1 H^* + \nu_1 & -\beta_2 H^* + \nu_2 & -\beta_1 I_1^* - \beta_2 I_2^* - d & 0 & 0 \\ \rho_1 & 0 & 0 & -\zeta_1 - d & 0 \\ 0 & \rho_2 & 0 & 0 & -\zeta_2 - d \end{pmatrix}.$$

Now we define a matrix

$$A \in ((a_{i,j})) \in \mathbb{R}^{3 \times 3} \tag{2}$$

to be the Jacobian matrix evaluated at equilibrium of the system without quiescent described in Appendix C. We introduce $B = G + dI$, such that the spectrum of B is just the shifted spectrum of G. Indeed, the stability of B implies stability of G.

Let

$$B = \begin{pmatrix} a_{11} - \rho_1 & a_{12} & a_{13} & \zeta_1 & 0 \\ a_{21} & a_{22} - \rho_2 & a_{23} & 0 & \zeta_2 \\ a_{31} & a_{32} & a_{33} & 0 & 0 \\ \rho_1 & 0 & 0 & -\zeta_1 & 0 \\ 0 & \rho_2 & 0 & 0 & -\zeta_2 \end{pmatrix}. \tag{3}$$

Proposition 1. *Let 3×3 matrix A be a Jacobian matrix of system without quiescence phase and we also define*

$$a_1 = -tr(A) = -a_{11} - a_{22} - a_{33},$$
$$a_2 = a_{11}a_{22} + a_{11}a_{33} + a_{22}a_{33} - a_{23}a_{32} - a_{12}a_{21} - a_{13}a_{31}, \quad (4)$$
$$a_3 = -det(A).$$

The matrix A in (2) is stable if and only if

$$tr(A) < 0, \quad det(A) < 0 \quad and \quad a_2 > 0. \quad (5)$$

The above Proposition 1 is simply a reformulation of the Routh-Hurwitz criteria (see details in [11,37,38]). We now find a criteria for stability of B under the following proposition.

Proposition 2. *The following three statements are equivalent for the matrix B above:*

- *Statement 1: The matrix B in (3) is stable for all $\rho_1, \rho_2, \zeta_1, \zeta_2 > 0$.*
- *Statement 2 : $b_1 > 0, \quad b_2 > 0, \quad b_3 > 0, \quad b_4 > 0, \quad b_5 > 0, \quad b_1 b_2 b_3 > b_3^2 + b_1^2 b_4$,*
  $(b_1 b_4 - b_5)(b_1 b_2 b_3 - b_3^2 - b_1^2 b_4) > b_5(b_1 b_2 - b_3)^2 + b_1 b_5^2 \quad$ for all $\quad \rho_1, \rho_2, \zeta_1, \zeta_2 > 0$.
- *Statement 3: $det(A) < 0, \quad tr(A) \leq 0, \quad a_2 > 0, \quad a_{11} \leq 0, \quad a_{22} \leq 0, a_{33} \leq 0$,*
  $a_{13}a_{31} \leq a_{11}a_{33}, a_{23}a_{32} \leq a_{22}a_{33}$.

The above statements are technically equivalent in the sense that for the system in (1) to be stable it must satisfy the given statements. We prove that *statement 1* implies *statement 2*, *statement 2* implies *statement 3* and *statement 3* implies *statement 1*. This proposition is a generalisation of the theorem in [11] and we use the same method as in [11] (see Appendix B for the proof of the Proposition 2 above, as we prove the stability of a generic matrix B as defined in (3)). The conditions in *statement 3* of the above proposition can be used to prove that the endemic equilibrium of (1) is locally asymptotically stable. Which means that if the system undergoes a perturbation (the system is set not too far away from its equilibrium) then the system eventually reaches its equilibrium. The local stability is not as strong as global stability, the latter meaning that the system returns to it equilibrium after whatever perturbation (without restriction). Note that we see the effect of local stability of the equilibrium solutions in the stochastic simulations using Gillespie's algorithm, as the realisations (sample paths) remain within the domain of attraction of the deterministic endemic equilibrium (Figure 1a,b).

As mentioned, the *statement 2* may sometimes be hard to apply, thus as an alternative, one can use *statement 3* to show that (1) is locally asymptotically stable. This is relatively easy as the dimension of the system is now reduced to 3×3, so that it is possible to compute the Jacobian matrix of the system without quiescence (A5) described in Appendix C to obtain the matrix A in (2). Then one can test the conditions described in *statement 3* above. Once those conditions are satisfied then the larger system (1) is also locally asymptotically stable.

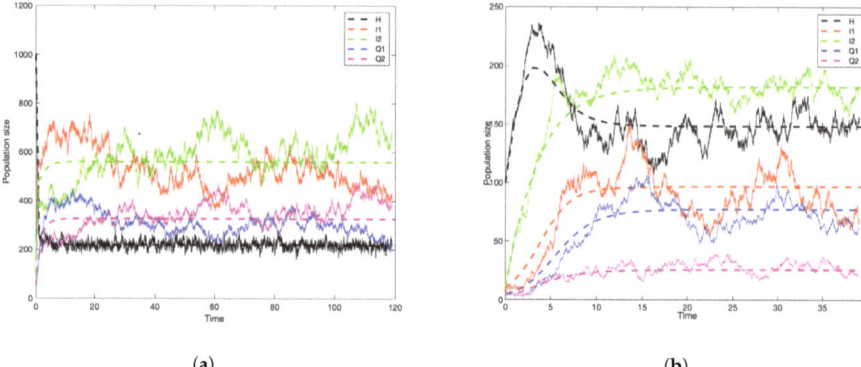

(a)   (b)

Figure 1. Numerical simulations of the deterministic model (1) compared with stochastic simulation using Gillespie's algorithm. In (**a**), the initial population size is $H = 1000, I_1 = 100, I_2 = 100, Q_1 = Q_2 = 50$. The values of the parameters are symmetrical; $\beta_1 = \beta_2 = 0.005, \Lambda = 1000, d = 0.5, \nu_1 = \nu_2 = 0.3, \gamma_1 = \gamma_2 = 0.003, \epsilon_1 = \epsilon_2 = 0.6, \zeta_1 = \zeta_2 = 0.7, \rho_1 = \rho_2 = 0.7$. While in (**b**), the initial population size is $H = 100, I_1 = 10, I_2 = 10, Q_1 = Q_2 = 5$. The values of the parameters are asymmetrical; $\beta_1 = 0.005, \beta_2 = 0.0005, \Lambda = 100, d = 0.3, \nu_1 = 0.3, \nu_2 = 0.003, \gamma_1 = \gamma_2 = 0.003, \epsilon_1 = 10, \epsilon_2 = 50, \zeta_1 = 0.2, \zeta_2 = 0.4, \rho_1 = 0.4, \rho_2 = 0.1$.

3. Stochastic Analysis

3.1. Transition Probabilities

This section defines a stochastic version to the deterministic model as described in Equation (1) of Section 2.1. We add stochasticity occurring at any of the possible transition of individuals between classes (birth and death). The transition probabilities of jumping from one state (e.g., infected quiescent) to the another state (e.g., infected) are defined bellow. We choose Δt very small so that during this time interval only one event occurs. The proportion of healthy population is H, the proportion of infected by parasite 1 population is I_1, the proportion of infected by parasite 2 population is I_2, the proportion of population in quiescence compartment infected by parasite 1 is Q_1 and the proportion of population in quiescence compartment infected by parasite 2 is Q_2. The possible changes are either $H + 1, H − 1, I_1 + 1, I_1 − 1, I_2 + 1, I_2 − 1, Q_1 + 1, Q_1 − 1, Q_2 + 1, Q_2 − 1$ or no change at all. Therefore, our stochastic process is a birth and death process. The one step transition probabilities are given in Table 1.

3.2. Stochastic Simulations

In order to test the validity of our assumptions to analyse the stochastic system, we used Gillespie's algorithm [39–41] to generate stochastic realisations/sample paths of the birth and death processes (Figure 1a,b). In (Figure 1a,b), the stochastic trajectories fluctuate around the deterministic equilibrium as predicted by Equation (1). Please note that in (Figure 1a) there are only three curves in the deterministic trajectories while there are five in the stochastic realisation. This is to due the fact that we chose symmetric parameter values of the model, so $I_1 = I_2$ and $Q_1 = Q_2$ in the deterministic setting, but not in the stochastic version.

Table 1. Transitions rates for the quiescence model 1.

Type	Transition	Rate
Birth of healthy host H	$(H_t, I_{1t}, I_{2t}, Q_{1t}, Q_{2t}) \to (H_t + 1, I_{1t}, I_{2t}, Q_{1t}, Q_{2t})$	$\Lambda \Delta t + o\Delta(t)$
Natural death of H	$(H_t, I_{1t}, I_{2t}, Q_{1t}, Q_{2t}) \to (H_t - 1, I_{1t}, I_{2t}, Q_{1t}, Q_{2t})$	$dH\Delta t + o\Delta(t)$
Infection of H by I_1	$(H_t, I_{1t}, I_{2t}, Q_{1t}, Q_{2t}) \to (H_t - 1, I_{1t} + 1, I_{2t}, Q_{1t}, Q_{2t})$	$\beta_1 H I_1 \Delta t + o\Delta(t)$
Infection of H by I_2	$(H_t, I_{1t}, I_{2t}, Q_{1t}, Q_{2t}) \to (H_t - 1, I_{1t}, I_{2t} + 1, Q_{1t}, Q_{2t})$	$\beta_2 H I_2 \Delta t + o\Delta(t)$
Death of I_1	$(H_t, I_{1t}, I_{2t}, Q_{1t}, Q_{2t}) \to (H_t, I_{1t} - 1, I_{2t}, Q_{1t}, Q_{2t})$	$(d + \gamma_1) I_1 \Delta t + o\Delta(t)$
Death of I_2	$(H_t, I_{1t}, I_{2t}, Q_{1t}, Q_{2t}) \to (H_t, I_{1t}, I_{2t} - 1, Q_{1t}, Q_{2t})$	$(d + \gamma_1) I_2 \Delta t + o\Delta(t)$
Recovery I_1 & replacement with H	$(H_t, I_{1t}, I_{2t}, Q_{1t}, Q_{2t}) \to (H_t + 1, I_{1t} - 1, I_{2t}, Q_{1t}, Q_{2t})$	$\nu_1 I_1 \Delta t + o\Delta(t)$
Recovery I_2 & replacement with H	$(H_t, I_{1t}, I_{2t}, Q_{1t}, Q_{2t}) \to (H_t + 1, I_{1t}, I_{2t} - 1, Q_{1t}, Q_{2t})$	$\nu_2 I_2 \Delta t + o\Delta(t)$
Immigration to I_1	$(H_t, I_{1t}, I_{2t}, Q_{1t}, Q_{2t}) \to (H_t, I_{1t} + 1, I_{2t}, Q_{1t}, Q_{2t})$	$\epsilon_1 \Delta t + o\Delta(t)$
Immigration to I_2	$(H_t, I_{1t}, I_{2t}, Q_{1t}, Q_{2t}) \to (H_t, I_{1t}, I_{2t} + 1, Q_{1t}, Q_{2t})$	$\epsilon_2 \Delta t + o\Delta(t)$
Go quiescent I_1 & birth of Q_1	$(H_t, I_{1t}, I_{2t}, Q_{1t}, Q_{2t}) \to (H_t, I_{1t} - 1, I_{2t}, Q_{1t} + 1, Q_{2t})$	$\rho_1 I_1 \Delta t + o\Delta(t)$
Go quiescent I_1 & birth of Q_1	$(H_t, I_{1t}, I_{2t}, Q_{1t}, Q_{2t}) \to (H_t, I_{1t}, I_{2t} - 1, Q_{1t}, Q_{2t} + 1)$	$\rho_2 I_2 \Delta t + o\Delta(t)$
Wake-up Q_1 & replacement with I_1	$(H_t, I_{1t}, I_{2t}, Q_{1t}, Q_{2t}) \to (H_t, I_{1t} + 1, I_{2t}, Q_{1t} - 1, Q_{2t})$	$\zeta_1 Q_1 \Delta t + o\Delta(t)$
Wake-up Q_2 & replacement with I_2	$(H_t, I_{1t}, I_{2t}, Q_{1t}, Q_{2t}) \to (H_t, I_{1t}, I_{2t} + 1, Q_{1t}, Q_{2t} - 1)$	$\zeta_2 Q_2 \Delta t + o\Delta(t)$
Natural death of Q_1	$(H_t, I_{1t}, I_{2t}, Q_{1t}, Q_{2t}) \to (H_t, I_{1t}, I_{2t}, Q_{1t} - 1, Q_{2t})$	$dQ_1 \Delta t + o\Delta(t)$
Natural death of Q_2	$(H_t, I_{1t}, I_{2t}, Q_{1t}, Q_{2t}) \to (H_t, I_{1t}, I_{2t}, Q_{1t}, Q_{2t} - 1)$	$dQ_2 \Delta t + o\Delta(t)$

3.3. Master Equation

The forward Kolmogorov differential equation also known as Master Equation, describes the rate of change of these probabilities is given in Table 1. The master equation describes the evolution of the disease individuals at the early times of the infection. To understand the long term dynamics, we need to derive its corresponding Fokker-Planck equation.

Let $p(i, j, k, l, m)(t) = \text{Prob}\{H(t) = i, I_1(t) = j, I_2(t) = k, Q_1(t) = l, Q_2(t) = m\}$, then

$$
\begin{aligned}
\frac{dp_{(i,j,k,l,m)}}{dt} =& \Lambda p_{(i-1,j,k,l,m)} + d(i+1)p_{(i+1,j,k,l,m)} + \beta_1(i+1)(j-1)p_{(i+1,j-1,k,l,m)} \\
&+ (d+\gamma_1)(j+1)p_{(i,j+1,k,l,m)} + \beta_2(i+1)(k-1)p_{(i+1,j,k-1,l,m)} \\
&+ (d+\gamma_2)(k+1)p_{(i,j,k+1,l,m)} + \nu_1(j+1)p_{(i-1,j+1,k,l,m)} + \nu_2(k+1)p_{(i-1,j,k+1,l,m)} \\
&+ \epsilon_1 p_{(i,j-1,k,l,m)} + \epsilon_2 p_{(i,j,k-1,l,m)} + \rho_1(j+1)p_{(i,j+1,k,l-1,m)} + \rho_2(k+1)p_{(i,j,k+1,l,m-1)} \\
&+ \zeta_1(l+1)p_{(i,j-1,k,l+1,m)} + \zeta_2(m+1)p_{(i,j,k-1,l,m+1)} \\
&+ d(l+1)p_{(i,j,k,l+1,m)} + d(m+1)p_{(i,j,k,l,m+1)} \\
&- \Big[\Lambda + di + \beta_1 ij + (d+\gamma_1)j + \beta_2 ik + (d+\gamma_2)k + \nu_1 j + \nu_2 k \\
&+ \epsilon_1 + \epsilon_2 + \rho_1 j + \rho_2 k + \zeta_1 l + \zeta_2 m + dl + dm\Big] p_{(i,j,k,l,m)}
\end{aligned}
\qquad (6)
$$

This master Equation (6) is then used to work out *Kramers-Moyal expansion* that led to the derivation of the *Fokker-Planck equation* below.

3.4. Fokker-Planck Equation of the Model

To understand the long term dynamics of the master Equation (6), we need to derive the corresponding Fokker-Planck equation. The Fokker-Planck equation describes further the rate of change of transitions probabilities described in Table 1. We can also find the long term distribution of variables.

Now, let

$$
p(i,j,k,l,m) = \int_{ih-\frac{h}{2}}^{ih+\frac{h}{2}} \int_{jh-\frac{h}{2}}^{jh+\frac{h}{2}} \int_{kh-\frac{h}{2}}^{kh+\frac{h}{2}} \int_{lh-\frac{h}{2}}^{lh+\frac{h}{2}} \int_{mh-\frac{h}{2}}^{mh+\frac{h}{2}} u(x_1, x_2, x_3, x_4, x_5) dx_1 dx_2 dx_3 dx_4 dx_5 + o(h^6),
$$

let also $x_1 = ih, x_2 = jh, x_3 = kh, x_4 = lh, x_5 = mh$ and $h = \frac{1}{N}$. We then performed *Kramers-Moyal expansion* to derived the following Fokker-Planck equation which is given as follows.

$$\begin{aligned}
\partial_t u(x_1,\ldots,x_5,t) = &-\partial_{x_1}\{h\lambda - dx_1 - \beta_1 x_1 x_2 - \beta_2 x_1 x_3 + \nu_1 x_2 + \nu_2 x_3\}u(x_1,\ldots,x_5,t)\\
&-\partial_{x_2}\{\beta_1 x_1 x_2 - (d+\gamma_1)x_2 - \nu_1 x_2 - \rho_1 x_2 + \zeta_1 x_4 + \epsilon_1\}u(x_1,\ldots,x_5,t)\\
&-\partial_{x_3}\{\beta_2 x_1 x_3 - (d+\gamma_2)x_2 - \nu_2 x_2 - \rho_2 x_3 + \zeta_2 x_5 + \epsilon_2\}u(x_1,\ldots,x_5,t)\\
&-\partial_{x_4}\{\rho_1 x_2 - \zeta_1 x_4 - dx_4\}u(x_1,\ldots,x_5,t)\\
&-\partial_{x_5}\{\rho_2 x_3 - \zeta_2 x_5 - dx_5\}u(x_1,\ldots,x_5,t)\\
&+\frac{h}{2}\partial_{x_1 x_1}\{h\lambda + dx_1 + \beta_1 x_1 x_2 + \beta_2 x_1 x_3 + \nu_1 x_2 + \nu_2 x_3\}u(x_1,\ldots,x_5,t)\\
&+\frac{h}{2}\partial_{x_2 x_2}\{\beta_1 x_1 x_2 + (d+\gamma_1)x_2 + \nu_1 x_2 + \rho_1 x_2 + h\epsilon_1\}u(x_1,\ldots,x_5,t)\\
&+\frac{h}{2}\partial_{x_3 x_3}\{\beta_2 x_1 x_3 + (d+\gamma_2)x_3 + \nu_2 x_3 + \rho_2 x_3 + h\epsilon_2\}u(x_1,\ldots,x_5,t)\\
&+\frac{h}{2}\partial_{x_4 x_4}\{\rho_1 x_2 + \zeta_1 x_4 + dx_4\}u(x_1,\ldots,x_5,t)\\
&+\frac{h}{2}\partial_{x_5 x_5}\{\rho_2 x_3 + \zeta_2 x_5 + dx_5\}u(x_1,\ldots,x_5,t)\\
&-h\partial_{x_1 x_2}\{\beta_1 x_1 x_2 + \nu_1 x_2\}u(x_1,\ldots,x_5,t)\\
&-h\partial_{x_1 x_3}\{\beta_2 x_1 x_3 + \nu_1 x_3\}u(x_1,\ldots,x_5,t)\\
&-h\partial_{x_2 x_4}\{\rho_1 x_2 + \zeta_1 x_4\}u(x_1,\ldots,x_5,t)\\
&-h\partial_{x_3 x_5}\{\rho_2 x_3 + \zeta_2 x_5\}u(x_1,\ldots,x_5,t)
\end{aligned} \quad (7)$$

3.5. Linear Transformation of the Fokker-Planck Equation

In order to solve the above Fokker-Planck Equation (7), we use the so-called asymptotic method (see for example [42]). The principle is to transform the multivariate Fokker-Planck equation to a linear Fokker-Planck equation which is linearised around the stationary state of the deterministic system (1). The solution of the linear Fokker-Planck is found to be normally distributed, the solution is given in the following two theorems (see chapter 8 of [43]). We numerically checked this results using our stochastic simulations and the comparison is shown in (Figure 2).

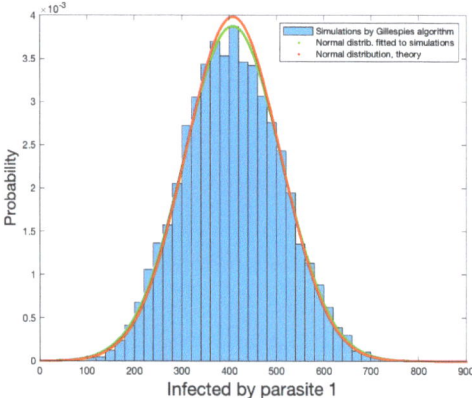

Figure 2. Histogram generated from simulations using Gillespie's algorithm is compared to the probability density with mean and variance obtained from simulation using Gillespie's algorithm and the probability density of normal distribution with mean and variance obtained from the theory of I_1, infected by parasite 1 compartment at time = 300 of the stochastic model with quiescence. The initial population sizes of the model are; $I_1 = 50,000$, $I_2 = 10,000$, $Q_1 = 5000$, $Q_2 = 5000$. The parameters of the model are $\beta_1 = \beta_2 = 0.05$, $\Lambda = 1000$, $d = 0.5$, $\nu_1 = \nu_2 = 0.3$, $\gamma_1 = \gamma_2 = 0.003$, $\zeta_1 = \zeta_2 = 0.1$, $\rho_1 = \rho_2 = 0.7$, $\epsilon_1 = \epsilon_2 = 10$.

Theorem 1. *The linear multivariate Fokker-Planck of (7) can be written as follows*

$$\frac{\partial P(y,t)}{dt} = -\sum_{ij}^{5} M_{ij} \frac{\partial}{\partial y_i} y_i P(y,t) + \frac{1}{2} \sum_{ij}^{5} N_{ij} \frac{\partial^2}{\partial y_i \partial y_j} P(y,t) \tag{8}$$

where $y = (y_1, \ldots, y_5)$, N_{ij} *is symmetric and positive definite, its solution is given as*

$$P(y,t) = (2\pi)^{\frac{1}{2}} det(\Sigma)^{\frac{1}{2}} exp(-\frac{1}{2} y \Sigma^{-1} y^T)$$

with

$$\Sigma^{-1} = 2 \int_0^\infty e^{-Mt} N e^{-Mt} dt.$$

The matrices N and M are defined explicitly in Appendix D.

Theorem 2. *For every matrix N which is symmetric and positive-definite, there a unique solution Σ^{-1} to the following equation known as Lyapunov equation*

$$M\Sigma^{-1} + \Sigma^{-1} M^T = N$$

where Σ^{-1} is symmetric, positive-definite and equal to

$$\Sigma^{-1} = \int_0^\infty e^{-Mt} N e^{-M^T t} dt.$$

Theorem 2 which is known as Lyapunov equation [44] allows us to compute the covariance matrix as found in the normal distribution shown in Theorem 1 fairly easily, this is due to the fact that matrices A and B are constant matrices, the only unknown is the Σ^{-1} matrix. The covariance matrix is of dimension 5 and tells us the degree at which each compartments namely healthy, infected by strain 1 and 2 and quiescence class 1 and 2 go together i.e., the relationship between each class. We use MATLAB to perform numerical calculations for the analytical solutions of the covariance matrix Σ^{-1}.

We also computed 10,000 independent stochastic realisations using Gillespie's algorithm. The probability histogram was plotted in (Figure 2) for the number of infected individuals by strain 1. This distribution is then compared with the probability density function of the normal distribution with mean and variance obtained from both Gilliespie's algorithm and the normal approximation method using linear multivariate Fokker-Planck Equation (7). The results are consistent which further validates our analytical result obtained using linear Fokker-Planck.

4. Covariance Matrix

In order to understand the effect of quiescence in our stochastic model, we need to compare the system with quiescence to that of the system without quiescence in terms of the number of infected by both parasites. To do the comparative study we need to collapse the covariance matrix for both models with and without quiescence so that we only have 2 covariance matrix of the infected individuals. For the model with quiescence, this is done by adding the number of individuals in the infected class and the number of individuals in the quiescence stage to obtain a total number of infected individuals (irrespective of their quiescence status). For the system without quiescence, it is straight forward, it is achieved by isolating the number of individuals in the infected compartment. This step is justified below, and the following results indicate how to compute the covariance matrix [45,46]. The obtained covariance matrix is denoted as the collapsed covariance matrix.

Let $\mathbf{Y} \sim \mathbf{N}_r(\mu, \Sigma)$ be r-variate multivariate normal distribution with mean μ and variance Σ, where

$$\mathbf{Y} = \begin{bmatrix} Y_1 \\ Y_2 \\ \vdots \\ Y_r \end{bmatrix} \quad \mu = \begin{bmatrix} \mu_1 \\ \mu_2 \\ \vdots \\ \mu_r \end{bmatrix} \quad \Sigma = \begin{bmatrix} \sigma_{1,1} & \sigma_{1,2} & \cdots & \sigma_{1,r} \\ \sigma_{2,1} & \sigma_{2,2} & \cdots & \sigma_{2,r} \\ \vdots & \vdots & \ddots & \vdots \\ \sigma_{r,1} & \sigma_{m,2} & \cdots & \sigma_{r,r} \end{bmatrix}$$

Any q linear combination of the Y_i, say $\mathbf{A}'\mathbf{Y}$, is (q-variate) multivariate normal. Let

$$\mathbf{A}'\mathbf{Y} = \begin{bmatrix} a_{11}Y_1 + a_{12}Y_2 + \cdots + a_{1r}Y_r \\ a_{21}Y_1 + a_{22}Y_2 + \cdots + a_{2r}Y_r \\ \cdots + \cdots + \cdots + \ldots \\ a_{q1}Y_1 + a_{q2}Y_2 + \cdots + a_{qr}Y_r \end{bmatrix},$$

then

$$\mathbf{A}'\mathbf{Y} \sim N_q(\mathbf{A}'\mu, \mathbf{A}'\Sigma\mathbf{A}). \tag{9}$$

Numerical examples of the collapsed covariance matrix are shown for various parameter combinations. The collapsed covariance matrix of the model with quiescence is denoted as E_q and the collapsed covariance matrix of the model without quiescence as E_{wq}. In an effort to understand the effect of quiescence on the stochastic process, we consider two different cases of parameter combinations: symmetric where the parameter values of strain 1 and 2 are exactly the same (Examples 1–3), and non-symmetric where the parameter values of stain 1 and 2 are different (for example $\rho_1 \neq \rho_2$, Examples 4–7).

Example 1. *We fix the following parameter values:* $\beta_1 = \beta_2 = 0.005, d = 0.5, \Lambda = 1000, \nu_1 = \nu_2 = 0.3, \rho_1 = \rho_2 = 0.7, \gamma_1 = \gamma_2 = 0.003, \zeta_1 = \zeta_2 = 0.1, \epsilon_1 = \epsilon_2 = 0.6$ *and the initial population sizes are* $H = 50,000, I_1 = 10,000, I_2 = 10,000, Q_1 = 5000, Q_2 = 5000, time = 300$. *We obtain the following collapsed covariance matrices:*

$$E_{q1} = \begin{pmatrix} 683,640 & -682,500 \\ -682,500 & 683,640 \end{pmatrix}, \quad E_{wq1} = \begin{pmatrix} 298,630 & -297,560 \\ -297,560 & 298,630 \end{pmatrix}.$$

Example 2. *We use the same parameter values as in example 1 only with a lower quiescence rate* $\rho_1 = \rho_2 = 0.4$

$$E_{q2} = \begin{pmatrix} 655,170 & -654,060 \\ -654,060 & 655,170 \end{pmatrix}, \quad E_{wq2} = E_{wq1}$$

We show in Example 1 that the model with quiescence exhibits a larger variance compared with the model without quiescence. When comparing Examples 1 and 2, we observe the effect of quiescence on reducing the variance of the number of infected individuals. When the rate of entering quiescence stage (ρ) decreases, the variance of the number of infected individuals decreases (E_{q1} versus E_{q2}).

Example 3. *The parameter and initial values are identical to Example 1 except that the disease transmission rates are now 10 times lower* $\beta_1 = \beta_2 = 0.0005$:

$$E_{q3} = \begin{pmatrix} 14.81 & -0.0388 \\ -0.0388 & 14.81 \end{pmatrix}, \quad E_{wq3} = \begin{pmatrix} 27,651 & -26,443 \\ -26,443 & 27,651 \end{pmatrix}.$$

In Example 3, we observe the effect of decreasing the transmission rate in reducing the variance and covariance of the collapsed covariance matrix. In contrast to example 1, in Example 3, we find that the model with quiescence has less variance compared to the model without quiescence.

We describe the effect of quiescence on variance by comparing Examples 1 and 3. In contrast to the absence of quiescence, quiescence generates two effects under low transmission rate: (1) a decrease of the number of infections, and (2) a decrease in the probability of extinction (in a small population stochasticity is important). Based on our simulations, it is indeed more likely for the parasite to go extinct in Example 3 than in Example 1. Therefore, both effects of quiescence in Example 3 concur to reduce the variance compared to the absence of quiescence. In Example 1, the population size of each parasite is high enough to be well approximated by a mean-field ODE, quiescence increases the number of infections and quiescence events produce additional randomness and simply inflate the variance (compared to the absence of quiescence).

Example 4. We use the same parameter values as in example 1 only with asymmetric rates of quiescence $\rho_1 = 0.3, \rho_2 = 0.5$

$$E_{q4} = \begin{pmatrix} 2251.9 & -57.42 \\ -57.42 & 64.35 \end{pmatrix}, \quad E_{wq4} = E_{wq1}$$

Now that we use asymmetrical rates of entering quiescence between the two strains in Example 4, the variance are much decreased compared to Examples 1 and 2. This further reduction in variance occurs because of the competition amongst the two parasite types in the model with quiescence (which was absent because of symmetrical rates in Examples 1–3). In other words, because the two parasite strains have different quiescence rates, there is also competition between them to infect host individuals. Furthermore, the strain with the largest rate of entering the quiescence stage (ρ) exhibits a smaller variance than the strain with a lower quiescent rate. By analogy, we call this phenomenon as moving average behaviour (see Section 5).

Example 5. We use the same parameter values as in Example 1 only with asymmetric rates of entering $\rho_1 = 0.8, \rho_2 = 0.4$ and exiting $\zeta_1 = 0.4, \zeta_2 = 0.8$ quiescence.

$$E_{q5} = \begin{pmatrix} 19.17 & -15.07 \\ -15.07 & 2187.1 \end{pmatrix}, \quad E_{wq5} = E_{wq1}.$$

In Example 5, we investigate the influence of asymmetric rates of entering and exiting the quiescent stage on the variance in infected individuals. We set the rate of entering quiescence of strain 1 to be larger than rate of strain 2, while the rate of exiting quiescence of strain 1 is smaller than that of strain 2. We still observe the so-called moving average effect, that is, the strain with the largest rate of entering the quiescence has the smaller variance. This example shows that entering quiescence has significant effect in changing the dynamics of the system.

Example 6. We use the same parameter values as in Example 1 only with asymmetric rates of entering $\rho_1 = 0.8, \rho_2 = 0.4$ and exiting $\zeta_1 = 0.8, \zeta_2 = 0.4$ quiescence.

$$E_{q6} = \begin{pmatrix} 164.04 & -151.92 \\ -151.92 & 2332.6 \end{pmatrix}, \quad E_{wq6} = E_{wq1}.$$

In Example 6, we take the rate of entering and exiting quiescence to be the same for each strain, that is, $\rho_1 = 0.8 = \zeta_1 = 0.8, \rho_2 = 0.4 = \zeta_2 = 0.4$, to ascertain if the moving average is determined by the rate of entering quiescence or the longest quiescence time. This example confirms that the moving average is determined by the rate of entering quiescence. We note by this example that rate of exiting quiescence stage doesn't effect the dynamic significantly as far as the moving average is concern.

Example 7. In Example 7, we increase the disease transmission rates and decrease the birth and death rate (compared to Example 1), while we assume asymmetric rates of entering quiescence (as in Example 5) but symmetric rates of exiting quiescence as well as the immigration rate. The following values are used $\beta_1 = \beta_2 = 0.05, d = 0.4, \Lambda = 100, \nu_1 = 0.03, \nu_2 = 0.3, \rho_1 = 0.8, \rho_2 = 0.4, \gamma_1 =$

$\gamma_2 = 0.03, \zeta_1 = \zeta_2 = 0.1, \epsilon_1 = \epsilon_2 = 0.6$ and the initial population sizes are as in Example 1. We obtain the following collapsed covariance matrices:

$$E_{q6} = \begin{pmatrix} 967.63 & -927.22 \\ -927.22 & 1151.1 \end{pmatrix}, \quad E_{wq6} = \begin{pmatrix} 245.56 & -3.6384 \\ -3.6384 & 5.8915 \end{pmatrix}.$$

From Example 7, here we use asymmetric values of parameters in both models, we see the influence of quiescence in reducing the variance of the collapsed covariance matrix whenever one of the rates of entering quiescence is high. In addition, we also see the effect of strain competition in the model without quiescence in reducing the variance of the number of infected individuals. In the model with quiescence we take the recovery rate of infected individuals by strain 1 to be 10 times smaller than those infected by strain 2, and observe our moving average effect.

As additional verification, we draw contour plots of the joint density of infected individuals by strain 1 and 2 in (Figure 3a,b) which compare the variance in the number of infected individuals by both strains. We confirm that the joint distribution of the number of infected individuals by parasite strain 1 and 2 have a smaller surface area, that is with less variance, under the model with quiescence than the absence of quiescence. In all examples, the values of the covariance (off-diagonal elements) are negative, and we observe this effect also in the contours (Figure 3a,b) because the number of infected individuals by parasite 1 and 2 are negatively correlated. This negative correlation is a result of the competition between the parasite types. We finally analyse the change in variance (Figure 4a) and covariance (Figure 4b) of the collapsed covariance matrix as a function of ρ_1 and ρ_2 (rates of entering quiescence). The effect of the transmission rates β_1 and β_2 is here again visible: when $\beta_1 = \beta_2$ are low, high rates of entering quiescence depletes the infected compartments so that the number of infected drops down and the infection decreases, which in turn reduces the variance. When $\beta_1 = \beta_2$ are high, there are enough infected to keep the infection spreading despite the rate of quiescence, hence the increases in the variance (under a fixed values of ζ_1 and ζ_2 (Figure 4a,b). The behaviour of the covariance is reversed as the infected classes are negatively correlated. Based on the examples above, increasing ζ_1 and ζ_2 would results in decreasing the difference between the variance (as well as for the covariance) for the different transmission rates β_1 and β_2.

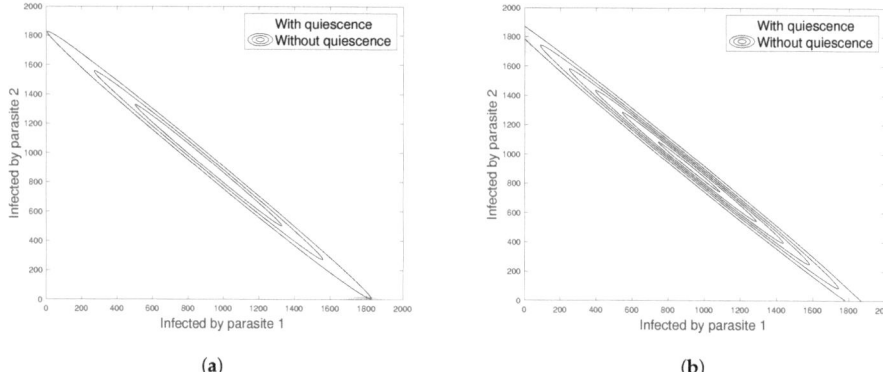

(a) (b)

Figure 3. Contour plots of the joint density of infected individuals by strain 1 and 2 based on simulations for (**a**) Example 4, and (**b**) Example 5 considered in the text. The *x*-axis is the number of infected individuals of strain 1 while the *y*-axis is the number of infected individuals by strain 2 based on the parameters stated in each example.

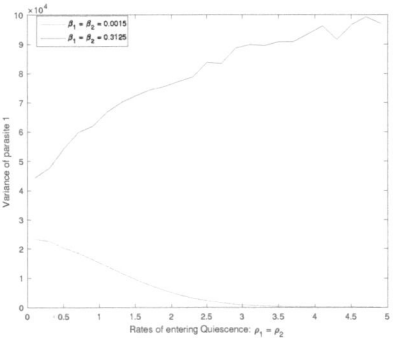 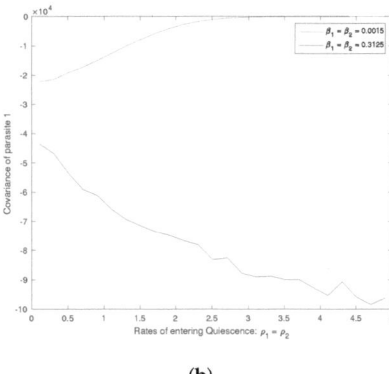

(a) (b)

Figure 4. Effect of quiescence, rates of entering the quiescence phase $\rho_1 = \rho_2$, and of transmission rates $\beta_1 = \beta_2$ on the (**a**) variance of parasite 1, and (**b**) covariance of parasite 1 of the collapsed covariance matrix. We use the following parameter values (symmetrical case): $d = 0.5, \Lambda = 1000, \nu_1 = \nu_2 = 0.3, \gamma_1 = \gamma_2 = 0.003, \zeta_1 = \zeta_2 = 0.1, \epsilon_1 = \epsilon_2 = 10$ and the initial population sizes are $H = 50,000$, $I_1 = 10,000, I_2 = 10,000, Q_1 = 5000, Q_2 = 5000$, time $= 300$. The blue line is for $\beta_1 = \beta_2 = 0.0015$, and the red line for $\beta_1 = \beta_2 = 0.3125$.

5. Discussion

In this study we aim to understand the effect of quiescence on the spread of infectious disease and with competition between parasite strains. Our study shows that introducing the pathogens ability to switch between an active and inactive (quiescence) phase can significantly impact the stochasticity in the system. In our system, when the invasion/immigration rates are turned off, one of the parasite type becomes extinct. However, when the invasion/immigration rates are turned on, coexistence of host and both parasite types is possible. If both strains show equal rates of infection, transmission and quiescence, there is no real competition and the system behaves as if only one parasite would be present. On other hand, when the parasite types have different characteristics, there is competition between them which generates various epidemiological dynamics.

Our collapsed covariance measure quantifies the infection load at the steady state of the system with and without quiescence. We measure this infection load for various parameter combinations of interest to understand the impact of quiescence on the stochastic process. Under symmetric quiescence rates and high transmission rates, quiescence increases the variance in infected individuals, while the quiescence reduces the variance in infected when transmission rates are low. When considering asymmetry in quiescence rates between parasite strains, we uncover a special phenomenon which we call by analogy to the moving average behaviour. Namely, the strain with the high rate of entering quiescence serves as moving average for the whole parasite population and buffers the effect of the second less quiescent strain. In other words, the strain with the higher quiescence determines the intensity of the noise in the stochastic infection process determining the variance of the number of infected individuals (lower variance under low disease transmission, higher variance under high disease transmission). Moving average is a well known concept in sound, signal, and image processing. In sound processing for example, moving average also known as low pass filter, filters the frequencies so that only low frequencies can be heard. The sound of noisy wave or distorted signal, is being smoothens by applying a moving average processing function because it assumes the areas of high frequencies as noise. We are not aware of the use of moving average in the field of disease epidemiology, and hence introduce it here as a consequence of quiescence in parasite. When different strains of parasite do show different quiescent rates, the competition between them under a stochastic epidemiological process reduces the number of infected individuals, as well as the virulence of the disease (number of host death). We theoretically predict that under competition between parasite types, the strain with the lower rate of entering quiescence gets fixed, however, if coexistence can be maintained by influx of parasite strains from outside, quiescence has the beneficial effect to reduce the stochasticity of the system. An extension for our work is to investigate if quiescence itself can evolve in such epidemiological setup as a bet-hedging strategy reducing stochasticity in transmission rates.

Due to the difficulty in the existing methods to analyse the stability of 5×5 matrix, we developed here a criterion for the study of stability of the system with quiescence for the deterministic system. Proposition 2 is important because it reduces the dimension of the system from 5 to 3. It is well known that studying the stability of the system with higher dimension is hard, often times impossible. While system with low dimension is easy and straight forward to study its stability. Thus the reduction in Proposition 2 is of significant importance that removes the difficulties of analysing matrix with high dimension.

We then extended our model to a stochastic version. We show that the analytic solution of the linear Fokker-Planck equation is normally distributed with mean around the equilibrium solution. We confirm this results by computing 10,000 independent stochastic realisations using Gillespie's algorithm (Figure 2). The probability histogram was plotted at a time equals to 300 generations. This distribution is then compared with the probability density function of the normal distribution with mean and variance as obtained from both Gilliespie's algorithm and the normal approximation method using linear multivariate Fokker-Planck Equation (7). The results are consistent which further validates our analytical result obtained using the linear Fokker-Planck equation.

As revealed by a wealth of recent studies on plant or animal, microbiomes are composed of multiple species and multiple strains per species. The composition of species and/or strains is governed by antagonistic, mutualistic or neutral inter- and intra-specific interactions along with stochastic processes such as birth and death, extinction-recolonization and migration of strains/species [see [30,47]]. We speculate that our results on quiescence should be affecting the dynamics in these multi-species systems. Moreover, many microbe, especially human parasites, enter quiescence stage as a mechanism of resistance against antibiotics [48]. This has important consequences for the management of infectious diseases. Furthermore, host bacteria can also enter quiescence upon contact with viruses [9], which can lead to changes in the expected population dynamics of the bacterial and virus populations [49]. It is therefore of paramount importance to understand the influence of the quiescence on the population of hosts and parasites, especially as coevolution between antagonistic species can drive the evolution of quiescence/dormancy [10].

6. Conclusions

We show in our study that quiescence reduces stochasticity and reduces the noise under strain competition. This principle is general enough and the same idea should be investigated for a model of bacteria submitted to stochasticity of antibiotic treatment. We speculate that quiescence is not only a bet-hedging strategy, but also influences the stochasticity of the population behaviour, namely the population size of bacteria becoming more stable in time and insensitive to antibiotic treatment. Our results also call for more in depth investigations of the quiescence behaviour upon infection, of the length and determinants of the quiescent stages and the effect of quiescence on stochastic disease transmission in human diseases.

Author Contributions: Conceptualization, U.S., J.M. and A.T.; methodology, U.S. and S.J.; formal analysis, U.S. and J.M.; investigation, U.S., J.M. and A.T.; writing—original draft preparation, U.S. and A.T.; writing—review and editing, S.J. and J.M. All authors have read and agreed to the published version of the manuscript.

Funding: U.S. is funded by Petroleum Technology Development Fund (PTDF) of Nigeria; S.J., J.M. and A.T. are supported by a grant from the Deutsche Forschungsgemeinschaft (DFG) through the TUM International Graduate School of Science and Engineering (IGSSE), GSC 81, within the project GENOMIE-QADOP.

Institutional Review Board Statement: Not applicable.

Informed Consent Statement: Not applicable.

Data Availability Statement: Not applicable.

Acknowledgments: The authors thank three reviewers for their useful comments. U.S. thanks Umaru Musa Yar'adua University Katsina (UMYUK), Nigeria for the opportunity to follow the TUM programme.

Conflicts of Interest: The authors declare no conflict of interest. The funders had no role in the design of the study; in the analyses, or interpretation of data; in the writing of the manuscript, or in the decision to publish the results.

Appendix A. Equilibrium Solution of the Model with Quiescent

From Equations (4) and (5) of system (1), the quiescence compartments, we find the equilibrium solutions and is given as follows

$$Q_1^* = \frac{\rho_1 I_1}{\zeta_1 + d}, Q_2^* = \frac{\rho_2 I_2}{\zeta_2 + d}. \quad \text{Let} \quad c_1 = \frac{\rho_1}{\zeta_1 + d}, c_2 = \frac{\rho_2}{\zeta_2 + d},$$

then the equilibrium solutions of the infected compartment (Equations (1) and (2) of system (1)) are given by

$$I_1^* = \frac{\epsilon_1}{d + \gamma_1 + \nu_1 + \rho_1 - \zeta_1 c_{11} - \beta_1 H^*}, I_2^* = \frac{\epsilon_2}{d + \gamma_2 + \nu_2 + \rho_2 - \zeta_2 c_{12} - \beta_2 H^*}.$$

Now we need to calculate the equilibrium solution in the healthy compartment, to do so we need the following propositions.

Proposition A1. *For $\epsilon_1, \epsilon_2 > 0$, there is at least one non-negative equilibrium solution in the healthy compartment.*

Proof. Substituting the equilibrium solutions of the quiescence and infected compartments as calculated above in the first equation of the system (1), we have

$P(H) = \Lambda(d + \gamma_1 + \nu_1 + \rho_1 - \zeta_1 c_1 - \beta_1 H)(d + \gamma_2 + \nu_2 + \rho_2 - \zeta_2 c_2 - \beta_2 H) - \beta_1 H \epsilon_1 (d + \gamma_2 + \nu_2 + \rho_2 - \zeta_2 c_2 - \beta_2 H) - \beta_2 H \epsilon_2 (d + \gamma_1 + \nu_1 + \rho_1 - \zeta_1 c_1 - \beta_1 H) - dH(d + \gamma_1 + \nu_1 + \rho_1 - \zeta_1 c_1 - \beta_1 H)(d + \gamma_2 + \nu_2 + \rho_2 - \zeta_2 c_2 - \beta_2 H) + \nu_1 \epsilon_1 (d + \gamma_2 + \nu_2 + \rho_2 - \zeta_2 c_2 - \beta_2 H) + \nu_2 \epsilon_2 (d + \gamma_1 + \nu_1 + \rho_1 - \zeta_1 c_1 - \beta_1 H),$

then

$P(0) = \Lambda(d + \gamma_1 + \nu_1 + \rho_1 - \zeta_1 c_1)(d + \gamma_2 + \nu_2 + \rho_1 - \zeta_1 c_1) + \nu_1 \epsilon_1 (d + \gamma_2 + \nu_2 + \rho_2 - \zeta_2 c_2) + \nu_2 \epsilon_2 (d + \gamma_1 + \nu_1 + \rho_1 - \zeta_1 c_1) > 0,$

because the terms inside brackets are all positive, and $P(H) \to -\infty$, then by intermediary value theorem there exist H^* such that

$$P(H^*) = 0, H^* > 0$$

Please observe that other compartments $(I_1^*, I_2^*, Q_1^*, Q_2^*)$ for H^* are non-negative, since

$$P\left(\frac{d + \gamma_1 + \nu_1 + \rho_1 - \zeta_1 c_1}{\beta_1}\right) < 0, \implies H^* \leq \frac{d + \gamma_1 + \nu_1 + \rho_1 - \zeta_1 c_1}{\beta_1} \implies I_1^* \geq 0,$$

by the same argument, we show that $I_2^* > 0$. Since $I_1^*, I_2^* > 0$, then $Q_1^*, Q_2^* > 0$ □

In the above Proposition A1, we find a polynomial of degree three in which we use intermediate value theorem to show that the polynomial has a solution.

Uniqueness of The Equilibrium Solution

We introduce the terms a, b, c, d defined bellow, with this notation, we obtain the following proposition

Proposition A2. *If $b^2 < 3ac$, then there is a unique non-negative equilibrium solution of $P(H)$.*

Proof. Let
$$P(H) = aH^3 + bH^2 + cH + d = 0,$$
$$\frac{dP}{dH} = 3aH^2 + 2bH^2 + c = 0. \quad (A1)$$

The solution of quadratic Equation (A1) is

$$H = \frac{-(2b) \pm \sqrt{(2b)^2 - 4(3a)c}}{2(3a)} \quad (A2)$$

where
$$a = -3\beta_1\beta_2 d,$$

$b = 2d\beta_1\rho_2 + 2d\beta_2\rho_1 + 2d\beta_1\nu_2 + 2d\beta_1\nu_1 - 2c_{12}d\beta_1\zeta_2 - 2c_{11}d\beta_2\zeta_1 + 2\beta_1\beta_2\epsilon_2 + 2\beta_1\beta_2\epsilon_1 + 2d\beta_1\gamma_2 + 2d\beta_1\gamma_1 + 2\Lambda\beta_1\beta_2 + 2d^2\beta_2 + 2d^2\beta_1$, $c = -\beta_1\epsilon_1\nu_2 - \Lambda\beta_1\nu_2 - \beta_2\epsilon_1\nu_1 - \Lambda\beta_2\nu_1 - d\rho_1\rho_2 - d\nu_1\rho_2 + c_{11}d\zeta_1\rho_2 - \beta_1\epsilon_1\rho_2 - d\gamma_1\rho_2 - \Lambda\beta_1\rho_2 - d^2\rho_2 - d\nu_2\rho_1 + c_{12}d\zeta_2\rho_1 - \beta_2\epsilon_2\rho_1 - d\gamma_2\rho_1 - \Lambda\beta_2\rho_1 - d^2\rho_1 - d\nu_1\nu_2 + c_{11}d\zeta_1\nu_2 - \beta_1\epsilon_2\nu_2 - d^2\nu_2 + c_{12}d\zeta_2\nu_1 - \beta_2\epsilon_2\nu_1 - d\gamma_2\nu_1 - d^2\nu_1 - c_{11}c_{12}d\zeta_1\zeta_2 + c_{12}\beta_1\epsilon_1\zeta_2 + c_{12}d\gamma_1\zeta_2 + c_{12}\Lambda\beta_1\zeta_2 + c_{12}d^2\zeta_2 + c_{11}\beta_2\epsilon_2\zeta_1 + c_{11}d\gamma_2\zeta_1 + c_{11}\Lambda\beta_2\zeta_1 + c_{11}d^2\zeta_1 - \beta_2\gamma_1\epsilon_2 - d\beta_2\epsilon_2 - \beta_1\gamma_2\epsilon_1 - d\beta_1\epsilon_1 - d\gamma_1\gamma_2 - \Lambda\beta_1\gamma_2 - d^2\gamma_2 - \Lambda\beta_2\gamma_1 - d^2\gamma_1 - \Lambda d\beta_1 - d^3$, choose parameter values so that

$$b^2 < 3ac,$$

then the quadratic Equation (A2) does not have real solution. □

In the above proof, we use calculus to find the maximum value of the polynomial. The analysis shows that the polynomial does not have a maximum or minimum value at the specified interval. This shows that the polynomial has only one root by Proposition A2 (existence of a solution) above.

Appendix B. Proof of Proposition 2

We now prove Proposition 2 stated in Section 2.3 above regarding the stability of the matrix B defined in (3).

Proof. The characteristics polynomial of B is given by

$$\lambda^5 + b_1\lambda^4 + b_2\lambda^3 + b_3\lambda^2 + b_4\lambda + b_5 = 0$$

where

$$b_1 = \rho_1 + \rho_2 + \zeta_1 + \zeta_2 - \text{tr}(A)$$

$$b_2 = \rho_1\rho_2 + \rho_1\zeta_1 + \rho_2\zeta_1 + \zeta_1\zeta_2 - \zeta_1\text{tr}(A) - \zeta_2\text{tr}(A) - (a_{11} + a_{33})\rho_2 - (a_{22} + a_{33})\rho_1 + a_2$$

$$b_3 = \zeta_1 a_2 + \zeta_2 a_2 + (a_{11}a_{33} - a_{13}a_{31})\rho_2 + (a_{22}a_{33} - a_{23}a_{32})\rho_1 - \det(A) - \zeta_1\zeta_2\text{tr}(A)$$
$$- (a_{22} + a_{33})\rho_1\zeta_2 - a_{33}\rho_1\rho_2 - a_{33}\rho_2\zeta_1 - a_{11}\rho_2\zeta_1$$

$$b_4 = \zeta_1\zeta_2 a_2 + (a_{22}a_{33} - a_{23}a_{32})\rho_1\zeta_2 + (a_{11}a_{33} - a_{13}a_{31})\rho_2\zeta_1 - (\zeta_1 + \zeta_2)\det(A)$$

$$b_5 = -\zeta_1\zeta_2\det(A)$$

- Step 1 By Routh-Hurwitz Criterion [11,37,38], the matrix B is stable if and only if the following conditions hold:
  - (i) $b_i > 0 \quad (i = 1,\ldots,5)$
  - (ii) $b_1 b_2 b_3 > b_3^2 + b_1^2 b_4$
  - (iii) $(b_1 b_4 - b_5)(b_1 b_2 b_3 - b_3^2 - b_1^2 b_4) > b_5(b_1 b_2 - b_3)^2 + b_1 b_5^2$
- Step 2
  Suppose that for all $\rho_1, \rho_2, \zeta_1, \zeta_2 > 0$
  - (iv) $b_1 > 0$

  $$= \rho_1 + \rho_2 + \zeta_1 + \zeta_2 - \text{tr}(A) > 0 \implies \text{tr}(A) \leq 0$$
  - (v) $b_2 > 0$

  $$= \rho_1\rho_2 + \rho_1\zeta_1 + \rho_2\zeta_1 + \zeta_1\zeta_2 - \zeta_1\text{tr}(A) - \zeta_2\text{tr}(A) - (a_{11} + a_{33})\rho_2 - (a_{22} + a_{33})\rho_1 + a_2 > 0$$

  $$\implies \text{tr}(A) \leq 0, \quad a_{11} \leq 0, \quad a_{22} \leq 0, \quad \text{and} \quad a_{33} \leq 0$$
  - (vi) $b_3 > 0$

  $$= \zeta_1 a_2 + \zeta_2 a_2 + (a_{11}a_{33} - a_{13}a_{31})\rho_2 + (a_{22}a_{33} - a_{23}a_{32})\rho_1 - \det(A) - \zeta_1\zeta_2\text{tr}(A)$$
  $$- (a_{22} + a_{33})\rho_1\zeta_2 - a_{33}\rho_1\rho_2 - a_{33}\rho_2\zeta_1 - a_{11}\rho_2\zeta_1 > 0$$

  $$\implies \det(A) < 0, \quad \text{tr}(A) \leq 0, \quad a_{11} \leq 0, \quad a_{22} \leq 0,$$

  $$a_{33} \leq 0, \quad a_{13}a_{31} \leq a_{11}a_{33}, \quad \text{and} \quad a_{23}a_{32} \leq a_{22}a_{33}$$
  - (vii) $b_4 > 0$

  $$\implies \zeta_1\zeta_2 a_2 + (a_{22}a_{33} - a_{23}a_{32})\rho_1\zeta_2 + (a_{11}a_{33} - a_{13}a_{31})\rho_2\zeta_1 > (\zeta_1 + \zeta_2)\det(A)$$

  $$\implies \det(A) < 0, \quad a_{13}a_{31} \leq a_{11}a_{33}, \quad \text{and} \quad a_{23}a_{32} \leq a_{22}a_{33}$$
  - (viii) $b_5 > 0$

  $$= -\zeta_1\zeta_2\det(A) > 0 \implies \det(A) < 0$$
- Step 3:
  Assume that $\det(A) < 0, \quad \text{tr}(A) \leq 0, \quad a_2 > 0, \quad a_{11} \leq 0, \quad a_{22} \leq 0, \quad a_{33} \leq 0,$

  $a_{13}a_{31} \leq a_{11}a_{33}, \quad a_{23}a_{32} \leq a_{22}a_{33}$. then for all $\rho_1, \rho_2, \zeta_1, \zeta_2 > 0$, we have

(ix) $\rho_1 + \rho_2 + \zeta_1 + \zeta_2 - \text{tr}(A) = b_1 > 0$

(x) $\rho_1\rho_2 + \rho_1\zeta_1 + \rho_2\zeta_1 + \zeta_1\zeta_2 - \zeta_1\text{tr}(A) - \zeta_2\text{tr}(A) - (a_{11} + a_{33})\rho_2 - (a_{22} + a_{33})\rho_1 + a_2 = b_2 > 0$

(xi) $\zeta_1 a_2 + \zeta_2 a_2 + (a_{11}a_{33} - a_{13}a_{31})\rho_2 + (a_{22}a_{33} - a_{23}a_{32})\rho_1 - \det(A) - \zeta_1\zeta_2\text{tr}(A) - (a_{22} + a_{33})\rho_1\zeta_2 - a_{33}\rho_1\rho_2 - a_{33}\rho_2\zeta_1 - a_{11}\rho_2\zeta_1 = b_3 > 0$

(xii) $\zeta_1\zeta_2 a_2 + (a_{22}a_{33} - a_{23}a_{32})\rho_1\zeta_2 + (a_{11}a_{33} - a_{13}a_{31})\rho_2\zeta_1 - (\zeta_1 + \zeta_2)\det(A) = b_4 > 0$

(xiii) $-\zeta_1\zeta_2\det(A) = b_5 > 0$

(xiv)
$$\begin{aligned}
&(\rho_1 + \rho_2 + \zeta_1 + \zeta_2 - \text{tr}(A))(\rho_1\rho_2 + \rho_1\zeta_1 + \rho_2\zeta_1 + \zeta_1\zeta_2 - \zeta_1\text{tr}(A) - \zeta_2\text{tr}(A) \\
&- (a_{11} + a_{33})\rho_2 - (a_{22} + a_{33})\rho_1 + a_2)(-\det(A) + \zeta_1 a_2 + \zeta_2 a_2 + (a_{11}a_{33} - a_{13}a_{31})\rho_2 \\
&+ (a_{22}a_{33} - a_{23}a_{32})\rho_1 - (a_{22} + a_{33})\rho_1\zeta_2 - a_{33}\rho_1\rho_2 - a_{33}\rho_2\zeta_1 - a_{11}\rho_2\zeta_1 - \zeta_1\zeta_2\text{tr}(A)) \\
&- (-\det(A) + \zeta_1 a_2 + \zeta_2 a_2 + (a_{11}a_{33} - a_{13}a_{31})\rho_2 + (a_{22}a_{33} - a_{23}a_{32})\rho_1 - (a_{22} + a_{33})\rho_1\zeta_2 \\
&- a_{33}\rho_1\rho_2 - a_{33}\rho_2\zeta_1 - a_{11}\rho_2\zeta_1 - \zeta_1\zeta_2\text{tr}(A))^2 - (\rho_1 + \rho_2 + \zeta_1 + \zeta_2 - \text{tr}(A))^2(-\zeta_1\det(A) \\
&- \zeta_2\det(A) + \zeta_1\zeta_2 a_2 + (a_{22}a_{33} - a_{23}a_{32})\rho_1\zeta_2 + (a_{11}a_{33} - a_{13}a_{31})\rho_2\zeta_1) \\
&= b_1 b_2 b_3 - b_3^2 - b_1^2 b_4 > 0 \\
&\implies b_1 b_2 b_3 > b_3^2 + b_1^2 b_4.
\end{aligned} \quad (A3)$$

For the full expansion of Equation (A3) for all $\rho_1 > 0, \rho_2 > 0, \zeta_1 > 0, \zeta_2 > 0$, see the wxMaxima output (as online available notebook).

(xv)
$$\begin{aligned}
&\Big((\rho_1 + \rho_2 + \zeta_1 + \zeta_2 - \text{tr}(A))(-\zeta_1\det(A) - \zeta_2\det(A) + \zeta_1\zeta_2 a_2 + (a_{22}a_{33} - a_{23}a_{32})\rho_1\zeta_2 \\
&+ (a_{11}a_{33} - a_{13}a_{31})\rho_2\zeta_1) - (\zeta_1\zeta_2\det(A))\Big)\Big((\rho_1 + \rho_2 + \zeta_1 + \zeta_2 - \text{tr}(A))(\rho_1\rho_2 + \rho_1\zeta_1 \\
&+ \rho_2\zeta_1 + \zeta_1\zeta_2 - \zeta_1\text{tr}(A) - \zeta_2\text{tr}(A) - (a_{11} + a_{33})\rho_2 - (a_{22} + a_{33})\rho_1 + a_2) \\
&(-\det(A) + \zeta_1 a_2 + \zeta_2 a_2 + (a_{11}a_{33} - a_{13}a_{31})\rho_2 \\
&+ (a_{22}a_{33} - a_{23}a_{32})\rho_1 - (a_{22} + a_{33})\rho_1\zeta_2 - a_{33}\rho_1\rho_2 - a_{33}\rho_2\zeta_1 - a_{11}\rho_2\zeta_1 - \zeta_1\zeta_2\text{tr}(A)) \\
&- (-\det(A) + \zeta_1 a_2 + \zeta_2 a_2 + (a_{11}a_{33} - a_{13}a_{31})\rho_2 + (a_{22}a_{33} - a_{23}a_{32})\rho_1 - (a_{22} + a_{33})\rho_1\zeta_2 \\
&- a_{33}\rho_1\rho_2 - a_{33}\rho_2\zeta_1 - a_{11}\rho_2\zeta_1 - \zeta_1\zeta_2\text{tr}(A)))^2 - (\rho_1 + \rho_2 + \zeta_1 + \zeta_2 - \text{tr}(A))^2 \\
&- (\rho_1 + \rho_2 + \zeta_1 + \zeta_2 - \text{tr}(A))(-\zeta_1\det(A) - \zeta_2\det(A) + \zeta_1\zeta_2 a_2 + (a_{22}a_{33} - a_{23}a_{32})\rho_1\zeta_2 \\
&+ (a_{11}a_{33} - a_{13}a_{31})\rho_2\zeta_1)\Big) \\
&- (\zeta_1\zeta_2\det(A))\Big((\rho_1 + \rho_2 + \zeta_1 + \zeta_2 - \text{tr}(A))(\rho_1\rho_2 + \rho_1\rho_1 + \rho_2\zeta_1 + \zeta_1\zeta_2 - \zeta_1\text{tr}(A) - \zeta_2\text{tr}(A) \\
&- (a_{11} + a_{33})\rho_2 - (a_{22} + a_{33})\rho_1 + a_2) - (-\det(A) + \zeta_1 a_2 + \zeta_2 a_2 + (a_{11}a_{33} - a_{13}a_{31})\rho_2 \\
&+ (a_{22}a_{33} - a_{23}a_{32})\rho_1 - (a_{22} + a_{33})\rho_1\zeta_2 - a_{33}\rho_1\rho_2 - a_{33}\rho_2\zeta_1 - a_{11}\rho_2\zeta_1 - \zeta_1\zeta_2\text{tr}(A))\Big)^2 \\
&- (\rho_1 + \rho_2 + \zeta_1 + \zeta_2 - \text{tr}(A))(-\zeta_1\zeta_2\det(A))^2 > 0
\end{aligned} \quad (A4)$$

$$= (b_1b_4 - b_5)(b_1b_2b_3 - b_3^2 - b_1^2b_4) - b_5(b_1b_2 - b_3)^2 - b_1b_5^2 > 0$$

$$\implies (b_1b_4 - b_5)(b_1b_2b_3 - b_3^2 - b_1^2b_4) > b_5(b_1b_2 - b_3)^2 + b_1b_5^2$$

For the full expansion of Equation (A4) for all $\rho_1 > 0, \rho_2 > 0, \zeta_1 > 0, \zeta_2 > 0$, see the wxMaxima output (as online available notebook). □

Appendix C. Description of the Model without Quiescence

In this section we will develop a mathematical model that describes the evolution of single Host- two parasites with constant recruitment rate. The model without quiescence is given by these set (system) of ordinary differential equations:

$$\frac{dI_1}{dt} = \beta_1 H I_1 - d I_1 - \gamma_1 I_1 - \nu_1 I_1 + \epsilon_1$$
$$\frac{dI_2}{dt} = \beta_2 H I_2 - d I_2 - \gamma_2 I_2 - \nu_2 I_2 + \epsilon_2 \qquad \text{(A5)}$$
$$\frac{dH}{dt} = \Lambda - \beta_1 H I_1 - \beta_2 H I_2 - d H + \nu_1 I_1 + \nu_2 I_2$$

Steady State Solution of the System

The analysis of steady state of the the system without quiescence (A5) has the same steps and similar results as for the system with quiescence.

Transition Probabilities

Table A1. Transitions rates of the model without quiescence (A5).

Type	Transition	Rate
birth of healthy host H	$(H_t, I_{1t}, I_{2t}) \to (H_t + 1, I_{1t}, I_{2t})$	$\Lambda \Delta t + o\Delta(t)$
natural death of H	$(H_t, I_{1t}, I_{2t}) \to (H_t - 1, I_{1t}, I_{2t})$	$dH\Delta t + o\Delta(t)$
infection of H by I_1	$(H_t, I_{1t}, I_{2t}) \to (H_t - 1, I_{1t} + 1, I_{2t})$	$\beta_1 H I_1 \Delta t + o\Delta(t)$
infection of H by I_2	$(H_t, I_{1t}, I_{2t}) \to (H_t - 1, I_{1t}, I_{2t} + 1)$	$\beta_2 H I_2 \Delta t + o\Delta(t)$
death of I_1	$(H_t, I_{1t}, I_{2t}) \to (H_t, I_{1t} - 1, I_{2t})$	$(d + \gamma_1) I_1 \Delta t + o\Delta(t)$
death of I_2	$(H_t, I_{1t}, I_{2t}) \to (H_t, I_{1t}, I_{2t} - 1)$	$(d + \gamma_1) I_2 \Delta t + o\Delta(t)$
recovery I_1 & replacement H	$(H_t, I_{1t}, I_{2t}) \to (H_t + 1, I_{1t} - 1, I_{2t})$	$\nu_1 I_1 \Delta t + o\Delta(t)$
recovery I_2 & replacement H	$(H_t, I_{1t}, I_{2t}) \to (H_t + 1, I_{1t}1, I_{2t} - 1)$	$\nu_2 I_2 \Delta t + o\Delta(t)$
immigration to I_1	$(H_t, I_{1t}, I_{2t}) \to (H_t, I_{1t} + 1, I_{2t})$	$\epsilon_1 \Delta t + o\Delta(t)$
immigration to I_2	$(H_t, I_{1t}, I_{2t}) \to (H_t, I_{1t}, I_{2t} + 1)$	$\epsilon_2 \Delta t + o\Delta(t)$

Master equation

Let $p(i,j,k)(t) = \text{Prob}\{H(t) = i, I_1(t) = j, I_2(t) = k\}$, then

$$\begin{aligned}\frac{dp_{(i,j,k)}}{dt} =& \Lambda p_{(i-1,j,k)} + d(i+1)p_{(i+1,j,k)} + \beta_1(i+1)(j-1)p_{(i+1,j-1,k)} \\ &+ (d+\gamma_1)(j+1)p_{(i,j+1,k)} + \beta_2(i+1)(k-1)p_{(i+1,j,k-1)} + (d+\gamma_2)(k+1)p_{(i,j,k+1)} \\ &+ \nu_1(j+1)p_{(i-1,j+1,k)} + \nu_2(k+1)p_{(i-1,j,k+1)} + \epsilon_1 p_{(i,j-1,k)} + \epsilon_2 p_{(i,j,k-1)} \\ &- [\Lambda + di + \beta_1 ij + (d+\gamma_1)j + \beta_2 ik + (d+\gamma_2)k + \nu_1 j + \nu_2 k + \epsilon_1 + \epsilon_2]p_{(i,j,k)}\end{aligned} \qquad \text{(A6)}$$

This master Equation (A6) is then used to work out the *Kramers-Moyal expansion* that led to the derivation of the *Fokker-Planck equation* below.

Derivation of Fokker-Planck Equation

Now, let

$$p(i,j,k) = \int_{ih-\frac{h}{2}}^{ih+\frac{h}{2}} \int_{jh-\frac{h}{2}}^{jh+\frac{h}{2}} \int_{kh-\frac{h}{2}}^{kh+\frac{h}{2}} u(x,y,z)dxdydz + o(h^4),$$

let also $x = ih, y = jh, z = kh$ and $h = \frac{1}{N}$. We then performed *Kramers-Moyal expansion* to derived the following Fokker-Planck equation which is given as follows.

$$\begin{aligned}\partial_t u(x,y,t) = &-\partial_x\{h\lambda - dx - \beta_1 xy - \beta_2 xz + v_1 y + v_2 z\}u(x,y,z)\\ &-\partial_y\{\beta_1 xy - (d+\gamma_1)y - v_1 y + h\epsilon_1\}u(x,y,z)\\ &-\partial_z\{\beta_2 xy - (d+\gamma_2)y - v_2 y + h\epsilon_2\}u(x,y,z)\\ &+\frac{h}{2}\partial_{xx}\{\lambda + dx + \beta_1 xy + \beta_2 xz + v_1 y + v_2 z\}u(x,y,z)\\ &-h\partial_{xy}\{\beta_1 xy + v_1 y\}u(x,y,z)\\ &+\frac{h}{2}\partial_{yy}\{\beta_1 xy + (d+\gamma_1)y + v_1 y + \epsilon_1\}u(x,y,z)\\ &-h\partial_{xz}\{\beta_2 xz + v_2 z\}u(x,y,z)\\ &+\frac{h}{2}\partial_{zz}\{\beta_2 xy + (d+\gamma_1)y + v_2 y + \epsilon_2\}u(x,y,z)\end{aligned} \quad (A7)$$

Linear Transformation of the Fokker-Planck equation

Theorem A1. *The linear Fokker-Planck equation for the above non-linear Fokker-Planck can be written more compactly as follows*

$$\frac{\partial P(y,t)}{dt} = -\sum_{ij}^{3} M_{ij}\frac{\partial}{\partial y_i}y_i P(y,t) + \frac{1}{2}\sum_{ij}^{3} N_{ij}\frac{\partial^2}{\partial y_i \partial y_j}P(y,t) \quad (A8)$$

where $y = (x,y,z)$, N_{ij} is symmetric and positive definite, its solution is give as

$$P(y,t) = (2\pi)^{\frac{1}{2}}det(\Sigma)^{\frac{1}{2}}exp(-\frac{1}{2}y\Sigma^{-1}y^T)$$

with

$$\Sigma^{-1} = 2\int_0^\infty e^{-Mt}Ne^{-Mt}dt.$$

Theorem A2. *For every matrix N which is symmetric and positive-definite, there a unique solution Σ^{-1} to the following equation known as Lyapunov equation*

$$M\Sigma^{-1} + \Sigma^{-1}M^T = N$$

where Σ^{-1} is symmetric, positive-definite and equal to

$$\Sigma^{-1} = \int_0^\infty e^{-Mt}Ne^{-M^T t}dt.$$

The above theorem known as Lyapunov theorem [44] gives us the opportunity to compute covariance matrix more easily since matrices M and N are constant matrices, the only unknown is Σ^{-1} matrix. We use MATLAB to obtain the covariance matrix Σ^{-1} numerically. The stochastic matrices M and N for the system without quiescence are similar to those that of the system with quiescence.

Appendix D. Stochastic Matrices of the Linear Fokker-Planck Equation

$$M = \begin{pmatrix} -d - \beta_1 I_1^* - \beta_1 I_2^* & -\beta_1 H^* + v_1 & -\beta_1 H^* + v_2 & 0 & 0 \\ \beta_1 I_1^* & \beta_1 H^* - d - \gamma_1 - v_1 - \rho_1 & 0 & \zeta_1 & 0 \\ \beta_1 I_2^* & 0 & \beta_1 H^* - d - \gamma_2 - v_2 - \rho_2 & 0 & \zeta_2 \\ 0 & \rho_1 & 0 & -\zeta_1 - d & 0 \\ 0 & 0 & \rho_2 & 0 & -\zeta_2 - d \end{pmatrix}$$

$$N = \begin{pmatrix} n_{11} & -(\beta_1 H^* I_1^* + \nu_1 I_1^*) & -(\beta_1 H^* I_2^* + \nu_1 I_2^*) & 0 & 0 \\ -(\beta_1 H^* I_1^* + \nu_1 I_1^*) & n_{22} & 0 & -(\rho_1 I_1^* + \zeta_1 Q_1^*) & 0 \\ -(\beta_1 H^* I_2^* + \nu_1 I_2^*) & 0 & n_{33} & 0 & -(\rho_2 I_2^* + \zeta_2 Q_2^*) \\ 0 & -(\rho_1 I_1^* + \zeta_1 Q_1^*) & 0 & n_{44} & 0 \\ 0 & 0 & -(\rho_2 I_2^* + \zeta_2 Q_2^*) & 0 & n_{55} \end{pmatrix}$$

where

$$n_{11} = \lambda + dH^* + \beta_1 H^* I_1^* + \beta_1 H^* I_2 + \nu_1 I_1^* + \nu_2 I_2^*,$$

$$n_{22} = \beta_1 H^* I_1^* + (d + \gamma_1) I_1^* + \nu_1 I_1^* + \rho_1 I_2^* + \zeta_1 Q_1^* + \epsilon_1,$$

$$n_{33} = \beta_1 H^* I_2^* + (d + \gamma_2) I_2^* + \nu_2 I_2^* + \rho_2 I_2^* + \zeta_2 Q_2^* + \epsilon_2,$$

$$n_{44} = \rho_1 I_1^* + \zeta_1 Q_1^* + dQ_1^*,$$

$$n_{55} = \rho_2 I_2^* + \zeta_2 Q_2^* + dQ_2^*$$

where $H^*, I_1^*, I_2^*, Q_1^*, Q_2^*$ are equilibrium solutions of (1) (rearranged in such away that healthy compartment comes first equation in the system. The order of the other compartments remains unchanged).

References

1. Cox, F.E. Well-temperate phage: Optimal bet-hedging against local environmental collapses. *Sci. Rep.* **2015**, *5*, 10523.
2. Lennon, J.T.; Jones, S.E. Microbial seed banks: The ecological and evolutionary implications of dormancy. *Nat. Rev. Microbiol.* **2011**, *9*, 119–130. [CrossRef] [PubMed]
3. Murphy, C.T.; Hu, P.J. Insulin/Insulin-Like Growth Factor Signaling in *C. elegans*. Available online: https://www.ncbi.nlm.nih.gov/books/NBK179230 (accessed on 27 June 2022).
4. Mélissa V.; Aurélien T. Host-parasite coevolution can promote the evolution of seed banking as a bet-hedging strategy. *Evolution* **2018**, *72*, 1362–1372.
5. Seger, J. What is bet-hedging? *Oxford Surv. Evol. Biol.* **1987**, *4*, 182–211.
6. Blath, J.; Hermann, F.; Slowik, M. A branching process model for dormancy and seed banks in randomly fluctuating environments. *arXiv* **2020**, arXiv:2007.06393.
7. Hamelin, F.M.; Allen, L.J.; Bokil, V.A.; Gross, L.J.; Hilker, F.M.; Jeger, M.J.; Manore, C.A.; Power, A.G.; Rúa, M.A.; Cunniffe, N.J. Coinfections by noninteracting pathogens are not independent and require new tests of interaction. *PLoS Biol.* **2019**, *17*, e3000551. [CrossRef]
8. Blath, J.; Tóbiás, A. Invasion and fixation of microbial dormancy traits under competitive pressure. *Stoch. Process. Appl.* **2020**, *130*, 7363–7395. [CrossRef]
9. Bautista, M.A.; Zhang, C.; Whitaker, R.J. Virus-induced dormancy in the archaeon Sulfolobus islandicus. *Am. Soc. Microbiol.* **2015**, *6*, e02565-14. [CrossRef]
10. Nil, G.; Liliana, M.-S.; Alex, B.M.; Ani, G.; Vincent, L.B.; Stuart, S.L.; Rapatbhorn, P.; Salil, P.D.; Sebastian, A.M.; Stefan, H.I.K.; et al. In Vitro Culture, Drug Sensitivity, and Transcriptome of Plasmodium Vivax Hypnozoites. *Cell Host Microbe* **2018**, *23*, 395–406.
11. Karl, P.H. *Topics in Mathematical Biology*, 1st ed.; Springer: Cham, Switzerland, 2017; pp. 1–68.
12. Thibaut, S.; Müller, J.; Hösel, V.; Aurélien, T. Are the better cooperators dormant or quiescent? *Math. Biosci.* **2019**, *318*, 108272.
13. Hairston, N.G., Jr.; De Stasio, B.T., Jr. Rate of evolution slowed by a dormant propagule pool. *Nature* **1988**, *336*, 239–242. [CrossRef]
14. Koopmann, B.; Johannes, M.; Aurélien, T.; Daniel, Ž. Fisher–Wright model with deterministic seed bank and selection. *Theor. Popul. Biol.* **2017**, *114*, 29–39. [CrossRef]
15. Templeton, A.R.; Levin, D.A. Evolutionary consequences of seed pools. *Theor. Am. Nat.* **1979**, *114*, 232–249. [CrossRef]
16. Blath, J.; Matthias, H.; Florian, N. The stochastic Fisher-KPP equation with seed bank and on/off branching coalescing Brownian motion. *Stoch. Partial. Differ. Equ. Anal. Comput.* **2022**, 1–46. [CrossRef]
17. Sorrell, I.; White, A.; Pedersen, A.B.; Hails, R.S.; Boots, M. The evolution of covert, silent infection as a parasite strategy. *Proc. R. Soc. B Biol. Sci.* **2009**, *276*, 2217–2226. [CrossRef] [PubMed]
18. Anthony, R.M.C. *Dormancy and Low Growth States in Microbial Disease*; Cambridge University Press: Cambridge, UK, 2003.
19. Cohen, N.R.; Lobritz, M.A.; Collins, J.J. Microbial persistence and the road to drug resistance. *Cell Host Microbe* **2013**, *13*, 632–642. [CrossRef] [PubMed]
20. Zhu, D.; Sorg, J.A.; Sun, X. Clostridioides difficile Biology: Sporulation, Germination, and Corresponding Therapies for C. difficile Infection. *Front. Cell. Infect.* **2018**, *8*, 29. [CrossRef]

21. Wood, T.K.; Knabel, S.J.; Kwan, B.W. Bacterial persister cell formation and dormancy. *Appl. Environ. Microbiol.* **2013**, *79*, 7116–7121. [CrossRef]
22. Cox, F.E. History of the discovery of the malaria parasites and their vectors. *BioMed Cent. Parasites Vectors* **2010**, *3*, 1–9. [CrossRef]
23. White, N.J. Determinants of relapse periodicity in Plasmodium vivax malaria. *Malar. J.* **2011**, *10*, 1–36. [CrossRef]
24. Aimee, R.T.; James, A.W.; Cindy, S.C.; Kanokpich, P.; Jureeporn, D.; Nicholas, P.J.D.; Francois, N.; Daniel, E.N.; Caroline, O.B.; Mallika, I.; et al. Resolving the cause of recurrent Plasmodium vivax malaria probabilistically. *Nat. Commun.* **2019**, *10*, 1–11.
25. Cindy, S.C.; Aung, P.P.; Claudia, T.; Htun, H.W.; Naw, P.P.; Widi, Y.; Suradet, T.; Pornpimon, W.; Rattanaporn, R.; Verena, I.C.; et al. Chloroquine Versus Dihydroartemisinin-Piperaquine With Standard High-dose Primaquine Given Either for 7 Days or 14 Days in Plasmodium vivax Malaria. *Clin. Infect. Dis.* **2018**, *68*, 1311–1319.
26. Balmer, O.; Tanner, M. Prevalence and implications of multiple-strain infections. *Lancet Infect. Dis.* **2011**, *11*, 868–878. [CrossRef]
27. Vaumourin, E.; Vourc'h, G.; Gasqui, P.; Vayssier-Taussat, M. The importance of multiparasitism: examining the consequences of co-infections for human and animal health. *BioMed Cent. Parasites Vectors* **2015**, *8*, 1–13. [CrossRef]
28. Minus, V.B.; Maurice, W.S. The Dynamics of Multiple Infection and the Evolution of Virulence. *Am. Nat.* **1995**, *146*, 881–910.
29. Matt, J.K.; Pejman, R. *Modeling Infectious Diseases in Humans and Animals*; Princeton University Press: Princeton, NJ, USA, 2011; pp. 15–52, 190–230.
30. Håkan, A.; Tom, B. *Stochastic Epidemic Models and Their Statistical Analysis*; Springer: New York, NY, USA, 2000; pp. 1–9.
31. Allen, L.J. *An Introduction to Stochastic Processes with Applications to Biology*, 2nd ed.; Chapman and Hall/CRC: New York, NY, USA, 2010; pp. 197–354.
32. Allen, L.J.; Brauer, F.; Van den Driessche, P.; Wu, J. *Mathematical Epidemiology*, 1st ed.; Springer: Berlin, Germany, 2010; pp. 81–128.
33. Daniel Ž.; Sona J.; Mélissa V.; Wolfgang S.; Aurélien T. Neutral genomic signatures of host-parasite coevolution. *BioMed Central Evol. Biol.* **2019**, *1*, 1–11.
34. Michael, S.; Lucía, P.; Nancy, W.B.; Philipp, D.; Jun, W.; Benedikt, M.; Sören, F.; Ruth, A.S.; John, F.B.; Sebastian, F.; et al. Neutrality in the Metaorganism. *PLoS Biol.* **2019**, *17*, e3000298.
35. Anderson, R.M.; May, R.M. *Infectious Diseases of Humans: Dynamics and Control*; Oxford University Press: New York, NY, USA, 1992; pp. 193–215.
36. Johan, G.; Onno, A. *Asymptotic Methods for the Fokker—Planck Equation and the Exit Problem in Applications*; Springer: Berlin, Germany, 1999.
37. Johannes, M.; Christina, K. *Methods and Models in Mathematical Biology*; Springer: Berlin/Heidelberg, Germany, 2015; pp. 1–115, 232–233.
38. Kestelman, H.; Gantmacher, F.R. The Theory of Matrices. *Biometrika* **1961**, *48*, 237. [CrossRef]
39. Gillespie, D.T. A general method for numerically simulating the stochastic time evolution of coupled chemical reactions. *J. Comput. Phys.* **1976**, *22*, 403–434. [CrossRef]
40. Gillespie, D.T. Exact stochastic simulation of coupled chemical reactions. *J. Phys. Chem.* **1977**, *81*, 2340–2361. [CrossRef]
41. Allen, L.J. A primer on stochastic epidemic models: Formulation, numerical simulation, and analysis. *Infect. Dis. Model.* **2017**, *2*, 128–142. [CrossRef] [PubMed]
42. Kogan, O.; Khasin, M.; Meerson, B.; Schneider, D.; Myers, C.R. Two-strain competition in quasineutral stochastic disease dynamics. *APS Phys. Rev. E.* **2014**, *90*, 042149. [CrossRef] [PubMed]
43. van Kampen, N.G. *Stochastic Processes in Physics and Chemistry*, 3rd ed.; Elsevier: Amsterdam, The Netherlands, 2007; pp. 193–218.
44. João, H.P. *Linear Systems Theory*, 2nd ed.; Princeton University Press: Princeton, NJ, USA, 2018; pp. 88–107.
45. Richard, A.J.; Dean, W.W. *Multivariate Analysis*, 6th ed.; Pearson Prentice Hall: Hoboken, NJ, USA, 2007; pp. 149–358.
46. Timm, N.H. *Applied Multivariate Analysis*; Springer: New York, NY, USA, 2002; pp. 79–90.
47. El, M.I.; Siu, Y.; Dunlop, M.J. Stochastic expression of a multiple antibiotic resistance activator confers transient resistance in single cells. *Sci. Rep.* **2016**, *1*, 1–9.
48. Balaban, N.Q.; Merrin, J.; Chait, R.; Kowalik, L.; Leibler, S. Bacterial persistence as a phenotypic switch. *Science* **2004**, *305*, 1622–1625. [CrossRef] [PubMed]
49. Blath, J.; Tóbiás, A. Virus dynamics in the presence of contact-mediated host dormancy. *arXiv* **2021**, arXiv:2107.11242.

Article

Mathematical Modelling of Harmful Algal Blooms on West Coast of Sabah

Fatin Nadiah Yussof [1], Normah Maan [1,*], Mohd Nadzri Md Reba [2] and Faisal Ahmed Khan [3]

[1] Department of Mathematics, Faculty of Science and Technology, Universiti Teknologi Malaysia, Skudai 81310, Malaysia
[2] Faculty of Geoinformation and Real Estate, Universiti Teknologi Malaysia, Skudai 81310, Malaysia
[3] Institute of Environmental Studies, University of Karachi, Karachi 75270, Pakistan
* Correspondence: normahmaan@utm.my

Citation: Yussof, F.N.; Maan, N.; Md Reba, M.N.; Khan, F.A Mathematical Modelling of Harmful Algal Blooms on West Coast of Sabah. *Mathematics* **2022**, *10*, 2836. https://doi.org/10.3390/math10162836

Academic Editors: Sophia Jang and Jui-Ling Yu

Received: 30 May 2022
Accepted: 5 August 2022
Published: 9 August 2022

Publisher's Note: MDPI stays neutral with regard to jurisdictional claims in published maps and institutional affiliations.

Copyright: © 2022 by the authors. Licensee MDPI, Basel, Switzerland. This article is an open access article distributed under the terms and conditions of the Creative Commons Attribution (CC BY) license (https://creativecommons.org/licenses/by/4.0/).

Abstract: Algal bloom is a condition in which there is a massive growth of algae in a certain region and it is said to be harmful when the bloom causes damage effects. Due to the tremendous impact of harmful algal bloom (HAB) on some aspects, this research proposes the mathematical modelling of an HAB model to describe the process of HAB together with population dynamics. This research considers the delay terms in the modelling since the liberation of toxic chemicals by toxin-producing phytoplankton (TPP) is not an instantaneous process in which the species need to achieve their maturity. A model of fish interaction is also being studied to show the effect of HAB on fish species. Time delay is incorporated for the mortality of fish due to the consumption of toxic zooplankton. Stability analysis is conducted and numerical simulations are applied to obtain the analytical results which highlight the critical values for the delay parameters. The existence of Hopf bifurcation is established when the delay passes the threshold value. The results of both models show that the inclusion of the delay term affects the model by stabilizing and destabilizing the model. Therefore, this research shows the effect of an inclusion delay term on the model and also gives knowledge and an understanding of the process of HAB occurrence as well as the effect of HAB on fish populations.

Keywords: harmful algal bloom; Hopf bifurcation; population dynamics; stability

MSC: 92D40

1. Introduction

Algal bloom is a situation wherein there is an abundance of algal cell density in a location of coastal water which is usually dominated by a single species or a few species. It is called harmful algal bloom (HAB) when the bloom has adverse effects on the marine ecosystem as well as on humans due to the natural toxin content in their body. HABs in Malaysian waters are quite worrying nowadays since the occurrence of blooms has been increasingly reported over the last decade. The natural toxins produced by the algal bloom may harm the marine ecosystem because it will accumulate in the filter-feeder shellfish and cause food poisoning to the human when they consumed shellfish.

Massive algal bloom can also kill fish or shrimp because they can barely breathe in the water to survive. High densities of algal blooms in water causes dissolved oxygen depletion. For example, in 2005, a fish killing event was reported in Penang which amounted to more than MYR 20 million in losses [1]. Therefore, it is necessary to have a good understanding and wide view of HAB dynamics and the study of marine plankton ecology is an important consideration.

HABs have regularly occurred in Sabah as early as 1976 eutrophication makes this area environmentally favourable for dinoflagellate to reproduce and grow. The water tends to be discoloured or murky, appearing red or green in colour and sometimes purple. The species of dinoflagellate that always causes bloom in Sabah seas is *Pyrodinium bahamense*.

Whatever feeds on *P. bahamense* accumulates PSTs transferred from the dinoflagellates. Toxic phytoplankton do not harm shellfish but can harm humans that have consumed the contaminated shellfish. It has been yearly reported that PSP in Sabah has been caused by toxins from *P. bahamense*. Some filter feeder fish such as *"ikan tamban, ikan basung"* and *"ikan rumahan"* take in the dinoflagellates as well when they feed on the zooplankton.

A broad classification of HABs species distinguishes two groups: (1) the toxin producers which can contaminate seafood and kill fish; (2) the high-biomass producers which are always associated with water discolouration (red tide) that can be caused hypoxia/anoxia and subsequently have a fatal impact on marine life after reaching dense concentrations [2].*Pyrodinium bahamense* is a well-known marine dinoflagellate and producer of paralytic shellfish toxin (PST) that is especially present in tropical waters [3], and which has caused more human illnesses and fatalities than any other PST-producing dinoflagellates. *P. bahamense* was first reported in 1976 along a 300-km-long stretch west coast of Sabah, Malaysia [4], and formed a toxic bloom in the Brunei Bay, Sabah, and resulted in human poisoning involving 202 people, with 7 casualties [4] due to paralytic shellfish poisoning (PSP). Toxic dinoflagellate *P. bahamense* has been a causative species for the occurrence of PSP events in Sabah annually since then [3,5,6].

Phytoplankton consists of two types which are toxic phytoplankton (TPP) and non-toxic phytoplankton (NTP). TPP have the ability to produce 'toxic' or 'allelopathic agents' that could harm the growth of other aquatic organisms [7,8], while NTP do not produce any toxic chemicals. NTP will become harmful if there is massive algal bloom that could cause a red tide. For example, when masses of algae die and decompose, the decaying process can deplete oxygen in the water, causing the water to become so low in oxygen that animals either leave the area or die. As such, phytoplankton could act as the indicator of the water quality as massive algae bloom will degrade the water quality [9].

HAB occurrences have recently alarmed the authorities to realize the need to raise awareness of HABs in Malaysia. For example, on 11th February 2014, due to the HAB bloom in Tanjung Kupang, there were massive fish kills and the operators reported losses of MYR 150,000. Fish stocks such as those of snappers, cods, seabass and threadfins in nine farms were wiped out during the event [10]. In Penang, the aquaculture operators also reported losses estimated around MYR 20 millions due to the fish kills during the period 2005–2006 [10]. Therefore, these losses could be prevented if there is an adequate monitoring program held by the relevant authorities. In addition to that, the safety of our seafood could also be guaranteed as well as our public health.

2. Materials and Methods

2.1. Nutrient-Phytoplankton-Zooplankton Interaction Model

Many researchers have constructed and studied the mathematical model of nutrient–phytoplankton–zooplankton interaction with different degrees of complexity. Mathematical modelling is important in order to improve our knowledge and understanding of the occurrence of HAB in relation to plankton ecology. This research incorporates a delay model to describe how toxin production by TPP is not an instantaneous process. This model explains how *Pyrodinium bahamense* sp. can cause HAB to occur.

$$\begin{aligned}
\frac{dN}{dt} &= D(N_0 - N) - \alpha_1 P_1 N - \alpha_2 P_2 N \\
\frac{dP_1}{dt} &= \theta_1 P_1 N - \beta_1 P_1 P_3 - m_1 P_1 - e_1 P_1 P_2 - D_1 P_1 \\
\frac{dP_2}{dt} &= \theta_2 P_2 N - \beta_2 P_2 P_3 - m_2 P_2 - e_2 P_1 P_2 - D_2 P_2 \\
\frac{dP_3}{dt} &= \gamma_1 P_1 P_3 - \gamma_2 P_2(t - \tau) P_3 - m_3 P_3 - D_3 P_3
\end{aligned} \quad (1)$$

where

$\alpha_1 = $ Nutrient uptake rate for the NTP
$\alpha_2 = $ Nutrient uptake rate for the TPP
$\theta_1 = $ Conversion rate of NTP for nutrient
$\theta_2 = $ Conversion rate of TPP for nutrient
$\beta_1 = $ Predation rate of NTP for zooplankton
$\beta_2 = $ Predation rate of TPP for zooplankton
$\gamma_1 = $ Conversion rate of zooplankton for NTP
$\gamma_2 = $ Death rate due to consumption of TPP
$m_1 = $ Natural death rate of NTP
$m_2 = $ Natural death rate of TPP
$m_3 = $ Natural death rate of zooplankton
$D = $ Dilution rate of nutrient
$D_1 = $ Dilution rate of NTP
$D_2 = $ Dilution rate of TPP
$D_3 = $ Dilution rate of zooplankton
$e_1 = $ Competition coefficient for NTP
$e_2 = $ Competition coefficient for TPP

- Time lag is considered for the maturation of the TPP population to produce toxin since the process is not instantaneous [3,11]. The mortality of the zooplankton population is described as $P_2(t-\tau)P_3$ [12,13].
- The functional response of Holling type I is applied for the functional response of phytoplankton to nutrients as it is used for lower organisms such as alga [14–16].
- The linear mass action law is used for the maximal zooplankton predation rate for NTP and TPP [17].
- The model considered interspecies competition to obtain nutrients [17].
- TPP do not harm NTP even though these contains high toxins at that time because the toxins do not secrete out into the environment [3,11,18].
- TPP harm the zooplankton whenever they are consumed and the toxin content is produced at a high level [18].

The system in (1) is rescaled by introducing new variables where

$$x = \frac{N}{N_0}, \quad y = \frac{P_1\alpha_1}{D}, \quad z = \frac{P_2\alpha_2}{D}, \quad w = \frac{P_3\beta_1}{D},$$
$$a = \frac{\theta_1}{\alpha_1}, \quad b = \frac{m_1}{D}, \quad c = \frac{e_1}{\alpha_2}, \quad d = \frac{D_1}{D},$$
$$f = \frac{\theta_2}{\alpha_2}, \quad g = \frac{m_2}{D}, \quad h = \frac{\beta_2}{\beta_1}, \quad m = \frac{e_1}{\alpha_1},$$
$$n = \frac{D_2}{D}, \quad p = \frac{\gamma_1}{\alpha_1}, \quad q = \frac{\gamma_2}{\alpha_2}, \quad r = \frac{m_3}{D},$$
$$s = \frac{D_3}{D}$$

Then system (1) becomes

$$\frac{dx}{dt} = 1 - x - xy - xz$$
$$\frac{dy}{dt} = axy - wy - by - cyz - dy$$
$$\frac{dz}{dt} = fxz - gz - hwz - myz - nz \tag{2}$$
$$\frac{dw}{dt} = pyw - qz(t-\tau)w - rw - sw$$

System (2) is linearized at $E^* = (x^*, y^*, z^*, w^*)$, in the form

$$\frac{dX}{dt} = MX(t) + NX(t-\tau) \tag{3}$$

where

$$M = \begin{bmatrix} H_1 & -x^* & -x^* & 0 \\ ay^* & H_2 & -cy^* & -y^* \\ fz^* & -mz^* & H_3 & -hz^* \\ 0 & pw^* & 0 & H_4 \end{bmatrix}, \tag{4}$$

$$N = \begin{bmatrix} 0 & 0 & 0 & 0 \\ 0 & 0 & 0 & 0 \\ 0 & 0 & 0 & 0 \\ 0 & 0 & qw^* & 0 \end{bmatrix} \tag{5}$$

and $X(.) = (x(.), y(.), z(.))^T$ is the state vector. The characteristic equation of (3) is as follows:

$$det(\lambda - M - Ne^{-\lambda \tau_1}) = 0 \tag{6}$$

which can be explicitly expressed as

$$F(\lambda, \tau) \equiv A(\lambda) + B(\lambda)e^{-\lambda \tau_1} = 0 \tag{7}$$

where $F = A, B$ are four-degree polynomials in λ in the form

$$F(\lambda, \tau) = \lambda^4 + J_1\lambda^3 + J_2\lambda^2 + J_3\lambda + J_4 + (K_1\lambda^2 + K_2\lambda + K_3)e^{-\lambda \tau_1} \tag{8}$$

where their coefficients are

$J_1 = -H_1 - H_2 - H_3 - H_4$
$J_2 = H_1H_2 + H_1H_3 + H_2H_3 + H_1H_4 + H_2H_4 + H_3H_4 + pw^*y^* + ax^*y^* - fx^*z^* - cmy^*z^*$
$J_3 = -H_1H_2H_3 - H_1H_2H_4 - H_1H_3H_4 - H_2H_3H_4 - pw^*y^* - H_3pw^*y^* - H_3ax^*y^* - H_4ax^*y^* + H_2fx^*z^* + H_4fx^*z^* - H_1cmy^*z^* - H_4cmy^*z^* - pchw^*y^*z^* - cfx^*y^*z^* - amx^*y^*z^*$
$J_4 = H_1H_2H_3H_4 + H_1H_3pw^*y^* + H_3H_4ax^*y^* - H_1H_4cmy^*z^* + H_2H_4fx^*z^* - H_1pchy^*w^*z^* + H_4cfx^*y^*z^* + H_4amx^*y^*z^* + pfw^*x^*y^*z^* - aphw^*x^*y^*z^*$
$K_1 = -qhw^*z^*$
$K_2 = H_1qhw^*z^* + H_2qhw^*z^* + qmw^*y^*z^*$
$K_3 = -H_1H_2qhw^*z^* - H_1qmw^*y^*z^* + qfw^*x^*y^*z^* - aqhw^*x^*y^*z^*$

where

$$H_1 = -1 - y^* - z^*$$
$$H_2 = ax^* - b - w^* - cz - d$$
$$H_3 = fx^* - g - hw^* - my - n$$
$$H_4 = py^* - qz^* - r - s$$

The Hopf bifurcation of the equilibrium is studied. If $\lambda = iw (w > 0)$ is a root of $F(\lambda, \tau) = 0$ for $\tau \neq 0$, the characteristic equation will undergo stability change such that

$$w^4 - J_1 i w^3 - J_2 w^2 + J_3(iw) + J_4 + [\cos(w\tau) - i\sin(w\tau)](-K_1 w^2 + K_2 iw + K_3) = 0 \quad (9)$$

The transcendental equations are obtained by separating the real and imaginary parts:

$$\begin{aligned} w^4 - J_2 w^2 + J_4 &= K_1 w^2 \cos(w\tau) + K_2 w \sin(w\tau) - K_3 \cos(w\tau) \\ -J_3 w - J_1 w^3 &= K_1 w^2 \sin(w\tau) - K_2 w \cos(w\tau) - K_3 \sin(w\tau) \end{aligned} \quad (10)$$

The squares of both equations are added up, thus becoming

$$w^8 + (J_1^2 - 2J_2)w^6 + (J_2^2 + 2J_4 - 2J_1 J_3 - K_1^2)w^4 + \\ (J_3^2 - 2J_2 J_4 - K_2^2 + 2K_1 K_3)w^2 + J_4^2 + K_3^2 = 0 \quad (11)$$

Substitute $n = w^2$ into (11) and obtain

$$n^4 + L_1 n^3 + L_2 n^2 + L_3 n + L_4 = 0 \quad (12)$$

where

$$\begin{aligned} L_1 &= J_1^2 - 2J_2 \\ L_2 &= J_2^2 + 2J_4 - 2J_1 J_3 - K_1^2 \\ L_3 &= J_3^2 + 2J_2 J_4 - K_2^2 + 2K_1 K_3 \\ L_4 &= J_4^2 - K_3^2 \end{aligned}$$

Theorem 1. *System (2) is stable with regard to the nontrivial equilibrium point $E^* = (x^*, y^*, z^*, w^*)$ if the characteristic Equation (12) satisfies the following Routh–Hurwitz conditions:*

1. $L_1 > 0$
2. $L_3 > 0$
3. $L_4 > 0$
4. $L_1 L_2 L_3 - (L_3^2 + L_1^2 L_4) > 0$

Therefore, by eliminating $\sin(n\tau)$ in (10), we have

$$\cos(n\tau) = \frac{-J_1 K_2 n^4 + J_3 K_2 n^2 - K_1 K_2 n^7 + J_2 K_1 K_2 n^5 - J_4 K_1 K_2 n^3 + K_2 K_3 n^5 + J_2 K_2 K_3 n^3 - J_4 K_2 K_3 n}{K_1 K_2 K_3 n^3 - K_1^2 K_2 n^5 - K_1 K_2 K_3 n^3 + K_2 K_3^2 n}$$

Then, we obtain

$$\tau = \frac{1}{w}[\arccos(\frac{-J_1 K_2 n^4 + J_3 K_2 n^2 - K_1 K_2 n^7 + J_2 K_1 K_2 n^5 - J_4 K_1 K_2 n^3 + K_2 K_3 n^5 + J_2 K_2 K_3 n^3 - J_4 K_2 K_3 n}{K_1 K_2 K_3 n^3 - K_1^2 K_2 n^5 - K_1 K_2 K_3 n^3 + K_2 K_3^2 n})] \quad (13)$$

Differentiate Equation (9) with respect to τ

$$\left(\frac{d\lambda}{d\tau}\right)^{-1} = \frac{(4\lambda^3 + 3J_1 \lambda^2 + 2J_2 \lambda + J_3)e^{\lambda\tau}}{\lambda(K_1 \lambda^2 + K_2 \lambda + K_3)} - \frac{2K_1 \lambda + K_2}{\lambda(K_1 \lambda^2 + K_2 \lambda + K_3)} + \frac{\tau}{\lambda}$$

$$e^{-\lambda\tau} = \frac{\lambda^4 + J_1 \lambda^3 + J_2 \lambda^2 + J_3 \lambda + J_4}{(K_1 \lambda^2 + K_2 \lambda + K_3)}$$

Substitute $e^{-\lambda\tau}$ into $\left(\frac{d\lambda}{d\tau}\right)^{-1}$,

$$\frac{4\lambda^3 + 3J_1 \lambda^2 + 2J_2 \lambda + J_3}{\lambda(\lambda^4 + J_1 \lambda^3 + J_2 \lambda^2 + J_3 \lambda + J_4)} - \frac{2K_1 \lambda + K_2}{\lambda(K_1 \lambda^2 + K_2 \lambda + K_3)} + \frac{\tau}{\lambda} \quad (14)$$

Hence,

$$\text{sign}\left\{\text{Re}\,\frac{d\lambda}{d\tau}\right\}^{-1}_{\lambda=iw} = \text{sign}\left\{\left[\frac{4\lambda^3+3\,J_1\lambda^2+2\,J_2\lambda+J_3}{\lambda(\lambda^4+J_1\lambda^3+J_2\lambda^2+J_3\lambda+J_4)}\right]_{\lambda=iw} - \left[\frac{2\,K_1\lambda+K_2}{\lambda(K_1\lambda^2+K_2\lambda+K_3)}\right]_{\lambda=iw}\right\}$$

Defining,

$$a_1 = 4\lambda^3 + 3\,J_1\lambda^2 + 2\,J_2\lambda + J_3$$
$$a_2 = 2\,K_1\lambda + K_2$$
$$b_1 = \lambda\left(\lambda^4 + J_1\lambda^3 + J_2\lambda^2 + J_3\lambda\right) + J_4$$
$$b_2 = \lambda\left(K_1\lambda^2 + K_2\lambda + K_3\right)$$

Therefore,

$$\text{sign}\left\{\text{Re}\,\frac{d\lambda}{d\tau}\right\}^{-1}_{\lambda=iw} = \text{sign}\left\{\left[\frac{a_1\,b_2 - a_2\,b_1}{b_1\,b_2}\right]_{\lambda=iw}\right\} \tag{15}$$

2.2. Plankton–Zooplankton–Fish Interaction Model

This model describes the effects of HABs on fish populations by providing knowledge and understanding on how the fish could die. A delay term is incorporated into the model to show that the mortality of the fish populations is not an instantaneous process. The developed model is as follows:

$$\frac{dx}{dt} = rx(t)(1 - x(t)/K) - c_1 x(t)y(t)$$
$$\frac{dy}{dt} = e_1 c_1 x(t)y(t) - c_2 y(t)z(t) - d_1 y(t) \tag{16}$$
$$\frac{dz}{dt} = e_2 c_2 y(t)z(t) - d_2 z(t) - fy(t)z(t-\tau)$$

The following set of assumptions is assumed to formulate the fish mathematical model:

- Let $x(t)$ be the toxin production phytoplankton (TPP) which are being consumed by the zooplankton population which in turn serves as food for the fish population, $f(t)$.
- Let r be the intrinsic growth rate of phytoplankton; K be the environmental capacity of phytoplankton; and c_1 be the predation rate of zooplankton while c_2 is the predation rate of fish.
- e_1 is the birth rate of zooplankton while e_2 is the birth rate of fish, d_1 is the mortality rate of zooplankton and d_2 is mortality rate of fish, and f is coefficient of toxin substance from TPP.
- Let τ be the time delay for the fish to die when feeding on the infected zooplankton as this is not an instantaneous process. The infected zooplankton become harmful to the fish when eaten.

$$J = \begin{bmatrix} -c_1 y - \frac{r(2x-K)}{K} & -c_1 x & 0 \\ e_1 c_1 y & e_1 c_1 x - c_2 z - d_1 & -c_2 y \\ 0 & e_2 c_2 z - fz & e_2 c_2 y - d_2 \end{bmatrix}, \tag{17}$$

where

$$H_1 = -\frac{rx}{K} + r(1 - \frac{x}{K}) - c_1 y$$
$$H_2 = -d_1 + c_1 e_1 x - c_2 z \tag{18}$$
$$H_3 = c_2 e_2 y - d_2$$

$$N = \begin{bmatrix} 0 & 0 & 0 \\ 0 & 0 & 0 \\ 0 & 0 & -fy \end{bmatrix} \tag{19}$$

The characteristic equation is

$$F(\lambda, \tau) = \lambda^3 + A_1\lambda^2 + A_2\lambda + A_3 + (B_1\lambda^2 + B_2\lambda + B_3)e^{-\lambda\tau} \tag{20}$$

where
$$A_1 = -H_1 - H_2 - H_3$$
$$A_2 = H_1H_2 + H_1H_3 + H_2H_3 + c_1^2 e_1 xy + c_2^2 e_2 yz$$
$$A_3 = -H_1H_2H_3 - c_1^2 e_1 H_3 xy - c_2^2 e_2 H_1 yz$$
$$B_1 = fx$$
$$B_2 = -fH_1 x - fH_2 x$$
$$B_3 = fxH_1H_2 + c_1^2 e_1 fx^2 y + c_1 c_2 fxyz$$

substitute $\lambda = iw$ into Equation (20)

$$(iw)^3 + A_1(iw)^2 + A_2(iw) + A_3 + (B_1(iw)^2 + B_2(iw) + B_3)e^{-iw\tau} = 0$$
$$-iw^3 - A_1w^2 + A_2iw + A_3 + (-B_1w^2 + B_2iw + B_3)(cosw\tau + isinw\tau) = 0 \quad (21)$$
$$-iw^3 - A_1w^2 + iA_2w + A_3 + (-B_1w^2 cosw\tau - iB_1w^2 sinw\tau + B_2iwcosw\tau - B_2wsinw\tau + B_3 cosw\tau + iB_3 sinw\tau = 0$$

separate imaginary and real parts

$$I: -w^3 + A_2w - B_1w^2 sinw\tau + B_2wcosw\tau + B_3 sinw\tau$$
$$R: -A_1w^2 + A_3 - B_1w^2 cosw\tau - B_2wsinw\tau + B_3 cosw\tau \quad (22)$$

$$-w^3 + A_2w = B_1w^2 sinw\tau - B_2wcosw\tau - B_3 sinw\tau$$
$$-A_1w^2 + A_3 = B_1w^2 cosw\tau + B_2wsinw\tau - B_3 cosw\tau \quad (23)$$

square and add up the equations
$$w^6 + (A_1^2 - 2A_2 - B_1^2 + 2B_1B_2)w^4 + (A_2^2 - 2A_1A_3 + 2B_1B_3 + B_2^2)w^2 + A_3^2 - B_3^2 = 0$$
where
$$C_1 = A_1^2 - 2A_2 - B_1^2 + 2B_1B_2$$
$$C_2 = A_2^2 - 2A_1A_3 + 2B_1B_3 + B_2^2 \quad (24)$$
$$C_3 = A_3^2 - B_3^2$$

let $u = w^2$
$$u^3 + C_1u^2 + C_2u + C_3 = 0 \quad (25)$$

then $H'(u) = 3u^2 + 2C_1u + C_2$

Hence, $H'(u) = 0$ has two roots which are given by

$$u_1^* = \frac{-C_1 + \sqrt{(C_1^2 - 3C_2)}}{3}$$
$$u_2^* = \frac{-C_1 - \sqrt{(C_1^2 - 3C_2)}}{3}$$

A hypothesis is formulated as below:

Hypothesis 1 (H1). $u_1^* > 0, H(u_1^*) < 0, C_1^2 - 3C_2 \geq 0$.

Since $C_3 > 0$, Equation (24) has no real positive roots if $C_1^2 - 3C_2 < 0$ (see Lemma 2.1 in [19]) and two real positive roots if Hypothesis 1 (H1) holds and these roots be ω_j (j = 1,2). Let $\omega_1 < \omega_2$ and then $H'(\omega_1) < 0$ and $H'(\omega_2) > 0$ (see Lemma 3.2 in [20]).

By Equation (23), we obtained following equation

$$sinw\tau = \frac{-A_1w^2 + A_3 + (-B_1w^2 + B_3)cosw\tau}{B_2w} \quad (26)$$

and substitute it into Equation (23).
$$-w^3 + A_2w = B_1w^2 \left[\frac{-A_1w^2 + A_3 + (-B_1w^2 + B_3)cosw\tau}{B_2w}\right] - B_2wcosw\tau - \left[\frac{-A_1w^2 + A_3 + (B_3 - B_1w^2)cosw\tau}{B_2w}\right]$$

$$cos w\tau = \frac{-B_2w^4 + B_2A_2w^2 + A_1B_1w^4 - A_3B_1w^2 - A_1B_3w^2 + A_3B_3}{B_1B_3 - B_1^2w^4 - B_2^2w^2 - B_3^2 + B_1B_3w^2}$$

$$\tau_j^k = \frac{1}{w_j}\left[arccos\left(\frac{-B_2w^4 + B_2A_2w^2 + A_1B_1w^4 - A_3B_1w^2 - A_1B_3w^2 + A_3B_3}{B_1B_3 - B_1^2w^4 - B_2^2w^2 - B_3^2 + B_1B_3w^2}\right) + 2k\pi\right] \quad (27)$$

where $j = 1, 2$ and $k = 0, 1, 2, ..$

Lemma 1. *If Hypothesis (H1) holds, then Equation (20) has a pair of pure imaginary roots $\mp iw$ and all other roots have non-zero real parts at $\tau = \tau_j^k$ ($j = 1,2, k = 0,1,2,...$)*

In addition, we define $\tau_0 = \min j = 1, 2\tau_j^0$, τ_0 represents the smallest positive value of $\tau_j^0, j = 1, 2$ given by Equation (26) and $w = w_j0$

Lemma 2. *If Hypothesis (H1) holds, then we have the following two transversality conditions:*

$$sign\left[\frac{dR\lambda(\tau)}{d\tau}\right]_\tau = \tau_1^k < 0, sign\left[\frac{dR\lambda(\tau)}{d\tau}\right]_\tau = \tau_1^k > 0 \quad (28)$$

where $k = 0, 1, 2, \ldots$

Therefore, the required transversality condition is obtained if $H'(\omega_1^2) < 0$, and $H'(\omega_2^2) > 0$.

3. Results

3.1. Nutrient–Phytoplankton–Zooplankton Interaction Model

A set of parameter values from the literature [17] was used to substantiate the analytical results obtained through numerical simulation (see Table 1). τ is considered a bifurcation parameter.

From the numerical simulations, it was found that, for $E^*(1.4653, 0.6618, 0.1647, 0.9806)$, the system is unstable for $\tau = 0$, which is without delay as in Figure 1. The assumption for the system without delay means that the produced toxin is an instantaneous process neglecting the maturity of the TPP population. Therefore, the absence of time lag in the system illustrates that HAB phenomena will occur faster and thus makes the system unstable. Figure 2 depicts the equilibrium between TPP and zooplankton populations loses its stability for $\tau = 0 < \tau_0$. This shows that an prey–predator interaction exists between TPP and zooplankton population. TPP do not secrete out the toxic substance into the environment but it will harm zooplankton if it is consumed when the toxin produced is at its peak. Meanwhile, Figure 3 shows that the equilibrium between NTP and TPP populations loses its stability for the non-delay system. The NTP and TPP populations interact during the interspecies competition for food hunting.

From the analytical findings, the value of the delay parameter of system (2) for the stability behaviour changes when $\tau_0 = 22.6841$. This finding is well supported by experimental research [3,11] where, in the batch culture of *Pyrodinium bahamense* in one month, the peak of the cell content is on the 22nd day. The toxin content rapidly peaks during the early exponential phase and rapidly declines prior to the onset of the plateau phase. This explains the reason behind the switching behaviour which occurred once in this research. We also remark that τ represents the time lag for the maturity of the TPP population for producing toxin.

Table 1. Parameter values used in the numerical simulation (Nutrient–Phytoplankton–Zooplankton Interaction Model).

Parameters	Symbols	Values
Dilution rate of nutrient	D	0.3 (h^{-1})
Constant input of nutrient concentration	N_0	1.58 (h^{-1})
Nutrient uptake rate for the NTP	α_1	0.03 (mL·h^{-1})
Nutrient uptake rate for the TPP	α_2	0.022 (mL·h^{-1})
Conversion rate of NTP	θ_1	0.02 (mL·h^{-1})
Conversion rate of TPP	θ_2	0.02 (mL·h^{-1})
Natural death rate of NTP	m_1	0.006 (h^{-1})
Natural death rate of TPP	m_2	0.006 (h^{-1})
Natural death rate of zooplankton	m_3	0.005 (h^{-1})
Competition coefficient	e_1	0.02 (mL·h^{-1})
Competition coefficient	e_2	0.02 (mL·h^{-1})
Predation rate of NTP	β_1	0.02 (mL·h^{-1})
Predation rate of TPP	β_2	0.01 (mL·h^{-1})
Conversion rate for NTP	γ_1	0.01 (mL·h^{-1})
Death rate due to consumption of TPP	γ_2	0.008 (mL·h^{-1})
Dilution rate of NTP	D_1	0.0004 (h^{-1})
Dilution rate of TPP	D_2	0.0004 (h^{-1})
Dilution rate of zooplankton	D_3	0.0003 (h^{-1})

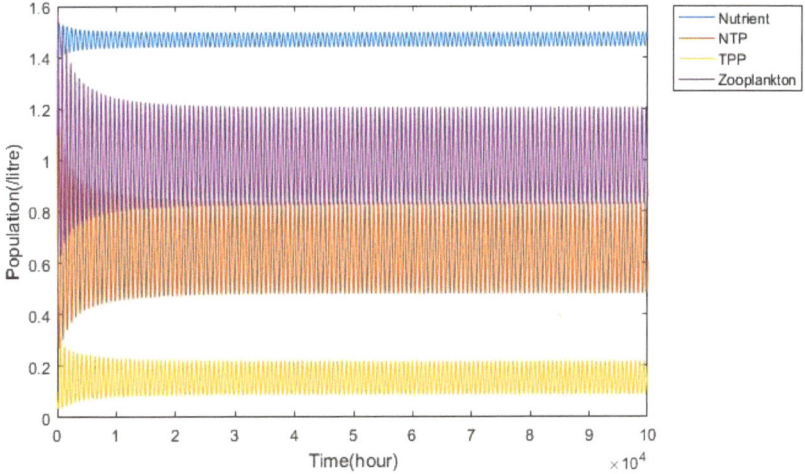

Figure 1. Simulation results of System (2) with $\tau = 0 < \tau_0$.

Therefore, as τ passes through the critical value of $\tau = \tau_0 = 22.6841$, the interior equilibrium point gains its stability and a Hopf bifurcation occurs as shown in Figure 4. It can be seen that the system switches from an unstable to stable system. Due to the time needed for the maturity of the TPP population, the system becomes locally stable since the HAB takes time to occur. Figures 5 and 6 illustrate the asymptotical stability of the equilibrium between the TPP with the zooplankton population and the NTP with the TPP populations, respectively. It was found that a stable Hopf-bifurcating periodic solution occurred in both figures.

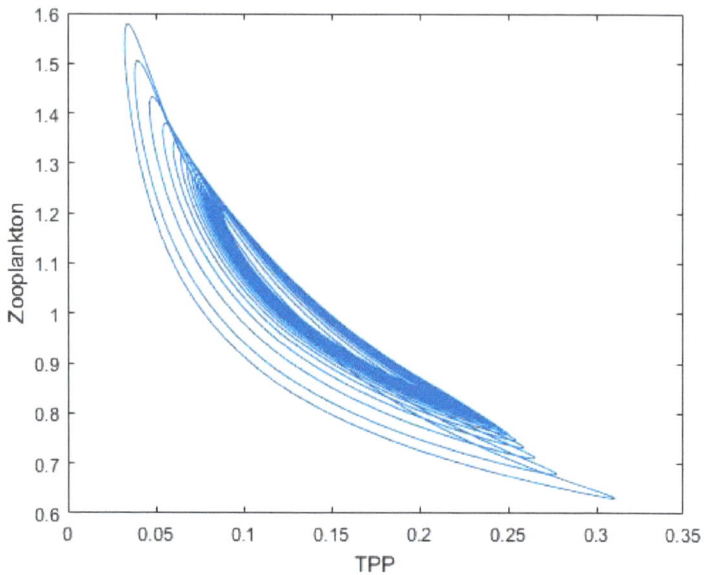

Figure 2. Equilibrium between the TPP and zooplankton populations loses its stability for $\tau = 0 < \tau_0$.

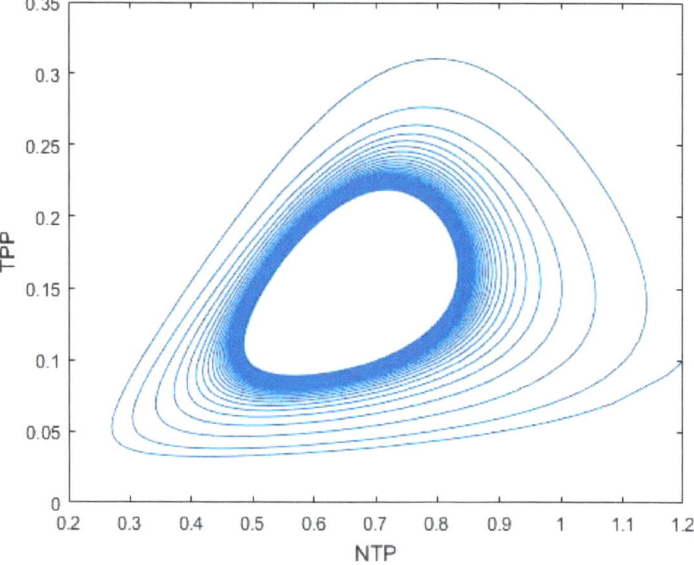

Figure 3. Equilibrium between the NTP and TPP populations loses its stability for $\tau = 0 < \tau_0$.

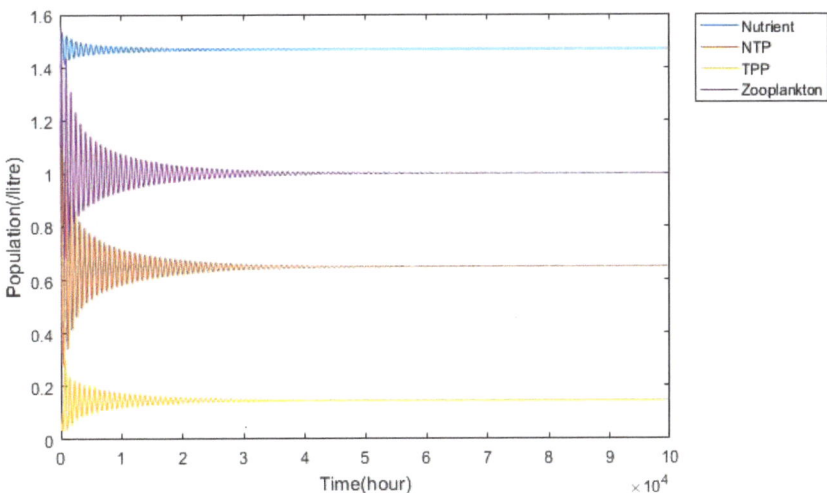

Figure 4. Simulation results of System (2) with $\tau = \tau_0 = 22.6841$.

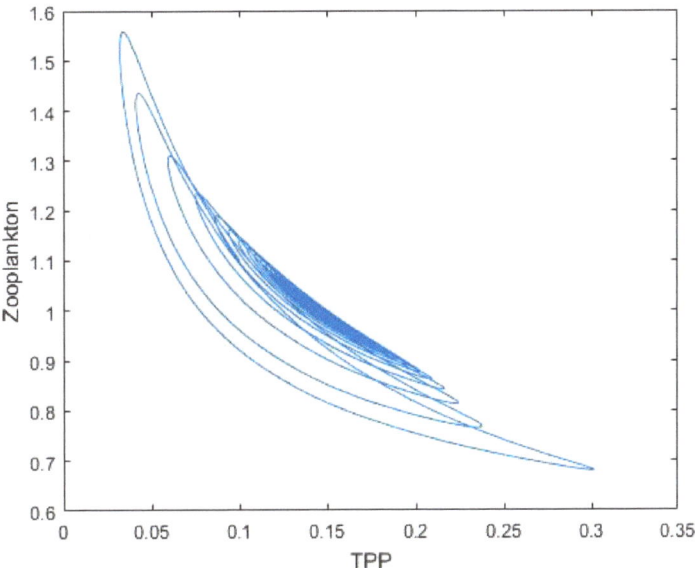

Figure 5. The asymptotical stability of equilibrium the between TPP and zooplankton populations for $\tau = \tau_0 = 22.6841$.

Then, the interior equilibrium point remains locally asymptotically stable whenever the value of $\tau = 30 > \tau_0$ increases, as shown in Figure 7. It can be seen that when the value τ is longer than τ_0, the unstable system becomes stable. A longer time lag describes that the TPP needs a longer time to mature and liberate toxic chemicals. Hence, the system becomes stable where, in this context, the HAB does not occur during the time lag because no toxic chemicals are released that could harm the marine ecosystem. Figures 8 and 9 depict the asymptotical stability of the equilibrium between TPP with the zooplankton populations and NTP with TPP populations for the solution of system (2) for $\tau = 30 > \tau_0$.

Figure 10 illustrates the simulation results of system (2) with $\tau = 20 < \tau_0$. The periodic solution occurs and the interior equilibrium point loses its stability as τ has a smaller value than the critical value τ_0. The time lag in this model represents the time taken for the TPP population to mature and produce toxin. Therefore, a shorter time lag results in an unstable system because TPP takes a shorter time to mature enough to produce toxin. This will promote the HAB to occur. Figures 11 and 12 show that the equilibrium loses its stability between TPP with zooplankton and NTP with TPP for $\tau < \tau_0$.

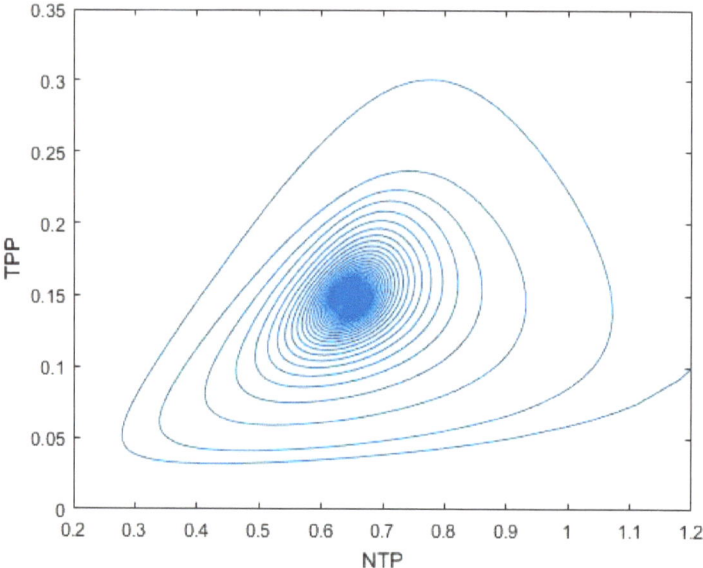

Figure 6. The asymptotical stability of the equilibrium between NTP and TPP populations for $\tau = \tau_0 = 22.6841$.

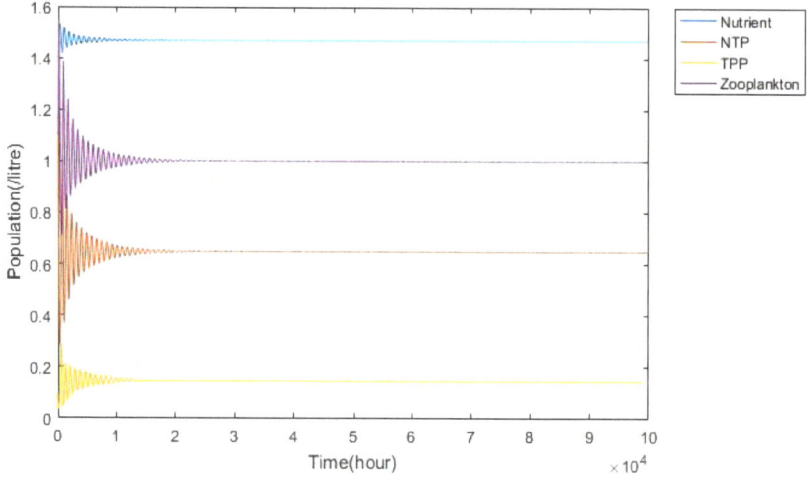

Figure 7. Simulation results of System (2) with $\tau = 30 > \tau_0$.

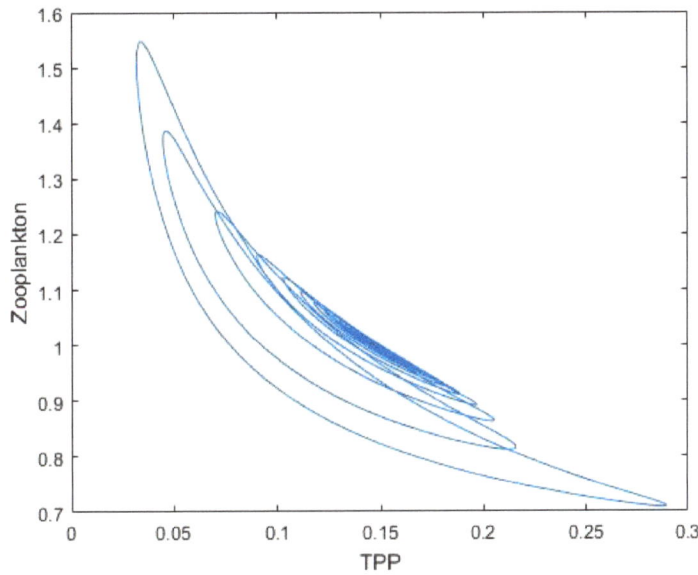

Figure 8. The asymptotical stability of the equilibrium between the TPP and zooplankton populations for $\tau = 30 > \tau_0$.

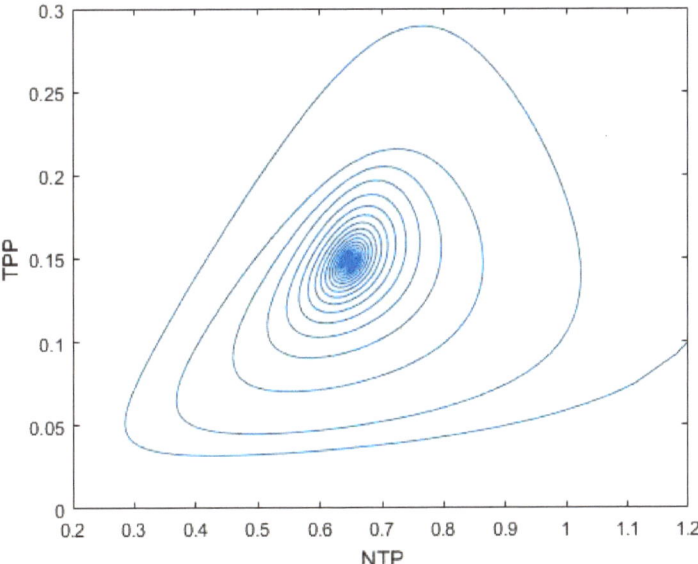

Figure 9. The asymptotical stability of the equilibrium between the NTP and TPP populations for $\tau = 30 > \tau_0$.

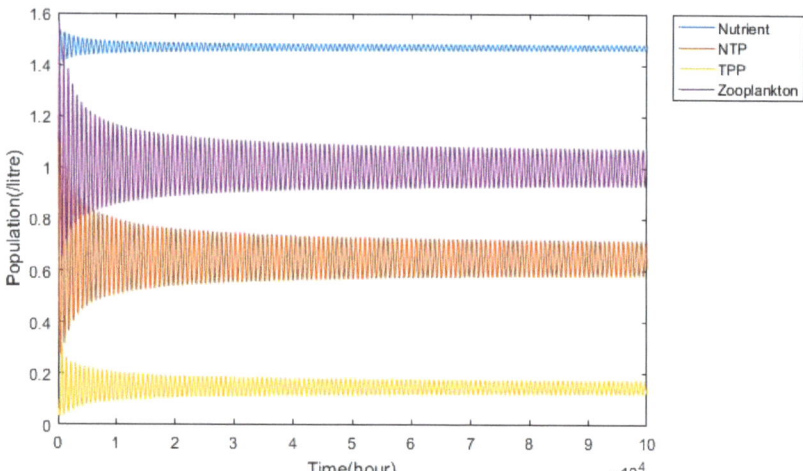

Figure 10. Simulation results of System (2) with $\tau < \tau_0$.

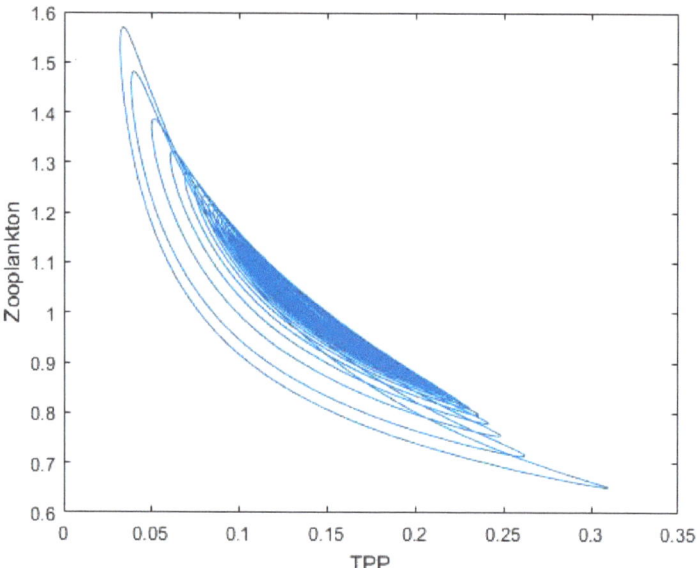

Figure 11. Equilibrium between the TPP and zooplankton populations loses its stability for $\tau < \tau_0$.

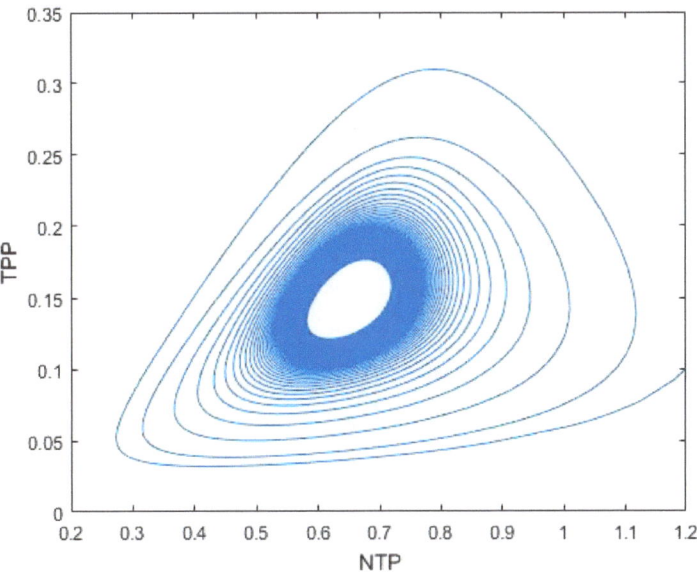

Figure 12. Equilibrium between the NTP and TPP populations loses its stability for $\tau < \tau_0$.

3.2. Plankton–Zooplankton–Fish Interaction Model

From the numerical simulations, it was found that, for $E^*(6.6731, 3.36538, 3.51923)$, the system is stable for $\tau = 0$, which means that there is no delay as in Figure 13. The parameter values used in the numerical simulation are as shown in Table 2.

Table 2. Parameter values used in the numerical simulation (Plankton–Zooplankton–Fish Interaction Model).

Parameters	Symbols	Values
Intrinsic growth rate	r	0.7 (mL·h^{-1})
Constant input of nutrient concentration	K	28 (h^{-1})
Mortality rate of zooplankton	d_1	0.23 (h^{-1})
Mortality rate of fish	d_2	0.15 (h^{-1})
Predation rate of zooplankton	c_1	0.65 (mL·h^{-1})
Predation rate of fish	c_2	0.45 (mL·h^{-1})
Birth rate of zooplankton	e_1	0.9 (mL·h^{-1})
Birth rate of fish	e_2	0.99 (mL·h^{-1})
Coefficient of toxicity	f	0.1 (h^{-1})

The asymptotical stability between TPP with fish, zooplankton with fish and among all populations for $\tau = 0$ is as shown in Figures 14–16. When the system is described as stable it means that fish kills occur in the water while the system is unstable when there no fish kills occur. This is because the objective of this model is to describe the fish kills due to HAB events. Meanwhile, the delay in this model indicates the time lag required for the fish to die after consuming the toxicated zooplankton. The values of τ are as in Table 3.

Table 3. τ values.

τ_j^+	τ_j^-
$\tau_0^+ = 1.37941$	$\tau_0^- = 5.39314$
$\tau_1^+ = 6.98104$	$\tau_1^- = 12.53884$
$\tau_2^+ = 12.58266$	$\tau_2^- = 19.6845$

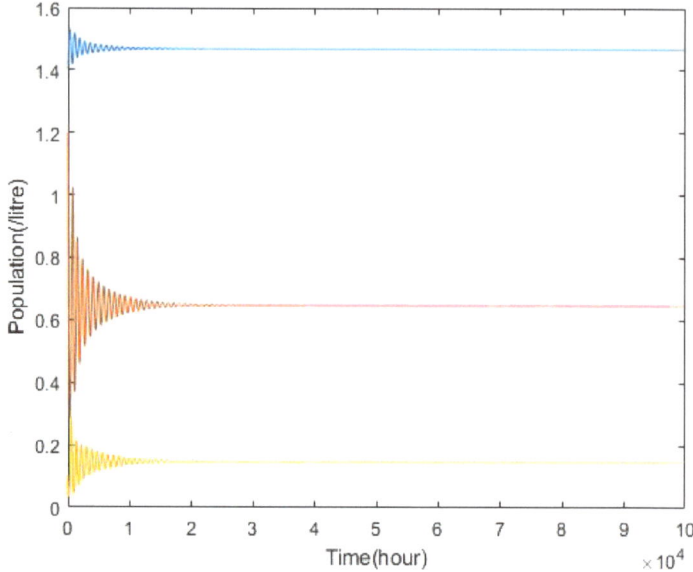

Figure 13. Simulation results of System (16) for $\tau = 0$.

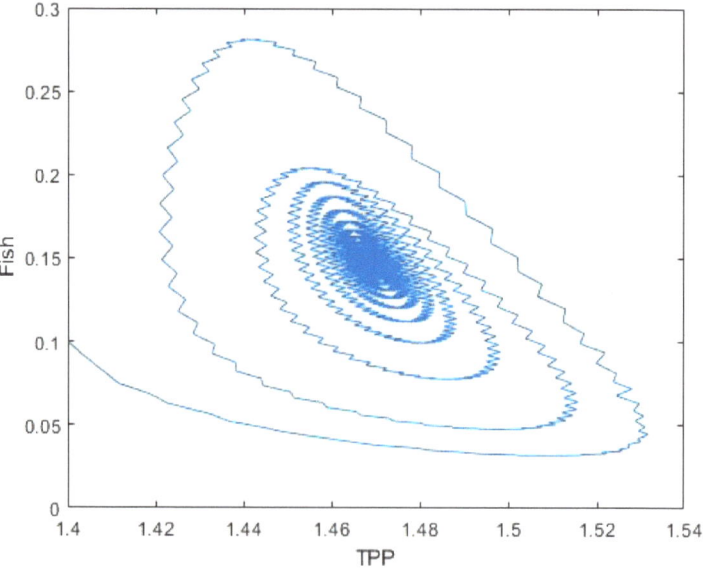

Figure 14. The asymptotical stability between the TPP and fish populations for $\tau = 0$.

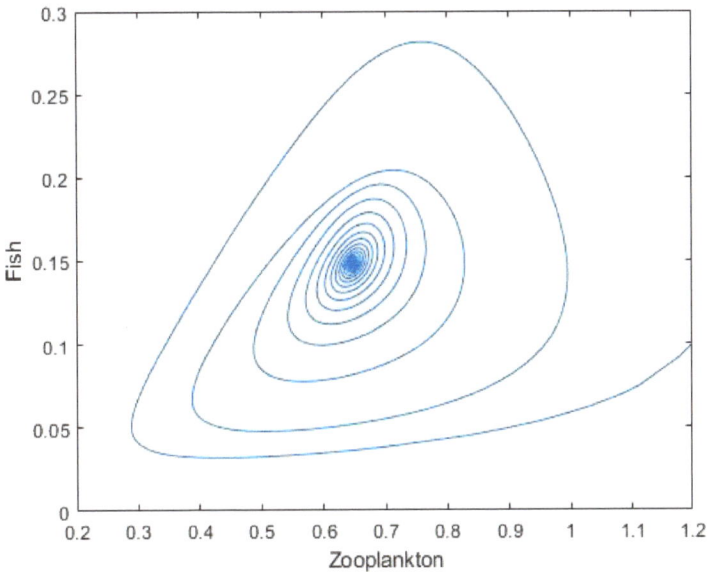

Figure 15. The asymptotical stability between the zooplankton and fish populations for $\tau = 0$.

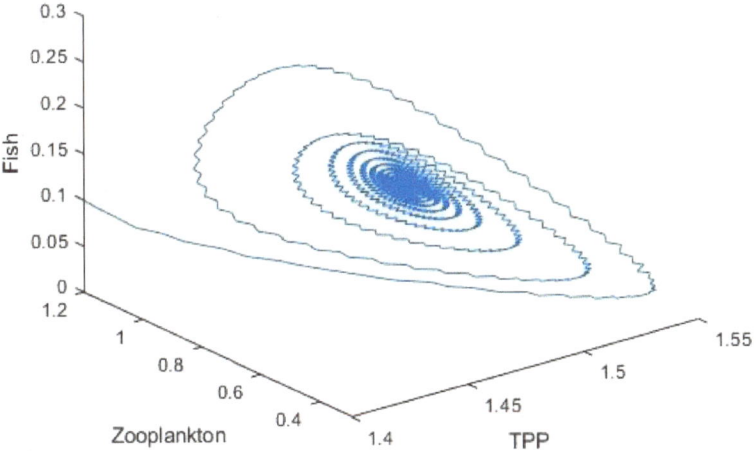

Figure 16. The asymptotical stability of all populations for $\tau = 0$.

From Figure 17, it can be seen that when the value of $\tau = \tau_0^+ = 1.37941$, the system becomes periodic and switches from a stable system to an unstable system and Hopf bifurcation occurs. This shows that the induced delay in this system affects the stability of the system. The equilibrium losing its stability between the TPP with fish, zooplankton with fish and among all populations are shown in Figures 18–20.

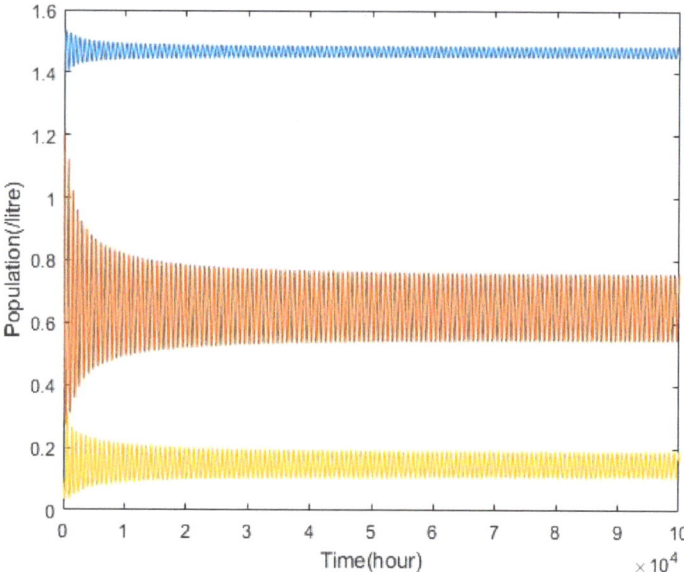

Figure 17. Simulation results of System (16) for $\tau = \tau_0^+$.

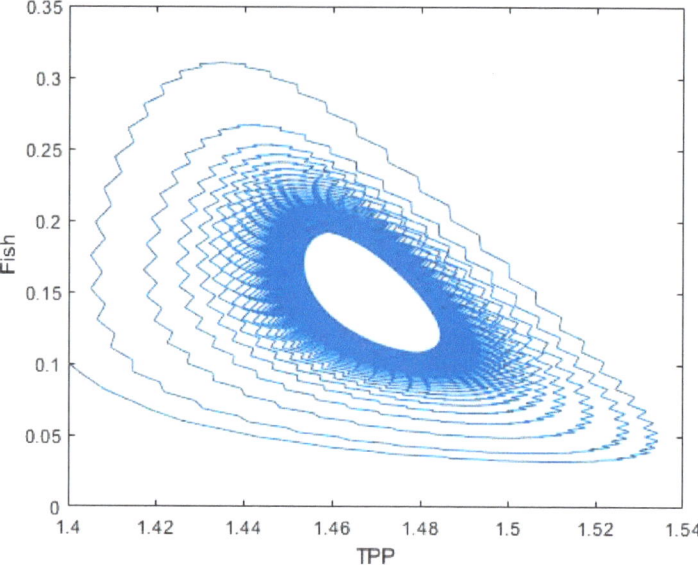

Figure 18. Equilibrium between the TPP and fish populations loses its stability for $\tau = \tau_0^+$.

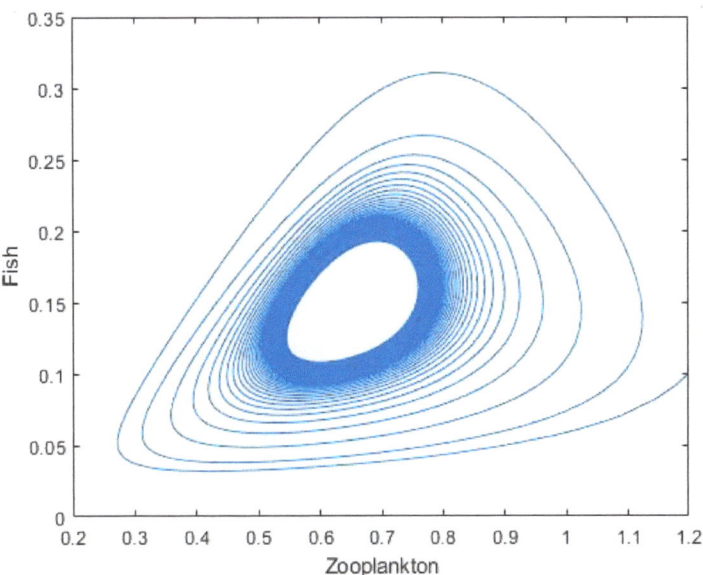

Figure 19. Equilibrium between the zooplankton and fish populations loses its stability for $\tau = \tau_0^+$.

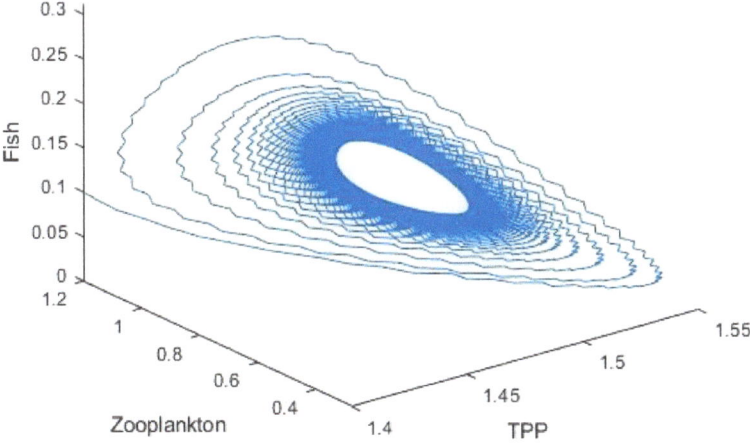

Figure 20. Equilibrium of all populations loses its stability for $\tau = \tau_0^+$.

However, Figure 21 illustrates that the system again switches to a stable system when the value of $\tau = \tau_0^- = 5.39314$. Thus, τ_0^- is the second bifurcation node in this system where the system changes from an unstable system to a stable system. The asymptotical stability between TPP with fish, zooplankton with fish and among all populations are as shown in Figures 22–24.

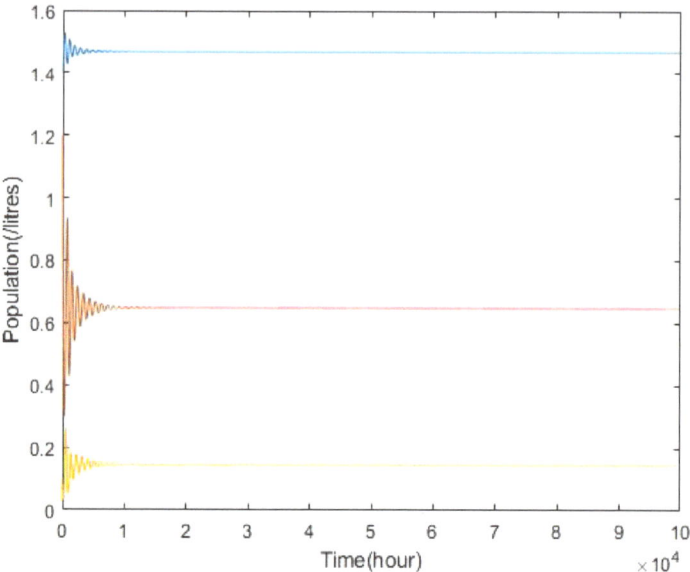

Figure 21. Simulation results of System (16) for $\tau = \tau_0^-$.

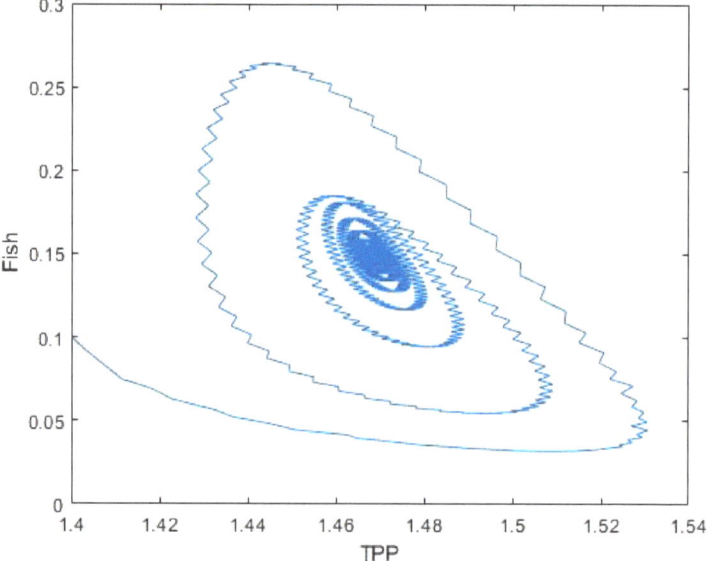

Figure 22. The asymptotical stability between the TPP and fish populations for $\tau = \tau_0^-$.

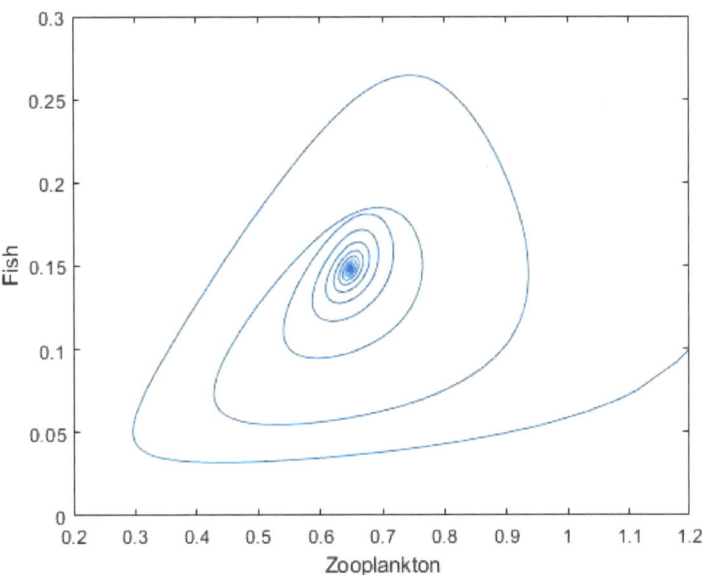

Figure 23. The asymptotical stability between the zooplankton and fish populations for $\tau = \tau_0^-$.

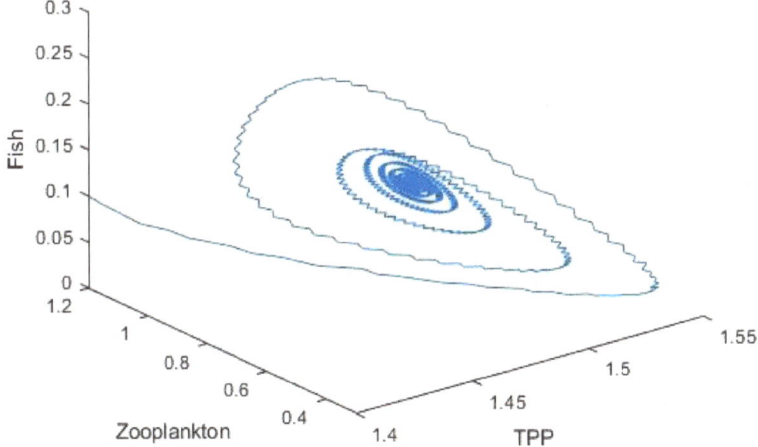

Figure 24. The asymptotical stability of all populations for $\tau = \tau_0^-$.

Meanwhile, Figure 25 shows that the system becomes unstable again when the value of $\tau = \tau_1^+ = 6.98104$. Therefore, this is the third bifurcation node in this system where the system switches from being a stable to unstable system. It can be seen that the system oscillates throughout the period. Equilibrium between the TPP with fish, zooplankton with fish and among all populations loses its stability as shown in Figures 26–28.

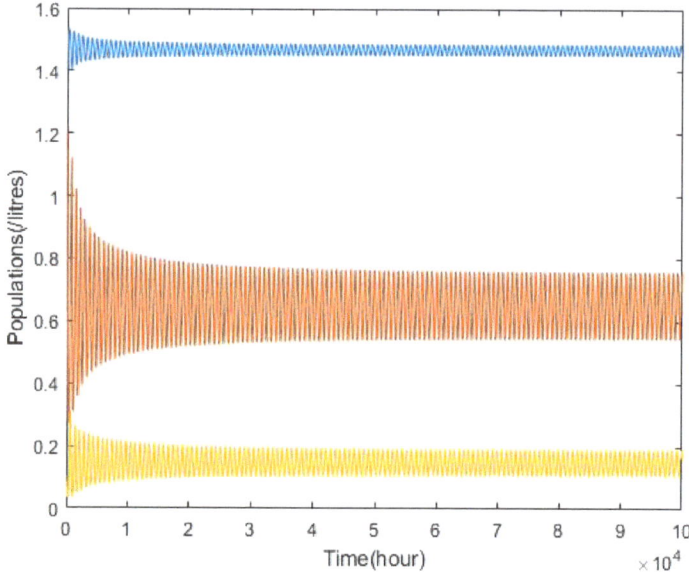

Figure 25. Simulation results of System (16) for $\tau = \tau_1^+$.

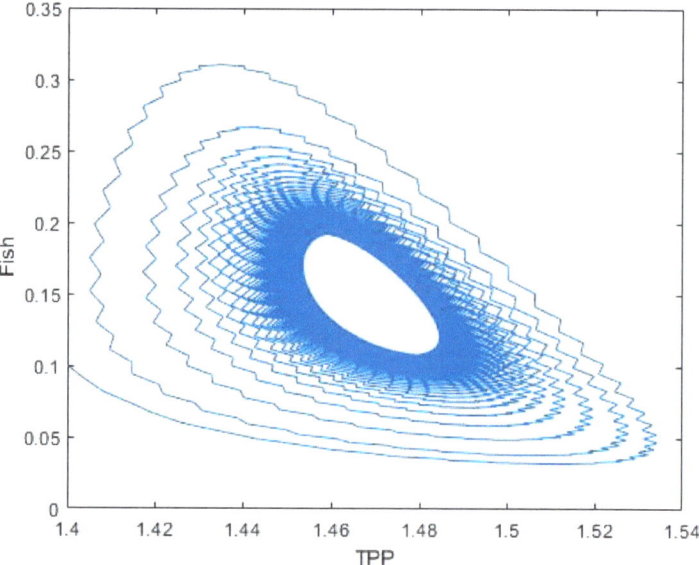

Figure 26. Equilibrium between the TPP and fish populations loses its stability for $\tau = \tau_1^+$.

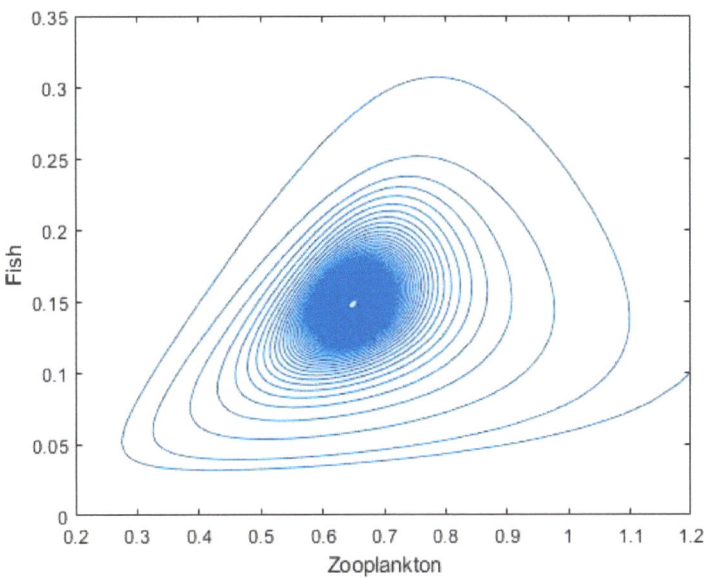

Figure 27. Equilibrium between the zooplankton and fish populations loses its stability for $\tau = \tau_1^+$.

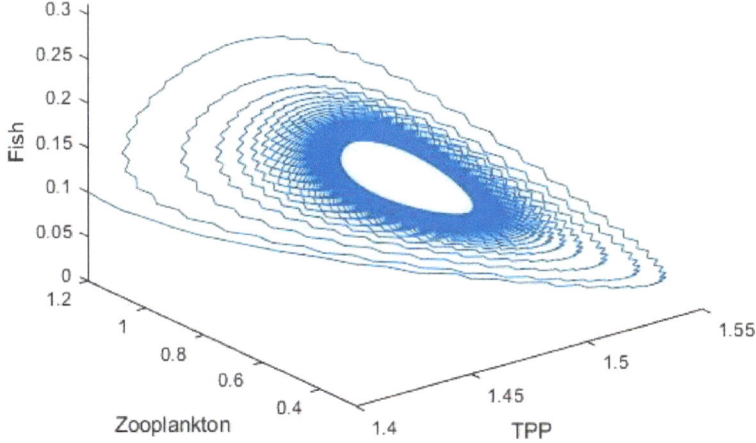

Figure 28. Equilibrium of all populations loses its stability for $\tau = \tau_1^+$.

However, the system remains unchanged when $\tau = \tau_1^- = 12.53884$, as shown in Figure 29. Thus, there is no Hopf bifurcation since there is no switching. The equilibrium between TPP with fish, zooplankton with fish and among all populations loses its stability for τ_1^- are shown as in Figures 30–32.

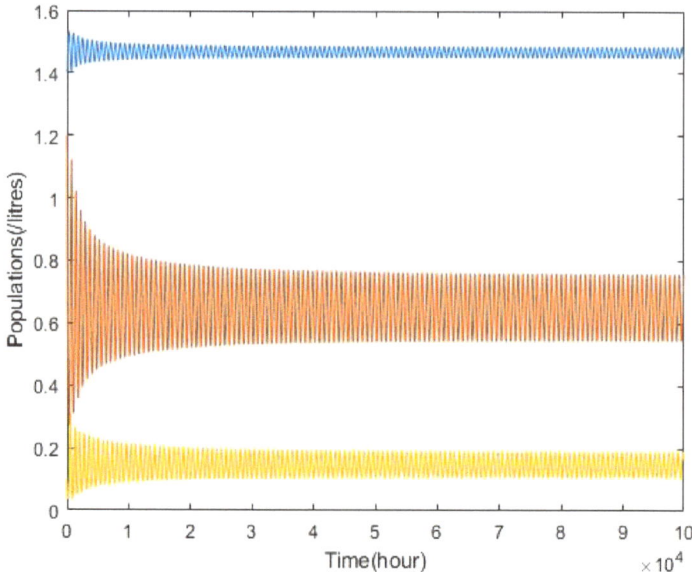

Figure 29. Simulation results of System (16) for $\tau = \tau_1^-$.

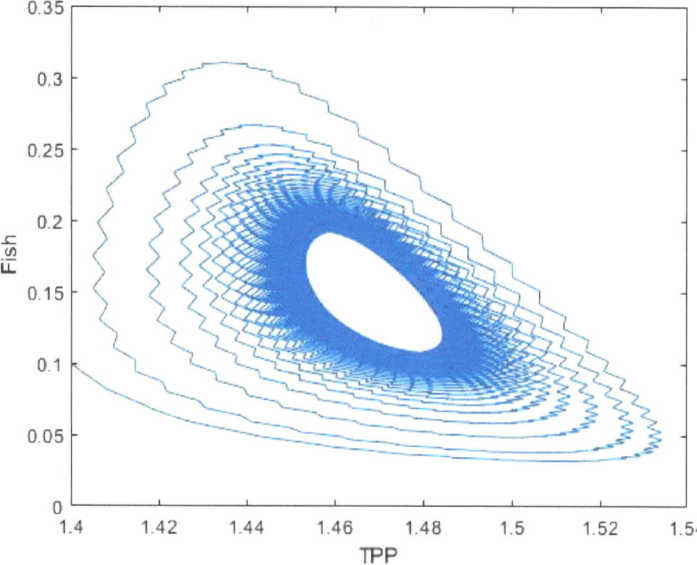

Figure 30. Equilibrium between the TPP and fish populations loses its stability for $\tau = \tau_1^-$.

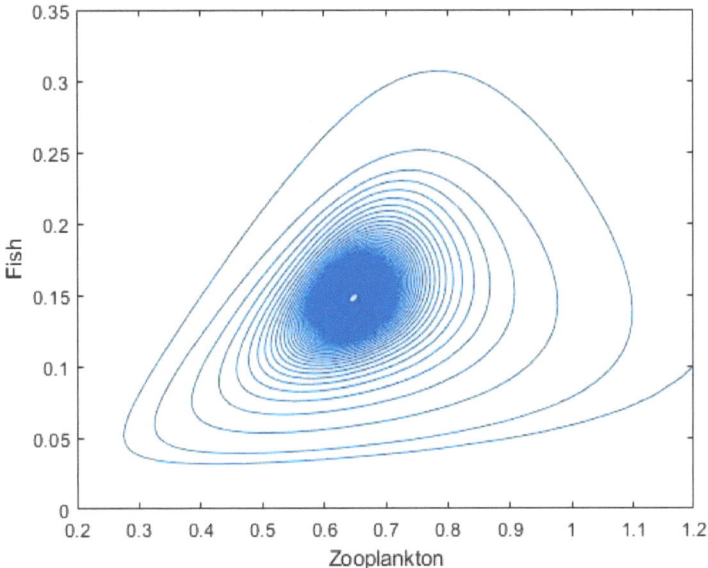

Figure 31. Equilibrium between the zooplankton and fish populations loses its stability for $\tau = \tau_1^-$.

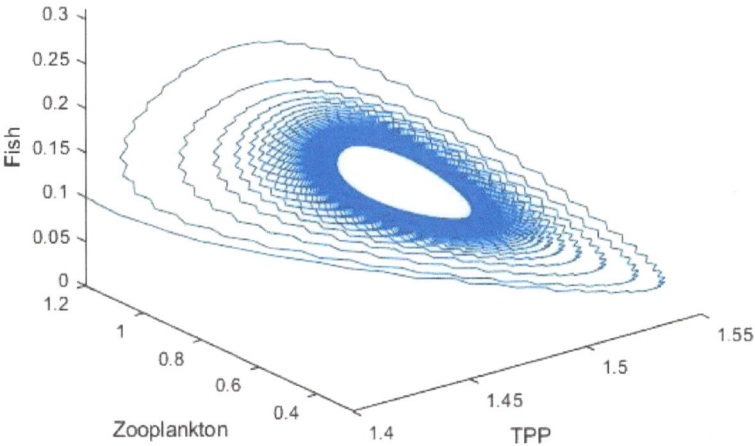

Figure 32. Equilibrium of all populations loses its stability for $\tau = \tau_1^-$.

Figure 33 illustrates the direction of Hopf while Figure 34 shows the stability information of System (16). It can be seen that for $\tau = 0$, which is without delay, the system is stable. However, the system switches to an unstable system for the first critical value of time delay which is $\tau = \tau_0^+ = 1.37941$. The system is asymptotically stable for $\tau < 1.37941$. Then, the system again switches to a stable system for the second critical value of the time delay, $\tau = \tau_0^- = 5.39314$. The system loses its stability when $\tau > 5.39314$ which is less than the third critical value $\tau > 6.98104$. However, the system remains unstable for $\tau > 6.98104$ which is less than the fourth critical value $\tau = 12.53884$.

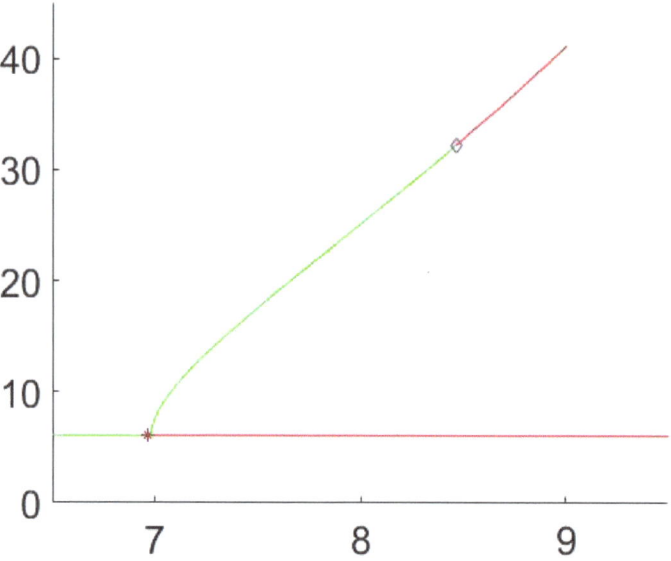

Figure 33. Direction of Hopf.

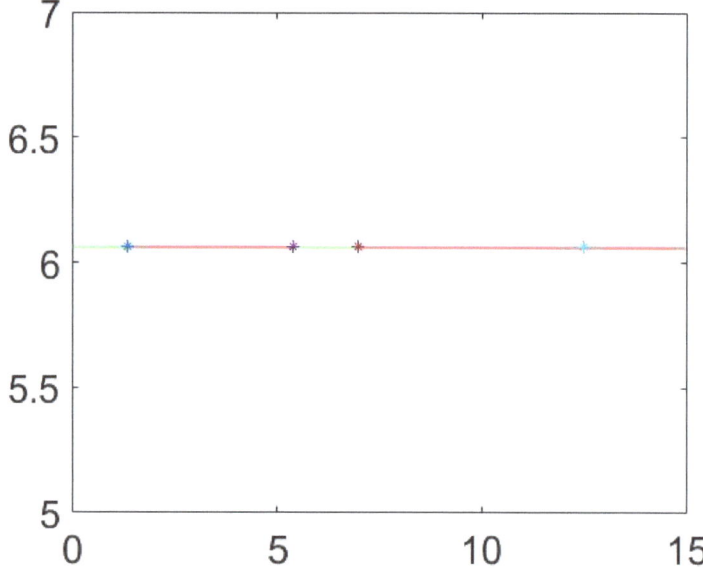

Figure 34. Stability information of System (16).

4. Discussion

In this research, the interactions between the nutrient, TPP population, NTP population, and zooplankton population were investigated to describe the occurrence of HAB events. The time delay is incorporated into this system to show that TPP species need to achieve their maturity before producing toxin. From the results, it can be seen that the unstable model becomes stable when delay is induced into the system. Whenever the time delay is equal to the critical value—which is $\tau_0 = 22.6841$—the system achieves its stability.

The value obtained is well supported by experimental findings [3,11] where in the batch culture of *Pyrodinium bahamense*, in a month, on the 22nd day, the toxin content is at its most. The toxin content rapidly peaks during the exponential phase and rapidly decline prior to the onset of a plateau phase.

The toxin released by the TPP population has had many detrimental consequences on marine creature, aquaculture sector, tourism, etc. In this research, the effect of toxin on fish populations is discussed where the interaction between TPP species, zooplankton and fish populations is well described. From the model, fish are affected by the toxin when they consumed toxicated zooplankton, which consumed the TPP population. However, the death of a fish population is not an instantaneous process but is mediated by some time lag. Therefore, delay in incorporated into this model to study the effect of delay into this system.

It can be seen that, for $\tau = 0$, which is without delay, the system is stable. However, the system switches to an unstable system for the first critical value of time delay which is $\tau = \tau_0^+ = 1.37941$. The system is asymptotically stable for $\tau < 1.37941$. Then, the system again switches to a stable system for the second critical value of time delay, $\tau = \tau_0^- = 5.39314$. The system loses back its stability when $\tau > 5.39314$ which is less than the third critical value $\tau > 6.98104$. However, the system remains unstable for $\tau > 6.98104$ but less than the fourth critical value $\tau = 12.53884$. Therefore, it can be concluded that there are two nodes of Hopf bifurcation which change the system from a stable system to an unstable system and switch back to a stable system and then remain unchanged. In an ecological sense, these results revealed that under certain parametric conditions, the delay of fish death can bring instability as well as stability in the planktonic food chain.

5. Conclusions

This study presented a mathematical model that describes the process of HAB with the presence of discrete delay. The inclusion of discrete delay is important to show that the production of toxin is not an instantaneous process where TPP species need to achieve their maturity before being able to produce toxin in their body. However, the produced toxin does not secrete out into the environment but is kept inside the cell body. *P.bahamense* becomes harmful to shellfish because shellfish act as a filter feeder and will filter the water going inside them. Thus, when there is massive bloom of *P.bahamense*, they get stuck in stomach of shellfish during filtration. The toxin does not harm the shellfish but it is harmful to human health whenever it is consumed. Moreover, when there is massive bloom, the decreased content of dissolved oxygen (DO) in the water kills fish because they can barely breathe to receive oxygen. Dinoflagellates have a rigid cell wall that also contains silica and they have two tiny whip-like structures known as flagellae to propel them through the water. Due to this rigid cell wall, it is hard to break but will accumulate in the fish gills and make it hard to breath. In some cases, when the cell wall touches the fish gills, it could explode and the toxin content released out of the cell. This toxin content is harmful to human health if it is consumed.

A delay model of plankton interaction is developed in which the time lag is incorporated for the maturity of TPP species to produce toxin. The stability behaviour of the system around the feasible steady states was investigated. The findings show that inducing discrete delay into the model has a stabilizing effect on the system. This result contradicts previous research wherein almost all of the previous research claimed that delay would stabilize their model system. Therefore, the delay can switch the system from unstable to stable or vice versa [21]. Our findings bring an ecological significance to the marine ecosystem, that is, if the time taken for the TPP to mature is longer, then the system is stable since no production of toxic chemicals could result from the occurrence of HAB. This research indicates that inducing discrete delay causes a stabilization effect in the system and shows the effect of dilution rate, nutrient concentration, and interspecies competition towards the model. This also demonstrates and gives information about the occurrence of HAB for a better understanding.

Furthermore, this study also presented a model of a plankton–fish–zooplankton interaction model which consist of three variables which are the TPP, zooplankton, and fish populations. In this model, the TPP population is being predated by the zooplankton population which in turn serves as food for the predator fish population. The time delay was incorporated into this model to show that the mortality of fish species due to the consumption of toxic zooplankton is not an instantaneous process but is mediated by some time lag. This model helps to understand and describe the effect of toxin liberation by the TPP population towards fish population where fish will die. This may harm the aquaculture sector where massive fish kills during HAB occurrence have occurred in Tanjung Kupang, Johor [10].

Therefore, this research gives knowledge and understanding of how HAB events occur due to *Pyrodinium bahamense* sp. and what factors are involved. Additionally, the second model describes the effect of HAB on the fish population in which it causes fish mortality. Hence, monitoring and awareness programs should be conducted to educate the public about the effects of HAB occurrence in order to minimize the loss.

Author Contributions: Conceptualization, N.M. and F.N.Y.; Data curation, M.N.M.R. and F.A.K.; Formal analysis, F.N.Y.; Methodology, F.N.Y.; Software, F.N.Y.; Supervision, N.M.; Validation, F.N.Y. and N.M.; Writing—original draft preparation, F.N.Y.; Writing—review and editing, F.N.Y., N.M., F.A.K., and M.N.M.R. All authors have read and agreed to the published version of the manuscript.

Funding: This research was funded by the Ministry of Higher Education, Malaysia, under Fundamental Research Grant Scheme (FRGS/1/2019/STG06/UTM/02/10), grant number R.J130000.7854.5F220.

Institutional Review Board Statement: Not applicable.

Informed Consent Statement: Not applicable.

Data Availability Statement: Data are available in a publicly accessible repository that does not issue DOIs. Publicly available datasets were analyzed in this study.

Acknowledgments: This research was supported by the Ministry of Higher Education, Malaysia, under Fundamental Research Grant Scheme (FRGS/1/2019/STG06/UTM/02/10), grant number R.J130000.7854.5F220. The authors are also thankful to Universiti Teknologi Malaysia for providing the facilities in this research.

Conflicts of Interest: The author declares no conflict of interest.

Abbreviations

The following abbreviations are used in this manuscript:

HAB	Harmful Algal Bloom
TPP	Toxin-Producing Phytoplankton
NTP	Non-Toxic Phytoplankton
PSP	Paralytic Shellfish Poisoning
PST	Paralytic Shellfish Toxin

References

1. Daily, S.C. Available online: http://sinchew-i.com (accessed on 23 January 2005).
2. Zingone, A.; Enevoldsen, O.H. The diversity of Harmful algal blooms: A challenge for science and management. *Ocean Coast. Manag.* **2000**, *43*, 725–748. [CrossRef]
3. Usup, G.; Ahmad, A.; Matsuoka, K.; Lim, P.T.; Leaw, C.P. Biology, ecology and bloom dynamics of the toxic marine dinoflagellate Pyrodinium bahamense. *Harmful Algae* **2012**, *14*, 301–312. [CrossRef]
4. Roy, R.N. Red tide and outbreak of paralytic shellfish poisoning in Sabah. *Med J. Malays.* **1977**, *31*, 247–251.
5. Suleiman, M.; Jelip, J.; Rundi, C.; Chua, T.H. Case report: Paralytic shellfish poisoning in Sabah, Malaysia. *Am. J. Trop. Med. Hyg.* **2017**, *97*, 1731–1736. [CrossRef] [PubMed]
6. Jipanin, S.J.; Muhamad-Shaleh, S.R.; Lim, P.T.; Leaw, C.P.; Mustapha, S. The Monitoring of Harmful Algae Blooms in Sabah, Malaysia. *J. Phys. Conf. Ser.* **2019**, *1358*, 012014. [CrossRef]
7. Arzul, G.; Seguel, M.; Guzman, L.; Denn, E.E. Comparison of allelopathic properties in threetoxic alexandrium species. *J. Exp. Mar. Biol. Ecol.* **1999**, *232*, 285–295. [CrossRef]

8. Hallam, T.; Clark, C.; Jordan, G. Effects of toxicants on populations: A qualitative approach. II. First order kinetics. *J. Theor. Biol.* **1983**, *18*, 25–37. [CrossRef] [PubMed]
9. Chakraborty, K.; Das, K. Modeling and analysis of a two-zooplankton one-phytoplankton system in the presence of toxicity. *Appl. Math. Model.* **2015**, *39*, 1241–1265. [CrossRef]
10. Teen, L.P.; Pin, L.C.; Gires, U. Harmful algal blooms in Malaysian waters. *Sains Malays.* **2012**, *41*, 1509–1515.
11. Usup, G.; Ahmad, A.; Ismail, N. Pyrodinium bahamense var. compressum red tides studies in Sabah, Malaysia. In *Biology, Epidemiology and Management of Pyrodinium Red Tides. Manila: ICLARM Conference Proceedings*; Hallegraeff, G.M., Maclean, J.L., Eds.; ICLARM: Bandar Seri Begawan, Brunei, 1989; pp. 97–110.
12. Rehim, M.; Zhang, Z.; Muhammadhaji, A. Mathematical Analysis of a Nutrient–Plankton System with Delay. *SpringerPlus* **2016**, *5*, 1055. [CrossRef] [PubMed]
13. Rehim, M.; Imran, M. Dynamical analysis of a delay model of phytoplankton-zooplankton interaction. *Appl. Math. Model.* **2012**, *36*, 638–647. [CrossRef]
14. Ma, Z. *Mathematical Modelling and Study of Population Ecology*; Anhui Education Publishing House: Hefei, China, 1996.
15. Holling, C.S. Some characteristics of simple types of predation and parasitism. *Can. Entomol.* **1959**, *91*, 385–398. [CrossRef]
16. Das, T.; Mukherjee, R.N.; Chaudhuri, K.S. Harvesting of a prey–predator fishery in the presence of toxicity. *Appl. Math. Model.* **2009**, *33*, 2282–2292. [CrossRef]
17. Bairagi, N.; Pal, S.; Chatterjee, S.; Chattopadhyay, J. Nutrient, non-toxic phytoplankton, toxic phytoplankton and zooplankton interaction in an open marine system. In *Aspects of Mathematical Modelling*; Birkhäuser: Basel, Switzerland, 2008; pp. 41–63.
18. Holmes, M.J.; Teo, S.L. Toxic marine dinoflagellates in Singapore waters that cause seafood poisonings. *Clin. Exp. Pharmacol. Physiol.* **2002**, *29*, 829–836. [CrossRef] [PubMed]
19. Ruan, S.; Wei, J. On the zeros of transcendental functions with applications to stability of delay differential equations with two delays. *Dyn. Contin. Discret. Impuls. Syst. Ser. A* **2003**, *10*, 863–874.
20. Li, M.Y.; Shu, H. Multiple stable periodic oscillations in a mathematical model of CTL response to HTLV-I infection. *Bull. Math. Biol.* **2011**, *73*, 1774–1793. [CrossRef] [PubMed]
21. Sipahi, R.; Niculescu, S.I.; Abdallah, C.T.; Michiels, W.; Gu, K. Stability and stabilization of systems with time delay. *IEEE Control Syst.* **2011**, *31*, 38–65.

Article

Predictability of Population Fluctuations

Rodrigo Crespo-Miguel [1] and Francisco J. Cao-García [1,2,*]

[1] Departamento de Estructura de la Materia, Física Térmica y Electrónica, Facultad de Ciencias Físicas, Universidad Complutense de Madrid, Plaza de Ciencias 1, 28040 Madrid, Spain
[2] Instituto Madrileño de Estudios Avanzados en Nanociencia (IMDEA-Nanociencia), Calle Faraday 9, 28049 Madrid, Spain
* Correspondence: francao@ucm.es

Abstract: Population dynamics is affected by environmental fluctuations (such as climate variations), which have a characteristic correlation time. Strikingly, the time scale of predictability can be larger for the population dynamics than for the underlying environmental fluctuations. Here, we present a general mechanism leading to this increase in predictability. We considered colored environmental fluctuation acting on a population close to equilibrium. In this framework, we derived the temporal auto and cross-correlation functions for the environmental and population fluctuations. We found a general correlation time hierarchy led by the environmental-population correlation time, closely followed by the population autocorrelation time. The increased predictability of the population fluctuations arises as an increase in its autocorrelation and cross-correlation times. These increases are enhanced by the slow damping of the population fluctuations, which has an integrative effect on the impact of correlated environmental fluctuations. Therefore, population fluctuation predictability is enhanced when the damping time of the population fluctuation is larger than the environmental fluctuations. This general mechanism can be quite frequent in nature, and it largely increases the perspectives of making reliable predictions of population fluctuations.

Keywords: population dynamics; predictability; anomalies; environmental fluctuations; population fluctuations; correlation times; temporal correlation; colored noise; colored environmental fluctuations

MSC: 92B05

Citation: Crespo-Miguel, R.; Cao-García, F.J. Predictability of Population Fluctuations. *Mathematics* 2022, 10, 3176. https://doi.org/10.3390/math10173176

Academic Editors: Sophia Jang and Jui-Ling Yu

Received: 2 August 2022
Accepted: 1 September 2022
Published: 3 September 2022

Publisher's Note: MDPI stays neutral with regard to jurisdictional claims in published maps and institutional affiliations.

Copyright: © 2022 by the authors. Licensee MDPI, Basel, Switzerland. This article is an open access article distributed under the terms and conditions of the Creative Commons Attribution (CC BY) license (https:// creativecommons.org/licenses/by/ 4.0/).

1. Introduction

Population dynamics is frequently affected by the randomness of the environmental fluctuations requiring the use of stochastic dynamics equations [1,2]. Environmental fluctuations have different sources including variability in resources needed by a population (e.g., food) [3]; unpredictability in weather or climate [4,5]; and natural disasters [6], which are usually considered extreme cases of environmental fluctuations [7]. Environmental fluctuations can alter the dynamics of a population, significantly impacting population fluctuations and their predictability [8], and even causing the extinction of otherwise stable populations [6,9,10]. Random environmental fluctuations can have an appreciable time correlation, requiring models with colored (temporally correlated) noise instead of white noise. Accurate prediction of the population dynamics requires using appropriate colored noise (i.e., with the correct correlation time function) to simulate the environmental fluctuations [11,12]. The color (or temporal correlation) of the environmental fluctuations has been shown to have relevant consequences for population dynamics and the population extinction risk [13–17]. The impact of colored noise on the dynamics has also been experimentally observed [11,18,19].

The environmental variability is especially critical in some species. For example, ectotherms are particularly sensitive to changes in temperature [20,21]. Ectotherms suffer important changes in growth [22] and development [23] depending on the circumstances given by the environment, and a study of the underlying mechanism describing the general effect of environmental variability can help to understand ectotherms' dynamics.

Here we are interested in using stochastic population dynamics models to obtain further insight into the predictability of the population fluctuations. It has been reported that the predictability of the population fluctuations can be larger than the underlying environmental fluctuations [11,24]. In particular, primary production fluctuations have been found to be predictable at larger time scales than the underlying sea surface temperature anomalies (environmental fluctuations) [25]. In the context of the study of the impact of El Niño teleconnections on the European climate variability, it was found that the predictability of the crop yield was higher than that of the underlying atmospheric variables affecting crop yield [26]. Analogous results have been found for the predictability of Malaria in Africa [27]. Similarly, higher predictability has been found for the Pacific fisheries anomalies than for the underlying Pacific sea surface temperatures (SSTs) when exploiting the Atlantic-Pacific teleconnection [28].

Here, we aim to apply stochastic population dynamics with colored environmental noise to understand population fluctuation predictability and its relations with environmental fluctuation predictability. In terms of temporal correlations, we aim to understand how the dynamics transform the temporal correlations of the environmental fluctuations into temporal correlations of the population fluctuations.

In Section 2, we present the population dynamics model (for small fluctuations around equilibrium) driven by colored environmental noise. In Section 3, we compute and compare the auto and cross-correlation functions between the environmental fluctuations and the population fluctuations. We compute their maxima and characteristic times, establishing their hierarchies, which provide insight into the propagation of the amplitude and temporal correlation of the fluctuations. Finally, the results are discussed in Section 4.

2. The Model: One Species with Temporally Correlated Noise

To study how temporal autocorrelated noise affects a single species, we begin by defining the differential equation that rules the evolution of fluctuations of a species around the equilibrium. For a population with size $N(t)$ (dimensionless) at a certain time t, evolving close to the equilibrium value N_{eq} of the population dynamics, we define the population fluctuations as $\varepsilon(t) = \frac{N(t) - N_{eq}}{N_{eq}}$, which are dimensionless. (When we assume small fluctuations, the effective equilibrium population size can be estimated with the average of the population size measured in a long enough time series). Close to equilibrium, this leads to the linear evolution equation

$$d\varepsilon = -\frac{\varepsilon}{T}dt + \lambda\, A dt \tag{1}$$

where T is the characteristic time of return to equilibrium (units of time), and $\gamma = 1/T$ is the rate of return to equilibrium (units of time^{-1}). λ is a coupling constant with units of $([A]\cdot\text{time})^{-1}$. The population is affected by environmental fluctuations A. Environmental fluctuations are random variations or anomalies in an environmental variable (such as temperature, humidity, or a resource needed by the population, and the units of A depend on the kind of environmental fluctuations considered) which influence the evolution of the population. Here, we consider environmental fluctuations A described by a positively-autocorrelated (red) noise defined as an Ornstein-Uhlenbeck process [29] such as

$$dA = -\frac{A}{\tau}dt + \frac{\sigma}{\tau}dW, \tag{2}$$

where τ is the characteristic correlation time of the noise (units of time), σ its amplitude (Units of $[A]\cdot\text{time}^{1/2}$), and dW the differential increment of a normalized Wiener process (i.e., $\xi = dW/dt$ is a normalized Gaussian white noise). $<dW(t)dW(t+t')> = c_{dWdW}(t') = 0$ for $t' \neq 0$ and $c_{dWdW}(t') = dt$ for $t' = 0$, with $<>$ the expectation value. All the variables used in this model are described in Table 1, as well as their units.

Table 1. Variables used with its description and units.

Variables	Description
$N(t)$	Population size at a given time t. Dimensionless.
$\varepsilon(t)$	Population density fluctuations around equilibrium $\varepsilon(t) = \frac{N(t)}{N_{(eq)}} - 1$. Dimensionless.
$A(t)$	Temporally autocorrelated environmental fluctuations at a given time t. Units $[A]$ depend on the kind of environmental fluctuations considered (e.g., temperature or humidity)
τ	Characteristic correlation time of the environmental fluctuations. Units of time.
T	Characteristic time of return to equilibrium of the population. Units of time.
$\gamma = 1/T$	Rate of returntoequilibrium. For the logistic equation and small fluctuations, it is equal to thegrowth rate r. Units of time^{-1}.
$\alpha = T/\tau = 1/(\gamma\tau)$	Ratio between the characteristic damping time of the population fluctuations T and the correlation time of the environmental fluctuations τ. Dimensionless.
σ	Amplitude of the noise. Units of $[A]\cdot$time$^{1/2}$.
λ	The coupling constant giving the impact of the environmental fluctuations A on the population dynamics ε. Units of $([A]\cdot$time$)^{-1}$.

Figure 1 shows a typical evolution for the environmental noise A and for the population fluctuation ε. Population fluctuations are compared for a lower (red) and a higher (green) damped population dynamics. The plot illustrates that higher damped population fluctuations present a smaller amplitude of population fluctuations. It also shows that peaks in environmental fluctuations A appear delayed and smoothed in the population fluctuations. This pattern anticipates the relevant and delayed temporal cross-correlations between the environmental and population fluctuations that we find in the next section.

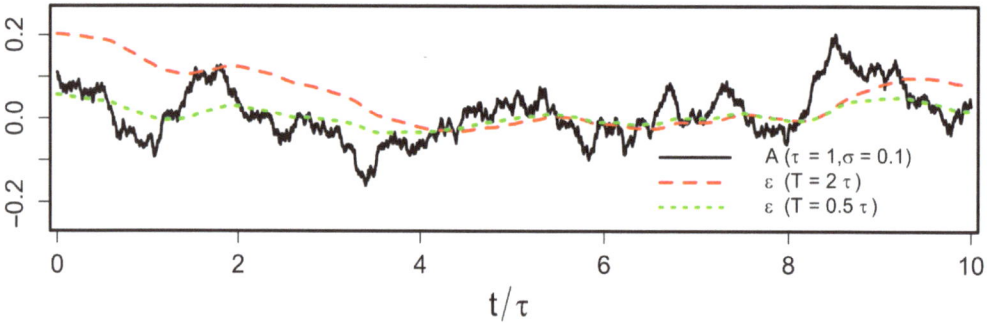

Figure 1. Evolution for the environmental fluctuations A (solid black line); and the population fluctuations for $T = 2\tau$ ($\Rightarrow \gamma = 0.5/\tau$) (red dashed line), and $T = 0.5\tau$ ($\Rightarrow \gamma = 2/\tau$) (green pointed line) for $\sigma = 0.1$, $\lambda = 1$ and $\tau = 1$. Population fluctuations peak a short time after environmental fluctuations peak, indicating a delayed correlation between environmental and population fluctuations.

3. Temporal Autocorrelations and Cross-Correlations

Once we have seen the behavior of the evolution before, our target is to calculate temporal correlations for a single species in the presence of temporally autocorrelated noise. We want to calculate environmental (noise) autocorrelation, species autocorrelation, and environmental-species correlation, as well as a correlation time.

The correlation between two magnitudes X and Y in two instants separated by a delay t' is given by the correlation function

$$c_{XY}(t') = <X(t)Y(t+t')>, \qquad (3)$$

where $<>$ means expected value. This correlation indicates how good is $X(t)$ as a predictor of $Y(t+t')$. Therefore, to understand the predictability of the population fluctuations, we have computed the correlations functions of the environmental fluctuations A and of the population fluctuations ε. See Appendix A for the detail of the computations. The correlation functions are

$$c_{AA}(t') = \frac{\sigma^2}{2\tau}e^{-|t'|/\tau} \qquad (4)$$

$$c_{\varepsilon\varepsilon}(t') = \begin{cases} \frac{\lambda^2\sigma^2\tau}{2}\frac{\alpha^2}{1-\alpha^2}\left(e^{-|t'|/\tau} - \alpha\, e^{-|t'|/T}\right), & T \neq \tau \\ \frac{\lambda^2\sigma^2\tau}{4}(1+|t'|/\tau)e^{-|t'|/\tau}, & T = \tau \end{cases} \qquad (5)$$

$$c_{A\varepsilon}(t') = \begin{cases} \frac{\lambda\sigma^2}{2}\frac{\alpha}{1+\alpha}e^{t'/\tau}, & t' \leq 0 \\ \frac{\lambda\sigma^2}{2}\frac{\alpha}{1-\alpha^2}\left((1+\alpha)e^{-t'/\tau} - 2\alpha\, e^{-t'/T}\right), & t' > 0 \text{ and } T \neq \tau \\ \frac{\lambda\sigma^2}{4}(1+2t'/\tau)e^{-t'/\tau}, & t' > 0 \text{ and } T = \tau \end{cases} \qquad (6)$$

$$c_{\varepsilon A}(t') = c_{A\varepsilon}(-t') \qquad (7)$$

where $\alpha = T/\tau = 1/(\gamma\tau)$ is the dimensionless ratio between the characteristic damping time of the population fluctuations T and the correlation time of the environmental fluctuations τ. We have represented these correlation functions in Figure 2A.

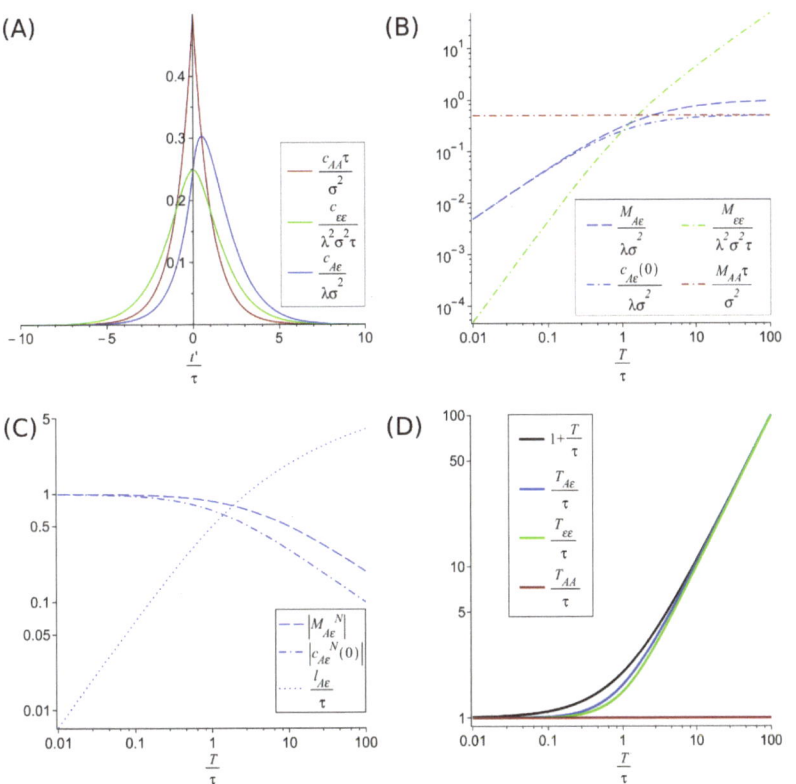

Figure 2. Correlation functions with their maximums and their values at $t' = 0$ and correlation times.

(**A**) represents the adimensionalized correlation functions $c_{\varepsilon\varepsilon}(t')$ (green), $c_{AA}(t')$ (red) and $c_{A\varepsilon}(t')$ (blue) adimensionalized for the case $\alpha = T/\tau = 1$. (**B**) compares the adimensionalized maxima of the autocorrelations function M_{AA} and $M_{\varepsilon\varepsilon}$ (which coincide with the value at $t' = 0$ of the respective autocorrelation) with the maxima of the adimensionalized crosscorrelation function $M_{A\varepsilon}$ and its value at zero delay $c_{A\varepsilon}(0)$. Their normalized values, $M_{A\varepsilon}^N = M_{A\varepsilon}/\sqrt{c_{AA}(0)c_{\varepsilon\varepsilon}(0)}$ and $c_{A\varepsilon}^N(0) = c_{A\varepsilon}(0)/\sqrt{c_{AA}(0)c_{\varepsilon\varepsilon}(0)}$ are shown in (**C**), with the delay of the cross-correlation maximum $l_{A\varepsilon}$. (**D**) compares the correlations times $T_{A\varepsilon}$, $T_{\varepsilon\varepsilon}$ and T_{AA}. These plots illustrate the hierarchies for temporal correlations and for the maxima of the correlations discussed in the main text. In particular, it shows that for low damping (large $\alpha = T/\tau$) the crosscorrelation time $T_{A\varepsilon}$ increases, allowing longer-term predictions, despite the decrease in accuracy that can be seen from the decay of the normalized maximum of the crosscorrelation $M_{A\varepsilon}^N$.

3.1. Maxima of the Correlation Functions

The autocorrelation function of the environmental fluctuations $c_{AA}(t')$ and the autocorrelation function of the species $c_{\varepsilon\varepsilon}(t')$, which are symmetric, have their maximum at the origin, $t' = 0$,

$$M_{AA} = c_{AA}(0) = \frac{\sigma^2}{2\tau} \tag{8}$$

$$M_{\varepsilon\varepsilon} = c_{\varepsilon\varepsilon}(0) = \frac{\lambda^2 \sigma^2 \tau}{2} \frac{\alpha^2}{1+\alpha} \tag{9}$$

The cross-correlation $c_{A\varepsilon}(t')$, has a value at the origin of

$$c_{A\varepsilon}(0) = \frac{\lambda \sigma^2}{2} \frac{\alpha}{1+\alpha}. \tag{10}$$

But the cross-correlation $c_{A\varepsilon}(t')$ has a lagged maximum (a minimum for negative coupling λ), see Figure 2A, situated at a time displacement $(t' = l_{A\varepsilon})$

$$l_{A\varepsilon} = \begin{cases} \tau \frac{\alpha}{1-\alpha} \ln\left(\frac{2}{1+\alpha}\right), & T \neq \tau \\ \frac{\tau}{2}, & T = \tau \end{cases} \tag{11}$$

This lag means that the population is more affected by the fluctuation after a certain time instead of instantly. Because of the basic property of correlations $c_{XY}(t') = c_{YX}(-t')$, the correlation function $c_{A\varepsilon}(t')$ has the maximum in $t' = -l_{A\varepsilon}$. This maximum is at $t' > 0$ for any $\alpha = T/\tau > 0$, and approaches the origin (smaller lag) as T/τ decreases. This dependence on T/τ causes the lag to tend to zero if the characteristic time of return to equilibrium of the population T is very short.

The cross-correlation $c_{A\varepsilon}(t')$ at this maximum located at $t' = l_{A\varepsilon}$ has a value

$$M_{A\varepsilon} = \begin{cases} \frac{\lambda \sigma^2}{2} \alpha \left(\frac{2}{1+\alpha}\right)^{\frac{\alpha}{\alpha-1}}, & T \neq \tau \\ \frac{\lambda \sigma^2}{2} e^{-1/2}, & T = \tau \end{cases} \tag{12}$$

It can be shown that the maximum correlation $M_{A\varepsilon}$ at most doubles the correlation at the origin $c_{A\varepsilon}(0)$, i.e., $1 \leq \frac{M_{A\varepsilon}}{c_{A\varepsilon}(0)} \leq 2$.

The maxima values can be adimensionalized and compared as in Figure 2B. This shows the following hierarchy

$$\begin{aligned} \frac{M_{\varepsilon\varepsilon}}{\sigma^2 \tau} &< \frac{M_{A\varepsilon}}{\lambda \sigma^2} < \frac{M_{AA}\tau}{\lambda^2 \sigma^2} \quad \text{for } T < \tau \\ \frac{M_{\varepsilon\varepsilon}}{\sigma^2 \tau} &\gtrsim \frac{M_{A\varepsilon}}{\lambda \sigma^2} \gtrsim \frac{M_{AA}\tau}{\lambda^2 \sigma^2} \quad \text{for } T \gtrsim \tau \end{aligned} \tag{13}$$

This hierarchy means that when the characteristic time scale of population fluctuations damping T is greater than the environmental fluctuations correlation time τ, the magnitude of the adimensionalized maxima increases as the fluctuation propagates (from the environment to the population). Conversely, when the population fluctuations dampen faster than the environmental fluctuations correlations time ($T < \tau$), the maxima decrease as the fluctuation propagates. Only in this later regime and when $T \ll \tau$ (i.e., on the constant environmental fluctuation limit) the normalized environment-population cross-correlation maximum reaches full correlation $M_{A\varepsilon}^N = 1$ (but at zero delay, $l_{A\varepsilon} = 0$). See Figure 2C. The normalized environment-population cross-correlation maximum and value at the origin are given by

$$M_{A\varepsilon}^N = \frac{M_{A\varepsilon}}{\sqrt{c_{AA}(0)c_{\varepsilon\varepsilon}(0)}} = \begin{cases} \text{sign}(\lambda)\sqrt{2}\left(\frac{2}{1+\alpha}\right)^{\frac{1+\alpha}{2(\alpha-1)}}, & T \neq \tau \\ \text{sign}(\lambda)\sqrt{2}\, e^{-1/2}, & T = \tau \end{cases} \quad (14)$$

$$c_{A\varepsilon}^N(0) = \frac{c_{A\varepsilon}(0)}{\sqrt{c_{AA}(0)c_{\varepsilon\varepsilon}(0)}} = \frac{\text{sign}(\lambda)}{\sqrt{1+\alpha}}. \quad (15)$$

3.2. Temporal Correlations

The characteristic time of temporal correlations gives the time extension of the predictability. For simple exponential decays of the correlation, the correlation time is just given by the characteristic decay factor in the exponential. For more general cases, we define the correlation time as

$$T_{XY} = \frac{\int_0^\infty t' |c_{XY}(t')| dt'}{\int_0^\infty |c_{XY}(t')| dt'}. \quad (16)$$

The absolute value allows incorporating the effects of negative correlations as predictors. For the autocorrelations and cross-correlations, we get

$$T_{AA} = T_{\varepsilon A} = \tau \quad (17)$$

$$T_{\varepsilon\varepsilon} = \tau\left[1 + \frac{\alpha^2}{1+\alpha}\right] = \tau + T\frac{1}{1+1/\alpha} \quad (18)$$

$$T_{A\varepsilon} = \tau\left[1 + \frac{2\alpha^2}{1+2\alpha}\right] = \tau + T\frac{1}{1+1/(2\alpha)} \quad (19)$$

In Figure 2D, these correlation times are plotted as functions of $\alpha = T/\tau$, the ratio between the damping time of the population fluctuations T and the correlation time of the environmental fluctuations τ. Figure 2D suggests a hierarchy of correlation times that can be proven from the previous expressions, i.e., Equations (17)–(19).

$$T_{AA} = T_{\varepsilon A} = \tau < T_{\varepsilon\varepsilon} < T_{A\varepsilon} < \tau + T \quad (20)$$

The difference between the last two is bounded by $0 < (T_{A\varepsilon} - T_{\varepsilon\varepsilon}) < \frac{\tau}{2}$.

This hierarchy of correlation times implies a longer correlation time, and therefore a larger scale of predictability, for population fluctuations than for environmental fluctuations.

4. Discussion

We aimed to understand the predictability of population fluctuations compared to environmental fluctuation predictability. To obtain an insight into the question, we computed the correlation functions of a population close to an equilibrium state in the presence of environmental colored noise. This computation allowed us to compute the correlation times and the maxima of the correlation functions, finding hierarchies for them, which gives general relations.

We found that the predictability of the population fluctuations is always higher than for the environmental fluctuations. Because of this, we have determined that the correlation time of the population fluctuations is always greater than the correlation time of the environmental fluctuations. The difference in correlation time increases with increased characteristic damping time of population fluctuations T. For example, for $T = 10\,\tau$ we have $T_{\varepsilon\varepsilon} = 10.1\ \tau$ and $T_{A\varepsilon} = 10.5\ \tau$; we also have that the maximum of the population-environment cross-correlation is at $l_{A\varepsilon} = 1.9\ \tau$ with a normalized correlation $M_{A\varepsilon}^N = 0.5$, showing a clear increase with respect to the correlation time for the environmental fluctuations T_{AA}. The underlying mechanism is analogous to the one described by Hasselmann for the integration of the fast weather components leading to the slow climate dynamics [30]. Our model stresses that the mechanism is general and time-scale independent. In practical cases times scales can range from days (for prey populations in agriculture) to years (for large species or ecosystems).

This study was inspired by our previous results on spatial population synchrony [31–34] and motivated by the findings that population fluctuations showed larger predictability than the underlying environmental variables. This was shown to happen for a wide range of systems: primary production in oceans [25], crop yield [26], malaria [27] and fisheries [28]. This higher predictability increases the prospects of predicting climatic variability effects on populations [26–28,35–37].

The determination of the effective equilibrium can be challenging in practical cases [24]. In general, the effective equilibrium is obtained from the time-average of the data in long-enough time series. However, sometimes the equilibrium can have seasonal oscillations or long-term trends. In this case, these variations in the equilibrium have to be taken into account, substracting them to obtain the correct fluctuations around equilibrium. Several model extensions are possible to obtain an insight into the scope of the results. The results have been obtained for a single-environmental variable acting on a single-species in the small fluctuation regime, which allows the linearization of the dynamical equations around the equilibrium. This model can be extended, including several interacting species and several environmental variables (which may also interact as wind stress and sea surface temperature). Another extension is including the division of species populations into distinct life stages, with some of them particularly affected by environmental fluctuations [38]. Our model considers small enough environmental fluctuations (which implies the population is close to equilibrium). This can be extended by studying larger environmental fluctuations in particularly relevant ecological models, which would clarify how the results in the present work are affected by the presence of nonlinearities.

The present study raises the question of how the propagation of fluctuations through the food webs impacts the predictability of the different species' population fluctuations. This more profound understanding of the population predictability will help to design improved conservation policies, particularly useful for species especially sensitive to environmental variability (represented in our model with great couplings λ), such as ectotherms.

Author Contributions: Conceptualization, F.J.C.-G.; Methodology, R.C.-M. and F.J.C.-G.; Software, R.C.-M.; Validation, R.C.-M. and F.J.C.-G.; Formal analysis, R.C.-M. and F.J.C.-G.; Investigation, R.C.-M. and F.J.C.-G.; Resources, R.C.-M. and F.J.C.-G.; Data curation, R.C.-M.; Writing-original draft preparation R.C.-M.; Writing-rewiew and editing, R.C.-M. and F.J.C.-G.; Visualization, R.C.-M.; Supervision, F.J.C.-G.; Project administration, F.J.C.-G.; Funding adquisition, F.J.C.-G. All authors have read and agreed to the published version of the manuscript.

Funding: This work was financially supported by 817578 TRIATLAS project of the Horizon 2020 Programme (EU) and RTI2018-095802-B-I00 of Ministerio de Economía y Competitividad (Spain) and Fondo Europeo de Desarrollo Regional (FEDER, EU).

Institutional Review Board Statement: Not applicable.

Informed Consent Statement: Not applicable.

Data Availability Statement: Not applicable.

Acknowledgments: We acknowledge early conversation with Emilia Sánchez (CERFACS) on predictability and temporal correlations, in relation with our previous results on spatial synchrony. We also acknowledge Belén Rodríguez-Fonseca and Iñigo Gómara for conversations on further applications of the presented framework.

Conflicts of Interest: The authors declare no conflict of interest.

Appendix A. Computation of Temporal Correlation Functions and Times

As the dynamics are time invariant, the asymptotic time correlations are stationary. The stationarity condition is

$$< X(t)Y(t+t') > = < X(t+dt)Y(t+t'+dt) >$$

where $X(t+dt) = X(t) + dX(t)$ and $Y(t+t'+dt) = Y(t+t') + dY(t+t')$. The application of this stationary condition provides relationships between time correlation, which allow computing them.

Appendix A.1. Wiener Process Temporal Autocorrelation

The temporal autocorrelation of the Wiener process (whose derivative gives the white noise) is known to be

$$c_{dWdW}(t') = \begin{cases} dt, & \text{for } t' = 0, \\ 0, & \text{for } t' \neq 0. \end{cases} \tag{A1}$$

Appendix A.2. Wiener—Colored-Noise Temporal Cross-Correlation

We now that $c_{dWA}(t') = < dW(t)A(t+t') >$ is zero for $t' \leq 0$, as there is no fluctuation propagation to the past. Therefore, we just have to make the computation for positive time displacement.

We compute $c_{dWA}(t') = < dW(t)A(t+t') >$ for $t' = dt, t' = 2dt, t' = 3dt, \ldots$

$$< dW(t)A(t+dt) > = < dW(t)\left(A(t) - \frac{A(t)}{\tau}dt + \frac{\sigma}{\tau}dW(t)\right) > = \frac{\sigma}{\tau}dt$$

$$< dW(t)A(t+2dt) > = < dW(t)\left(A(t+dt) - \frac{A(t+dt)}{\tau}dt + \frac{\sigma}{\tau}dW(t+dt)\right) > = \frac{\sigma}{\tau}\left(1 - \frac{dt}{\tau}\right)dt$$

$$< dW(t)A(t+3dt) > = < dW(t)\left(A(t+2dt) - \frac{A(t+2dt)}{\tau}dt + \frac{\sigma}{\tau}dW(t+2dt)\right) > = \frac{\sigma}{\tau}\left(1 - \frac{dt}{\tau}\right)^2 dt$$

These results allow us to get the general expression

$$c_{dWA}(ndt) = < dW(t)A(t+ndt) > = \frac{\sigma}{\tau}\left(1 - \frac{dt}{\tau}\right)^{n-1} dt$$

In the large n limit, we get the exponential expression

$$c_{dWA}(t') = \frac{\sigma}{\tau}e^{-t'/\tau}dt \text{ if } t' > 0$$

Therefore, we have

$$c_{dWA}(t') = \begin{cases} 0 & \text{if } t' \leq 0 \\ \frac{\sigma}{\tau}e^{-t'/\tau} dt & \text{if } t' > 0 \end{cases} \tag{A2}$$

Appendix A.3. Wiener—Population Temporal Cross-Correlation

There is no propagation of the fluctuations to the past. Thus, $c_{dW\varepsilon}(t') = < dW(t)\varepsilon(t+t') >$ is zero for $t' \leq 0$, and we only have to compute the correlation for positive time displacement. The same procedure used for $c_{dWA}(t')$ allows obtaining $c_{dW\varepsilon}(t')$

$$< dW(t)\varepsilon(t+dt) > = < dW(t)\cdot(\varepsilon(t) - \gamma\varepsilon(t)dt + \lambda A(t)dt) > = 0$$

$$< dW(t)\varepsilon(t+2dt) > = < dW(t)\cdot(\varepsilon(t+dt) - \gamma\varepsilon(t+dt)dt + \lambda A(t+dt)dt) > = \frac{\lambda\sigma}{\tau}dt^2$$

$$< dW(t)\varepsilon(t+3dt) > = < dW(t)\cdot(\varepsilon(t+2dt) - \gamma\varepsilon(t+2dt)dt + \lambda A(t+2dt)dt) > = \frac{\lambda\sigma}{\tau}(1-\gamma dt)dt^2 + \frac{\lambda\sigma}{\tau}\left(1-\frac{dt}{\tau}\right)dt^2$$

$$< dW(t)\varepsilon(t+4dt) > = < dW(t)\cdot(\varepsilon(t+3dt) - \gamma\varepsilon(t+3dt)dt + \lambda A(t+3dt)dt) >$$
$$= \frac{\lambda\sigma}{\tau}(1-\gamma dt)^2 dt^2 + \frac{\lambda\sigma}{\tau}(1-\gamma dt)\left(1-\frac{dt}{\tau}\right)dt^2 + \frac{\lambda\sigma}{\tau}\left(1-\frac{dt}{\tau}\right)^2 dt^2$$

$$< dW(t)\varepsilon(t+ndt) > = \frac{dt^2}{\tau}\lambda\sigma \sum_{i=0}^{n-2}(1-\gamma dt)^{n-2-i}\left(1-\frac{dt}{\tau}\right)^i = \frac{\lambda\sigma}{\tau}dt^2(1-\gamma dt)^{n-2}\sum_{i=1}^{n-1}\left(\frac{1-\frac{dt}{\tau}}{1-\gamma dt}\right)^{i-1}$$

The later expression gives, when $\gamma\tau = 1$

$$\frac{\lambda\sigma}{\tau}dt^2(1-\gamma dt)^{n-2}\sum_{i=1}^{n-1} 1 = \frac{\lambda\sigma}{\tau}dt^2(1-\gamma dt)^{n-2}\cdot(n-1) \approx \frac{\lambda\sigma}{\tau}t' e^{-\gamma t'}dt = \frac{\lambda\sigma}{\tau}t' e^{-t'/\tau}dt,$$

while for $\gamma\tau \neq 1$

$$\frac{\lambda\sigma}{\tau}dt^2(1-\gamma dt)^{n-2}\sum_{i=1}^{n-1}\left(\frac{1-\frac{dt}{\tau}}{1-\gamma dt}\right)^{i-1} = \frac{\lambda\sigma}{\tau}dt^2(1-\gamma dt)^{n-2}\cdot\frac{1-\left(\frac{1-\frac{dt}{\tau}}{1-\gamma dt}\right)^{n-1}}{1-\frac{1-\frac{dt}{\tau}}{1-\gamma dt}} = \frac{\lambda\sigma dt}{1-\gamma\tau}\left((1-\gamma dt)^{n-1} - \left(1-\frac{dt}{\tau}\right)^{n-1}\right)$$
$$\approx \frac{\lambda\sigma}{1-\gamma\tau}\left(e^{-\gamma t'} - e^{-t'/\tau}\right)dt.$$

(Note that in the limit $\gamma\tau \to 1$, the results for $\gamma\tau = 1$ are recovered, indicating the continuity of the solution on $\gamma\tau$.)

Therefore, we have the temporal correlation

$$c_{dW\varepsilon}(t') = \begin{cases} 0 & \text{if } t' < 0 \\ \frac{\lambda\sigma}{1-\gamma\tau}\left(e^{-\gamma t'} - e^{-t'/\tau}\right)dt & \text{if } t' > 0 \text{ and } \gamma\tau \neq 1 \\ \frac{\lambda\sigma}{\tau}t' e^{-t'/\tau}dt & \text{if } t' > 0 \text{ and } \gamma\tau = 1 \end{cases} \quad (A3)$$

Appendix A.4. Colored-Noise Autocorrelations

The computation of this (and the following) temporal correlations relies on the time invariance of the dynamics, which leads to the stationarity of the asymptotic temporal correlations.

We begin calculating the temporal autocorrelation for the environmental autocorrelations, $c_{AA}(t') = < A(t)A(t+t') >$, whose stationary condition implies

$$< A(t)A(t+t') > = < (A(t)+dA(t))\cdot(A(t+t')+dA(t+t')) > =$$
$$< (A(t) - A(t)/\tau\, dt + \sigma/\tau\, dW(t))\cdot(A(t+t') - A(t+t')/\tau\, dt + \sigma/\tau\, dW(t+t')) >$$

Expanding up to the first order in dt we get

$$< A(t)A(t+t') > = < A(t)A(t+t') > - \frac{2}{\tau}< A(t)A(t+t') > dt$$
$$+ \frac{\sigma}{\tau}\left(1-\frac{dt}{\tau}\right)< A(t)dW(t+t') > + \frac{\sigma}{\tau}\left(1-\frac{dt}{\tau}\right)< dW(t)A(t+t') >$$
$$+ \frac{\sigma^2}{\tau^2}< dW(t)dW(t+t') >,$$

which gives the equation

$$\frac{2}{\tau}c_{AA}(t')dt = \frac{\sigma}{\tau}\left(1-\frac{dt}{\tau}\right)c_{AdW}(t') + \frac{\sigma}{\tau}\left(1-\frac{dt}{\tau}\right)c_{dWA}(t') + \frac{\sigma^2}{\tau^2}c_{dWdW}(t').$$

As we have shown that $c_{dWA} \sim dt$ and $c_{dW\varepsilon} \sim dt$ [Equations (A2) and (A3)], which indicates that there are still terms of second order in the previous equation. Keeping only the first order terms in dt and using $c_{AdW}(t') = c_{dWA}(-t')$, the equation becomes

$$c_{AA}(t') = \frac{\sigma}{2\,dt}\left(c_{dWA}(t') + c_{dWA}(-t')\right) + \frac{\sigma^2}{2\tau}\frac{c_{dWdW}(t')}{dt}$$

This later equation gives $c_{AA}(t')$, in terms of the cross-correlations of the white noise with the colored noise and with the population fluctuations.

Substituting Equation (A2), we get environmental autocorrelation

$$c_{AA}(t') = \frac{\sigma^2}{2\tau}e^{-|t'|/\tau} \tag{A4}$$

Appendix A.5. Colored-Noise—Population Cross-Correlation

We continue with the environment-species temporal cross-correlation $c_{A\varepsilon}(t') = <A(t)\varepsilon(t+t')>$, whose stationary condition gives

$$<A(t)\varepsilon(t+t')> = <(A(t)+dA(t))\cdot(\varepsilon(t+t')+d\varepsilon(t+t'))> =$$
$$<(A(t) - A(t)/\tau\,dt + \sigma/\tau\,dW(t))\cdot(\varepsilon(t+t') - \gamma\varepsilon(t+t')dt + \lambda A(t+t')\,dt)>$$

Again, up to the first order in dt, we get

$$<A(t)\varepsilon(t+t')> = <A(t)\varepsilon(t+t')> - \left(\gamma + \frac{1}{\tau}\right)<A(t)\varepsilon(t+t')>dt$$
$$+\frac{\sigma}{\tau}(1-\gamma dt)<dW(t)\varepsilon(t+t')> + \lambda <A(t)A(t+t')>dt + \frac{\lambda\sigma}{\tau}<dW(t)A(t+t')>dt,$$

resulting in the second relation,

$$-\left(\gamma + \frac{1}{\tau}\right)c_{A\varepsilon}(t')dt + \frac{\sigma}{\tau}(1-\gamma dt)c_{dW\varepsilon}(t') + \lambda c_{AA}(t')dt + \frac{\lambda\sigma}{\tau}c_{dWA}(t')dt = 0.$$

Recalling again that $c_{dWA} \sim dt$ and $c_{dW\varepsilon} \sim dt$, fewer terms are of the first order in dt, leading to

$$c_{A\varepsilon}(t') = \frac{1}{\gamma + 1/\tau}\left(\frac{\sigma}{\tau}\frac{c_{dW\varepsilon}(t')}{dt} + \lambda c_{AA}(t')\right)$$

Substituting Equations (A3) and (A4), we can calculate the environmental-population fluctuations cross-correlation

$$c_{A\varepsilon}(t') = \begin{cases} \frac{\lambda\sigma^2}{2(1+\gamma\tau)}e^{t'/\tau}, & t' \leq 0 \\ \frac{\lambda\sigma^2}{2((\gamma\tau)^2-1)}\left((1+\gamma\tau)e^{-t'/\tau} - 2e^{-\gamma t'}\right), & t' > 0 \text{ and } \gamma\tau \neq 1 \\ \frac{\lambda\sigma^2}{4\tau}(\tau + 2t')e^{-t'/\tau}, & t' > 0 \text{ and } \gamma\tau = 1 \end{cases} \tag{A5}$$

while $c_{\varepsilon A}(t') = c_{A\varepsilon}(-t')$.

Appendix A.6. Autocorrelations of the Population Fluctuations

We finally compute the temporal autocorrelation for the population fluctuations of the species $c_{\varepsilon\varepsilon}(t') = <\varepsilon(t)\varepsilon(t+t')>$, whose stationary condition implies

$$<\varepsilon(t)\varepsilon(t+t')> = <(\varepsilon(t)+d\varepsilon(t))\cdot(\varepsilon(t+t')+d\varepsilon(t+t'))> =$$
$$<(\varepsilon(t) - \gamma\varepsilon(t)dt + \lambda A(t)\,dt)\cdot(\varepsilon(t+t') - \gamma\varepsilon(t+t')dt + \lambda A(t+t')\,dt)>.$$

Keeping terms up to first order in dt, we obtain the following expression:

$$<\varepsilon(t)\varepsilon(t+t')> = <\varepsilon(t)\varepsilon(t+t')> - 2\gamma<\varepsilon(t)\varepsilon(t+t')>dt$$
$$+\lambda<\varepsilon(t)A(t+t')>dt + \lambda<A(t)\varepsilon(t+t')>dt$$

In terms of correlations and using the relation $c_{XY}(t') = c_{YX}(-t')$, we have

$$c_{\varepsilon\varepsilon}(t') = \frac{\lambda}{2\gamma}\left(c_{A\varepsilon}(t') + c_{A\varepsilon}(-t')\right).$$

Substituting Equation (A5), we get for the population fluctuations autocorrelation

$$c_{\varepsilon\varepsilon}(t') = \begin{cases} \frac{\lambda^2 \sigma^2 \tau}{2\gamma\tau((\gamma\tau)^2 - 1)}\left(\gamma\tau e^{-\frac{|t'|}{\tau}} - e^{-\gamma|t'|}\right), & \gamma\tau \neq 1 \\ \frac{\lambda^2 \sigma^2}{4}(\tau + |t'|)e^{-|t'|/\tau}, & \gamma\tau = 1 \end{cases} \quad (A6)$$

Appendix A.7. Maxima

The environmental noise autocorrelation $c_{AA}(t')$ and of the population fluctuations autocorrelation $c_{\varepsilon\varepsilon}(t')$ have their maximum at the origin $t' = 0$. The environment-population cross-correlation has a lagged maximum at a time $t' = l_{A\varepsilon}$ with

$$l_{A\varepsilon} = \begin{cases} \frac{\ln\left(\frac{2\gamma\tau}{\gamma\tau+1}\right)}{\gamma\tau - 1}\tau, & \gamma\tau \neq 1 \\ \frac{\tau}{2}, & \gamma\tau = 1 \end{cases} \quad (A7)$$

with a magnitude $M_{A\varepsilon} = c_{A\varepsilon}(l_{A\varepsilon})$ given by

$$M_{A\varepsilon} = \begin{cases} \frac{\lambda\sigma^2 \left(\frac{2\gamma\tau}{1+\gamma\tau}\right)^{\frac{1}{1-\gamma\tau}}}{2\gamma\tau}, & \gamma\tau \neq 1 \\ \frac{\lambda\sigma^2}{2} e^{-\frac{1}{2}}, & \gamma\tau = 1. \end{cases} \quad (A8)$$

These expressions are also given in the main text in terms of $\alpha = \frac{T}{\tau} = \frac{1}{\gamma\tau}$, the ratio of the population relaxation time T and the correlation time of environmental fluctuations τ.

Appendix A.8. Correlation Times

The previous explicit expression for the time correlation function allows computing their respective correlation times

$$T_{AA} = \frac{\int_0^\infty t' c_{AA}(t')dt'}{\int_0^\infty c_{AA}(t')dt'} = \frac{\int_0^\infty t' \frac{\sigma^2}{2\tau} e^{-t'/\tau}dt'}{\int_0^\infty \frac{\sigma^2}{2\tau} e^{-t'/\tau}dt'} = \frac{\int_0^\infty t' e^{-t'/\tau}dt'}{\int_0^\infty e^{-t'/\tau}dt'} = \tau, \quad (A9)$$

$$T_{\varepsilon A} = \tau, \quad (A10)$$

$$T_{\varepsilon\varepsilon} = \tau \frac{(\gamma\tau)^2 + \gamma\tau + 1}{\gamma\tau(\gamma\tau + 1)} = \tau\left[1 + \frac{1}{\gamma\tau(\gamma\tau + 1)}\right] = \tau\left[1 + \frac{\alpha^2}{1+\alpha}\right] = \tau + T\frac{\alpha}{1+\alpha}, \quad (A11)$$

$$T_{A\varepsilon} = \tau \frac{(\gamma\tau)^2 + 2\gamma\tau + 2}{\gamma\tau(\gamma\tau + 2)} = \tau\left[1 + \frac{2}{\gamma\tau(\gamma\tau + 2)}\right] = \tau\left[1 + \frac{2\alpha^2}{1+2\alpha}\right] = \tau + T\frac{2\alpha}{1+2\alpha}, \quad (A12)$$

where $\alpha = \frac{T}{\tau} = \frac{1}{\gamma\tau}$ is the ratio of the population relaxation time T and the correlation time of environmental fluctuations τ.

References

1. Gotelli, N.J. *A Primer of Ecology*, 4th ed.; Sinauer Associates: Sunderland, MA, USA, 2008.
2. Lande, R.; Engen, S.; Saether, B.-E. Stochastic Population Dynamics in Ecology and Conservation. In *Oxford Series in Ecology and Evolution*; Oxford University Press: Oxford, UK, 2003. [CrossRef]
3. Fujiwara, M.; Takada, T. Environmental Stochasticity. *eLS* **2017**, 1–8. [CrossRef]
4. Nowicki, P.; Bonelli, S.; Barbero, F.; Balletto, E. Relative Importance of Density-Dependent Regulation and Environmental Stochasticity for Butterfly Population Dynamics. *Oecologia* **2009**, *161*, 227–239. [CrossRef] [PubMed]
5. Saltz, D.; Rubenstein, D.I.; White, G.C. The Impact of Increased Environmental Stochasticity Due to Climate Change on the Dynamics of Asiatic Wild Ass. *Conserv. Biol.* **2006**, *20*, 1402–1409. [CrossRef] [PubMed]

6. Mangel, M.; Tier, C. Dynamics of Dynamics of Metapopulations with Demographic Stochasticity and Environmental Catastrophes. *Theor. Popul. Biol.* **1993**, *44*, 1–31. [CrossRef]
7. Shaffer, M. Minimum Viable Populations: Coping with Uncertainty. In *Viable Populations for Conservation*; Cambridge University Press: Cambridge, UK, 1987; pp. 69–86. [CrossRef]
8. Luis, A.D.; Douglass, R.J.; Mills, J.N.; Bjørnstad, O.N. Environmental Fluctuations Lead to Predictability in Sin Nombre Hantavirus Outbreaks. *Ecology* **2015**, *96*, 1691–1701. [CrossRef]
9. Schreiber, S.J. Interactive Effects of Temporal Correlations, Spatial Heterogeneity and Dispersal on Population Persistence. *Proc. R. Soc. B Biol. Sci.* **2010**, *277*, 1907–1914. [CrossRef]
10. Crespo-Miguel, R.; Jarillo, J.; Cao-García, F.J. Dispersal-induced resilience to stochastic environmental fluctuations in populations with Allee effect. *Phys. Rev. E* **2022**, *105*, 014413. [CrossRef]
11. Petchey, O.L. Environmental Colour Affects Aspects of Single-Species Population Dynamics. *Proc. R. Soc. B Boil. Sci.* **2000**, *267*, 747–754. [CrossRef]
12. Halley, J.M. Ecology, Evolution and 1f-Noise. *Trends Ecol. Evol.* **1996**, *11*, 33–37. [CrossRef]
13. Ripa, J.; Lundberg, P. Noise Colour and the Risk of Population Extinctions. *Proc. R. Soc. London* **1996**, *263*, 1751–1753. [CrossRef]
14. Heino, M.; Ripa, J.; Kaitala, V. Extinction Risk under Coloured Environmental Noise. *Ecography* **2000**, *23*, 177–184. [CrossRef]
15. Greenman, J.V.; Benton, T.G. The Amplification of Environmental Noise in Population Models: Causes and Consequences. *Am. Nat.* **2003**, *161*, 225–239. [CrossRef] [PubMed]
16. Kamenev, A.; Meerson, B.; Shklovskii, B. How Colored Environmental Noise Affects Population Extinction. *Phys. Rev. Lett.* **2008**, *101*, 268103. [CrossRef] [PubMed]
17. Spanio, T.; Hidalgo, J.; A Muñoz, M. Impact of Environmental Colored Noise in Single-Species Population Dynamics. *Phys. Rev. E* **2017**, *96*, 042301. [CrossRef] [PubMed]
18. Laakso, J.; Löytynoja, K.; Kaitala, V. Environmental Noise and Population Dynamics of the Ciliated Protozoa Tetrahymena Thermophila in Aquatic Microcosms. *Oikos* **2003**, *102*, 663–671. [CrossRef]
19. Reuman, D.C.; Costantino, R.F.; Desharnais, R.A.; Cohen, J.E. Colour of Environmental Noise Affects the Nonlinear Dynamics of Cycling, Stage-Structured Populations. *Ecol. Lett.* **2008**, *11*, 820–830. [CrossRef] [PubMed]
20. Zuo, W.; Moses, M.E.; West, G.B.; Hou, C.; Brown, J.H. A General Model for Effects of Temperature on Ectotherm Ontogenetic Growth and Development. *Proc. R. Soc. B Boil. Sci.* **2011**, *279*, 1840–1846. [CrossRef]
21. Paaijmans, K.P.; Heinig, R.L.; Seliga, R.A.; Blanford, J.I.; Blanford, S.; Murdock, C.C.; Thomas, M.B. Temperature Variation Makes Ectotherms More Sensitive to Climate Change. *Glob. Chang. Biol.* **2013**, *19*, 2373–2380. [CrossRef]
22. Atkinson, D. Temperature and Organism Size—A Biological Law for Ectotherms? *Adv. Ecol. Res.* **1994**, *25*, 1–58. [CrossRef]
23. De Jong, G.; van der Have, T.M. Temperature Dependence of Development Rate, Growth Rate and Size: From Biophysics to Adaptation. In *Phenotypic Plasticity of Insects: Mechanisms and Consequence*; Science Publishers, Inc.: Plymouth, UK, 2009; pp. 461–526.
24. Pimm, S.L.; Redfearn, A. The Variability of Population Densities. *Nature* **1988**, *334*, 613–614. [CrossRef]
25. Séférian, R.; Bopp, L.; Gehlen, M.; Swingedouw, D.; Mignot, J.; Guilyardi, E.; Servonnat, J. Multiyear Predictability of Tropical Marine Productivity. *Proc. Natl. Acad. Sci. USA* **2014**, *111*, 11646–11651. [CrossRef] [PubMed]
26. Capa-Morocho, M.; Rodríguez-Fonseca, B.; Ruiz-Ramos, M. Crop Yield as a Bioclimatic Index of El Niño Impact in Europe: Crop Forecast Implications. *Agric. For. Meteorol.* **2014**, *198–199*, 42–52. [CrossRef]
27. Diouf, I.; Suárez-Moreno, R.; Rodríguez-Fonseca, B.; Caminade, C.; Wade, M.; Thiaw, W.M.; Deme, A.; Morse, A.P.; Ndione, J.-A.; Gaye, A.T.; et al. Oceanic Influence on Seasonal Malaria Incidence in West Africa. *Weather Clim. Soc.* **2022**, *14*, 287–302. [CrossRef]
28. Gómara, I.; Rodríguez-Fonseca, B.; Mohino, E.; Losada, T.; Polo, I.; Coll, M. Skillful prediction of tropical Pacific fisheries provided by Atlantic Niños. *Environ. Res. Lett.* **2021**, *16*, 054066. [CrossRef]
29. García-Ojalvo, J.; Sancho, J.M.; Ramírez-Piscina, L. Generation of spatiotemporal colored noise. *Phys. Rev. A* **1992**, *46*, 4670–4675. [CrossRef]
30. Hasselmann, K. Stochastic Climate Models Part I. Theory. Theory. *Tellus* **1976**, *28*, 473–485. [CrossRef]
31. Jarillo, J.; Saether, B.-E.; Engen, S.; Cao, F.J. Spatial Scales of Population Synchrony of Two Competing Species: Effects of Harvesting and Strength of Competition. *Oikos* **2018**, *127*, 1459–1470. [CrossRef]
32. Jarillo, J.; Sæther, B.-E.; Engen, S.; Cao-García, F.J. Spatial Scales of Population Synchrony in Predator-Prey Systems. *Am. Nat.* **2020**, *195*, 216–230. [CrossRef]
33. Lee, A.; Jarillo, J.; Peeters, B.; Hansen, B.; Cao-García, F.; Sæther, B.; Engen, S. Population Responses to Harvesting in Fluctuating Environments. *Clim. Res.* **2022**, *86*, 79–91. [CrossRef]
34. Fernández-Grande, M.A.; Cao-García, F.J. Spatial Scales of Population Synchrony Generally Increases as Fluctuations Propagate in a Two Species Ecosystem. *arXiv* **2020**, arXiv:2012.11043. Available online: https://arxiv.org/ftp/arxiv/papers/2012/2012.11043.pdf (accessed on 1 August 2022).
35. Iizumi, T.; Luo, J.-J.; Challinor, A.; Sakurai, G.; Yokozawa, M.; Sakuma, H.; Brown, M.; Yamagata, T. Impacts of El Niño Southern Oscillation on the global yields of major crops. *Nat. Commun.* **2014**, *5*, 3712. [CrossRef] [PubMed]
36. Watters, G.M.; Olson, R.J.; Francis, R.C.; Fiedler, P.C.; Polovina, J.J.; Reilly, S.B.; Aydin, K.Y.; Boggs, C.H.; E Essington, T.; Walters, C.J.; et al. Physical Forcing and the Dynamics of the Pelagic Ecosystem in the Eastern Tropical Pacific: Simulations with ENSO-Scale and Global-Warming Climate Drivers. *Can. J. Fish. Aquat. Sci.* **2003**, *60*, 1161–1175. [CrossRef]

37. Christensen, V.; Coll, M.; Buszowski, J.; Cheung, W.W.L.; Frölicher, T.; Steenbeek, J.; Stock, C.A.; Watson, R.; Walters, C.J. Oceanic Influence on Seasonal Malaria Incidence in West Africa. *Glob. Ecol. Biogeogr.* **2015**, *24*, 507–517. [CrossRef]
38. Lowe, W.H.; Martin, T.E.; Skelly, D.K.; Woods, H.A. Metamorphosis in an Era of Increasing Climate Variability. *Trends Ecol. Evol.* **2021**, *36*, 360–375. [CrossRef] [PubMed]

Article

Optimal Treatment of Prostate Cancer Based on State Constraint

Wenhui Luo [1,†], Xuewen Tan [1,*,†], Xiufen Zou [2,*] and Qing Tan [2]

[1] School of Mathematics and Computer Science, Yunnan Minzu University, Kunming 650500, China; 21213037570009@ymu.edu.cn
[2] School of Mathematics and Statistics, Wuhan University, Wuhan 430072, China; qtan@whu.edu.cn
* Correspondence: tanxw0910@ymu.edu.cn (X.T.); xfzou@whu.edu.cn (X.Z.)
† These authors contributed equally to this work.

Abstract: As a new tumor therapeutic strategy, adaptive therapy involves utilizing the competition between cancer cells to suppress the growth of drug-resistant cells, maintaining a certain tumor burden. However, it is difficult to determine the appropriate time and drug dose. In this paper, we consider the competition model between drug-sensitive cells and drug-resistant cells, propose the problem of drug concentration, and provide two state constraints: the upper limit of the maximum allowable drug concentration and the tumor burden. Using relevant theories, we propose the best treatment strategy. Through a numerical simulation and quantitative analysis, the effects of drug concentrations and different tumor burdens on treatments are studied, and the effects of cell-to-cell competitive advantage on cell changes are taken into account. The clinical dose titration method is further simulated; the results show that our therapeutic regimen can better suppress the growth of drug-resistant cells, control the tumor burden, limit drug toxicity, and extend the effective treatment time.

Keywords: problems in pharmacology; drug toxicity; tumor burden; state constraints; optimal control

MSC: 37M05

1. Introduction

In most countries and regions across the world, cancer is the leading cause of death; prostate cancer is the second largest cancer in men. How to better treat it has become a long-standing problem. The maximum tolerated dose (MTD) treatment is commonly used in clinics, but MTD treatment leads to massive drug-sensitive cell death and a significant increase in drug-resistant cells, ultimately leading to treatment failure [1]. After continuous studies, Gatenby et al. [2] proposed adaptive therapy to exploit competition between cancer cells, maintain a certain tumor burden, and suppress the growth of drug-resistant cells. For adaptive therapy [3], compared with MTD, the administration resulted in a decrease in drug-sensitive cells, an increase in drug-resistant cells and drug withdrawal, an increase in sensitive cells, a decrease in drug-resistant cells, and the use of drugs to control the number of drug-sensitive cells, further affecting drug-resistant cells. Therefore, by choosing the appropriate dose and treatment time, we maintain a certain tumor burden, suppress drug-resistant cells, and extend the effective treatment time. However, it is difficult to determine the drug dose and treatment period.

Cunningham et al. [4] proposed the Lotka–Volterra model of the interaction between cancer cells, and analyzed an optimal control problem to reach a certain stable point, providing the optimal dose. Liu et al. [5] established a competition model between drug-sensitive and drug-resistant cancer cells and proposed a new dynamic optimization problem with constraints to establish an adaptive treatment scheme for prostate cancer; the control variable was the drug dose and the drug dose played a role in the kinetics as well as in the concentration. However, in the actual course of treatment, the drug may have to reach a certain level to have an effect; the drug concentration is not equal to the drug dose. Therefore, it is necessary to consider the drug concentration, but the competition model ignored the drug concentration factor. In fact, most prostate cancer treatment models do not take this into account [6,7].

Drugs not only kill cancer cells but also affect healthy cells. Therefore, in the process of treatment, one also needs to consider drug toxicity. Ledzewicz et al. [8] analyzed cancer chemotherapy models in which the pharmacokinetics equation was introduced to minimize damage to myeloid cells from chemotherapy; they analyzed the effect of the pharmacokinetics equation on chemotherapy dose. Urszula et al. [9] modified the mathematical model; they mainly considered the tumor volume and angiogenesis ability, using multiple treatment schemes to minimize the tumor volume. They provided the solutions of several potential mathematical models. Liadis et al. [10] used mathematical models to describe the pharmacokinetics, antitumor efficacy, and toxicity of anticancer drugs, providing a schedule for administration, optimizing drug doses, minimizing tumor burden, and limiting toxicity. Poh Ling Tan et al. [11] considered a mathematical model of cancer chemotherapy, proposed an objective, provided several different constraint conditions, proposed two control problems, and obtained the satisfied exact solution.

Therefore, in the course of cancer treatment, one needs to consider how to determine the dose and treatment time, take into account the drug toxicity, suppress the number of drug-resistant cells, and extend the limited treatment time. Based on Liu et al. [5], we describe the drug concentration effect on treatment. Because of the side effects of the drug, we consider the toxicity of the drug, and provide the maximum allowable drug concentration. At the same time, because excessive tumor burden will lead to treatment failure, the maximum tolerable tumor burden is presented. Therefore, the treatment process is constrained by drug toxicity and tumor burden. Under the two constraints, the optimal control problem is proposed to optimize the drug dose and treatment time, so that the number of drug-resistant cells at the terminal time and the drug cost are the lowest in the limited time. Using the numerical simulation and quantitative analysis, the optimal treatment time and dose are obtained. The number of tumor cells, optimal dose, and treatment time are analyzed at different tumor-loading levels, further simulating the dose titration protocol proposed by Cunningham et al. [4]. The results show that when the tumor burden is 150%, treatment starts, with the maximum tolerated dose initially administered. When the maximum allowable drug concentration is reached, the dose is reduced; with intermittent dosing at moderate doses, this is optimal. It can maintain a certain tumor burden, reduce the number of drug-resistant cells at the terminal moment, and reduce drug costs, further limiting drug toxicity.

The structure of this article is as follows. In the second part, we propose a Lotka–Volterra model to describe the interaction between cancer cells, consider the drug concentration problem, present the first-order linear pharmacokinetics equation, present two state constraints, and propose an optimal control problem. In the third part, the state constraints are analyzed and the optimal control structure is given. In the fourth part, through the numerical simulation, we present the best treatment time and the drug dose, analyze the different cancer cell upper-limit levels, consider the effects of intercellular competition and drug concentration on cells, compare the dose titration method, and present a summary. In the fifth part, we present a conclusion.

2. Optimal Control Problem with Control Variables and Two State Constraints

First, Liu et al. [5] established a Lotka–Volterra model between drug-sensitive and drug-resistant prostate cells.

$$\begin{cases} \dfrac{dT_1(t)}{dt} = \lambda_1 T_1 \left[1 - \dfrac{(a_{11}T_1 + a_{12}T_2)(1 + \alpha\beta(t))}{K_1}\right] - \mu_1 T_1, \\ \dfrac{dT_2(t)}{dt} = \lambda_2 T_2 \left[1 - \dfrac{a_{21}T_1 + a_{22}T_2}{K_2}\right] - \mu_2 T_2, \end{cases} \quad (1)$$

where T_1 represents drug-sensitive cells, T_2 represents drug-resistant cells, λ_1 and λ_2 represent the net growth rate of cells, K_1 represents the environmental capacity of drug-sensitive cancer cells, K_2 represents the environmental capacity of drug-resistant cancer cells, μ_1 and μ_2 represent the natural mortality of cells, α represents the patient's sensitivity to the targeted drug, β is the drug dose, $(a_{ij})_{2\times 2}$ represents competition between sensitive and resistant cells.

In cancer treatment, medication is a drug dose. In the above model, the effect of the drug dose is considered; that is, after medication, the number of sensitive cells is reduced, thus affecting the drug-resistant cells. Drug concentration refers to the constant accumulation of drug doses in the body's blood. When the drug concentration is too low, it may not be enough to kill enough sensitive cells. When the drug concentration is too high, it may affect normal cells and harm the human body. Therefore, it is essential to consider the effect of drug concentration on treatment. We propose the following model.

$$\begin{cases} \dfrac{dT_1(t)}{dt} = \lambda_1 T_1 \left[1 - \dfrac{(a_{11}T_1 + a_{12}T_2)(1+\alpha c(t))}{K_1}\right] - \mu_1 T_1, \\ \dfrac{dT_2(t)}{dt} = \lambda_2 T_2 \left[1 - \dfrac{a_{21}T_1 + a_{22}T_2}{K_2}\right] - \mu_2 T_2, \\ \dfrac{dc(t)}{dt} = -fc + k\beta. \end{cases} \quad (2)$$

For drug concentration and continuous drug dose infusion, a process of self-clearance and accumulation occurs, so the corresponding model is proposed, where f and k represent kinetics of drug concentration c in vivo,

Optimal Control of Prostate Cancer

The state equation is constrained by the control variable

$$0 \leq \beta(t) \leq 1, \quad (3)$$

considering drug toxicity limits and tumor burden, the following two state constraints are proposed:

$$c - c_{\max} \leq 0, \quad (4)$$

$$T_1 + T_2 - \theta \leq 0, \quad (5)$$

where $c_{\max}$ is the maximum allowable drug concentration, θ is the initial maximum tumor burden (the drug-sensitive and drug-resistant cell numbers indicate the tumor burden). Hansen et al. [12] proposed that, in adaptive therapy, according to the PSA's (prostate cancer index) 50% rule treatment, and inspired by this, we propose that the initial maximum tumor burden is 150% of the initial tumor burden (the values for $c_{\max}$ and θ are given below).

Denote the state variable $x = (T_1(t), T_2(t), c(t)) \in R^3$ by considering the objective

$$J(x, \beta) = \phi\left(T_2(t_f)\right) + \int_0^{t_f} \beta(t) dt. \quad (6)$$

where ϕ represents the number of resistant cells at the end of treatment. t_f represents the number of resistant cells at the end of treatment.

This objective function (6) represents the number of drug-resistant cells and the cost of the drug to be minimized at the end of a limited treatment time.

Then, we consider the optimal control problem. We minimize the objective function under state Equation (2), control variable (3), and state constraints (4) and (5).

3. Minimum Principle: Necessary Optimality Condition

Gollmann et al. [13,14] proposed a method to extend the state constraint from hybrid control to a pure state constraint. Buskens et al. [15] provided the necessary optimality conditions for optimal control problems. Poh Ling Tan et al. [11] obtained the augmented Hamiltonian function by directly connecting the state constraints with the multipliers η_1 and η_2. Referring to the correlation theory, we consider the state constraint problem and obtain the optimality conditions of the optimal control problem by using the correlation theory.

3.1. State Constraints

For the drug concentration constraint $c - c_{\max} \leq 0$, consider the equation of state

$$\dot{c} = -fc + k\beta,$$

it can explicitly contain the control variable and satisfy the regularity condition

$$\frac{\partial}{\partial \beta} \dot{c}(t) = k \neq 0,$$

for the drug concentration constraint, the maximum allowable drug concentration is reached when the drug is continuously administered, $c = c_{\max}$, we can obtain $\dot{c}(t) = 0$. We obtain the boundary drug dose

$$\beta_1 = \frac{f}{k} c_{\max}.$$

For the cancer cells constraint, $T_1 + T_2 - \theta \leq 0$. We introduce a new variable $S(x)$. Let $S(x) = T_1 + T_2 - \theta$. We consider the first derivative:

$$\begin{aligned}
0 = S'(t) &= T_1'(t) + T_2'(t) \\
&= \lambda_1 T_1 \left[1 - \frac{(a_{11}T_1 + a_{12}T_2)(1 + \alpha c(t))}{K_1}\right] - \mu_1 T_1 \\
&\quad + \lambda_2 T_2 \left[1 - \frac{a_{21}T_1 + a_{22}T_2}{K_2}\right] - \mu_2 T_2 \\
&= (\lambda_1 - \mu_1)T_1 + (\lambda_2 - \mu_2)T_2 - \frac{\lambda_1 a_{11} T_1^2}{K_1} - \frac{\lambda_1 a_{11} T_1^2 \alpha c}{K_1} \\
&\quad - \frac{\lambda_1 a_{12} T_1 T_2}{K_1} - \frac{\lambda_1 a_{12} T_1 T_2 \alpha c}{K_1} - \frac{\lambda_2 a_{21} T_1 T_2}{K_2} - \frac{\lambda_2 a_{22} T_2^2}{K_2},
\end{aligned}$$

from the first derivative of the number of cancer cells, we can see that the control variable $\beta(t)$ does not appear. We consider the second derivative:

$$\begin{aligned}
0 = S''(t) &= (\lambda_1 - \mu_1)T_1' + (\lambda_2 - \mu_2)T_2' - \frac{2\lambda_1 a_{11} T_1}{K_1} \\
&\quad - \frac{2\lambda_1 a_{11} T_1 \alpha c}{K_1} + \frac{\lambda_1 a_{11} T_1^2 \alpha c f}{K_1} - \frac{\lambda_1 a_{11} T_1^2 \alpha k \beta}{K_1} \\
&\quad - \frac{\lambda_1 a_{12} T_1' T_2}{K_1} - \frac{\lambda_1 a_{12} T_2' T_1}{K_1} - \frac{\lambda_2 a_{21} T_1' T_2}{K_2} \\
&\quad - \frac{\lambda_2 a_{21} T_2' T_1}{K_2} - \frac{2\lambda_2 a_{22} T_2}{K_2} - \frac{\lambda_1 a_{12} T_1' T_2 \alpha c}{K_1} \\
&\quad - \frac{\lambda_1 a_{12} T_2' T_1 \alpha c}{K_1} + \frac{\lambda_1 a_{12} T_1 T_2 \alpha f c}{K_1} - \frac{\lambda_1 a_{12} T_1 T_2 \alpha k \beta}{K_1},
\end{aligned}$$

$$\begin{aligned}
S''(t) &= (\lambda_1 - \mu_1)^2 T_1 + (\lambda_2 - \mu_2)^2 T_2 - \frac{(\lambda_1 - \mu_1)\lambda_1 a_{11} T_1^2}{K_1} - \frac{(\lambda_1 - \mu_1)\lambda_1 a_{11} T_1^2 \alpha c}{K_1} \\
&\quad - \frac{(\lambda_1 - \mu_1)\lambda_1 a_{12} T_1 T_2}{K_1} - \frac{(\lambda_1 - \mu_1)\lambda_1 a_{12} T_1 T_2 \alpha c}{K_1} - \frac{(\lambda_2 - \mu_2)\lambda_2 a_{21} T_1 T_2}{K_2}
\end{aligned}$$

$$
\begin{aligned}
&- \frac{(\lambda_2 - \mu_2)\lambda_2 a_{22} T_2^2}{K_2} - \frac{2\lambda_1 a_{11} T_1}{K_1} - \frac{2\lambda_1 a_{11} T_1 \alpha c}{K_1} + \frac{\lambda_1 a_{11} T_1^2 \alpha c f}{K_1} \\
&- \frac{(\lambda_1 - \mu_1)\lambda_1 a_{12} T_1 T_2}{K_1} - \frac{\lambda_1 a_{11} T_1^2 \alpha k \beta}{K_1} - \frac{(\lambda_1 - \mu_1)\lambda_1 a_{12} T_1 T_2 \alpha c}{K_1} \\
&+ \frac{\lambda_1 a_{12} T_2}{K_1}\left(\frac{\lambda_1 a_{11} T_1^2}{K_1} + \frac{\lambda_1 a_{11} T_1^2 \alpha c}{K_1} + \frac{\lambda_1 a_{12} T_1 T_2}{K_1} + \frac{\lambda_1 a_{12} T_1 T_2 \alpha c}{K_1}\right) \\
&- \frac{(\lambda_2 - \mu_2)\lambda_1 a_{12} T_1 T_2}{K_1} + \frac{\lambda_1 a_{12} T_1}{K_1}\left(\frac{\lambda_2 a_{21} T_1 T_2}{K_2} + \frac{\lambda_2 a_{22} T_2^2}{K_2}\right) - \frac{2\lambda_2 a_{22} T_2}{K_2} \\
&+ \frac{\lambda_1 a_{12} T_1 T_2 \alpha f c}{K_1} - \frac{\lambda_1 a_{12} T_1 T_2 \alpha k \beta}{K_1} - \frac{(\lambda_1 - \mu_1)\lambda_2 a_{21} T_1 T_2}{K_2} \\
&+ \frac{\lambda_2 a_{21} T_2}{K_2}\left(\frac{\lambda_1 a_{11} T_1^2}{K_1} + \frac{\lambda_1 a_{11} T_1^2 \alpha c}{K_1} + \frac{\lambda_1 a_{12} T_1 T_2}{K_1} + \frac{\lambda_1 a_{12} T_1 T_2 \alpha c}{K_1}\right) \\
&- \frac{(\lambda_2 - \mu_2)\lambda_2 a_{21} T_1 T_2}{K_2} + \frac{\lambda_2 a_{21} T_1}{K_2}\left(\frac{\lambda_2 a_{22} T_2^2}{K_2} + \frac{\lambda_2 a_{21} T_1 T_2}{K_2}\right) \\
&+ \frac{\lambda_1 a_{12} T_2 \alpha c}{K_1}\left(\frac{\lambda_1 a_{11} T_1^2}{K_1} + \frac{\lambda_1 a_{11} T_1^2 \alpha c}{K_1} + \frac{\lambda_1 a_{12} T_1 T_2}{K_1} + \frac{\lambda_1 a_{12} T_1 T_2 \alpha c}{K_1}\right) \\
&- \frac{(\lambda_2 - \mu_2)\lambda_1 a_{12} T_1 \alpha c}{K_1} + \frac{\lambda_1 a_{12} T_1 \alpha c}{K_1}\left(\frac{\lambda_2 a_{21} T_1 T_2}{K_2} + \frac{\lambda_2 a_{22} T_2^2}{K_2}\right),
\end{aligned}
$$

furthermore, we find that the control variable $\beta(t)$ appears explicitly in the second derivative. Therefore, there exists a second-order state constraint satisfying the regularity condition.

$$\frac{\partial}{\partial \beta} S''(t) = -\frac{\lambda_1 a_{11}\alpha k T_1^2 + \lambda_1 a_{12}\alpha k T_1 T_2}{K_1} \neq 0,$$

hence, for boundary control $T_1 + T_2 = \theta$, we have $S''(t) = 0$, and obtain the dose:

$$
\begin{aligned}
\beta_2 =\ & \frac{K_1}{\lambda_1 a_{11}\alpha T_1^2 k + \lambda_1 a_{12}\alpha T_1 T_2 k}(\lambda_1 - \mu_1)^2 T_1 + (\lambda_2 - \mu_2)^2 T_2 - \frac{(\lambda_1 - \mu_1)\lambda_1 a_{11} T_1^2}{K_1} \\
&- \frac{(\lambda_1 - \mu_1)\lambda_1 a_{11} T_1^2 \alpha c}{K_1} - \frac{(\lambda_1 - \mu_1)\lambda_1 a_{12} T_1 T_2}{K_1} - \frac{(\lambda_1 - \mu_1)\lambda_1 a_{12} T_1 T_2 \alpha c}{K_1} \\
&- \frac{(\lambda_2 - \mu_2)\lambda_2 a_{21} T_1 T_2}{K_2} - \frac{(\lambda_2 - \mu_2)\lambda_2 a_{22} T_2^2}{K_2} - \frac{2\lambda_1 a_{11} T_1}{K_1} - \frac{2\lambda_1 a_{11} T_1 \alpha c}{K_1} \\
&+ \frac{\lambda_1 a_{11} T_1^2 \alpha c f}{K_1} - \frac{(\lambda_1 - \mu_1)\lambda_1 a_{21} T_1 T_2}{K_1} - \frac{(\lambda_2 - \mu_2)\lambda_1 a_{12} T_1 T_2}{K_1} \\
&+ \frac{\lambda_1 a_{12} T_2}{K_1}\left(\frac{\lambda_1 a_{11} T_1^2}{K_1} + \frac{\lambda_1 a_{11} T_1^2 \alpha c}{K_1} + \frac{\lambda_1 a_{12} T_1 T_2}{K_1} + \frac{\lambda_1 a_{12} T_1 T_2 \alpha c}{K_1}\right) \\
&+ \frac{\lambda_1 a_{12} T_1}{K_1}\left(\frac{\lambda_2 a_{21} T_1 T_2}{K_2} + \frac{\lambda_2 a_{22} T_2^2}{K_2}\right) - \frac{2\lambda_2 a_{22} T_2}{K_2} + \frac{\lambda_1 a_{12} T_1 T_2 \alpha f c}{K_1} \\
&+ \frac{\lambda_2 a_{21} T_2}{K_2}\left(\frac{\lambda_1 a_{11} T_1^2}{K_1} + \frac{\lambda_1 a_{11} T_1^2 \alpha c}{K_1} + \frac{\lambda_1 a_{12} T_1 T_2}{K_1} + \frac{\lambda_1 a_{12} T_1 T_2 \alpha c}{K_1}\right) \\
&+ \frac{\lambda_2 a_{21} T_1}{K_2}\left(\frac{\lambda_2 a_{22} T_2^2}{K_2} + \frac{\lambda_2 a_{21} T_1 T_2}{K_2}\right) - \frac{(\lambda_1 - \mu_1)\lambda_1 a_{12} T_1 T_2 \alpha c}{K_1} \\
&- \frac{(\lambda_1 - \mu_1)\lambda_2 a_{21} T_1 T_2}{K_2} - \frac{(\lambda_2 - \mu_2)\lambda_2 a_{21} T_1 T_2}{K_2}
\end{aligned}
$$

$$+ \frac{\lambda_1 a_{12} T_2 \alpha c}{K_1} \left(\frac{\lambda_1 a_{11} T_1^2}{K_1} + \frac{\lambda_1 a_{11} T_1^2 \alpha c}{K_1} + \frac{\lambda_1 a_{12} T_1 T_2}{K_1} + \frac{\lambda_1 a_{12} T_1 T_2 \alpha c}{K_1} \right)$$
$$- \frac{(\lambda_2 - \mu_2) \lambda_1 a_{12} T_1 \alpha c}{K_1} + \frac{\lambda_1 a_{12} T_1 \alpha c}{K_1} \left(\frac{\lambda_2 a_{21} T_1 T_2}{K_2} + \frac{\lambda_2 a_{22} T_2^2}{K_2} \right).$$

The drug dose in the boundary state is obtained.

3.2. Optimal Control Structure

Let us denote $\sigma = (\sigma_1, \sigma_2, \sigma_3) \in R^3$. References [9,16]. The Hamilton function is given by the Pontryagin's minimum principle.

$$H(x, \sigma, \beta) = \beta(t) + \sigma_1(t) \left(\lambda_1 T_1 \left(1 - \frac{(a_{11} T_1 + a_{12} T_2)(1 + \alpha c(t))}{K_1} \right) - \mu_1 T_1 \right)$$
$$+ \sigma_2(t) \left(\lambda_2 T_2 \left(1 - \frac{a_{12} T_1 + a_{22} T_2}{K_2} \right) - \mu_2 T_2 \right)$$
$$+ \sigma_3(t)(-fc + k\beta),$$

connect the state constraints using multipliers η_1 and η_2 to the Hamiltonian mechanics:

$$H(x, \sigma, \beta, \eta_1, \eta_1) = H(x, \sigma, \beta) + \eta_1(c - c_{\max}) + \eta_2(T_1 + T_2 - \theta),$$

let (x, β) be the optimal solution. Then, there are adjoint functions and multiplier functions satisfying the following conditions:

(I) Adjoint differential equations

$$\dot{\sigma}(t) = -H_x(t, x, \beta(t), \sigma(t), \eta(t)).$$

(II) Transversality conditions

$$\sigma(t_f) = \frac{\partial \phi(t_f)}{\partial x}.$$

(III) Minimizing conditions

$$H(t, x, \beta^*(t), \sigma(t), \eta(t)) \leq H(t, x, \beta(t), \sigma(t), \eta(t)).$$

(IV) Complementarity conditions

$$\eta_1(t) \geq 0, \quad \eta_1(t)(c - c_{\max}) = 0,$$
$$\eta_2(t) \geq 0, \quad \eta_2(t)(T_1 + T_2 - \theta) = 0.$$

The adjoint equation is obtained via the above theoretical analysis

$$\dot{\sigma_1}(t) = -1 - \sigma_1(t)(\lambda_1 - \mu_1) + \sigma_1(t) \frac{2\lambda_1 a_{11} T_1 (1 + \alpha c)}{K_1}$$
$$+ \sigma_1(t) \frac{\lambda_1 a_{12} T_2 (1 + \alpha c)}{K_1} + \sigma_2(t) \frac{\lambda_2 a_{21} T_2}{K_2} - \eta_2,$$

$$\dot{\sigma_2}(t) = -1 - \sigma_1(t) \frac{\lambda_1 a_{12} T_1 (1 + \alpha c)}{K_1} - \sigma_2(t)(\lambda_2 - \mu_2)$$
$$+ \sigma_2(t) \frac{\lambda_2 a_{21} T_1}{K_2} + \sigma_2(t) \frac{\lambda_2 a_{22} T_2}{K_2} - \eta_2,$$

$$\dot{\sigma_3}(t) = -\sigma_1(t)\frac{\lambda_1 a_{11} T_1^2 \alpha}{K_1} + \sigma_1(t)\frac{\lambda_1 a_{12} T_1 T_2 \alpha}{K_1} + \sigma_3(t)f - \eta_1, \quad (7)$$

the optimal control structure is obtained via the Pontryagin's minimum principle

$$\frac{\partial H}{\partial \beta} = 0,$$

we can obtain the switching function

$$\gamma(t) = 1 + \lambda_3(t)k,$$

we further obtain the control structure

$$\beta^*(t) = \begin{cases} 1 & \gamma(t) > 0, \\ \beta_i & \gamma(t) = 0, \\ 0 & \gamma(t) < 0. \end{cases}$$

For the control problem mentioned in the study, we consider the initial number of cancer cells. Step 1. First, the maximum dose is administered. As a result, the number of sensitive cells decreases, drug-resistant cells increase, and the drug concentration goes up. When drug concentration reaches the maximum allowable drug concentration, the drug is withdrawn, and the time is recorded. At this time, the number of sensitive cells increases and the number of drug-resistant cells decreases. Step 2. When the number of cancer cells reaches the initial maximum tumor burden, the drug is re-administered. This leads to a decrease in the number of sensitive cells, an increase in the number of drug-resistant cells, output time, continuous circulation, and intermittent treatment of cancer. This approach takes into account the concentration of the drug, avoids high or low doses, and takes into account the burden on the tumor. The number of sensitive cells is controlled by selecting the optimal treatment time and drug dosage, which further inhibits the number of drug-resistant cells and prolongs the effective treatment time.

In this paper, three treatment cycles are considered, and the following control structures are given:

$$\beta(t) = \begin{cases} 1 & 0 \leq t < t_1, \\ \beta_1 & t_1 \leq t < t_2, \\ 0 & t_2 \leq t < t_3, \\ \beta_2 & t_3 \leq t < t_4, \\ 0 & t_4 \leq t < t_5, \\ \beta_3 & t_5 \leq t < t_6, \\ 0 & t_6 \leq t < t_7, \\ \beta_4 & t_7 \leq t < t_8, \\ 0 & t_8 \leq t < t_f. \end{cases} \quad (8)$$

4. Numerical Simulation

Li et al. [17] proposed a control parameter vectorization method to solve the final control problem of free time. Feng et al. [18] proposed a visual version of MISER software 3.3, which is convenient for the practical application of optimal control theory and technology. There are many studies on how to solve nonlinear optimal control problems [19–21]. We use the discretization method to deal with the optimal control problem. We consider the optimal duration of the treatment and dosage in a limited period of time.

In the therapeutic period $[t_0, t_f]$, we solve the state equation in the forward direction and the co-state equation in the reverse direction. Refer to the parameter mentioned by Liu et al. [5], $\mu_1 = 0.001$, $\mu_2 = 0.0005$, $a_{12} = 0.1$. Some are not given and we set $\lambda_1 = 0.26$,

$\lambda_2 = 0.3, a_{11} = 0.1, a_{21} = 0.58, a_{22} = 0.2, K_1 = 5000, K_2 = 500, f = 1.4657, k = 5, \eta_1 = 0.1, \eta_2 = 0.1, T_1(0) = 1000, T_2(0) = 50, c_{\max} = 2.68, \theta = 1575, t_0 = 0, t_f = 42$.

The optimal treatment time and dose are obtained via a numerical simulation.

Optimal dose: $\beta_1 = 0.7856, \beta_2 = 0.7857, \beta_3 = 0.7857, \beta_4 = 0.7857$.

Optimal treatment time: $t_1 = 0.8, t_2 = 3.4, t_3 = 8.8, t_4 = 14, t_5 = 19.8, t_6 = 25, t_7 = 31, t_8 = 36.2$.

We can obtain $T_2(t_f) = 91.7164, J = 106.9731$.

Among them, Figure 1 shows the time-varying curves for the drug concentration and drug dose, Figure 2 shows the time-varying curves for the number of sensitive versus resistant cells, and Figure 3 shows the tumor burden change curves. Using the necessary optimality condition, the terminal time covariance is obtained via the covariance equation.

$$\lambda_1(t_f) = 0, \lambda_2(t_f) = 1, \lambda_3(t_f) = 0,$$

the initial value of the covariant is obtained via the numerical simulation,

$$\lambda_1(0) = -1.2372, \lambda_2(0) = -8.9337, \lambda_3(0) = -199.7054,$$

and the adjoint variables $\lambda_k(t), k = 1, 2, 3$, are displayed in Figures 4 and 5.

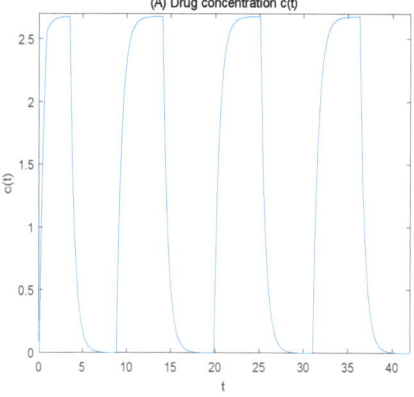
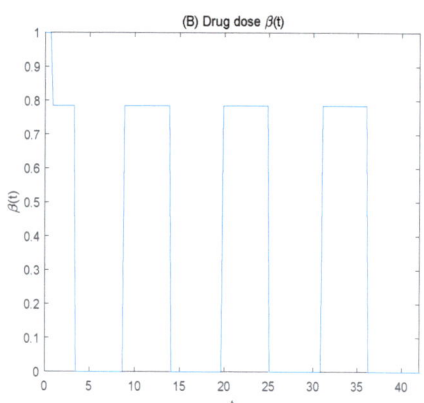

Figure 1. (**A**) Denotes the drug concentration, (**B**) denotes the drug dose.

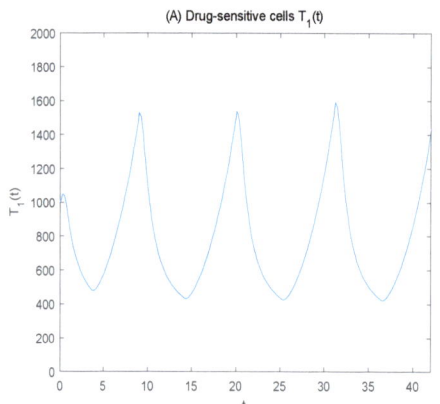
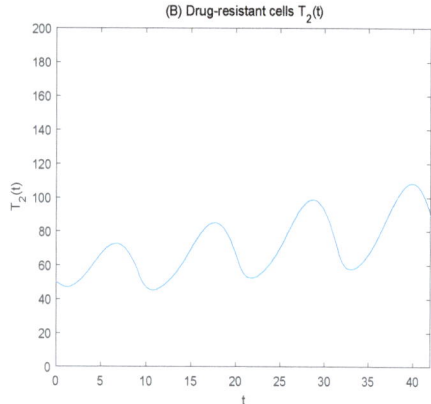

Figure 2. (**A**) Denotes the drug-sensitive cells, (**B**) denotes the drug-resistant cells (tumor burden is 150%).

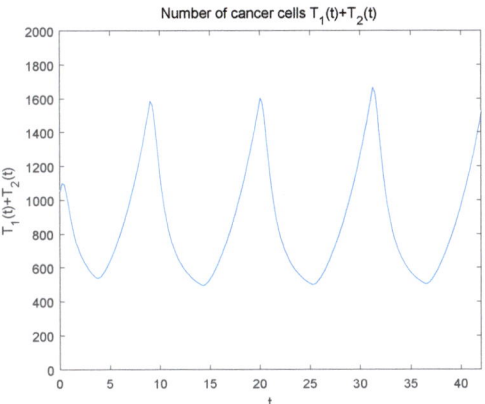

Figure 3. Number of cancer cells.

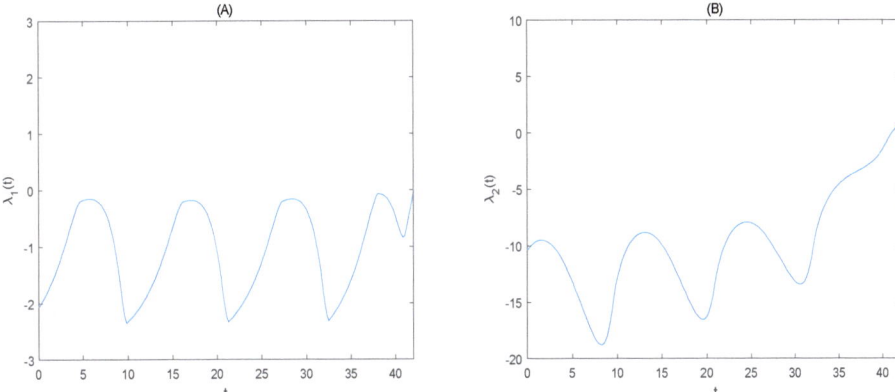

Figure 4. (**A**) Denotes adjoint variables λ_1, (**B**) denotes adjoint variables λ_2.

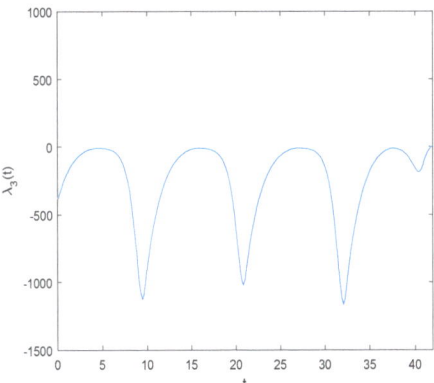

Figure 5. Denotes adjoint variables λ_3.

Figure 1B shows that the drug dose was initially presented at the maximum tolerated dose; when the maximum allowable drug concentration was reached, the drug dose was reduced with intermittent dosing, controlling for the number of cancer cells. Figure 2 shows that the number of sensitive cells decreased and the number of resistant cells increased after administration. After drug withdrawal, sensitive cells increased, resistant cells decreased, the number of cancer cells showed periodic changes, drug-resistant cells increased slowly with the prolongation of treatment time. Figure 3 shows that the tumor burden is maintained at a certain level.

Competition between cancer cells.

Adaptive therapy utilizes competition among cancer cells to maintain a certain tumor burden. Thus, we think more about competition between cells. When $a_{11} = 0.8$, there is too much competition between sensitive cells; as shown in Figure 6, we can see that sensitive cells can inhibit drug-resistant cells during the initial phase of treatment, and the number of drug-resistant cells slowly increases. In the later period of treatment, the number of sensitive cells decreased sharply and the number of drug-resistant cells increased because of the competition between sensitive cells.

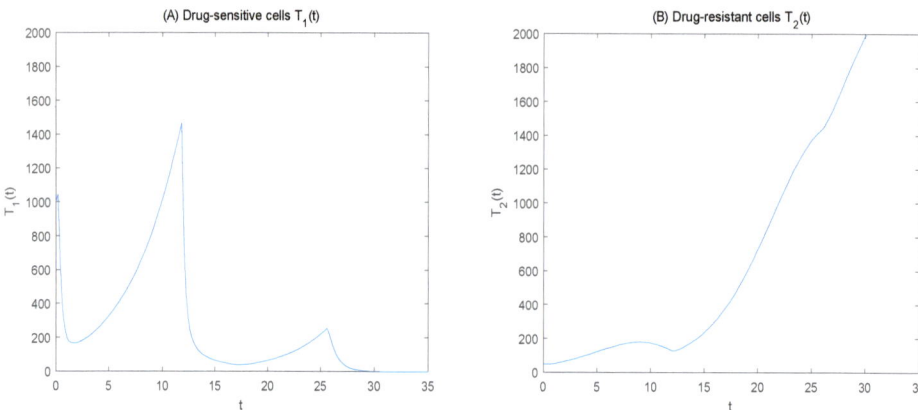

Figure 6. (**A**) Denotes drug-sensitive cells, (**B**) denotes drug-resistant cells (when $a_{11} = 0.8$).

When $a_{12} = 0.8$, as shown in Figure 7, we can see that at the initial stage of treatment, sensitive cells show cyclical changes, and resistant cells slowly increase; at later stages of treatment, sensitive cells lose their competitive advantage, and drug-resistant cells increase.

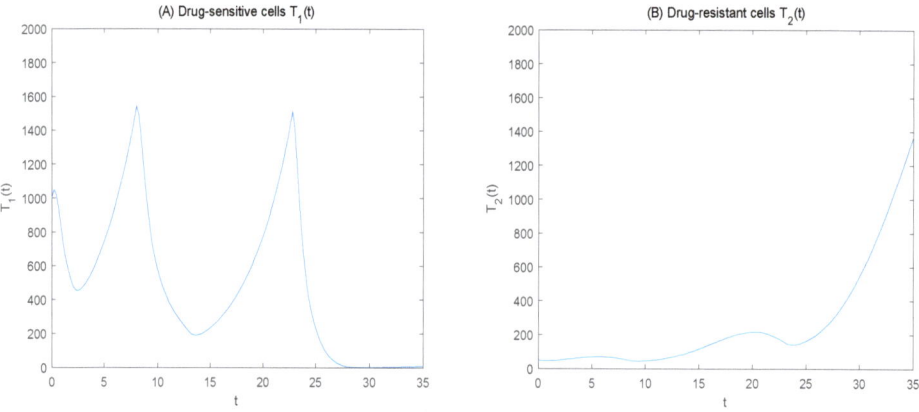

Figure 7. (**A**) Denotes drug-sensitive cells, (**B**) denotes drug-resistant cells (when $a_{12} = 0.8$).

When $a_{21} = 0.2$, as shown in Figure 8, we can see that sensitive cells can inhibit drug-resistant cells at the initial stage of treatment, and at the later stage of treatment, drug-resistant cells increase dramatically; compared with a_{12}, drug-resistant cells are more numerous, reducing the duration of treatment.

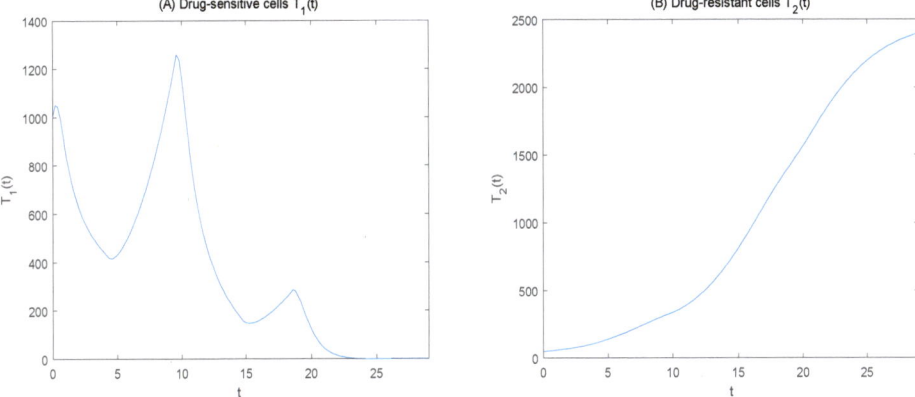

Figure 8. (**A**) Denotes drug-sensitive cells, (**B**) denotes drug-resistant cells (when $a_{21} = 0.2$).

When $a_{22} = 0.8$, as shown in Figure 9, it shows a downward trend in the number of drug-resistant cells but an increase in the number of sensitive cells, resulting in a rapid reach of the tumor burden and subsequent treatment failure.

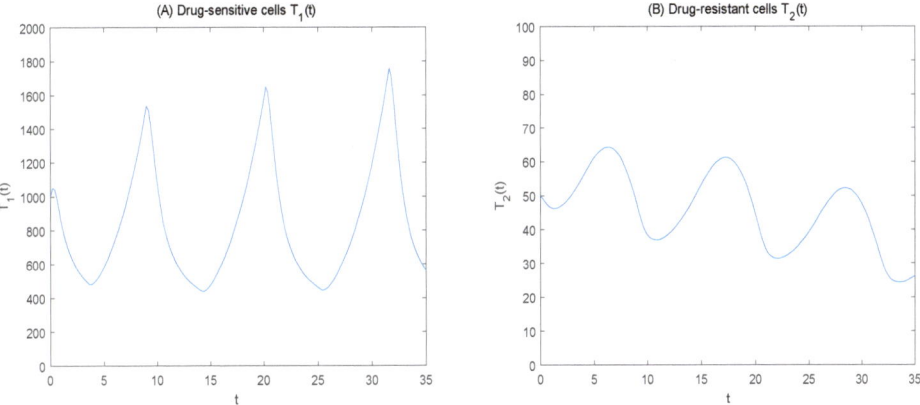

Figure 9. (**A**) Denotes drug-sensitive cells, (**B**) denotes drug-resistant cells (when $a_{22} = 0.8$).

Drug concentration

This study proposed the effect of drug concentration on therapy. We further considered the model proposed by Liu et al, considering only the effect of drug dose on therapy. Adjusting for $\lambda_1 = 0.1$, as shown in Figure 10, we found an overall upward trend in sensitive cells and a decrease in drug-resistant cells, this resulted in the sensitive cells rapidly reaching the maximum tumor burden, leading to treatment failure. The results showed that the drug was not enough to kill a large number of sensitive cells, resulting in a competitive advantage of sensitive cells over drug-resistant cells. Compared with Figure 9, we can see that the number of drug-resistant cells can be more effectively controlled and the stable tumor burden can be maintained by considering the drug concentration.

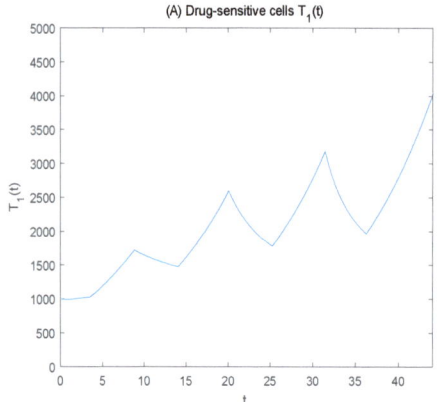
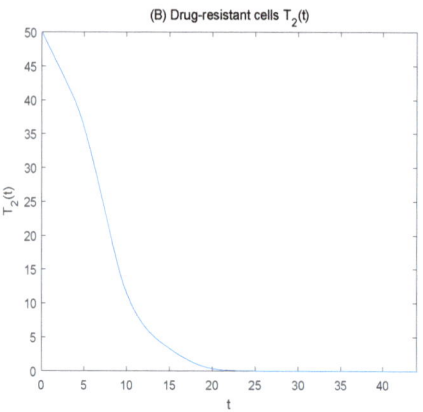

Figure 10. (**A**) Denotes drug-sensitive cells, (**B**) denotes drug-resistant cells.

4.1. Consider the Tumor Burden as 110%

The drug dosage is unchanged and the treatment time is optimized.

Optimal treatment time. $t_1 = 0.8$, $t_2 = 3.4$, $t_3 = 7.4$, $t_4 = 12.6$, $t_5 = 17.4$, $t_6 = 22.6$, $t_7 = 27.8$, $t_8 = 33$.

We can obtain $T_2(t_f) = 471.0447$, $J = 486.1442$.

Figure 11 shows the curve of sensitive and resistant cells over time at 110% tumor burden; we can see that the killing rate of drug-sensitive cells increases with the prolongation of treatment time, and the number of drug-resistant cells shows an overall declining trend. The number of drug-resistant cells increases, which indicates that the sensitive cells do not inhibit the drug-resistant cells well in the later stage of treatment.

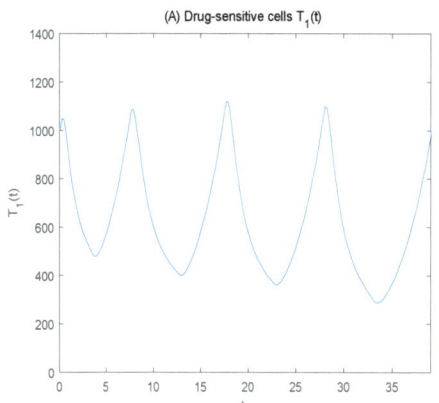
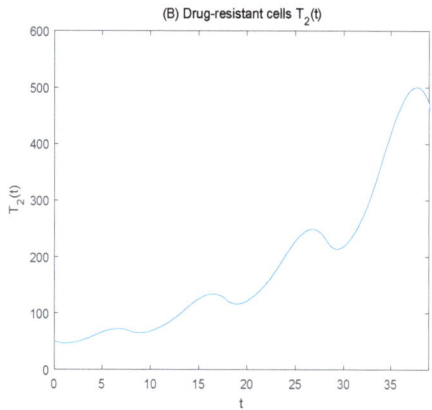

Figure 11. (**A**) Denotes drug-sensitive cells, (**B**) denotes drug-resistant cells (tumor burden is 110%).

Compared to a starting treatment, when the tumor burden is 150%, the treatment time is shortened and more resistant cells are generated. The reason for the significant increase in the number of drug-resistant cells may be that the drug dose is too large, killing too many sensitive cells, resulting in the later period of treatment, cell-to-cell competition weakens, and the number of drug-resistant cells increases. Therefore, we further optimize the drug dose.

Drug dose. $\beta_1 = 0.7856$, $\beta_2 = 0.7$, $\beta_3 = 0.7$, $\beta_4 = 0.7$.

We can obtain $T_2(t_f) = 143.3169$, $J = 157.0795$.

Changes in drug-sensitive cells affect drug-resistant cells because high doses kill too many drug-sensitive cells. Therefore, we reduce the drug dose, as shown in Figure 12, as the drug dose decreases over time. The number of drug-sensitive cells shows an upward trend, while the number of drug-resistant cells significantly decreases. Therefore, when the patient's maximum tolerated tumor burden is small, the dose is relatively small, suppressing the number of resistant cells. However, compared with 150% tumor burden, the number of drug-resistant cells remain larger at the end of the treatment period, despite the reduced cost of the drug.

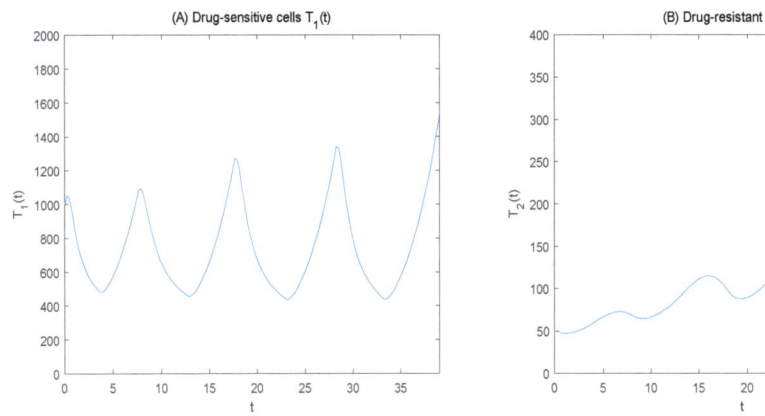

Figure 12. (**A**) Denotes drug-sensitive cells, (**B**) denotes drug-resistant cells (tumor burden is 110%).

4.2. Consider the Tumor Burden as 170%

The drug dosage is unchanged and the treatment time is optimized.

Optimal treatment time $t_1 = 0.8$, $t_2 = 3.8$, $t_3 = 10$, $t_4 = 15.2$, $t_5 = 21.8$, $t_6 = 27$, $t_7 = 33.8$, $t_8 = 39.2$.

We can obtain $T_2(t_f) = 23.8859$, $J = 39.4568$.

Figure 13 shows the curve of sensitive and resistant cells over time at 170% tumor burden. It shows that the number of sensitive cells increases significantly with the time of treatment, showing an overall upward trend. The number of drug-resistant cells increases at the beginning of treatment, decrease significantly at the end of treatment, and are even lower than the initial resistant cells. This indicates that, at this time, there are too many sensitive cells and competitive enhancements of the inhibition of drug-resistant cells.

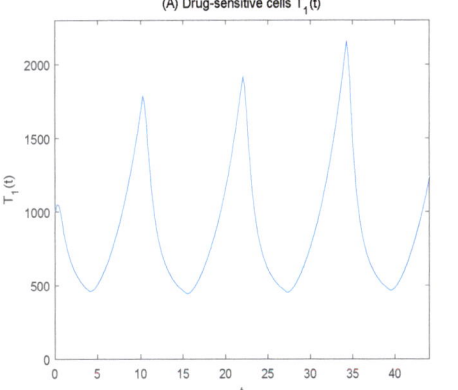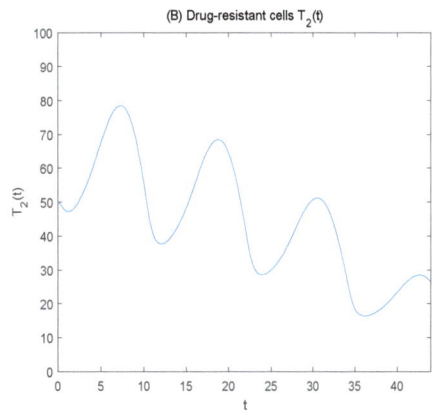

Figure 13. (**A**) Denotes drug-sensitive cells, (**B**) denotes drug-resistant cells (tumor burden is 170%).

Compared to a tumor burden of 150%, the number of drug-resistant cells is significantly lower, but the number of drug-sensitive cells is significantly increased. This could cause the tumor to reach the maximum tolerable burden more quickly, resulting in treatment failure The reason for this change may be that the drug did not kill enough sensitive cells, causing the sensitive cells to grow too quickly, so we further optimize the drug dose.

Drug dose. $\beta_1 = 0.7856$, $\beta_2 = 0.84$, $\beta_3 = 0.84$, $\beta_4 = 0.84$.

We can obtain $T_2(t_f) = 64.5510$, $J = 80.9798$.

To control drug-sensitive cells, we adjust the drug dose, as shown in Figure 14; as the drug dose increases, the number of sensitive cells decreases and the number of drug-resistant cells increases. As a result, the tumor burden increases and the drug dose increases. Compared with a tumor burden of 150%, during longer treatment periods, the number of drug-resistant cells is less, but the increasing dose of the drug and the rising cost of the drug, to some extent, break the limit of drug toxicity and affect normal cells.

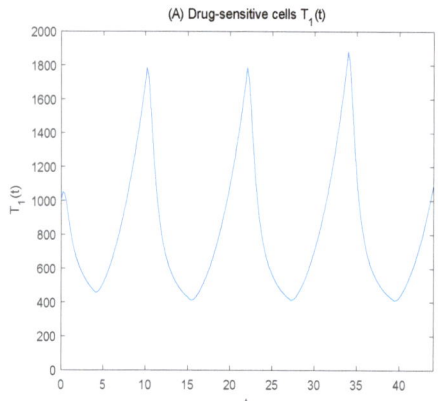
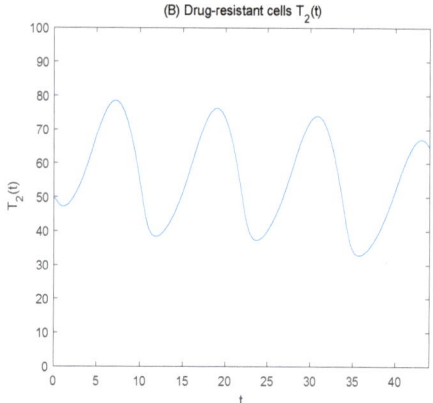

Figure 14. (**A**) Denotes drug-sensitive cells, (**B**) denotes drug-resistant cells (tumor burden is 170%).

At the same time, we further simulate the maximum tolerated dose commonly used in clinical practice.

4.3. Dose Titration Protocol

Cunningham et al. [4] analyzed a widely-used regimen, specifically a dose-titration treatment approach. In this regimen, the dose is increased by 0.1 when the tumor volume rises to more than 110% of the target tumor volume. Conversely, if the tumor volume drops below 90% of the intended maintenance volume, the dose is decreased by 0.1. They determined the optimal treatment strategy for the drug obtained using the optimization theory. With reference to the dose titration protocol described above, our study treats the number of cancer cells as the tumor burden; thus, given an initial dose, if the tumor burden increases to 150%, the dose increases by 0.1; if it decreases to 50%, the dose decreases by 0.1.

Let us think about a cycle; consider the issue of drug toxicity.

Drug dose: $b_1 = 0.8$, $b_2 = 0.7$,

Drug time: $t_1 = 4$, $t_2 = 22.2$,

We can obtain $T_2(t_f) = 1595.4672$, $J = 1687.6672$.

The change in the number of cancer cells is shown in Figure 15.

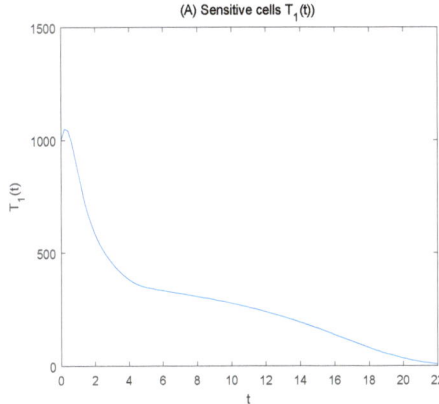
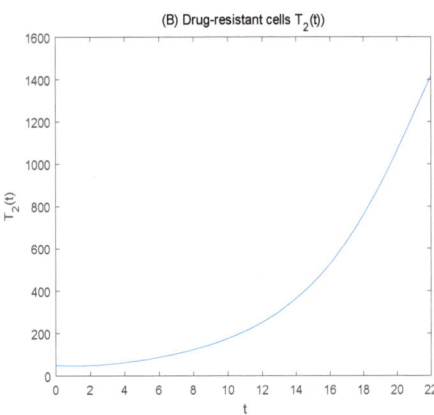

Figure 15. (**A**) Denotes drug-sensitive cells, (**B**) denotes drug-resistant cells (dose titration protocol).

As shown in Figure 15, when the initial dose is set at the maximum tolerated dose and considering the tumor burden, the number of drug-dose-sensitive cells was effectively reduced. However, due to a slow reduction in the dose, the number of drug-resistant cells increased significantly within a shorter treatment period.

Therefore, using dose titration to determine the most beneficial dose might lead to the rapid killing of sensitive cells, resulting in a loss of competitiveness. Our treatment protocol, through numerical simulation, directly provides the optimal drug dose. This controls the number of sensitive cells, inhibits the rapid proliferation of drug-resistant cells, and extends the treatment time.

Summary

The numerical simulation results show that when the tumor burden is 150%, within the permissible limit of drug toxicity, the administration of the drug causes drug-sensitive cells to decrease and drug-resistant cells to increase. Upon withdrawal of the drug, the sensitive cells increase, and the drug-resistant cells decrease. Throughout the treatment period, the number of drug-resistant cells increased slowly, and the tumor burden was maintained at a certain level. The competition between cells affects cell changes, and further analysis does not take into account the problem of drug concentration when it is not sufficient to kill sensitive cells, resulting in a significant increase in drug-resistant cells. When the tumor burden is 110%, the drug dose is reduced, the drug cost is reduced, the treatment time is shortened, and more resistant cells are produced. When the tumor load is 170%, the treatment time is prolonged, the number of drug-resistant cells is relatively small, but it is easy to reach the maximum drug-resistant load. Further increasing the drug dose will lead to breaking the limit of drug toxicity, affecting healthy cells. For dose-titration problems, given an initial dose and considering the drug toxicity issue, the strategy involves gradually increasing or decreasing the drug dose to find the most beneficial amount. When the initial dose is high, using the magnitude of the tumor burden to adjust the dose might result in extensive death of sensitive cells, a loss of competitiveness, and a significant rise in the number of drug-resistant cells. If the initial dose is low, the gradual increase in dose and failure to eliminate sensitive cells can lead to the rapid proliferation of these cells, which soon reach the maximum tolerance of the tumor load, leading to treatment failure. Therefore, the maximum tolerated tumor burden is too large or too small, and the drug dose is too large or too small, which will affect the effect of treatment. Using mathematical simulation, our study shows that the initial maximum drug resistance dose is given first; the drug is discontinued when the maximum allowable drug concentration is reached. When 150% of the initial tumor burden is reached, the drug is administered, and with the prolongation of the treatment period, it is optimal to give the drug intermittently at a moderate dose, which not only maintains a certain tumor burden and inhibits the rapid growth of drug-resistant cells, but also limits the drug toxicity and reduces the cost of the drug; the duration of treatment is prolonged effectively.

However, the maximum tolerable tumor burden varies from patient to patient, and we only considered the general case. Therefore, how to monitor the patient's maximum tolerable tumor burden according to clinical practice is important. Choosing the optimal treatment time and dosage and implementing individualized treatments are the issues that will be studied next.

5. Conclusions

During the course of tumor treatment, the generation of drug-resistant cells leads to the failure of treatment. With adaptive therapy, the goal is to maintain a certain number of sensitive cells, competitive inhibition resistance, a certain tumor burden, and extend the duration of treatment. Therefore, it is critical to select the appropriate treatment time and drug dose. If the dose is too low, it might fail to kill enough sensitive cells, leading to the quick attainment of the maximum tolerated tumor burden. Conversely, an excessively high dose may result in the death of a large number of sensitive cells, reducing competition and inhibiting the growth of drug-resistant cells less effectively. Additionally, an accumulation of too many drugs could have adverse side effects on the body. We took into consideration the model of competition between drug-sensitive and drug-resistant cells proposed by Liu et al. [5], and introduced a pharmacokinetics equation to describe the time course of drug concentrations in vivo. Because the drug not only kills cancer cells but also has an effect on healthy ones, it is not possible to cure cancer cells in sufficient doses. Therefore, in the process of cancer treatment, the issue of drug toxicity is proposed. We look at how to achieve the ideal cancer cell-killing rate and inhibit the growth of drug-resistant cells without damaging the healthy cells, and how to select the treatment time and dose to achieve the optimal therapeutic effect. We propose optimal control problems with two state constraints: the maximum allowable drug concentration and the maximum tolerated tumor burden. Firstly, the optimal control structure was obtained by using the optimal control theory to analyze the control problems. Secondly, the optimal treatment time and drug dose were obtained by numerical simulation, and the change rule of tumor cells under different tumor loads and the optimal treatment time and drug dose were given; a dose titration protocol was further simulated. The results show that when the tumor burden is at 150%, it is optimal to administer the maximum tolerated dose. Once the maximum allowable drug concentration is attained, the drug should be given intermittently at a moderate dose. This strategy helps maintain the tumor burden at a stable level, inhibit the growth of drug-resistant cells, reduce drug costs, and prolong the drug's efficacy. These findings offer insights into the treatment of prostate cancer.

However, our study relies on initial values while focusing on the effects of intercellular competition factors on treatment, so that initial values and competition coefficients have a greater impact on treatment outcomes than other factors. At the same time, the drug concentration change in the human body is worthy of further study. For the treatment approach proposed in this paper, determining how to tailor it to the individual patient's situation remains a topic for a follow-up study.

Author Contributions: W.L.: conceptualization, methodology, formal analysis, investigation, software, writing—original draft, writing—review and editing. X.T.: conceptualization, methodology, validation, writing—review and editing. X.Z.: validation, formal analysis, investigation, writing—review and editing. Q.T.: validation, formal analysis, methodology, writing—review and editing. All authors have read and agreed to the published version of the manuscript.

Funding: This work is supported by the Youth Talent of Xingdian Talent Support Program (Xuewen Tan) and the National Natural Science Foundation of China (no. 12261104).

Data Availability Statement: Data sharing is not applicable to this article as no data sets were generated or analyzed in the current study.

Conflicts of Interest: The authors declare that they have no competing interest.

References

1. Gatenby, R.A. A change of strategy in the war on cancer. *Nature* **2009**, *459*, 508–509. [CrossRef]
2. Gatenby, R.A.; Silva, A.S.; Gillies, R.J.; Frieden, B.R. Adaptive therapy. *Cancer Res.* **2009**, *69*, 4894–4903. [CrossRef]
3. Zhang, J.; Fishman, M.N.; Brown, J.; Gatenby, R.A. Integrating evolutionary dynamics into treatment of metastaticcastrate-resistant prostate cancer (mCRPC): Updated analysis of the adaptive abiraterone (abi) study (NCT02415621). *J. Clin. Oncol.* **2019**, *37*, 5041–5041. [CrossRef]
4. Cunningham, J.; Thuijsman, F.; Peeters, R.; Viossat, Y.; Brown, J.; Gatenby, R.; Staňková, K. Optimal control to reach eco-evolutionary stability in metastatic castrate-resistant prostate cancer. *PLoS ONE* **2020**, *15*, e0243386. [CrossRef]
5. Liu, R.; Wang, S.; Tan, X.; Zou, X. Identifying optimal adaptive therapeutic schedules for prostate cancer through combining mathematical modeling and dynamic optimization. *Appl. Math. Model.* **2022**, *107*, 688–700. [CrossRef]
6. West, J.B.; Dinh, M.N.; Brown, J.S.; Zhang, J.; Anderson, A.R.; Gatenby, R.A. Multidrug cancer therapy in metastatic castrate-resistant prostate cancer: An evolution-based strategy. *Clin. Cancer Res.* **2019**, *25*, 4413–4421. [CrossRef]
7. Strobl, M.A.R.; West, J.; Viossat, Y.; Damaghi, M.; Robertson-Tessi, M.; Brown, J.S.; Gatenby, R.A.; Maini, P.K.; Anderson, A.R. Turnover modulates the need for a cost of resistance in adaptive therapy. *Cancer Res.* **2021**, *81*, 1135–1147. [CrossRef]
8. Ledzewicz, U.; Schättler, H. Optimal controls for a model with pharmacokinetics maximizing bone marrow in cancer chemotherapy. *Math. Biosci.* **2007**, *206*, 320–342. [CrossRef]
9. Ledzewicz, U.; Maurer, H.; Schättler, H. Optimal and suboptimal protocols for a mathematical model for tumor anti-angiogenesis in combination with chemotherapy. *Math. Biosci. Eng.* **2011**, *8*, 307–323.
10. Iliadis, A.; Barbolosi, D. Optimizing drug regimens in cancer chemotherapy by an efficacy-toxicity mathematical model. *Comput. Biomed. Res.* **2000**, *33*, 211–226. [CrossRef]
11. Tan, P.L.; Maurer, H.; Kanesan, J.; Chuah, J.H. Optimal Control of Cancer Chemotherapy with Delays and State Constraints. *J. Optim. Theory Appl.* **2022**, *194*, 749–770. [CrossRef]
12. Hansen, E.; Read, A.F. Modifying adaptive therapy to enhance competitive suppression. *Cancers* **2020**, *12*, 35–56. [CrossRef]
13. Göllmann, L.; Kern, D; Maurer, H. Optimal control problems with delays in state and control variables subject to mixed control-state constraints. *Optim. Control Appl. Methods* **2009**, *30*, 341–365. [CrossRef]
14. Göllmann, L.; Maurer, H. Theory and applications of optimal control problems with multiple time-delays. *J. Ind. Manag. Optim.* **2014**, *10*, 413–441. [CrossRef]
15. Büskens, C.; Maurer, H. SQP-methods for solving optimal control problems with control and state constraints: Adjoint variables, sensitivity analysis and real-time control. *J. Comput. Appl. Math.* **2000**, *120*, 85–108. [CrossRef]
16. Tan, J.; Zou, X. Optimal control strategy for abnormal innate immune response. *Comput. Math. Methods Med.* **2015**, *2015*, 386235. [CrossRef] [PubMed]
17. Li, S.; Zhao, R.; Zhang, Q. Optimization method for solving bang-bang and singular control problems. *J. Control Theory Appl.* **2012**, *10*, 559–564. [CrossRef]
18. Yang, F.; Teo, K.L.; Loxton, R.; Rehbock, V.; Li, B.; Yu, C.; Jennings, L. VISUAL MISER: An efficient user-friendly visual program for solving optimal control problems. *J. Ind. Manag. Optim. JIMO* **2016**, *12*, 781–810.
19. Maurer, H.; Büskens, C.; Kim, J.H.R.; Kaya, C.Y. Optimization methods for the verification of second order sufficient conditions for bang-bang controls. *Optim. Control Appl. Methods* **2005**, *26*, 129–156. [CrossRef]
20. Kaya, C.Y.; Noakes, J.L. Computational method for time-optimal switching control. *J. Optim. Theory Appl.* **2003**, *117*, 69–92. [CrossRef]
21. Lee, H.W.J.; Teo, K.L.; Rehbock, V.; Jennings, L.S. Control parametrization enhancing technique for time optimal control problems. *Dyn. Syst. Appl.* **1997**, *6*, 243–262.

Disclaimer/Publisher's Note: The statements, opinions and data contained in all publications are solely those of the individual author(s) and contributor(s) and not of MDPI and/or the editor(s). MDPI and/or the editor(s) disclaim responsibility for any injury to people or property resulting from any ideas, methods, instructions or products referred to in the content.

Article

Mathematical Model Predicting the Kinetics of Intracellular LCMV Replication

Julia Sergeeva [1,2,†], Dmitry Grebennikov [3,4,5,†], Valentina Casella [6], Paula Cebollada Rica [6], Andreas Meyerhans [6,7] and Gennady Bocharov [3,4,8,*]

1. Moscow Institute of Physics and Technology (National Research University), 141700 Dolgoprudny, Russia; sergeeva.iud@phystech.edu
2. Skolkovo Institute of Science and Technology, 121205 Moscow, Russia
3. Marchuk Institute of Numerical Mathematics of the RAS, 119333 Moscow, Russia; grebennikov_d_s@staff.sechenov.ru
4. Moscow Center of Fundamental and Applied Mathematics at INM RAS, 119234 Moscow, Russia
5. World-Class Research Center "Digital Biodesign and Personalized Healthcare", Sechenov First Moscow State Medical University, 119991 Moscow, Russia
6. Infection Biology Laboratory, Universitat Pompeu Fabra, 08003 Barcelona, Spain; valentina.casella@upf.edu (V.C.); paula.cebollada@upf.edu (P.C.R.); andreas.meyerhans@upf.edu (A.M.)
7. ICREA, Pg. Lluis Companys 23, 08010 Barcelona, Spain
8. Institute for Computer Science and Mathematical Modelling, Sechenov First Moscow State Medical University, 119991 Moscow, Russia
* Correspondence: g.bocharov@inm.ras.ru
† These authors contributed equally to this work.

Abstract: The lymphocytic choriomeningitis virus (LCMV) is a non-cytopathic virus broadly used in fundamental immunology as a mouse model for acute and chronic virus infections. LCMV remains a cause of meningitis in humans, in particular the fatal LCMV infection in organ transplant recipients, which highlights the pathogenic potential and clinical significance of this neglected human pathogen. Paradoxically, the kinetics of the LCMV intracellular life cycle has not been investigated in detail. In this study, we formulate and calibrate a mathematical model predicting the kinetics of biochemical processes, including the transcription, translation, and degradation of molecular components of LCMV underlying its replication in infected cells. The model is used to study the sensitivity of the virus growth, providing a clear ranking of intracellular virus replication processes with respect to their contribution to net viral production. The stochastic formulation of the model enables the quantification of the variability characteristics in viral production, probability of productive infection and secretion of protein-deficient viral particles. As it is recognized that antiviral therapeutic options in human LCMV infection are currently limited, our results suggest potential targets for antiviral therapies. The model provides a currently missing building module for developing multi-scale mathematical models of LCMV infection in mice.

Keywords: LCMV; intracellular replication; mathematical model; stochastic description; sensitivity analysis

MSC: 92-10; 92B05; 92C45; 92C70

1. Introduction

Infectious diseases caused by viruses (e.g., HIV-1, HBV or SARS-CoV-2) present a serious problem to human health worldwide. To understand their pathogenesis, infections are studied experimentally and by mathematical modelling approaches. The current technologies including multiplex analyses, microscopic and mesoscopic visualization, "omics-" technologies and bioinformatic analyses now allow for a multi-physics assessment of the processes regulating virus–host interactions at molecular-, cellular-, and systemic levels [1–3]. However, the adequate construction of mathematical models for studying the course and outcome of infectious diseases in terms of the description details to the level of understanding of its structure and functional components remains to be a great challenge. Indeed, models need to consider (1) virus replication at a single cell level, (2) spatial infection spreading across cell populations and (3) the systemic dynamics of disease characteristics. At present, mostly the population dynamics of antiviral immune responses has received substantial attention (e.g., [4–6]), while the development of integrative models is in its infancy. The latter requires models of intracellular virus life cycles, as single infected cells are the initiating and fuelling events in systemic virus spreading and key targets for combination therapies.

The lymphocytic choriomeningitis virus (LCMV) is a non-cytopathic virus broadly used in fundamental immunology as a mouse model for acute and chronic virus infections [7]. Based on the experimental LCMV infection model system, many conceptual discoveries in immunology have been made ranging from Major Histocompatibility Complex (MHC)-mediated immunological restriction to T-lymphocyte exhaustion (we refer to [8] for a comprehensive overview). Surprisingly, the intracellular kinetics of LCMV replication remains poorly understood. Modern experimental developments have enabled a high-dimensional characterization of LCMV infection across a number of scales [9,10]. To quantitatively describe, analyse and predict the LCMV-host interaction under various manipulations, consistent multi-scale mathematical models are required. So far, the population dynamics of CTL responses to LCMV infection were considered [8,11]. However, a quantitative understanding of the LCMV life cycle is lacking.

1.1. Molecular and Genome Structure of LCMV

LCMV has a bi-segmented, linear, negative strand RNA genome ((-)RNA) with ambisense coding of the viral proteins [12]. The ambisense coding strategy implies that virus proteins are coded in different directions (+polarity and -polarity). This means that the gene encoded on the -RNA strand needs to be transcribed into the +strand before it could be translated into protein. This type of coding strategy is believed to enable the temporal control of gene expression by regulating the two genes of an ambisense RNA segment differently.

The organization of LCMV is shown in Figure 1.

The LCMV RNA genome consists of two single-stranded RNA species: large L (7.2 kb) [13] and small S (3.4 kb) [14]. Each segment carries two viral genes in opposite orientation and is separated by an intergenic noncoding region (IGR) [15,16]. The IGR forms a relatively stable stem-loop structure, which functions as a transcription terminator and in virus assembly [17]. All proteins are translated from subgenomic viral-complementary mRNAs.

The L segment encodes the L protein (200 kDa) and the Z protein (11 kDa). The L protein is a RNA-dependent RNA polymerase (RdRp). It produces subgenomic mRNAs as well as full-length genomic and antigenomic RNAs via transcription and replication [18]. The viral RNA polymerase RdRp generates mostly encapsidated, uncapped full length (+)strand and (-)strand RNA species. The encapsidated RNAs are the templates for the synthesis of subgenomic, capped and non-polyadenylated mRNAs that are translated into viral proteins.

The Z protein is a matrix protein with multiple essential functions. In large concentrations, it inhibits replication and transcription by direct association with RdRp [19,20], facilitating assembly. Z plays a significant role in viral budding [21]: it interacts with the cellular ESCRT machinery and with virion components [22], and thus mediates their incorporation into nascent virions. In addition, Z interacts with several host cell proteins, such as the oncoprotein promyelocytic leukemia protein (PML), ribosomal P proteins, and the eukaryotic translation initiation factor 4E (eIF-4E) [23–25].

The S segment encodes the virus nucleoprotein (NP) and the glycoprotein precursor (GP-C). The NP protein associates with the viral RNA genome to form the nucleocapsid. This interacts with the viral polymerase and constitutes the viral ribonucleoprotein (RNP). This complex mediates transcription and replication, and is considered as the minimum unit of LCMV infectivity. NP availability determines the transition of the polymerase from transcription to replication by attenuating the structure-dependent transcription termination of the intergenome region (IGR) located between the encoded genes [26].

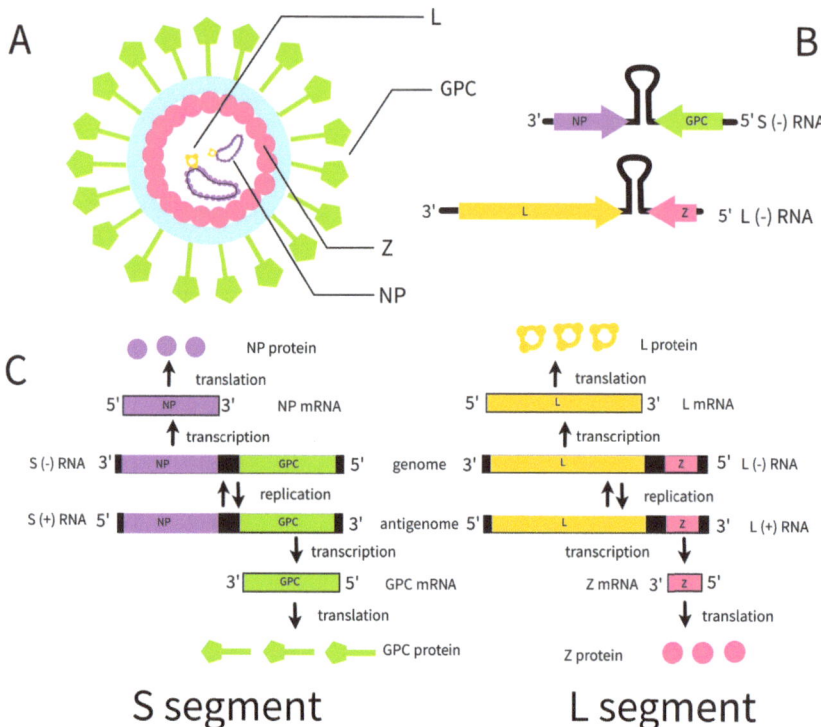

Figure 1. Virion structure and genome organization. (**A**) Schematic representation of a lymphocytic choriomeningitis virus (LCMV) virion. It consists of a lipid bilayer (light blue) from the host cell plasma membrane in which glycoprotein spikes (green) are incorporated. The glycoprotein mediates virus entry into target cells after receptor binding. The Z protein (pink) builds a matrix structure below the lipid bilayer. The nucleoprotein NP (violet) in association with the polymerase L (yellow) and the genomic RNA form the ribonucleoprotein (RNP) complex. (**B**) Genome organization of LCMV. LCMV has a bi-segmented (-)RNA genome that is composed of small S and large L RNA segments. The respective segments encode viral proteins in ambisense orientation. Intergenic regions (black) separate the open reading frames. The S segment encodes the virus nucleoprotein (NP) and the glycoprotein precursor (GP-C). The L segment encodes the L protein and the Z protein. (**C**) LCMV replication and transcription stages. The NP mRNA is transcribed from S (-)RNA, the GPC mRNA is transcribed from S (+)RNA, L mRNA is transcribed from L (-)RNA and Z is transcribed from L (+)RNA. Intergenic and non-coding regions are in black.

GP-Cs undergo post-translational modifications, which include glycosylation and then proteolytic cleavages. Firstly, the stable signal peptide (SSP) is cleaved within the endoplasmic reticulum by a cellular signal peptidase. This 58-amino-acid long SSP is then retained as a stable subunit. It is a critical component for downstream, mature glycoprotein complex formation [27]. In addition, SSP interacts with the immature GP1/2 precursor, which is cleaved by the cellular protease SKI-1/S1P in the Golgi complex to produce the GP1 and GP2 subunits [28]. The three subunits, SSP, GP1, and GP2, then traffic to the cellular plasma membrane where virus assembly and egress occurs. GP-1, GP-2 and SSP associate non-covalently. They form club-shaped projections on virions and mediate cell entry. GP-1 is a peripheral membrane protein and is responsible for binding to the virus receptor α-Dystroglycan (α-DG) [29]. GP-2 is an integral membrane protein and it, in concert with SSP, mediates the fusion of the viral envelope with the cellular membrane.

1.2. Intracellular Replication of LCMV

The LCMV life cycle starts with the infection of target cells. For this, the virion surface GP-1 protein interacts with cell surface α-DG that is mainly expressed on dendritic cells (DCs) [30–32]. The virion then enters target cells via non-coated vesicles that direct it to late endosomes [33–35]. This internalization process is cholesterol-dependent but clathrin-independent. At the late endosomes, a pH-dependent fusion between virion and endosome membranes occurs which releases virus genomic RNAs and L proteins into the cytoplasm. The L protein then initiates virus genome replication and viral mRNA generation. Subsequent translation of NP, L and Z mRNAs occurs in the cytoplasm while GPC mRNA is translated at the endoplasmic reticulum. The precursor GPC protein is post-translationally cleaved in the Golgi apparatus into the stable signal peptide SSP and the glycoproteins GP-1 and GP-2. The increase in Z protein concentration leads to the inhibition of the L polymerase and a shift towards virus assembly and release. The genomic RNAs are coated with NP proteins and transported with GP, Z and L proteins to the cell membrane, where virions are assembled and released from the infected cell by budding. The overall scheme of the intracellular LCMV replication stages is presented in Figure 2. The scheme is used to formulate the mathematical model of the LCMV life cycle.

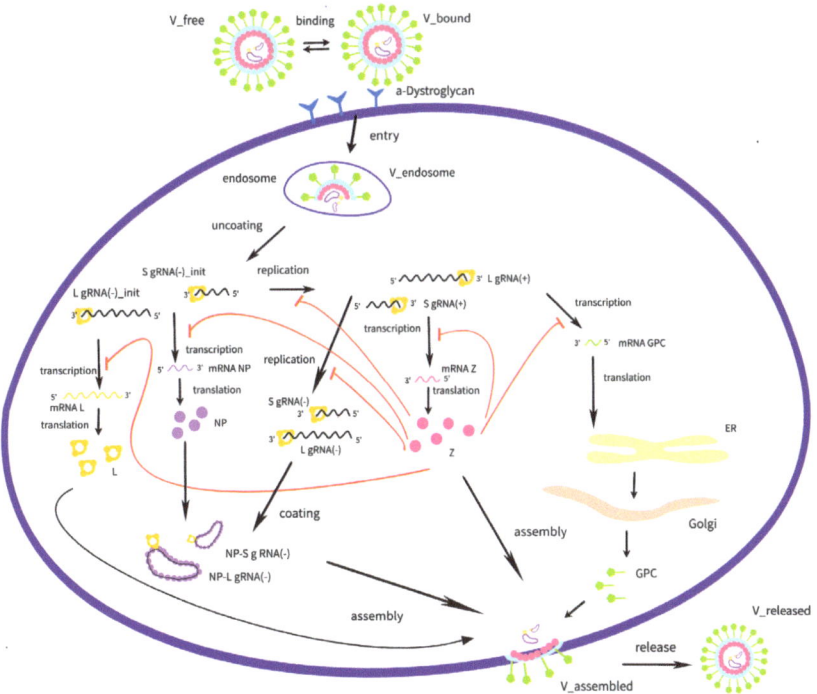

Figure 2. Biochemical scheme of the LCMV life cycle. The individual steps in the LCMV life cycle that are incorporated into the mathematical model are shown schematically. Details are described in the text. "init" refers to initial incoming virus genome.

In Section 2, we present the reference data available for model calibration and the computation tools used for simulations and analysis. In Section 3, the mathematical model is constructed both in deterministic and stochastic formulations. Section 4 presents the model-based prediction of the parameter sensitivity of net single cell LCMV production and the characteristics of the variability in viral production, including the secretion of protein-deficient viral particles. The study results are discussed in Section 5.

2. Experimental Data and Methods

2.1. Kinetics of Virion Components in the Cell

Experiments on the kinetics of LCMV were examined in [19]. RNAs were isolated at 6 time points between 0 and 72 h after infection, and the NP mRNA, Z mRNA, L RNA, and S RNA levels were analyzed using Northern blot hybridization. The level of the Z protein was analyzed by Western blotting. Some qualitative conclusions can be drawn from these experiments:

1. At all time points, the number of S RNA was significantly larger than L RNA. During the first hours of infection, S RNA was observed in large numbers, whereas L RNA abundance was characterized by undetectable numbers;
2. NP mRNA reaches peak concentration in the early hours of cell infection;
3. Z mRNA and Z protein concentrations increase at the end of the virus life cycle.

The growth curves, i.e., the time-dependence of the number of virions released from the infected cells in an in vitro culture, were obtained in a number of studies [34,36–38]. To obtain the kinetics of virion production per cell, growth curves were normalized by dividing the growth curve values by the respective MOI and the estimated total number of cells in the plate, assuming that all cells were infected simultaneously at the beginning, and no secondary infection occurred. The following re-scaling formula was used:

$$V_{cell} = \frac{V_{total}}{\text{estimated number of cells in plate} \cdot \text{MOI}}$$

where V_{cell} is the number of virions per cell, V_{total} stands for the number of virions in the entire culture, and MOI is the multiplicity of infection. According to the known ratios of protein concentrations during infection in the cell for the arenavirus family [39], and the numbers of each protein in the LCMV virion [40], one can generate the expected curves for proteins. To do this, the growth curves must be multiplied by the number of proteins. From the obtained kinetic curves and the known quantitative data, the following general conclusions can be drawn:

1. At the end of the life cycle, the expected number of LCMV virions is estimated to be about several hundreds;
2. The ratio of protein components should be as follows: NP > GPC > Z > L;
3. The LCMV life cycle lasts from 20 to 40 h.

The resulting empirical data summarized in Figure 3 were used to calibrate the model solution $V_{released}(t)$.

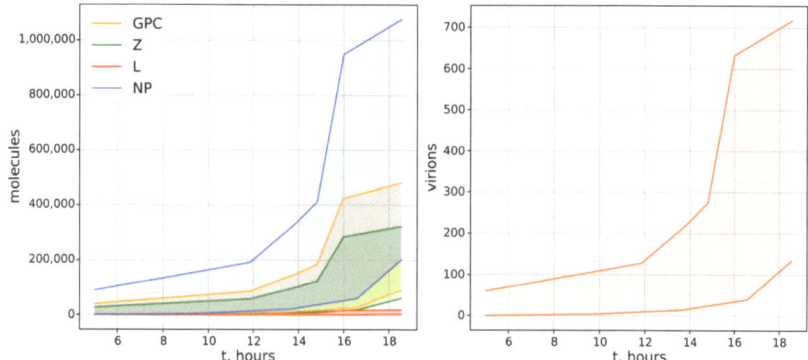

Figure 3. Generalized kinetics of LCMV growth in an infected cell. Estimates of the number of the LCMV proteins (**left**) and released virions (**right**) as a function of time after infection derived from [18–20,34,36–41]. The shaded areas represent observed ranges of abundances.

2.2. Z Protein-Mediated Inhibition Kinetics

A number of studies explore the kinetics and mechanisms of Z-protein-based regulation [19,20,41]. As previously described, Z inhibits RNA-dependent RNA polymerase L at high concentrations, which leads to the inhibition of transcription and replication and promotes the transition to assembly and budding. According to [20], it is known from studies of Machupo virus (MACV), another arenavirus, that untagged MACV Z inhibits the viral RNA synthesis in the mid-nanomolar range ($IC_{50} = 0.32$ µM), and GST-tagged MACV Z has a slightly higher IC_{50} (1.36 µM), due to an altered protein solubility. It can be assumed for LCMV that Z protein-inhibition occurs over the same concentration range. Multiplied by the characteristic cell volume (1 pL), the number of Z molecules required for half-maximal inhibition can be estimated as $K_I \approx 0.32 \cdot 10^{-18} \cdot 6 \cdot 10^{23} \approx 192000$ molecules for Machupo virus. Based on the above arguments, we take the inhibition constant for LCMV as $K_I = 50000$ molecules.

2.3. Basic Computational Tools

The following libraries in Julia language were used to simulate and analyze the model: DifferentialEquations v7.10.0 (numerical solution of the deteministic model), SciMLSensitivity v7.46.0 (local sensitivity analysis), JumpProcesses v9.8.0 (numerical solution of the stochastic model), PyPlot v2.11.2 and Plots v1.39.0 (visualizations).

2.4. Stochastic Modelling Algorithm

The deterministic model of LCMV replication described by a system of ODEs is translated into a stochastic Markov chain-based description following the dynamic Monte Carlo approach. To implement the dynamic MC description numerically, a number of methods (stochastic simulation algorithms) are available, including the popular Gillespie's direct method [42,43] and a number of exact and approximate SSA variations [44]. Previously, we proposed the hybrid stochastic-deterministic approximate method [45] to accelerate computations. Here, we use the rejection SSA (RSSA) with composition-rejection search (RSSA-CR) [46] implemented in JumpProcesses Julia library. In contrast to Gillespie's direct method, the rejection-based SSA delays the need to update the propensity rates (which is conducted after each transition in the direct method), which can be time-consuming for systems with many complex nonlinear processes.

Table 1 lists the propensities of all transitions that take place in the Markov chain-based stochastic system. The variables of the stochastic model can have only nonnegative integer values. The transitions correspond to increments and decrements of variable values by one unit (particle or molecule), except for the transition processes number 15 and 18 (which correspond to $[NP\text{-}LgRNA_{(-)}]$ and $[NP\text{-}SgRNA_{(-)}]$ formation) and the process number 38 (which corresponds to virion assembly with production of $[V_{assembled}]$). In these transitions, the number of NP, GPC, Z and L proteins is reduced by n_{NP}, n_{GPC}, n_Z and n_L, which are the number of protein molecules required for packing the ribonucleocapsids and for the assembly of LCMV virions. Therefore, if the current number of molecules in the cell is less than the required amount for these events, the ribonucleocapsids and the assembled virions are packed with an incomplete number of constitutive protein molecules, while the corresponding protein molecules in the cell are reduced to zero, as indicated in Table 1. This MC formulation allows us to analyse the production kinetics and protein content distribution in protein-deficient particles (see Section 4.5).

Table 1. Stochastic model formulated as a Markov chain showing the reactions (transition processes) and their propensities (intensities). The biological meaning of the time-dependent variables of the model is explained in Table 2 and the parameters are determined in Table 3.

m	Elementary Reaction	Transition Intensity, a_m
	Cell entry	
1	$[V_{free}] \to [V_{free}] - 1, [V_{bound}] \to [V_{bound}] + 1$	$k_{bind}[V_{free}]$
2	$[V_{free}] \to [V_{free}] - 1$	$d_V[V_{free}]$
3	$[V_{free}] \to [V_{free}] + 1, [V_{bound}] \to [V_{bound}] - 1$	$k_{diss}[V_{bound}]$
4	$[V_{bound}] \to [V_{bound}] - 1, [V_{endosome}] \to [V_{endosome}] + 1$	$k_{fuse}[V_{bound}]$
5	$[V_{bound}] \to [V_{bound}] - 1$	$d_V[V_{bound}]$
6	$[V_{endosome}] \to [V_{endosome}] - 1,$ $[LgRNA_{(-)}^{init}] \to [LgRNA_{(-)}^{init}] + 1, [SgRNA_{(-)}^{init}] \to [SgRNA_{(-)}^{init}] + 1,$ $[GPC] \to [GPC] + m_{GPC}, [Z] \to [Z] + m_Z, [L] \to [L] + m_L$	$k_{uncoat}[V_{endosome}]$
7	$[V_{endosome}] \to [V_{endosome}] - 1$	$d_{endosome}[V_{endosome}]$
	Replication	
8	$[LgRNA_{(-)}^{init}] \to [LgRNA_{(-)}^{init}] - 1$	$d_{LgRNA_{(-)}}[LgRNA_{(-)}^{init}]$
9	$[SgRNA_{(-)}^{init}] \to [SgRNA_{(-)}^{init}] - 1$	$d_{SgRNA_{(-)}}[SgRNA_{(-)}^{init}]$
10	$[LgRNA_{(+)}] \to [LgRNA_{(+)}] + 1$	$k_{repl_{(+)}}(l_{LgRNA})^{-1}[LgRNA_{(-)}^{init}]$
11	$[LgRNA_{(+)}] \to [LgRNA_{(+)}] - 1$	$d_{LgRNA_{(+)}}[LgRNA_{(+)}]$
12	$[SgRNA_{(+)}] \to [SgRNA_{(+)}] + 1$	$k_{repl_{(+)}}(l_{SgRNA})^{-1}[SgRNA_{(-)}^{init}]$
13	$[SgRNA_{(+)}] \to [SgRNA_{(+)}] - 1$	$d_{SgRNA_{(+)}}[SgRNA_{(+)}]$
14	$[LgRNA_{(-)}] \to [LgRNA_{(-)}] + 1$	$k_{repl_{(-)}}(l_{LgRNA})^{-1}[LgRNA_{(+)}]\theta_{RdRp}\theta_{inhib}$
15	$[LgRNA_{(-)}] \to [LgRNA_{(-)}] - 1,$ $[NP] \to ([NP] - n_{NP}) \vee 0,$ $[N\text{-}LgRNA_{(-)}] \to [N\text{-}LgRNA_{(-)}] + 1$	$k_{complex}\theta_{complex}[LgRNA_{(-)}]$
16	$[LgRNA_{(-)}] \to [LgRNA_{(-)}] - 1$	$d_{LgRNA_{(-)}}[LgRNA_{(-)}]$
17	$[SgRNA_{(-)}] \to [SgRNA_{(-)}] + 1$	$k_{repl_{(-)}}(l_{SgRNA})^{-1}[SgRNA_{(+)}]\theta_{RdRp}\theta_{inhib}$
18	$[SgRNA_{(-)}] \to [SgRNA_{(-)}] - 1,$ $[NP] \to ([NP] - n_{NP}) \vee 0,$ $[NP\text{-}SgRNA_{(-)}] \to [NP\text{-}SgRNA_{(-)}] + 1$	$k_{complex}\theta_{complex}[SgRNA_{(-)}]$
19	$[SgRNA_{(-)}] \to [SgRNA_{(-)}] - 1$	$d_{SgRNA_{(-)}}[SgRNA_{(-)}]$
	Transcription	
20	$[RNA_{NP}] \to [RNA_{NP}] + 1$	$k_{transcr_{NP}}(l_{NP})^{-1}[SgRNA_{(-)}^{init}]\theta_{RdRp}\theta_{inhib}$
21	$[RNA_{NP}] \to [RNA_{NP}] - 1$	$d_{RNA_{NP}}[RNA_{NP}]$
22	$[RNA_{GPC}] \to [RNA_{GPC}] + 1$	$k_{transcr}(l_{GPC})^{-1}[SgRNA_{(+)}]\theta_{RdRp}\theta_{inhib}$
23	$[RNA_{GPC}] \to [RNA_{GPC}] - 1$	$d_{RNA_{GPC}}[RNA_{GPC}]$
24	$[RNA_Z] \to [RNA_Z] + 1$	$k_{transcr}(l_Z)^{-1}[LgRNA_{(+)}]\theta_{RdRp}\theta_{inhib}$
25	$[RNA_Z] \to [RNA_Z] - 1$	$d_{RNA_Z}[RNA_Z]$
26	$[RNA_L] \to [RNA_L] + 1$	$k_{transcr}(l_L)^{-1}[LgRNA_{(-)}^{init}]\theta_{RdRp}\theta_{inhib}$
27	$[RNA_L] \to [RNA_L] - 1$	$d_{RNA_L}[RNA_L]$

Table 1. Cont.

m	Elementary Reaction	Transition Intensity, a_m
		Translation
28	$[NP] \to [NP] + 1$	$k_{transl}(l_{NP})^{-1}[RNA_{NP}]$
29	$[NP] \to [NP] - 1$	$d_{NP}[NP]$
30	$[GPC] \to [GPC] + 1$	$k_{transl}(l_{GPC})^{-1}[RNA_{GPC}]$
31	$[GPC] \to [GPC] - 1$	$d_{GPC}[GPC]$
32	$[Z] \to [Z] + 1$	$k_{translZ}(l_Z)^{-1}[RNA_Z]$
33	$[Z] \to [Z] - 1$	$d_Z[Z]$
34	$[L] \to [L] + 1$	$k_{transl}(l_L)^{-1}[RNA_L]$
35	$[L] \to [L] - 1$	$d_L[L]$
		Assembly and release
36	$[NP\text{-}LgRNA_{(-)}] \to [NP\text{-}LgRNA_{(-)}] - 1$	$d_{NP\text{-}LgRNA_{(-)}}[NP\text{-}LgRNA_{(-)}]$
37	$[NP\text{-}SgRNA_{(-)}] \to [NP\text{-}SgRNA_{(-)}] - 1$	$d_{NP\text{-}SgRNA_{(-)}}[NP\text{-}SgRNA_{(-)}]$
38	$[GPC] \to ([GPC] - n_{GPC}) \vee 0$, $[Z] \to ([Z] - n_Z) \vee 0$, $[L] \to ([L] - n_L) \vee 0$, $[NP\text{-}LgRNA_{(-)}] \to [NP\text{-}LgRNA_{(-)}] - 1$, $[NP\text{-}SgRNA_{(-)}] \to [NP\text{-}SgRNA_{(-)}] - 1$, $[V_{assembled}] \to [V_{assembled}] + 1$	$k_{assemb}\theta_{assemb}[NP\text{-}SgRNA_{(-)}][NP\text{-}LgRNA_{(-)}]$
39	$[V_{assembled}] \to [V_{assembled}] - 1$, $[V_{released}] \to [V_{released}] - 1$	$k_{release}[V_{assembled}]$
40	$[V_{assembled}] \to [V_{assembled}] - 1$	$d_{assembled}[V_{assembled}]$
41	$[V_{released}] \to [V_{released}] - 1$	$d_V[V_{released}]$

2.5. Sensitivity Analysis

To examine the relationship between the net production of LCMV and the parameters of the intracellular biochemical reactions, we used the sensitivity analysis. Two characteristics of the virus net growth were considered: (i) The cumulative number of released virions and (ii) the total number of new virions secreted by an infected cell during time T (20 h) from the beginning of infection (thus, disregarding their degradation). The first one is denoted as $\Phi_{AUC}(\mathbf{y}(\mathbf{p}))$ and is calculated as an area under the model solution $\mathbf{y}(\mathbf{p})$ component curve, i.e., the integral of the solution component $[V_{released}]$ with respect to the time variable t on an interval $[0, T]$. The second characteristic is denoted $\Phi_{total}(\mathbf{y}(\mathbf{p}))$ and is calculated as the integral of the release rate of assembled virions $k_{release}[V_{assembled}]$. Computationally, we follow our previous approach [47] to analyse the local sensitivity of the total number of released virions, i.e., functional $\Phi_{AUC}(\mathbf{y}(\mathbf{p})) = \int_0^T [V_{released}]dt = [V_{AUC}(T)]$, and the total number of produced virions, functional $\Phi_{total}(\mathbf{y}(\mathbf{p})) = \int_0^T k_{release}[V_{assembled}]dt = [V_{total}(T)]$, for $T = 20$ h. The local sensitivity analysis was performed via the adjoint equations method implemented in Julia using the DiffEqSensitivity library. To compare contributions of the biochemical processes, the sensitivity coefficients were multiplied by the corresponding parameter values. The results were ranked by decreasing absolute values and visualized as histograms (separately for negative and positive derivatives).

3. Mathematical Model

In this section, we present the deterministic ODE-based model of the LCMV life cycle by adapting the approach used in our previous work, which focused on modeling the ontogeny of another RNA virus, namely SARS-CoV-2 [48]. The notation for the time-dependent variables is introduced that is lately used for the formulation of the stochastic model. The calibrated deterministic model parameters and functional forms of the calibrated reaction kinetics are transformed into the propensities of the respective transitions of the MCMC-based stochastic model, as described in Section 2.4.

3.1. Deterministic Model of Intracellular LCMV Replication

The LCMV life cycle shown in Figure 2 suggests the following set of time-dependent variables listed in Table 2. The ordinary differential equations (ODEs) are used to model the key replication steps, which include: (a) cell entry, (b) replication, (c) transcription, (d) translation of proteins, and (e) assembly and release of virions. The system of equations was formulated using the basic principles of chemical kinetics, especially the mass action law and Michaelis–Menten parameterization for describing the assembly, coating, replication and transcription processes.

Table 2. Time-dependent variables and their biochemical meaning.

Variable	Meaning
$[V_{free}]$	Free virions outside the cell membrane
$[V_{bound}]$	Virions bound to α-DG receptor
$[V_{endosome}]$	Virions in endosomes
$[LgRNA_{(-)}^{init}]$	L negative genomic RNAs, released from virions, that infect the cell
$[SgRNA_{(-)}^{init}]$	S negative genomic RNAs, released from virions, that infect the cell
$[LgRNA_{(+)}]$	L positive genomic RNAs
$[SgRNA_{(+)}]$	S positive genomic RNAs
$[LgRNA_{(-)}]$	L negative genomic RNAs
$[SgRNA_{(-)}]$	S negative genomic RNAs
$[RNA_{NP}]$	NP RNAs
$[RNA_{GPC}]$	GPC RNAs
$[RNA_Z]$	Z RNAs
$[RNA_L]$	L RNAs
$[NP]$	NP proteins
$[Z]$	Z proteins
$[L]$	L proteins
$[GPC]$	GPC proteins
$[NP\text{-}LgRNA_{(-)}]$	$LgRNA_{(-)}$ coated with NP
$[NP\text{-}SgRNA_{(-)}]$	$SgRNA_{(-)}$ coated with NP
$[V_{assembled}]$	Assembled virions in endosomes
$[V_{released}]$	Virions released via exocytosis

3.2. Cell Entry

The rate of change of the number of free, bound and endosome virions is described by the following three ODEs.

$$\frac{d[V_{free}]}{dt} = -k_{bind}[V_{free}] - d_V[V_{free}] + k_{diss}[V_{bound}] \quad (1)$$

The first term describes binding free virions to the receptor; it means that $[V_{free}]$ become $[V_{bound}]$ with constant k_{bind}. The second one corresponds to free virion degradation with constant d_V. The last term depicts the dissociation of bound virions from the receptor; it means that $[V_{bound}]$ become $[V_{free}]$ with rate constant k_{diss}.

$$\frac{d[V_{bound}]}{dt} = k_{bind}[V_{free}] - \left(k_{fuse} + k_{diss} + d_V\right)[V_{bound}] \quad (2)$$

The first term describes binding free virions to the receptor; it means that $[V_{free}]$ become $[V_{bound}]$ with constant k_{bind}. The second term explains the fusion of bound virions; it means that $[V_{bound}]$ become $[V_{endosome}]$ with constant k_{fuse}. The third term depicts dissociation of bound virions from the receptor; it means that $[V_{bound}]$ become $[V_{free}]$ with constant k_{diss}. The last term illustrates the degradation rate of bound virions with constant d_V.

$$\frac{d[V_{endosome}]}{dt} = k_{fuse}[V_{bound}] - (k_{uncoat} + d_{endosome})[V_{endosome}] \tag{3}$$

The first term describes the fusion of bound virions; it means that $[V_{bound}]$ become $[V_{endosome}]$ with constant k_{fuse}. The second term explains the uncoating of virions in endosomes; it means that $[V_{endosome}]$ uncoat with constant k_{uncoat}; thus, the number of virions in endosomes decreases. The last term depicts the degradation of viruses in endosomes with constant $d_{endosome}$.

3.3. Replication of Genomic RNAs

The rate of change of the number of L negative genomic RNAs, S negative genomic RNAs, L positive genomic RNAs, L positive genomic RNAs, L negative genomic RNAs and S negative genomic RNAs is modelled using the equations listed below.

$$\frac{d\left[LgRNA_{(-)}^{init}\right]}{dt} = k_{uncoat}[V_{endosome}] - d_{LgRNA_{(-)}}\left[LgRNA_{(-)}^{init}\right] \tag{4}$$

The first term describes the uncoating of viruses in endosomes; it results in the $[V_{endosome}]$ decline and appearance of $[LgRNA_{(-)}^{init}]$ with constant k_{uncoat}. The second term depicts the degradation of $[LgRNA_{(-)}^{init}]$ with the rate constant $d_{LgRNA_{(-)}}$.

$$\frac{d\left[SgRNA_{(-)}^{init}\right]}{dt} = k_{uncoat}[V_{endosome}] - d_{SgRNA_{(-)}}\left[SgRNA_{(-)}^{init}\right] \tag{5}$$

The first term describes the uncoating of viruses in endosomes; it results in $[V_{endosome}]$ decline and appearance of $[SgRNA_{(-)}^{init}]$ with constant k_{uncoat}. The second term depicts degradation of $[SgRNA_{(-)}^{init}]$ with constant $d_{SgRNA_{(-)}}$.

$$\frac{d\left[LgRNA_{(+)}\right]}{dt} = k_{repl_{(+)}}(l_{LgRNA})^{-1}\left[LgRNA_{(-)}^{init}\right] - d_{LgRNA_{(+)}}\left[LgRNA_{(+)}\right] \tag{6}$$

The first term describes replication; L protein (RdRp) produces $[LgRNA_{(+)}]$ using $[LgRNA_{(-)}^{init}]$ as a template in the Michaelis–Menten type of reaction with constant $k_{repl_{(+)}}$ and K_{RdRp} (Michaelis constant—concentration of RNA at which the reaction rate is half-maximal). Also, the term is normalized by the length of the L segment l_{LgRNA}; since we obtain the length of the synthesized chain in nucleotides to obtain the number of copies, we need to divide by the length of the chain. The second term describes the degradation of $[LgRNA_{(+)}]$ with constant $d_{LgRNA_{(+)}}$.

$$\frac{d\left[SgRNA_{(+)}\right]}{dt} = k_{repl_{(+)}}(l_{SgRNA})^{-1}\left[SgRNA_{(-)}^{init}\right] - d_{SgRNA_{(+)}}\left[SgRNA_{(+)}\right] \tag{7}$$

The first term describes replication; the initial L protein (RdRp) produces $[SgRNA_{(+)}]$ using $[SgRNA_{(-)}^{init}]$ as a template in reaction with constant $k_{repl_{(+)}}$. Also, the term is normalized by the length of the S segment l_{SgRNA}; since we obtain the length of the synthesized chain in nucleotides to obtain the number of copies, we need to divide by the length of the chain. The second term describes the degradation rate of $[SgRNA_{(+)}]$ with constant $d_{SgRNA_{(+)}}$.

$$\frac{d[LgRNA_{(-)}]}{dt} = k_{repl_{(-)}}(l_{LgRNA})^{-1}[LgRNA_{(+)}]\theta_{RdRp}\theta_{inhib} \\ - \left(d_{LgRNA_{(-)}} + k_{complex}\theta_{complex}\right)[LgRNA_{(-)}] \qquad (8)$$

The first term describes replication; the initial L protein (RdRp) produces $[LgRNA_{(-)}]$ using $[LgRNA_{(+)}]$ as a template with constant $k_{repl_{(-)}}$. Also, this term is multiplied by θ_{inhib}. It indicates that Z inhibits L. Then, the term is normalized by the length of the L segment l_{LgRNA}, since we obtain the length of the synthesized chain in nucleotides to obtain the number of copies, we need to divide by the length of the chain. The second term explains the degradation rate of $[LgRNA_{(-)}]$ with constant $d_{LgRNA_{(-)}}$. The third term depicts the coating of RNA with a NP protein; the number of $[LgRNA_{(-)}]$ declines because it is coated with NP protein in the Michaelis–Menten type of reaction with reaction constant $k_{complex}$ and K_{NP} (Michaelis constant—concentration of NP protein at which the reaction rate is half-maximal). The following notation is used for taking into account saturation effects:

$$\theta_{inhib} = \frac{K_I}{K_I + Z}, \quad \theta_{RdRp} = \frac{[L]}{[L] + K_{RdRp}}, \quad \theta_{complex} = \frac{[NP]}{[NP] + K_{NP}}. \qquad (9)$$

$$\frac{d[SgRNA_{(-)}]}{dt} = k_{repl_{(-)}}(l_{SgRNA})^{-1}[SgRNA_{(+)}]\theta_{RdRp}\theta_{inhib} \\ - \left(d_{SgRNA_{(-)}} + k_{complex}\theta_{complex}\right)[SgRNA_{(-)}] \qquad (10)$$

In the above equation, the first term describes replication; the L protein (RdRp) produces $[SgRNA_{(-)}]$ using $[SgRNA_{(+)}]$ as a template in the Michaelis–Menten type of reaction with constant $k_{repl_{(-)}}$ and K_{RdRp} (Michaelis constant—concentration of RNA at which the reaction rate is half-maximal). Also, this term is multiplied by θ_{inhib}. It indicates that Z inhibits L. Also, the term is normalized by the length of the S segment l_{SgRNA}; since we obtain the length of the synthesized chain in nucleotides, to obtain the number of copies, we need to divide by the length of the chain. The second term describes the degradation of $[SgRNA_{(-)}]$ with constant $d_{SgRNA_{(-)}}$. The last term depicts the coating of RNA with NP protein, $[SgRNA_{(-)}]$ declines, because it coats with the NP protein in the Michaelis–Menten type of reaction with reaction constant $k_{complex}$ and K_{NP} (Michaelis constant—concentration of NP protein at which the reaction rate is half-maximal).

3.4. Transcription

To describe the transcription of matrix RNAs, the following equations are used.

$$\frac{d[RNA_{NP}]}{dt} = k_{transcrNP}(l_{NP})^{-1}\left[SgRNA_{(-)}^{init}\right]\theta_{RdRp}\theta_{inhib} - d_{RNA_{NP}}[RNA_{NP}] \qquad (11)$$

The first term accounts for transcription; the L protein (RdRp) produces NP RNA using $[SgRNA_{(-)}]$ as a template in the Michaelis–Menten type of reaction with constant $k_{transcrNP}$ and K_{RdRp} (Michaelis constant—concentration of RNA at which the reaction rate is half-maximal). Also, the term is normalized by the length of the NP RNA l_{NP}, since we obtain the length of the synthesized chain in nucleotides; to obtain the number of RNAs, we need to divide by the length of the RNA. In addition, this term is multiplied by θ_{inhib}. It indicates that Z inhibits L. The second term is responsible for the degradation of NP RNA with rate constant $d_{RNA_{NP}}$.

$$\frac{d[RNA_{GPC}]}{dt} = k_{transcr}(l_{GPC})^{-1}[SgRNA_{(+)}]\theta_{RdRp}\theta_{inhib} - d_{RNA_{GPC}}[RNA_{GPC}] \qquad (12)$$

The first term corresponds to transcription; the L protein (RdRp) produces GPC RNA using $[SgRNA_{(+)}]$ as a template in the Michaelis–Menten type of reaction with constant $k_{transcr}$ and K_{RdRp} (Michaelis constant—concentration of RNA at which the reaction rate is half-maximal). Also, this term is multiplied by θ_{inhib}. It indicates that Z inhibits L. Also, the term is normalized by the length of the GPC RNA l_{GPC}, since we obtain the length of the synthesized chain in nucleotides; to obtain the number of RNAs, we need to divide by the length of the RNA. The second term depicts the degradation rate of GPC RNA with constant $d_{RNA_{GPC}}$.

$$\frac{d[RNA_Z]}{dt} = k_{transcr}(l_Z)^{-1}\left[LgRNA_{(+)}\right]\theta_{RdRp}\theta_{inhib} - d_{RNA_Z}[RNA_Z] \qquad (13)$$

The first term accounts for transcription; the L protein (RdRp) produces Z RNA using $[LgRNA_{(+)}]$ as a template in the Michaelis–Menten type of reaction with constant $k_{transcr}$ and K_{RdRp} (Michaelis constant—concentration of RNA at which the reaction rate is half-maximal). Also, this term is multiplied by θ_{inhib}. It indicates that Z inhibits L. Also, the term is normalized by the length of the Z RNA l_Z, since we obtain the length of the synthesized chain in nucleotides; to obtain the number of RNAs, we need to divide by the length of the RNA. The second term is responsible for the degradation of Z RNA with constant d_{RNA_Z}.

$$\frac{d[RNA_L]}{dt} = k_{transcr}(l_L)^{-1}\left[LgRNA_{(-)}^{init}\right]\theta_{RdRp}\theta_{inhib} - d_{RNA_L}[RNA_L] \qquad (14)$$

The first term describes transcription; the L protein (RdRp) produces L RNA using $[LgRNA_{(-)}]$ as a template in the Michaelis–Menten type of reaction with constant $k_{transcr}$ and K_{RdRp} (Michaelis constant—concentration of RNA at which the reaction rate is half-maximal). Also, this term is multiplied by θ_{inhib}. It indicates that Z inhibits L. Also, the term is normalized by the length of the L RNA l_L, since we obtain the length of the synthesized chain in nucleotides; to obtain the number of RNAs, we need to divide by the length of the RNA. The second term describes the degradation rate of L RNA with constant d_{RNA_L}.

3.5. Translation

The rate of change of the abundance of viral proteins is modelled using the equations listed below.

$$\frac{d[NP]}{dt} = k_{transl}(l_{NP})^{-1}[RNA_{NP}] - d_{NP}[NP]$$
$$-k_{complex}n_{NP}\theta_{complex}\left(\left[LgRNA_{(-)}\right] + \left[SgRNA_{(-)}\right]\right) \qquad (15)$$

The first term is responsible for the translation of the NP protein from NP RNA: ribosomes synthesize the NP protein using the NP RNA with constant k_{transl} that characterizes the general rate of translation in the number of nucleotides passed per hour, which is divided by the length of NP RNA l_{NP} to specify that the production of one protein is equal to passing through that particular protein's RNA (through its length). The second term corresponds to the degradation of the NP protein with constant d_{NP}. The third term accounts for the coating of RNA with the NP protein; NP coats $[SgRNA_{(-)}]$ and $[LgRNA_{(-)}]$ in the Michaelis–Menten type of reaction with reaction constant $k_{complex}$ and K_{NP} (Michaelis constant—concentration of NP protein at which the reaction rate is half of the maximum). Also, the term is multiplied by n_{NP}, because this term describes the rate of genome RNA decline; thus, to turn it to the NP decline rate, the term should be multiplied by the number of NP proteins per virion (one virion—one L and one S genome RNA).

$$\frac{d[Z]}{dt} = k_{uncoat}m_Z[V_{endosome}] + k_{translZ}(l_Z)^{-1}[RNA_Z] - d_Z[Z]$$
$$-k_{assemb}n_Z\theta_{assemb}\left[NP\text{-}SgRNA_{(-)}\right]\left[NP\text{-}LgRNA_{(-)}\right] \qquad (16)$$

The first term describes the unpackaging of the initial Z protein from the $[V_{endosome}]$ ($m_Z = n_Z$ number of Z proteins per virion) with constant k_{uncoat}. The second term describes the translation of the Z protein from the Z RNA: ribosomes synthesize the Z protein using Z RNA with constant $k_{translZ}$, which characterizes the general rate of translation in the number of nucleotides passed per hour; this is divided by the length of Z RNA l_Z, specifying that the production of one protein is equal to passing through particular protein's RNA (through its length). The third term describes the degradation rate of the Z protein with constant d_Z. The last term accounts for virion assembly—it is regarded as a reaction with constant k_{assemb} between all components of the virion (coated RNA and all proteins). Also, the term is multiplied by n_Z; because this term describes the assembled virions' production rate, to turn it to the Z decline rate, the term should be multiplied by the number of Z proteins per virion. The saturation of the assembly process is parameterized using the product of Michaelis–Menten type functions:

$$\theta_{assemb} = \frac{[Z]}{[Z] + K_Z} \frac{[L]}{[L] + K_L} \frac{[GPC]}{[GPC] + K_{GPC}}. \qquad (17)$$

$$\begin{aligned}\frac{d[L]}{dt} &= k_{uncoat} m_L [V_{endosome}] + k_{transl}(l_L)^{-1}[RNA_L] - d_L[L] \\ &\quad - k_{assemb} n_L \theta_{assemb} \left[NP\text{-}SgRNA_{(-)}\right]\left[NP\text{-}LgRNA_{(-)}\right]\end{aligned} \qquad (18)$$

The first term describes the unpackaging of the initial L protein from $[V_{endosome}]$ ($m_L = n_L$ number of L proteins per virion) with constant k_{uncoat}. The second term is responsible for the translation of the L protein from L RNA. Ribosomes synthesize the L protein using the L RNA with constant k_{transl} that characterizes the general rate of translation in the number of nucleotides passed per hour, which is divided by the length of L RNA l_L to specify that the production of one protein is equal to passing through the particular protein's RNA (through its length). The third term accounts for the degradation rate of the L protein with constant d_L. The last term describes virion assembly—it is regarded as a reaction with constant k_{assemb} between all components of virion (coated RNA and all proteins). Also, the term is multiplied by n_L, because this term describes assembled virions' production rate; thus, to turn it to the L decline rate, the term should be multiplied by the number of L proteins per virion.

$$\begin{aligned}\frac{d[GPC]}{dt} &= k_{uncoat} m_{GPC} [V_{endosome}] + k_{transl}(l_{GPC})^{-1}[RNA_{GPC}] - d_{GPC}[GPC] \\ &\quad - k_{assemb} n_{GPC} \theta_{assemb} \left[NP\text{-}SgRNA_{(-)}\right]\left[NP\text{-}LgRNA_{(-)}\right]\end{aligned} \qquad (19)$$

The first term describes the unpackaging of the initial GPC protein from $[V_{endosome}]$ ($m_{GPC} = n_{GPC}$ is the number of GPC proteins per virion) with constant k_{uncoat}. The second term describes the translation of the GPC protein from GPC RNA; ribosomes synthesize the GPC protein using GPC RNA with constant k_{transl} that characterizes the general rate of translation in the number of nucleotides passed per hour, which is divided by the length of GPC RNA l_{GPC} to specify that the production of one protein is equal to passing through the particular protein's RNA (through its length). The third term depicts the degradation rate of the GPC protein with constant d_{GPC}. The last term indicates the virion assembly—it is regarded as a reaction with constant k_{assemb} between all components of the virion (coated RNA and all proteins). Also, the term is multiplied by n_{GPC}, because this term describes the assembled virions' production rate; thus, to relate to the GPC decline rate, the term should be multiplied by the number of GPC proteins per virion.

3.6. Assembly and Release of Virions

To model the rate of change of the assembled and released virions, we formulate the following equations.

$$\frac{d[NP\text{-}LgRNA_{(-)}]}{dt} = -k_{assemb}\theta_{assemb}\left[NP\text{-}SgRNA_{(-)}\right]\left[NP\text{-}LgRNA_{(-)}\right] \\ - d_{NP\text{-}LgRNA_{(-)}}[NP\text{-}LgRNA_{(-)}] + k_{complex}\theta_{complex}[LgRNA_{(-)}] \quad (20)$$

The first term describes the virion assembly—it is regarded as a reaction with constant k_{assemb} between all components of the virion (coated RNA and all proteins). This term describes the assembled virions' production rate; thus, it is equal to the coated RNA decline rate. The second term describes the degradation rate of coated $[LgRNA_{(-)}]$ with constant $d_{NP\text{-}LgRNA_{(-)}}$. The third term indicates the coating of $[LgRNA_{(-)}]$ with the NP protein: the number of $[NP\text{-}LgRNA_{(-)}]$ increases because $[LgRNA_{(-)}]$ coats with the NP protein in the Michaelis–Menten type of reaction with reaction constant $k_{complex}$ and K_{NP} (Michaelis constant—concentration of NP protein at which the reaction rate is half-maximal).

$$\frac{d[NP\text{-}SgRNA_{(-)}]}{dt} = -k_{assemb}\theta_{assemb}\left[NP\text{-}SgRNA_{(-)}\right]\left[NP\text{-}LgRNA_{(-)}\right] \\ - d_{NP\text{-}SgRNA_{(-)}}[NP\text{-}SgRNA_{(-)}] + k_{complex}\theta_{complex}[SgRNA_{(-)}] \quad (21)$$

The first term is responsible for virion assembly—it is regarded as a reaction with constant k_{assemb} between all components of virion (coated RNA and all proteins). This term describes the assembled virions' production rate; thus, it is equal to the coated RNA decline rate. The second term indicates the degradation rate of coated $[SgRNA_{(-)}]$ with constant $d_{NP\text{-}SgRNA_{(-)}}$. The third term describes the coating of $[SgRNA_{(-)}]$ with the NP protein: the number of $[NP\text{-}SgRNA_{(-)}]$ increases because $[SgRNA_{(-)}]$ coats with the NP protein in the Michaelis–Menten type of reaction with reaction constant $k_{complex}$ and K_{NP} (Michaelis constant—concentration of NP protein at which the reaction rate is half-maximal).

$$\frac{d[V_{assembled}]}{dt} = k_{assemb}\theta_{assemb}\left[NP\text{-}SgRNA_{(-)}\right]\left[NP\text{-}LgRNA_{(-)}\right] \\ - (k_{release} + d_{assembled})[V_{assembled}] \quad (22)$$

The first term is responsible for virion assembly—it is regarded as the reaction with constant k_{assemb} between all components of virion (coated RNA and all proteins), but the Z protein is considered as the main assembly protein; therefore, it was used as an "enzyme" in the Michaelis–Menten equation. The second term depicts the release of assembled virions: $[V_{assembled}]$ turn to $[V_{released}]$ with constant $k_{release}$. The third term indicates the degradation rate of assembled virions with constant $d_{assembled}$.

$$\frac{d[V_{released}]}{dt} = k_{release}[V_{assembled}] - d_V[V_{released}] \quad (23)$$

The first term describes the release of assembled virions: $[V_{assembled}]$ turn to $[V_{released}]$ with constant $k_{release}$. The second term accounts for the degradation of released virions with constant d_V.

3.7. Calibration of LCMV Replication Model

The parameters of the model were quantified to match the model solution to empirical data described in Section 2, with the initial guesses for model parameters based on our previous models of SARS-CoV-2 and HIV-1 replication [47,48]. There are no experimental data for the degradation kinetics of LCMV virions in free, bound and endosomal states. We have, therefore, used the simplifying assumption that the degradation rates of free and bound virions are the same, and similar to those estimated for SARS-CoV-2, as described in reference [48]. This assumed rate then matches the description for Influenza viruses, for which around 50% of virions fail to release the virus genome upon cell entry [49].

The overall set of parameters is presented in Table 3.

Table 3. Description of the model parameters.

Parameter	Description, Units	Value	Refs.
k_{bind}	Rate of virion binding to α-DG receptor, h^{-1}	10	[48]
d_V	Clearance rate of extracellular virions, h^{-1}	0.1	[48]
k_{diss}	Dissociation rate constant of bound virions, h^{-1}	0.51	[48]
k_{fuse}	Fusion rate constant, h^{-1}	0.52	[48]
k_{uncoat}	Uncoating rate constant, h^{-1}	0.49	[48]
$d_{endosome}$	Degradation rate of virions in endosomes, h^{-1}	0.05	[48]
$d_{LgRNA_{(-)}}$	Degradation rate of negative sense L RNAs in cell, h^{-1}	0.1	[48]
$d_{SgRNA_{(-)}}$	Degradation rate of negative sense S RNAs in cell, h^{-1}	0.1	[48]
$d_{LgRNA_{(+)}}$	Degradation rate of positive sense L RNAs in cell, h^{-1}	0.1	[48]
$d_{SgRNA_{(+)}}$	Degradation rate of positive sense S RNAs in cell, h^{-1}	0.1	[48]
$k_{repl(+)}$	Replication rate of positive sense RNAs, copies · nt/(mRNA · h)	340	[48]
$k_{repl(-)}$	Replication rate of negative sense RNAs, copies · nt/(mRNA · h)	$13.6 \cdot 10^6$	[48]
$k_{complex}$	Rate of the nucleocapsid formation $[NP\text{-}gRNA]$, h^{-1}	0.3	[48]
K_{NP}	Threshold number of NP proteins at which nucleocapsid formation slows down, molecules	$5 \cdot 10^6$	[48]
K_Z	Threshold number of Z proteins at which assembly slows down, molecules	450	[40]
K_L	Threshold number of L proteins at which assembly slows down, molecules	25	[40]
K_{GPC}	Threshold number of GPC proteins at which assembly slows down, molecules	670	[40]
K_{RdRp}	Threshold number of RNA enhancing RNA transcription and replication, molecules	20	[40]
K_I	Threshold number of Z molecules for half-maximal inhibition of L, molecules	$5 \cdot 10^4$	[20]
$k_{transcr}$	Transcription rate of RNAs, copies copies · nt/(mRNA · h)	$7 \cdot 10^5$	adjusted
$k_{transcrNP}$	Transcription rate of NP RNAs, copies copies · nt/(mRNA · h)	$2.1 \cdot 10^6$	adjusted
$d_{RNA_{NP}}$	Degradation rate of NP RNA in cell, h^{-1}	0.31	[48]
d_{RNA_Z}	Degradation rate of Z RNA in cell, h^{-1}	0.3	[48]
d_{RNA_L}	Degradation rate of L RNA in cell, h^{-1}	0.32	[48]
$d_{RNA_{GPC}}$	Degradation rate of GPC RNA in cell, h^{-1}	0.29	[48]
k_{assemb}	Rate of virion assembly, h^{-1}	1	[48]
k_{transl}	Translation rate, nt/mRNA h^{-1}	$4.5 \cdot 10^4$	[48]
$k_{translZ}$	Translation rate of Z, nt/mRNA h^{-1}	2250	[48]
d_{NP}	Degradation rate of NP protein in cell, h^{-1}	0.021	[48]
d_Z	Degradation rate of Z protein in cell, h^{-1}	0.03	[48]
d_L	Degradation rate of L protein in cell, h^{-1}	0.04	[48]
d_{GPC}	Degradation rate of GPC protein in cell, h^{-1}	0.022	[48]
$d_{NP\text{-}LgRNA_{(-)}}$	Degradation rate of ribonucleoprotein of $LgRNA_{(-)}$, h^{-1}	0.2	[48]
$d_{NP\text{-}SgRNA_{(-)}}$	Degradation rate of ribonucleoprotein of $SgRNA_{(-)}$, h^{-1}	0.2	[48]
$k_{release}$	Rate of virion release via exocytosis, h^{-1}	7	[48]
$d_{assembled}$	Assembled virion degradation rate, h^{-1}	0.07	[48]
n_{NP}	Number of NP protein per virion, molecules	1500	[40]
n_Z	Number of Z protein per virion, molecules	450	[40]

Table 3. *Cont.*

Parameter	Description, Units	Value	Refs.
n_L	Number of L protein per virion, molecules	25	[40]
n_{GPC}	Number of GPC protein per virion, molecules	670	[40]
l_{NP}	Length of RNA genome coding NP protein, nt	1674	[50]
l_Z	Length of RNA genome coding Z protein, nt	270	[50]
l_L	Length of RNA genome coding L protein, nt	6630	[50]
l_{GPC}	Length of RNA genome coding GPC protein, nt	1494	[50]
l_{SgRNA}	Length of S segment of genomic RNA, nt	3400	[50]
l_{LgRNA}	Length of L segment of genomic RNA, nt	7200	[50]
m_Z	Number of Z proteins, initially released to the cell from $V_{endosome}$, molecules	450	[40]
m_L	Number of L proteins, initially released to the cell from $V_{endosome}$, molecules	25	[40]
m_{GPC}	Number of GPC proteins, initially released to the cell from $V_{endosome}$, molecules	670	[40]

The corresponding solution of the deterministic model predicting the replication dynamics of LCMV in a single replication cycle is shown in Figure 4.

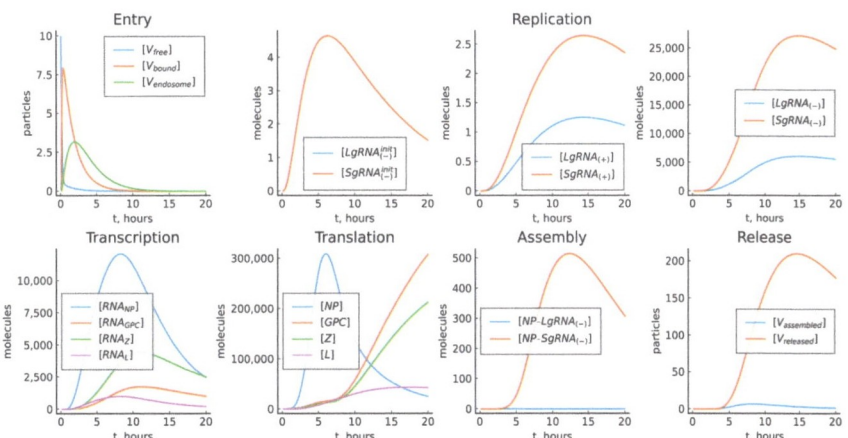

Figure 4. Reference model solution with parameters estimated in Table 3, $[V_{free}](0) = 10$.

3.8. Stochastic Model

The Gillespie-based stochastic model of LCMV replication is derived using the elementary reactions terms of the deterministic equations as shown in Table 1.

The summary statistics of an ensemble of 10,000 realizations of the stochastic model is shown in Figure 5.

The predicted variability of the LCMV replication indicates that the uncertainty in the dynamics of released virions is much larger than that of the assembled ones. The same observation applies to $[SgRNA_{(-)}]$ versus $[LgRNA_{(-)}]$ and $[NP\text{-}SgRNA_{(-)}]$ versus $[NP\text{-}LgRNA_{(-)}]$.

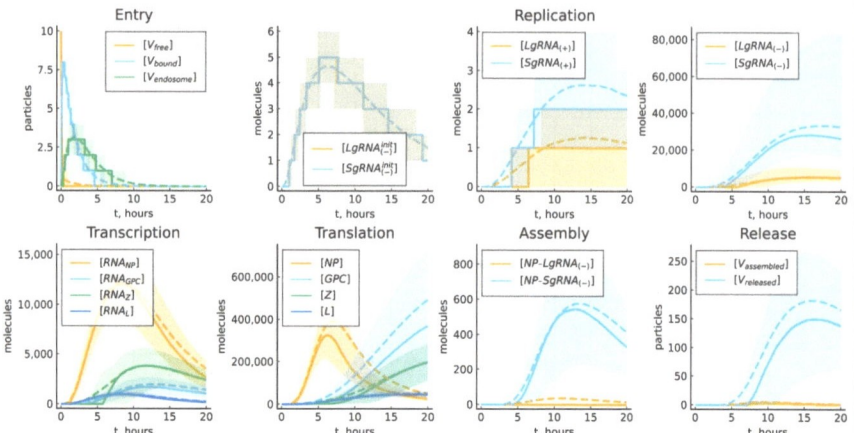

Figure 5. Statistics of an ensemble of 10,000 realizations of the stochastic model. Solid lines indicate the medians, dashed lines—mean values, and filled area—interquartile ranges.

4. Results

4.1. Implications of the Model Calibration Uncertainty

The model was calibrated to match the experimental LCMV growth curves under the assumptions that the number of the produced proteins should be determined by their presence in the infectious virions. As a consequence, we had two different values for the transcription rate constants $k_{transcr}$ and $k_{transcrNP}$, as well as for the translation rate constants k_{transl} and $k_{translZ}$. If these rate constants are set to be the same, the kinetics of the replication of viral components changes, as shown in Figure 6.

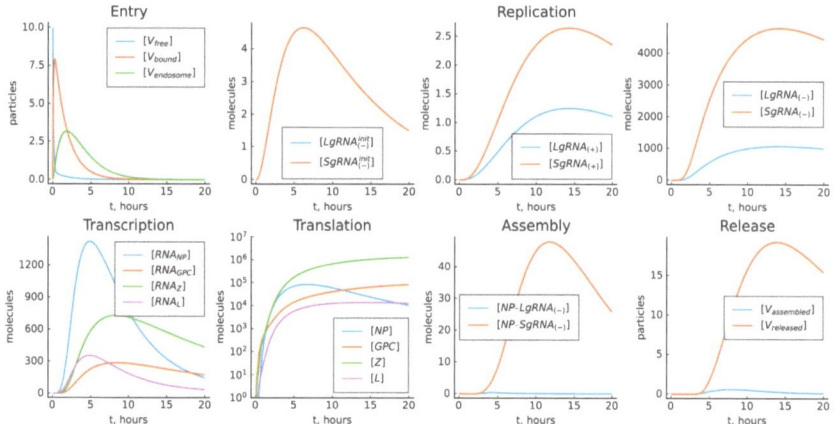

Figure 6. Model solution with parameters estimated in Table 3 except for $k_{transcr} = k_{transcrNP}$ and $k_{transl} = k_{translZ}$, $[V_{free}](0) = 10$.

4.2. Sensitivity Analysis of the Deterministic Model

By conducting a local sensitivity analysis, we can determine which parameters cause significant changes to the value of the $\Phi(y)$ functional in a small vicinity of the baseline parameters. Figure 7 displays the sensitivity indices that are normalized for their comparison by the baseline parameter values and have both negative and positive effects on the functional. The results of the local sensitivity analysis predict that the following processes have the greatest effect on the total number of produced virions:

- Translation (negative effect for Z, positive for the rest);
- Transcription (positive effect for NP, negative for the rest);
- Degradation of NP mRNA (negative effect);
- Degradation of free virions (negative effect);
- Fusion with endosomal membrane (positive effect);
- Unpacking (positive effect);
- Replication (positive effect for (+)RNA replication, negative effect for (−)RNA).

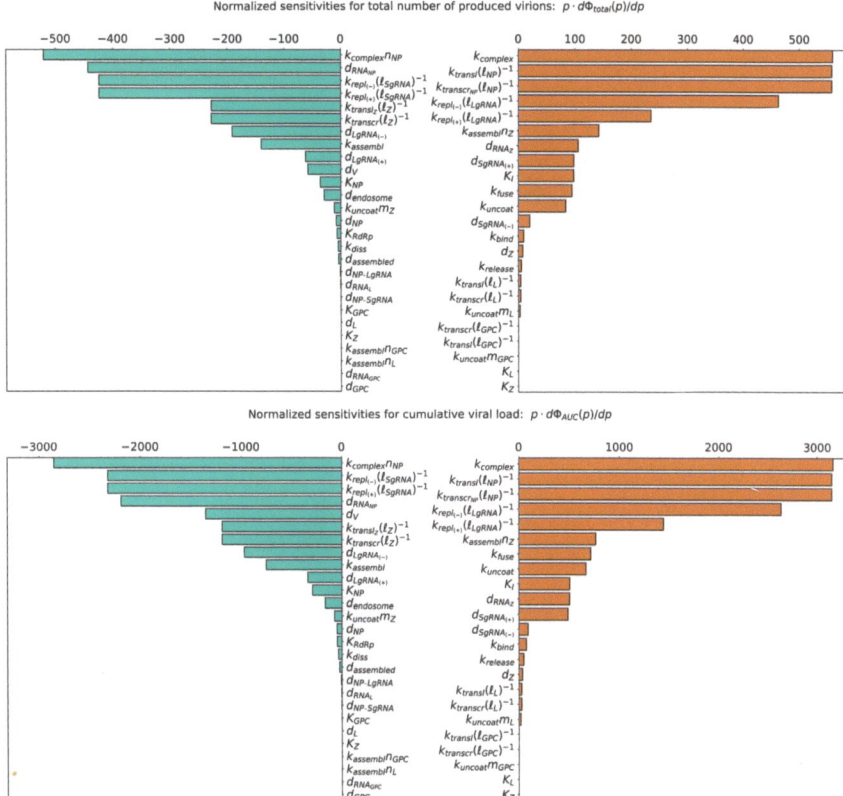

Figure 7. Model parameters ranked according to their normalized sensitivity indices. (**Top**): sensitivity towards the total number of produced virions Φ_{total}. (**Bottom**): sensitivity towards the cumulative viral load Φ_{AUC}. (**Left**): indices having negative effect. (**Right**): indices having positive effect.

4.3. Kinetic Variability of the LCMV Life Cycle

The low numbers of reaction constituents and the fluctuations in the reaction processes imply variability in the production of LCMV by an infected cell. Using the stochastic model, we estimated the uncertainty by plotting the histograms of the number of released virions, the area under the curve and the total number of produced virions over 20 h post infection, as presented in Figure 8. They indicate that a certain proportion of cell infections goes extinct (left vertical column in each histogram). Indeed, the initial stages of LCMV replication are characterized by small abundances of the reactants and a greater impact of random fluctuations on the reaction rates. In certain realizations, the degradation events can be more frequent than that of the sustaining/expanding reaction events, e.g., the turnover of genomic strands, thus resulting in an abortive infection.

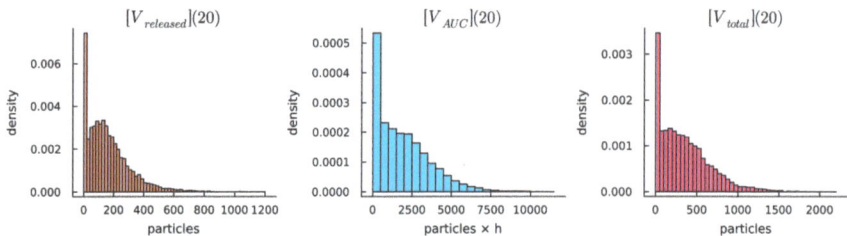

Figure 8. Variability of the virus production indices estimated by 10^4 realizations of the stochastic model. (**Left**): number of released virions. (**Center**): area under the curve. (**Right**): total number of produced virions.

4.4. Probability of Productive Infection

As some of the simulated infections of the target cells go extinct, we further quantified the probability of the productive infection for various numbers of LCMV entering the target cell, also known as MOI. The results are shown in Figure 9 (left). It is close to 0.9 for MOI = 10 and then saturates. The values of MOI affect the efficiency of the LCMV replication cycle, as one can observe from Figure 9 for the number of released (middle) and total number of produced (right) virions by 20 h.

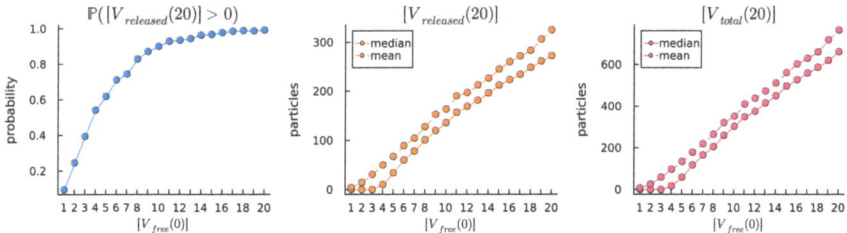

Figure 9. Probability of productive infection (**left**) and produced infectious viruses (**middle** and **right**) for various MOI estimated by 10^4 realizations of the stochastic model.

4.5. Protein-Deficient Virions

The life cycle of LCMV is characterized by some imbalance of the relative abundance of the viral proteins and genomic RNAs. As a consequence, a certain number of the secreted virions are non-infectious because of a deficiency in some of the constitutive components. The stochastic model allows one to evaluate the fraction of the respective particles known in virology as defective interfering viruses (DIPs) and the nature of the deficiency. Our model does not describe the mutations of viral RNA but only the level of completeness in the number of proteins in the assembled virions; see method details in Section 2.4. The plots in Figure 10 specify the corresponding estimates of incomplete particles in an ensemble of 10,000 realizations of the stochastic model for the baseline set of model parameter values listed in Table 3. The variability of assembled particles with respect to their protein levels is shown in Figure 11. One can observe that the assembly of complete virions is limited by the availability of GPC and Z molecules.

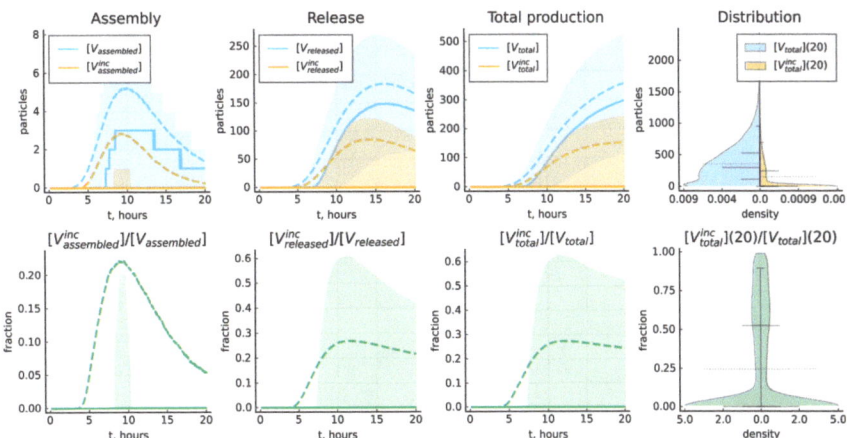

Figure 10. The kinetics of complete and incomplete virion production. **Top** panel shows the number of assembled and released virions and total number of produced virions as function of time, as well as the distribution of the total number of complete and incomplete virions throughout 20 h. **Bottom** panel shows the fraction of incomplete virions as function of time, as well as the distribution of the total number of complete and incomplete virions throughout 20 h. Solid lines indicate the median values, dashed lines—mean values and filled areas—interquartile ranges. Violin plots indicate the estimated probability density, as well as the mean values (dashed), median values and the following percentiles: 0.05, 0.25, 0.75 and 0.95. Baseline set of parameters from Table 3 is considered.

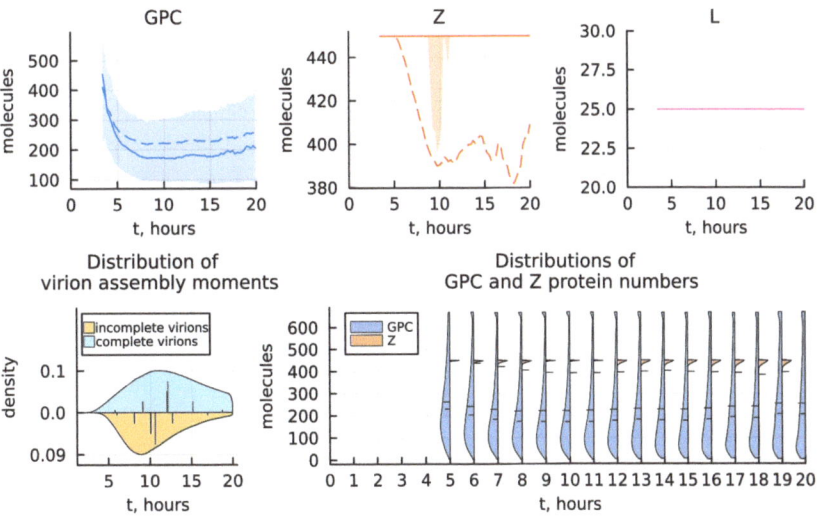

Figure 11. The kinetics of protein number distribution in incomplete virions. **Top** panel shows the number of GPC, Z and L proteins in the assembled incomplete virions as function of time. **Bottom** panel shows the distribution of virion assembly moments for complete and incomplete particles, as well as evolution of the distributions of GPC and Z protein numbers in incompletely assembled virions. Solid lines indicate the median values, dashed lines—mean values and filled areas—interquartile ranges. Violin plots indicate the estimated probability density, as well as the mean values (dashed), median values and the following percentiles: 0.05, 0.25, 0.75 and 0.95. Baseline set of parameters from Table 3 is considered.

As noted before, in calibrating the model, we assumed that the number of viral proteins should follow that of the infectious virions according to the composition of mature LCMV. To implement this assumption, the transcription and translation rates of some proteins are fixed to be different. If the assumption is relaxed, i.e., if the transcription and translation rates of all viral proteins are set to be the same, then the ensemble of stochastic realizations becomes different. The fraction of DIPs as well as the nature of the protein-related deficiencies is shown in Figures 12 and 13, respectively. In this model modification, the assembly of complete virions is limited by the availability of only GPC molecules.

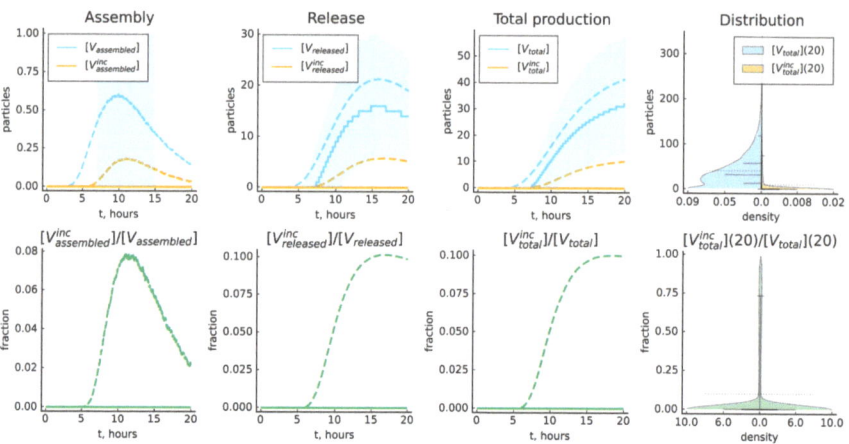

Figure 12. The kinetics of complete and incomplete virion production. **Top** panel shows the number of assembled, released virions and total number of produced virions as function of time, as well as the distribution of the total number of complete and incomplete virions throughout 20 h. **Bottom** panel shows the fraction of incomplete virions as function of time, as well as the distribution of the total number of complete and incomplete virions throughout 20 h. Solid lines indicate the median values, dashed lines—mean values and filled areas—interquantile ranges. Violin plots indicate the estimated probability density, as well as the mean values (dashed), median values and the following percentiles: 0.05, 0.25, 0.75 and 0.95. Modified set of parameters with the transcription and translation rates of all proteins being the same is considered.

Paradoxically, the fraction of incomplete particles is reduced when the protein transcription and translation rates are set as equal, i.e., ad hoc constraints are not applied. This can be linked to the fact that the assembly events by themselves are rare in this modification of the model, and the sum of incompletely and completely assembled particles which are still not released does not exceed one virion throughout the moments of the life cycle (Figure 12). The distribution of the virion assembly event moments is also altered compared to the other version of the model (Figure 13).

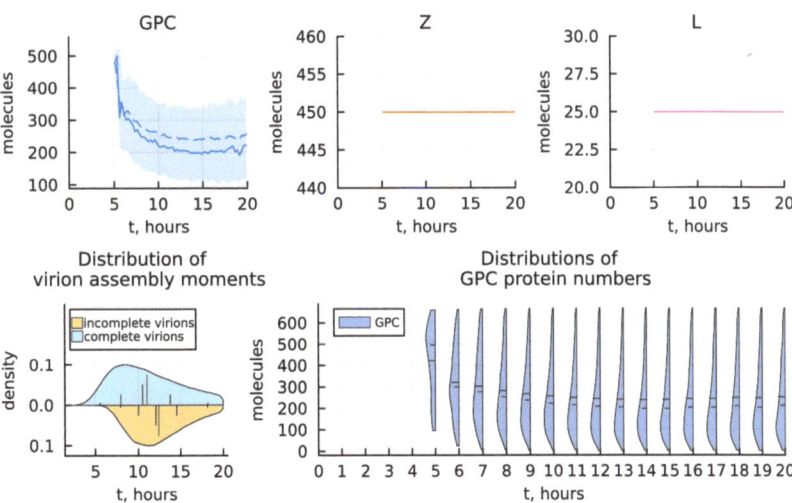

Figure 13. The kinetics of protein number distribution in incomplete virions. **Top** panel shows the number of GPC, Z and L proteins in the assembled incomplete virions as function of time. **Bottom** panel shows the distribution of virion assembly moments for complete and incomplete particles, as well as evolution of the distributions of GPC protein numbers in incompletely assembled virions. Solid lines indicate the median values, dashed lines—mean values and filled areas—interquantile ranges. Violin plots indicate the estimated probability density, as well as the mean values (dashed), median values and the following percentiles: 0.05, 0.25, 0.75 and 0.95. Modified set of parameters with the transcription and translation rates of all proteins being the same is considered.

5. Discussion

The aim of our study is to provide a complete quantitative description of the LCMV life cycle steps within an infected cell. This enables us to predict the robustness and fragility of each step with respect to the overall virus production, thus helping to identify weak spots that could be efficient targets for antiviral therapies. To generate the model, experimental data on LCMV growth in cell cultures, LCMV genome structure and replication steps, protein composition of LCMV virions as well as known rates of elementary biochemical reaction steps were used. The knowledge generated by our model goes far beyond the current qualitative understanding of the LCMV life cycle and includes novel quantitative characteristics such as the probability of productive infection, fraction of secreted protein-deficient virus particles and the variability of virus production between individual cells. Furthermore, we predict, via sensitivity analysis of the model, the particularly vulnerable steps that should be best targeted by antiviral drugs. This enables an informed screening for antiviral drugs and may reduce the underlying experimental work.

Viruses are very simple biological entities and thus share many common biochemical reaction steps in their life cycles, including viral genome replication, transcription, translation, virus particle assembly and virus release from the cell. However, they differ in genome length and arrangement, protein composition and structure. All these commonalities and differences were taken into account for the LCMV model presented here. Parameter values of the model, therefore, are a mix of some LCMV-specific parameters like protein composition, genome structure, replication stages and more general parameters that also characterise other viruses. The calibration of our model was conducted by a manual adjustment of parameter values to match the generalized kinetics of LCMV production illustrated in Figure 3 and described in Sections 2.1 and 2.2. This was necessary because detailed single-cell experimental data are lacking and thus we could not apply a maximum likelihood approach. Moreover, some aspects of the LCMV replication cycle kinetics have not been empirically observed which resulted in a calibration uncertainty, as estimated in Section 4. As a starting point for model calibration, the parameter estimates from the previously developed mathematical models of IAV, HIV-1 and SARS-CoV-2 life cycles have been used, as well as the functional dependencies for the nonlinear regulation processes.

To assess the sensitivity of the model performance to parameter variations, we implemented the traditional deterministic local analysis. A complementary global sensitivity analysis method treats model parameters as random variables, and therefore, requires making certain assumptions on the distributions of the parameter values. In practice, uniform distributions in plausible parameter ranges are frequently used, as well as triangular and normal distributions. The results of the global sensitivity analysis, therefore, will depend on these additional assumptions, which cannot be robustly specified now due to the lack of respective quantitative experimental data on each model parameter. This aspect deserves further attention in future work.

To parameterize the assembly kinetics, we assumed that the assembly rate is proportional to all the components that constitute a viral particle, i.e., to the ribonucleocapsids [NP-LgRNA(-)] and [NP-SgRNA(-)], as well as to Z, L and GPC proteins. The dependence on protein concentration is nonlinear and is given by a product of Michaelis–Menten functions. This implies a saturation in the rate based on the availability of proteins. This parameterization of the assembly process has been previously used in models for IAV [51], HIV-1 [45] and SARS-CoV-2 [52] life cycles.

In our study, both deterministic and stochastic models are used. They should be considered as complementary to each other. The use of the ODE-based deterministic formulation for the biochemical species concentrations assumes that they vary continuously according to the Mass Action Law. This enables a calibration of the model parameters. However, when considering single cell infections, some of the LCMV replication steps may proceed with low numbers of reactants. In this case, the random fluctuations of the reaction rates are more prominent, thus invalidating to a certain degree the deterministic modelling approach. These limitations can be overcome by the stochastic re-formulation of the deterministic model. This can be achieved by considering the transitions that take place between the variables as Markov processes. Specifically, the discrete-state continuous-time Markov chain-based model can be formulated (in which individual simulation paths can be numerically implemented using Monte-Carlo techniques), in which the model variables can take discrete integer numbers, and the propensities of the individual reactions are defined through probabilities that the respective transitions would take place in an infinitesimal increment of time. Importantly, the probabilities are defined by the abundances of the chemical species, while the reaction rate constants are derived directly from the underlying deterministic model. To note, some predictions of the deterministic model might vary substantially from that of the stochastic model. The stochastic model enables one to quantify and explain the emergence of heterogeneities in the virus life cycle, including the variability in net viral progeny and the probability of a productive infection.

6. Conclusions

LCMV is a prototypic arenavirus which provides a widely used experimental model to investigate the pathogenesis of both acute and persistent virus infections [53]. It is applied to study the molecular biology of other arenaviruses, such as the important human pathogens Lassa virus and Junin virus, which can cause hemorrhagic fever disease with high mortality [54]. In our study, we formulated and calibrated a mathematical model predicting the kinetics of biochemical processes, including the transcription, translation and degradation of molecular components of LCMV underlying its replication in infected cells. To the best of our knowledge, it is the first quantitative mathematical model of intracellular LCMV growth. The model provides a building module for developing multiscale mathematical models of LCMV infection in mice. The existing models for other viruses including HIV-1, Influenza A virus and SARS-CoV-2 are referenced in the discussion section, and distinctive features between these are mentioned.

LCMV remains an important cause of meningitis in humans, the fatal LCMV infection in organ transplant recipients in particular, which highlights the pathogenic potential and clinical significance of this neglected human pathogen [7]. It is recognized that antiviral therapeutic options in human LCMV infection are currently limited [7]. Our study provides a clear ranking of intracellular virus replication processes with respect to their contribution to the net viral production, thus suggesting potential targets for antiviral therapies.

Our mathematical model predicts the variability of the replication process and the probability of productive infection. The stochastic model enables us to predict the production of LCMV virions that are deficient in protein content. The predictions of our study require further experimental validation. The best option would be an experimental analysis of the LCMV life cycle, i.e., to follow the virus infections with simultaneous measurements of viral replication intermediates and host transcriptional changes as was previously made for other viruses, e.g., for HIV-1 [55], poliovirus [49].

Author Contributions: Conceptualization, J.S., D.G., A.M. and G.B.; Methodology, D.G., A.M. and G.B.; Software, J.S. and D.G.; Validation, J.S., D.G., V.C., P.C.R. and A.M.; Formal analysis, D.G.; Investigation, J.S., D.G. and G.B.; Data curation, J.S., D.G., V.C., P.C.R. and A.M.; Writing—original draft, J.S., D.G. and G.B.; Writing—review & editing, J.S., D.G., V.C., P.C.R., A.M. and G.B.; Visualization, J.S., D.G., V.C. and P.C.R.; Supervision, G.B.; Funding acquisition, G.B. All authors have read and agreed to the published version of the manuscript.

Funding: The work of G. Bocharov and A. Meyerhans was supported by the Russian Science Foundation according to the research project number 23-11-00116 (deterministic model development, calibration and sensitivity analysis presented in Sections 1; 2.1 and 2.2, 2.5; 3.1–3.7; 4.2; 5) and performed at Marchuk Institute of Numerical Mathematics of the Russian Academy of Sciences. A. Meyerhans is also supported by the Spanish Ministry of Science and Innovation grant no. PRPPID2022-141395OB-I00, and "Unidad de Excelencia María de Maeztu", funded by the AEI (CEX2018-000792-M). The work of D. Grebennikov (stochastic model development and numerical simulations presented in Sections 2.3 and 2.4; 3.8; 4.1, 4.3–4.5) was financed by the Ministry of Science and Higher Education of the Russian Federation within the framework of state support for the creation and development of World-Class Research Centers "Digital biodesign and personalized healthcare" No. 075-15-2022-304 and performed at Sechenov First Moscow State Medical University.

Data Availability Statement: No new data were created.

Conflicts of Interest: The authors declare no conflict of interest.

Abbreviations

The following abbreviations are used in this manuscript:

LCMV	Lymphocytic choriomeningitis virus
RING	Really interesting gene
ESCRT	Endosomal sorting complexes required for transport
α-DG	α-Dystroglycan
RdRp	RNA-dependent RNA polymerase
RNP	Ribonucleoprotein
SSP	Stable signal peptide
SSA	Stochastic simulation algorithm
ODE	Ordinary differential equation
MC	Markov chain

References

1. Poon, M.M.L.; Farber, D.L. The Whole Body as the System in Systems Immunology. *iScience* **2020**, *23*, 101509. [CrossRef] [PubMed]
2. Germain, R.N.; Radtke, A.J.; Thakur, N.; Schrom, E.C.; Hor, J.L.; Ichise, H.; Arroyo-Mejias, A.J.; Chu, C.J.; Grant, S. Understanding immunity in a tissue-centric context: Combining novel imaging methods and mathematics to extract new insights into function and dysfunction. *Immunol. Rev.* **2022**, *306*, 8–24. [CrossRef] [PubMed]

3. Hor, J.L.; Germain, R.N. Intravital and high-content multiplex imaging of the immune system. *Trends Cell Biol.* **2022**, *32*, 406–420. [CrossRef]
4. Cardozo-Ojeda, E.F.; Perelson, A.S. Modeling HIV-1 Within-Host Dynamics After Passive Infusion of the Broadly Neutralizing Antibody VRC01. *Front. Immunol.* **2021**, *12*, 710012. [CrossRef]
5. Sanche, S.; Cassidy, T.; Chu, P.; Perelson, A.S.; Ribeiro, R.M.; Ke, R. A simple model of COVID-19 explains disease severity and the effect of treatments. *Sci. Rep.* **2022**, *12*, 14210. [CrossRef] [PubMed]
6. Nikas, A.; Ahmed, H.; Moore, M.R.; Zarnitsyna, V.I.; Antia, R. When does humoral memory enhance infection? *PLoS Comput Biol.* **2023**, *19*, e1011377. [CrossRef] [PubMed]
7. Vilibic-Cavlek, T.; Savic, V.; Ferenc, T.; Mrzljak, A.; Barbic, L.; Bogdanic, M.; Stevanovic, V.; Tabain, I.; Ferencak, I.; Zidovec-Lepej, S. Lymphocytic Choriomeningitis—Emerging Trends of a Neglected Virus: A Narrative Review. *Trop. Med. Infect. Dis.* **2021**, *6*, 88. [CrossRef] [PubMed]
8. Bocharov, G.; Argilaguet, J.; Meyerhans, A. Understanding Experimental LCMV Infection of Mice: The Role of Mathematical Models. *J. Immunol. Res.* **2015**, *2015*, 739706. [CrossRef]
9. Argilaguet, J.; Pedragosa, M.; Esteve-Codina, A.; Riera, G.; Vidal, E.; Peligero-Cruz, C.; Casella, V.; Andreu, D.; Kaisho, T.; Bocharov, G.; et al. Systems analysis reveals complex biological processes during virus infection fate decisions. *Genome Res.* **2019**, *29*, 907–919. [CrossRef]
10. Pedragosa, M.; Riera, G.; Casella, V.; Esteve-Codina, A.; Steuerman, Y.; Seth, C.; Bocharov, G.; Heath, S.; Gat-Viks, I.; Argilaguet, J.; et al. Linking Cell Dynamics With Gene Coexpression Networks to Characterize Key Events in Chronic Virus Infections. *Front. Immunol.* **2019**, *10*, 1002. [CrossRef]
11. Bocharov, G.A. Modelling the dynamics of LCMV infection in mice: Conventional and exhaustive CTL responses. *J. Theor. Biol.* **1998**, *192*, 283–308. [CrossRef] [PubMed]
12. Nguyen, M.; Haenni, A.L. Expression strategies of ambisense viruses. *Virus Res.* **2003**, *93*, 141–150. [CrossRef] [PubMed]
13. Salvato, M.S.; Shimomaye, E.M. The completed sequence of lymphocytic choriomeningitis virus reveals a unique RNA structure and a gene for a zinc finger protein. *Virology* **1989**, *173*, 1–10. [CrossRef] [PubMed]
14. Southern, P.J.; Singh, M.K.; Riviere, Y.; Jacoby, D.R.; Buchmeier, M.J.; Oldstone, M.B. Molecular characterization of the genomic S RNA segment from lymphocytic choriomeningitis virus. *Virology* **1987**, *157*, 145–155. [CrossRef] [PubMed]
15. Meyer, B.J.; De La Torre, J.C.; Southern, P.J. Arenaviruses: Genomic RNAs, Transcription, and Replication. *Curr. Top. Microbiol. Immunol.* **2002**, *262*, 139–157. [CrossRef] [PubMed]
16. Salvato, M.S.; Clegg, J.C.S.; Buchmeier, M.J.; Charrel, R.N.; Gonzales, J.P.; Lukashevich, I.S.; Peters, C.J.; Rico-Hesse, R.; Romanowski, V. Family Arenaviridae. In *Virus Taxonomy: Ninth Report of the International Committee on Taxonomy of Viruses*; King, A.M.Q.; Adams, M.J.; Carstens, E.B.; Lefkowitz, E.F., Eds.; Elsevier: San Diego, CA, USA, 2012; pp. 715–723.
17. Pinschewer, D.D.; Perez, M.; de la Torre, J.C. Dual role of the lymphocytic choriomeningitis virus intergenic region in transcription termination and virus propagation. *J. Virol.* **2005**, *79*, 4519–4526. [CrossRef] [PubMed]
18. Lee, K.J.; Novella, I.S.; Teng, M.N.; Oldstone, M.B.; de la Torre, J.C. NP and L proteins of lymphocytic choriomeningitis virus (LCMV) are sufficient for efficient transcription and replication of LCMV genomic RNA analogs. *J. Virol.* **2000**, *74*, 3470–3477. [CrossRef] [PubMed]
19. Cornu, T.I.; de la Torre, J.C. RING finger Z protein of lymphocytic choriomeningitis virus (LCMV) inhibits transcription and RNA replication of an LCMV S-segment minigenome. *J. Virol.* **2001**, *75*, 9415–9426. [CrossRef]
20. Kranzusch, P.J.; Whelan, S.P. Arenavirus Z protein controls viral RNA synthesis by locking a polymerase–promoter complex. *Proc. Natl. Acad. Sci. USA* **2011**, *108*, 19743–19748. [CrossRef]
21. Perez, M.; Craven, R.C.; de la Torre, J.C. The small RING finger protein Z drives arenavirus budding: Implications for antiviral strategies. *Proc. Natl. Acad. Sci. USA* **2003**, *100*, 12978–12983. [CrossRef]
22. Fehling, S.K.; Lennartz, F.; Strecker, T. Multifunctional nature of the arenavirus RING finger protein Z. *Viruses* **2012**, *4*, 2973–3011. [CrossRef] [PubMed]
23. Borden, K.L.; Campbell Dwyer, E.J.; Salvato, M.S. An arenavirus RING (zinc-binding) protein binds the oncoprotein promyelocyte leukemia protein (PML) and relocates PML nuclear bodies to the cytoplasm. *J. Virol.* **1998**, *72*, 758–766. [CrossRef] [PubMed]
24. Borden, K.L.; CampbellDwyer, E.J.; Carlile, G.W.; Djavani, M.; Salvato, M.S. Two RING finger proteins, the oncoprotein PML and the arenavirus Z protein, colocalize with the nuclear fraction of the ribosomal P proteins. *J. Virol.* **1998**, *72*, 3819–3826. [CrossRef] [PubMed]
25. Campbell, D.E.J.; Lai, H.; MacDonald, R.C.; Salvato, M.S.; Borden, K.L. The lymphocytic choriomeningitis virus RING protein Z associates with eukaryotic initiation factor 4E and selectively represses translation in a RING-dependent manner. *J. Virol.* **2000**, *74*, 3293–3300. [CrossRef]
26. Pinschewer, D.D.; Perez, M.; de la Torre, J.C. Role of the virus nucleoprotein in the regulation of lymphocytic choriomeningitis virus transcription and RNA replication. *J. Virol.* **2003**, *77*, 3882–3887. [CrossRef] [PubMed]
27. Bederka, L.H.; Bonhomme, C.J.; Ling, E.L.; Buchmeier, M.J. Arenavirus stable signal peptide is the keystone subunit for glycoprotein complex organization. *MBio* **2014**, *5*, e02063-14. [CrossRef] [PubMed]
28. Wright, K.E.; Spiro, R.C.; Burns, J.W.; Buchmeier, M.J. Post-translational processing of the glycoproteins of lymphocytic choriomeningitis virus. *Virology* **1990**, *177*, 175–183. [CrossRef]

29. Cao, W.; Henry, M.D.; Borrow, P.; Yamada, H.; Elder, J.H.; Ravkov, E.V.; Nichol, S.T.; Compans, R.W.; Campbell, K.P.; Oldstone, M.B.A. Identification of α-dystroglycan as a receptor for lymphocytic choriomeningitis virus and Lassa fever virus. *Science* **1998**, *282*, 2079–2081. [CrossRef]
30. Sevilla, N.; Kunz, S.; Holz, A.; Lewicki, H.; Homann, D.; Yamada, H.; Campbell, K.P.; de la Torre, J.C.; Oldstone, M.B.A. Immunosuppression and resultant viral persistence by specific viral targeting of dendritic cells. *J. Exp. Med.* **2000**, *192*, 1249–1260 [CrossRef]
31. Kunz, S.; Sevilla, N.; McGavern, D.B.; Campbell, K.P.; Oldstone, M.B.A. Molecular analysis of the interaction of LCMV with its cellular receptor α-dystroglycan. *J. Cell Biol.* **2001**, *155*, 301–310. [CrossRef]
32. Oldstone, M.B.; Campbell, K.P. Decoding arenavirus pathogenesis: Essential roles for alpha-dystroglycan-virus interactions and the immune response. *Virology* **2011**, *411*, 170–179. [CrossRef]
33. Quirin, K.; Eschli, B.; Scheu, I.; Poort, L.; Kartenbeck, J.; Helenius, A. Lymphocytic choriomeningitis virus uses a novel endocytic pathway for infectious entry via late endosomes. *Virology* **2008**, *378*, 21–33. [CrossRef] [PubMed]
34. Rojek, J.M.; Sanchez, A.B.; Nguyen, N.T.; de la Torre, J.C.; Kunz, S. Different mechanisms of cell entry by human-pathogenic Old World and New World arenaviruses. *J. Virol.* **2008**, *82*, 7677–7687. [CrossRef] [PubMed]
35. Rojek, J.M.; Perez, M.; Kunz, S. Cellular entry of lymphocytic choriomeningitis virus. *J. Virol.* **2008**, *82*, 1505–1517. [CrossRef] [PubMed]
36. Lehmann-Grube, F.; Slenczka, W. Über die Vermehrung von LCM-Virus (Stamm WE3) in Zell-kulturen. *Zentralblatt Bakteriol. Infekt.* **1967**, *206*, 525.
37. Sullivan, B.M.; Emonet, S.F.; Welch, M.J.; Lee, A.M.; Campbell, K.P.; de la Torre, J.C.; Oldstone, M.B. Point mutation in the glycoprotein of lymphocytic choriomeningitis virus is necessary for receptor binding, dendritic cell infection, and long-term persistence. *Proc. Natl. Acad. Sci. USA* **2011**, *108*, 2969–2974. [CrossRef]
38. Wen, Y.; Xu, H.; Wan, W.; Shang, W.; Jin, R.; Zhou, F.; Mei, H.; Wang, J.; Xiao, G.; Chen, H.; et al. Visualizing lymphocytic choriomeningitis virus infection in cells and living mice. *iScience* **2022**, *25*, 105090. [CrossRef] [PubMed]
39. Strecker, T.; Eichler, R.; Meulen, J.T.; Weissenhorn, W.; Dieter Klenk, H.; Garten, W.; Lenz, O. Lassa virus Z protein is a matrix protein sufficient for the release of virus-like particles. *J. Virol.* **2003**, *77*, 10700–10705. [CrossRef] [PubMed]
40. Salvato, M.S.; Schweighofer, K.J.; Burns, J.; Shimomaye, E.M. Biochemical and immunological evidence that the 11 kDa zinc-binding protein of lymphocytic choriomeningitis virus is a structural component of the virus. *Virus Res.* **1992**, *22*, 185–198. [CrossRef]
41. Kang, H.; Cong, J.; Wang, C.; Ji, W.; Xin, Y.; Qian, Y.; Li, X.; Chen, Y.; Rao, Z. Structural basis for recognition and regulation of arenavirus polymerase L by Z protein. *Nat. Commun.* **2021**, *12*, 4134. [CrossRef]
42. Gillespie, D.T. A general method for numerically simulating the stochastic time evolution of coupled chemical reactions. *J. Comput. Phys.* **1976**, *22*, 403–434. [CrossRef]
43. Gillespie, D.T. Exact stochastic simulation of coupled chemical reactions. *J. Phys. Chem.* **1977**, *81*, 2340–2361. [CrossRef]
44. Marchetti, L.; Priami, C.; Thanh, V.H. *Simulation Algorithms for Computational Systems Biology*; An EATCS Series; Texts in Theoretical Computer Science; Springer International Publishing: Cham, Switzerland, 2017; ISBN 9783319631110.
45. Sazonov, I.; Grebennikov, D.; Meyerhans, A.; Bocharov, G. Markov Chain-Based Stochastic Modelling of HIV-1 Life Cycle in a CD4 T Cell. *Mathematics* **2021**, *9*, 2025. [CrossRef]
46. Thanh, V.H.; Zunino, R.; Priami, C. Efficient Constant-Time Complexity Algorithm for Stochastic Simulation of Large Reaction Networks. *IEEE/ACM Trans. Comput. Biol. Bioinf.* **2017**, *14*, 657–667. [CrossRef] [PubMed]
47. Shcherbatova, O.; Grebennikov, D.; Sazonov, I.; Meyerhans, A.; Bocharov, G. Modeling of the HIV-1 life cycle in productively infected cells to predict novel therapeutic targets. *Pathogens* **2020**, *9*, 255. [CrossRef] [PubMed]
48. Grebennikov, D.; Kholodareva, E.; Sazonov, I.; Karsonova, A.; Meyerhans, A.; Bocharov, G. Intracellular life cycle kinetics of SARS-CoV-2 predicted using mathematical modelling. *Viruses* **2021**, *13*, 1735. [CrossRef] [PubMed]
49. Heldt, F.S.; Kupke, S.Y.; Dorl, S.; Reichl, U.; Frensing, T. Single-cell analysis and stochastic modelling unveil large cell-to-cell variability in influenza A virus infection. *Nat. Commun.* **2015**, *6*, 8938. [CrossRef]
50. UniProt Consortium. UniProt: A worldwide hub of protein knowledge. *Nucleic Acids Res.* **2019**, *47*, D506–D515. [CrossRef]
51. Heldt, F.S.; Frensing, T.; Reichl, U. Modeling the intracellular dynamics of influenza virus replication to understand the control of viral RNA synthesis. *J. Virol.* **2012**, *86*, 7806–7817. [CrossRef]
52. Sazonov, I.; Grebennikov, D.; Meyerhans, A.; Bocharov, G. Sensitivity of SARS-CoV-2 Life Cycle to IFN Effects and ACE2 Binding Unveiled with a Stochastic Model. *Viruses* **2022**, *14*, 403. [CrossRef]
53. Zhou, X.; Ramach, R.S.; Mann, M.; Popkin, D.L. Role of lymphocytic choriomeningitis virus (LCMV) in understanding viral immunology: Past, present and future. *Viruses* **2012**, *4*, 2650–2669. [CrossRef]
54. Lee, A.M.; Cruite, J.; Welch, M.J.; Sullivan, B.; Oldstone, M.B. Pathogenesis of Lassa fever virus infection: I. Susceptibility of mice to recombinant Lassa Gp/LCMV chimeric virus. *Virology* **2013**, *442*, 114–121. [CrossRef]
55. Mohammadi, P.; Desfarges, S.; Bartha, I.; Joos, B.; Zangger, N.; Muñoz, M.; Günthard, H.F.; Beerenwinkel, N.; Telenti, A.; Ciuffi, A. 24 hours in the life of HIV-1 in a T cell line. *PLoS Pathog.* **2013**, *9*, e1003161. [CrossRef]

Disclaimer/Publisher's Note: The statements, opinions and data contained in all publications are solely those of the individual author(s) and contributor(s) and not of MDPI and/or the editor(s). MDPI and/or the editor(s) disclaim responsibility for any injury to people or property resulting from any ideas, methods, instructions or products referred to in the content.

Article

Modelling Infectious Disease Dynamics: A Robust Computational Approach for Stochastic SIRS with Partial Immunity and an Incidence Rate

Amani S. Baazeem [1,*], Yasir Nawaz [2], Muhammad Shoaib Arif [2,3,*], Kamaleldin Abodayeh [3] and Mae Ahmed AlHamrani [1]

1. Department of Mathematics and Statistics, College of Science, Imam Mohammad Ibn Saud Islamic University (IMSIU), P.O. Box 90950, Riyadh 11623, Saudi Arabia
2. Department of Mathematics, Air University, PAF Complex E-9, Islamabad 44000, Pakistan
3. Department of Mathematics and Sciences, College of Humanities and Sciences, Prince Sultan University, Riyadh 11586, Saudi Arabia
* Correspondence: asbaazeem@imamu.edu.sa (A.S.B.); marif@psu.edu.sa (M.S.A.)

Abstract: For decades, understanding the dynamics of infectious diseases and halting their spread has been a major focus of mathematical modelling and epidemiology. The stochastic SIRS (susceptible–infectious–recovered–susceptible) reaction–diffusion model is a complicated but crucial computational scheme due to the combination of partial immunity and an incidence rate. Considering the randomness of individual interactions and the spread of illnesses via space, this model is a powerful instrument for studying the spread and evolution of infectious diseases in populations with different immunity levels. A stochastic explicit finite difference scheme is proposed for solving stochastic partial differential equations. The scheme is comprised of predictor–corrector stages. The stability and consistency in the mean square sense are also provided. The scheme is applied to diffusive epidemic models with incidence rates and partial immunity. The proposed scheme with space's second-order central difference formula solves deterministic and stochastic models. The effect of transmission rate and coefficient of partial immunity on susceptible, infected, and recovered people are also deliberated. The deterministic model is also solved by the existing Euler and non-standard finite difference methods, and it is found that the proposed scheme forms better than the existing non-standard finite difference method. Providing insights into disease dynamics, control tactics, and the influence of immunity, the computational framework for the stochastic SIRS reaction–diffusion model with partial immunity and an incidence rate has broad applications in epidemiology. Public health and disease control ultimately benefit from its application to the study and management of infectious illnesses in various settings.

Keywords: stochastic numerical scheme; stability; consistency; diffusive SIRS model; partial immunity; incidence rate and disease spread

MSC: 35R60; 65C30; 65M12

1. Introduction

For the stochastic diffusive epidemic model with partial immunity and an incidence rate, a finite difference approach is a numerical method for solving the partial differential equation (PDE). The PDE describes time- and space-variant population dynamics of the susceptible, infected, and recovered groups. The model's incidence rate term describes how quickly new infections spread. At the same time, the partial immunity factor considers that not everyone is vulnerable to the disease. The finite difference method transforms the PDE into a set of ODEs, which can then be solved numerically. The spatial domain is grid-divided, and finite difference operators are used to approximate the PDE derivatives. Multiple numerical techniques can then be used to solve the resulting system of ODEs.

The Euler technique is frequently used to resolve the system of ODEs. The Euler method's simplicity and explicitness may lead to inaccuracies when dealing with enormous time increments. The Crank–Nicolson approach is more precise. However, it is implicit. Compared to the Euler method, the Crank–Nicolson approach is more stable but demands more processing power.

Using a stochastic solver is an alternative method for resolving the system of ODEs. A stochastic solver would consider the unpredictability of the disease's spread. Diseases with low transmission rates or those whose prevalence is influenced by environmental variables may benefit from this type of modelling.

When simulating the spread of infectious disease, stochastic modelling is a common approach for examining the underlying dynamics of the disease. More so, it has been seen that stochastic models are typically more illuminating than deterministic ones since the latter can only predict one outcome given a particular set of conditions. A stochastic model, on the other hand, forecasts several different possibilities. Using stochastic differential equations, numerous scholars have suggested numerous mathematical models to characterize the dynamics of epidemics in recent years (e.g., Refs. [1–4]). To obtain more realistic systems of population interactions, authors have inserted temporal delays into such models and explored their dynamical properties (see, for example, Refs. [5–7]).

Vaccination has the potential to play a significant role in disease control by reducing the rate of reproduction and, consequently, the number of sick people in an endemic region. It is well established that certain vaccines produce just transitory immunity while others provide lifelong protection. Thus, the time it takes for an individual to develop immunity to an infection or vaccine is considered a delay factor in many published works' construction of epidemic models (for example, refer to Refs. [8–10]). Based on the equivalent deterministic model developed and explored in [11], the authors in [12] devised the stochastic SVIR epidemic model. This was carried out because vaccinations are such an efficient technique for reducing diseases.

It is common knowledge that accurate epidemic modelling relies heavily on accurate incidence rates to explain infectious disease dynamics. Many researchers have advocated nonlinear incidence rates as a more flexible model for dealing with genuine data and a more nuanced approach to analyzing disease transmission than bilinear and standard incidence rates [13].

A universal functional response $F(S,\tau) = \frac{\beta S}{1+\lambda_1 S + \lambda_2 \tau + \lambda_3 S \tau}$ was recently introduced by Hattaf et al. [14], where $\lambda_1, \lambda_2, \lambda_3 \geq 0$ are saturation factors assessing the psychological or inhibitory effect. Using this equation, we can extrapolate from the literature a wide variety of incidence rates. If $\lambda_1 = \lambda_2 = \lambda_3 = 0$, for instance (see [15]), we obtain the bilinear incidence rate $F(S,\tau) = \beta S$. If $\lambda_2 = \lambda_3 = 0$, or if $\lambda_1 = \lambda_3 = 0$, the saturated incidence function $F(S,\tau) = \frac{\beta S}{1+\lambda_1 S}$ is produced (see [16,17]). If $\lambda_3 = 0$, the Beddington–DeAngelis functional response $F(S,\tau) = \frac{\beta S}{1+\lambda_1 S + \lambda_2 \tau}$ is achieved (see [18,19] for details). If $\lambda_3 = \lambda_1 \lambda_2$, the Crowley–Martin functional response $F(S,\tau)$ is found to be $F(S,\tau) = \frac{\beta S}{1+\lambda_1 S + \lambda_2 \tau + \lambda_1 \lambda_2 S \tau}$.

However, the influence of vaccinations on public health in populations is significantly impacted by the duration of immunity, making it one of the most crucial components of disease and vaccines. Individual immunity to infectious diseases was shown to last anywhere from a few months to a lifetime [20]. For instance, the protection afforded by the varicella [21] and pertussis [22] vaccines against infectious diseases is only brief. Loss of immunological memory and the evolution of the disease are two key reasons why immunity (whether infection-induced or vaccination-induced) diminishes for many infectious disorders [23].

A few researchers have worked on numerical solutions to the epidemic models. While Nowak et al. [24] proposed a deterministic model for the simulation of hepatitis B virus infection, Wang and Wang [25] proposed an alternative model in which the virus moves randomly, and the concentration gradient is assumed to be proportional to the virus's population flux. Suryanto et al. provided a non-standard FDS for the numerical approximation of the SIR epidemic model with a saturated incidence rate. The scheme results are dynamically consistent with the continuous model [26]. Naik et al. assumed a Crowley–Martin functional response and a Holling type-II treatment rate for the SIR epidemic model. They turned to homotopy analysis for the analytical solutions of the provided model. The authors consider the model's stability and find it can exist in two distinct states: disease-free and endemic [27].

Physical phenomenon modelling is a fascinating field of study and practice. Partial differential equations (PDEs) are utilized because they accurately describe the underlying physical behavior [28–31]. There is a lot of research in the field of solving PDEs, and many different methods are used [32–38]. Forty years ago, it was widely believed that advances in nutrition, pharmaceuticals, and vaccines were largely responsible for the dramatic drop in the human mortality rate that occurred then. Infectious infections have always been a major problem for people and cattle. Traditional epidemic models cannot capture how illnesses behave. As a result, it is crucial to think about epidemic models within a stochastic framework. Therefore, fresh case-specific literature is necessary. The dynamics of stochastic partial differential equations are the subject of many recent investigations. The authors performed in-depth analyses of several physical phenomena using the finite difference scheme [39–41]. Macas-Daz et al. [42] studied the stochastic epidemiology model using a non-traditional finite difference approach. The dynamics of a stochastic model of smoking were investigated by Raza et al., who devised a non-standard finite difference to do so [43]. The stochastic fractional epidemic model was numerically approximated by Nauman et al. [44]. The stochastic dengue epidemic model was solved by Raza et al. [45]. Alkhazzan et al. [46] examined and discussed the dynamics of an SVIR epidemic model. The utilization of the fractional order Caputo fractional derivative co-infection illness epidemic model has been examined in previous studies [47–50]. In chemistry, MiR-17-92 is critical in regulating the Myc/E2F protein. A novel fractional-order delayed Myc/E2F/miR-17-92 network model revealing their relationship is proposed in [51].

There are several potential uses for the computational scheme developed for the stochastic (SIRS) reaction–diffusion model with partial immunity and an incidence rate in epidemiology and other fields of study. Some important information about its uses is as follows:

1. Epidemiological Modelling: The primary use of this computational framework is the modelling of infectious disease dynamics in populations. Because it allows researchers to examine the impact of partial immunity on disease transmission and prevalence, it is especially helpful when thinking about diseases with various levels of immunity. This is particularly important in the case of influenza, where immunity can shift from season to season due to strain changes.

2. Geographical Spread Analysis: Because this model includes diffusion, it can be used to analyze the geographical spread of diseases. The ability to optimize healthcare resource allocation and implement effective control measures relies on researchers thoroughly understanding how diseases spread across geographic regions.

3. Vaccination Strategy: Vaccination techniques can be tested using the model. It is useful for calculating the effects of vaccination rates, waning immunity, and partial immunity on the overall disease burden in a community. Policymakers might use these data as a reference when deciding how to proceed with vaccination drives.

4. Public Health Policy Planning: Infectious disease dynamics knowledge is essential for public health policymaking. This model can shed light on how factors like incidence rates and geographic location influence the spread of disease. It is useful for determining how to allocate resources best and implement intervention techniques to reduce disease spread.

5. Disease Evolution: By adding partial immunity, the model may also be used to examine how diseases change over time. The immune response to diseases like HIV is

complex and changes over time, which is particularly relevant. The model can show how the disease may evolve and how therapies may alter its course.

Suppose you want to simulate the spread of disease. In that case, you can use the finite difference approach or a computational methodology for a stochastic diffusive epidemic model with partial immunity and an incidence rate. This technique can examine how changing certain variables impacts disease transmission and how efficient certain preventative strategies are.

Researchers and public health officials can use the finite difference approach or computational scheme for a stochastic diffusive epidemic model with partial immunity and an incidence rate to better understand and manage disease transmission.

The solutions to the epidemic models can be found by applying analytical and numerical methods. The analytical methods sometimes take more time to converge than numerical methods when applied to nonlinear problems. Different methods exist to handle nonlinear term(s) in differential equations. However, nonlinear terms are linearized using implicit finite difference methods. However, for the explicit methods, linearization is not required. So, linear finite difference schemes are sometimes useful for solving nonlinear differential equations. An iterative method can also be adopted to overcome the deficiency of explicit schemes when applied to problems having Neumann-type boundary conditions. An iterative scheme is also employed in this work to manage such cases. The stopping criteria of the iterative scheme for the deterministic model are also provided, and the iterative will be stopped if this criterion is met. The Wiener process term is approximated by the MATLAB built-in function of using normal distribution with mean zero. So, the MATLAB built-in facility is adopted for solving the stochastic diffusive epidemic model.

Public Health Benefits:

As a powerful tool for comprehending and controlling infectious diseases, the suggested computational framework for the stochastic SIRS reaction–diffusion model with partial immunity and an incidence rate provides substantial advantages to public health. By including an incidence rate and partial immunity, the model provides a more accurate portrayal of disease dynamics in populations with different immunity levels. By taking into account the inherent unpredictability in the interactions between individuals and the distribution of diseases over space, the computational scheme's stochastic explicit finite difference method helps to model the dynamics of infectious disease transmission and evolution.

An effective strategy for disease control can be developed with the use of the model's findings. Key parameters impacting disease dynamics can be identified by studying the influence of transmission rates and coefficients of partial immunity on susceptible, infected, and recovered people using the model. With this information, we may better develop public health plans and tailored interventions to reduce the transmission of infectious illnesses in various environments. In the end, public health authorities and lawmakers can make better disease prevention and control decisions because of the computational framework's extensive use in epidemiology.

Limitations of the Study:

Even though the suggested computational paradigm sheds light on the dynamics of infectious diseases, its limits must be recognized. The mathematical model's assumptions regarding homogenous mixing and constant parameters, among other simplifications, are restricted. Complex real-world interactions and population-level fluctuations may be beyond the scope of these assumptions.

Furthermore, the model assumes partial immunity, the integrity of which depends on the accessibility of pertinent data and the thoroughness of immunity-related elements taken into account.

Validation of Methods:

It is necessary to validate the stability and consistency of the suggested computational strategy in the mean square sense and apply it to diffusive epidemic models with incidence rates and partial immunity. To further explore the process of validation, the subsequent variables are examined:

Stability: The scheme's stability is guaranteed by a thorough analysis that considers the predictor–corrector stages. Establishing stability criteria demonstrates that the numerical solution exhibits convergence towards the accurate solution when the discretization parameters progressively decrease.

Consistency: verifying consistency in the mean square sense demonstrates that as the grid spacing decreases, the numerical solution converges to the theoretical solution of the stochastic partial differential equations.

Comparison with existing model: The new technique is evaluated using the existing Euler method and a non-standard finite difference method. The suggested technique is demonstrated to be superior to the existing non-standard finite difference method in solving the deterministic model through the provision of well-defined metrics and performance indicators.

The reliability and correctness of the proposed computational scheme in capturing the dynamics of infectious diseases within the stochastic SIRS reaction–diffusion model framework with partial immunity and an incidence rate are ensured by implementing a complete validation technique.

2. Stochastic Computational Scheme

An explicit two-stage scheme is proposed that can solve stochastic differential equations. Both stages of the scheme are explicit. The scheme consists of a fixed step size. The first stage of the scheme is the Euler–Maruyama method, and the second stage contains parameters that will be found later by comparing Taylor series expansion. For starting the constructing procedure of the scheme, consider the following stochastic partial differential equation:

$$dv = G\left(v, \frac{\partial^2 v}{\partial x^2}\right)dt + \sigma v dW \tag{1}$$

where σ is a constant, and $W(t)$ represents a Winner process.

The proposed scheme will be constructed for the deterministic model (1). i.e., $\sigma = 0$. Later on, the scheme will be constructed for the stochastic model (1).

The first stage of the scheme is expressed as:

$$\overline{v}_i^{n+1} = v_i^n + dv_i^n \tag{2}$$

where $\overline{v}_i^{n+1}$ represents the solutions of Equation (1) computed at ith grid point and at an arbitrary time level. The solution computed at the first stage should not considered as a final solution at $(n+1)th$ level. Stage (2) can also be considered as the predictor stage. The corrector stage can be expressed as:

$$v_i^{n+1} = \frac{1}{3}\left(2v_i^n + \overline{v}_i^{n+1}\right) + a\, dv_i^n + b\, d\overline{v}_i^{n+1} \tag{3}$$

The values of parameters a and b can be determined by considering the Taylor series expansion of v_i^{n+1} as:

$$v_i^{n+1} = v_i^n + dv_i^n + \frac{1}{2}d^2v_i^n + \cdots \tag{4}$$

By substituting Equation (4) into Equation (3), the following is obtained:

$$v_i^n + dv_i^n + \frac{1}{2}d^2v_i^n + \cdots = \frac{1}{3}\left(2v_i^n + \overline{v}_i^{n+1}\right) + a\, dv_i^n + b\, d\overline{v}_i^{n+1} \tag{5}$$

By using (2) into Equation (5):

$$v_i^n + dv_i^n + \frac{1}{2}d^2v_i^n + \cdots = \frac{1}{3}(3v_i^n + dv_i^n) + a\, dv_i^n + b\, dv_i^n + bd^2v_i^n \tag{6}$$

Equating coefficients of dv_i^n and $d^2v_i^n$ on both sides of Equation (6) yields:

$$\left. \begin{array}{l} 1 = \frac{1}{3} + a + b \\ \frac{1}{2} = b \end{array} \right\} \tag{7}$$

Solving Equation (7), the values of a and b can be expressed as:

$$a = \frac{1}{6} \quad \text{and} \quad b = \frac{1}{2} \tag{8}$$

The semi-discretization for stochastic Equation (1) is given by:

$$\overline{v}_i^{n+1} = v_i^n + G\left(v_i^n, \left.\frac{\partial^2 v}{\partial x^2}\right|_i\right)^n \Delta t + \sigma v_i^n \Delta W \tag{9}$$

and

$$v_i^{n+1} = \frac{1}{3}\left(2v_i^n + \overline{v}_i^{n+1}\right) + a\left(G\left(v_i^n, \left.\frac{\partial^2 v}{\partial x^2}\right|_i\right)^n \Delta t + \sigma v_i^n \Delta W\right) + b\left(G\left(\overline{v}_i^{n+1}, \left.\frac{\partial^2 \overline{v}}{\partial x^2}\right|_i\right)^{n+1} \Delta t + \sigma \overline{v}_i^{n+1} \Delta W\right) \tag{10}$$

where a and b will be chosen from Equation (8) and $\Delta W \sim N(0, \Delta t)$.

Letting $G = d_1 \frac{\partial^2 v}{\partial x^2}$ in Equation (1), the fully discretized equations are:

$$\overline{v}_i^{n+1} = v_i^n + d_1 \left(\frac{v_{i+1}^n - 2v_i^n + v_{i-1}^n}{(\Delta x)^2}\right) \Delta t + \sigma v_i^n \Delta W \tag{11}$$

and

$$v_i^{n+1} = \frac{1}{3}\left(2v_i^n + \overline{v}_i^{n+1}\right) + a\left\{d_1 \left(\frac{v_{i+1}^n - 2v_i^n + v_{i-1}^n}{(\Delta x)^2}\right)\Delta t + \sigma v_i^n \Delta W\right\} + b\left\{d_1 \left(\frac{\overline{v}_{i+1}^{n+1} - 2\overline{v}_i^{n+1} + \overline{v}_{i-1}^{n+1}}{(\Delta x)^2}\right)\Delta t + \sigma \overline{v}_i^{n+1} \Delta W\right\} \tag{12}$$

3. Stability Analysis

The stability analysis of the proposed scheme for stochastic parabolic linear equations will be performed by applying Fourier series analysis. The analysis provides the conditions on step size and involved parameters. The stability analysis assumes the dependent variable by the component of the Fourier series. The transformations are given as:

$$\left. \begin{array}{l} \overline{v}_i^{n+1} = \overline{Q}^{n+1} e^{i\overline{I}\psi}, \; v_i^{n+1} = Q^{n+1} e^{i\overline{I}\psi} \\ v_{i\pm 1}^n = Q^n e^{(i\pm 1)\overline{I}\psi}, \; \overline{v}_{i\pm 1}^{n+1} = \overline{Q}^{n+1} e^{(i\pm 1)\overline{I}\psi} \end{array} \right\} \tag{13}$$

where $\overline{I} = \sqrt{-1}$.

It yields by substituting some of the transformations from Equation (13) into the first stage of the proposed scheme (11).

$$\overline{Q}^{n+1} e^{i\overline{I}\psi} = Q^n e^{i\overline{I}\psi} + \frac{d_1 \Delta t}{(\Delta x)^2}\left(e^{(i+1)\overline{I}\psi} - 2e^{i\overline{I}\psi} + e^{(i-1)\overline{I}\psi}\right)Q^n + \sigma e^{i\overline{I}\psi} \Delta W Q^n \tag{14}$$

Dividing both sides of Equation (14) by $e^{i\overline{I}\psi}$ yields:

$$\overline{Q}^{n+1} = Q^n + d\left(e^{\overline{I}\psi} - 2 + e^{-\overline{I}\psi}\right)Q^n + \sigma \Delta W Q^n$$

where $d = \frac{d_1 \Delta t}{(\Delta x)^2}$.

Using trigonometric identities yields:

$$\overline{Q}^{n+1} = (1 + 2d(\cos\psi - 1) + \sigma \Delta W)Q^n \tag{15}$$

Similarly, upon substituting some of the transformations from Equation (13) into the second stage of the proposed scheme (12), it gives:

$$Q^{n+1}e^{i\bar{I}\psi} = \tfrac{1}{3}\left(2Q^n e^{i\bar{I}\psi} + \overline{Q}^{n+1}e^{i\bar{I}\psi}\right) + a\left\{d_1\left(\frac{e^{(i+1)\bar{I}\psi} - 2e^{i\bar{I}\psi} + e^{(i-1)\bar{I}\psi}}{(\Delta x)^2}\right)Q^n \Delta t + \sigma e^{i\bar{I}\psi} Q^n \Delta W\right\} + b\left\{d_1\left(\frac{e^{(i+1)\bar{I}\psi} - 2e^{i\bar{I}\psi} + e^{(i-1)\bar{I}\psi}}{(\Delta x)^2}\right)\overline{Q}^{n+1} \Delta t + \sigma e^{i\bar{I}\psi} \overline{Q}^{n+1} \Delta W\right\} \qquad (16)$$

Dividing both sides of Equation (16) by $e^{i\bar{I}\psi}$ yields:

$$Q^{n+1} = \tfrac{1}{3}\left(2Q^n + \overline{Q}^{n+1}\right) + a\left\{2d_1 \frac{(\cos\psi - 1)}{(\Delta x)^2}\Delta t + \sigma \Delta W\right\}Q^n + b\left\{2d_1 \frac{(\cos\psi - 1)}{(\Delta x)^2}\Delta t + \sigma \Delta W\right\}\overline{Q}^{n+1} \qquad (17)$$

Using Equation (15) in Equation (17) produces:

$$Q^{n+1} = \left[\tfrac{2}{3} + 2ad(\cos\psi - 1) + \sigma \Delta W\right]Q^n + \left[\tfrac{1}{3} + 2bd(\cos\psi - 1) + \sigma \Delta W\right][1 + 2d(\cos\psi - 1) + \sigma \Delta W]Q^n \qquad (18)$$

The amplification factor for the scheme is given as:

$$\frac{Q^{n+1}}{Q^n} = \left(\tfrac{2}{3} + 2ad(\cos\psi - 1) + \left(\tfrac{1}{3} + 2bd(\cos\psi - 1)\right)(1 + 2d(\cos\psi - 1))\right) + (\tfrac{1}{3} + 2bd(\cos\psi - 1) + 1 + 2d(\cos\psi - 1) + 1)\sigma \Delta W + \sigma^2(\Delta W)^2 \qquad (19)$$

Applying the expected value on the square of amplitudes of the two consecutive Fourier components of the solution of the differential equations using the proposed scheme and also using the inequality give the stability condition for the proposed stochastic scheme as:

$$E\left|\frac{Q^{n+1}}{Q^n}\right|^2 \leq 2E|\tfrac{2}{3} + 2ad(\cos\psi - 1) + \left(\tfrac{1}{3} + 2bd(\cos\psi - 1)\right)(1 + 2d(\cos\psi - 1))|^2 + 2|2bd(\cos\psi - 1) + \tfrac{7}{3} + 2d(\cos\psi - 1)|^2 E|\sigma \Delta W|^2 + 2\sigma^4 E|(\Delta W)^2|^2 \qquad (20)$$

If

$$2|\tfrac{2}{3} + 2ad(\cos\psi - 1) + \left(\tfrac{1}{3} + 2bd(\cos\psi - 1)\right)(1 + 2d(\cos\psi - 1))|^2 < 1$$

and let

$$\lambda = 2\sigma^2|\tfrac{7}{3} + 2bd(\cos\psi - 1) + 2d(\cos\psi - 1)|^2 + 6\Delta t$$

Then, inequality (20) can be expressed as:

$$\left|\frac{Q^{n+1}}{Q^n}\right|^2 \leq 1 + \lambda \Delta t \qquad (21)$$

Therefore, the proposed stochastic numerical scheme is conditionally stable.

Theorem 1. *The proposed stochastic numerical scheme (11)–(12) is consistent in the mean square sense.*

Proof. Let P be the smooth function:

$$L(P)_i^n = P((n+1)\Delta t, i\Delta x) - P(n\Delta t, i\Delta x) - d_1 \int_{n\Delta t}^{(n+1)\Delta t} P_{xx}(s, i\Delta x)ds - \sigma \int_{n\Delta t}^{(n+1)\Delta t} P(s, i\Delta x)dW(s) \qquad (22)$$

$$L_i^n P = P((n+1)\Delta t, i\Delta x) - P(n\Delta t, i\Delta x) - \Delta t \left[\frac{d_1(a+\frac{1}{3})}{(\Delta x)^2}(P(n\Delta t, (i+1)\Delta x) - 2P(n\Delta t, i\Delta x) + \right.$$
$$P(n\Delta t, (i-1)\Delta x)) + \frac{d_1 b}{(\Delta x)^2}\left(\overline{P}((n+1)\Delta t, (i+1)\Delta x) - 2\overline{P}((n+1)\Delta t, i\Delta x) + \overline{P}((n+1)\Delta t, (i-1)\Delta x)\right) \right] -$$
$$\sigma\left(a+\tfrac{1}{3}\right)P(n\Delta t, i\Delta x)(W((n+1)\Delta t) - W(n\Delta t)) - \sigma b \overline{P}((n+1)\Delta t, i\Delta x)(W((n+1)\Delta t) - W(n\Delta t)) \quad (23)$$

where $\overline{P}((n+1)\Delta t, i\Delta x) = P(n\Delta t, i\Delta x) + \frac{d_1 \Delta t}{(\Delta x)^2}(P(n\Delta t, (i+1)\Delta x) - 2P(n\Delta t, i\Delta x) + P(n\Delta t, (i-1)\Delta x)) + \sigma P(n\Delta t, i\Delta x)(W((n+1)\Delta t) - W(n\Delta t))$.

The following equations can be obtained from Equations (22) and (23):

$$E|L(P)_i^n - L_i^n P|^2 = E| - d_1 \int_{n\Delta t}^{(n+1)\Delta t} P_{xx}(s, i\Delta x)ds - \sigma \int_{n\Delta t}^{(n+1)\Delta t} P(s, i\Delta x)dW(s) +$$
$$\frac{d_1(a+\tfrac{1}{3})}{(\Delta x)^2}(P(n\Delta t, (i+1)\Delta x) - 2P(n\Delta t, i\Delta x) + P(n\Delta t, (i-1)\Delta x)) +$$
$$\frac{d_1 b}{(\Delta x)^2}(\overline{P}((n+1)\Delta t, (i+1)\Delta x) - 2\overline{P}((n+1)\Delta t, i\Delta x) + \overline{P}((n+1)\Delta t, (i-1)\Delta x)) \quad (24)$$
$$+\sigma(a+\tfrac{1}{3})P(n\Delta t, i\Delta x)(W((n+1)\Delta t) - W(n\Delta t))$$
$$+\sigma b\overline{P}((n+1)\Delta t, i\Delta x)(W((n+1)\Delta t) - W(n\Delta t))|^2$$

Equation (24) can be rewritten as:

$$E|L(P)_i^n - L_i^n P|^2 \le 2d_1^2 E\left|\int_{n\Delta t}^{(n+1)\Delta t} P_{xx}(s, i\Delta x)ds\right.$$
$$-\frac{\Delta t}{(\Delta x)^2}\{(a+\tfrac{1}{3})(P(n\Delta t, (i+1)\Delta x) - 2P(n\Delta t, i\Delta x) + P(n\Delta t, (i-1)\Delta x)) +$$
$$b(\overline{P}((n+1)\Delta t, (i+1)\Delta x) - 2\overline{P}((n+1)\Delta t, i\Delta x) + \overline{P}((n+1)\Delta t, (i-1)\Delta x))\} \quad (25)$$
$$|^2 + 2\sigma^2 E\left|\int_{n\Delta t}^{(n+1)\Delta t} P(s, i\Delta x)dW(s) - (a+\tfrac{1}{3})P(n\Delta t, i\Delta x)(W((n+1)\Delta t) - W(n\Delta t)) -\right.$$
$$b\overline{P}((n+1)\Delta t, i\Delta x)(W((n+1)\Delta t) - W(n\Delta t))|^2$$

Now, the following result is used:

$$E\left|\int_{t_o}^t f(s, w)dW_s\right|^{2m} \le (t - t_o)^{n-1}[m(2m-1)]^m \int_{t_o}^t E\left[|f(s,w)|^{2m}\right]ds \quad (26)$$

where t_o is the initial time.

By using the result (26) in (25), the following inequality can be obtained:

$$E|L(P)_i^n - L_i^n P|^2 \le 2d_1^2 E\left|\int_{n\Delta t}^{(n+1)\Delta t} P_{xx}(s, i\Delta x)ds - \frac{\Delta t}{(\Delta x)^2}\{(a+\tfrac{1}{3})(P(n\Delta t, (i+1)\Delta x)\right.$$
$$-2P(n\Delta t, i\Delta x) + P(n\Delta t, (i-1)\Delta x)) + b(\overline{P}((n+1)\Delta t, (i+1)\Delta x) - 2\overline{P}((n+1)\Delta t, i\Delta x) + \quad (27)$$
$$\overline{P}((n+1)\Delta t, (i-1)\Delta x))\}|^2 + 2\sigma^2 \Delta t \int_{n\Delta t}^{(n+1)\Delta t} E[|P(s, i\Delta x) - (a+\tfrac{1}{3})P(n\Delta t, i\Delta x) - b\overline{P}((n+1)\Delta t, i\Delta x)|^2]ds$$

Thus, implementation of limits when $\Delta x \to 0$, $\Delta t \to 0$ and $(n\Delta t, i\Delta x) \to (t, x)$ then results in:

$$E|L(P)_i^n - L_i^n P|^2 \to 0 \quad (28)$$

Therefore, the proposed stochastic numerical scheme is consistent in the mean square sense. □

4. Diffusive Stochastic Epidemic Model

Let S, I, and R represent the densities of susceptible, infectious, and recovered people at location x and time t. Letting $\beta(x)$ represent the transmission rate and $\mu(x)$ denote the natural mortality of people, $\alpha(x)$ is used for mortality caused by the disease, $\gamma(x)$ denotes the rate of losing of immunity, $\wedge(x)$ denotes the birth rate of susceptible people, $\delta(x)$ represents the recovery rate, and these functions are positive Holder continuous functions. By following [52] for the deterministic model, the stochastic SIRS model is expressed as:

$$\frac{\partial S}{\partial t} = d_1 \frac{\partial^2 S}{\partial x^2} + \wedge(x) - \beta(x)\frac{S(t,x)I(t,x)}{1 + mI(t,x)} - \mu(x)S + \gamma(x)R + (1-p)\delta(x)I + \sigma_1 SW(t) \tag{29}$$

$$\frac{\partial I}{\partial t} = d_2 \frac{\partial^2 I}{\partial x^2} + \frac{SI}{1+mI} - (\delta(x) + \mu(x) + \alpha(x))I + \sigma_2 IW(t) \tag{30}$$

$$\frac{\partial R}{\partial t} = d_3 \frac{\partial^2 R}{\partial x^2} + p\delta(x)I - (\mu(x) + \gamma(x))R + \sigma_3 RW(t) \tag{31}$$

Subject to the boundary conditions:

$$\frac{\partial S}{\partial x} = 0, \frac{\partial I}{\partial x} = 0, \frac{\partial R}{\partial x} = 0 \text{ for } t > 0, x \epsilon \partial\Omega \tag{32}$$

and initial conditions are given as:

$$S(0,x) = f_1(x), I(0,x) = f_2(x), R(0,x) = f_3(x) \tag{33}$$

For $d_1 = d_2 = d_3 = 0$ and $\sigma_1 = \sigma_2 = \sigma_3 = 0$, the disease-free equilibrium points can be determined from the following equations:

$$\wedge(x) - \beta(x)\frac{SI}{1+mI} - \mu(x)S + r(x)R + (1-p)\delta(x)I = 0 \tag{34}$$

$$\frac{SI}{1+mI} - (\delta(x) + \mu(x) + \alpha(x))I = 0 \tag{35}$$

$$p\delta(x)I - (\mu(x) + \gamma(x))R = 0 \tag{36}$$

By solving Equations (34)–(36), the disease-free equilibrium points are found as:

$$B(\frac{\wedge(x)}{\mu(x)}, 0, 0)$$

Theorem 2. *The system of Equations (29)–(31) with $d_1 = d_2 = d_3 = 0$ and $\sigma_1 = \sigma_2 = \sigma_3 = 0$ is locally stable if $\beta(x) \wedge (x) < \alpha(x)\mu(x) + \delta(x)\mu(x)$.*

Proof. The Jacobian of the system (29)–(31) with $d_S = d_I = d_R = 0$ and $\sigma_1 = \sigma_2 = \sigma_3 = 0$ is given as:

$$J = \begin{bmatrix} -\frac{\beta(x)I}{1+mI} - \mu & (1-p)\delta(x) + \frac{\beta(x)mSI}{(1+mI)^2} - \frac{\beta S}{1+mI} & \gamma(x) \\ \frac{\beta(x)I}{1+mI} & -\alpha(x) - \delta(x) - \mu(x) - \frac{\beta(x)mIS}{(1+mI)^2} + \frac{\beta(x)S}{1+mI} & 0 \\ 0 & \delta(x)p & -\gamma(x) - \mu(x) \end{bmatrix} \tag{37}$$

The Jacobian at the disease-free equilibrium point B is given by:

$$J|_B = \begin{bmatrix} -\mu(x) & (1-\rho)\delta(x) - \frac{\beta(x)\bigwedge(x)}{\mu(x)} & \gamma(x) \\ 0 & -\alpha(x) - \delta(x) - \mu(x) - \frac{\beta(x)\bigwedge(x)}{\mu(x)} & 0 \\ 0 & \delta(x)\rho & -\gamma(x) - \mu(x) \end{bmatrix} \quad (38)$$

The Eigenvalue of $J|_B$ is found to be:

$$\lambda_1 = -\mu(x), \lambda_2 = -\gamma(x) - \mu(x), \lambda_3 = \frac{-\alpha(x)\mu(x) - \delta(x)\mu(x) - \mu^2(x) + \beta(x)\bigwedge(x)}{\mu(x)}$$

Since λ_1 and λ_2 are negative, and λ_3 will be negative if:

$$-\alpha(x)\mu(x) - \delta(x)\mu(x) - \mu^2(x) + \beta(x)\bigwedge(x) < 0$$

it is implied that:

$$\beta(x)\bigwedge(x) < \alpha(x)\mu(x) + \delta(x)\mu(x) + \mu^2(x)$$

□

5. Discussions

A stochastic finite difference method is proposed, which is an explicit scheme. The scheme can be applied to discretize time variables in the considered stochastic parabolic equations. The second-order central difference formulas discretize the space terms since the considered diffusive epidemic model consists of the second-order spatial derivatives. The scheme is conditionally stable, and it is conditionally convergent. The scheme can be used for both classical and stochastic parabolic equations. The stability condition of the scheme depends upon both the time and space step sizes and the contained parameters in the epidemic diffusive model. For the adopted model, the boundary conditions are Neumann type. So, to handle these boundary conditions using the finite difference explicit scheme, an additional iterative scheme is also employed. The iterative scheme requires an initial guess to start the solution procedure. It also requires a stopping criterion for breaking the loop over the iterations. The outer loop is employed for using the iterative scheme that will be stopped if the maximum of norms of solutions computed on two consecutive iterations will be less than some tolerance. The iterative scheme will be stopped if the solution satisfies the mentioned criterion. Otherwise, it will continue to find the solution over the new iteration. So, the convergence of the solution depends on the employed numerical schemes for discretizing the stochastic partial differential equations and stopping or converging the criteria of the iterative scheme.

Given the abundance of mathematical models about epidemic diseases documented in the literature, employing an approximate analytical or numerical scheme to solve even the most complex ones is necessary. A numerical scheme for solving deterministic and stochastic models is proposed in this work. Additionally, existing numerical schemes for deterministic cases are contrasted to the scheme. The scheme under consideration is capable of solving both deterministic and stochastic models. The Euler–Maruyama technique is available as a method for solving stochastic differential equations. The method applies stochastic models to the classical forwards Euler method for deterministic models. If the coefficient of the Weiner process term remains constant, the method precisely integrates it. However, it approximates the integral of the Weiner process term with respect to the variable coefficient. The proposed methodology yields a more precise solution for deterministic models than the Euler method. Approximating the integral of the stochastic component of the differential equation is the function of the stochastic component of the scheme.

6. Results

There exist numerical schemes for finding solutions to epidemic models and providing a guarantee for obtaining positive solutions. Among these schemes, the non-standard finite difference method (NSFD) can be used to solve epidemic models and guarantee the positivity of the solution. Among the existing NSFD methods, one provides an unconditionally stable solution and gives surety for the positive solution. In this work, a comparison of the proposed numerical scheme is made with the existing NSFD method. Figure 1 compares the stochastic and deterministic solutions using the proposed scheme. Figures 2–4 show this comparison, and the first-order forward Euler method obtains the solution. Due to the lack of first-order accuracy of the NSFD, the obtained solution deviates slightly from the first- or second-order solutions. The first-order solution is obtained by employing the forward Euler method, and the second-order solution is obtained by the proposed scheme for the deterministic model. This deficiency in existing finite difference has also been proved in [53] for the diffusive models. Since the solutions to an epidemic remain positive for some chosen values of parameters, any numerical scheme can be considered for those cases. Therefore, the proposed scheme and first-order Euler methods are also employed for the epidemic model. Figure 5 shows the effect of the transmission rate parameter on the susceptible people. The susceptible people grow by rising transmission rate parameters. The effect of the transmission rate parameter on infected people can be seen in Figure 6. The infected people grow as the transmission rate parameter enhances. The effect of the transmission rate parameter on recovered people can be seen in Figure 7. The recovered people are also grown by rising transmission rate parameters. Since recovered people become susceptible, when recovered people grow, the susceptible people also grow. The number of infected people increases because susceptibility converts to infection by rising transmission rate parameters. The effect of the coefficient of partial immunity on susceptible individuals is shown in Figure 8. The susceptible people decay by the rising coefficient of the partial immunity parameter. Figures 9 and 10 show the effect of the coefficient of partial immunity on infected and recovered people. The infected people decay, and the recovered people grow by enhancing the coefficient of partial immunity. The coefficient of partial immunity produces growth in the body's immune system, leading to decay in infected people and growth in recovered people. Figures 11–13 show the contour plots for susceptible, infected, and recovered people for the deterministic model. The variation in both space coordinates can be seen in these contour plots. The mesh plots underneath the contours are also displayed in Figures 14–16 for the stochastic model. The effect of the Wiener process term can be seen in the mesh underneath the contour plots. The large coefficient of the Wiener process term gives more oscillation-type solutions than those with a small coefficient of Weiner process terms.

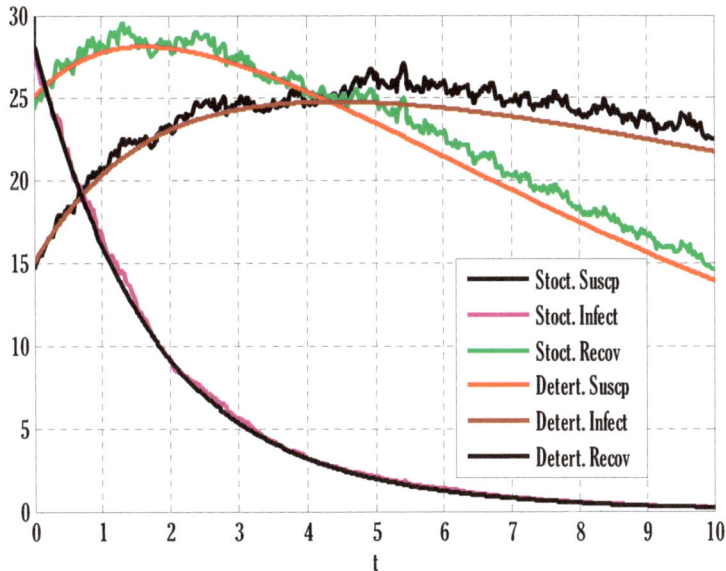

Figure 1. Comparison of stochastic and deterministic solutions of the considered model using $d_1 = 0.3, d_2 = 0.1, d_3 = 0.3, \Lambda = 0.7, \beta = 0.01, p = 0.5, m = 0.5, \delta = 0.5, \mu = 0.07, \alpha = 0.05, \gamma = 0.03, S_0 = 15, I_0 = 30, N = 70, \sigma_1 = 0.1, \sigma_2 = 0.1, \sigma_3 = 0.1$.

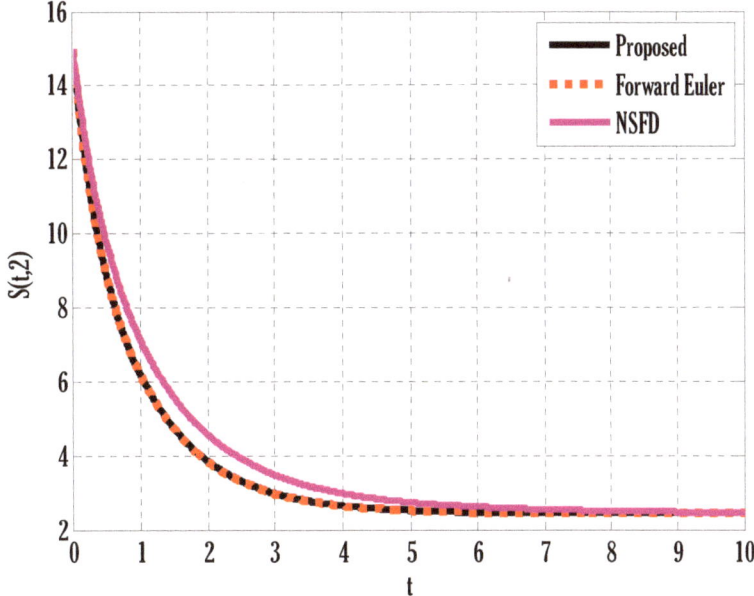

Figure 2. Comparison of proposed, Euler, and NSFD methods for susceptible people in the deterministic model using $d_1 = 0.3, d_2 = 0.1, d_3 = 0.3, \Lambda = 1.7, \beta = 0.3, p = 0. m = 0.1, \delta = 0.5, \mu = 0.5, \alpha = 0.5, \gamma = 0.3, S_0 = 15, I_0 = 30, N = 70$.

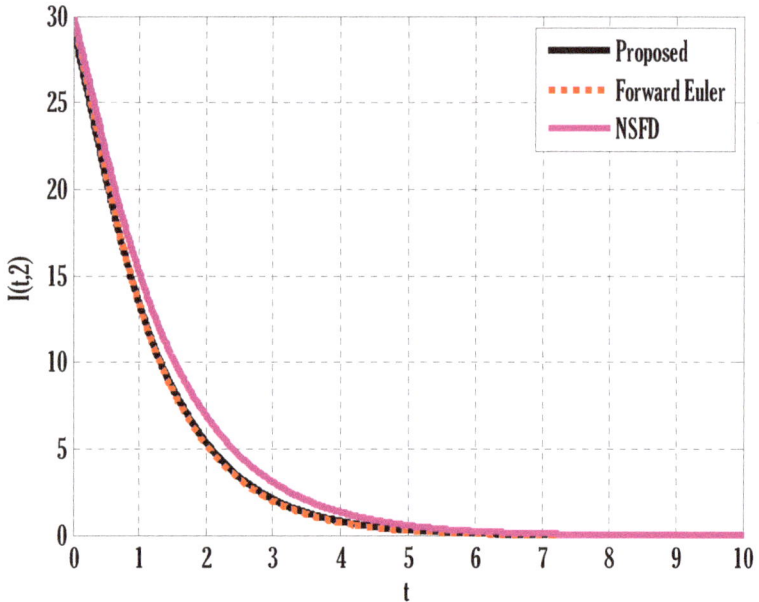

Figure 3. Comparison of proposed, Euler, and NSFD methods for infected people in the deterministic model using $d_1 = 0.3, d_2 = 0.1, d_3 = 0.3, \Lambda = 1.7, \beta = 0.3, p = 0. m = 0.1, \delta = 0.5, \mu = 0.5, \alpha = 0.5, \gamma = 0.3, S_0 = 15, I_0 = 30, N = 70$.

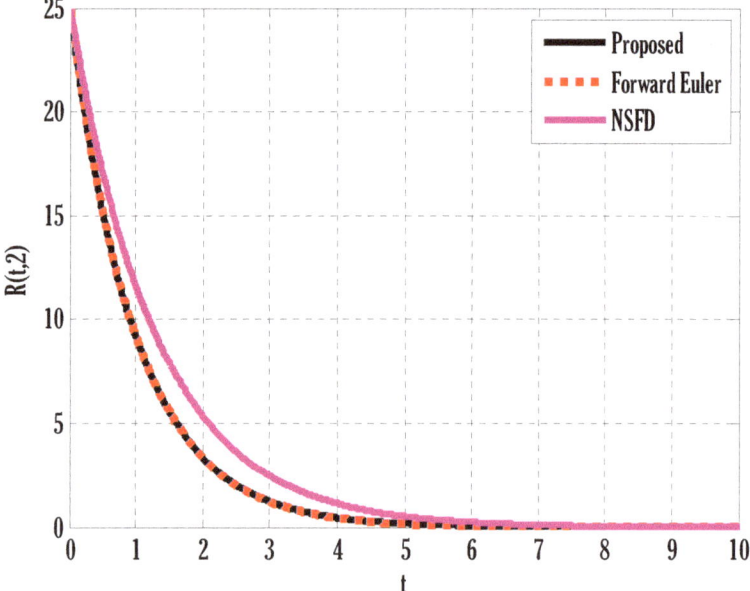

Figure 4. Comparison of proposed, Euler, and NSFD methods for recovered people in the deterministic model using $d_1 = 0.3, d_2 = 0.1, d_3 = 0.3, \Lambda = 1.7, \beta = 0.3, p = 0, m = 0.1, \delta = 0.5, \mu = 0.5, \alpha = 0.5, \gamma = 0.3, S_0 = 15, I_0 = 30, N = 70$.

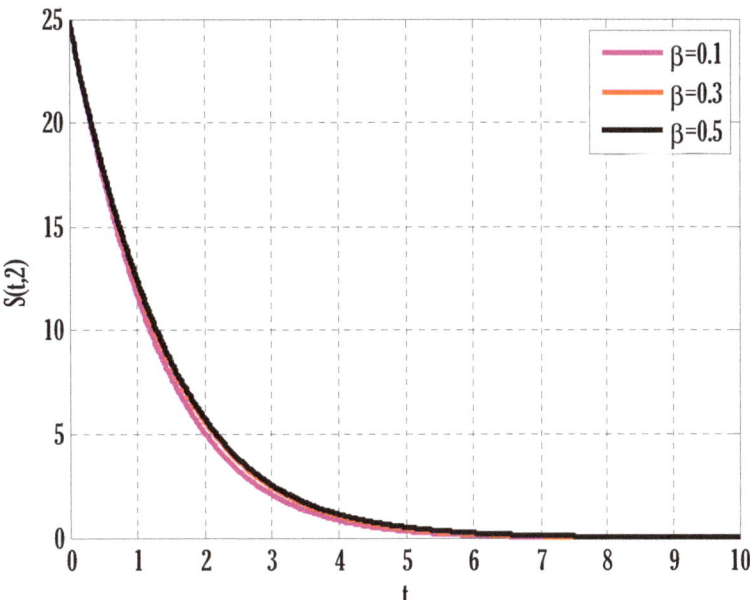

Figure 5. Effect of transmission rate on susceptible people in the deterministic model using $d_1 = 0.3, d_2 = 0.1, d_3 = 0.3, \Lambda = 1.7, p = 0.5, m = 0.1, \delta = 0.5, \mu = 0.7, \alpha = 0.5, \gamma = 0.3, S_0 = 15, I_0 = 30, N = 70$.

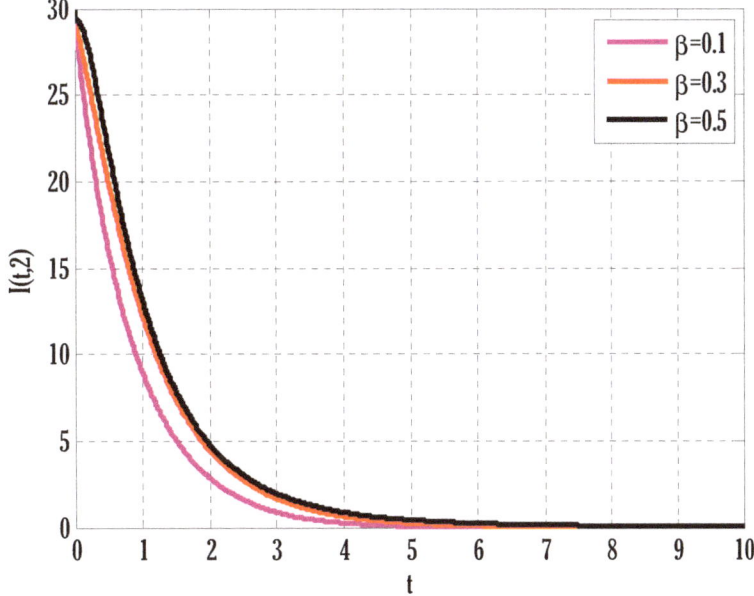

Figure 6. Effect of transmission rate on infected people in the deterministic model using $d_1 = 0.3, d_2 = 0.1, d_3 = 0.3, \Lambda = 1.7, p = 0.5, m = 0.1, \delta = 0.5, \mu = 0.7, \alpha = 0.5, \gamma = 0.3, S_0 = 15, I_0 = 30, N = 70$.

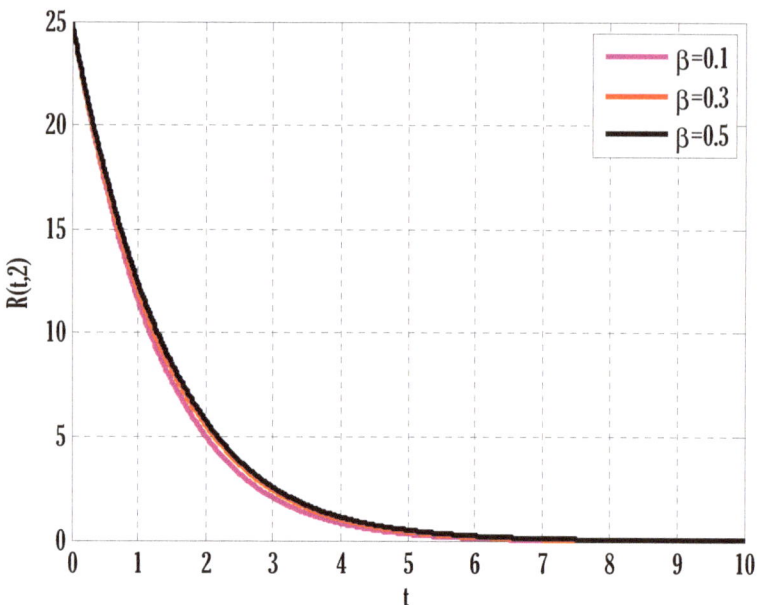

Figure 7. Effect of transmission rate on recovered people in the deterministic model using $d_1 = 0.3, d_2 = 0.1, d_3 = 0.3, \Lambda = 1.7, p = 0.5, m = 0.1, \delta = 0.5, \mu = 0.7, \alpha = 0.5, \gamma = 0.3, S_0 = 15, I_0 = 30, N = 70$.

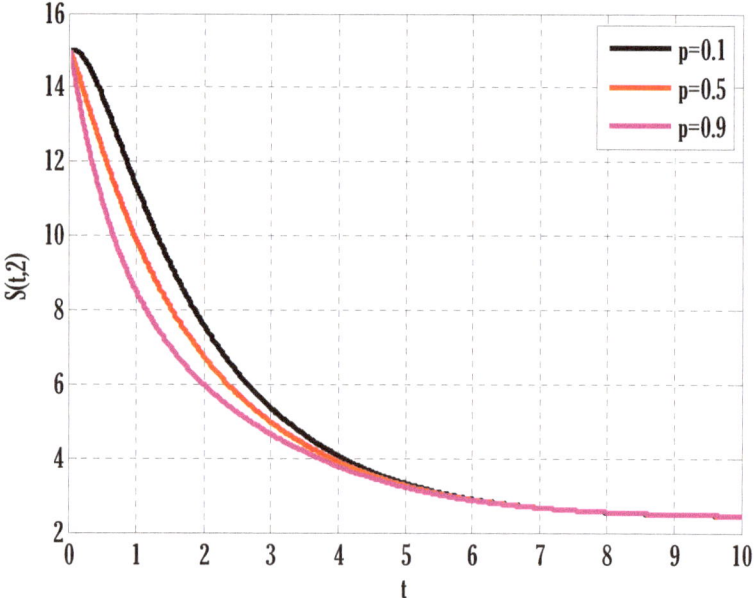

Figure 8. Effect of coefficient of partial immunity on susceptible people in the deterministic model using $d_1 = 0.3, d_2 = 0.1, d_3 = 0.3, \Lambda = 1.7, \beta = 0.1, m = 0.1, \delta = 0.5, \mu = 0.7, \alpha = 0.5, \gamma = 0.3, S_0 = 15, I_0 = 30, N = 70$.

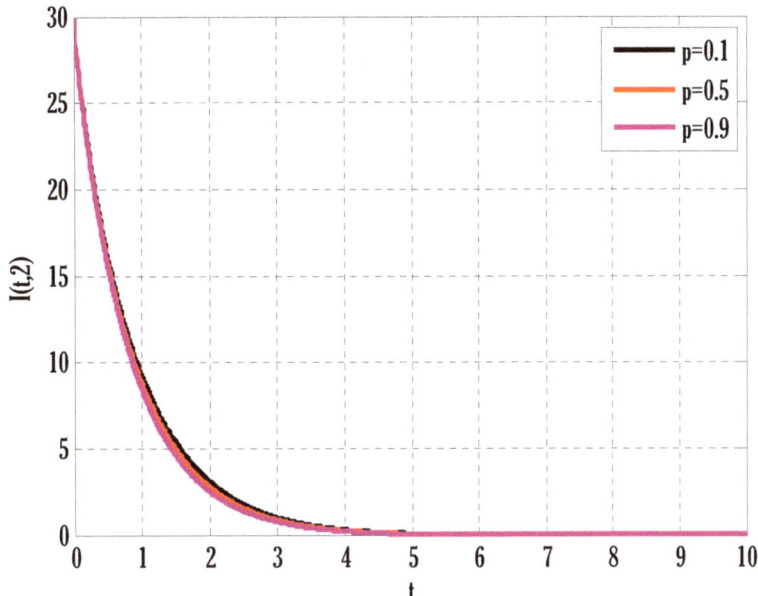

Figure 9. Effect of coefficient of partial immunity on infected people in the deterministic model using $d_1 = 0.3, d_2 = 0.1, d_3 = 0.3, \Lambda = 1.7, \beta = 0.1, m = 0.1, \delta = 0.5, \mu = 0.7, \alpha = 0.5, \gamma = 0.3, S_0 = 15, I_0 = 30, N = 70$.

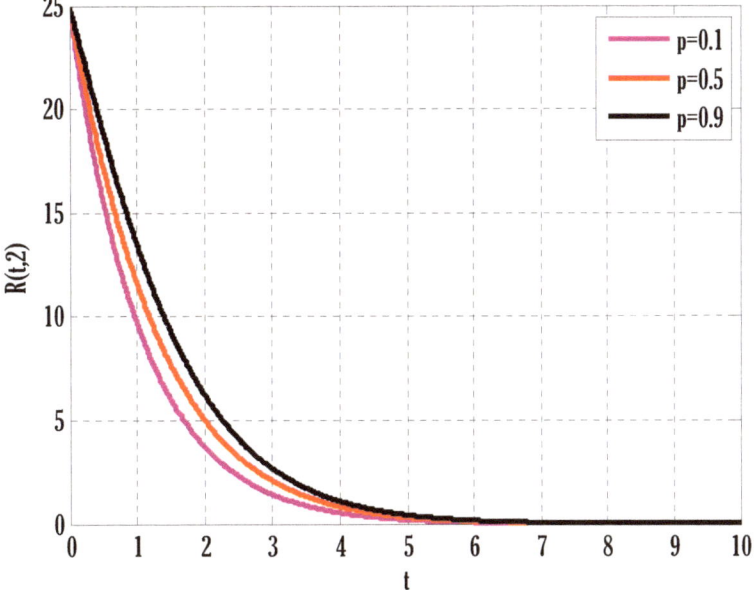

Figure 10. Effect of coefficient of partial immunity on recovered people in the deterministic model using $d_1 = 0.3, d_2 = 0.1, d_3 = 0.3, \Lambda = 1.7, \beta = 0.1, m = 0.1, \delta = 0.5, \mu = 0.7, \alpha = 0.5, \gamma = 0.3, S_0 = 15, I_0 = 30, N = 70$.

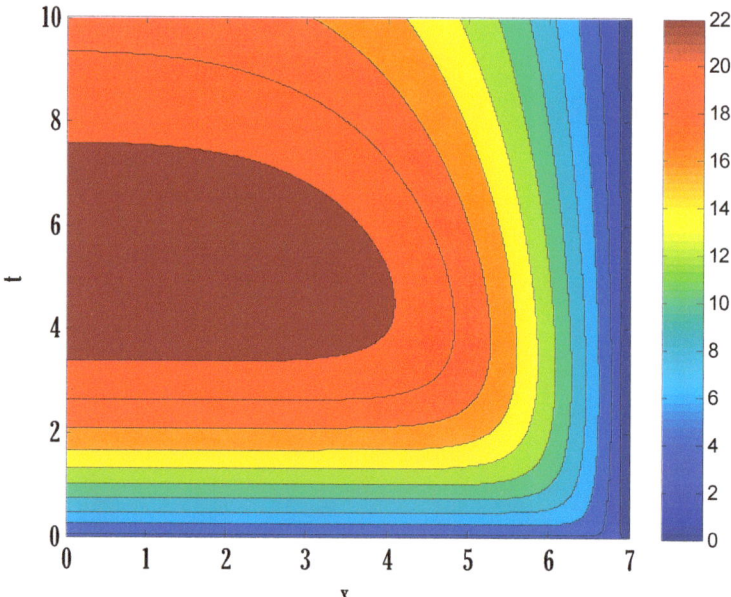

Figure 11. Contour plot on susceptible people in the deterministic model using $d_1 = 0.3$, $d_2 = 0.1, d_3 = 0.3, \Lambda = 0.7, \beta = 0.1, m = 0.4, p = 0.2, \delta = 0.5, \mu = 0.1, \alpha = 0.5, \gamma = 0.1$, $S_0 = 3.5, I_0 = 1.702, N = 100$.

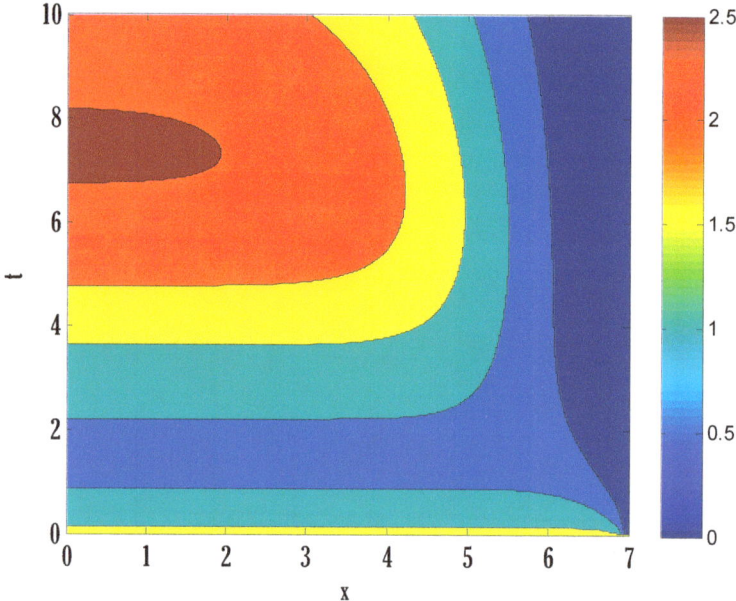

Figure 12. Contour plot on infected people in the deterministic model using $d_1 = 0.3$, $d_2 = 0.1$, $d_3 = 0.3, \Lambda = 0.7, \beta = 0.1, m = 0.4, p = 0.2, \delta = 0.5, \mu = 0.1, \alpha = 0.5, \gamma = 0.1, S_0 = 3.5$, $I_0 = 1.702, N = 100$.

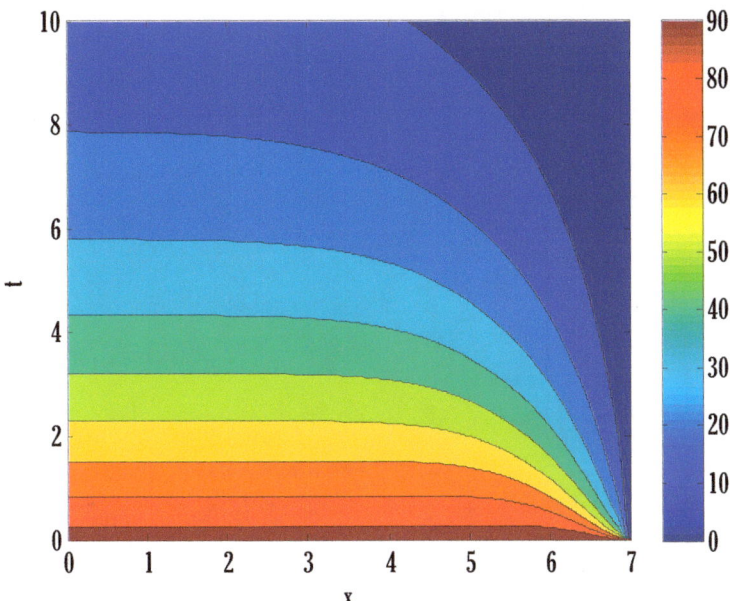

Figure 13. Contour plot on recovered people in the deterministic model using $d_1 = 0.3, d_2 = 0.1, d_3 = 0.3, \Lambda = 0.7, \beta = 0.1, m = 0.4, p = 0.2, \delta = 0.5, \mu = 0.1, \alpha = 0.5, \gamma = 0.1, S_0 = 3.5, I_0 = 1.702, N = 100$.

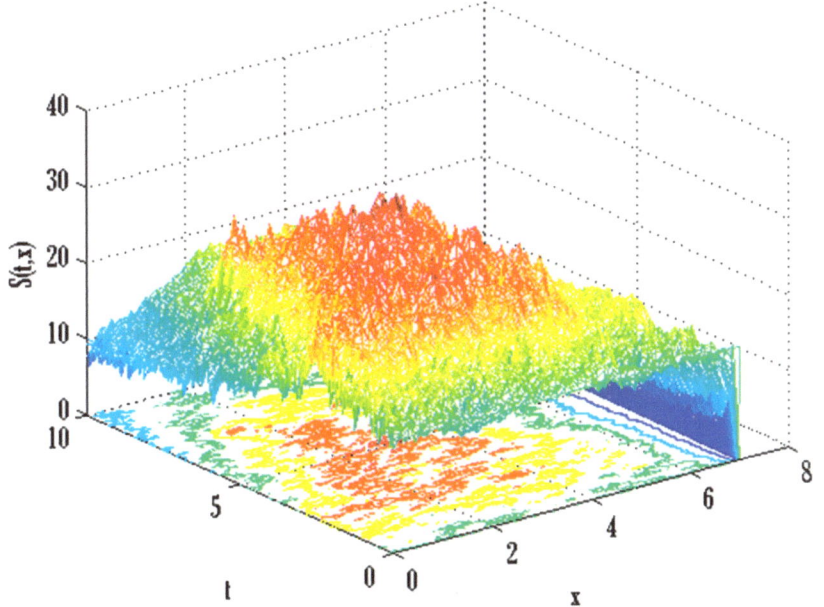

Figure 14. Mesh plot underneath contours for susceptible people of the stochastic model using $d_1 = 0.3, d_2 = 0.1, d_3 = 0.3, \Lambda = 0.7, \beta = 0.1, m = 0.5, p = 0.9, \delta = 0.5, \mu = 0.1, \alpha = 0.1, \gamma = 0.3, S_0 = 15, I_0 = 30, N = 70, \sigma_1 = 0.5, \sigma_2 = 0.1, \sigma_3 = 0.1$.

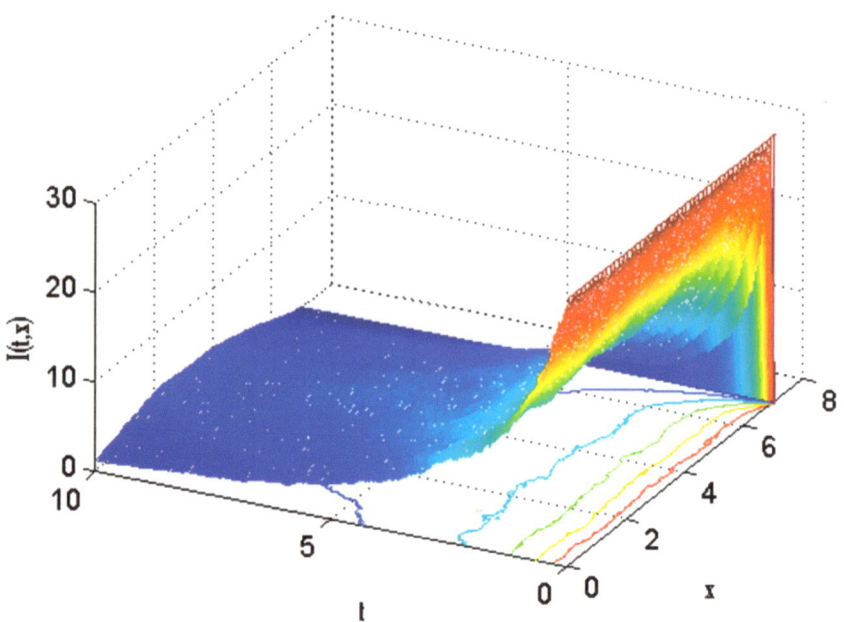

Figure 15. Mesh plot underneath contours for infected people of the stochastic model using $d_1 = 0.3, d_2 = 0.1, d_3 = 0.3, \Lambda = 0.7, \beta = 0.1, m = 0.5, p = 0.9, \delta = 0.5, \mu = 0.1, \alpha = 0.1, \gamma = 0.3, S_0 = 15, I_0 = 30, N = 70, \sigma_1 = 0.5, \sigma_2 = 0.1, \sigma_3 = 0.1$.

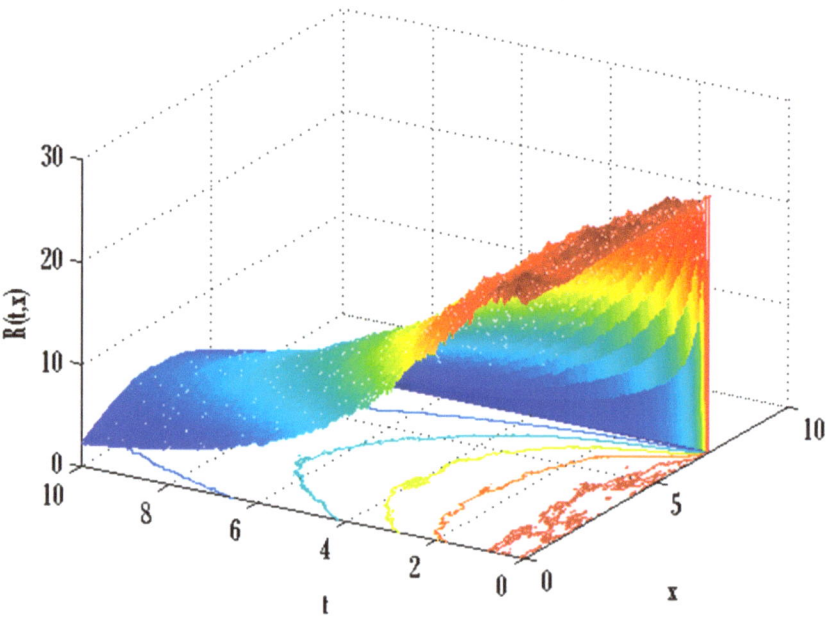

Figure 16. Mesh plot underneath contours for recovered people of the stochastic model using $d_1 = 0.3, d_2 = 0.1, d_3 = 0.3, \Lambda = 0.7, \beta = 0.1, m = 0.5, p = 0.9, \delta = 0.5, \mu = 0.1, \alpha = 0.1, \gamma = 0.3, S_0 = 15, I_0 = 30, N = 70, \sigma_1 = 0.5, \sigma_2 = 0.1, \sigma_3 = 0.1$.

7. Conclusions

A computational scheme has been proposed for solving the stochastic diffusive SIRS model with an incidence rate and partial immunity. An additional iterative scheme has also been employed for handling Neumann-type boundary conditions applied on each domain end. So, a stopping criterion was also set up to stop the iterative procedure for the deterministic model. The computational framework utilized for the stochastic SIRS reaction–diffusion model with partial immunity and an incidence rate holds significant potential and adaptability within epidemiology and mathematical modelling. It has wide-ranging uses and can improve our understanding of infectious disease dynamics and help us create better prevention and treatment methods. Due to its ability to account for factors including partial immunity, regional diffusion, and changing incidence rates, this model is invaluable for public health planning and disease management. This computational technique adds to our understanding of infectious diseases in various populations and geographical locations by examining the complex relationship between immunity, spatial spread, and disease transmission. In the face of new infectious diseases and endemic pathogens, it is crucial to assess immunization tactics, research disease evolution, and forecast future trends. Because of its stochastic nature, the model more accurately represents epidemiological processes, which is important because of the inherent uncertainty in disease transmission. This is of great use when the spread of a disease is heavily influenced by chance and the activities of individuals. This method links theoretical epidemiological studies and real-world public health policymaking. The concluding points can be expressed as:

1. Comparison showed that the proposed scheme was more accurate than the existing NSFD scheme for the deterministic model.
2. Susceptible, infected, and recovered people were seen to grow by enhancing transmission parameters.
3. Infected and recovered people were also grown by raising the coefficient of partial immunity.
4. The proposed scheme performed better than the existing non-standard finite difference method in order of accuracy.

The stochastic SIRS reaction–diffusion model with partial immunity and an incidence rate is useful for researchers, politicians, and medical professionals in a world where infectious illnesses threaten public health systems. Using it, we may better manage infectious disease outbreaks, distribute scarce resources, and prepare for emergencies, all of which improve public health and lessen these crises' toll on the world's population. Upon the conclusion of this project, it is possible to propose further applications for the existing strategy [54–56]. This model will continue to be at the forefront of attempts to address the ever-changing environment of infectious illnesses as research in this field develops.

Author Contributions: Conceptualization, methodology, and analysis, A.S.B.; funding acquisition, A.S.B.; investigation, Y.N.; methodology, Y.N.; visualization, M.S.A.; writing—review and editing, M.S.A.; resources, K.A.; supervision, K.A.; data curation, M.A.A.; formal analysis, M.A.A. All authors have read and agreed to the published version of the manuscript.

Funding: This work was supported and funded by the Deanship of Scientific Research at Imam Mohammad Ibn Saud Islamic University (IMSIU) (grant number IMSIU-RG23014).

Data Availability Statement: The manuscript includes all required data and implementing information.

Acknowledgments: This research was supported by the Deanship of Scientific Research, Imam Mohammad Ibn Saud Islamic University (IMSIU), Saudi Arabia, Grant No. (IMSIU-RG23014).

Conflicts of Interest: The authors declare no conflict of interest to report regarding the present study.

References

1. Adnani, J.; Hattaf, K.; Yousfi, N. Stability Analysis of a Stochastic SIR Epidemic Model with Specific Nonlinear Incidence Rate. *Int. J. Stoch. Anal.* **2013**, *2013*, 431257. [CrossRef]

2. Jehad, A.; Ghada, A.; Shah, H.; Elissa, N.; Hasib, K. Stochastic dynamics of influenza infection: Qualitative analysis and numerical results. *Math. Biosci. Eng.* **2022**, *19*, 10316–10331.
3. Shah, H.; Elissa, N.; Hasib, K.; Haseena, G.; Sina, E.; Shahram, R.; Mohammed, K. On the Stochastic Modeling of COVID-19 under the Environmental White Noise. *J. Funct. Spaces* **2022**, *2022*, 4320865.
4. Miaomiao, G.; Daqing, J.; Tasawar, H. Stationary distribution and periodic solution of stochasticchemostat models with single-species growthon two nutrients. *Int. J. Biomath.* **2019**, *12*, 1950063.
5. Liu, Q.; Jiang, D.; Shi, N.; Hayat, T.; Alsaedi, A. Asymptotic behavior of a stochastic delayed SEIR epidemic model with nonlinear incidence. *Phys. A* **2016**, *462*, 870–882. [CrossRef]
6. Tailei, Z.; Zhidong, T. Global asymptotic stability of a delayed SEIRS epidemic model with saturation incidence. *Chaos Solitons Fractals* **2008**, *37*, 1456–1468.
7. Rui, X.; Zhien, M. Global stability of a SIR epidemic model with nonlinear incidence rate and time delay. *Nonlinear Anal. Real World Appl.* **2009**, *10*, 3175–3189.
8. Hattaf, K.; Mahrouf, M.; Adnani, J.; Yousfi, N. Qualitative analysis of a stochastic epidemic model with specific functional response and temporary immunity. *Phys. A* **2018**, *490*, 591–600. [CrossRef]
9. Pitchaimani, M.; Brasanna, D.M. Stochastic dynamical probes in a triple delayed SICR model with general incidence rate and immunization strategies. *Chaos Solitons Fractals* **2021**, *143*, 110540.
10. Xu, C.; Li, X. The threshold of a stochastic delayed SIRS epidemic model with temporary immunity and vaccination. *Chaos Solitons Fractals* **2018**, *111*, 227–234. [CrossRef]
11. Xianning, L.; Yasuhiro, T.; Shingo, I. SVIR epidemic models with vaccination strategies. *J. Theoret. Biol.* **2008**, *253*, 1–11.
12. Zhang, X.; Jiang, D.; Hayat, T.; Ahmad, B. Dynamical behavior of a stochastic SVIR epidemic model with vaccination. *Phys. A* **2017**, *483*, 94–108. [CrossRef]
13. Li, F.; Zhang, S.Q.; Meng, X.Z. Dynamics analysis and numerical simulations of a delayed stochastic epidemic model subject to a general response function. *Comput. Appl. Math.* **2019**, *38*, 95. [CrossRef]
14. Hattaf, K.; Yousfi, N.; Tridane, A. Stability analysis of a virus dynamics model with general incidence rate and two delays. *Appl. Math. Comput.* **2013**, *221*, 514–521. [CrossRef]
15. Wang, J.; Zhang, J.; Jin, Z. Analysis of an SIR model with bilinear incidence rate. *Nonlinear Anal. Real World Appl.* **2010**, *11*, 2390–2402. [CrossRef]
16. Liu, X.; Yang, L. Stability analysis of an SEIQV epidemic model with saturated incidence rate. *Nonlinear Anal. Real World Appl.* **2012**, *13*, 2671–2679. [CrossRef]
17. Zhao, Y.; Jiang, D. The threshold of a stochastic SIRS epidemic model with saturated incidence. *Appl. Math. Lett.* **2014**, *34*, 90–93. [CrossRef]
18. Cantrell, R.; Cosner, C. On the dynamics of predator-prey models with the Beddington–DeAngelis functional response. *J. Math. Anal. Appl.* **2001**, *257*, 206–222. [CrossRef]
19. Zhou, X.; Cui, J. Global stability of the viral dynamics with Crowley–Martin functional response. *Bull. Korean Math. Soc.* **2011**, *48*, 555–574. [CrossRef]
20. Anderson, R.; Garnett, G. Low-efficacy HIV vaccines: Potential for community-based intervention programmes. *Lancet* **1996**, *348*, 1010–1013. [CrossRef]
21. Chaves, S.; Gargiullo, P.; Zhang, J.; Civen, R.; Guris, D.; Mascola, L.; Seward, J. Loss of vaccine-induced immunity to varicella over time. *N. Engl. J. Med.* **2007**, *356*, 1121–1129. [CrossRef] [PubMed]
22. Wendelboe, A.; Van Rie, A.; Salmaso, S.; Englund, J. Duration of immunity against pertussis after natural infection or vaccination. *Pediatr. Infect. Dis. J.* **2005**, *24*, 58–61. [CrossRef] [PubMed]
23. Craig, M.P. An evolutionary epidemiological mechanism, with applications to type a influenza. *Theor. Popul. Biol.* **1987**, *31*, 422–452.
24. Nowak, M.A.; Bonhoeffer, S.; Hill, A.M.; Boehme, R.; Thomas, H.C.; McDade, H. Viral dynamics in hepatitis B virus infection. *Proc. Natl. Acad. Sci. USA* **1996**, *93*, 4398–4402. [CrossRef]
25. Wang, K.; Wang, W. Propagation of HBV with spatial dependence. *Math. Biosci.* **2007**, *210*, 78–95. [CrossRef] [PubMed]
26. Suryanto, A.; Darti, I. On the non-standard numerical discretization of SIR epidemic model with a saturated incidence rate and vaccination. *AIMS Math.* **2021**, *6*, 141–155. [CrossRef]
27. Naik, P.A.; Zu, J.; Ghoreishi, M. Stability analysis and approximate solution of SIR epidemic model with Crowley–Martin type functional response and holling type-II treatment rate by using homotopy analysis method. *J. Appl. Anal. Comput.* **2020**, *10*, 1482–1515.
28. Ahmad, I.; Khan, M.N.; Inc, M.; Ahmad, H.; Nisar, K.S. Numerical simulation of simulate an anomalous solute transport model via local meshless method. *Alex. Eng. J.* **2020**, *59*, 2827–2838. [CrossRef]
29. Ahmad, H.; Akgül, A.; Khan, T.A.; Stanimirovic, P.S.; Chu, Y.M. New perspective on the conventional solutions of the nonlinear time-fractional partial differential equations. *Complexity* **2020**, *2020*, 8829017. [CrossRef]
30. Ahmad, H.; Khan, T.A.; Stanimirovic, P.S.; Ahmad, I. Modified variational iteration technique for the numerical? solution of fifth order KdV-type equations. *J. Appl. Comput. Mech.* **2020**, *6*, 1220–1227.
31. Ahmad, H.; Seadawy, A.R.; Khana, T.A. Modified variational iteration algorithm to find approximate solutions of nonlinear Parabolic equation. *Math. Comput. Simul.* **2020**, *177*, 13–23. [CrossRef]

32. Ahmad, I.; Ahmad, H.; Inc, M.; Yao, S.W.; Almohsen, B. Application of local meshless method for the solution of two term time fractional-order multi-dimensional PDE arising in heat and mass transfer. *Therm. Sci.* **2020**, *24* (Suppl. S1), 95–105. [CrossRef]
33. Inc, M.; Khan, M.N.; Ahmad, I.; Yao, S.W.; Ahmad, H.; Thounthong, P. Analysing time-fractional exotic options via efficient local meshless method. *Results Phys.* **2020**, *19*, 103385. [CrossRef]
34. Khan, M.N.; Ahmad, I.; Ahmad, H. A Radial Basis Function Collocation Method for Space-dependent? Inverse Heat Problems. *J. Appl. Comput. Mech.* **2020**. Available online: https://jacm.scu.ac.ir/article_15512_e7b25d7b217ff1267e45fc596fbfa54b.pdf (accessed on 22 November 2023).
35. Shah, N.A.; Ahmad, I.; Bazighifan, O.; Abouelregal, A.E.; Ahmad, H. Multistage optimal homotopy asymptotic method for the nonlinear Riccati ordinary differential equation in nonlinear physics. *Appl. Math.* **2020**, *14*, 1009–1016.
36. Wang, F.; Ali, S.N.; Ahmad, I.; Ahmad, H.; Alam, K.M.; Thounthong, P. Solution of Burgers' equation appears in fluid mechanics by multistage optimal homotopy asymptotic method. *Therm. Sci.* **2022**, *26* 1 Pt B, 815–821. [CrossRef]
37. Liu, X.; Ahsan, M.; Ahmad, M.; Nisar, M.; Liu, X.; Ahmad, I.; Ahmad, H. Applications of Haar wavelet-finite difference hybrid method and its convergence for hyperbolic nonlinear Schrö dinger equation with energy and mass conversion. *Energies* **2021**, *14*, 7831. [CrossRef]
38. Ahsan, M.; Lin, S.; Ahmad, M.; Nisar, M.; Ahmad, I.; Ahmed, H.; Liu, X. A Haar wavelet-based scheme for finding the control parameter in nonlinear inverse heat conduction equation. *Open Phys.* **2021**, *19*, 722–734. [CrossRef]
39. Yasin, M.W.; Ahmed, N.; Iqbal, M.S.; Rafiq, M.; Raza, A.; Akgül, A. Reliable numerical analysis for stochastic reaction–diffusion system. *Phys. Scr.* **2022**, *98*, 015209. [CrossRef]
40. Wang, X.; Yasin, M.W.; Ahmed, N.; Rafiq, M.; Abbas, M. Numerical approximations of stochastic Gray–Scott model with two novel schemes. *AIMS Math.* **2023**, *8*, 5124–5147. [CrossRef]
41. Yasin, M.W.; Ahmed, N.; Iqbal, M.S.; Raza, A.; Rafiq, M.; Eldin, E.M.T.; Khan, I. Spatio-temporal numerical modeling of stochastic predator–prey model. *Sci. Rep.* **2023**, *13*, 1990. [CrossRef] [PubMed]
42. Macías-Díaz, J.E.; Raza, A.; Ahmed, N.; Rafiq, M. Analysis of a non-standard computer method to simulate a nonlinear stochastic epidemiological model of coronavirus-like diseases. *Comput. Methods Prog. Biomed.* **2021**, *204*, 106054. [CrossRef] [PubMed]
43. Raza, A.; Rafiq, M.; Ahmed, N.; Khan, I.; Nisar, K.S.; Iqbal, Z. A structure preserving numerical method for solution of stochastic epidemic model of smoking dynamics. *Comput. Mater. Contin.* **2020**, *65*, 263–278. [CrossRef]
44. Ahmed, N.; Macías-Díaz, J.E.; Raza, A.; Baleanu, D.; Rafiq, M.; Iqbal, Z.; Ahmad, M.O. Design analysis and comparison of a non-standard computational method for the solution of a general stochastic fractional epidemic model. *Axioms* **2021**, *11*, 10. [CrossRef]
45. Raza, A.; Arif, M.S.; Rafiq, M. A reliable numerical analysis for stochastic dengue epidemic model with incubation period of virus. *Adv. Differ. Equ.* **2019**, *2019*, 32. [CrossRef]
46. Alkhazzan, A.; Wang, J.; Nie, Y.; Hattaf, K. A new stochastic split-step θ-nonstandard finite difference method for the developed SVIR epidemic model with temporary immunities and general incidence rates. *Vaccines* **2022**, *10*, 1682. [CrossRef]
47. Ali, A.; Alshammari, F.S.; Islam, S.; Khan, M.A.; Ullah, S. Modeling and analysis of the dynamics of novel coronavirus (COVID-19) with Caputo fractional derivative. *Results Phys.* **2021**, *20*, 103669. [CrossRef]
48. Ali, A.; Islam, S.; Rasheed, S.; Allehiany, F.; Baili, J.; Khan, M.A.; Ahmad, H. Dynamics of a fractional order Zika virus model with mutant. *Alex. Eng. J.* **2022**, *61*, 4821–4836. [CrossRef]
49. Aba Oud, M.A.; Ali, A.; Alrabaiah, H.; Ullah, S.; Khan, M.A.; Islam, S. A fractional order mathematical model for COVID-19 dynamics with quarantine, isolation, and environmental viral load. *Adv. Differ. Equ.* **2021**, *2021*, 106. [CrossRef]
50. Ali, A.; Ullah, S.; Khan, M.A. The impact of vaccination on the modeling of COVID-19 dynamics: A fractional order model. *Nonlinear Dyn.* **2022**, *110*, 3921–3940. [CrossRef]
51. Li, P.; Peng, X.; Xu, C.; Han, L.; Shi, S. Novel extended mixed controller design for bifurcation control of fractional-order Myc/E2F/miR-17-92 network model concerning delay. *Math. Methods Appl. Sci.* **2023**, *46*, 18878–18898. [CrossRef]
52. Wang, J.; Teng, Z.; Dai, B. Qualitative analysis of a reaction-diffusion SIRS epidemic model with nonlinear incidence rate and partial immunity. *Infect. Dis. Model.* **2023**, *8*, 881e911. [CrossRef] [PubMed]
53. Pasha, S.A.; Nawaz, Y.; Arif, M.S. On the non-standard finite difference method for reaction–diffusion models. *Chaos Solitons Fractals* **2023**, *166*, 112929. [CrossRef]
54. Arif, M.S.; Abodayeh, K.; Nawaz, Y. *Construction of a Computational Scheme for the Fuzzy HIV/AIDS Epidemic Model with a Nonlinear Saturated Incidence Rate*; Tech Science Press: Norwood, MA, USA, 2023. [CrossRef]
55. Arif, M.S.; Abodayeh, K.; Nawaz, Y. A Reliable Computational Scheme for Stochastic Reaction–Diffusion Nonlinear Chemical Model. *Axioms* **2023**, *12*, 460. [CrossRef]
56. Nawaz, Y.; Arif, M.S.; Bibi, K.A.A.M. Finite Difference Schemes for Time-Dependent Convection q-Diffusion Problem. *AIMS Math.* **2022**, *7*, 16407–16421. [CrossRef]

Disclaimer/Publisher's Note: The statements, opinions and data contained in all publications are solely those of the individual author(s) and contributor(s) and not of MDPI and/or the editor(s). MDPI and/or the editor(s) disclaim responsibility for any injury to people or property resulting from any ideas, methods, instructions or products referred to in the content.

Article

Antiangiogenic Therapy Efficacy Can Be Tumor-Size Dependent, as Mathematical Modeling Suggests

Maxim Kuznetsov [†] and Andrey Kolobov *

Division of Theoretical Physics, P.N. Lebedev Physical Institute of the Russian Academy of Sciences,
53 Leninskiy Prospekt, 119991 Moscow, Russia; kuznetsovmb@mail.ru
* Correspondence: scilpi@mail.ru
[†] Current address: Division of Mathematical Oncology and Computational Systems Biology, City of Hope, Duarte, CA 91010, USA.

Abstract: Antiangiogenic therapy (AAT) is an indirect oncological modality that is aimed at the disruption of cancer cell nutrient supply. Invasive tumors have been shown to possess inherent resistance to this treatment, while compactly growing benign tumors react to it by shrinking. It is generally accepted that AAT by itself is not curative. This study presents a mathematical model of non-invasive tumor growth with a physiologically justified account of microvasculature alteration and the biomechanical aspects of importance during tumor growth and AAT. In the untreated setting, the model reproduces tumor growth with saturation, where the maximum tumor volume depends on the level of angiogenesis. The outcomes of the AAT simulations depend on the tumor size at the moment of treatment initiation. If it is close to the stable size of an avascular tumor grown in the absence of angiogenesis, then the tumor is rapidly stabilized by AAT. The treatment of large tumors is accompanied by the displacement of normal tissue due to tumor shrinkage. During this, microvasculature undergoes distortion, the degree of which depends on the displacement distance. As it affects tumor nutrient supply, the stable size of a tumor that undergoes AAT negatively correlates with its size at the beginning of treatment. For sufficiently large initial tumors, the long-term survival of tumor cells is compromised by competition with normal cells for the severely limited inflow of nutrients, which makes AAT effectively curative.

Keywords: mathematical oncology; biomechanics; partial differential equations

MSC: 34Q92; 92C05

1. Introduction

1.1. Biological Background

Cancer currently remains a major cause of morbidity and mortality worldwide [1]. New methods for its treatment, as a rule, have limited efficacy, target only a narrow range of cancer types, and have limited availability to the general public due to their high cost. Therefore, an important challenge in oncology is the optimization of the types of anticancer therapy that are already introduced into clinical practice.

Standard and long-established types of anticancer treatment, such as chemotherapy and radiotherapy, lead to the eradication of actively proliferating cells subject to therapeutic action. The non-selectivity of these treatments inevitably leads to the damage of healthy cells that are reached by chemotherapeutic drugs or are traversed by radiation beams. Recently, a group of radically different anticancer modalities has emerged that perform indirect interference with the mechanisms sustaining the existence of cancer as a complex organ embedded in a host organism [2]. Prominent examples of such approaches are immunotherapy and antiangiogenic therapy. Immunotherapy is an umbrella term for a group of medical interventions aimed at the disruption of the ability of cancer cells to evade immune surveillance [3]. The goal of antiangiogenic therapy (AAT) is breaking the process of tumor angiogenesis, i.e., the formation of blood vessels (in particular, capillaries that provide nutrient exchange [4]). These therapies are not devoid of side-effects, which are, nevertheless, usually more moderate and affect other organs than the standard treatments.

Enabling the process of tumor angiogenesis is a crucial step in cancer progression. In its absence, tumors generally cannot grow beyond the size of 1–2 mm [5]. Further tumor growth is restricted by limited nutrient supply from capillaries located in normal tissues that are pushed away by a growing tumor mass. Thus, an avascular tumor eventually reaches a stable state in which the ongoing proliferation of its cells in the tumor periphery is compensated for by the death of nutrient-deprived cells in its core.

One way for the tumor cells to overcome nutrient deficiency is to invade nearby tissues and co-opt existing capillaries. Enabling invasion is a crucial hallmark of malignant tumors [6]. However, it is a complex process that requires the accumulation of a sufficient number of cell mutations [7]. Since the overall frequency of mutations correlates with the rate of tumor cell divisions, acquiring an invasive phenotype is a long process for small tumors. Angiogenic switching is a faster process that generally manifests itself while a tumor is still benign and lacks invasive properties.

In healthy tissues the process of angiogenesis takes place, e.g., during wound healing, and it leads to an ordered vascular system, finely tuned for each organ. Tumor cells, however, produce angiogenic molecules excessively, which results in the formation of chaotically organized and highly permeable capillary networks. AAT neutralizes the action of angiogenic molecules. This leads to the cessation of the formation of new capillaries, the normalization of the structure of already formed tumor capillaries [8], the further normalization of the density of the capillary network [9], and the alleviation of tumor-associated edema [10].

The restriction of nutrient supply caused by AAT limits the growth of tumors and can yield their shrinkage but generally does not lead to a tumor being cured. This provides ground for the use of AAT in combination with other modalities. In clinical practice, AAT is generally paired with chemotherapy (CT) [11]. There are multiple factors that influence the efficacy of AAT by itself and in combination with CT. In particular, AAT entails the reduced inflow of chemotherapeutic drugs into a tumor, which was observed experimentally [12,13]. This renders the problem of the optimization of AAT-based treatments in clinical practice, which is a highly nontrivial task. Its solution is heavily compromised by the impossibility of testing all the feasible treatment alterations due to logistical and ethical reasons.

1.2. Mathematical Background

A methodology that can point at the potential biomarkers of treatment efficacy and that can significantly narrow down the range of potentially effective therapeutic protocols is mechanistic mathematical modeling. It envisions the tumor and its microenvironment as a single complex system that, contrary to a real-life situation, can be reproduced under a broad variation of parameters and treatment approaches.

Several methods exist for modeling tumor growth when taking into account angiogenesis and AAT. The simplest method relies on the system of ordinary differential equations. The models of this kind generally include an equation for the logistic growth of the tumor volume, with its maximum value being a variable that is dependent on the concentration of the antiangiogenic drug [14]. Although such phenomenological models can be convenient for preclinical and clinical studies, they clearly represent oversimplifications that omit spatial aspects and neglect many of the physiological processes that can influence treatment outcomes.

The most popular approach for modeling angiogenesis and AAT is agent-based modeling, which involves a detailed reproduction of capillary networks and, as is frequently the case, explicit consideration of blood flow maps [15,16]. Such models can provide elegant visualizations of microvasculature remodeling and can yield useful insights. However, they require significant computational costs, which increase with tumor size. That crucially limits the practical use of such models. Up to date, they have not been used to simulate an entire course of AAT.

The use of continuous, spatially distributed models based on partial differential equations can provide a compromise between computational cost and physiological validity [17,18]. Although such models are unable to reproduce the microscopic aspects of a capillary network, they allow for the consideration of the crucial dynamic features of tumor microvasculature under unperturbed tumor growth and under the course of therapy. However, the related models presented nowadays in the literature focus on invasive tumors, and they ignore the biomechanical aspects crucial for the reproduction of tumor response to alterations in microvasculature.

On the other hand, there exists a sufficient amount of modeling studies devoted to the biomechanical aspects accompanying tumor growth and treatment, which do not account for dynamically changing tumor microvasculature. In particular, consideration of interstitial fluid dynamics and their influence on drug delivery is a well-researched problem in the case of static tumors [19–21]. In the case of a dynamic tumor that can both grow and shrink during therapy, a physiologically correct approach to modeling is the simultaneous account of the stress arising in the solid phase of the tissue (cells and extracellular matrix) along with the dynamics of the interstitial fluid since they are closely interrelated. In particular, the deformation of the solid component of the tissue affects fluid flow, while the outflow of fluid from the tumor leads to its shrinkage and to the alleviation of stress exerted by the surrounding normal tissue.

The related works that account for solid stress using mathematical modeling are less numerous. The methods used range from relatively simple to complex. The complex methods are generally adapted from the area of solid mechanics, based on the multiplicative decomposition of the tissue strain gradient tensor into components corresponding to different physical processes [22,23]. The use of such methods is associated with great computational costs but is justified, e.g., if any quantitative agreement with the experimental results is pursued. For qualitative studies, however, a more practical approach is the use of simpler methods that regard tumors as a liquid-like or linearly elastic medium [24,25]. Such methods have been repeatedly proven to be able to qualitatively reproduce experimental observations, e.g., the decrease in maximum tumor size with the increase in applied external pressure [26] and the oozing of liquid from a large tumor due to the elevated pressure in its core [27].

1.3. Current Study

The current study simultaneously considers both the alterations in microvasculature and the evolution of biomechanical aspects during tumor growth and AAT. To the best of our knowledge, this is the first work of this kind to provide simulations of the entire course of AAT. This study is based on our previous works on the mathematical modeling of tumor angiogenesis and AAT [28–30] and on our works focused on the biomechanical properties of tumors and normal tissues [31–34].

Section 2 introduces the mathematical model, providing its crucial assumptions, equations, parameters, and aspects of numerical solving. The model is implemented in C++ computational code (with the use of Dev-C++, version 5.11), which can be downloaded from the Supplementary Materials section. The results are presented in Section 3. Section 3.1 considers free tumor growth with and without angiogenesis. The model reproduced the layered structures of proliferating, quiescent, and dead tumor cells, which are characteristic of non-invasive tumors that yield growth when under saturation. The maximum tumor volume increases with the initiation of angiogenesis. Section 3.2 is devoted to modeling AAT and shows that its effect depends on the tumor size at the moment of its administration. Small tumors are quickly stabilized by AAT, while the treatment of sufficiently large tumors is accompanied by the displacement of normal tissue due to tumor shrinkage, which causes the rupture of capillaries and, thus, effectively provides an additional decrease in tumor nutrient supply. To the best of our knowledge, such qualitative outcomes have not been shown previously in the literature. Section 3.3 is devoted to the study of the combination of AAT with chemotherapy. Its results suggest that the delay of AAT administration within this combination can compromise the potential curative effect of the treatment. Section 4 finalizes this study with an overview of the main results and a discussion of their clinical significance, as well as the future scope of our work.

2. Model

2.1. Equations

The investigated model is presented in the system of Equation (1). It has nine partial differential equations controlling the dynamics of spatially distributed variables. Each of them depends on one spatial co-ordinate, r, and a temporal co-ordinate, t. The block scheme of the main model interactions is presented in Figure 1. For a detailed description of the interactions of the model, we refer the readers to our previous work [33]. The crucial model aspects are as follows.

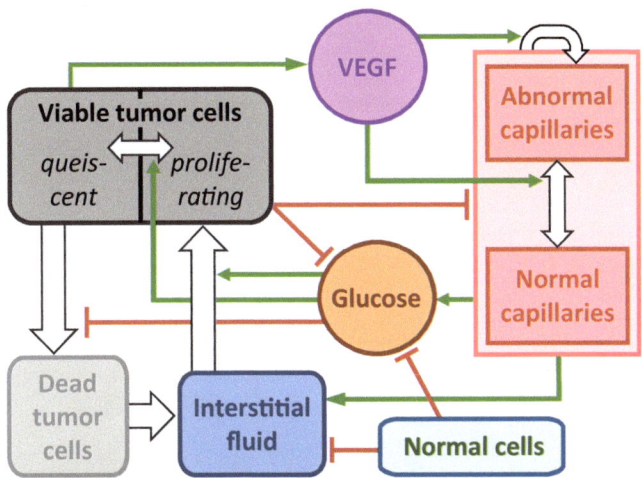

Figure 1. Scheme of the main interactions of the model governed by Equation (1). The green arrows denote the stimulating interactions, the red lines show the inhibiting interactions, and the white arrows correspond to the transitions of the variables.

The model reproduces the spherically symmetric growth of a non-invasive tumor within a normal tissue. Under sufficient levels of glucose, g, tumor cells maintain the proliferative state, n_p, in which their number grows exponentially. Cells use interstitial fluid, f, as the mass source. In the absence of glucose, they transit reversibly to the quiescent state, n_q, under which nutrient deficiency tumor cells die; this is reflected by their transition into the dead state, m. In this, they gradually degrade and transform into interstitial fluid.

The tumor cells are surrounded by normal cells, h, and they collectively constitute the porous solid phase fraction of the tissue, denoted as $s = n_p + n_q + m + h$. The interstitial fluid represents its second phase, which is capable of viscous flow through the pores within the solid fraction. The tissue is assumed to be saturated and incompressible, which implies that the total density of the cells and fluid together remains constant.

The rate of cell proliferation is influenced by both local glucose level and local solid stress, denoted as $\sigma(s)$. The solid stress function is built on the assumption that the volume fraction of cells correlates with the average distance between them [35]. When the cell fraction is at its normal value ($s = s_0$), the interactions among cells result in zero solid stress. Cells in close proximity tend to repel each other, while cells at a distance tend to attract. With increasing distance, the interaction strength eventually vanishes.

$$
\begin{aligned}
\text{proliferating tumor cells:} \quad & \frac{\partial n_p}{\partial t} = \overbrace{B n_p \cdot \Theta_p(\sigma) \frac{g}{g+g^*}}^{\text{proliferation}} \overbrace{- B \cdot [1 - \Theta_{tr}(g)] n_p + B \cdot \Theta_{tr}(g) n_q}^{\text{transition}} \overbrace{- \frac{1}{r^2} \frac{\partial (I_s n_p r^2)}{\partial r}}^{\text{advection}}; \\
\text{quiescent tumor cells:} \quad & \frac{\partial n_q}{\partial t} = \overbrace{B \cdot [1 - \Theta_{tr}(g)] n_p - B \cdot \Theta_{tr}(g) n_q}^{\text{transition}} \overbrace{- v n_q \cdot \Theta_d(g)}^{\text{death by starvation}} \overbrace{- \frac{1}{r^2} \frac{\partial (I_s n_q r^2)}{\partial r}}^{\text{advection}}; \\
\text{normal cells:} \quad & \frac{\partial h}{\partial t} = \overbrace{- \frac{1}{r^2} \frac{\partial (I_s h r^2)}{\partial r}}^{\text{advection}}; \\
\text{dead tumor cells:} \quad & \frac{\partial m}{\partial t} = \overbrace{v n_q \cdot \Theta_d(g)}^{\text{death by starvation}} \overbrace{- M m}^{\text{degradation}} \overbrace{- \frac{1}{r^2} \frac{\partial (I_s m r^2)}{\partial r}}^{\text{advection}}; \\
\text{interstitial fluid:} \quad & \frac{\partial f}{\partial t} = \overbrace{[L_n c_n + L_a c_a] \cdot [p_c - p]}^{\text{inflow}} \overbrace{- L_l h [p - p_l]}^{\text{outflow}} \overbrace{+ M m}^{\text{cell degradation}} \overbrace{- B n_p \cdot \Theta_p(\sigma) \frac{g}{g+g^*}}^{\text{cell proliferation}} \overbrace{- \frac{1}{r^2} \frac{\partial (I_f f r^2)}{\partial r}}^{\text{advection}}; \\
\text{VEGF:} \quad & \begin{cases} \frac{\partial v}{\partial t} = \overbrace{S_v n_q}^{\text{secretion}} \overbrace{- \omega [c_n + c_a] v}^{\text{internalization}} \overbrace{- M_v v}^{\text{degradation}} \overbrace{+ D_v \Delta v}^{\text{diffusion}} & \text{if AAT is off,} \\ v = 0 & \text{if AAT is on;} \end{cases} \\
\text{normal capillaries:} \quad & \frac{\partial c_n}{\partial t} = \overbrace{- M_c [n_q + m] c_n}^{\text{degradation}} + \overbrace{\frac{V_n v^*}{v + v^*} c_a}^{\text{normalization}} \overbrace{- \frac{V_d v}{v + v^*} c_n}^{\text{denormalization}} \overbrace{- \mu [c_n - 1] \cdot \Theta(c_n - 1)}^{\text{pruning}} \overbrace{- \frac{1}{r^2} \frac{\partial (I_s c_n r^2)}{\partial r}}^{\text{advection}} \\
\text{abnormal capillaries:} \quad & \frac{\partial c_a}{\partial t} = \overbrace{- M_c [n_p + k_M \{n_q + m\}] c_a}^{\text{degradation}} + \overbrace{\frac{R v}{v + v^*} [c_n + c_a] [1 - \frac{c_n + c_a}{c_{max}}]}^{\text{angiogenesis}} \overbrace{- \frac{V_n v^*}{v + v^*} c_a}^{\text{normalization}} + \overbrace{\frac{V_d v}{v + v^*} c_n}^{\text{denormalization}} \\
& \quad + \underbrace{\frac{D_c}{r^2} \frac{\partial^2 (g r^2)}{\partial r^2}}_{\text{active motion}} \underbrace{- \frac{1}{r^2} \frac{\partial (I_s c_a r^2)}{\partial r}}_{\text{advection}}; \\
\text{glucose:} \quad & \frac{\partial g}{\partial t} = \overbrace{[P_n^g c_n + P_a^g c_a] \cdot [1 - g]}^{\text{inflow}} \\
& \quad \overbrace{- [\{v_g B\} n_p \Theta_p(\sigma) + Q_h^g \{n_q + h + n_p [1 - \Theta_p(\sigma)]\}] \frac{g}{g+g^*}}^{\text{consumption}} + \overbrace{\frac{D_g}{r^2} \frac{\partial^2 (g r^2)}{\partial r^2}}^{\text{diffusion}}; \\
\text{where} \quad & s + f = 1, \ s = n_p + n_q + h + m, \\
& \Theta_p(\sigma) = [1 + \tanh(\epsilon\{\sigma_p - \sigma\})]/2, \ \Theta_{tr}(g) = [1 + \tanh(\epsilon\{g - g^*\})]/2, \\
& \Theta_d(g) = [1 + \tanh(\epsilon\{g_d - g\})]/2, \\
& f(I_f - I_s) = -K \frac{\partial p}{\partial r}, \ \frac{\partial p}{\partial r} = -\frac{\partial \sigma}{\partial r}, \\
\text{solid stress:} \quad & \sigma \equiv \sigma(s) = k \frac{[s - s_0][s - s_s]^2}{[1 - s]^{0.1}} \cdot \Theta(s - s_s).
\end{aligned}
\tag{1}
$$

Interstitial fluid enters the tissue from capillaries, two types of which are taken into account: normal, c_n, and abnormal, c_a. Abnormal capillaries possess increased permeability to fluid and glucose due to the influence of vascular endothelial growth factor (VEGF) v. It is produced by nutrient-deprived quiescent cells. It also stimulates the formation of new capillaries in the abnormal state. At low VEGF concentrations, capillaries normalize, which implies a decrease in their permeability. Normalized excessive capillaries tend to return to their basal physiological density, which reflects the process of the pruning of microvasculature in healthy tissues. Interstitial fluid drains into the lymphatic system, which is not considered explicitly but is assumed to have a density proportional to that of normal cells. Consequently, the lymphatic capillaries are absent within the tumor. Blood capillaries degrade within the tumor due to implicit factors, such as rupture caused by their displacement and due to biochemical reasons [36].

We model the action of AAT as having the maximum theoretically possible efficacy. When the treatment begins, all the present VEGF is implied to become immediately bound to the antiangiogenic drug and, therefore, is neutralized. The following normalization of microvasculature, however, is not immediate. The dynamics of the accompanying processes happen at physiologically justified rates, as described above.

2.2. Parameters

The parameters of the model were determined based on the outcomes of the experiments (of different types) presented in the literature (if available) or estimated in order to reproduce the well-established features accompanying tumor growth. The basic set of parameters is provided in Table 1, where the following normalization parameters were used to obtain their model values: 1 h for time; 10^{-2} cm for length; $3 \cdot 10^8$ cells/mL for maximum cell density; 10^{-11} mol/mL for VEGF concentration; 100 cm^2/cm^3 for capillary surface area density; 1 mg/mL for glucose concentration. The choice of the majority of model parameters is justified in our work [33].

Table 1. Model parameters.

Parameter	Description	Value	Based on
Cells:			
B	maximum rate of cell proliferation	0.01	[37]
σ_p	critical stress for cell proliferation	15	[35]
ϵ	smoothing parameter of Heaviside function	500	[33]
ν	rate of death by starvation	0.003	[33,38]
g_d	critical level of glucose for survival	0.001	[33]
M	rate of degradation of dead cells	0.01	[33]
Stress:			
k	solid stress coefficient	500	[33]
s_s	minimum fraction of interacting cells	0.3	[26]
s_0	initial fraction of cells	0.8	[26]
Interstitial fluid:			
L_n	hydraulic conductivity of normal capillaries	0.1	[22]
L_a	hydraulic conductivity of abnormal capillaries	0.22	[33]
p_c	fluid pressure in capillaries	4	[22]
L_l	hydraulic conductivity of lymphatic capillaries	1300	[22]
p_l	lymph pressure	0	[22]
K	tissue hydraulic conductivity	0.1	[39]
VEGF:			
S_v	secretion rate	1	[40]
ω	internalization rate	1	[41]
M_v	degradation rate	0.01	[42]
D_v	diffusion coefficient	21	[42]
Capillaries:			
R	maximum rate of angiogenesis	0.008	[43]
c_{max}	maximum surface area density	5	[43]
M_c	characteristic degradation rate	0.03	[43,44]
k_M	coefficient of degradation in the tumor core	2	[43,44]
V_n	normalization rate	0.1	[45]
V_d	denormalization rate	0.1	[45]
μ	pruning rate	0.002	[45]
v^*	Michaelis constant for VEGF action	0.001	[33]
D_c	coefficient of active movement	0.03	[43,44]
Glucose:			
g^*	Michaelis constant for consumption	0.01	[46]
P_n^g	permeability of normal capillaries	4	[47]
P_a^g	permeability of abnormal capillaries	10	[48]
ν_g	parameter of consumption by proliferating cells	1200	[37]
Q_h^g	rate of consumption by normal tissue	0.5	[49]
D_g	diffusion coefficient	100	[50]

2.3. Numerical Solving

During the numerical simulation of Equation (1), intercellular fluid, f, was not explicitly taken into account, given the conservation law $f = 1 - s$. The kinetic, diffusion, and advection equations for the other variables were solved sequentially at each time step. The explicit Euler method was employed to solve the kinetic equations. The use of this straightforward approach is justified by the relatively small time steps that guide the solving of advective equations. For the diffusion equations, the implicit Crank–Nicholson scheme was implemented. These classical methods are described, e.g., in [51]. In order to solve the advective equations, the conservative flux-corrected transport algorithm (incorporating an implicit antidiffusion stage) was used [52]. However, this method introduces a minor amount of uncorrectable diffusion, leading to the artificial invasion of normal tissue by the tumor. A similar challenge arises in modeling the normal tissue boundary. In order to address this issue, two additional floating points were introduced on the computational grid, marking the positions of the tumor-normal tissue interface and the normal tissue boundary. The co-ordinates of these points were computed by ensuring the conservation of total cell volume when solving advection equations at each time step.

The following initial conditions were used, which represent a spherical section of normal tissue of an initial radius of $r_0^N = 3$ mm, with a small spherical colony of tumor cells that have a radius of $r_0^T = 0.2$ mm and are located in its center at $r = 0$:

$$\begin{cases} n_p(r,0) = s_{st}, \\ h(r,0) = 0, \\ g(r,0) = 1, \\ c_n(r,0) = 0 \end{cases} \text{for } r \leq r_0^T; \quad \begin{cases} n_p(r,0) = 0, \\ h(r,0) = s_{st}, \\ g(r,0) = 1, \\ c_n(r,0) = 1 \end{cases} \text{for } r_0^T < r \leq r_0^N; \quad (2)$$

$$\forall r, \, n_q(r,0) = m(r,0) = v(r,0) = c_a(r,0) = 0.$$

Here, s_{st} is the steady state value for the fraction of cells. It is only slightly smaller than s_0, which corresponds to a minor stretching of the network of interconnected cells due to the pressure of the surrounding fluid. The following boundary conditions were used, where r^T is the changing radius of the tumor, and r^N is the changing outer radius of normal tissue:

$$\forall t, \, \frac{\partial n_p}{\partial r}|_0 = \frac{\partial n_q}{\partial r}|_0 = \frac{\partial m}{\partial r}|_0 = \frac{\partial v}{\partial r}|_0 = \frac{\partial c_n}{\partial r}|_0 = \frac{\partial c_a}{\partial r}|_0 = \frac{\partial g}{\partial r}|_0 = 0;$$

$$\frac{\partial [n_p + n_q + m]}{\partial r}|_{r^T} = \frac{\partial h}{\partial r}|_{r^T}; \, \frac{\partial g}{\partial r}|_{r^N} = 0; \quad (3)$$

$$h(r^N, t) = s_0; \, v(r^N, t) = c_a(r^N, t) = 0, \, c_n(r^N, t) = 1.$$

There are two separate advective motions in this model: $I_f = I_f(r,t)$ denotes the absolute velocity of the fluid, and $I_s = I_s(r,t)$ denotes the velocity of the solid phase. By summing up the equations of the dynamics of all cells and assuming both flow velocities to be zero at $r = 0$, Equation (4) is obtained. This was used to define advective velocities during numerical solution.

$$I_s = K \frac{\partial p}{\partial r} + \frac{1}{r^2} \int_0^r \{[L_n c_n + L_a c_a] \cdot [p_c - p] - L_l h[p - p_l]\} z^2 dz;$$

$$I_f = I_s - \frac{K}{f} \frac{\partial p}{\partial r}. \quad (4)$$

3. Results

3.1. Free Tumor Growth with and without Angiogenesis

Figure 2 compares the cases of free tumor growth with and without the initiation of angiogenesis under the same values of model parameters, as presented in Table 1. Initially, the tumor consists entirely of proliferating cells, with their number growing exponentially. However, within a few hours, some tumor cells start experiencing a deficiency of nutrients, which are supplied to the tumor mass from surrounding capillaries that are pushed away by the expanding tumor. Consequently, tumor growth slows down, and the tumor obtains a layered structure. Its inner core becomes predominantly occupied by quiescent cells, and the outer rim by proliferating cells. This structure is characteristic of tumor spheroids in experimental settings and non-invasive tumors in vivo. As the total number of tumor cells keeps increasing, the further exacerbation of nutrient deficiency results in the appearance of dead cells in the tumor core. Their degradation turns them into a viscous liquid, which, from a modeling point of view, is indistinguishable from the rest of the interstitial fluid. The decrease in the number of tumor cells in the central part of the tumor implies the stretching of the solid phase of the tumor tissue. This, in accordance with the biomechanical terms in Equation (1), underlies the elevated fluid pressure in the tumor core compared to the surrounding normal tissue. Therefore, fluid oozes from the tumor mass, contributing to a further decrease in its growth rate. When the total rates of tumor cell proliferation and death equate, the tumor reaches a stable state.

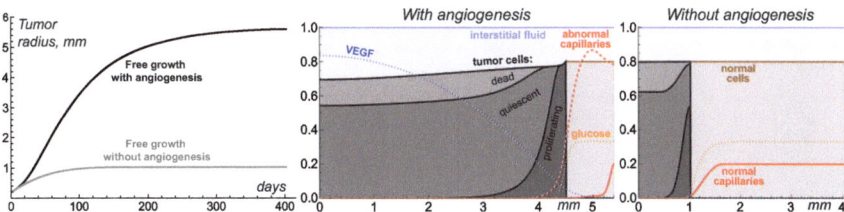

Figure 2. Left: tumor growth curves produced by Equations (1)–(4) with and without angiogenesis. **Middle** and **Right**: distributions of model variables for these simulations. The values of the variables for glucose, VEGF, and capillaries are renormalized for better visualization.

In the case without angiogenesis, the avascular tumor growth stops at ≈1 mm in radius. This is consistent with clinical observations [5]. In the presence of angiogenesis, the formation of new capillaries is stimulated by VEGF secreted by quiescent tumor cells. Capillaries influenced by VEGF have greater permeability, which, along with the increase in microvascular density, contributes to the increased inflow of glucose to the tumor. The vascularized tumor has a larger pool of proliferating cells, which means that a greater total rate of outflow of dead cells is required to compensate for it, yielding a stable tumor. In the considered simulation, the corresponding maximum tumor radius is ≈5.6 mm. This model is restricted, with consideration given to a homogeneous, nonmutating tumor. In a more realistic scenario, further tumor growth would be ensured, in particular, by the continuous selection of cells that proliferate faster and are more tolerant to nutrient deficiency and the initiation of tumor cell invasion into surrounding tissue accompanied by the co-opting of capillaries located there.

Despite the variety of considered physiological processes and the nontrivial pattern of the distribution of the model variables produced by this model, on a higher level of consideration, the simulations of free tumor growth provide quite classical S-shaped growth curves [53]. Such curves by themselves can be qualitatively reproduced by much simpler models based on a few ordinary differential equations. In the corresponding models, the dependence of tumor growth on angiogenesis is generally reproduced via the introduction of the dependence of maximum tumor volume on the amount of secreted proangiogenic signals [14]. In such simpler approaches, the cessation of angiogenesis results in the gradual decrease in tumor volume down to the value corresponding to the case of the initially avascular tumor. The current model, however, yields a more intricate pattern of tumor response to AAT, as discussed in further sections.

3.2. Antiangiogenic Therapy Beginning at Different Moments of Tumor Growth

Figure 3 illustrates the nontrivial nature of tumor response to AAT under the variation in tumor radius at which the treatments begin. The elimination of VEGF for the 1 mm tumor yields its quick growth saturation. The capillary system that undergoes degradation within the tumor volume, normalization, and pruning is eventually stabilized with a slightly greater total amount of capillaries than in the case of the avascular tumor. Therefore, it can support the existence of a stable tumor slightly greater than 1 mm in radius.

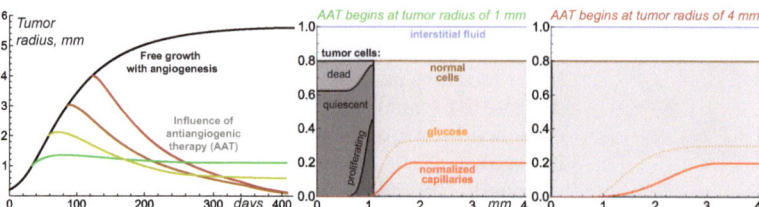

Figure 3. Left: tumor growth curves produced by Equations (1)–(4) under free tumor growth and with antiangiogenic therapy (AAT) starting at four different moments. **Middle** and **Right**: stable distributions of model variables for the simulations of AAT starting when the tumor reaches 1 mm and 4 mm in radius. The values of the variables for glucose and capillaries are renormalized for better visualization.

AAT performed for larger tumors does not result in tumor stabilization at this radius. For a 2 mm tumor, the treatment yields a final tumor radius of 0.6 mm. For 3 mm and 4 mm tumors, their sizes steadily decrease through the simulations, tending toward negligible values. From the modeling point of view, although the tumor always has some finite radius, the interpretation of such qualitative results may imply the complete cure of the tumor.

The reasons behind this nontrivial pattern of tumor response to AAT lie in the processes accompanying tumor shrinkage and the consequent remodeling of displaced normal tissue and microvasculature. In the case of a small vascularized tumor, the displacement of the capillary system is only minor. Therefore, the final tumor size is almost not affected by the physiological processes that happen along with tissue displacement. From the general mathematical point of view, the system state right before the antiangiogenic treatment is, by itself, close to the stable state that would be achieved in the absence of angiogenesis. Thus, the treatment imposes only a comparably small perturbation to tumor dynamics.

In contrast, large vascularized tumors have evolved to states that are significantly different from the stable state of an initially avascular tumor. The rapid normalization of microvessel structure and density in response to the elimination of VEGF entails a quick decrease in the total volume of proliferative tumor cells that can be sustained by microvasculature. In a short period, the overall tumor cell proliferation rate becomes unable to compensate for the rate of ongoing loss of tumor volume due to the outflow of dead cell remnants. As the difference between the absolute rates of these processes keeps increasing, the tumor undergoes rapid shrinkage.

The displacement of the interface between the tumor and normal tissue pulls the normal cells and microvasculature towards the center of the tumor, which is in accordance with the advection terms presented in Equation (1). The spherical geometry of the system means that this forced motion of capillaries is more active in the regions with greater curvature, i.e., near the tumor. As the normalized capillary system undergoes rupture and pruning, its overall volume continuously decreases. Eventually, the microvasculature system ends up in a state in which its density is close to its initial value at the outer side of the normal tissue, but it falls down to negligible values towards the tumor surface. The total volume of a stable microvasculature depends on the degree of its displacement and remodeling that it has undergone in response to treatment. Therefore, initially, larger tumors end up having smaller volumes of surrounding microvasculature.

The stable volume of a tumor that can be supported by the nutrient supply from the resulting microvasculature depends not only on the total volume of the latter but also on its configuration within the normal tissue. The pool of normal cells represents the active consumers of nutrients and, therefore, the competitors of tumor cells. Large gaps between the tumor surface and the areas with physiologically normal capillary density are detrimental to tumor size since the nutrients that are supplied from the capillaries and that diffuse toward the tumor undergo active consumption by normal cells. In extreme cases, the level of glucose entering the tumor rim is, by itself, not sufficient to ensure tumor cell survival, which results in a steady decrease in tumor volume down to negligible values.

Overall, the complexity of the intertwined physiological processes results in the observed hysteresis effect, in which the final state of the tumor after AAT depends on the previous history of tumor progression.

3.3. Combining Antiangiogenic Therapy with Chemotherapy

The above-described nature of tumor response to the cessation of angiogenesis should also affect the combined types of treatment involving AAT. Previously, we hypothesized that in combination with chemotherapy (CT), the delay of administration of the antiangiogenic drug can be beneficial when compared to the case of the simultaneous initiation of CT and AAT. The rationale behind this hypothesis was that such an approach could exploit the increased permeability of the angiogenic capillary network in the peritumoral region, which is in contrast to the normalized network that forms as a result of AAT. Thus, it should ensure the enhanced penetration of the cytotoxic agent into the tumor. The account for the biomechanical properties of the tissues, however, suggests that the alternation of the scheduling of combined AAT and CT may yield more nontrivial consequences.

In order to illustrate this idea, let's consider an augmented version of the model expressed by Equations (1)–(4), which also considers the intravenous injections of chemotherapeutic drugs. Equation (5) lists the additional terms introduced in the model to account for the chemotherapeutic drug and its action. Chemotherapy is assumed to affect only proliferating cells. One newly introduced partial differential equation governs the distribution of chemotherapeutic agents in the tissue, and a new ordinary differential equation governs its temporal dynamics in blood.

$$
\begin{aligned}
\text{proliferating tumor cells:} \quad & \frac{\partial n_p}{\partial t} = \overbrace{\ldots}^{\text{previously considered processes}} \overbrace{-\chi u n_p}^{\text{death by CT}} ; \\
\text{dead tumor cells:} \quad & \frac{\partial m}{\partial t} = \overbrace{\ldots}^{\text{previously considered processes}} \overbrace{+\chi u n_p}^{\text{cell death by CT}} ; \\
\text{chemotherapeutic agent in tissue:} \quad & \frac{\partial u}{\partial t} = \overbrace{\{[L_n \gamma_n^u c_n + L_a \gamma_a^u c_a] \cdot [p_c - p]\}[u_{bl} \cdot \Theta(p_c - p) + u \cdot \Theta(p - p_c)]}^{\text{advective inflow/outflow}} \\
& + \overbrace{[P_n^u c_n + P_a^u c_a] \cdot [u_{bl} - u]}^{\text{diffusive inflow/outflow}} \\
& \overbrace{-L_l h[p - p_l]u}^{\text{lymphatic outflow}} + \overbrace{\frac{D_u}{r^2} \frac{\partial^2 (u r^2)}{\partial r^2}}^{\text{diffusion}} - \overbrace{\frac{1}{r^2} \frac{\partial (I_f u r^2)}{\partial r}}^{\text{advection}} ; \\
\text{chemotherapeutic agent in blood:} \quad & \frac{\partial u_{bl}}{\partial t} = \overbrace{\sum_{i=1}^{I} \delta(t - t_i)}^{\text{injections}} \overbrace{-C_u u_{bl}}^{\text{clearance}} .
\end{aligned}
\qquad (5)
$$

The term "drug injections" represents the external control that increases the concentration of a chemotherapeutic drug in the blood by a normalized unit at designated moments. In this work, we simulate a protocol with $I = 6$ injections separated by 3-week intervals. The beginning of CT takes place when a tumor achieves a 4 mm radius.

Additional model parameters are presented in Table 2. The estimation of the parameters related to the chemotherapeutic agent was performed using our approach presented previously in [33]. We refer the reader to it for the corresponding details. Here, we consider a chemotherapeutic agent with a 5 nm hydrodynamic radius. It is well-known that substances with a low-molecular weight move through the pores in capillary walls via diffusion, while the process of advection dominates for high-molecular-weight agents [54]. The same reasoning applies to their movement through the tissue. Both diffusion and advection physiological processes are accounted for herein. The sensitivity of cells to the drug corresponds to a moderate CT, which, by itself, can not eradicate the tumor.

Table 2. Additional parameters of the model, accounting for chemotherapy.

Parameter	Description	Value
Cells:		
χ	sensitivity to chemotherapeutic agent	0.05
Chemotherapeutic agent:		
γ_n^u	fraction of available pore cross-section area, normal capillaries	0.09
γ_a^u	fraction of available pore cross-section area, abnormal capillaries	0.58
P_n^u	diffusive permeability, normal capillaries	0.007
P_a^u	diffusive permeability, abnormal capillaries	0.25
D_u	diffusion coefficient	13
C_u	clearance rate	0.0015

The following initial and boundary conditions were used for the chemotherapeutic drug:

$$\forall r,\ u(r,0) = 0,\ u_{bl} = 0;$$
$$\forall t,\ \frac{\partial u}{\partial r}|_0 = \frac{\partial u}{\partial r}|_{r^T} = 0. \quad (6)$$

Figure 4 illustrates the tumor dynamics in the resulting system under the treatment of a relatively large tumor using CT, AAT, and their combination, with AAT taking place at different moments. Chemotherapy by itself results in significant tumor shrinkage, which, however, is followed by tumor regrowth after the treatment is halted. The case of mono-AAT has already been demonstrated above, and it effectively results in the eradication of the tumor.

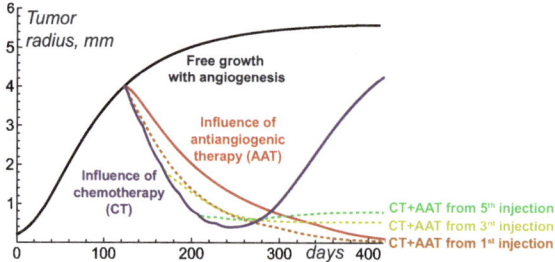

Figure 4. Tumor growth curves produced by Equations (1)–(6) under free tumor growth, antiangiogenic therapy (AAT), chemotherapy (CT), and their combination, with AAT starting at the times of the different injections of the chemotherapeutic drug.

The combination of CT and AAT starting simultaneously leads to the faster shrinkage of the tumor than mono-AAT. This happens because the tumor cells, in this case, are subject not only to a similar depletion of nutrients but also to direct cytotoxic action. However, the case of mono-CT initially leads to even faster tumor shrinkage. This reflects the above-mentioned fact that the normalization of capillaries results in a reduced decrease in cytotoxic agents in the tumor. In the case of the high-molecular-weight chemotherapeutic agent considered herein, this reduction is very well pronounced and is eventually reflected in these high-level tumor growth curves. However, in the long term, the combination of simultaneously initiated CT and AAT proves to be more efficient than mono-CT due to the eventual critical shortage of nutrient supply to the tumor as their competition with normal cells exacerbates under capillary network scarcity.

A delay to the beginning of AAT within its combination with CT ensures the faster initial shrinkage of the tumor. The seeming benefit of such an approach, nevertheless, is deceptive. At the moment of the third and fifth injections of the chemotherapeutic drug, the tumors have radii of ≈1.9 mm and ≈0.7 mm, respectively. In accordance with the simulations presented in the previous section, the AAT initiated for such tumors results in their stabilization at small but notable sizes. Thus, the delay in AAT administration in combination with CT compromises the potential curative effect of the treatment.

4. Conclusions and Discussion

4.1. Overview of Main Results

This paper presented a mathematical modeling study of the non-invasive solid tumor response to antiangiogenic therapy (AAT), taking into account the biomechanical aspects. The tumor in the considered model represents a compact object embedded in normal tissue. An increase in tumor volume and the displacement of normal tissue are ensured by the gradients of solid stress that arise due to tumor cell proliferation. The tumor pushes microvasculature away during its growth, compromising its own supply of nutrients, which are necessary for cell proliferation and survival. The degradation and outflow of dead cells eventually compensate for tumor proliferation, yielding tumor growth stabilization.

The initiation of angiogenesis by tumor cells experiencing metabolic stress results in the augmentation of microvasculature permeability and surface area. The resulting abnormal microvasculature can support the existence of larger stable tumors.

Simulations of AAT show that the outcome of the elimination of proangiogenic factors depends on the proximity of the current tumor size to the size of the stable avascular tumor grown without the initiation of angiogenesis. For a tumor with close size, AAT yields a minor perturbation to its dynamics and leads to its rapid stabilization. For larger tumors, however, the quick fall in nutrient supply significantly affects their dynamics. The domination of outflow of dead cell mass over cell proliferation causes the displacement of the interface between the tumor and the normal tissue, which pulls the normal cells and microvasculature towards the core of the tumor. As the capillary system undergoes rupture and pruning during this movement, the system eventually stabilizes at notably decreased volumes regarding the capillary system, the density of which falls toward the tumor surface. The degree of distortion of microvasculature depends on the distance of its displacement. Therefore, the stable sizes of tumors that underwent AAT negatively correlate with their sizes at the beginning of AAT. For sufficiently large initial tumors, the destruction of microvasculature is so crucial that, eventually, it is able to support the survival of not only normal but non-normal tumor cells. Thus, in such cases, AAT is effectively curative as long as it blocks all the possible mechanisms of angiogenesis.

4.2. Clinical Significance

The idea that AAT can be curative is an intriguing outcome of this study; however, to the best of our knowledge, there are no clinical cases supporting it. The very possibility of obtaining such confirmation is significantly compromised by the fact that AAT is rarely used in the mono regime. It is generally combined with other modalities, including the surgical removal of the tumor after its shrinkage caused by AAT. Moreover, the model used herein assumes compactly growing benign tumors, while invasive tumors have been shown on numerous occasions to possess inherent resistance to AAT due to the ability of motile cancer cells to actively escape nutrient-deficient regions [55]. Therefore, for invasive tumors, the possibility of the curative effect of AAT seems highly unlikely. It should also be noted that, in reality, other signaling molecules (other than VEGF) can be involved in the stimulation of microvessel growth, although they are generally assumed to be much less important. Further aid from experimental and clinical researchers can shed light on the possibility of the validation of the concept of curative AAT.

4.3. Future Prospects

The designed approach considers the physiological processes accompanying the dynamics of a tumor and its microenvironment during AAT in detail. It largely determines the efficacy of the delivery of concomitantly administrated drugs to the tumor. The consideration of tissue as a porous biphasic media with solid and liquid components is crucial for a physiologically adequate reproduction of the dynamics of high-molecular-weight drugs, which is dominated by advective motion. This study provides example simulations of AAT combined with chemotherapy (CT). One of the qualitative outcomes of administrating AAT simultaneously with CT, as suggested by the modeling, is the notable reduction in the inflow of the chemotherapeutic drug into the tumor, which compromises initial tumor shrinkage. Given these intriguing results, we will use the developed model as the basis for future studies on the optimization of combined types of antitumor therapy with the use of antiangiogenic drugs.

The results of this work were obtained by using simulations of a spherically symmetric tumor, which effectively renders the model one-dimensional and, thus, drastically reduces computational complexity. Such an approach facilitates the ability to simulate the long-term behavior of a tumor and its microenvironment in response to treatment, thus making the reconstruction of this behavior during the entire course of a prolonged treatment practically feasible. The obtained qualitative results are expected to be preserved under sufficiently moderate perturbations of spherical symmetry in a more realistic three-dimensional setting. Nevertheless, conducting the three-dimensional modeling study, especially based on patient imaging data, represents an intriguing future prospect. Such work, in particular, would allow for exploring the limits of the applicability of the results for tumors of varying sizes and shapes.

Supplementary Materials: The C++ computational code can be downloaded at: https://www.mdpi.com/article/10.3390/math12020353/s1.

Author Contributions: Conceptualization, M.K. and A.K.; methodology, M.K. and A.K.; software, M.K.; investigation, M.K.; writing—original draft preparation, M.K.; writing—review and editing, M.K. and A.K.; visualization, M.K.; supervision, A.K.; funding acquisition, M.K. and A.K. All authors have read and agreed to the published version of the manuscript.

Funding: This work is supported by the Russian Science Foundation under grant 22-21-00835.

Data Availability Statement: The data presented in this study are available on request from the corresponding author.

Conflicts of Interest: The authors declare no conflicts of interest.

Abbreviations

The following abbreviations are used in this manuscript:

CT   chemotherapy
AAT   antiangiogenic therapy
VEGF vascular endothelial growth factor

References

1. Siegel, R.L.; Miller, K.D.; Wagle, N.S.; Jemal, A. Cancer statistics, 2023. *CA Cancer J. Clin.* **2023**, *73*, 17–48. [CrossRef] [PubMed]
2. Hanahan, D.; Weinberg, R.A. Hallmarks of cancer: The next generation. *Cell* **2011**, *144*, 646–674. [CrossRef] [PubMed]
3. Chen, D.S.; Mellman, I. Oncology meets immunology: The cancer-immunity cycle. *Immunity* **2013**, *39*, 1–10. [CrossRef] [PubMed]
4. Jayson, G.C.; Kerbel, R.; Ellis, L.M.; Harris, A.L. Antiangiogenic therapy in oncology: Current status and future directions. *Lancet* **2016**, *388*, 518–529. [CrossRef] [PubMed]
5. Naumov, G.N.; Akslen, L.A.; Folkman, J. Role of angiogenesis in human tumor dormancy: Animal models of the angiogenic switch. *Cell Cycle* **2006**, *5*, 1779–1787. [CrossRef] [PubMed]
6. Lazebnik, Y. What are the hallmarks of cancer? *Nat. Rev. Cancer* **2010**, *10*, 232–233. [CrossRef]
7. Kalluri, R.; Weinberg, R.A. The basics of epithelial-mesenchymal transition. *J. Clin. Investig.* **2009**, *119*, 1420–1428. [CrossRef] [PubMed]
8. Gee, M.S.; Procopio, W.N.; Makonnen, S.; Feldman, M.D.; Yeilding, N.M.; Lee, W.M. Tumor vessel development and maturation impose limits on the effectiveness of anti-vascular therapy. *Am. J. Pathol.* **2003**, *162*, 183–193. [CrossRef]
9. Yuan, F.; Chen, Y.; Dellian, M.; Safabakhsh, N.; Ferrara, N.; Jain, R.K. Time-dependent vascular regression and permeability changes in established human tumor xenografts induced by an anti-vascular endothelial growth factor/vascular permeability factor antibody. *Proc. Natl. Acad. Sci. USA* **1996**, *93*, 14765–14770. [CrossRef]

10. Jain, R.K.; Di Tomaso, E.; Duda, D.G.; Loeffler, J.S.; Sorensen, A.G.; Batchelor, T.T. Angiogenesis in brain tumours. *Nat. Rev. Neurosci.* **2007**, *8*, 610–622. [CrossRef]
11. Garcia, J.; Hurwitz, H.I.; Sandler, A.B.; Miles, D.; Coleman, R.L.; Deurloo, R.; Chinot, O.L. Bevacizumab (Avastin®) in cancer treatment: A review of 15 years of clinical experience and future outlook. *Cancer Treat. Rev.* **2020**, *86*, 102017. [CrossRef] [PubMed]
12. Claes, A.; Wesseling, P.; Jeuken, J.; Maass, C.; Heerschap, A.; Leenders, W.P. Antiangiogenic compounds interfere with chemotherapy of brain tumors due to vessel normalization. *Mol. Cancer Ther.* **2008**, *7*, 71–78. [CrossRef] [PubMed]
13. Ma, J.; Pulfer, S.; Li, S.; Chu, J.; Reed, K.; Gallo, J.M. Pharmacodynamic-mediated reduction of temozolomide tumor concentrations by the angiogenesis inhibitor TNP-470. *Cancer Res.* **2001**, *61*, 5491–5498. [PubMed]
14. Hahnfeldt, P.; Panigrahy, D.; Folkman, J.; Hlatky, L. Tumor development under angiogenic signaling: A dynamical theory of tumor growth, treatment response, and postvascular dormancy. *Cancer Res.* **1999**, *59*, 4770–4775. [PubMed]
15. McDougall, S.R.; Anderson, A.R.; Chaplain, M.A. Mathematical modelling of dynamic adaptive tumour-induced angiogenesis: Clinical implications and therapeutic targeting strategies. *J. Theor. Biol.* **2006**, *241*, 564–589. [CrossRef] [PubMed]
16. Stéphanou, A.; McDougall, S.R.; Anderson, A.R.; Chaplain, M.A. Mathematical modelling of the influence of blood rheological properties upon adaptative tumour-induced angiogenesis. *Math. Comput. Model.* **2006**, *44*, 96–123. [CrossRef]
17. Swanson, K.R.; Rockne, R.C.; Claridge, J.; Chaplain, M.A.; Alvord Jr, E.C.; Anderson, A.R. Quantifying the role of angiogenesis in malignant progression of gliomas: In silico modeling integrates imaging and histology. *Cancer Res.* **2011**, *71*, 7366–7375. [CrossRef]
18. Alfonso, J.C.L.; Köhn-Luque, A.; Stylianopoulos, T.; Feuerhake, F.; Deutsch, A.; Hatzikirou, H. Why one-size-fits-all vaso-modulatory interventions fail to control glioma invasion: In silico insights. *Sci. Rep.* **2016**, *6*, 37283. [CrossRef]
19. Welter, M.; Rieger, H. Interstitial fluid flow and drug delivery in vascularized tumors: A computational model. *PLoS ONE* **2013**, *8*, e70395. [CrossRef]
20. Steuperaert, M.; Debbaut, C.; Carlier, C.; De Wever, O.; Descamps, B.; Vanhove, C.; Ceelen, W.; Segers, P. A 3D CFD model of the interstitial fluid pressure and drug distribution in heterogeneous tumor nodules during intraperitoneal chemotherapy. *Drug Deliv.* **2019**, *26*, 404–415. [CrossRef]
21. Zhan, W. Convection enhanced delivery of anti-angiogenic and cytotoxic agents in combination therapy against brain tumour. *Eur. J. Pharm. Sci.* **2020**, *141*, 105094. [CrossRef] [PubMed]
22. Stylianopoulos, T.; Martin, J.D.; Snuderl, M.; Mpekris, F.; Jain, S.R.; Jain, R.K. Coevolution of solid stress and interstitial fluid pressure in tumors during Pprogression: Implications for vascular collapse evolution of solid and fluid stresses in tumors. *Cancer Res.* **2013**, *73*, 3833–3841. [CrossRef]
23. Preziosi, L.; Ambrosi, D.; Verdier, C. An elasto-visco-plastic model of cell aggregates. *J. Theor. Biol.* **2010**, *262*, 35–47. [CrossRef] [PubMed]
24. Byrne, H.M.; King, J.R.; McElwain, D.S.; Preziosi, L. A two-phase model of solid tumour growth. *Appl. Math. Lett.* **2003**, *16*, 567–573. [CrossRef]
25. Franks, S.; King, J. Interactions between a uniformly proliferating tumour and its surroundings: Stability analysis for variable material properties. *Int. J. Eng. Sci.* **2009**, *47*, 1182–1192. [CrossRef]
26. Byrne, H.; Preziosi, L. Modelling solid tumour growth using the theory of mixtures. *Math. Med. Biol. J. IMA* **2003**, *20*, 341–366. [CrossRef]
27. Jain, R.K.; Tong, R.T.; Munn, L.L. Effect of vascular normalization by antiangiogenic therapy on interstitial hypertension, peritumor edema, and lymphatic metastasis: Insights from a mathematical model. *Cancer Res.* **2007**, *67*, 2729–2735. [CrossRef]
28. Kolobov, A.; Kuznetsov, M. Investigation of the effects of angiogenesis on tumor growth using a mathematical model. *Biophysics* **2015**, *60*, 449–456. [CrossRef]
29. Kuznetsov, M.; Kolobov, A. Optimization of Combined Antitumor Chemotherapy with Bevacizumab by Means of Mathematical Modeling. In *Trends in Biomathematics: Modeling, Optimization and Computational Problems: Selected Works from the BIOMAT Consortium Lectures, Moscow 2017*; Springer: Cham, Switzerland, 2018 ; pp. 347–363.
30. Kuznetsov, M. Mathematical modeling shows that the response of a solid tumor to antiangiogenic therapy depends on the type of growth. *Mathematics* **2020**, *8*, 760. [CrossRef]
31. Kuznetsov, M. Combined influence of nutrient supply level and tissue mechanical properties on benign tumor growth as revealed by mathematical modeling. *Mathematics* **2021**, *9*, 2213. [CrossRef]
32. Kuznetsov, M.; Kolobov, A. Agent-Based Model for Studying the Effects of Solid Stress and Nutrient Supply on Tumor Growth. *Mathematics* **2023**, *11*, 1900. [CrossRef]
33. Kuznetsov, M.; Kolobov, A. Optimization of size of nanosensitizers for antitumor radiotherapy using mathematical modeling. *Int. J. Mol. Sci.* **2023**, *24*, 11806. [CrossRef] [PubMed]
34. Kuznetsov, M.; Kolobov, A. Mathematical modelling for spatial optimization of irradiation during proton radiotherapy with nanosensitizers. *Russ. J. Numer. Anal. Math. Model.* **2023**, *38*, 303–321. [CrossRef]
35. Mascheroni, P.; Stigliano, C.; Carfagna, M.; Boso, D.P.; Preziosi, L.; Decuzzi, P.; Schrefler, B.A. Predicting the growth of glioblastoma multiforme spheroids using a multiphase porous media model. *Biomech. Model. Mechanobiol.* **2016**, *15*, 1215–1228. [CrossRef]
36. Holash, J.; Maisonpierre, P.; Compton, D.; Boland, P.; Alexander, C.; Zagzag, D.; Yancopoulos, G.; Wiegand, S. Vessel cooption, regression, and growth in tumors mediated by angiopoietins and VEGF. *Science* **1999**, *284*, 1994–1998. [CrossRef]

37. Freyer, J.; Sutherland, R. A reduction in the in situ rates of oxygen and glucose consumption of cells in EMT6/Ro spheroids during growth. *J. Cell. Physiol.* **1985**, *124*, 516–524. [CrossRef] [PubMed]
38. Izuishi, K.; Kato, K.; Ogura, T.; Kinoshita, T.; Esumi, H. Remarkable tolerance of tumor cells to nutrient deprivation: Possible new biochemical target for cancer therapy. *Cancer Res.* **2000**, *60*, 6201–6207. [PubMed]
39. Netti, P.A.; Berk, D.A.; Swartz, M.A.; Grodzinsky, A.J.; Jain, R.K. Role of extracellular matrix assembly in interstitial transport in solid tumors. *Cancer Res.* **2000**, *60*, 2497–2503.
40. Kelm, J.M.; Sanchez-Bustamante, C.D.; Ehler, E.; Hoerstrup, S.P.; Djonov, V.; Ittner, L.; Fussenegger, M. VEGF profiling and angiogenesis in human microtissues. *J. Biotechnol.* **2005**, *118*, 213–229. [CrossRef]
41. Mac Gabhann, F.; Popel, A.S. Interactions of VEGF isoforms with VEGFR-1, VEGFR-2, and neuropilin in vivo: A computational model of human skeletal muscle. *Am. J. Physiol.-Heart Circ. Physiol.* **2007**, *292*, H459–H474. [CrossRef]
42. Köhn-Luque, A.; De Back, W.; Yamaguchi, Y.; Yoshimura, K.; Herrero, M.; Miura, T. Dynamics of VEGF matrix-retention in vascular network patterning. *Phys. Biol.* **2013**, *10*, 066007. [CrossRef] [PubMed]
43. Dickson, P.V.; Hamner, J.B.; Sims, T.L.; Fraga, C.H.; Ng, C.Y.; Rajasekeran, S.; Hagedorn, N.L.; McCarville, M.B.; Stewart, C.F.; Davidoff, A.M. Bevacizumab-induced transient remodeling of the vasculature in neuroblastoma xenografts results in improved delivery and efficacy of systemically administered chemotherapy. *Clin. Cancer Res.* **2007**, *13*, 3942–3950. [CrossRef] [PubMed]
44. Stamatelos, S.K.; Kim, E.; Pathak, A.P.; Popel, A.S. A bioimage informatics based reconstruction of breast tumor microvasculature with computational blood flow predictions. *Microvasc. Res.* **2014**, *91*, 8–21. [CrossRef]
45. Dings, R.P.; Loren, M.; Heun, H.; McNiel, E.; Griffioen, A.W.; Mayo, K.H.; Griffin, R.J. Scheduling of radiation with angiogenesis inhibitors Anginex and Avastin improves therapeutic outcome via vessel normalization. *Clin. Cancer Res.* **2007**, *13*, 3395–3402. [CrossRef] [PubMed]
46. Casciari, J.; Sotirchos, S.; Sutherland, R. Mathematical modelling of microenvironment and growth in EMT6/Ro multicellular tumour spheroids. *Cell Prolif.* **1992**, *25*, 1–22. [CrossRef] [PubMed]
47. Clough, G.; Smaje, L. Exchange area and surface properties of the microvasculature of the rabbit submandibular gland following duct ligation. *J. Physiol.* **1984**, *354*, 445–456. [CrossRef] [PubMed]
48. Kuznetsov, M.B.; Kolobov, A.V. Transient alleviation of tumor hypoxia during first days of antiangiogenic therapy as a result of therapy-induced alterations in nutrient supply and tumor metabolism—Analysis by mathematical modeling. *J. Theor. Biol.* **2018**, *451*, 86–100. [CrossRef] [PubMed]
49. Baker, P.G.; Mottram, R. Metabolism of exercising and resting human skeletal muscle, in the post-prandial and fasting states. *Clin. Sci.* **1973**, *44*, 479–491. [CrossRef]
50. Tuchin, V.; Bashkatov, A.; Genina, E.; Sinichkin, Y.P.; Lakodina, N. In vivo investigation of the immersion-liquid-induced human skin clearing dynamics. *Tech. Phys. Lett.* **2001**, *27*, 489–490. [CrossRef]
51. Press, W.H.; Teukolsky, S.A.; Vetterling, W.T.; Flannery, B.P. *Numerical Recipes, 3rd Edition: The Art of Scientific Computing*; Cambridge University Press: Cambridge, UK, 2007.
52. Boris, J.P.; Book, D.L. Flux-corrected transport. I. SHASTA, a fluid transport algorithm that works. *J. Comput. Phys.* **1973**, *11*, 38–69. [CrossRef]
53. Kuznetsov, M.; Clairambault, J.; Volpert, V. Improving cancer treatments via dynamical biophysical models. *Phys. Life Rev.* **2021**, *39*, 1–48. [CrossRef] [PubMed]
54. Herring, N.; Paterson, D.J. *Levick's Introduction to Cardiovascular Physiology*; CRC Press: Boca Raton, FL, USA, 2018.
55. Bergers, G.; Hanahan, D. Modes of resistance to anti-angiogenic therapy. *Nat. Rev. Cancer* **2008**, *8*, 592–603. [CrossRef] [PubMed]

Disclaimer/Publisher's Note: The statements, opinions and data contained in all publications are solely those of the individual author(s) and contributor(s) and not of MDPI and/or the editor(s). MDPI and/or the editor(s) disclaim responsibility for any injury to people or property resulting from any ideas, methods, instructions or products referred to in the content.

Article

Mathematical Analysis of Four Fundamental Epidemiological Models for Monkeypox Disease Outbreaks: On the Pivotal Role of Human–Animal Order Parameters—In Memory of Hermann Haken

Till D. Frank [1,2]

[1] Psychological Sciences, University of Connecticut, 406 Babbidge Road, Storrs, CT 06269, USA; till.frank@uconn.edu
[2] Physics Department, University of Connecticut, 179 Auditorium Road, Storrs, CT 06269, USA

Abstract: Four fundamental models that describe the spread of Monkeypox disease are analyzed: the SIR-SIR, SEIR-SIR, SIR-SEIR, and SEIR-SEIR models. They form the basis of most Monkeypox diseases models that are currently discussed in the literature. It is shown that the way the model subpopulations are organized in disease outbreaks and evolve relative to each other is determined by the relevant unstable system eigenvectors, also called order parameters. For all models, analytical expressions of the order parameters are derived. Under appropriate conditions these order parameters describe the initial outbreak phases of exponential increase in good approximation. It is shown that all four models exhibit maximally two order parameters and maximally one human–animal order parameter. The human–animal order parameter firmly connects the outbreak dynamics in the animal system with the dynamics in the human system. For the special case of the SIR-SIR model, it is found that the two possible order parameters completely describe the dynamics of infected humans and animals during entire infection waves. Finally, a simulation of a Monkeypox infection wave illustrates that in line with the aforementioned analytical results the leading order parameter explains most of the variance in the infection dynamics.

Keywords: monkeypox virus; infectious disease; mathematical modelling; order parameters

MSC: 15A18; 34A34; 92D25; 92D30

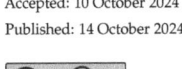

1. Introduction

Monkeypox (Mpox) disease is an infectious disease that is endemic in several African countries [1]. During the last five decades, Mpox infection waves have repeatedly occurred in those countries [2,3]. In this context, understanding the initial outbreak phases of Mpox infection waves is of particular importance because these initial phases offer the opportunity for ad hoc interventions that may dramatically reduce the infection dynamics [4]. In particular, in line with previous works on COVID-19 waves [4], a vital step to understand the emergence of Mpox infection waves is to conduct model-based analyses that determine the initial organization of such waves. Insights obtained from such endeavors are not only relevant for the aforementioned African countries. Rather, due to international travel, Mpox infection waves can spread out to non-endemic countries as it was observed recently during the global 2022–2023 Mpox epidemic [5,6].

Mpox disease comes with symptoms like fever, rash, sore throat, and respiratory distress [7] and can lead to death [1–3]. The disease is caused by the Monkeypox virus that is transmitted from animals to humans [1,8]. In particular, rodents such as squirrels, rats, and mice can carry the virus but also certain monkeys (whence the name Monkeypox) [8]. However, once the virus has invaded a particular human population it can also spread out within the population by means of human to human transmissions [1]. Temporal limited outbreaks of Monkeypox disease have been observed since 1970 [1–3]. Such waves are typically observed in the human population, whereas the infection dynamics in the animal population is unobserved. During the period 2000–2009, when taking all observed disease outbreaks together, it is estimated that there had been about 10,000 cases of Monkeypox disease. For the period of 2010–2019, this estimate is higher at about 19,000 cases [3]. In particular, from September 2017 to April 2018 an infection wave spread out through several regions of Nigeria [2,8,9]. The wave in the human population was probably triggered by multiple, independent animal to human transmissions of the Monkeypox virus [8]. In addition, it was confirmed that human to human transmissions were involved in the disease outbreak [9]. Since January 2023, cases of Monkeypox disease started to rise dramatically in the Democratic Republic of the Congo (DRC). As of August 2024, the infection surge is still ongoing [10,11] and is about to spread out to several neighboring countries of the DRC [12]. Within the DRC the surge reached the 20,000 mark of suspected cases [13] that had never been reached before. In view of those developments, on 14 August 2024, the WHO announced its highest level of alert for Mpox and declared the Mpox outbreak as a health emergency of international concern [12]. Finally, as mentioned above, in several instances international travel brought the Mpox disease to non-endemic countries [2,3]. Most dramatically, during the period of 2022–2023 Mpox disease spread out globally (primarily in South, Middle, and North America and Europe [5,6]) and produced almost 100,000 infected cases worldwide [14]. While the 2022–2023 global epidemic eventually subsided due to intervention and prevention measures and in the absence of an animal reservoir, the situation in the endemic African countries and, in particular, the current DRC-centered outbreak are highly unpredictable.

For the time being, Mpox disease waves in endemic African countries triggered by waves in the respective animal reservoirs are likely to occur and they may or may not spill over to non-endemic countries [11].

Several efforts have been made to describe the emergence of Mpox disease in human–animal systems with the help of epidemiological models [15]. At the heart of these efforts are models that describe susceptible (S), infected (I), and recovered (R) individuals [4,16]. Such SIR models can describe both the human and animal populations of interest. Adding exposed (E) individuals that have been infected but are not yet infectious leads to SEIR models [4,16] that again may be used to describe both the human and animal populations of interest. Combining these two types of models, SIR and SEIR, we arrive at four fundamental models: SIR-SIR, SEIR-SIR, SIR-SEIR, and SEIR-SEIR models, where the first acronym describes the animal system, while the latter refers to the human system. An SIR-SIR Monkeypox model has been studied by Bhunu and Mushayabasa [17]. SIR-SIR Monkeypox models were also used by Emeka et al. [18] and Somma et al. [19] and have been slightly generalized to take vaccinated [18] and quarantined [19] individuals into account, respectively. Madubueze et al. [20] based their Monkeypox model on an SIR-SEIR system and fine-grained the human SEIR infection dynamics, among other things, by taking again the possibility of vaccination into account. Usman and Adamu [21], Peter et al. [22], Bankuru et al. [23], and Collins and Duffy [24] used Mpox SEIR-SEIR approaches featuring additional groups of quarantined [22] or vaccinated [21,23] individuals. A plenitude of highly detailed epidemiological models for the spread of Mpox disease in human–animal systems has been proposed in the literature. Such models include, for example, individuals with different degree of infectiousness [25,26], quarantined and isolated individuals [27], clinically ill or hospitalized individuals [25,26,28], and detected versus undetected cases [29]. All these models have in common that they are based on one of the aforementioned four fundamental models.

Despite these modeling efforts, what is missing is an analysis of the multi-compartmental components involved in Mpox outbreaks. Such multi-compartmental components describe compartments bound together to entities and are determined by stable and unstable eigenvectors of the respective human–animal systems. Multi-compartmental component analyses have been conducted for various epidemiological models describing COVID-19 outbreaks during the COVID-19 pandemic [4,30] and several virus dynamics models describing SARS-CoV-2 infections [31] and the human immune reaction [32]. In particular, the leading components that describe the initial organizations of COVID-19 outbreaks in populations have been determined in terms of so-called order parameters [33–35] for SIR systems, SEIR systems, and some higher-dimensional models [4]. As mentioned above, a comparable analysis is missing in the modeling literature on Mpox disease outbreaks. That is, the above reviewed studies on epidemiological Mpox disease models did not present any analysis of relevant Mpox disease order parameters. Therefore, the current study supplements the existing literature and adds a novel aspect to it. In the context of the COVID-19 pandemic, benefits of the order parameter perspective have been demonstrated. For example, it has been demonstrated that the impact of intervention measures can be conveniently analyzed when focusing on the leading building-blocks or order parameters of COVID-19 waves. Explicitly, using this approach, COVID-19 waves observed in the USA [36], Europe [37], China [38], Thailand [39], and Pakistan [40] have been analyzed. Interestingly, all systems investigated in those studies on COVID-19 waves exhibited only a single leading multi-compartmental component or order parameter. In contrast, as it will be shown below, Mpox infection dynamics in general is characterized by two order parameters. In anticipation of this novel aspect and in view of the absence of studies devoted to determine Mpox order parameters, the aim of the current study is to identify and compute the leading organizational elements or order parameters of the four fundamental models listed above and to interpret their qualitative and quantitative aspects. The aim is to demonstrate that they dominate and determine the initial phase dynamics of Mpox outbreaks. In doing so, it will be determined how compartments or subpopulations evolve relative to each other. In addition, the objective is to identify the remaining multi-compartmental components given in terms of (neutrally) stable eigenvectors and to explore their roles as well for the enfolding of Mpox infection waves.

The remainder of this study is structured as follows. The four fundamental models will be introduced in Section 2. The models will be analyzed in Section 3. In particular, key results regarding the multi-compartmental building-blocks in terms of order parameters and their amplitudes will be obtained in Section 3.1 and implications of those results will be discussed in Section 3.2. Section 3.3 will briefly exemplify that under certain conditions the dynamics along the aforementioned remaining eigenvectors makes essential contributions to the overall dynamics as well. In Section 3.4, some findings will be illustrated with the help of a simulated Mpox infection wave. Some conclusions will be drawn in Section 4. Certain limitations of the current study will be addressed in this section as well.

2. Methods

2.1. Four Fundamental Models

Let us define the four fundamental epidemiological models for Mpox infection dynamics.

2.1.1. Model A (SIR-SIR Model)

Let S_a, I_a, and R_a denote the number of individuals in the subpopulations of susceptible, infected, and recovered animals, respectively. Likewise, let S_h, I_h, and R_h denote the number of humans in the susceptible, infected, and recovered subpopulations, respectively. The evolution equations of the population variables read [17]

$$\frac{d}{dt}S_a = -\frac{\beta_a}{N_a}I_a S_a ,$$
$$\frac{d}{dt}I_a = \frac{\beta_a}{N_a}I_a S_a - \gamma_a I_a ,$$
$$\frac{d}{dt}R_a = \gamma_a I_a ,$$
$$\frac{d}{dt}S_h = -\left(\frac{\beta_h}{N_h}I_h + \frac{\beta_{12}}{N_a}I_a\right)S_h ,$$

$$\begin{aligned}
\frac{d}{dt}I_h &= \left(\frac{\beta_h}{N_h}I_h + \frac{\beta_{12}}{N_a}I_a\right)S_h - \gamma_h I_h, \\
\frac{d}{dt}R_h &= \gamma_h I_h,
\end{aligned} \qquad (1)$$

where $N_a = S_a + I_a + R_a$ and $N_a = S_a + I_a + R_a$ denote the total animal and human populations, respectively. In Equation (1), β_a, β_{12}, and β_h denote the effective contact rates (also called infection rates or transmission rates) of animal to animal, animal to human, and human to human transmissions, respectively. The parameters γ_a and γ_h denote recovery rates of infected animal and human individuals, respectively. The current study focuses on infection waves that take place on relatively short durations of a few months such that birth and death processes can be neglected. Moreover, deaths due to Mpox disease are neglected as well. The populations are assumed to be constant at least in good approximation such that variations in N_a and N_h can be neglected. Consequently, the evolution equations for R_a and R_h can be eliminated by putting $R_a = N_a - S_a - I_a$ and $R_h = N_h - S_h - I_h$. Moreover, in the current study, for the sake of simplicity, epidemiological models will be formulated in rescaled variables (i.e., with the help of fractions) as defined by [41]

$$s_j = S_j/N_j, \, i_j = I_j/N_j, \, r_j = R_j/N_j \qquad (2)$$

for $j = a, h$. The SIR-SIR model (model A) defined by Equation (1) then becomes

$$\begin{aligned}
\frac{d}{dt}s_a &= -\beta_a i_a s_a, \\
\frac{d}{dt}i_a &= \beta_a i_a s_a - \gamma_a i_a, \\
\frac{d}{dt}s_h &= -(\beta_h i_h + \beta_{12} i_a)s_h, \\
\frac{d}{dt}i_h &= (\beta_h i_h + \beta_{12} i_a)s_h - \gamma_h i_h
\end{aligned} \qquad (3)$$

with $r_a = 1 - s_a - i_a$ and $r_h = 1 - s_h - i_h$. The state vector of model A reads $\mathbf{x} = (s_a, i_a, s_h, i_h)$. As mentioned in the introduction, Bhunu and Mushayabasa [17], Emeka et al. [18], and Somma et al. [19] based their studies on SIR-SIR models as described by Equation (1).

2.1.2. Model B (SEIR-SIR Model)

The SEIR-SIR model involves the class of exposed animals (E_a) that are infected but not yet infectious. The relative size of the exposed animal subpopulation is denoted by $e_a = E_a/N_a$. The evolution equations for the rescaled model variables read

$$\begin{aligned}
\frac{d}{dt}s_a &= -\beta_a i_a s_a, \\
\frac{d}{dt}e_a &= \beta_a i_a s_a - \alpha_a e_a, \\
\frac{d}{dt}i_a &= \alpha_a e_a - \gamma_a i_a, \\
\frac{d}{dt}s_h &= -(\beta_h i_h + \beta_{12} i_a)s_h, \\
\frac{d}{dt}i_h &= (\beta_h i_h + \beta_{12} i_a)s_h - \gamma_h i_h
\end{aligned} \qquad (4)$$

and involve in addition to the SIR-SIR model parameters the parameter α_a, which describes the transition rate of animals from being infected and non-infectious to being infected and infectious. For the fraction variables of recovered animal and human individuals, the following relations hold: $r_a = 1 - s_a - e_a - i_a$ and $r_h = 1 - s_h - i_h$. The state vector of the SEIR-SIR model defined by Equation (4) reads $\mathbf{x} = (s_a, e_a, i_a, s_h, i_h)$. Note that in what follows we will refer to the population variables i_a and i_h as infectious populations rather than infected populations in order to highlight the distinction between the variables e_j and i_j for $j = a, h$ that describe both infected individuals.

2.1.3. Model C (SIR-SEIR Model)

Like model B, model C involves a class of exposed individuals. Unlike model B, in model C this class (E_h) shows up in the human subsystem. The relative size is denoted by $e_h = E_h/N_h$. The evolution equations of the rescaled model variables read

$$\begin{aligned}
\frac{d}{dt} s_a &= -\beta_a i_a s_a, \\
\frac{d}{dt} i_a &= \beta_a i_a s_a - \gamma_a i_a, \\
\frac{d}{dt} s_h &= -(\beta_h i_h + \beta_{12} i_a) s_h, \\
\frac{d}{dt} e_h &= (\beta_h i_h + \beta_{12} i_a) i_h - \alpha_h e_h, \\
\frac{d}{dt} s_h &= \alpha_h e_h - \gamma_h i_h
\end{aligned} \qquad (5)$$

and are complemented by the relations $r_a = 1 - s_a - i_a$ and $r_h = 1 - s_h - e_h - i_h$. In Equation (5) the parameter α_h describes the transition rate of infected but non-infectious humans (i.e., exposed humans) to become infectious. The model state vector reads $\mathbf{x} = (s_a, i_a, s_h, e_h, i_h)$. As mentioned in the introduction, Madubueze et al. [20] based their study on a Monkeypox model of the SIR-SEIR system type.

2.1.4. Model D (SEIR-SEIR Model)

The SEIR-SEIR model (model D) takes the possibility of exposed individuals into account both for the human and animal populations of interest. Accordingly, the model reads

$$\begin{aligned}
\frac{d}{dt} s_a &= -\beta_a i_a s_a, \\
\frac{d}{dt} e_a &= \beta_a i_a s_a - \alpha_a e_a, \\
\frac{d}{dt} i_a &= \alpha_a e_a - \gamma_a i_a, \\
\frac{d}{dt} s_h &= -(\beta_h i_h + \beta_{12} i_a) s_h, \\
\frac{d}{dt} e_h &= (\beta_h i_h + \beta_{12} i_a) i_h - \alpha_h e_h, \\
\frac{d}{dt} s_h &= \alpha_h e_h - \gamma_h i_h
\end{aligned} \qquad (6)$$

with $r_a = 1 - s_a - e_a - i_a$ and $r_h = 1 - s_h - e_h - i_h$ and all parameters as defined for the previous models A,B, C. The state vector of the SEIR-SEIR model defined by Equation (6) reads $\mathbf{x} = (s_a, e_a, i_a, s_h, e_h, i_h)$. Various authors have used the SEIR-SEIR model defined by Equation (6) as a departure point to model the spread of Mpox disease [21–24] (see also the Introduction).

2.2. Admissible Model Parameters

In what follows it is assumed that all model parameters are positive like

$$\beta_a, \beta_h, \beta_{12}, \gamma_a, \gamma_h, \alpha_a, \alpha_h > 0. \qquad (7)$$

That is, degenerated special cases of models exhibiting vanishing model parameters are ignored.

3. Results
3.1. Potential Order Parameters

Order parameters are known to describe the emerging order of multi-component systems in various disciplines [33,35] and have recently been determined for various epidemiological models describing the COVID-19 pandemic [4]. In the context of the current study, it is useful to discuss order parameters in the context of potential order parameters—as they will be defined next.

Definition 1. *A potential order parameter is an eigenvector associated with an eigenvalue that for appropriate model parameters assumes positive values.*

In other words, in general, dynamical systems exhibit two types of eigenvalues: eigenvalues that are negative or zero in any case and eigenvalues that for appropriate model parameters become positive (but may become negative or zero for other parameter values). Eigenvectors associated with the second type of eigenvalues will be called potential order parameters. The implication of the definition is that for those model parameters that make the eigenvalue in fact positive the potential order parameter is an order parameter or unstable eigenvector [33,35]. In contrast, for model parameters that make the eigenvalue negative the potential order parameter corresponds to a stable eigenvector [33,35].

Theorem 1. *All four models A–D defined by Equations (3)–(6) exhibit two potential order parameters for the admissible model parameters listed in Section 2.2.*

Proof. It is sufficient to show that each model exhibits two eigenvalues that for appropriate, admissible model parameters can become positive.

The model A (SIR-SIR model) exhibits the disease-free fixed points $s_a^* \in [0,1]$, $i_a^* = 0$, $s_h^* \in [0,1]$, $i_h^* = 0$. Let us introduce the following two relative variables describing differences with respect to fixed point variables $\delta_j = s_j - s_j^*$ for $j = a, h$. Note that i_a and i_h already can be regarded as relative variables because the respective fixed point values read $i_a^* = 0$ and $i_h^* = 0$. The model A state vector of relative variables reads $\mathbf{u} = (\delta_a, i_a, \delta_h, i_h)$. The eigenvalues of model A are obtained from a linear stability analysis for which it is assumed that all entries of the relative state vector are small quantities (i.e., the state of the epidemiological system is close to a fixed point of the system). Then, Equation (3) becomes a linear evolution equation of the form [4,33]

$$\frac{d}{dt}\mathbf{u} = L\mathbf{u} \tag{8}$$

with the linearization matrix L defined by

$$L = \begin{pmatrix} 0 & -\beta_a^* & 0 & 0 \\ 0 & \beta_a^* - \gamma_a & 0 & 0 \\ 0 & -\beta_{12}^* & 0 & -\beta_h^* \\ 0 & \beta_{12}^* & 0 & \beta_h^* - \gamma_h \end{pmatrix} \tag{9}$$

and $\beta_a^* = \beta_a s_a^*$, $\beta_h^* = \beta_h s_h^*$, and $\beta_{12}^* = \beta_{12} s_h^*$. The matrix L exhibits the eigenvalues $\lambda_1 = 0$, $\lambda_2 = \beta_a^* - \gamma_a$, $\lambda_3 = 0$, and $\lambda_4 = \beta_h^* - \gamma_h$. The pair of eigenvalues λ_1 and λ_2 (and likewise the pair λ_3 and λ_4) are known as eigenvalues of SIR systems [4,42]. As will be shown below in the context of Theorem 2, the eigenvalues λ_3 and λ_4 can indeed be interpreted as eigenvalues of the SIR human subsystem. In contrast, while λ_1 and λ_2 formally correspond to SIR system eigenvalues such that it would be tempting to interpret them as SIR animal subsystem eigenvalues, as it will be shown below, at least for λ_2 such an interpretation is misleading. Rather, it is more appropriate to interpret λ_2 (in line with its derivation from matrix (9)) as an eigenvalue of the entire SIR-SIR system. λ_2 and λ_4 for appropriate, admissible model parameters (namely, $\beta_a^* > \gamma_a > 0$ and $\beta_h^* > \gamma_h > 0$, respectively) assume positive values. Therefore, the corresponding eigenvectors are the potential order parameters of the SIR-SIR system. They will be derived explicitly below.

For model B (SEIR-SIR model) the fixed points are given by $s_a^* \in [0,1]$, $e_a^* = 0$, $i_a^* = 0$, $s_h^* \in [0,1]$, $i_h^* = 0$. The state vector of relative variables with respect to those fixed points reads $\mathbf{u} = (\delta_a, e_a, i_a, \delta_h, i_h)$. For states sufficiently close to a given fixed point Equation (4) can be linearized and becomes Equation (8) with L defined by

$$L = \begin{pmatrix} 0 & 0 & -\beta_a^* & 0 & 0 \\ 0 & -\alpha_a & \beta_a^* & 0 & 0 \\ 0 & \alpha_a & -\gamma_a & 0 & 0 \\ 0 & 0 & -\beta_{12}^* & 0 & -\beta_h^* \\ 0 & 0 & \beta_{12}^* & 0 & \beta_h^* - \gamma_h \end{pmatrix}. \tag{10}$$

The matrix L exhibits the eigenvalues $\lambda_1 = 0$ and

$$\lambda_{2,3} = -\frac{\gamma_a + \alpha_a}{2} \pm \sqrt{\frac{(\gamma_a + \alpha_a)^2}{4} + \alpha_a(\beta_a^* - \gamma_a)}, \tag{11}$$

where the upper (lower) sign holds for λ_2 (λ_3). These eigenvalues are known as eigenvalues of epidemiological SEIR models [4,42]. However, as will be shown in the context of Theorem 2 with respect to model B they actually describe eigenvalues of the entire SEIR-SIR model. The two remaining eigenvalues of L read $\lambda_4 = 0$ and $\lambda_5 = \beta_h^* - \gamma_h$ and denote SIR-human subsystem eigenvalues (as will be shown below). λ_2 assumes positive values for admissible parameters if $\beta_a^* > \gamma_a > 0$ holds, whereas λ_3 is negative for all admissible model parameters [4]. λ_5 is positive for admissible parameters if $\beta_h^* > \gamma_h > 0$ holds. In summary, λ_2 and λ_5 may assume positive values for admissible model parameters. By Definition 1, the corresponding eigenvectors describe the potential order parameters of the epidemiological SEIR-SIR system (4). They will be derived below.

In the case of model C (SIR-SEIR model) the fixed points are given by $s_a^* \in [0,1]$, $i_a^* = 0$, $s_h^* \in [0,1]$, $e_h^* = 0$, and $i_h^* = 0$. Accordingly, the state vector of relative variables reads $\mathbf{u} = (\delta_a, i_a, \delta_h, e_h, i_h)$ and satisfies Equation (8), which is again close to the aforementioned fixed points. For model C the linearization matrix L reads

$$L = \begin{pmatrix} 0 & -\beta_a^* & 0 & 0 & 0 \\ 0 & \beta_a^* - \gamma_a & 0 & 0 & 0 \\ 0 & -\beta_{12}^* & 0 & 0 & -\beta_h^* \\ 0 & \beta_{12}^* & 0 & -\alpha_h & \beta_h^* \\ 0 & 0 & 0 & \alpha_h & -\gamma_h \end{pmatrix}. \tag{12}$$

A detailed calculation shows that the five eigenvalues of L are given in terms of three SEIR-human subsystem eigenvalues and two eigenvalues that formally look like SIR system eigenvalues. The SIR-system-like eigenvalues read $\lambda_1 = 0$ and $\lambda_2 = \beta_a^* - \gamma_a$. The SEIR-human subsystem eigenvalues read $\lambda_3 = 0$ and

$$\lambda_{4,5} = -\frac{\gamma_h + \alpha_h}{2} \pm \sqrt{\frac{(\gamma_h + \alpha_h)^2}{4} + \alpha_h(\beta_h^* - \gamma_h)}, \tag{13}$$

where the upper (lower) sign holds for λ_4 (λ_5). λ_2 is positive if $\beta_a^* > \gamma_a > 0$, λ_4 assumes positive values if $\beta_h^* > \gamma_h > 0$, and λ_5 is negative for all admissible model parameters. In summary, only two eigenvalues may become positive: λ_2 and λ_4. The corresponding eigenvectors denote the potential order parameters of the SIR-SEIR system (5).

Finally, the fixed points of model D (SEIR-SEIR model) are described by $s_a^* \in [0,1]$, $e_a = 0$, $i_a^* = 0$, $s_h^* \in [0,1]$, $e_h = 0$, and $i_h^* = 0$. The model D state vector of relative variables reads $\mathbf{u} = (\delta_a, e_a, i_a, \delta_h, e_h, i_h)$ and satisfies Eq. (8) in the linear domain dynamics with L given by

$$L = \begin{pmatrix} 0 & 0 & -\beta_a^* & 0 & 0 & 0 \\ 0 & -\alpha_a & \beta_a^* & 0 & 0 & 0 \\ 0 & \alpha_a & -\gamma_a & 0 & 0 & 0 \\ 0 & 0 & -\beta_{12}^* & 0 & 0 & -\beta_h^* \\ 0 & 0 & \beta_{12}^* & 0 & -\alpha_h & \beta_h^* \\ 0 & 0 & 0 & 0 & \alpha_h & -\gamma_h \end{pmatrix}. \quad (14)$$

It can be shown that the six eigenvalues of L are given in terms of three SEIR eigenvalues for the human subsystem and three eigenvalues that again at least formally look like SEIR eigenvalues and only involve animal subsystem parameters. They are listed above already in the context of the SEIR-SIR and SIR-SEIR models. For the sake of clarity they are explicitly listed here. Those related to the animal subsystem parameters read $\lambda_1 = 0$ and

$$\lambda_{2,3} = -\frac{\gamma_a + \alpha_a}{2} \pm \sqrt{\frac{(\gamma_a + \alpha_a)^2}{4} + \alpha_a(\beta_a^* - \gamma_a)}, \quad (15)$$

where the upper (lower) sign holds for λ_2 (λ_3). The three SEIR-human subsystem eigenvalues read $\lambda_4 = 0$ and

$$\lambda_{5,6} = -\frac{\gamma_h + \alpha_h}{2} \pm \sqrt{\frac{(\gamma_h + \alpha_h)^2}{4} + \alpha_h(\beta_h^* - \gamma_h)}, \quad (16)$$

where again the upper (lower) sign holds for λ_5 (λ_6). In line with the previous discussion, it follows that λ_3 and λ_6 are always negative. In contrast, λ_2 and λ_5 are positive if $\beta_a^* - \gamma_a > 0$ and $\beta_h^* - \gamma_h > 0$ holds, respectively. In other words, for model D, λ_2 and λ_5 may assume positive values and the corresponding eigenvectors denote the potential order parameters of the SEIR-SEIR system (6).

In summary, all four fundamental models A, B, C, and D exhibit two potential order parameters. □

Corollary 1. *The four fundamental models A, B, C, and D defined by Equations (3)–(6) exhibit maximally two order parameters for the admissible model parameters listed in Section 2.2.*

Proof. If the eigenvalues of both potential order parameters assume positive values, then the model under consideration exhibits two order parameters. This is the maximal number. □

Definition 2. *A human–animal order parameter is an order parameter (unstable eigenvector) that exhibits non-vanishing components both in the animal and human subsystems.*

As we will see below there are eigenvectors that only exhibit components in either the animal subsystem or the human subsystem. Their coordinates (or amplitudes) describe dynamics in either of the two systems. In contrast, eigenvectors that exhibit components in both system connect the animal subsystem dynamics with the human subsystem dynamics. In particular, unstable eigenvectors (order parameters) with that property are of interest because they describe the emerging order of an Mpox outbreak in terms of multi-compartmental components that link both subsystems with each other. By Definition 2 these multi-compartmental components will be called human–animal order parameters.

Theorem 2. *All four fundamental models A, B, C, and D defined by Equations (3)–(6) exhibit maximally one human–animal order parameter for the admissible model parameters listed in Section 2.2.*

Proof. In what follows, the eigenvectors of all four models will be derived and, in doing so, a constructive proof of Theorem 2 will be given. Eigenvectors will be denoted by $\mathbf{v}_j$ with $j = 1, \ldots, 4$ for model A, $j = 1, \ldots, 5$ for models B and C, and $j = 1, \ldots, 6$ for model D.

For model A, from matrix (9) it follows that eigenvectors related to $\lambda_1 = 0$ and λ_3 read $\mathbf{v}_1 = (1,0,0,0)$ and $\mathbf{v}_3 = (0,0,1,0)$. The eigenvector of $\lambda_4 = \beta_h^* - \gamma_h$ reads

$$\mathbf{v}_4 = \frac{1}{Z_4} \begin{pmatrix} 0 \\ 0 \\ -\beta_h^* \\ \lambda_4 \end{pmatrix} \quad (17)$$

with $Z_4 = \sqrt{(\beta_h^*)^2 + \lambda_4^2}$. In order to derive $\mathbf{v}_2$ associated to $\lambda_2 = \beta_a^* - \gamma_a$ note that $\mathbf{v}_2$ satisfies

$$\begin{pmatrix} -\lambda_2 & -\beta_a^* & 0 & 0 \\ 0 & 0 & 0 & 0 \\ 0 & -\beta_{12}^* & -\lambda_2 & -\beta_h^* \\ 0 & \beta_{12}^* & 0 & \lambda_4 - \lambda_2 \end{pmatrix} \mathbf{v}_2 = 0 \quad (18)$$

Consequently, the first two components of $\mathbf{v}_2$ have the same structure as the two non-vanishing components of $\mathbf{v}_4$ such that $\mathbf{v}_2 = (-\beta_a^*, \lambda_2, a, b)/Z_2$ holds, where a and b (and Z_2) are still to be determined. Substituting this ansatz into Equation (18), and exploiting the third and fourth rows of the matrix equation, yields a and b (and Z_2). The result reads

$$\mathbf{v}_2 = \frac{1}{Z_2} \begin{pmatrix} -\beta_a^* \\ \lambda_2 \\ -\beta_{12}^*\left(1 + \frac{\beta_h^*}{\lambda_2 - \lambda_4}\right) \\ \beta_{12}^* \frac{\lambda_2}{\lambda_2 - \lambda_4} \end{pmatrix} \quad (19)$$

with $Z_2 = \sqrt{(\beta_a^*)^2 + \lambda_2^2 + (\beta_{12}^*)^2 \xi}$ and $\xi = [1 + \beta_h^*/(\lambda_2 - \lambda_4)]^2 + [\lambda_2/(\lambda_2 - \lambda_4)]^2$. The eigenvectors $\mathbf{v}_2$ and $\mathbf{v}_4$ correspond to the potential order parameters of the SIR-SIR model (3). However, $\mathbf{v}_4$ exhibits non-vanishing components only in the human subsystem. In contrast, $\mathbf{v}_2$ exhibits non-vanishing components in both subsystems and, consequently, can describe an emerging order involving both subsystems. For $\lambda_2 > 0$, it follows from Definition 2 that $\mathbf{v}_2$ is the human–animal order parameter of the SIR-SIR system. Accordingly, the corresponding eigenvalue λ_2 should be interpreted as eigenvalue of the entire SIR-SIR system (as anticipated above). Note that the two non-vanishing components of $\mathbf{v}_4$ are known as components of the order parameter of SIR models [4]. Accordingly, for $\lambda_4 > 0$, on the one hand, the eigenvector $\mathbf{v}_4$ constitutes an order parameter of the epidemiological system (3). On the other hand, while it does not qualify as a human–animal order parameter, it may be regarded as the SIR order parameter of the human subsystem of Equation (3). Likewise, λ_4 may be regarded as an SIR human subsystem eigenvalue (as anticipated above)—in addition to its original role as eigenvalue of the model matrix (9) of model (3). In summary, the SEIR-SIR model (model A) maximally exhibits one human–animal order parameter.

For the SEIR-SIR model (model B) defined by Equation (4), the eigenvectors associated to $\lambda_1 = 0$ and $\lambda_4 = 0$ read $\mathbf{v}_1 = (1,0,0,0,0)$ and $\mathbf{v}_4 = (0,0,0,1,0)$. For $\lambda_5 = \beta_h^* - \gamma_h$ from the matrix (10) we obtain again an eigenvector with the components of an SIR order parameter:

$$\mathbf{v}_5 = \frac{1}{Z_5} \begin{pmatrix} 0 \\ 0 \\ 0 \\ -\beta_h^* \\ \lambda_5 \end{pmatrix} \qquad (20)$$

with $Z_5 = \sqrt{(\beta_h^*)^2 + \lambda_5^2}$. The eigenvectors of $\lambda_{2,3}$ can be obtained using the ansatz $\mathbf{v}_{2,3} = (x, y, z, e, f)$. From Equation (10), it follows that the first three components x, y, z can be determined independently from the remaining two. They address the animal SEIR subsystem. The solution reads

$$\begin{pmatrix} x \\ y \\ z \end{pmatrix} = \frac{1}{Z_j} \begin{pmatrix} -\beta_a^*(\lambda_j + \alpha_a) \\ \beta_a^* \lambda_j \\ \lambda_j(\lambda_j + \alpha_a) \end{pmatrix} \qquad (21)$$

for $j = 2, 3$, where Z_j has still to be determined. Using the ansatz $\mathbf{v}_{2,3} = (x, y, z, e, f)$ in combination with the matrix (10) the remaining components e, f can be determined. The result reads

$$\mathbf{v}_j = \frac{1}{Z_j} \begin{pmatrix} -\beta_a^*(\lambda_j + \alpha_a) \\ \beta_a^* \lambda_j \\ \lambda_j(\lambda_j + \alpha_a) \\ -\beta_{12}^*(\lambda_j + \alpha_a)\left(1 + \frac{\beta_h^*}{\lambda_j - \lambda_5}\right) \\ \beta_{12}^*(\lambda_j + \alpha_a)\frac{\lambda_j}{\lambda_j - \lambda_5} \end{pmatrix} \qquad (22)$$

for $j = 2, 3$ and Z_j defined such that $|\mathbf{v}_j| = 1$. The eigenvectors $\mathbf{v}_2$ and $\mathbf{v}_5$ correspond to the potential order parameters of the SEIR-SIR model (4). However, $\mathbf{v}_5$ exhibits non-vanishing components only in the human subsystem. In contrast, $\mathbf{v}_2$ exhibits non-zero components in both subsystems. Consequently, for $\lambda_2 > 0$ it follows that $\mathbf{v}_2$ is the human–animal order parameter of the SEIR-SIR system. Furthermore, note that the subvector defined by Equation (21) is known as the order parameter of SEIR models [4]. This implies that the human–animal order parameter $\mathbf{v}_2$ exhibits in the animal subsystem the ordinary order parameter of epidemiological SEIR models. Finally, for $\lambda_5 > 0$ the eigenvector $\mathbf{v}_5$ is an order parameter of the SEIR-SIR model and may be regarded as the SIR order parameter of the human subsystem. λ_5 may be regarded as the corresponding eigenvalue of the SIR human subsystem (as anticipated above). In summary, the SEIR-SIR model (model B) maximally exhibits one human–animal order parameter.

The SIR-SEIR model (model C) exhibits the eigenvectors $\mathbf{v}_1 = (1, 0, 0, 0, 0)$ and $\mathbf{v}_3 = (0, 0, 1, 0, 0)$ associated to $\lambda_1 = 0$ and $\lambda_3 = 0$. From matrix (12), it follows that the eigenvectors $\mathbf{v}_{4,5}$ related to the eigenvalues $\lambda_{4,5}$ assume the form $\mathbf{v}_{4,5} = (0, 0, x', y', z')$. Since they address exclusively the human SEIR subsystem, the components should constitute an SEIR order parameter as shown in Equation (21). A detailed calculation shows that this is indeed the case:

$$\mathbf{v}_j = \frac{1}{Z_j} \begin{pmatrix} 0 \\ 0 \\ -\beta_h^*(\lambda_j + \alpha_h) \\ \beta_h^* \lambda_j \\ \lambda_j(\lambda_j + \alpha_h) \end{pmatrix} \qquad (23)$$

for $j = 4, 5$ with Z_j such that $|\mathbf{v}_j| = 1$. The derivation of $\mathbf{v}_2$ associated to $\lambda_2 = \beta_a^* - \gamma_a$ follows in part the derivation of $\mathbf{v}_2$ of the SIR-SIR model. As such, $\mathbf{v}_2$ satisfies

$$\begin{pmatrix} -\lambda_2 & -\beta_a^* & 0 & 0 & 0 \\ 0 & 0 & 0 & 0 & 0 \\ 0 & -\beta_{12}^* & -\lambda_2 & 0 & -\beta_h^* \\ 0 & \beta_{12}^* & 0 & -(\alpha_h + \lambda_2) & \beta_h^* \\ 0 & 0 & 0 & \alpha_h & -(\gamma_h + \lambda_2) \end{pmatrix} \mathbf{v}_2 = 0. \qquad (24)$$

Accordingly, the first two components of $\mathbf{v}_2$ constitute an SIR order parameter for the animal subsystem such that $\mathbf{v}_2 = (-\beta_a^*, \lambda_2, x'', y'', z'')/Z_2$ holds. A detailed calculation yields the remaining components x'', y'', z''. The result reads

$$\mathbf{v}_2 = \frac{1}{Z_2} \begin{pmatrix} -\beta_a^* \\ \lambda_2 \\ -\beta_{12}^* \frac{(\lambda_2 + \alpha_h)(\lambda_2 + \gamma_h)}{P_h(\lambda_2)} \\ \beta_{12}^* \frac{\lambda_2(\lambda_2 + \gamma_h)}{P_h(\lambda_2)} \\ \beta_{12}^* \frac{\lambda_2 \alpha_h}{P_h(\lambda_2)} \end{pmatrix} \qquad (25)$$

with the polynomial $P_h(\phi)$ involving only human subsystem model parameters defined by

$$P_h(\phi) = (\phi + \alpha_h)(\phi + \gamma_h) - \alpha_h \beta_h^* \qquad (26)$$

and Z_2 chosen such that $|\mathbf{v}_2| = 1$. Note that $P_h(\lambda) = 0$ is the characteristic equation of $\lambda_{4,5}$ and yields the eigenvalues (13) of the SIR-SEIR model. However, in the context of $\mathbf{v}_2$, P_h is applied to λ_2 rather than $\lambda_{4,5}$; see Equation (25). The eigenvectors $\mathbf{v}_2$ and $\mathbf{v}_4$ correspond to the potential order parameters of the SIR-SEIR model (5). $\mathbf{v}_4$ addresses only the human subsystem. In contrast, $\mathbf{v}_2$ addresses both subsystems. Consequently, for $\lambda_2 > 0$ we see that $\mathbf{v}_2$ is the human–animal order parameter of the SIR-SEIR system. For $\lambda_4 > 0$ the eigenvector $\mathbf{v}_4$ is an order parameter of the system and may be regarded as the SEIR order parameter of the human subsystem. However, it does not qualify as a human–animal order parameter. In summary, for the SIR-SEIR model (model C) there is maximally one human–animal order parameter.

The eigenvectors $\mathbf{v}_j$ of the SEIR-SEIR model (model D) defined by Equation (6) satisfy

$$\begin{pmatrix} -\lambda_j & 0 & -\beta_a^* & 0 & 0 & 0 \\ 0 & -(\alpha_a + \lambda_j) & \beta_a^* & 0 & 0 & 0 \\ 0 & \alpha_a & -(\gamma_a + \lambda_j) & 0 & 0 & 0 \\ 0 & 0 & -\beta_{12}^* & -\lambda_j & 0 & -\beta_h^* \\ 0 & 0 & \beta_{12}^* & 0 & -(\alpha_h + \lambda_j) & \beta_h^* \\ 0 & 0 & 0 & 0 & \alpha_h & -(\gamma_h + \lambda_j) \end{pmatrix} \mathbf{v}_j = 0; \qquad (27)$$

see also Equation (14). The eigenvalues $\lambda_1 = 0$ and $\lambda_4 = 0$ are associated with the eigenvectors $\mathbf{v}_1 = (1, 0, 0, 0, 0, 0)$ and $\mathbf{v}_4 = (0, 0, 0, 1, 0, 0)$. The 3×3 matrix in the right-bottom corner defines eigenvectors of the form $\mathbf{v}_j = (0, 0, 0, x''', y''', z''')$. They have components like SEIR order parameter eigenvectors as in Equation (21) but describe the human subsystem. That is, for $j = 5, 6$ the eigenvectors read

$$\mathbf{v}_j = \frac{1}{Z_j} \begin{pmatrix} 0 \\ 0 \\ 0 \\ -\beta_h^*(\lambda_j + \alpha_h) \\ \beta_h^* \lambda_j \\ \lambda_j(\lambda_j + \alpha_h) \end{pmatrix} \qquad (28)$$

with Z_j such that $|\mathbf{v}_j| = 1$. Not surprisingly, they resemble the eigenvectors of the SEIR system of the SIR-SEIR model (compare Equations (23) and (28)). In view of the left-upper 3×3 matrix in Equation (27), the remaining eigenvectors $\mathbf{v}_{2,3}$ assume the form

$$\mathbf{v}_j = \frac{1}{Z_j} \begin{pmatrix} -\beta_a^*(\lambda_j + \alpha_a) \\ \beta_a^* \lambda_j \\ \lambda_j(\lambda_j + \alpha_a) \\ a'' \\ b'' \\ c'' \end{pmatrix}, \qquad (29)$$

where a'', b'', c'' still need to be determined. Substituting Equation (29) into Equation (27) allows one to determine those components, which leads to

$$\mathbf{v}_j = \frac{1}{Z_j} \begin{pmatrix} -\beta_a^*(\lambda_j + \alpha_a) \\ \beta_a^* \lambda_j \\ \lambda_j(\lambda_j + \alpha_a) \\ -\beta_{12}^*(\lambda_j + \alpha_a) \frac{(\lambda_j+\alpha_h)(\lambda_j+\gamma_h)}{P_h(\lambda_j)} \\ \beta_{12}^*(\lambda_j + \alpha_a) \frac{\lambda_j(\lambda_j+\gamma_h)}{P_h(\lambda_j)} \\ \beta_{12}^*(\lambda_j + \alpha_a) \frac{\lambda_j \alpha_h}{P_h(\lambda_j)} \end{pmatrix}, \qquad (30)$$

with P_h defined by Equation (26) and Z_j such that $|\mathbf{v}_j| = 1$. The last three components in Equation (30) related to the human subsystem resemble the human subsystem components of $\mathbf{v}_2$ of the SIR-SEIR model. As indicated in Equation (30) they are identical except for the pre-factor $\lambda_j + \alpha_a$ (compare Equations (25) and (30)). The eigenvectors $\mathbf{v}_2$ and $\mathbf{v}_5$ correspond to the potential order parameters of the SEIR-SEIR model (6). $\mathbf{v}_5$ addresses only the human subsystem, while $\mathbf{v}_2$ addresses both subsystems. Consequently, $\mathbf{v}_2$ for $\lambda_2 > 0$ is the human–animal order parameter of the SEIR-SEIR model (model D). For $\lambda_5 > 0$ the eigenvector $\mathbf{v}_5$ is also an order parameter of the SEIR-SEIR model. It may be regarded as the SEIR order parameter of the human subsystem (but not as a human–animal order parameter). In summary, for the SEIR-SEIR model (model D) there is maximally one human–animal order parameter.

In conclusion, all four models exhibit maximally one human–animal order parameter. □

3.2. Implications: Amplitude Dynamics and the Role of Human–Animal Order Parameters

Let us define the amplitudes $A_1, \ldots, A_m$ of the model eigenvectors $\mathbf{v}_j$ implicitly by the expansion [4]

$$\mathbf{u} = \sum_{j=1}^{m} \mathbf{v}_j A_j \qquad (31)$$

with $m = 4$ for model A, $m = 5$ for models B and C, and $m = 6$ for model D, where it is assumed that the eigenvectors are linearly independent from each other and form a complete vector basis (i.e., degenerated, special cases may be discussed separately). The expansion (31) holds for arbitrary $\mathbf{u}$ (i.e., it holds beyond the linear initial phase dynamics that will be defined below) [4]. In line with Equation (31), the state vector of the model under consideration can be expressed like

$$\mathbf{x} = \mathbf{x}^* + \sum_{j=1}^{m} \mathbf{v}_j A_j, \qquad (32)$$

where $\mathbf{x}^*$ denotes the fixed point of interest (see also Section 3.1). Explicitly, the amplitudes A_j can be computed from either $\mathbf{u}$ or $\mathbf{x}$ like

$$A_j = \mathbf{w}_j \cdot \mathbf{u} = \mathbf{w}_j \cdot (\mathbf{x} - \mathbf{x}^*), \tag{33}$$

where the dot denotes the scalar product and $\mathbf{w}_j$ the bi-orthogonal vector associated to $\mathbf{v}_j$ [4]. In general, the bi-orthogonal vectors $\mathbf{w}_j$ can be determined numerically with the help of the analytical expressions for $\mathbf{v}_j$ [4]. As mentioned in the introduction, initial phases are crucial phases of infection waves. The expansion defined by Equation (32) can be discussed for such initial phases in the context of the four fundamental models A, B, C, and D. To this end, it is helpful to make the following definition.

Definition 3. *The linearized initial phase dynamics is the dynamics of the state vector $\mathbf{x}$ as defined by the linearized evolution Equation (8) with $\mathbf{x} = \mathbf{x}^* + \mathbf{u}$ and an initial state $\mathbf{x}(t = 0)$ in an ϵ-environment of the fixed point $\mathbf{x}^*$ such that $|\mathbf{u}(t = 0)| < \epsilon$.*

The idea here is that infection waves typically start with a small number of infected individuals such that the human–animal system initially is close to a fixed point. Mathematically, this property of the initial state to be in a close vicinity of a fixed point can be expressed by requiring that the initial state is in an ϵ-environment of a fixed point and by choosing a small value for ϵ. If ϵ is sufficiently small, the linearized model defined by (8) describes a good approximation of its original nonlinear model (either A, B, C, or D). It is beyond the current study to define precisely what is meant by a good approximation. It is sufficient to note that on the one hand the accuracy of the linear approximation solution as measured by reasonably defined quantities typically improves when ϵ is made smaller and smaller. On the other hand, for Mpox infection waves, at a certain point in time, the nonlinear aspects of the models A, B, C, and D will become relevant. At that point in time, the linear approximate model (8) will fail to give an accurate description of the infection dynamics. In summary, Equation (8) is tailored to describe the initial phase dynamics, as it is also pointed out in Definition 3. Solutions of the initial phase dynamics as defined in Definition 3 and by Equation (8) are given in terms of the superposition

$$\mathbf{x} = \mathbf{x}^* + \sum_{j=1}^{m} \mathbf{v}_j A_j(0) \exp\{\lambda_j t\}, \tag{34}$$

where $A_j(0)$ denotes the initial amplitudes at the initial time point $t = 0$. The initial amplitudes can be computed from the initial state $\mathbf{x}(0)$ with the help of Equation (33) [4]. For example, for the SIR-SIR model (3) the superposition solution (34) reads

$$\mathbf{x} = \mathbf{x}^* + \mathbf{v}_2 A_2(0) \exp\{\lambda_2 t\} + \mathbf{v}_4 A_4(0) \exp\{\lambda_4 t\} + \mathbf{h}_0, \ \mathbf{h}_0 = \mathbf{v}_1 A_1(0) + \mathbf{v}_3 A_3(0). \tag{35}$$

Theorem 3. *For the admissible model parameters listed in Section 2.2 the initial phase dynamics of any Mpox outbreak dynamics as described by the four fundamental models A, B, C, and D defined by Equations (3)–(6) and the linearized evolution Equation (8) corresponds to one of three qualitatively different scenarios.*

In other words, despite the differences across the four models, there exist only three qualitatively different scenarios how Mpox disease outbreaks (as described by those models) initially evolve.

Proof. Let $\lambda^{(h,X)}$ and $\mathbf{v}^{(h,X)}$ denote the eigenvalue and eigenvector of the potential order parameter of the human subsystem of the model X with $X = A, B, C, D$. Likewise, let $\lambda^{(12,X)}$ and $\mathbf{v}^{(12,X)}$ denote the eigenvalue and eigenvector of the potential human–animal order parameter of the model X. Let us next turn to Equation (34). All four models exhibit two neutrally stable eigenvectors that are associated with zero eigenvalues and point into the directions of s_a and s_h, respectively. Since we consider an Mpox disease outbreak, the disease-free fixed point under consideration must be unstable [4], which implies that at least one of the two eigenvalues $\lambda^{(h,X)}$ and $\lambda^{(12,X)}$ must be positive. Furthermore, there are maximally two positive eigenvalues. In total, these considerations lead to the following three Mpox disease outbreak scenarios:

$$\begin{aligned} Scenario(i) &: \lambda^{(h,X)} > 0 \, , \lambda^{(12,X)} < 0 \, , \\ Scenario(ii) &: \lambda^{(h,X)} < 0 \, , \lambda^{(12,X)} > 0 \, , \\ Scenario(iii) &: \lambda^{(h,X)} > 0 \, , \lambda^{(12,X)} > 0. \end{aligned} \quad (36)$$

In scenario (i), the outbreak dynamics is characterized by two neutrally stable directions (see above) and one unstable direction given by the SIR ($X = A, C$) or SEIR ($X = B, D$) human subsystem order parameter $\mathbf{v}^{(h,X)}$. The remaining directions are given in terms of stable eigenvectors. In scenario (ii), the outbreaks dynamics is characterized again by two neutrally stable directions. There is one unstable direction given by the human–animal order parameter $\mathbf{v}^{(12,X)}$. The remaining directions are given in terms of stable eigenvectors. Although scenario (i) and (ii) have in common that they both feature only a single unstable direction, scenarios (i) and (ii) differ from each other qualitatively because they involve different types of order parameters. Further details about this difference will be discussed below. Finally, scenario (iii) describes an outbreak dynamics that is characterized by two neutrally stable directions and two unstable directions given in terms of the two maximally possible order parameters discussed in Section 3.1. The remaining directions for the models B, C, and D are given by stable eigenvectors. Scenario (iii) differs from scenarios (i) and (ii) qualitatively by the number of unstable directions. □

In what follows, the scenarios will be discussed in more detail. In scenario (i) we have $\lambda^{(h,X)} > 0$ and $\lambda^{(12,X)} < 0$. The state $\mathbf{x}$ of the system under consideration evolves away from the fixed point along the direction $\mathbf{v}^{(h,X)}$, which has only non-vanishing components in the space of the human system (e.g., for model A: $\mathbf{v}^{(h,X)} = \mathbf{v}_4$ with $v_{4,1} = v_{4,2} = 0$, $v_{4,3} = -\beta_h^*/Z_4$ and $v_{4,4} = \lambda_4/Z_4$). That is, $A^{(h,X)}(t) = A^{(h,X)}(0) \exp\{\lambda^{(h,X)}t\}$ holds and describes an exponential increase in the amplitude related to $\mathbf{v}^{(h,X)}$. In contrast, let $\xi(X)$ denote the index of the human subsystem order parameter $\mathbf{v}^{(h,X)}$ of scenario (i) (e.g., $\xi(A) = 4$ for model A). Then, components of the initial state $\mathbf{x}(0)$ in all other directions as measured by $A_j(0) = \mathbf{w}_j(\mathbf{x}(0) - \mathbf{x}^*)$ for $j \neq \xi$ and $j = 1, \ldots, m$ either decay in magnitude or remain constant. More precisely, let $s(i)$ denote the indices of negative eigenvalues associated with stable eigenvectors with $i = 1$ for model A, $i = 1, 2$ for models B and C, and $i = 1, 2, 3$ for model D. Then $A_{s(i)}(t) = A_{s(i)}(0) \exp\{\lambda_{s(i)}t\}$ describes a dynamics towards the fixed point. Let us split the overall dynamics into three components: an outwards dynamics ($\mathbf{x}_{out}$) describing the dynamics away from the fixed point along unstable eigenvectors (i.e., order parameters), an inwards dynamics ($\mathbf{x}_{in}$) describing the dynamics towards the fixed point along stable directions, and $\mathbf{h}_0$ describing the constant part of the dynamics related to the two neutrally stable directions. Accordingly, Equation (34) for all three scenarios (i), (ii), and (iii) becomes

$$\mathbf{x} = \mathbf{x}^* + \mathbf{x}_{out} + \mathbf{x}_{in} + \mathbf{h}_0 \, . \quad (37)$$

Specifically, for scenario (i), we obtain

$$\begin{aligned} \mathbf{x}_{out} &= \mathbf{v}^{(h,X)} A^{(h,X)}(0) \exp\{\lambda^{(h,X)}t\} \, , \lambda^{(h,X)} > 0 \, , \\ \mathbf{x}_{in} &= \sum_{i=1}^{m-3} \mathbf{v}_{s(i)} A_{s(i)}(0) \exp\{\lambda_{s(i)}t\} \, , \lambda_{s(i)} < 0 \, . \end{aligned} \quad (38)$$

The component $\mathbf{x}_{out}$ is most relevant for the disease outbreak. As mentioned above, $\mathbf{v}^{(h,X)}$, addresses only the human subsystem. Consequently, scenario (i) describes an outbreak due to human to human transmissions (while the infection dynamics in the animal subsystem subsides). In line with earlier studies on COVID-19 outbreaks [4], $\mathbf{v}^{(h,X)}$ describes the organization of this type of Mpox outbreak. For example, for the SIR-SIR model (3) (model A), from the order parameter $\mathbf{v}_4$ defined by Equation (17) it follows that during the initial phase of an Mpox outbreak as a result of the outwards dynamics $\mathbf{x}_{out}$ changes Δs_h and Δi_h in the relative sizes of the susceptible and infected populations satisfy

$$\mathbf{x}_{out} \Rightarrow \frac{\Delta i_h}{\Delta s_h} = \frac{v_{4,4}}{v_{4,3}} = -\frac{\lambda_4}{\beta_h^*}. \tag{39}$$

Accordingly, a decay of susceptibles by $\Delta s_h < 0$ comes with an increase in infectious individuals by $\Delta i_h = -\lambda_4 \Delta s_h / \beta_h^* > 0$ and vice versa an increase in infectious individuals by $\Delta i_h > 0$ is associated with a decrease in susceptibles of $\Delta s_h = -\beta_h^* \Delta i_h / \lambda_4 < 0$. Similar considerations can be made for models B, C, and D based on the human subsystem order parameters defined by Equations (20), (23), and (28), respectively. For example, for the SIR-SEIR model (5) (model C), due to the outwards dynamics $\mathbf{x}_{out}$ the populations e_h and i_h change relative to each other like

$$\mathbf{x}_{out} \Rightarrow \frac{\Delta i_h}{\Delta e_h} = \frac{v_{4,5}}{v_{4,4}} = \frac{\lambda_4 + \alpha_h}{\beta_h^*}. \tag{40}$$

Any increase in exposed humans by $\Delta E_h = 100$ individuals implies an increase in infectious individuals by $\Delta I_h = (\lambda_4 + \alpha_h)/\beta_h^* \cdot 100$ individuals (where we have used that $\Delta I_h / \Delta E_h = \Delta i_h / \Delta e_h$ holds). In summary, during the initial phase of a scenario (i) outbreak the component $\mathbf{x}_{out}$ that drives the outbreak establishes rigid relationships between the dynamics of the subpopulations s_h and i_h (all models) and e_h (models C,D). These relationships, in turn, are determined by the model-specific human subsystem order parameter $\mathbf{v}^{(h,X)}$.

The Mpox outbreak scenario (ii) is characterized by $\lambda^{(h,X)} < 0$ and $\lambda^{(12,X)} > 0$. The system state $\mathbf{x}$ evolves away from the fixed point along the direction of the human–animal order parameter $\mathbf{v}^{(12,X)}$. Equation (37) holds with

$$\begin{aligned}
\mathbf{x}_{out} &= \mathbf{v}^{(12,X)} A^{(12,X)}(0) \exp\{\lambda^{(12,X)} t\}, \quad \lambda^{(12,X)} > 0, \\
\mathbf{x}_{in} &= \sum_{i=1}^{m-3} \mathbf{v}_{s(i)} A_{s(i)}(0) \exp\{\lambda_{s(i)} t\}, \quad \lambda_{s(i)} < 0.
\end{aligned} \tag{41}$$

By Definition 2, the human–animal order parameter $\mathbf{v}^{(12,X)}$ exhibits components both in the animal and human subsystems (e.g., see Equation (19) for model A). Consequently, scenario (ii) describes Mpox outbreaks that involve infection outbreaks in the animal subsystems that drive Mpox outbreaks in the corresponding human subsystems. While in the previously discussed scenario, scenario (i), the infection dynamics in an animal subsystem immediately subsides and the initial phase of a wave is caused by human to human virus transmissions, in the scenario (ii) the infection dynamics in a human subsystem would subside immediately if the system would be decoupled from its animal reservoir. More precisely, if we would put $\beta_{12} = 0$, then due to the fact that in scenario (ii) we have $\lambda^{(h,X)} < 0$ the disease-free fixed points of the human subsystem under consideration are neutrally stable. In other words, due to the coupling with $\beta_{12} > 0$ the infection wave of the animal subsystem under consideration drives an infection wave in the corresponding human subsystem. Moreover, $\mathbf{v}^{(12,X)}$ describes the organization of scenario (ii) outbreaks caused by the outwards dynamics $\mathbf{x}_{out}$. For example, for model A from Equation (19) it follows that during the initial phase of such outbreaks changes Δs_a and Δi_a in the relative sizes of the susceptible and infectious animal populations satisfy

$$\mathbf{x}_{out} \Rightarrow \frac{\Delta i_a}{\Delta s_a} = \frac{v_{2,2}}{v_{2,1}} = -\frac{\lambda_2}{\beta_a^*}. \tag{42}$$

Accordingly, a decrease in susceptibles animals as measured by $\Delta s_a < 0$ comes with an increase in infectious animals as measured by Δi_a with $\Delta i_a = -\lambda_2 \Delta s_a / \beta_a^* > 0$ and vice versa an increase in infectious animals $\Delta i_a > 0$ is associated with an decrease in susceptible animals like $\Delta s_a = -\beta_a^* \Delta i_a / \lambda_2 < 0$. Importantly, the human–animal order parameter $\mathbf{v}_2$ of model A also describes the coupling between the animal and human subsystems. For example, changes Δi_h and Δi_s due to the outwards dynamics component $\mathbf{x}_{out}$ are given by

$$\mathbf{x}_{out} \Rightarrow \frac{\Delta i_h}{\Delta i_a} = \frac{v_{2,4}}{v_{2,2}} = \frac{\beta_{12}^*}{\lambda_2 - \lambda_4} > 0 . \qquad (43)$$

That is, the outwards dynamics exhibits the property that an increase in infectious animals, say, by 1% is associated with an increase in the population of infectious human individuals by $1\% \cdot \beta_{12}^* / (\lambda_2 - \lambda_4)$. This example and Equation (43) illustrate that there is a rigid coupling between the animal and the human subsystems, which in the case of SIR-SIR systems (model A) is described in detail by the human–animal order parameter $\mathbf{v}_2$. With the help of the previously derived human–animal order parameters defined by Equations (22), (25), and (30) for models B, C, and D, respectively, similar explicit conclusions can be drawn about the emerging order involved in Mpox waves as described by those models.

The third scenario, scenario (iii), is characterized by two positive eigenvalues, $\lambda^{(h,X)} > 0$ and $\lambda^{(12,X)} > 0$, and describes Mpox infection waves established by an interplay (or coexistence) of two order parameters: $\mathbf{v}^{(h,X)}$ and $\mathbf{v}^{(h,12)}$. Accordingly, the outwards dynamics away from the fixed point does not take place along a single direction. Rather, it takes place in a plane spanned by the vectors $\mathbf{v}^{(h,X)}$ and $\mathbf{v}^{(h,12)}$. More precisely, Equation (37) holds with

$$\begin{aligned}
\mathbf{x}_{out} &= \mathbf{v}^{(h,X)} A^{(h,X)}(0) \exp\{\lambda^{(h,X)} t\} \\
&\quad + \mathbf{v}^{(12,X)} A^{(12,X)}(0) \exp\{\lambda^{(12,X)} t\} , \ \lambda^{(h,X)} > 0 , \ \lambda^{(12,X)} > 0 , \\
\mathbf{x}_{in} &= \sum_{i=1}^{m-4} \mathbf{v}_{s(i)} A_{s(i)}(0) \exp\{\lambda_{s(i)} t\} , \ \lambda_{s(i)} < 0 ,
\end{aligned} \qquad (44)$$

where $A^{(h,X)}$ and $A^{(12,X)}$ denote the amplitudes of the eigenvectors $\mathbf{v}^{(h,X)}$ and $\mathbf{v}^{(h,12)}$. According to the initial phase dynamics described by the linearized Equation (8), the amplitudes $A^{(h,X)}$ and $A^{(12,X)}$ measuring distances along the order parameter directions increase exponentially in magnitude over time. In doing so, the state of the system evolves further and further away from the disease-free fixed point in the 2D plane spanned by the two order parameters. The precise trajectory depends on the model parameters $\lambda^{(h,X)} > 0$, $\lambda^{(12,X)} > 0$ and initial conditions $A^{(h,X)}(0), A^{(12,X)}(0)$. As indicated in Equation (44), an inward dynamics does not exist for model A, while for models B and C we have $i = 1$ and for model D we have $i = 1, 2$.

For all three scenarios and all four models, during an initial interval $[0, T]$ Equation (37) may be used to compute approximative solutions to the exact solutions of the nonlinear models. That is, let $\mathbf{x}$ denote the solution of one of the models A, B, C, or D. Then, Equation (37) may be used to describe an approximative relationship like

$$\mathbf{x} \approx \mathbf{x}^* + \mathbf{x}_{out} + \mathbf{x}_{in} + \mathbf{h}_0 . \qquad (45)$$

The power of this approximation comes for situations in which the inwards dynamics is negligible. Such situations may arise when the eigenvalues of the inwards dynamics are relatively large in the amount such that $\mathbf{x}_{in}$ decays rapidly towards zero or when the initial amplitudes $A_s(i)(0)$ are relatively small compared to the order parameter amplitudes $A^{(h,X)}(0)$ and $A^{(12,X)}(0)$. If $\mathbf{x}_{in}$ can be neglected, then Equation (45) simplifies to yield

$$\mathbf{x} \approx \mathbf{x}^* + \mathbf{x}_{out} + \mathbf{h}_0 . \qquad (46)$$

For the three scenarios, Equation (46) reads explicitly

$$
\begin{aligned}
(i) &: \quad \mathbf{x} \approx \mathbf{x}^* + \mathbf{v}^{(h,X)} A^{(h,X)}(0) \exp\{\lambda^{(h,X)} t\} + \mathbf{h}_0, \\
(ii) &: \quad \mathbf{x} \approx \mathbf{x}^* + \mathbf{v}^{(12,X)} A^{(12,X)}(0) \exp\{\lambda^{(12,X)} t\} + \mathbf{h}_0, \\
(iii) &: \quad \mathbf{x} \approx \mathbf{x}^* + \mathbf{v}^{(h,X)} A^{(h,X)}(0) \exp\{\lambda^{(h,X)} t\} + \mathbf{v}^{(12,X)} A^{(12,X)}(0) \exp\{\lambda^{(12,X)} t\} \\
&\quad + \mathbf{h}_0.
\end{aligned}
\qquad (47)
$$

The discussion so far focused on the initial phase dynamics. This discussion was centered around the order parameters and their amplitudes. As mentioned above in the context of the Definition 3, when looking at the later stages of an infection wave, then, in general, nonlinear aspects of epidemiological models become relevant. At those later stages, all amplitudes may make considerable contributions to the infection dynamics. This issue will be illustrated in Section 3.3.

In closing this section, let us point out that for the SIR-SIR model there exists a peculiarity that does not exist for the higher-dimensional models B, C, and D. The two potential order parameters $\mathbf{v}_2$ and $\mathbf{v}_4$ of the SIR-SIR model and their amplitudes completely describe the populations of infectious individuals i_a and i_h. That is, let P_i the projection of the state $\mathbf{x}$ in the subspace of i_a and i_h, then

$$
\begin{pmatrix} i_a(t) \\ i_h(t) \end{pmatrix} = P_i(\mathbf{x}^* + \mathbf{v}_2 A_2(t) + \mathbf{v}_4 A_4(t))
\qquad (48)
$$

holds. Equation (48) holds for any time point t and is not an approximation. Equation (48) follows from the fact that $\mathbf{v}_1$ and $\mathbf{v}_3$ do not have any components in the subspace of i_a and i_h.

3.3. Role of the Neutrally Stable Eigenvectors and Their Amplitudes

Let $\mathbf{v}^{(a,0,X)}$ and $\mathbf{v}^{(h,0,X)}$ denote the eigenvectors of model X that exhibit only an s_a or s_h component, respectively. For example, for model A we have $\mathbf{v}^{(a,0,X)} = \mathbf{v}_1 = (1,0,0,0)$ and $\mathbf{v}^{(h,0,X)} = \mathbf{v}_3 = (0,0,1,0)$ (see Section 3.1). Let $\lambda^{(a,0,X)}$ and $\lambda^{(h,0,X)}$ denote the zero eigenvalues associated with those eigenvectors. Likewise, let $A^{(a,0,X)}$ and $A^{(h,0,X)}$ denote the amplitudes of $\mathbf{v}^{(a,0,X)}$ and $\mathbf{v}^{(h,0,X)}$.

Theorem 4. *For the admissible model parameters listed in Section 2.2, any Mpox infection wave as described by the four fundamental models A, B, C, or D defined by Equations (3)–(6) exhibits the following final stage properties. All amplitudes converge to zero expect for the amplitudes $A^{(a,0,X)}$ and $A^{(h,0,X)}$ associated with the zero eigenvalues $\lambda^{(a,0,X)} = \lambda^{(h,0,X)} = 0$. The final fixed point values of $A^{(a,0,X)}$ and $A^{(h,0,X)}$ for $t \to \infty$ correspond to the decay of the respective susceptible subpopulations s_a and s_h over the entire course of the infection wave like $A^{(a,0,X)}(t \to \infty) = s_a^*(t \to \infty) - s_a^*(0) < 0$ and $A^{(h,0,X)}(t \to \infty) = s_h^*(t \to \infty) - s_h^*(0) < 0$.*

In Theorem 4, $s_a^*(0)$ and $s_h^*(0)$ denote the fixed point values s_a^* and s_h^*, respectively, considered in Section 3.1. The specifier (0) has been added to distinguish more clearly between the final and initial fixed point values of a wave. Theorem 4 illustrates that while the order parameters and their amplitudes are the key building-blocks that describe the initial phase of an Mpox infection wave, the remaining amplitudes can play crucial roles at later stages during the time course of an infection wave. Theorem 4 highlights the role of the neutrally stable eigenvectors and their amplitudes.

Proof. As worked out in Section 3.1 in the context of Theorem 2, the neutrally stable eigenvectors are the only eigenvectors that do not exhibit components of infected individuals whether exposed or infectious, human or animal (i.e., they do not exhibit components such as e_a, i_a, e_h, i_h). They only exhibit components in the direction of susceptible populations. This implies that all other eigenvectors feature at least one component that describes an infected subpopulation. Furthermore, as discussed in Section 3.1 in the context of Theorem 1, the models A, B, C, and D only exhibit disease-free fixed points. Consequently, any wave dynamics eventually approaches a disease-free fixed point that features zero infected individuals [4,41]. This implies that in the long term

$$\lim_{t \to \infty} A_j(t) = 0 \ \forall j : j = 1, \ldots, m, \ j \neq n(a, 0, X), \ j \neq n(h, 0, X), \tag{49}$$

where $n(a, 0, X)$ and $n(h, 0, X)$ correspond to the indices j of the eigenvalues $\lambda^{(a,0,X)}$ and $\lambda^{(h,0,X)}$, respectively. That is, all amplitudes vanish expect for those related to the neutrally stable eigenvectors. From Equations (32) and (49), it then follows that the state vector in the long term satisfies

$$\mathbf{x}^*(\infty) = \mathbf{x}^*(0) + \mathbf{v}^{(a,0,X)} A^{(a,0,X)}(\infty) + \mathbf{v}^{(h,0,X)} A^{(h,0,X)}(\infty), \tag{50}$$

where $\mathbf{x}^*(0)$ denotes the initial fixed point vector under consideration and $\mathbf{x}^*(\infty)$ denotes the new fixed point vector that the wave assumes when it has completely subsided (i.e., for $t \to \infty$). From Equation (50) and the definition of $\mathbf{v}^{(a,0,X)}$ and $\mathbf{v}^{(h,0,X)}$ it follows that

$$\Delta s_{a,\infty} = s_a^*(t \to \infty) - s_a^*(0) = A^{(a,0,X)}(t \to \infty),$$
$$\Delta s_{h,\infty} = s_h^*(t \to \infty) - s_h^*(0) = A^{(h,0,X)}(t \to \infty), \tag{51}$$

which is the statement made in Theorem 4. □

Equation (51) in combination with the results presented in Section 3.2 points out that changes in susceptibles Δs can be determined by different types of eigenvectors and their amplitudes. During initial stages, changes Δs in relation to changes of other populations are determined by order parameters (see, e.g., Equations (39) and 42)). During these initial stages, the exponential decay of susceptible populations again is determined by order parameters (see Equation (47)). In contrast, the final stage values of susceptibles are determined by the amplitudes of the neutrally stable eigenvectors. This also implies that during the course of an infection wave at some point in time the amplitudes $A^{(a,0,X)}$ and $A^{(h,0,X)}$ of the neutrally stable eigenvectors make essential contributions to the infection wave dynamics. This issue will be illustrated in Section 3.4 below.

3.4. Simulation

In this section some aspects of the aforementioned results will be illustrated by means of a simulation. For the sake of brevity, only a simulation for the simplest model, the SIR-SIR model defined by Equation (3), will be presented. The following model parameters were used: $\beta_a = 40/y$, $\gamma_a = 12/y$, $\beta_h = 32.85/y$, and $\gamma_h = 28.08/y$ [23], where "y" stands for one year. The goal was to simulate a wave with a peak at about 2 months after wave onset. Such a 2-months-peak has been observed during the 2017 Monkeypox outbreak in Nigeria [8,9]. To this end, β_{12} was assumed to be $\beta_{12} = 10/y$, which produced the intended 2-months peak (see below). For the selected model parameters the two non-zero eigenvalues of the SIR-SIR model were found to be $\lambda_2 = 24.0/y$ and $\lambda_4 = 4.44/y$. That is, the model described a scenario (iii) outbreak involving two order parameters: the human–animal order parameter $\mathbf{v}^{(12,A)} = \mathbf{v}_2$ associated with $\lambda_2^{(12,A)} = 24.0/y$ and the human subsystem order parameter $\mathbf{v}^{(h,A)} = \mathbf{v}_4$ associated with $\lambda_4^{(h,A)} = 4.4/y$.

Equation (3) was solved numerically (using a Euler forward method with a time step τ of $\tau = 0.01$ days $= 2.74 \cdot 10^{-5}$ years) to obtain trajectories for the state variables s_a, i_a, s_h, s_i. From the trajectories of the state variables thus obtained the trajectories of the amplitude variables $A_1, \ldots A_4$ were computed. To this end, the explicit expression for $\mathbf{v}_2$ and $\mathbf{v}_4$ (see Equations (19) and (17), respectively) were used and $\mathbf{w}_j$ for $j = 1, \ldots, 4$ were computed numerically [4]. The amplitudes A_j were then obtained from Equation (33) for $j = 1, \ldots, 4$.

A noted in Sections 3.2 and 3.3, while the order parameter amplitudes $A_2^{(12,A)}$ and $A_4^{(h,A)}$ initially increase exponentially, the increase eventually is stopped and they decay to zero when the wave eventually subsides. This is consistent with the fact that the evolution equations of amplitudes of epidemiological models in general are nonlinear [4]. In this context, it is important to point out that even when order parameter amplitudes (such as $A_2^{(12,A)}$ and $A_4^{(h,A)}$) stop to increase exponentially and nonlinear effects become relevant, then still for some period order parameter amplitudes continue to make the main contributions to the infection dynamics. The reason for this is that initially the remaining amplitudes either decayed in magnitude or remained constant. In order to illustrate the role of the two order parameters $\mathbf{v}_2^{(12,A)}$ and $\mathbf{v}_4^{(h,A)}$ and their amplitudes of the SIR-SIR model for the entire duration of the simulated scenario (iii) infection wave, an approximation $\mathbf{x}_{app}$ of $\mathbf{x}$ was used that was based on the two order parameters like

$$\mathbf{x}_{app} = \mathbf{x}^* + \mathbf{v}_2^{(12,A)} A_2^{(12,A)}(t) + \mathbf{v}_4^{(h,A)} A_4^{(h,A)}(t) + \mathbf{h}_0 \qquad (52)$$

with $\mathbf{h}_0$ as defined in Equation (35). Note that this approximation goes beyond the initial phase approximations given by Equation (47) for scenario (iii) outbreaks of models A, B, C, and D. In Equation (52), the amplitudes do not necessarily increase in an exponential manner.

Finally, in order to quantify the contributions that the order parameter amplitudes $A_2^{(12,A)}$ and $A_4^{(h,A)}$ as well as the neutrally stable amplitudes $A_1^{(a,0,A)}$ and $A_3^{(h,0,A)}$ make towards the infection dynamics of the simulated wave, an amplitude space perspective was taken with the amplitude space defined by the four-dimensional space spanned by the amplitude variables $A_1, \ldots, A_4$ [4]. For each amplitude at each time point t the variance explained by that amplitude at that time point t was determined. More precisely, explained variance scores were computed like $\text{Score}_j(t) = \text{var}(A_j)(t) / \sum_{k=1}^{4} \text{var}(A_k)(t)$, where $\text{var}(A_j)(t)$ denotes the variance of the amplitude trajectory up to time point t (i.e., $\text{var}(A_j)(t) = (T-1)^{-1} \sum_{k=1}^{k^*} [A_j(t_k) - M_{j,t}]^2$ with $M_{j,t}$ being the mean $M_{j,t} = T^{-1} \sum_{k=1}^{k^*} A_j(t_k)$ with $t = t_{k^*}$ and $T = k^*$). Note that this is a time series framework where mean values and variances are computed from samples that consists of data taken from trajectories at discrete time points t_k.

Figure 1 presents some of the simulation results. Panels (a) and (b) show the four state variables s_a, i_a, s_h, and i_h from top to bottom as solid black lines. Panel (a) shows the first 60 days. This period describes the simulated initial outbreak and the increase in the size of human infectious population towards its peak value. In contrast, panel (b) shows the total simulation period of 180 days and includes later stages of the simulated infection wave that describe the subsiding of the infection dynamics. As expected from the model equations of s_a and s_h, the populations s_a and s_h decayed monotonically. In contrast, i_a and i_h formed infection waves. For the selected parameters, both populations reached peak values at approximately the same time.

Panel (c) shows the amplitudes $A_1, \ldots, A_4$ as functions of time during the entire 180 days simulation period with $A_2^{(12,A)}$ and $A_4^{(h,A)}$ given as solid black and gray lines, respectively, and $A_1^{(a,0,A)}$ and $A_3^{(h,0,A)}$ given as dotted black and gray lines, respectively. As can be seen in panel (c), during the first 60 days the human-environment order parameter amplitude $A_2^{(12,A)}$ (solid black) increased monotonically and played the dominant role among all four amplitudes. The human subsystem order parameter amplitude $A_4^{(h,A)}$ (solid gray) also varied over time during that 60 days interval but its variations were relatively small as compared to $A_2^{(12,A)}$. This is not surprising, because for the selected model parameters λ_2 was about 5.5 times larger than λ_4. The remaining two (neutrally stable) amplitudes $A_1^{(a,0,A)}$ and $A_3^{(h,0,A)}$ (dotted lines) stayed almost constant during the initial 60 days period. After 60 days, the amplitudes $A_1^{(a,0,A)}$ and $A_3^{(h,0,A)}$ started to make essential contributions to the infection dynamics. The values of $A_1^{(a,0,A)}$ and $A_3^{(h,0,A)}$ at the simulation stop of $t = 180$ describe in good approximation the drop in susceptibles s_a and s_h as discussed in the context of Theorem 4 (compare panels (b) and (c)).

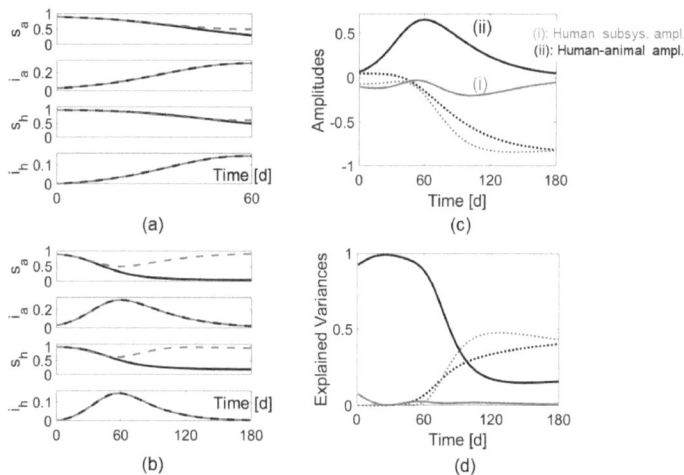

Figure 1. State space and amplitude space description of a simulated Mpox wave. Panels (**a**) and (**b**) show the state variables as solid black lines for the first 60 days (panel (**a**)) and the entire simulation period of 180 days (panel (**b**)). Gray dashed lines show state variables as described by the two order parameter description x_{app} defined by Equation (52). Panel (**c**) shows the order parameter amplitudes A_2 (solid black) and A_4 (solid gray) as well as the remaining amplitudes A_1 (dotted black) and A_3 (dotted gray) as functions of time. Panel (**d**) shows the explained variance scores of the amplitudes $A_1, \ldots, A_4$. For model parameters see text.

The relative importance of the four amplitudes during different stages of the simulated infection wave can also be explained with the help of their explained variance scores shown in panel (d). Panel (d) shows the explained variance scores for $A_2^{(12,A)}$ and $A_4^{(h,A)}$ given as solid black and gray lines, respectively, and $A_1^{(a,0,A)}$ and $A_3^{(h,0,A)}$ given as dotted black and gray lines, respectively. That is, in panel (d) the same color coding is used as in panel (c). Accordingly, during the first 60 days, the human–animal order parameter amplitude $A_2^{(12,A)}$ (solid black) explained most of the variance. During the first 20 days, the human subsystem order parameter amplitude $A_4^{(h,A)}$ (solid gray) also played a role such that during that period the two order parameter amplitudes taken together explain almost 100 percent of the variance in the infection dynamics. After 60 days, the explained variance score of $A_2^{(12,A)}$ decayed sharply, indicating that $A_2^{(12,A)}$ stopped playing the dominant role. For that later stages of the wave the neutrally stable amplitudes $A_1^{(a,0,A)}$ and $A_3^{(h,0,A)}$ explained most of the infection dynamics variance.

The gray dashed lines plotted in panels (a) and (b) show the state variable approximation x_{app} defined by Equation (52). As can be seen, the solutions for the infectious populations i_a and i_h as described by x_{app} were found to be identical to the exact solutions i_a and i_h (i.e., the gray dashed lines run exactly on top of the solid black lines). This illustrates the peculiarity of the SIR-SIR model expressed by Equation (48), namely, that the two potential order parameters (which are both actual order parameters for the simulated scenario (iii) outbreak) describe exactly the dynamics of i_a and i_h. That is, as far as state variables i_a and i_h are concerned, x_{app} is not an approximation but an exact description of the infection dynamics. Moreover, during the initial period of 60 days x_{app} is a fair approximation of the state dynamics of s_a and s_h (see panel (a)). However, the simulation revealed that after that period $\mathbf{x}_{app}$ became a poor approximation of the dynamics of s_a and s_h. This is consistent with the results presented in panels (c) and (d) and also illustrates what has been discussed previously in the context of Theorem 4. Panels (c) and (d) demonstrate that for the simulated Mpox infection wave the neutrally stable amplitudes $A_1^{(a,0,A)}$ and $A_3^{(h,0,A)}$ indeed became important after the initial phase passed by. Since $\mathbf{x}_{app}$ neglects these amplitude contributions and $A_1^{(a,0,A)}$ and $A_3^{(h,0,A)}$ are associated with eigenvectors that point into the direction of the susceptible populations s_a and s_h, it is not surprising that $\mathbf{x}_{app}$ did not adequately capture the dynamics of the susceptibles of the simulated wave during the entire course of the wave.

In summary, it was found that the two order parameters and their amplitudes provided an exact description of the infectious human and animal populations (which is a peculiarity of the SIR-SIR model that does not hold for the remaining models B, C, and D). Furthermore, for the selected model parameters the order parameter approximation $\mathbf{x}_{app}$ also provided a good fit of the susceptible population dynamics during the initial increasing phase of the wave. For the selected model parameters, the human–animal order parameter amplitude $A_2^{(12,A)}$ made the main contribution, while the human subsystem order parameter amplitude $A_4^{(h,A)}$ made only a secondary contribution. At later time points the neutrally stable amplitudes $A_1^{(a,0,A)}$ and $A_3^{(h,0,A)}$ became important.

Finally, as mentioned above, for the simulated wave the human–animal order parameter amplitude dominated over the human subsystem order parameter amplitude. Therefore, changes in the population sizes of i_a and i_h should be determined approximately by $\mathbf{v}_2^{(12,A)}$ as described by Equation (43). Graphically speaking, the phase curve $i_h(i_a)$ in the 2D subspace spanned by i_a and i_h should follow the projection of the order parameter $\mathbf{v}_2^{(12,A)}$ into that subspace. Figure 2 shows the phase curve $i_h(i_a)$ of the simulated infection wave for the first 60 days (panel (a)) and for the entire simulation period (panel (b)) as solid black lines. The phase curves shown in Figure 2 were drawn from the solutions i_a and i_h presented in panels (a) and (b) of Figure 1. The phase curves were also drawn from the solution given by $\mathbf{x}_{app}$ (see the dashed gray lines). As expected (see Equation (48) again), the phase curves computed from $\mathbf{x}_{app}$ were identical to the phase curves obtained directly from the SIR-SIR model solutions. Importantly, panels (a) and (b) present the projection of the order parameter $\mathbf{v}_2^{(12,A)}$ into the 2D plane of i_a and i_h as red dotted lines. As can be seen in panel (a), the phase curve initially followed closely the order parameter $\mathbf{v}_2^{(12,A)}$. However, when the infection wave was about to reach the infection peak (i.e., towards the end of the 60-day period) the phase curve started to deviate from $\mathbf{v}_2^{(12,A)}$. The initial part during which the phase curve followed $\mathbf{v}_2^{(12,A)}$ is consistent with the scenario (ii) approximation shown in Equation (47). The deviation from $\mathbf{v}_2^{(12,A)}$ at the end of the 60-day period demonstrates the role of the second order parameter $\mathbf{v}_4^{(h,A)}$. In this context, note again that when taking this second order parameter $\mathbf{v}_4^{(h,A)}$ into account, we obtain the gray dashed line that runs on top of the exact solution. That is, the difference between a phase space dynamics along the red straight line and the actual dynamics indicated by the dashed gray line was entirely due to the contribution of the secondary order parameter: the human subsystem order parameter $\mathbf{v}_4^{(h,A)}$. Panel (b) demonstrates that for the subsiding part of the infection wave from 60 days to 180 days in crude approximation the phase curve $i_h(i_a)$ followed the direction defined by $\mathbf{v}_2^{(12,A)}$ (dotted red line). However, $i_h(i_a)$ deviated clearly from $\mathbf{v}_2^{(12,A)}$. As argued above, this deviation was due to the the term $\mathbf{v}_4^{(h,A)} A_4^{(h,A)}(t)$. In the interval from 60 to 180 days, the amplitude $A_4^{(h,A)}(t)$ formed a very shallow U-shaped curve (see the solid gray line in panel (c) of Figure 1). In line with this U-shape curve, the subsiding branch of the phase curve $i_h(i_a)$ in panel (b) of Figure 2 running from the top-right corner towards the fixed point $i_a^* = i_h^* = 0$ first deviated slightly, subsequently reached a maximal deviation from $\mathbf{v}_4^{(12,A)}$, and finally approached again the direction specified by $\mathbf{v}_4^{(12,A)}$. In this context, note that $\mathbf{v}_4^{(12,A)}$ is attached in the 2D space at $\mathbf{x}(0)$ with $i_a(0) \neq 0$, $i_h(0) \neq 0$. Consequently, close to simulation stop at $t = 180$ days when the phase curve $i_h(i_a)$ was about to approach the fixed point $i_a^* = i_h^* = 0$ the phase curve crossed the $\mathbf{v}_4^{(12,A)}$-line.

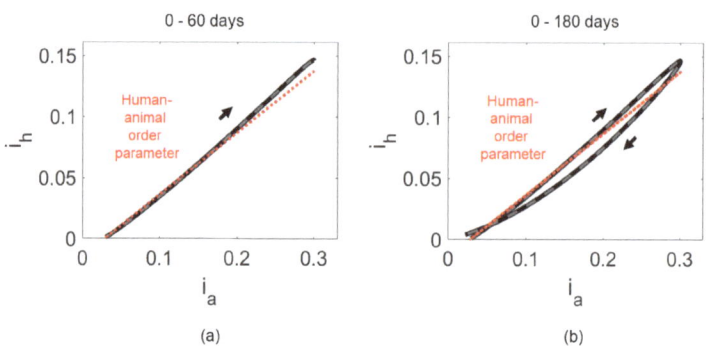

(a)　　　　　　　　　　　　　　(b)

Figure 2. Illustration of the role of the human–animal order parameter for the simulated Mpox wave. Panels (**a**,**b**) show the phase curve $i_h(i_a)$ for the first 60 days (panel (**a**)) and the entire simulation period of 180 days (panel (**b**)) as solid black lines. Phase curve solutions obtained from $\mathbf{x}_{app}$ are shown as well as dashed gray lines. The direction of the human–animal order parameter $\mathbf{v}_2$ is indicated as a dotted red line.

4. Conclusions

Mpox outbreaks in endemic countries are typically initiated by animal to human transmissions of the Monkeypox virus [1,8]. However, once the Monkeypox virus has arrived in a particular human population, human to human transmissions may make a crucial contribution to the infection dynamics as well [1]. The current study is the first study that takes an order parameter approach that has been developed in the wake of the COVID-19 pandemic [4] to the field of Mpox infection outbreaks in order to address these two mechanisms. In four fundamental epidemiological models for Mpox outbreaks, two types of multi-compartmental components or building-blocks have been identified that shape and determine Mpox outbreaks. They are given in terms of human subsystem order parameters, on the one hand, and human–animal order parameters, on the other hand (see Section 3.1). The latter multi-compartmental components link the dynamics in animal subsystems rigidly with the dynamics in human subsystems during initial phases of Mpox outbreaks (see Section 3.2). The mathematical analysis revealed that each of the four fundamental models exhibits maximally only one human–animal order parameter and maximally only one human subsystem order parameter (see Theorems 1 and 2).

Previous work by Ma [42] pointed out the role of eigenvalues describing the temporal aspects of the initial phases of infectious disease outbreaks. Among other things, in the study by Ma [42] it has been assumed that the observable at hand, $X(t)$, increases exponentially according to a simple exponential function like $X(t) = X(0) \exp(\lambda t)$. This situation holds for scenarios (i) and (ii) assuming that the approximations shown in Equation (47) hold. In contrast, as such, the single-parameter exponential increase model does not hold for scenario (iii) even under the simplified conditions described in Equation (47). Having said that, the simulation study presented in Section 3.4 showed that a scenario (iii) outbreak may effectively look like a scenario (i) or (ii) outbreak when one of the two relevant positive eigenvalues is relatively large with respect to the other. That is, the current study supplements the study by Ma [42] by identifying conditions under which single-parametric laws like $X(t) = X(0) \exp(\lambda t)$ hold.

The current study focused on four fundamental Mpox models that effectively exhibit between four (SIR-SIR model) and six (SEIR-SEIR model) state variables. As mentioned in the introduction, more sophisticated models based on those four fundamental models have been proposed that feature relatively high-dimensional state spaces. In this context, Al-Shomrani et al. [25] proposed a 12-dimensional model based on the SEIR-SEIR model (6). Importantly, at the bifurcation point when the disease-free fixed point becomes unstable the authors were able to derive an analytical expression for the leading eigenvector (which in this case is the eigenvector associated with a zero eigenvalue). While the study by Al-Shomrani et al. was not tailored to discuss order parameters, it nevertheless shows that discussions as presented in the current study and calculations as carried out in Section 3 are not limited to the fundamental models defined by Equations (3)–(6): high-dimensional models may be analyzed in a similar way as the fundamental models have been analyzed in the current study.

Various studies as mentioned in the introduction have studied the impact of prevention and intervention measures on the spread of Mpox disease (see, e.g., [19–23]). In the context of early COVID-19 outbreaks in China [38], USA [40], and Thailand [39] during the year 2020, model-based analyses have found some evidence that intervention measures resulted in changes in the order parameters that shaped the respective outbreaks. Order parameters either changed their orientations [38,39] and/or qualitatively switched from unstable eigenvectors to stable eigenvectors [38–40] resulting in a subsiding of the COVID-19 surges of interest. The current study provides a basis to discuss similar impacts of prevention and intervention measures on the order parameters of Mpox infection models such as the fundamental models defined by Equations (3)–(6). While a detailed discussion is beyond the scope of this study, it should only be pointed out that in the context of Mpox waves intervention measures may result in a switch between different types of outbreak scenarios. More precisely, it is plausible to assume that in an endemic country witnessing a scenario (iii) outbreak, interventions may considerably reduce human to human transmission such that the eigenvalue $\lambda^{(h,X)}$ turns from a positive to a negative value. Since $\lambda^{(12,X)}$ would be not affected by such intervention measures, the outbreak may continue in the human subsystem (as long as $\beta_{12} > 0$) in terms of a scenario (ii) outbreak. In doing so, a switch from a scenario (iii) to a scenario (ii) would occur. The remaining scenario (ii) outbreak could only be entirely stopped in the human subsystem by de-coupling the human population under consideration completely from the infectious animal reservoir (i.e., by administering intervention measures that lead to $\beta_{12} = 0$).

In the four fundamental models that were examined in the current study, demographic terms were neglected. The reason for this was that the primary aim of the current study was to study the emergence of relative short-lived Mpox infection waves during which variations of population sizes due to birth and deaths can be assumed to be negligibly small. In future work, our analysis may be generalized to take the vital dynamics of populations into account. However, when demographic terms and/or variations in the total sizes of populations are taken into account, then the resulting epidemiological models typically increase in complexity, that is, they become higher-dimensional as compared to models that perform without those features. The aim of the current study was to discuss the main idea, namely, the existence of certain multi-compartmental components or building-blocks that shape and determine Mpox infection outbreaks with the help of analytical expressions. Such analytical expressions can be derived conveniently for relatively low-dimensional models as those discussed in the current study. In contrast, taking demographic terms and/or variations in population sizes into account may come at the cost that considerations have to be based on numerical approaches, that is, at the cost of losing concreteness.

Funding: This research received no external funding.

Data Availability Statement: The original contributions presented in the study are included in the article, further inquiries can be directed to the corresponding author.

Conflicts of Interest: The author declares no conflicts of interest.

References

1. World Health Organization. Monkeypox Key Facts as of 19 May 2022. 2022. Available online: https://www.who.int/news-room/fact-sheets/detail/mpox (accessed on 25 May 2024).
2. Sklenovska, N.; Ranst, M.V. Emergence of monkeypox as the most important orthopoxvirus infection in humans. *Front. Public Health* **2018**, *6*, 241. [CrossRef]
3. Bunge, E.M.; Hoet, B.; Chen, L.; Lienert, F.; Weidenthaler, H.; Bear, L.R.; Steffen, R. The changing epidemiology of human monkeypox: A potential threat? A systematic review. *PLoS Neglected Trop. Dis.* **1996**, *16*, e0010141. [CrossRef]
4. Frank, T.D. *COVID-19 Epidemiology and Virus Dynamics: Nonlinear Physics and Mathematical Modeling*; Springer: Berlin/Heidelberg, Germany, 2022.
5. Laurenson-Schafer, H.; Sklenovska, N.; Hoxha, A.; Kerr, S.M.; Ndumbi, P.; Fitzner, J.; Almiron, M.; de Sousa, L.A.; Briand, S.; Cenciarelli, O.; et al. Description of the first global outbreak of mpox: An analysis of global surveillance data. *Lancet Glob. Health* **2023**, *11*, e1012–e1023. [CrossRef]
6. Munir, T.; Khan, M.; Cheema, S.A.; Khan, F.; Usmani, A.; Nazir, M. Time series analysis and short-term forecasting of monkeypox outbreaks trends in the 10 major affected countries. *BMC Infect. Dis.* **2024**, *24*, 16. [CrossRef]
7. Oladoye, M.J. Monkeypox: A neglected viral zoonotic disease. *Eur. J. Med. Educ. Technol.* **2021**, *14*, em2108. [CrossRef]
8. Petersen, E.; Abubukar, I.; Ihekweazu, C.; Heymann, D.; Ntoumi, F.; Blumberg, L.; Asogun, D.; Mukonka, V.; Lule, S.A.; Bates, M.; et al. Monkeypox: Enhancing public health preparedness for an emerging lethal human zoonotic epidemic threat in the wake of the smallpox post-eradication era. *Int. J. Infect. Dis.* **2019**, *78*, 78–84. [CrossRef]
9. Yinka-Ogunleye, L.; Aruna, O.; Dalhat, M.; Ogoina, D.; McCollum, A.; Disu, Y.; Mamadu, I.; Akinpelu, A.; Ahmad, A.; Burga, J.; et al. Outbreak of human monkeypox in Nigeria in 2017–2018: A clinical and epidemiological report. *Lancet Infect. Dis.* **2019**, *19*, 872–879. [CrossRef] [PubMed]
10. World Health Organization. 2022–2024 Mpox (Monkeypox) Outbreak: Global Trends Report from 22 August 2024. 2024. Available online: https://worldhealthorg.shinyapps.io/mpx_global/ (accessed on 25 August 2024).
11. Mbala-Kingebeni, P.; Rimoin, A.W.; Kacita, C.; Liesenborghs, L.; Nachega, J.B.; Kindrachuk, J. The time is now (again) for mpox containment and elimination in Democratic Republic of the Congo. *PLoS Glob. Public Health* **2024**, *4*, e0003171. [CrossRef]
12. World Health Organization. WHO Director-General Declares Mpox Outbreak a Public Health Emergency of International Concern. 2024. Available online: https://www.who.int/news/item/14-08-2024-who-director-general-declares-mpox-outbreak-a-public-health-emergency-of-international-concern (accessed on 26 August 2024).
13. Center for Disease Control and Prevention. 2023 Outbreak in Democratic Republic of the Congo as of 30 May 2024. Available online: https://www.who.int/emergencies/disease-outbreak-news/item/2024-DON522 (accessed on 30 July 2024).
14. Center for Disease Control and Prevention. Ongoing 2022 Global Outbreak Cases and Data as of 5 March 2024. Available online: https://www.cdc.gov/mpox/outbreaks/2022/index-1.html (accessed on 30 July 2024).
15. Banuet-Martinez, M.; Yang, Y.; Jafari, B.; Kaur, A.; Butt, Z.A.; Chen, H.H.; Yanushkevich, S.; Moyles, I.R.; Heffernan, J.M.; Korosec, C.S. Monkeypox: A review of epidemiological modelling studies and how modelling has led to mechanistic insight. *Epidemiol. Infect.* **2023**, *151*, e121. [CrossRef]
16. Rock, K.; Brand, S.; Moir, J.; Keeling, M.J. Dynamics of infectious diseases. *Rep. Prog. Phys.* **2014**, *77*, 026602. [CrossRef] [PubMed]
17. Bhunu, C.P.; Mushayabasa, S. Modelling the Transmission Dynamics of Pox-like Infections. *IAENG Int. J. Appl. Math.* **2011**, *41*, 1–9.
18. Emeka, P.C.; Ounorah, M.O.; Eguda, F.Y.; Babangida, B.G. Mathematical model for monkeypox virus transmission dynamics. *Epidemiology* **2018**, *8*, 1000348.
19. Somma, S.A.; Akinwande, N.I.; Chado, U.D. A mathematical model of monkey pox virus transmision dynamics. *Ife J. Sci.* **2019**, *21*, 195–204. [CrossRef]
20. Madubueze, C.E.; Onwubuya, I.O.; Nkem, G.N.; Chazuka, Z. The transmission dynamics of the monkeypox virus in the presence of environmental transmission. *Front. Appl. Math. Stat.* **2022**, *8*, 1061546. [CrossRef]
21. Usman, S.; Adamu, I.I. Modeling the transmission dynamics of the monkeypox virus infection with treatment and vaccination interventions. *J. Appl. Math. Phys.* **2017**, *5*, 2335–2353. [CrossRef]
22. Peter, O.J.; Kumar, S.; Kumari, N.; Obuntolu, F.A.; Oshinubi, K.; Musa, R. Transmission dynamics of monkeypox virus: A mathematical modelling approach. *Model. Earth Syst. Environ.* **2022**, *8*, 3423–3434. [CrossRef]
23. Bankuru, S.V.; Kossol, S.; Hou, W.; Mahmoudi, P.; Rychtar, J.; Taylor, D. A game-theoretic model of monkeypox to access vaccination strategies. *PeerJ* **2020**, *8*, e9272. [CrossRef] [PubMed]
24. Collins, O.C.; Duffy, K.J. Dynamics and control of mpox using two modelling approaches. *Model. Earth Syst. Environ.* **2024**, *10*, 1657–1669. [CrossRef]
25. Al-Shomrani, M.M.; Musa, S.S.; Yusuf, A. Unfolding the transmission dynamics of monkeypox virus: An epidemiological modelling analysis. *Mathematics* **2023**, *11*, 1121. [CrossRef]
26. Okongo, W.; Abonyo, J.O.; Kioi, D.; Moore, S.E.; Agueghoh, S.N. Mathematical modeling and optimal control analysis of monkeypox virus in contaminated environment. *Model. Earth Syst. Environ.* **2024**, *10*, 3969–3994. [CrossRef]
27. Peter, O.J.; Abidemi, A.; Ojo, M.M.; Ayoola, T.A. Mathematical model and analysis of monkeypox with control strategies. *Eur. Phys. J. Plus* **2023**, *138*, 242. [CrossRef]

28. Samreen; Ullah, S.; Nawaz, R.; Alshehri, A. Mathematical modeling of monkeypox infection with optimized preventive control analysis: A case study with 2022 outbreak. *Eur. Phys. J. Plus* **2023**, *138*, 689. [CrossRef]
29. Chatuvedi, M.; Rodiah, I.; Kretzschmar, M.; Scholz, S.; Lange, B.; Karch, A.; Jaeger, V. Estimating the relative importance of epidemioligcal and behavioral parameters for epidemic mpox transmission: A modelling study. *BMC Med.* **2024**, *22*, 297.
30. Das, A.; Dhar, A.; Goyal, S.; Kundu, A.; Pandey, S. COVID-19: Analytical results from a modified SEIR model and comparison of different intervention strategies. *Chaos Solitons Fractals* **2021**, *144*, 110595. [CrossRef] [PubMed]
31. Frank, T.D. SARS-coronavirus-2 infections: Biological instabilities characterized by order parameters. *Phys. Biol.* **2022**, *19*, 036001. [CrossRef]
32. Frank, T.D. Amplitude equations and order parameters of human SARS-COV-2 infections and immune reactions: A model-based approach. *Adv. Complex Syst.* **2024**, *27*, 2450001. [CrossRef]
33. Haken, H. *Synergetics: An Introduction*; Springer: Berlin/Heidelberg, Germany, 1977.
34. Wunner, G.; Pelster, A. *Self-Organization in Complex Systems: The Past, Present, and Future of Synergetics*; Springer: Berlin/Heidelberg, Germany, 2016.
35. Frank, T. *Determinism and Self-Organization of Human Perception and Performance*; Springer: Berlin/Heidelberg, Germany, 2019.
36. Frank, T.D. Rise and decay of the COVID-19 epidemics in the USA and the State of New York in the first half of 2020: A nonlinear physics perspective yielding novel insights. *BioMed Res. Int.* **2021**, *2021*, 6645688. [CrossRef]
37. Frank, T.D. COVID-19 interventions in some European countries induced bifurcations stabilizing low death states against high death states: An eigenvalue analysis based on the order parameter concept of synergetics. *Chaos Solitons Fractals* **2020**, *140*, 110194. [CrossRef] [PubMed]
38. Frank, T.D. COVID-19 order parameters and order parameter time constants of Italy and China: A modeling approach based on synergetics. *J. Biol. Syst.* **2020**, *28*, 589–608. [CrossRef]
39. Frank, T.D.; Chiangga, S. SEIR order parameters and eigenvectors of the three stages of completed COVID-19 epidemics: With an illustration for Thailand January to May 2020. *Phys. Biol.* **2021**, *18*, 046002. [CrossRef]
40. Frank, T.D.; Smucker, J. Characterizing stages of COVID-19 epidemics: A nonlinear physics perspective based on amplitude equations. *Eur. Phys. J. Spec. Top.* **2022**, *231*, 3403–3418. [CrossRef] [PubMed]
41. Hethcote, H.W. The mathematics of infectious diseases. *SIAM Rev.* **2000**, *42*, 599–653. [CrossRef]
42. Ma, J. Estimating epidemic exponential growth rate and basic reproduction number. *Infect. Dis. Model.* **2020**, *5*, 129–141. [CrossRef] [PubMed]

Disclaimer/Publisher's Note: The statements, opinions and data contained in all publications are solely those of the individual author(s) and contributor(s) and not of MDPI and/or the editor(s). MDPI and/or the editor(s) disclaim responsibility for any injury to people or property resulting from any ideas, methods, instructions or products referred to in the content.

MDPI AG
Grosspeteranlage 5
4052 Basel
Switzerland
Tel.: +41 61 683 77 34

Mathematics Editorial Office
E-mail: mathematics@mdpi.com
www.mdpi.com/journal/mathematics

Disclaimer/Publisher's Note: The title and front matter of this reprint are at the discretion of the Guest Editors. The publisher is not responsible for their content or any associated concerns. The statements, opinions and data contained in all individual articles are solely those of the individual Editors and contributors and not of MDPI. MDPI disclaims responsibility for any injury to people or property resulting from any ideas, methods, instructions or products referred to in the content.

www.ingramcontent.com/pod-product-compliance
Lightning Source LLC
LaVergne TN
LVHW072330090526
838202LV00019B/2384